CONTEMPORARY CHALLENGES TO CRIMINAL JUSTICE: LIBER AMICORUM FOR RALPH HENHAM

This study provides a critical examination of seminal issues within the main areas of criminal justice: its theoretical framework, domestic and comparative criminal justice, transnational and international criminal law. Exploring some of the most interesting challenges arising in these fields, it examines the impact of 'public morality' on sentencing policy, murder and the mandatory life sentence, genocide and the notion of magnitude and incitement to terrorism. Taking an approach that is fully integrated in contemporary criminal justice scholarship, it offers a diverse and expert perspective. With a comprehensive introduction and conclusion drawing the various strands together, it offers a rigorous, coherent overview of the key issues in play in contemporary international criminal justice. This diversity and expertise ensures its appeal to a large audience of students, scholars and practitioners of criminal justice around the world.

**Volume 23 in the series Studies in International
and Comparative Criminal Law**

Studies in International and Comparative Criminal Law

General Editor: Michael Bohlander

Criminal law had long been regarded as the preserve of national legal systems, and comparative research in criminal law for a long time had something of an academic ivory tower quality. However, in the past 15 years it has been transformed into an increasingly, and moreover practically, relevant subject of study for international and comparative lawyers. This can be attributed to numerous factors, such as the establishment of ad hoc international criminal tribunals and the International Criminal Court, as well as to developments within the EU, the UN and other international organisations. There is a myriad of initiatives related to tackling terrorism, money laundering, organised crime, people trafficking and the drugs trade, and the international 'war' on terror. Criminal law is being used to address global or regional problems, often across the borders of fundamentally different legal systems, only one of which is the traditional divide between common and civil law approaches. It is therefore no longer solely a matter for domestic lawyers. The need exists for a global approach which encompasses comparative and international law.

Responding to this development this new series will include books on a wide range of topics, including studies of international law, EU law, the work of specific international tribunals, and comparative studies of national systems of criminal law. Given that the different systems to a large extent operate based on the idiosyncracies of the peoples and states that have created them, the series will also welcome pertinent historical, criminological and socio-legal research into these issues.

Editorial Committee:

Recent titles in this series:

Contemporary Challenges to Criminal Justice

Liber Amicorum for Ralph Henham

Edited by
Paul Behrens

·HART·

OXFORD · LONDON · NEW YORK · NEW DELHI · SYDNEY

HART PUBLISHING

Bloomsbury Publishing Plc

Kemp House, Chawley Park, Cumnor Hill, Oxford, OX2 9PH, UK

1385 Broadway, New York, NY 10018, USA

29 Earlsfort Terrace, Dublin 2, Ireland

HART PUBLISHING, the Hart/Stag logo, BLOOMSBURY and the Diana logo are
trademarks of Bloomsbury Publishing Plc

First published in Great Britain 2023

A catalogue record for this book is available from the British Library.

A catalogue record for this book is available from the Library of Congress.

Library of Congress Control Number: 2023944927

ISBN: HB: 978-1-50994-862-8
       ePDF: 978-1-50994-864-2
       ePub: 978-1-50994-863-5

Typeset by Compuscript Ltd, Shannon

To find out more about our authors and books visit www.hartpublishing.co.uk.
Here you will find extracts, author information, details of forthcoming events
and the option to sign up for our newsletters.

Professor Ralph Jean Henham
(May 2023)

Picture credit: Annemarie Henham

Table of Contents

Notes on Contributors

Noah Al-Malt, LLM, JD, is a former Senior Legal Consultant for the defence in the case of *Prosecutor v Meas Muth* at the Extraordinary Chambers in the Courts of Cambodia (Case 003) and the defence in the case of *Prosecutor v Paul Gicheru* at the International Criminal Court. He has previously worked for the defence team in Case 004 at the Extraordinary Chambers in the Courts of Cambodia (*Prosecutor v Yim Tith*), for the Kilolo defence team in *Prosecutor v Bemba et al* at the International Criminal Court, and for the Prlić defence team in the case of *Prosecutor v Jadranko Prlić* at the International Criminal Tribunal for the Former Yugoslavia. Mr Al-Malt is a graduate of Barry University School of Law and Leiden University and is a member of the New York Bar.

Paul Behrens, PhD, LLM, is Reader (Associate Professor) in Law at the University of Edinburgh, where he teaches courses on International Criminal Law and Diplomatic Law. He was *amicus curiae* in the *Ongwen* case before the Appeals Chamber of the International Criminal Court. He is also member of the Expert Advisory Group to the Scottish Government on Ending Conversion Practices and has provided evidence to committees of the Scottish Parliament and the German Bundestag. Dr Behrens is member of the Edinburgh Centre for International and Global Law, the Centre for Criminal Law and Criminal Justice (Durham), the Surrey International Law Centre and Associate of the Stanley Burton Centre for Holocaust and Genocide Studies (Leicester). He has held visiting appointments at the law schools of Uppsala (Sweden), Stockholm (Sweden), Kiel (Germany) and other universities.

Dr Behrens is co-editor of *Elements of Genocide* (Routledge, 2012), *Holocaust and Genocide Denial* (Routledge, 2017) and *The Criminal Law of Genocide* (Ashgate, 2007) and has published also widely on diplomatic law, including the books *Diplomatic Interference and the Law* (Hart, 2016) and (ed) *Diplomatic Law in a New Millennium* (Oxford University Press, 2017) and on LGBT matters, including (with Sean Becker, eds) *Justice After Stonewall: LGBT Life Between Challenge and Change* (Routledge, 2023). Dr Behrens also contributes regularly to newspapers (including *The Guardian*, *The Scotsman*, *The Herald*, *Süddeutsche Zeitung*, *Frankfurter Rundschau*) and gives media interviews on legal subjects.

Roger Cotterrell, LLD, MSc, FBA, is Anniversary Professor of Legal Theory at Queen Mary University of London, and a Fellow of both the British Academy and the UK Academy of Social Sciences. He was Dean of the Faculty of Laws at Queen Mary University of London from 1993 to 1996 and Professor of Legal Theory from 1990 to 2005. In 2013 he was awarded the Socio-Legal Studies Association lifetime achievement award for contributions to the sociolegal community. Professor Cotterrell has held visiting academic positions at the University of Texas at Austin, Lund University, the Catholic University of Brussels, the University of California at Berkeley, the Onati

Institute for the Sociology of Law, the European University Institute and the University of Hong Kong. His books include *Sociological Jurisprudence: Juristic Thought and Social Inquiry* (2018), *Emile Durkheim: Justice, Morality and Politics* (2010), *Living Law: Studies in Legal and Social Theory* (2008), *Law, Culture and Society: Legal Ideas in the Mirror of Social Theory* (2006), *The Politics of Jurisprudence: A Critical Introduction to Legal Philosophy*, 2nd edn (2003), *Emile Durkheim: Law in a Moral Domain* (1999), *Law's Community: Legal Theory in Sociological Perspective* (1995), and *The Sociology of Law: An Introduction*, 2nd edn (1992).

Jonathan Doak, PhD, FRSA, LLB is Professor of Criminal Justice and Associate Dean for Research in Nottingham Law School. He is a member for the Centre of Rights and Justice, the Centre for Advocacy, and the Centre for Legal Education. His research focuses on issues relating to the rights of vulnerable parties within the criminal trial, and wider issues relating to criminal procedure (particularly evidence, cross-examination and restorative justice) and transitional justice (particularly in relation to process and reparation). Professor Doak is currently a co-investigator on *Mapping the Changing Face of Cross-Examination* (Nuffield award 2020–23). He is coauthor (with David O'Mahony) of *Reimagining Restorative Justice: Agency and Accountability in the Criminal Process* (Hart, 2017) as well as (with Claire McGourlay and Mark Thomas) *Evidence in Context* (Routledge, 2018, 2015, 2012, 2008, 2005) and *Victims' Rights, Human Rights and Criminal Justice: Reconceiving the Role of Third Parties* (Hart, 2008). Professor Doak was formerly editor-in-chief of the *International Journal of Evidence and Proof* (2015–2019) and is member of the editorial boards of the *Journal of Criminal Law* and the *British Journal of Community Justice*. He also sits on the Advisory Board for the Palgrave Series in *Victims and Victimology*.

He has previously taught at Durham University, the University of Sheffield and Ulster University and is a graduate of Queen's University Belfast.

Mark Drumbl, SJD, LLM, JD, MA, BA, is the Class of 1975 Alumni Professor at Washington & Lee University School of Law, where he also serves as Director of the Transnational Law Institute. He has held visiting appointments on several law faculties, including Queen's University Belfast, Oxford University, Université de Paris II (Panthéon-Assas), University of Melbourne, University of Sydney, University of Ottawa, Monash University, Free University of Amsterdam, and Trinity College Dublin. Professor Drumbl's research and teaching interests include public international law, international criminal law, global environmental governance and transitional justice. His book *Atrocity, Punishment, and International Law* (Cambridge University Press, 2007) has received critical acclaim and has won commendations from the International Association of Criminal Law (US national section) and the American Society of International Law. In 2012, he published *Reimagining Child Soldiers in International Law and Policy* (Oxford University Press), which has also been extensively and enthusiastically reviewed. He coedited the *Research Handbook on Child Soldiers* (Elgar, 2019). Professor Drumbl has worked in criminal defence in Rwanda, lectures widely, and serves as an expert in US courts; his research also has been cited by courts in Canada, the United States and the United Kingdom.

Caroline Fournet, PhD, LLM, is Professor of Law at the University of Exeter. Previously, she was Professor of Comparative Criminal Law and International Justice at the Department of Criminal Law and Criminology at the University of Groningen. She is editor-in-chief of the *International Criminal Law Review* (Brill) and one of the coeditors of the academic journal *Human Remains and Violence: An Interdisciplinary Journal* (Manchester University Press). In 2016, she took up a Visiting Professional position in Chambers at the International Criminal Court. In 2012–16, she was co-investigator on the European Research Council-funded multidisciplinary research programme 'Corpses of Genocide and Mass Violence'. Her current research focuses on the dual use of forensic evidence in the investigation and prosecution of mass violence crimes on one hand and in the identification of victims and the building of post-atrocity memory on the other. Her publications include *Biolaw and International Criminal Law: Towards Interdisciplinary Synergies* coedited with Professor Anja Matwijkiw (Brill, 2020) and '"Face to Face with Horror": The Tomašica Mass Grave and the Trial of Ratko Mladić' (2020) 6(2) *Human Remains and Violence* 23–41.

Michael G Karnavas is a criminal defence lawyer with over forty years of experience, appearing before state and federal courts in the United States, the International Criminal Tribunal for the Former Yugoslavia, the International Criminal Tribunal for Rwanda, the Extraordinary Chambers in the Courts of Cambodia and the International Criminal Court.

Klearchos A Kyriakides, PhD, MPhil, LLB is a non-practising solicitor in England and Wales as well as a Senior Visiting Fellow in the School of Law of the Cyprus Campus of the University of Central Lancashire, his academic home since 2015. From 2004 until 2015, he was Senior Lecturer at the School of Law of the University of Hertfordshire, where he taught inter alia ethics, professional conduct and regulation. Since 2006, he has been an executive committee member of the West London Law Society, for whom he served as Vice-President from 2008 until 2010 and as President from 2010 until 2011. From 2005 until 2013, he also served as an executive committee member of the Hertfordshire Law Society. His recent publications include 'Survivor-Centered Approaches to Conflict-Related Sexual Violence in International Humanitarian and Human Rights Law' (2022) 24(6) *AMA (American Medical Association) Journal of Ethics* 495–517 (https://doi.org.10.1001/amajethics.2022.495), an article co-written with Andreas K Demetriades, and 'The Akkuyu Nuclear Power Plant in Turkey: Some Causes for Concern' (2023) 25 (3) *Journal of Balkan and Near Eastern Studies* 340–377 (https://doi.org/10.1080/19448953.2022.2143855). He was educated at the universities of Birmingham, Cambridge and Westminster.

Candace McCoy, PhD, JD, is Professor of Criminal Justice at the City University of New York, with appointments at the CUNY Graduate Center and the doctoral programme at John Jay College. Previously, she was on the faculty of Rutgers University – Newark. Professor McCoy specialises in the study of criminal justice policies. A generalist, she teaches and publishes on such topics as bail, police practices, plea bargaining, jury decision-making, sentencing, drug courts and criminal justice ethics. While on leave from teaching duties, she has served in government posts; from

2016 to 2018, she was the Director of Policy Analysis for the Inspector General over the New York City Police Department. Professor McCoy's research on police reform concentrates on the role of law and courts in encouraging community engagement in police accountability. She edited the book *Holding Police Accountable* (Urban Institute Press, 2012) and wrote *How Lawsuits Improve American Policing*, a study of the impact of section 1983 litigation on police practices over the past three decades. She publishes in periodicals such as *Law and Society Review*, the *Journal of Legislation*, and law reviews such as *UCLA Journal of Law and Criminal Justice*. Reforming plea bargaining has been a scholarly and policy concern throughout her career, beginning with publication of *Politics and Plea Bargaining* (University of Pennsylvania Press, 1992) and reports for bar association studies. Professor McCoy is a graduate of the school of law at the University of Cincinnati and is a member of the Ohio bar. She received a doctorate in Jurisprudence and Social Policy from the University of California, Berkeley.

Some points and portions of McCoy's chapter in this volume were also published in the United States as 'The Coercive Trial Penalty: Timing Is Everything' (2022) 35(2) *Federal Sentencing Reporter*.

Barry Mitchell is a former Professor of Criminal Law and Criminal Justice at Coventry University School of Law where he specialised in all aspects of homicide law in England and Wales. He carried out both theoretical and empirical research and worked with government departments such as the Ministry of Justice, the Home Office, the Crown Prosecution Service and the Law Commission. In collaboration with Professor Julian V Roberts (University of Oxford) Professor Mitchell conducted innovative public survey research into murder, manslaughter and the punishment of offenders (see *Exploring the Mandatory Life Sentence for Murder* (Hart, 2012)). His particular interests included the operation of the plea of diminished responsibility in murder cases (in collaboration with Professor RD Mackay), the punishment of the most serious instances of murder, the imposition and review of whole life orders, and the liability of those who cause death through the use of minimal violence. Professor Mitchell retired in 2016.

David Nelken, PhD, LLD is Professor of Comparative and Transnational Law (and a former Vice-Dean and Head of Research) at the Dickson Poon School of Law, King's College London. He is a Fellow of the British Academy and of the UK Academy of Social Sciences. He taught at Cambridge, Edinburgh and University College, London, before moving to Italy in 1989 as Distinguished Professor of Legal Institutions and Social Change at the University of Macerata. From 1995 until 2013 he was Distinguished Research Professor of Law at Cardiff University, and, from 2010 until 2014, Visiting Professor of Criminology at Oxford University.

His work, covering both theoretical enquiry and empirical investigation, is in the areas of comparative sociology of law, criminology, and legal and social theory. Awards he has received include the American Sociological Association Distinguished Scholar Award (1985), the Sellin–Glueck International Award of the American Criminological Society (2009), the Podgorecki Distinguished Senior Scholar Award from the International Sociological Association (2011) and the (US) Law & Society Association's

International Scholar Award (2013). Authored and edited books include *The Limits of the Legal Process* (Academic Press, 1985), *Adapting Legal Cultures* (Hart, 2001, with Johannes Feest), *Beyond the Study of Law in Context* (Ashgate, 2009), *Comparative Criminal Justice: Making Sense of Difference* (Sage, 2010), *Comparative Criminal Justice and Globalisation* (Ashgate, 2011), *Using Legal Culture* (Wildy, Simmonds and Hill, 2012), *Globalisation and Crime* (Ashgate, 2013, with Susanne Karstedt) and the *Elgar Handbook of Comparative Criminal Justice* (Elgar, 2022, with Claire Hamilton).

Tanya Pettay, JD, is a former Senior Legal Consultant for the defence in the case of *Prosecutor v Meas Muth* at the Extraordinary Chambers in the Courts of Cambodia (Case 003). She has previously worked for the Ieng Sary defence team (*Prosecutor v Nuon Chea, Khieu Samphan Ieng Sary and Ieng Thirith*, Case 002). She has also worked for the defence in the case of *Prosecutor v Jadranko Prlić* at the International Criminal Tribunal for the Former Yugoslavia. Ms Pettay is a graduate of Indiana University Maurer School of Law and was admitted to the Bar in Indiana in 2007.

Paul Roberts, BCL, MA (Oxon), MPhil (Cantab), FBA, is Professor of Criminal Jurisprudence at the University of Nottingham School of Law, and an Adjunct Professor of Law at China University of Political Science and Law (CUPL), Beijing. His teaching and research focus on criminal evidence and procedure, incorporating philosophical, sociolegal, international and comparative perspectives and with a strong accent on methodology and interdisciplinarity. His major publications include *Roberts and Zuckerman's Criminal Evidence*, 3rd edn (Oxford University Press, 2022); Roberts and Stockdale (eds), *Forensic Science Evidence and Expert Witness Testimony: Reliability Through Reform?* (Edward Elgar, 2018); Hunter, Roberts, Young and Dixon (eds), *The Integrity of Criminal Process: From Theory into Practice* (Hart, 2016); Roberts (ed), *Theoretical Foundations of Criminal Trial Procedure* (Ashgate, 2014); Roberts and Hunter (eds), *Criminal Evidence and Human Rights: Reimagining Common Law Procedural Traditions* (Hart, 2012); and Roberts and Redmayne (eds), *Innovations in Evidence and Proof: Integrating Theory, Teaching and Research* (Hart, 2007). Roberts has held visiting positions or given keynote conference papers and invited lectures in over twenty countries in Africa, the Americas, Asia, Australasia and Europe, and his work has been translated into Chinese and Spanish. He has also served as consultant to the English and Scottish Law Commissions, the Crown Prosecution Service, and the Forensic Science Regulator.

William Schabas OC, LLD, LLM, LLB, BA, is Professor of International Law at Middlesex University, London, Emeritus Professor of International Human Law and Human Rights at Leiden University, Emeritus Professor of Human Rights Law at the University of Galway, Honorary Chairman of the Irish Centre for Human Rights, and invited visiting scholar at the Paris School of International Affairs (Sciences Po). He is also 'door tenant' at the chambers of 9 Bedford Row, in London.

Professor Schabas is author of one of the principal texts on the subject of genocide (*Genocide in International Law: The Crime of Crimes*, Cambridge University Press, 2009), and his writings have been frequently cited by the Trial and Appeals Chambers of the International Criminal Tribunal for the Former Yugoslavia. His other writings include twenty-one books and more than 350 articles in academic journals, principally in the fields of international criminal law and international human rights law. These include *The Colour Line and the Law of Nations: Racism and Racial Discrimination in the Making of International Law* (Oxford University Press, 2023), *The Customary International Law of Human Rights* (Oxford University Press, 2021), *Introduction to the International Criminal Court* (Cambridge University Press, 2020), *The Abolition of the Death Penalty in International Law* (Cambridge University Press, 2002). He has twice received the Certificate of Merit of the American Society of International Law for his books, *The UN International Criminal Tribunals: Former Yugoslavia, Rwanda and Sierra Leone* (Cambridge University Press, 2006) and *The European Convention on Human Rights: A Commentary* (Oxford University Press, 2015). His writings have been translated into several languages, including Russian, German, Spanish, Portuguese, Chinese, Japanese, Arabic, Persian, Turkish, Nepali and Albanian.

In 2009, Professor Schabas was elected President of the International Association of Genocide Scholars. He was a delegate of the International Centre for Criminal Law Reform and Criminal Justice Policy to the United Nations Diplomatic Conference of Plenipotentiaries on the Establishment of an International Criminal Court, Rome, 15 June–17 July 1998. He has often been invited to participate in international human rights missions on behalf of non-governmental organisations and is the chair and president of the International Institute for Criminal Investigation.

Professor Schabas served as one of three international members of the Sierra Leone Truth and Reconciliation Commission. Professor Schabas has worked as a consultant on capital punishment for the United Nations Office of Drugs and Crime, and drafted the 2010, 2015 and 2020 reports of the Secretary-General on the status of the death penalty.

Professor Schabas was named an Officer of the Order of Canada in 2006. He was elected a member of the Royal Irish Academy in 2007. He has been awarded the Vespasian V Pella Medal for International Criminal Justice of the Association internationale de droit pénal, and the Gold Medal in the Social Sciences of the Royal Irish Academy.

Sten Verhoeven, PhD, LLM, LLB is a member of the Faculty of Law of Hangzhou City University in Hangzhou, China. His research focuses on international criminal law, international humanitarian law, and international constitutionalism. Dr Verhoeven's publications include (with Wouters) 'The Prohibition of Genocide as a Norm of Ius Cogens and its Implications for the Enforcement of the Law of Genocide' [2005] *International Criminal Law Review* 401–16; (with Wouters and DeMeyere) 'The International Criminal Court's Office of the Prosecutor: Navigating between Independence and Accountability' [2008] *International Criminal Law Review* 273–317; (with Wouters) 'The Domestic Prosecution of Genocide' in Behrens and Henham (eds), *Elements of Genocide* (Routledge, 2012). Dr Verhoeven is a graduate of the Katholieke Universiteit Leuven in Belgium.

Stuart Weinstein, MBA, BA, JD, non-practising solicitor and attorney in several US jurisdictions, is Reader in Legal Risk Management at Aston Law School, Aston University, Birmingham where his research interests focus on international business law (with an emphasis on legal risk management, governance and compliance) and the impact of technology on legal practice.

Zhang Yi, PhD in Law, was born in 1990, Xi'an, Shaanxi Province. He graduated from Northwest University of Political Science and Law in 2012 with a bachelor's degree in law. He graduated from the Law School of University of Macau in 2014 and 2019 with master's and doctor's degrees in comparative criminal law. He was a Visiting Scholar at the Max-Planck-Institute for Foreign and International Criminal Law in 2016.

He is currently an Assistant Professor of Criminal Procedure Law at the Northwest University of Political Science and Law, China and Director of the Shaanxi Provincial Criminal Law Society. His research interests include criminal law and criminal procedure law.

He has published five academic papers independently and cooperatively in journals such as the *Journal of National Prosecutors College*, *Criminal Law Review* and the *Bulletin of Faculty of Law of the University of Macau*. He has participated in the writing of two books. He has participated in the Key Project of National Philosophy and Social Science Foundation (Study on the Prevention of Religious Extreme Terrorism (17AFX007)), participated in the Western Project of National Philosophy and Social Science Foundation (Study on the Particularity of the Investigation Method of Trial Evidence in Guilty Plea Cases (20XFX010)) and the University-Procuratorate Cooperation Project (Study on the Standardization of Supplementary Investigation Under the Background of the Integration of Arrest and Prosecution (2020LXJC002)) as a major participant.

Ralph Henham – A Homage*

PAUL BEHRENS

IT IS ONE of the great pleasures of editing a *liber amicorum* that it offers an opportunity to reflect on the achievements of the colleague in whose honour the book is written.

That is an uplifting task. In the case of Ralph Henham, it is aided also by the fact that his research has found reception in the writings of scholars from a wide range of backgrounds and has attracted their respect throughout his career.

1. RALPH HENHAM THROUGH HIS WORKS

The rigour which Henham brought to his work and which would characterise his research throughout the years, was unmistakable even in his early monographs. *Sentencing Principles and Magistrates' Sentencing Behaviour*, which investigates the approaches that magistrates take to the sentencing task and the aspects underlying their decisions, was based on work that had begun a decade before its publication and which involved interviews and questionnaires with 149 magistrates and eleven court clerks.[1] In the literature, the importance of this study was emphasised, with reviewers comparing it to Roger Hood's work on the magistracy in the 1960s.[2] *Sentence Discounts and the Criminal Process*,[3] a book that reflected on the practice relating to guilty pleas with sentence discounts in the Crown Court and the Magistrates' courts, was researched with no less discipline, exploring the transcripts of sentencing remarks by judges in 310 guilty plea cases, and gaining applause for tackling a subject of such significance and for ensuring the cooperation of the courts in this task.[4]

But Henham did not limit himself to the exploration of criminal justice on the domestic plane. In *Transforming International Criminal Justice*,[5] together with Mark

---

*I am indebted to Jonathan Doak, Paul Roberts and Roger Cotterrell for their insightful comments on Ralph Henham's work. All remaining mistakes are, of course, mine.

[1] Ralph Henham, *Sentencing Principles and Magistrates' Sentencing Behaviour* (Aldershot, Avebury, 1990).

[2] Martin Wasik, '*Sentencing Principles and Magistrates' Sentencing Behaviour*. Ralph J Henham. Aldershot: Avebury (1990) [Book Review]' (1991) 30 *Howard Journal of Criminal Justice* 250–51.

[3] Ralph Henham, *Sentence Discounts and the Criminal Process* (Aldershot, Ashgate, 2001).

[4] Richard Young, 'Ralph J Henham, *Sentence Discounts and the Criminal Process*. Ashgate: Aldershot, 2001 [Book Review]' (2003) 7(2) *Edinburgh Law Review* 264, 267–68.

[5] Mark Findlay and Ralph Henham, *Transforming International Criminal Justice: Retributive and Restorative Justice in the Trial Process* (Cullompton, Willan; Abingdon, Routledge, 2005).

Findlay, he set out to examine theoretical models of international criminal justice and proposed the transformation of international criminal trials and the delivery of justice to victim communities through the harmonisation of restorative and retributive justice paradigms to achieve a 'collaborative justice' framework.[6] The authors suggested a repositioning of the role of victims in criminal justice – not only by giving them a greater voice in trial proceedings, but also by introducing more restorative elements into the system, by enhancing the options at its disposal and including consequences that involve stakeholders from various sides to the relevant debate.[7]

It was not only the ambitious aims that set this work aside from its competitors – objectives which were hailed as admirable and laudable[8] – but also its employment of a new method at the core of which was the exploration of local, regional and global contexts to offer a critical examination of the structural, organisational and discretionary levels of the trial process;[9] an approach which was to become known under the name of 'comparative contextual analysis'.[10]

Transforming International Criminal Justice was received with high praise: Williams called it an 'original, extremely thought provoking work' and referred to its use as a source to 'support wider understanding of the principles of retributive and restorative justice' as 'excellent';[11] Sedgwick, in the *International Criminal Law Review*, hailed its meticulous scholarship and noted that the authors' suggestions were 'adaptable and innovative'.[12]

In the same year, Henham published another volume that took international criminal justice as its core concern: *Punishment and Process in International Criminal Trials*.[13] With this, he returned to essential aspects of sentencing and provided a critical analysis of the rationale underlying sentencing considerations on the international plane, but also of the philosophical challenges which punishment for international crimes encounters.[14] The book also raised important questions about the best mechanisms to realise international criminal justice[15] and explored the adequacy of the existing procedures.

Henham's conclusions revealed that many of the traits which have caused grief to scholars of criminology and criminal justice on the domestic level for decades were

---

[6] ibid, in particular at xv, xvii, chs 7 and 8 and see also James Burnham Sedgwick, 'Mark Findlay/Ralph Henham, *Transforming International Criminal Justice: Retributive and Restorative Justice in the Trial Process* [Book Review]' (2007) 7 *International Criminal Law Review* 549, 553.

[7] See Findlay and Henham (n 5), in particular xix, xxx, and chs 7 and 8, and see also Louise Mallinder, '*Transforming International Criminal Justice: Retributive and Restorative Justice in the Trial Process*. By Mark Findlay and Ralph Henham (Cullompton, Willan Publishing, 2005) [Book Review]' (2006) 46 *British Journal of Criminology* 156.

[8] Mallinder (n 7) and see Sedgwick (n 6) 553.

[9] Sedgwick (n 6) 553.

[10] See Findlay and Henham (n 5) in particular at xv, xvii and ch 1.

[11] Dewi Williams, '*Transforming International Criminal Justice, Retributive and Restorative Justice in the Trial Process* by Mark Findlay and Ralph Henham [Book Review]' (2006) 40 *Law Teacher* 366–68, 367–68.

[12] Sedgwick (n 6) 554.

[13] Ralph Henham, *Punishment and Process in International Criminal Trials* (Aldershot, Ashgate, 2005).

[14] ibid, in particular ch 5.

[15] ibid, in particular 10, and ch 8.

all too common on the international plane as well, including the dominating position of retribution as the main rationale for sentencing, with rehabilitation being often relegated to secondary place.[16] But Henham also offered recommendations for the future, such as the adoption of a statement of purposes for sentencing and the development of norms that address victims' concerns,[17] and he argued in favour of an understanding of international sentencing that would make it 'socially responsive, morally sensitive and culturally relevant'.[18]

Reviewers observed that *Punishment and Process* was a book that made a timely contribution to the scholarship in the field[19] and led the reader in a 'logical and coherent procession of argument through the chapters'.[20] The author's extensive employment of material also found praise – not least because he managed, at the same time, to present an accessible overview of the existing literature.[21]

Six years later, there followed a book which may well be considered the magnum opus in Henham's writing – *Sentencing and the Legitimacy of Trial Justice*,[22] a work in which he provided a critical examination of the gap between legitimacy and the sentencing decisions of criminal courts. While the focus in previous monographs had been on criminal justice primarily in a particular legal system, *Sentencing and the Legitimacy of Trial Justice* took a wider perspective and thus offered insights for national criminal courts and for the International Criminal Court (ICC) alike. At the same time, Henham was well aware and took account of the fact that 'very different opinions of what justice should consist of and how it should be delivered' exist in contemporary societies.[23]

The subjects addressed in the book included salient aspects of the criminal justice system, such as the very question of the rationales for punishment[24] and the relationship between victimisation and sentencing (which also explored the question of morality in the context of the understanding of punishment from the perspective of victims);[25] but it also provided an exploration of selected domestic criminal justice systems and the lessons that could be drawn from them, in particular in view of sentencing and public perception.[26]

Henham's conclusions appeared to confirm the fear which the research question foreshadowed: to the degree at least that the aims of punishment and their realisation are not in alignment with what people perceive as justice, a gap between legitimacy

---

[16] See ibid 21.
[17] ibid, in particular 17 and 41; see also Firew Kebede Tiba, 'Ralph Henham: *Punishment and Process in International Criminal Trials* [Book Review]' (2007) 2 *Asian Journal of Criminology* 75.
[18] Henham (n 13) 209.
[19] Tiba (n 17) 77.
[20] Sophie Rigney, '*Punishment and Process in International Criminal Trials*, Ralph Henham, Aldershot: Ashgate Publishing Limited, 2005 [Book Review]' (2006) 25:1 *University of Tasmania Law Review* 100–02, 101.
[21] ibid.
[22] Ralph Henham, *Sentencing and the Legitimacy of Trial Justice* (Abingdon, Routledge, 2011).
[23] ibid 2.
[24] ibid ch 3, and see also 170.
[25] ibid ch 7.
[26] ibid ch 8.

and sentencing decisions seems to exist,[27] leading, where the judiciary is concerned, to a loss of credibility in relation to the administration of justice.[28]

But Henham did not leave his readers without a candle in the dark. Guidance to more promising paths was offered throughout the book; on the one hand, in the shape of references to the significance of a moral legitimacy of the criminal justice system that is derived from social context[29] and, on the other hand, in a call for penal norms to be 'sensitive to maintaining the appropriate balance between social control and subjugation and how this balance is perceived by different social groups and communities'.[30]

Sentencing and the Legitimacy of Trial Justice was hailed as a 'well written, informative' text which offered a 'wealth of comparative and crossdisciplinary assessments'.[31] Reviewers praised the fascinating discussions its chapters offered,[32] and found the argument convincing that responsibility for causes and consequences of criminality should be shared between individuals and communities.[33] The book as a whole was considered an 'insightful analysis of sentencing and public perception',[34] and as 'valuable' and 'thought-provoking'.[35] Doak, writing in *Punishment and Society*, called it a 'primary reference point for those seeking an in-depth analysis of the relationship between legitimacy and sentencing' and highly recommended it 'to criminologists with an interest in punishment theory, as well as to legal academics who seek broader moral and sociological insights into the operation of the penal law'.[36]

At the time of writing, Henham's most recent monograph is *Sentencing Policy and Social Justice*.[37] In this work, he addresses various challenges that arise in sentencing policy and practice in England and Wales and engages in particular with prominent controversies that have emerged in this field – such as those kindled by the sentencing of irregular migrants, sentencing for financial crime and the sentencing of women.

The book offers critical conclusions on contemporary sentencing policy and challenges in particular the view that the current sentencing practice responds adequately to social realities and their impact on criminality and victimisation. The existing strong position of retribution and deterrence in particular led, in the author's view, to the fact that current policy finds it difficult to obtain the legitimacy

---

[27] ibid, particularly at 13, 112, and see also Nicola Padfield, '*Sentencing and the Legitimacy of Trial Justice*, by R. Henham [Book Review]' (2012) 51(5) *Howard Journal of Criminal Justice* 540, 541.

[28] See Henham (n 23), particularly at 22, 110, 112; see also Patrick Webb, '*Sentencing and the Legitimacy of Trial Justice* [Book Review]' (2012) 58(5) *Crime, Law and Social Change* 576.

[29] Henham (n 23), in particular 57, 173, 242 and ch 1.

[30] ibid 316.

[31] Webb (n 28) 577, 578.

[32] See Jonathan Doak, 'Ralph Henham, *Sentencing and the Legitimacy of Trial Justice*. Abingdon: Routledge, 2012 [Book Review]' (2012) 14:5 *Punishment and Society* 626–28, 627.

[33] Padfield (n 27) 541.

[34] Webb (n 28) 578.

[35] Padfield (n 27) 544.

[36] Doak (n 32) 628.

[37] Ralph Henham, *Sentencing Policy and Social Justice* (Oxford, Oxford University Press, Clarendon Studies in Criminology, 2018).

that is required as the basis for support of the law.[38] What is required, he suggests, is an understanding of the values underpinning punishment that allows the State to engage more effectively with the justice needs and the expectations of communities. Henham outlines practical reforms to sentencing, including the suggestion of regional branches of the Sentencing Council that would be able to adapt sentencing to local conditions.[39]

Sentencing Policy and Social Justice, too, received praise for the 'insights and well-judged reflections' that the text contained; Canton, writing in the *Howard Journal of Crime and Justice*, thus noted among its 'most commendable achievements' the fact that it opened up 'questions about what other values sentencing does, and ought to, express and with what effect'.[40]

2. COMMON THEMES IN HENHAM'S RESEARCH

The depth of engagement with which Henham addressed his research is, without doubt, a characterising feature of his entire work and has been recognised as such by reviewers across the years who emphasised his 'rigorous methodology',[41] extensive use of material[42] and 'mastery of [the] research'.[43] One example among many may suffice as an illustration: in *Sentencing and the Legitimacy of Trial Justice*, Henham explored not only the sentencing practices of the International Criminal Tribunal for the Former Yugoslavia, the International Criminal Tribunal for Rwanda, the ICC, the Kosovo Specialist Chambers, the Special Court for Sierra Leone and the East Timor Tribunal, but also included, on the domestic plane, case studies from three different jurisdictions.[44]

It is, at the same time, this very rigour that allowed him to introduce new perspectives without having to fear criticism about potential cracks in the foundations of his arguments. His work was thus lauded for his 'novel framework' of analysis,[45] for the valuable contribution it made to existing literature,[46] and for its original and innovative nature.[47]

It was and is truly pioneering, in more than one respect. What Tiba noted, with regard to the inclusion of restorative themes in the discretionary powers of judges (a topic addressed in *Punishment and Process*) holds true for other fields as well:

---

[38] ibid, eg 83, 168, 201 and see also Rob Canton, '*Sentencing Policy and Social Justice* (Clarendon Studies in Criminology) R. Henham. Oxford: Oxford University Press (2018) [Book Review]' (2019) 58(1) *Howard Journal of Crime and Justice* 129, 130.

[39] Henham (n 37) 12–14, 21 and ch 7.

[40] Canton (n 38) 130.

[41] Sedgwick (n 6) 554.

[42] Rigney (n 20) 101.

[43] Williams (n 11) 367.

[44] Henham (n 22), in particular chs 3 and 6 regarding international criminal courts and tribunals, and see ch 8 for comparisons with national jurisdictions outside England and Wales.

[45] Rigney (n 20) 101.

[46] Doak (n 32) 628.

[47] See Williams (n 11) 367; Sedgwick (n 6) 554.

Henham's 'work sets a future agenda'[48] which scholars in the field may well find worth pursuing. It was pioneering also with regard to the consideration of values – '[m]ost discussions' in criminal law, as Canton remarked, are limited to those values expressed in the law, at the expense of other values that 'bind us as a society', yet in *Sentencing Policy and Social Justice*, Henham opened up the discussion to include those 'other values' that sentencing does or should express.[49] And Doak, writing about *Sentencing and the Legitimacy of Trial Justice*, commented that the questions explored were 'fundamental' yet relatively rarely addressed in detail by commentators to date: '[c]ertainly', he added, 'none have done so in such a holistic and thorough manner as Henham' who advanced the case for closer examination of the moral and social context of sentencing by law and policymakers.[50]

The life of a pioneer is not always easy – all too often, those who spearhead new approaches have to contend with criticism based on little more than the fact that colleagues are not quite prepared to leave their comfort zones. Henham was somewhat more fortunate in that regard – to the degree at least that his innovative efforts received appreciation by colleagues who acknowledged the shortcomings manifested in traditional approaches[51] but also understood that Henham was the right person to address the matters subjected to examination. Padfield speaks for many when she highlights this particular aspect with regard to the relationship between diverse fields of criminal justice: 'too long', she noted, 'many of us who are engaged with the study of domestic criminal justice have ignored what has been going on in the world of international criminal justice, and the opposite is also true', before concluding that 'Ralph Henham stands in that rare place: a scholar, whose work spans these two very different worlds, and who can with credibility use examples from both the international and the domestic context to develop an important argument for both.'[52] Credibility is the essential word: Henham's own background and scholarship made him eminently qualified to be a wanderer between the worlds – not only between different criminal justice systems, but even between academic disciplines (on this, more below).

From an early stage, reviewers also noted the accessible manner in which his research was presented.[53] The topics he addresses are, by their very nature, complex, and that makes it all the more remarkable that he managed to convey them in an engaging way to a wide readership – often with the help of narrative or bullet-point summaries, with diagrams and, in particular, through the use of examples from areas with which readers could claim familiarity or case studies which were fascinating in their own right. Plea bargaining was thus employed to demonstrate challenges that arise in the application of fairness in trial justice,[54] the harsh sentences given to participants in riots that took place in England in 2011 to illuminate questions of estrangement

---

[48] Tiba (n 17) 76.

[49] Canton (n 38) 129.

[50] Doak (n 32) 628.

[51] See Sedgwick (n 6) 554 on the question of context.

[52] Padfield (n 27) 540.

[53] See Paul Cooper, '*Sentencing Principles and Magistrates Sentencing Behaviour*, by Ralph Henham, Gower, 1990 [Book Review]' (1991) 13 *Liverpool Law Review* 99, 100.

[54] Henham (n 22), in particular ch 5.

and discrimination,[55] the rebuilding of the Mostar Bridge in Bosnia-Herzegovina in illustration of the 'holistic sharing of moral consciousness'.[56]

In conjunction with the commitment to a clear and disciplined structure which has been a hallmark of Henham's work throughout the years, these are features whose helpfulness in guiding the reader through the topics at hand has found appreciation within the academic community.[57]

Where the subject matter is concerned, one would not go far wrong by observing that the interrelationship between society and the criminal justice system as well as the dialogue between societal values and judicial decisions, and in particular between decision-makers and community expectations in the sentencing process, forms a prevailing concern of Henham's work. Attention to social inclusiveness is frequently at the core of this, a factor that allows the repositioning of sentencing policy to include options that advance not only interests of disadvantaged minorities but social equality in general. The right of victims in particular, the importance of the representation of their interests in the judicial process and of judicial options that allow the voice of victims to be heard, are features that occupy positions of particular importance in his writings.

At the same time, he does not lose sight of human rights considerations and the place they merit in penological analysis. In that regard, in championing a rights-based methodology for the analysis of the sentencing process in lieu of the more traditional 'crime control' and 'due process' models, Henham's approach – advocated by him more than twenty years ago[58] – can again, without exaggeration, lay claim to the title of a truly pioneering initiative.

In scrutinising the judicial rationale behind sentencing, further considerations emerge that constitute common themes. An essential place is occupied here by a reiterated critique of the retributive approach that so often characterises sentencing both in the domestic and the international context.[59] The manifest shortcomings of retributivism apart,[60] what Henham's work reveals is also the negative force that an exclusionary focus on this rationale exerts on the development of criminal justice in general[61] and its counterproductive effects on the acquisition of legitimacy and on the required engagement with the social realities[62] as well as, at the international level, on the promotion of peace and reconciliation.[63]

Rather, however, than proposing a 'silver bullet' solution by claiming an inherent superiority of one rationale over another, Henham's solutions are based on the realities of sentencing considerations and their social perception – advocating, for instance, in *Transforming International Criminal Justice*, a model that relies on the harmonisation of restorative and retributive justice within the international criminal trial process.[64]

---

[55] Henham (n 37), in particular 71–84.
[56] Henham (n 22) 143.
[57] See Williams (n 11) 367; Rigney (n 20) 101.
[58] See Ralph Henham, 'Human Rights, Due Process and Sentencing' (1998) 38(4) *British Journal of Criminology* 592–610.
[59] See at n 16 above. See also Tiba (n 17) 75.
[60] See on this also Paul Behrens, 'Criminal Justice in an Age of Uncertainty' (ch 17 in this volume).
[61] Findlay and Henham (n 5) in particular 255, 257, chs 7 and 8; and see also Mallinder (n 7) 157.
[62] See above at n 38.
[63] See Henham (n 13), in particular 97 and 100. See also Tiba (n 17) 75.
[64] See Findlay and Henham (n 5), in particular xiv, 281, 313, and see above at n 6.

Throughout his publications, Henham's work also testifies to its author's refusal to be restricted by arbitrary (but traditionally accepted) limitations of one academic perspective or one particular jurisdiction – and indeed, to his capacity to recognise the dangers that such parochialism brings in its train. His work adopts a comparative approach – most clearly perhaps in *Sentencing and the Legitimacy of Trial Justice*, in which important insights are gained from sentencing practice and considerations in France and Italy,[65] but also in his earlier articles on victim participation in England and Italy.[66] But his writings also reach beyond the consideration of related issues in diverse national jurisdictions: one factor that makes works such as *Sentencing and the Legitimacy of Trial Justice* and *Transforming International Criminal Justice* truly unique is the fact that they deliberately include domestic as well as international perspectives and critically explore the insights that, especially with regard to considerations underlying decision-making in criminal justice, either system offers for the other.[67]

From the vantage point of academic categorisation, an interdisciplinary approach has always been a key aspect of Henham's considerations, and his writings attest in particular to the incorporation of insights that a sociological perspective can bring to the field of criminal justice and penology. It is a welcome change from existing approaches: the incorporation of analyses of scholars from the field of sociology amounts to a holistic procedure which one reviewer of *Punishment and Process in International Criminal Trials* appreciated as 'refreshing'.[68] But it was more than that. Where sentencing is concerned, which is so intimately related to the message that criminal law disseminates to victims and perpetrators, to perpetrator subgroups, victim communities and society as a whole, the argument may well be advanced that neither the cognitive processes underlying sentencing decisions nor the effects of sentencing can be adequately approached from the perspective of one discipline alone, and that sociology, more than many other fields, is eminently suited to render an appropriate understanding of the challenges that arise and to offer apposite critique to decision-making in the area of criminal justice.

It also meant that the appeal of Henham's work went beyond that of writings targeted at one particular group of readers alone. Reviewers have thus noted the helpfulness of his work to scholars and analysts alike,[69] and it is clear that the insights gained from his research benefit in equal measure practitioners at domestic as well as international criminal courts and tribunals, but also academics (and students new to their relevant disciplines) who approach the criminal justice process from a range of perspectives, including law, sociology, history and politics.

---

[65] Henham (n 22) ch 8; see also Padfield (n 27) 543 and Webb (n 28) 577.

[66] See Ralph Henham and Grazia Mannozzi, 'Victim Participation and Sentencing in England and Italy: A Legal and Policy Analysis' (2003) 11(3) *European Journal of Crime, Criminal Law and Criminal Justice* 278–317 and Ralph Henham and Grazia Mannozzi, 'Il ruolo delle vittime nel processo penale e nella commisurazione della pena: un'analisi delle scelte normative e politico-criminali effettuate nell'ordinamento inglese e in quello italiano' (2005) 2 *Rivista Italiana di diritto e procedura penale* 706–38.

[67] See Henham (n 44). For domestic perspectives in Findlay and Henham (n 5) see, in particular, 201–14.

[68] Rigney (n 20) 100.

[69] Cooper (n 53) 100.

Not every writer could have addressed such a wide range of topics, across diverse jurisdictions and from the perspectives of various disciplines, in a convincing manner. Henham was exactly the right person to do it. His academic and professional training and his extensive work in the field made him eminently qualified to engage in this task – he was as much at home in the field of legal scrutiny as in sociological analysis. Rigney had a point when she noted that 'theorists may be wary of extending beyond their field of specialty', while highlighting the expertise that Henham possesses in the field of sociology of law.[70] And Canton's verdict can stand for the views of many: 'Ralph Henham', he wrote, 'combines the rigour of a legal scholar with the critical and discursive reflections of a social scientist to consider the relationship between sentencing and social justice.'[71] At a time which knows of institutional pressures to abandon the ideal of *universitas* in favour of the myopic focus on ever more minute specialisation, this is a compliment that cannot apply to many.

3. RECOGNITION AND COOPERATION

In light of these achievements it is, perhaps, not surprising that Henham's work was recognised by academic and professional bodies and exerted a clear influence on the development of criminal law.

It was cited in case law – in England, for instance, the High Court referred in the case of *Gemmell v HM Advocate* to his 1999 article 'Bargain Justice or Justice Denied?', which engaged with the relationship between sentence discounts and the criminal process.[72] Ten years earlier, the Constitutional Court of South Africa had already made reference, in *S v Dodo*, to *Criminal Justice and Sentencing Policy*, a monograph in which Henham had investigated sentencing powers and the considerations underlying them with regard to a range of crucial areas, including drug offences, white-collar crime, violent crime, dangerous offenders and offenders with mental health conditions.[73]

In the academic field, Henham has held numerous visiting positions at universities within and outside the United Kingdom, including as Visiting Fellow at the Centre for Criminology at the University of Oxford in 2007; as Visiting Scholar at the University of Cambridge in 2010 and from 2015 to 2016 and at the Washington and Lee University School of Law in 2013; as International Visiting Research Fellow at the University of Sydney in 2008; as Visiting Professor at the University of Sussex from 2012 to 2015; and as Visiting Lecturer at the University of Loughborough from 1990 to 1992.

---

[70] Rigney (n 20) 101.

[71] Canton (n 38) 130.

[72] *Gemmell v HM Advocate* 2012 JC 223, para 45 (per Lord Justice-Clerk Gill), with reference to Ralph Henham, 'Bargain Justice or Justice Denied? Sentence Discounts and the Criminal Process' (1999) 62(4) *MLR* 515.

[73] *S v Dodo* (South Africa, Constitutional Court), Judgment, 5 April 2001, 2001 (5) BCLR 423 (CC) (per Ackermann J), with reference to Ralph Henham, *Criminal Justice and Sentencing Policy* (Dartmouth, Aldershot 1996) 9–10 and 131.

Recognition also came through membership in scholarly organisations, such as the European Society of Criminology Working Groups on Sentencing and Penal Decision-Making (from 2011) and on Restorative Justice (from 2019), the Centre for Rights and Justice at Nottingham Trent University (from 2013), Associate Membership of the Criminal Justice Research Centre of Nottingham University (from 2014) and Council Membership of the Society of Public Teachers of Law (1997–2002). In 2017, he was made a Fellow of the Royal Society of Arts.

A particular aspect which many of Ralph Henham's colleagues came to cherish was his significant capacity to engage in scholarly cooperation, an ability that manifested itself in research initiatives, joint funding projects and in the publication of scholarly works based on joint efforts. Such cooperation extended not only to colleagues already established in the field, but also to those relatively new to academia, to whom he gave generously of his time and counsel.

Nor were such efforts 'one-off pieces' whose impact was limited to the particular publication – they did, instead, continue to inform his thinking and writing on the relevant areas of criminal justice, and those who had toiled with him on previous works could often find themselves credited in later works that took into account insights gained in these earlier stages. His work with Grazia Mannozzi at the University of Insubria on victim participation and sentencing is an example: its direct outcome were two articles, one published in English, the other in Italian,[74] but reference to it was also made in *Punishment and Process in International Criminal Trials*, where questions arising from these matters emerged in the context of comparisons between Italian and English criminal justice processes.[75]

His cooperation with Mark Findlay, similarly, led not only to an article and a book chapter,[76] but also to two co-written books, of which the latter – *Beyond Punishment* – was nominated for the SLS Hart Socio-Legal Book Prize in 2011.[77]

And in the field of restorative justice, his work with Jonathan Doak and Barry Mitchell resulted in a 2009 article in which the authors explored several matters arising from the decision to roll out the 'Victims' Focus Scheme' across England and Wales and the difficulty of accommodating victims' interests within the framework of the adversarial system.[78]

Henham's considerable editorial work resulted in cooperation with a larger range of scholars and practitioners. His credentials in this field are impressive and embrace numerous positions on editorial boards of journals – including membership of the

---

[74] See Ralph Henham and Grazia Mannozzi (2003) (n 66) and Ralph Henham and Grazia Mannozzi (2005) (n 66).

[75] See Henham (n 13), in particular 68–70, 215, 217–19.

[76] Ralph Henham and Mark Findlay, 'Criminal Justice Modelling and the Comparative Contextual Analysis of Trial Process' (2002) 2 *International Journal of Comparative Criminology* 162; Mark Findlay and Ralph Henham, 'Integrating Theory and Method in the Comparative Contextual Analysis of Trial Process' in M McConville and WH Chui (eds), *Research Methods for Law* (Edinburgh, Edinburgh University Press, 2007).

[77] Findlay and Henham (n 5) and Mark Findlay and Ralph Henham, *Beyond Punishment: Achieving International Criminal Justice* (Basingstoke, Palgrave Macmillan, 2010). The authors also published an edited book, see below (n 79).

[78] Ralph Henham, Jonathan Doak and Barry Mitchell, 'Victims and the Sentencing Process: Developing Participatory Rights?' (2009) 29 *Legal Studies* 651.

editorial advisory group of the *Howard Journal of Criminal Justice* from 2000 to 2012, membership of the editorial board of the *International Journal of the Sociology of Law* (now *International Journal of Law, Crime and Justice*) from 1998 to 2022, as well as the series editorship (with Findlay) of the International and Comparative Criminal Justice series of Routledge (from 2004). His co-editorship of three books also gave him the opportunity to select and work directly with a wide range of talent, from academia and practice alike, from early researchers to scholars of long standing.[79] *The Criminal Law of Genocide* (2007) provides an illustration. It was a book whose outlook was deliberately broad – both regarding the subject area and the background of its contributors. It investigated the crime of genocide from historical perspectives, but also analysed case studies, aspects of the crime, its international and domestic prosecution as well as questions of prevention, alternative justice solutions and sentencing.

For this, the editors brought together twenty-four authors who were scholars, judges, practising lawyers and activists and included some of the most prominent names in the field. On the history of the crime, Henry T. King, a former Nuremberg Prosecutor, provided an engaging discussion of the treatment of genocide at Nuremberg, in which he also reflected on meeting Raphael Lemkin, the creator of the word 'genocide'.[80] Roméo Dallaire, former head of the United Nations Assistance Mission for Rwanda at the time when the atrocities against the Tutsis in that country began, co-wrote a chapter on the major powers and the Rwandan genocide;[81] Tuiloma Neroni Slade, a former Presiding Judge of Pre-Trial Chamber II of the ICC, contributed an analysis of the prohibition of genocide within the ICC framework,[82] and Juan E. Méndez, the first UN Special Adviser on the Prevention of Genocide, examined the United Nations' role in the prevention of genocide.[83]

The wide remit of the book and the extensive range of its authors account for much of the praise the work received. Swatek-Evenstein thus commented on the 'highly readable selection of engaging views by scholars as well as practitioners on the crime of genocide';[84] Sloan on the 'remarkable variety of areas' and the fascinating issues the book explored;[85] Khemoni noted the 'thorough approach' which it took and found that,

---

[79] Ralph Henham and Paul Behrens, *The Criminal Law of Genocide: International, Comparative and Contextual Aspects* (Aldershot, Ashgate, 2007); Ralph Henham and Mark Findlay, *Exploring the Boundaries of International Criminal Justice* (Aldershot, Ashgate, 2011); Paul Behrens and Ralph Henham, *Elements of Genocide* (Abingdon, Routledge, 2012).

[80] Henry T King Jr, 'Genocide and Nuremberg', in Henham and Behrens (n 79) 29–35.

[81] Roméo Dallaire and Kishan Manocha, 'The Major Powers and the Genocide in Rwanda' in Henham and Behrens (n 79) 61–71.

[82] Tuiloma Neroni Slade, 'The Prohibition of Genocide under the Legal Instruments of the International Criminal Court' in Henham and Behrens (n 79) 155–64.

[83] Juan E Méndez, 'The United Nations and the Prevention of Genocide' in Henham and Behrens (n 79) 225–30.

[84] Mark Swatek-Evenstein, '*The Criminal Law of Genocide: International, Comparative and Contextual Aspects*. Ralph Henham and Paul Behrens (eds.) [Book Review]' (2009) 11(4) *Journal of Genocide Research* 516–19, 516.

[85] J Sloan, 'Review of *The Criminal Law of Genocide: International, Comparative and Contextual Aspects*, by Ralph Henham and Paul Behrens (Eds.)' (2008) 18(5) *Law and Politics Book Review* 444–48, 447.

due to its interdisciplinary analyses, it would 'appeal to not only legal practitioners but also to policy-makers, historians, academics and scholars'[86] (it has, in fact, since then been adopted as a textbook on university courses on genocide). Henham's own chapter was praised as a 'careful and scholarly legal discussion of the difficult and controversial sentencing procedures of the ad hoc tribunals in the context of genocide'.[87]

4. CONCLUSION

Any attempt to mirror the life and work of a person whose scholarly achievement extends to such a vast range of academic fields and jurisdictions is a challenging task. Even this volume, largely limited to the legal aspects of the criminal justice system, cannot hope to embrace all the areas which are reflected in Henham's work just within these parameters.

The fact, however, that authors from the theory of the criminal justice system, from domestic, transnational and international perspectives have come together to engage, in honour of Ralph Henham, with aspects that extend from questions of public morality and sentencing to the criminal justice system of the former Soviet Union, from the strict liability system of the Office of Foreign Asset Control of the United States to the feasibility of a universal criminal code, tells a story in itself. Many authors contributed to works edited by Henham in the past, others are friends and colleagues with whom he engaged in an exchange of scholarly ideas over the years, in private settings as well as expert meetings, and none had to be asked twice when first approached with the idea of a *liber amicorum*. In that regard, Henham's great capacity to engage in scholarly cooperation also translates into a capacity to inspire joint initiatives of this nature; but one ventures to guess that there is another aspect that is at the root of such willingness to honour him as a scholar and friend.

It is certainly true that, in his reflections on the criminal justice systems, Henham did not shy away from criticism where he felt that it was merited. But his look went to the future as well; and he provided suggestions to address the prevailing problems – as apparent in his calls for social justice to be a key objective of sentencing policy, for a balancing of retributive and reconciliatory demands,[88] for a better understanding of the connection between trial justice and its actual effects,[89] for a sharing of responsibility of the causes and consequences of criminality between individuals and communities,[90] but also in rather more specific recommendations, such as the suggestion of principles for sentencing purposes in international criminal justice[91] and the use of regional branches of the Sentencing Council to adapt policy to locally prevailing conditions.[92]

---

[86] Melissa Khemoni, '*The Criminal Law of Genocide: International, Comparative and Contextual Aspects*. Ralph Henham and Paul Behrens (Eds) [Book Review]' (2008) 34(4) *Commonwealth Law Bulletin* 941, 943.

[87] Sloan (n 85) 447.

[88] Henham (n 13), in particular 23, 130–31, 197.

[89] Henham (n 22) 295; see also Padfield (n 27) 243.

[90] Henham (n 22) 3.

[91] Henham (n 13), in particular 17 and 41; see also Tiba (n 17) 75.

[92] See above at n 39.

That is not the perspective of a scholar who has given up on criminal justice. On the contrary, what shines through his work is an irrepressibly positive message in the face of the sometimes daunting challenges and deficiencies of the contemporary criminal justice system. Nor are we the only ones to notice that – reviewers have indeed referred to his works as optimistic;[93] and Canton, writing about his views on the required (and suggested) link between sentencing practices and 'common good' values, values that benefit everybody, notes that his considerations are 'all the more salient in times of cynical political populism and a "post-truth" era'.[94] Salient, too, is his message of hope and encouragement. It is this which provides ample explanation for the desire of his friends to honour him – and for harbouring, perhaps, the wish, that, especially in times in which the ideal of criminal justice has come under attack from so many sides, the example of Ralph Henham's life and work may serve as an inspiration to others.

[93] Tiba (n 17) 76.
[94] Canton (n 38) 130.

Part 1

Introduction and Foundations

1

Challenges to Contemporary Criminal Justice

PAUL BEHRENS

1. INTRODUCTION

T HE MISCHIEFS WHICH inform criminal law today appear to be children of the new millennium. Previous generations did not have to deal with cybercrime, with biometric fraud or (at least to the same degree) with crimes against the environment and protected species. On the international level, the long history of certain crimes would be difficult to deny, but permanent structures to interpret their elements and to evaluate the conduct of defendants came into place only with the establishment of the International Criminal Court (ICC). Similarly, corruption and transnational organised crime are by no means new manifestations, but treaties of transnational criminal law to address them on a universal basis were concluded only at the beginning of this century.

The way in which criminal law interacts with those who have to engage with its rules likewise shows features that at first sight appear to be wedded to the modern age. The conflict, for instance, between the wish to take into account the demands of constituents lobbying for new crimes or harsher sentences and the legal requirement of proportionality could only have emerged in the age of representative democracy and has been given added impetus through the rise of activist groups and social media. At the same time, the proliferation of crimes that stands at the end of that process develops its own impact on the perception of criminal law by the general public, leading to an increasing difficulty on the part of individuals to gauge what exactly is required of them, but also to an intensified alienation of society from the mandates devised by the drafters of the law. Nor is the task of the legal profession made easier by these developments: apart from the additional burden that they place on traditional methods of interpretation, the voice of other systems that may have an impact on the same situation – in particular, human rights law – increases the difficulties that inhabit the construction of the law today.

And yet, once contemporary challenges are subjected to closer analysis, their appearance as entirely modern phenomena invites repositioning: in many instances, the finding appears justified that their precursors can be traced to earlier ages.

The scholars at the court of Hammurabi did not have to concern themselves with computer hacking. But it is not the creation of a new crime that causes challenges. The aspects that often give cause for debate – the question, say, whether a new law is still sufficiently accessible, or questions about its moral foundations, including the subjectivity inherent in that concept and the possibility of diachronic splits in its assessment – are older than that.

If the genesis of seemingly modern challenges is reduced to its foundations, it often will have to be concluded that they are rooted in the very nature of the law itself, in what makes the crime a crime. What gives them a modern veneer is the shape they receive in the contemporary age and the extent to which some of these elementary aspects have been allowed to manifest themselves.

Three challenges in particular appear to fall in this category, and it seems apposite to consider them within the framework of the characteristics which the concept of criminal law itself dictates. They relate to the regulatory nature of the law, to its reflection of moral values and to its discriminatory character, where 'discrimination' is understood in the original sense of the term, ie relating to the performance of distinctions along the lines of specific parameters. The result cannot strive to offer an exhaustive list of contemporary challenges, but it highlights aspects of criminal law which, while finding their origins in the very nature of the system, have attained particular pertinence in recent years.

2. THE CHALLENGES

2.1. Criminal Law as a Regulatory Mechanism

The understanding of crime, in the old Halsbury definition, as 'an unlawful act or default which is an offence against the public [and which] renders the person guilty of the act or default liable to legal punishment',[1] has, in its emphasis on the interrelationship between crime and societal interests, lost little of its force. Contemporary scholars are likewise keen to underline this aspect of the concept of crime;[2] and the European Court of Human Rights (ECtHR), when assessing whether charges brought against a person were criminal charges in the meaning of Article 6(1) of the European Convention on Human Rights (ECHR) will take into account whether the relevant matters concern 'general interests of society, usually protected by criminal law'.[3]

It is, however, this very aspect that must be considered to be at the root of some of the most tangible problems which the criminal justice system and those subjected to its application face today. With its availability as a tool for social regulation, the State has at its disposal a mechanism that appears to provide a suitable remedy for

---

[1] Earl of Halsbury et al, *Laws of England: Being a Complete Statement of the Whole Law of England* (London, Butterworth & Co, 1909) 232.
[2] See David Ormerod and Karl Laird, *Smith and Hogan's Criminal Law*, 14th edn (Oxford, Oxford University Press, 2015) 5.
[3] ECtHR, *Produkcija Plus Storitveno Podjetje DOO v Slovenia* (Appl No 47072/15), Judgment, 23 October 2018, para 42.

a large number of societal problems, and there is evidence that it is seen as such not only by parts of public and the media, but by legislators as well. The understanding of criminal law as a panacaea is arguably more pronounced today than it has ever been.

Stories of overzealous legislators make headlines on a regular basis,[4] and with good reason: laws (passed by the Westminster Parliament) which prohibit the sale of grey squirrels[5] or entry into the hull sections of the Titanic[6] do, at the very least, raise the question whether the legislative aim could not have been achieved through measures other than criminalisation. In spite of the ridicule that such efforts evoke, criminal law has lost none of its popularity as a regulatory instrument: towards the end of the New Labour administration in the United Kingdom, it was reported that in excess of 3,600 crimes had been enacted in the Blair and Brown years;[7] the total number of crimes estimated to be on the statute books stood, in 2015, at more than 10,000 offences – '[n]ot including the thousands of bye-laws created at a local level'.[8] Not including, also, common law offences that never received codification.

This inflation of crimes invites paradoxical consequences. The adoption of new offences may well correspond to a (perceived) societal need for regulation; but the frequent resort to criminal law to address societal problems[9] may disadvantage the constituency whom this approach is meant to benefit. Green, talking about the multiplication of narrowly defined offences, notes with some justification that 'greater specificity also has its costs' and that 'the greater the number of offenses, the more complicated the Code becomes and the greater the amount of cognitive resources that must be expended on it'.[10]

It is a challenge which translates into human rights concerns as well. In its interpretation of Article 7 ECHR (*nullum crimen sine lege*), the ECtHR clarified that it understood the concept of law to imply certain 'qualitative requirements, notably those of accessibility and foreseeability'.[11] Yet even if each of the newly minted offences were specific enough to 'enable individuals to regulate their conduct',[12] their sheer number makes it increasingly likely that their addressees will be caught by a normative prohibition which had not been foreseeable for them.

That far, the law seems uncharitable towards defendants wishing to claim ignorance in this respect. The ECtHR at any rate observed that a law is not deprived of

---

[4] See eg Nigel Morris, 'Blair's "Frenzied Law Making": A New Offence for Every Day Spent in Office', *Belfast Telegraph*, 16 August 2006.

[5] See s 14ZA(1)(a) in conjunction with Sch 9, Wildlife and Countryside Act 1981, c 69.

[6] Art 6(1) in conjunction with Art 4 Protection of Wrecks (RMS Titanic) Order 2003, SI 2003/2496.

[7] Nigel Morris, 'More than 3,600 New Offences under Labour', *Independent*, 4 September 2008.

[8] Ormerod and Laird (n 2) 3 and n 2. Similar developments can be observed in other jurisdictions as well, see eg William J Stuntz, 'The Pathological Politics of Criminal Law' (2001) 100 *Michigan Law Review* 505, 508 and Stuart Weinstein, 'OFAC's Strict Liability Regime: Blackstone and Holmes Were Right' (ch 8 in this volume) at n 53.

[9] See also AP Simester, JP Spencer, F Stark, GR Sullivan and GJ Virgo, *Simester and Sullivan's Criminal Law*, 6th edn (Oxford, Hart, 2016) 21.

[10] Stuart P Green, 'Prototype Theory and the Classification of Offenses in a Revised Model Penal Code: A General Approach to the Special Part' (2000) 4 *Buffalo Criminal Law Review* 301, 312.

[11] ECtHR, *Cantoni v France* (Appl No 17862/91), Judgment, 11 November 1996, para 29.

[12] ECtHR, *Bakir v Turkey* (Appl No 46713/10), Judgment 10 July 2018, para 53.

the above-named qualities even if a person has to take 'appropriate legal advice' to ascertain its requirements.[13] Yet at a time when 'not all crimes are readily identifiable even to the lawyer',[14] this qualification seems to make a mockery of the requirement of foreseeability.

International criminal law had courted its own problems in this regard – due, in particular, to the fact that, for long periods of its history, it had to rely on customary international law and thus on a source that can be vague, difficult to access and possessed of ill-defined boundaries. But within the last generation – through the adoption of the Statute of the ICC – it witnessed a considerable effort at reform, from whose insights domestic law can benefit.

The ICC Statute may invite criticism too, and from opposing corners at that. It seems too narrow, because it does not include classic crimes such as piracy or more contemporary crimes like ecocide. It seems too extensive, because of its unwieldy Article 8, which includes more than fifty individual war crimes. At the same time, it brings all offences which the Prosecution can charge under one roof, within the four corners of one and the same Statute. Each crime has its particular, well-specified characteristics, which are accessible through the Statute itself and through the Elements of Crimes, the authoritative commentary to the crimes under the jurisdiction of the Court.

That does not mean that all difficulties relating to the application of the principle of *nullum crimen sine lege* have disappeared. The recent *Ongwen* case, in which the defendant was charged inter alia with the crime of forced marriage and in which the Trial Chamber agreed to subsume this under the more general category of 'other crimes against humanity',[15] shows that reliance on customary international law and the debate it invites in relation to foreseeability and accessibility have not entirely disappeared. By and large, however, the drafters of the ICC Statute have managed to respect the concerns that had arisen in relation to other institutions of international criminal law and thus presented a code which, in its comprehensive and accessible nature, reflects a drafting effort which other jurisdictions may find worthy of emulation.

2.2. Criminal Law and Morality

The second characteristic of criminal law to which reference has been made above relates to the fact that it gives expression to moral sentiments; that crime, in the words of Henry Hart, is conduct which incurs 'a formal and solemn pronouncement of the moral condemnation of the community'.[16]

---

[13] *Cantoni* (n 11) para 35.
[14] Ormerod and Laird (n 2) 3.
[15] See ICC (Trial Chamber), *Prosecutor v Dominic Ongwen*, ICC-02/04-01/15, Judgment, 4 February 2021, paras 2747–2748, 3116.
[16] Henry M Hart Jr, 'The Aims of the Criminal Law' (1958) 23 *Law & Contemporary Problems* 401, 405.

The validity of this understanding has attracted doubt. In that regard, Ormerod and Laird point out that some forms of conduct attract sanction under the criminal justice system for reasons of 'social expediency and not because of their immoral nature' and go so far as to conclude that the 'test of immorality is not a very helpful one in seeking to identify *universal* characteristics of a crime'.[17]

A distinction along the lines of immorality and 'social expediency' is tempting where certain crimes are concerned – the above named examples of selling grey squirrels and entering the Titanic[18] appear to fall squarely in the latter category. But it is difficult to escape the conclusion that such an allocation is ultimately an arbitrary choice. Endangering historical monuments or wilfully introducing invasive species may, after all, be seen as immoral choices by sections of society. Even the consideration of the criminal legal system per se as embodying moral values cannot easily be dismissed. It is that understanding which not only informed the system of natural law, but which still survives in commonly employed phrases like those of the 'sanctity of the law' or of 'law-abiding citizens' which, it is submitted, encompass more than references to an accepted code of purely administrative character.

It may be recalled, also, that, as late as 1999, the ECtHR had to decide a case, brought against the United Kingdom, in which conduct *contra bonos mores* was at the core of the relevant domestic law; behaviour which case law had helpfully defined as conduct with the property of being 'wrong rather than right in the judgment of the majority of contemporary fellow citizens'.[19] That could not only have encompassed the entire breadth of criminal law, but, in so doing, the law employed the very etymon (*mos*) of the word 'moral'. Such considerations blur the boundary between so-called *mala prohibita* and *mala in se* and highlight the artificiality of distinctions along these lines.

But criminal law as a moral construct invites challenges which still persist. The fact that the understanding of morals is subject to temporal parameters is well known, and current developments substantiate this observation. Germany which, as late as 1994, criminalised certain same-sex activities,[20] became in 2020 one of the first European States to criminalise conversion 'treatment' – ie practices that seek to change or suppress a person's sexual orientation or gender identity.[21] Such changes in moral perceptions seem to be part of the natural evolution of criminal law, and there is good reason to welcome them when they lead to a better alignment of domestic law with human rights mandates, as was certainly the case in this particular matter.[22]

---

[17] Ormerod and Laird (n 2) 8–9 (emphasis in original).

[18] See above at nn 5 and 6.

[19] See on this ECtHR, *Hashman and Harrup v The United Kingdom* (Appl No 25594/94), Judgment, 25 November 1999, para 13.

[20] S 175 of the German Criminal Code, which initially outlawed male homosexual acts in general, underwent several revisions. By 1994, it still enshrined an age of consent for male same-sex activities that was higher than that for heterosexual acts. See JMT Labuschangne, 'Sexual Orientation, Sexual Autonomy and Discrimination in Definition of Crime' (1996) 12 *South African Journal on Human Rights* 321. Strafgesetzbuch, 13 November 1998 (BGBl I/3322).

[21] See ss 1 and 2 Gesetz zum Schutz vor Konversionsbehandlungen, 12 June 2020 (BGBl I/1285).

[22] See, on the impact of conversion practices on the human rights of the victims, Independent Expert on Protection against Violence and Discrimination Based on Sexual Orientation and Gender Identity,

But the pendulum can, of course, swing the other way. That States would seek to employ a seemingly altered perception of morality as a basis for legislative changes to restrict human rights is not hypothetical – especially in cases in which the allegation is advanced that the security of the State itself is in danger. The evaluation of 'Extinction Rebellion' – a movement that demonstrates against climate change – by British authorities in 2019 illustrates that point. After, in April of that year, Extinction Rebellion had caused obstruction to traffic in London,[23] several of its members were charged with public order offences,[24] and the name of the group later appeared, along those of neo-Nazi and Islamist militant organisations, in a document with which the British counterterrorism police sought to help the public recognise 'when young people or adults may be vulnerable to extreme or violent ideologies'.[25]

These events represent more than a diachronic development. They took place at the same time at which the climate emergency had already been employed in the courtroom as a basis for the necessity defence, with varying degrees of sympathy by the judges. When the 'Delta 5' – environmental activists who in 2014 had caused an obstruction to railway trucks in Washington State that were used to transport crude oil[26] – were put on trial, their judge eventually allowed the necessity defence;[27] and while he ultimately concluded that its conditions were not met, he showed great understanding for the defendants, describing them as 'tireless advocates of the kind that we need more of in this society'.[28]

Even though it is entirely possible that such different understandings on the morality of the relevant conduct arise within one and the same jurisdiction, the fact that moral perceptions may be strongly informed by cultural parameters constitutes a problem that has gained prominence in a world which has witnessed the rise of institutions seeking to establish standards that are applicable with universal force.

The field of international criminal law exemplifies this problem. The subjective and culturally dependent nature of perceptions of morality gained particular clarity where the concept of child soldiers was concerned. There is evidence that, for instance, in parts of Sierra Leone the moral evaluation of enlisting child soldiers – a crime for which the Special Court for Sierra Leone (SCSL) stipulated the component of 'volunteering to join an armed force or group'[29] – is subject to cultural parameters.

Practices of So-Called 'Conversion Therapy', Report to the Human Rights Council, A/HRC/44/53 (1 May 2020) ('Independent Expert'), paras 59–74.

[23] Aamna Mohdin, Matthew Taylor, Molly Blackall, 'Extinction Rebellion Protesters Stop Traffic in City of London', *The Guardian*, 25 April 2019.

[24] Amy Walker, 'Extinction Rebellion Protesters Appear in Court in London', *The Guardian*, 12 July 2019.

[25] Iliana Magra, 'British Police Said Watch Out for Extremists – Like Climate Activists', *New York Times*, 13 January 2020.

[26] Julia Carrie Wong, 'Activists Lose Criminal Case on Climate Change Defense – But Judge Praises Effort', *The Guardian*, 15 January 2016.

[27] Abigail J Fallon, 'Break the Law to Make the Law: The Necessity Defense in Environmental Civil Disobedience Cases and Its Human Rights Implications' (2018) 33 *Journal of Environmental Law & Litigation* 375, 380–81.

[28] Wong (n 26) and see Fallon (n 27).

[29] SCSL, Trial Chamber, *Prosecutor v Alex Tamba Brima, Brima Bazzy Kamara and Santigie Borbor Kanu*, SCSL-04-16-T, Judgment 20 June 2007, para 735 ('*Brima et al*'). This sets enlistment apart from the crime of conscription of child soldiers, see ibid para 734.

Kelsall thus quotes an outreach worker in Kenema town as noting that '[i]f some young fellow of thirteen or fourteen years is very courageous and says "let me go and fight" no-one is going to stop him. The community doesn't think anyone should be held responsible for that.'[30] It is an understanding that differs markedly from the evaluation the SCSL adopted which does not accept consent of the enlisted person as a defence.[31]

While such a reading is certainly compatible with the objective of protecting the rights of the child – not least with regard to obligations pertaining to children's rights to life, to their survival and development[32] – it too raises challenges relating to the foreseeability of the law.[33] The question, in particular, whether defendants had 'fair warning' of the criminalisation of the relevant conduct cannot easily be dismissed.

The problem is exacerbated by the fact that differing moral perceptions manifest themselves not only at the codification level, but also at the level of interpretation. The UK case of *R v Brown* (1993) which arose from prosecution for consensual sado-masochistic acts, is an illustration.[34] In the House of Lords judgment, the question of consent and its position in criminal law played an important role; but the fact that the judges were divided serves as an indication that a measure of subjectivity inhabited the evaluation. Lord Templeman's view that society was 'entitled and bound to protect itself against a cult of violence' and that '[c]ruelty is uncivilised'[35] may, prima facie, appear to have persuasive force. But it did not prevent the assessment of violent sports such as boxing from benefitting from a more generous understanding of the application of consent,[36] which ultimately found its basis in a different appreciation of the moral position of this particular justification for the relevant conduct.[37]

Similar situations are known in international criminal law, where, for instance, the question of the availability of the defence of duress for soldiers charged with a crime involving the killing of innocent victims led, likewise, to a 3:2 split in the ICTY Appeals Chamber (and, on the basis of that narrow majority, to a negative decision).[38] That this problem involves considerations intimately linked to moral appraisal is undeniable; in fact, the concept of the 'moral choice', as apparent from available case law in the field, was invoked by judges on both sides of the divide.[39]

---

[30] Tim Kelsall, *Culture under Cross-Examination: International Justice and the Special Court for Sierra Leone* (Cambridge, Cambridge University Press, 2009) 154, 155, with reference to an interview conducted in 2008.

[31] *Brima et al* (n 29), para 735.

[32] See Art 6 Convention on the Rights of the Child, 20 November 1989, 1577 UNTS 3.

[33] See above at n 11. See also SCSL, Appeals Chamber, *Prosecutor v Sam Hinga Norman*, SCSL-04-14-AR72(E), Decision on preliminary motion based on lack of jurisdiction (child recruitment) 31 May 2004, Dissenting Opinion of Justice Robertson, para 6.

[34] *R v Brown* [1994] 1 AC 212 (1993).

[35] ibid 237.

[36] See on this, Lord Templeman, ibid 231, and, with regard to the inconsistencies in this field, Lord Slynn, ibid 278.

[37] cf, however, Lord Mustill, ibid 273, and Lord Slynn, ibid 282.

[38] See ICTY Appeals Chamber, *Prosecutor v Drazen Erdemović*, IT-96-22-A, Judgment, 7 October 1997, para 21.

[39] See eg ibid, Joint Separate Opinion of Judge McDonald and Judge Vorah, para 45; Joint and Dissenting Separate Opinion of Judge Cassese, para 45 and n 107.

Yet what that means for individual defendants is that the judicial assessment of their conduct in these situations is deprived of much of its objectivity. Whether a conviction is entered can, even where grave international crimes are concerned, depend on the method of moral assessment which individual judges apply. The close connection between criminal law and morality, while unavoidable, also opens the door to arbitrariness and has the capacity of significantly reducing the capacity of the law's addressees to determine with certainty what exactly the law expects of them.

2.3. Criminal Law and Discrimination

Where a State is prepared to bestow on certain interests the safeguards of criminal law, it also affirms the fact that they merit an elevation of that kind. In their totality, they are values that bind the inhabitants of a State together; they do, indeed, go some way in defining the society in question.

By the same token, it is this aspect of criminal law that allows its divisive force to assert itself. Criminal law establishes an 'us group' against a 'them group': those who are not law-abiding are ipso facto on the other side of the divide.

It is a perception which is based on the highly comforting (and highly misleading) understanding that such a division is possible, with the consequence that the removal of lawbreakers from society will suffice to keep 'the rest of us' safe.

As such, it can look back on a long history. It is this retributive understanding of the law that must be held accountable for the, at times, inflationary use of capital punishment[40] – an option which to its advocates must have appeared the 'most reliable' way of removing perpetrators from society. In the nineteenth century, the discriminating force of criminal law found its manifestation in Franz von Liszt's theory of 'criminal types', which later developed into the theory of perpetrator types.[41] This concept of the ideal *typus* of perpetrators in turn would, in its most excessive form, wield considerable influence on the National Socialist concept of criminal law.[42]

But even in liberal democracies, the apparent need to make distinctions between 'us' and 'them' has not disappeared. It finds expression inter alia in the United Kingdom in the phenomenon of newspaper articles dedicated to criminals who were 'put behind bars' in a particular month[43] – articles far removed from lofty aims of rehabilitation and reintegration and which, with their publication of the relevant names and pictures, are not all that distant from the pillory in the market square.

---

[40] See, for historical excessive use in England, CH O'Halloran, 'Development of the Right of Appeal in England in Criminal Cases' (1949) 27 *Canadian Bar Review* 153, 159–60; for a critical overview of its use in the United States, see Rob Warden and Daniel Lennard, 'Death in America under Color of Law: Our Long, Inglorious Experience with Capital Punishment' (2018) 13 *Northwestern Journal of Law & Social Policy* 194–306.

[41] Thomas Vormbaum, *Einführung in die moderne Strafrechtsgeschichte* (Heidelberg, Springer, 2011) 188.

[42] ibid 206, and see Alessandro Spena, 'Iniuria Migrandi: Criminalization of Immigrants and the Basic Principles of the Criminal Law' (2014) 8 *Criminal Law & Philosophy* 635, 642–43.

[43] See, among others, Cameron Rutherford, 'The Names and Faces of All the Criminals Jailed Across Hertfordshire in October 2022', *HertsLive*, 2 November 2022, at https://www.hertfordshiremercury.co.uk/news/hertfordshire-news/names-faces-criminals-jailed-across-7766843.

From the perspective of comparative criminal law, however, even the seemingly unifying aspect of domestic criminal law can serve to enhance divisions. Where it characterises the values of one society, it also sets them apart from others. Provisions that appear more closely connected to the political and cultural framework of a jurisdiction – the prohibition of same-sex activities, say, or of blasphemy or restrictions on political opposition – seem to divide, rather than unite, the international community. They underline, at least prima facie, the discriminatory aspect of criminal law.[44]

A feature closely linked to this discriminatory characteristic are the particular consequences that those in violation of criminal law face. It is true that the objective of rehabilitation occupies an increasingly significant position in the criminal laws especially of Europe.[45] That, however, does not mean that the retributive character has disappeared altogether. The point can, in fact, be made that it is that which sets criminal law apart from other parts of the legal system:[46] it is here that the sharp edge of the sword of State is felt. To speak with Simester and Sullivan, it is the criminal justice system which constitutes the 'most potent peace-time threat to the civil rights of those citizens suspected of and prosecuted for crimes'.[47]

That also means that criminal law inevitably attracts questions which attach to the very nature of its mandate. The severity of its sanctions raises questions about its legitimacy: Radbruch's famous observation that a good jurist, at every moment of his professional life, had to be conscious not only of the need, but also of the 'profoundly questionable nature' of his vocation[48] applies with much greater force where long-term imprisonment looms than where the legal issue is a contract for a Holstein cow.

Nor can questions about the effects of a system of this kind be easily resolved. For one, the acknowledgement of its inherent discrimination makes it all too easy for society to abdicate its own responsibility in relation to the collective difficulties that the phenomenon of crime invokes.[49] But the marginalisation and alienation of perpetrators from mainstream society is capable of inviting another effect which is counterproductive to efforts to counteract crime: when faced with exclusion, there is a temptation for perpetrators and former perpetrators to turn to societal subgroups that treat them differently – such as delinquent peer groups, in which their past conduct and imprisonment may even be reason for a higher status in the group's internal order.[50]

In light of these considerations, it is understandable that criminal law has encountered attempts to establish limitations on its use – efforts to define when the sword is

---

[44] But see also, for a more detailed consideration, Paul Behrens, 'Towards a Criminal Code for the World?' (ch 16 in this volume).

[45] See on this ECtHR, *Dickson v United Kingdom* (Appl No 44362/04), Judgment, 4 December 2007, para 75.

[46] See on this Paul Behrens, 'Criminal Justice in an Age of Uncertainty' (ch 17 in this volume) at n 46.

[47] Simester et al (n 9) 21.

[48] Gustav Radbruch, *Rechtsphilosophie*, 4th edn (Stuttgart, KF Koehler, 1950) 208.

[49] See on this Erin I Kelly, 'What Is Justice?' (2020) 18 *Georgetown Journal of Law & Public Policy* 902.

[50] See Paul Behrens, 'Why Not the Law? Options for Dealing with Genocide and Holocaust Denial' in Paul Behrens, Nicholas Terry and Olaf Jensen (eds), *Holocaust and Genocide Denial. A Contextual Perspective* (Abingdon, Routledge, 2017) 241.

allowed to strike. In continental European States in particular, but also in European Criminal Law, the understanding of criminal law as '*ultima ratio*' has gained a place of prominence;[51] but restrictions can also be derived from the impact that criminalisation may have on individual human rights. Where, for instance, it affects the right to respect for private and family life, freedom of religion, freedom of expression or freedom of assembly and association, the ECHR provides that such interference must pursue a recognised legitimate interest and be 'necessary in a democratic society',[52] thus requiring the performance of a proportionality assessment.[53]

Proportionality, however, invites a more detailed consideration of the tools that are being used to achieve the relevant aim – at the very least, the methods which the State employs must constitute a suitable way of reaching the goal.[54] If that were not the case – if (*horribile dictu*!) the measures of criminal law were not suitable instruments to begin with – the relevant balancing exercise would raise uncomfortable questions going to the very raison d'être of criminal justice in its contemporary form.

3. ABOUT THIS BOOK

An analysis of contemporary challenges to criminal justice demonstrates that their assessment is insufficiently done if it limits itself to a consideration of the framework of the particular jurisdiction in which a certain form of misconduct has been addressed. The proliferation of legal mandates under English criminal law cannot appropriately be evaluated without an understanding of the impact which this may have on the requirement of foreseeability, nor can the charging before international criminal tribunals of offences derived from customary international law be adequately evaluated without an investigation of the demands of *nullum crimen sine lege*. In these cases, it is only through an examination of mandates derived from human rights law that the necessary positioning of the relevant norms can be performed.

At the same time, the look at other legal systems not only imposes a burden on those tasked with the interpretation of their own normative framework; it opens opportunities too. Difficulties which may seem germane to domestic law often make an appearance in international or transnational criminal law as well – the impact of morality and its concomitant challenges are certainly not unknown in any of the three systems. And while none of them can lay claim to perfection, each benefits from a consideration of the others.

---

[51] See Sakari Melander, 'Ultima Ratio in European Criminal Law' (2013) 3 *European Criminal Law Review* 45, in particular at 46–47.

[52] See Arts 8(2), 9(2), 10(2) and 11(2) European Convention for the Protection of Human Rights and Fundamental Freedoms (ECHR), 4 April 1950, 213 UNTS 221.

[53] ECtHR, *Olsson v Sweden (No 1)* (Appl No 10465/83), Judgment, 24 March 1988, para 67; ECtHR, *Eweida and Others v United Kingdom* (Appl Nos 48420/10, 59842/10, 51671/10 and 36516/10), Judgment, 15 January 2013, para 83; ECtHR, *Handyside v United Kingdom* (Appl No 5493/72), Judgment, 7 December 1976, para 49; ECtHR, *Chassagnou and Others v France* (Appl Nos 25088/94, 28331/95 and 28443/95), Judgment, 29 April 1999, para 112.

[54] See on this Paul Behrens, *Diplomatic Interference and the Law* (Oxford, Hart, 2016) 119.

What is required, therefore, is a study that opens the way to a dialogue between diverse criminal justice systems, to a discussion of the challenges they have encountered and of the approaches each developed to address them, while giving due consideration to the foundations and principles that underlie them.

That is the path which *Contemporary Challenges to Criminal Justice* follows. In the following chapters, experts from all three fields provide a critical analysis of seminal topics in their areas. Where appropriate, the contributors take the opportunity to draw insights from each other's chapters and to critique each other's findings. The result is an approach in which the weight often shifts from introspective analysis to intradisciplinary communication with the aim of identifying and critically evaluating solutions to challenges which transcend boundaries.

The first part (Introduction and Foundations) is dedicated to the investigation of aspects which carry application to several systems of criminal law and are of significance for an understanding of some of the more fundamental aspects of criminal justice.

Chapter 2 (Cotterrell) thus engages with the different understandings of crime – in particular, the differentiation between crime as declared by the State and its popular understanding. It also explores the need for solidarity in a network of community as a basis for the popular understanding of crime and questions its existence on the international level. Chapter 3 (Drumbl) examines the relationship between social morality and penal ideology and raises the question whether a restorative and empathetic sentencing policy may more firmly be based on grounds other than victims' rights. Chapter 4 (Kyriakides) is dedicated to questions that arise in the teaching of law and its engagement with ethical challenges, exploring the recommendations of the 2013 Legal Education and Training Review and the professional duties of solicitors in this area.

The second part (Domestic and Comparative Criminal Justice) considers challenges of criminal justice that primarily emerged in particular national jurisdictions as well as aspects related to a comparative approach to the field.

Chapter 5 (Doak) engages with the right to redress and raises the question whether this right may exist for victims of 'ordinary' crime. It reflects on various legal systems in which aspects of redress were incorporated in justice processes and calls for a reorientation of criminal justice which would allow for the integration of reparatory interests. Chapter 6 (Mitchell) analyses existing problems with the law's attempt at encapsulating the most serious homicides, with particular emphasis on the sentencing of convicted murderers. It critically examines the situation arising through the Criminal Justice Act 2003 and explores questions relating to the legitimacy of sentencing of murderers. Chapter 7 (McCoy) is dedicated to the topic of plea bargaining. While the practice is based on considerations of expediency, the plea process raises concerns relating to the 'trial penalty' – the possibility that defendants may face a significantly higher sentence if a case goes to trial. Chapter 8 (Weinstein) engages with aspects of the US Office of Foreign Asset Control (OFAC) and its sanctions system. It discusses in particular the challenges that arise from the strict liability regime that applies and proposes the availability of a mistake of law defence that would require OFAC to prove that the relevant party knowingly violated the law. Chapter 9 (Nelken) critically analyses recent research into the criminal justice system in States formerly members of the Soviet Union. It explores issues such as efforts to reform criminal justice procedures and State manipulation of self-governance by prisoners and offers an analysis highlighting the significance of a methodology based on parameters which appreciate the temporal and regional framework and the cultural context of the relevant system.

The third part (International Criminal Justice) deals with challenges that arise, both on the substantive and the procedural side, in the fields of international criminal law and international criminal trials.

Chapter 10 (Schabas) investigates a charge made in relation to several institutions of international criminal justice – that they do in fact engage in 'victor's justice'. It analyses efforts at the depoliticisation of international criminal justice, but also raises the question whether equivalence, regardless of the circumstances of a specific situation, can be a justifiable goal. Chapter 11 (Roberts) explores the way in which the consultation of trial transcripts can allow conclusions on the decision-making processes of those involved in the administration of justice, but also investigates the importance of the cultural contextualisation of evidence. Chapter 12 (Karnavas, Pettay and Al-Malt) analyses challenges that arise from the fact that the Extraordinary Chambers in the Courts of Cambodia were established to bring 'senior leaders' of the Khmer Rouge and those 'most responsible' for the relevant crimes to justice. It explores the conceptual difficulties that arise in that context, but also reflects on the insights that can be drawn from these challenges for the jurisdictional contours of future tribunals and courts. Chapter 13 (Fournet) explores the difficulties that arise from the limitations inherent in the definition of genocide and reflects on the creativity which judicial construction has brought to issues such as actus reus, the group element, and the mens rea of the crime, highlighting advantages and dangers inherent in such approaches. Chapter 14 (Behrens) is dedicated to the threshold criterion which manifests itself on the subjective side of the crime of genocide. The chapter critically evaluates various approaches to the determination of substantiality and highlights the significance of the individualised approach, which permits the adoption of preventive steps at a stage when the crime has not yet developed dimensions where objective substantiality is an inevitable consequence.

The fourth part (Transnational Criminal Justice) explores aspects which have caused controversies in the field of transnational criminal law and investigates the insights that can be gained from their treatment in judicial decisions and scholarly debate.

Chapter 15 (Verhoeven and Yi) deals with the offence of incitement to terrorism. It addresses challenges caused by the lack of a universally accepted definition of terrorism and the fact that questions relating to the subjective aspects of the conduct of incitement remain unresolved, but also explores the potential for conflicts between offences of incitement and the human right of freedom of speech. Chapter 16 (Behrens) raises the question whether transnational crimes can provide indication of a consensus within the international community on shared values and potentially serve as a precursor to a universal criminal code. The chapter analyses the criticisms that such a perspective encounters and reflects on insights that are to be gained from the current status of selected instruments of transnational criminal law in this field.

Chapter 17 (Behrens) revisits some of the seminal questions that attach to contemporary criminal law and summarises certain key findings reached in the chapters of this book. In so doing, it highlights difficulties that attach to some of the principal aspirations of criminal law but also reflects on the way in which different criminal justice systems influence one another and can provide solutions to difficulties which are common to all of them.

The book concludes with some of the authors' personal reflections on Professor Ralph Henham, to whom this study is dedicated, and with a brief biography of the friend and colleague whom they honour.

For the purposes of this book, and unless otherwise specified by the authors, the following definitions have been adopted. 'International Criminal Law' refers to the legal system relating to international and internationalised criminal courts and tribunals and their procedure. On the substantive side, it refers to the rules relating to international crimes (regardless of their forum of adjudication). 'Transnational Criminal Law' refers to international instruments under which the parties assume the duty to adopt, in their domestic legal systems, provisions criminalising certain forms of conduct. On the substantive side, it refers to rules relating to the relevant crimes themselves. The term 'domestic criminal law' refers to a national criminal justice system (not necessarily that of the country of the contributor) and its procedural and substantive rules.

Opinions expressed by the individual authors are their own; they are not necessarily indicative of the opinions of the institutions of which they may be members or of other authors of this work.

Particular thanks go to Sinead Moloney and Sasha Jawed at Hart Publishing for all their work and helpful counsel during the production process, as well as to Professor Michael Bohlander for accepting this volume in the Studies in International & Comparative Criminal Law series.

Unless otherwise noted the cut-off point for the consideration of factual and legal developments was 1 September 2021.

2

The Concept of Crime in Transnational Perspective

ROGER COTTERRELL

1. INTRODUCTION

I S THERE A need for a concept of crime? Surely debates around this issue have now been played out? Louk Hulsman notes that 'there is no "ontological reality" of crime'.[1] That is, the term seems to refer to no irreducible, distinctive social phenomenon existing independently of legal definition. Crime is what the state (or some international agency authorised by states) declares it to be through law. By designating an offence as 'criminal', state law links it to established assumptions about kinds of punishment appropriate for criminal behaviour. And, it seems, *any* conduct might be so designated. Crime is what the criminal law in a given society at a given time states it to be. For criminal lawyers in general what matters is the procedure and substance of this law. And juristically rationalising it is not the same as conceptualising 'crime' as a social entity.

Yet the immense variety of kinds of conduct labelled as criminal sometimes attracts comment and even concern[2] because 'the sheer number of criminal offences has grown exponentially'.[3] In this situation, doubts about the coherence of 'crime' as a category have tended to be pushed aside in practice – so William Stuntz has suggested – by making criminal law

> not one field but two. The first [field] consists of a few core crimes. ... The second consists of everything else. Criminal law courses, criminal law literature, and popular conversations about crime focus heavily on the first. The second dominates criminal codes.[4]

---

[1] Louk HC Hulsman, 'Critical Criminology and the Concept of Crime' (abridged) in J Muncie, E McLaughlin and M Langan (eds), *Criminological Perspectives: A Reader* (London, Sage, 1996) 300.

[2] William J Stuntz, 'The Pathological Politics of Criminal Law' (2001) 100 *Michigan Law Review* 505–600.

[3] Douglas Husak, 'Crimes Outside the Core' (2004) 39 *Tulsa Law Review* 755–79, 768.

[4] Stuntz (n 2) 512.

In other words, crime as a basic social category is assumed to be well understood; but perhaps that understanding depends on generalising from a few seemingly prominent kinds of criminalisation, often leaving aside much else.

Whatever the truth of this as regards juristic and popular perspectives, criminologists have been concerned to conceptualise crime and have divided mainly into two broad camps in doing so. One camp expressly or tacitly adopts a broadly *legal* demarcation of crime as its practical focus: what the state, through its law, marks out as crime provides criminology with its basic subject matter and its scholarly field. But, for strong intellectual and moral-political reasons, many other criminologists have rejected the idea that the subject matter of their field is given to them by legal-political fiat. Fearing to be 'kings without a country',[5] they have wanted to produce their own concept of crime, or to discard crime as a concept in favour of a more independent focus for their knowledge field.[6] Alongside this, efforts have been made for moral and political reasons to open up or replace the idea of crime, so as to cover types of behaviour typically not criminalised by state law, or thought to be treated insufficiently seriously by the state, or in which the state and its agents are themselves implicated.[7]

Until recently, such efforts to escape the state law focus have surely had limited effect. If the state is not to hold a monopoly in declaring what is to count as crime, where else can the authority to define crime be found? If critical criminologists, setting out to challenge state law definitions of crime, have sometimes found a hearing, it is because they have appealed to widespread concerns about serious wrongdoing. They have aimed to link established popular notions about the seriousness of 'crime' to other widely felt social concerns. Beyond popular assumptions that crime is what criminal law says it is, other popular ideas exist as to what are serious social wrongs, about what *should* be treated as criminal, or about what is 'really' criminal even if law does not declare it to be so. But what authoritative conceptualisations of crime could come from such diffuse popular understandings?

Is it possible to speak of a *cultural* authority underpinning ideas of crime, as contrasted with the *political* authority of the state and its juristic servants – 'cultural' referring here broadly to bonds of shared tradition, interests, beliefs, values or emotional allegiance that may hold people together in conditions of relatively stable social coexistence? In some circumstances can this cultural authority be important? Studying its character would be an essentially sociological enterprise.

Where the state extends criminalisation beyond certain limits cultural attitudes might not support this; popular ideas of crimes as *mala in se* (wrong by nature) might be significantly out of alignment with the scope and character of some state *mala prohibita* (that is, acts that are wrongs merely because prohibited). The same position might arise where the state is seen to 'undercriminalise', to condone impunity or provide inadequate punishments. More generally, it might arise where the state,

---

[5] cf JM Van Bemmelen, 'The "Criminologist": A King Without a Country?' (1951) 63 *Juridical Review* 24–38.

[6] Stuart Henry and Mark M Lanier (eds), *What Is Crime? Controversies over the Nature of Crime and What to Do about It* (Boulder, CO, Rowman and Littlefield, 2001).

[7] Dawn L Rothe and David O Friedrichs, 'The State of the Criminology of Crimes of the State' (2006) 33 *Social Justice* 147–61.

in punishing or not punishing, is seen to serve special interests rather than a broad public interest – or where the very idea of public interest becomes confused. Cultural definitions of crime might matter when the state's general practice in criminalising begins to be questioned.

Thus, when cultural authority *does* largely support the state's political authority in treating crime, this may depend on the state being seen as a secure, reliable regulator – as holding what Max Weber called a monopoly of legitimate violence in its territory[8] – together with a popular sense that the state and its law represent a relatively stable sociopolitical and economic order against which crime is easily seen as a serious threat that the state identifies and addresses.

In this chapter I shall argue that the state monopoly of defining crime is being weakened, especially by the transnational spread of criminal jurisdiction – that is, by the increasingly felt need to apply ideas of crime coherently across and irrespective of national boundaries.[9] If this is so, the question of how and by whom the meaning of 'crime' is to be settled assumes renewed importance. Cultural authority (the authority of popular ideas arising in everyday social life) to shape the concept of crime may have new significance as the political authority to shape it becomes less clear. So, in what follows, suggestions are made of ways in which the state's independent power to determine what is criminal is becoming destabilised or restricted. The question then arises: where can the idea of crime in transnational context find a supporting input of cultural authority? The answer suggested is in emerging transnational networks of communal relations – networks that now extend beyond the various social networks from which national popular ideas about crime have arisen.

2. STATE AND CRIME: PERSPECTIVES FROM SOCIAL THEORY

If the state's sole authority to criminalise has usually been popularly accepted this is surely partly because no other authority has seemed sufficiently focused to compete with it. But it may also be because popular assumptions about what the state criminalises have tended to conform to popular views about what crime is. In this respect Stuntz's idea of 'two fields' of criminal law, one known, the other unknown, seems important. What has been popularly seen as the state's management of the idea of crime – and accepted as legitimate as such – has actually been *only a part of its extensive practice of criminalisation.*

Some warrant for this view might be found in Weberian and Durkheimian sociolegal theories.[10] Weber has little to say directly about crime, presumably because in his perspective the state's power to criminalise is just one of many regulatory techniques

---

[8] Max Weber, 'Politics as a Vocation' in HH Gerth and C Wright Mills (eds and transl), *From Max Weber: Essays in Sociology* (London: Routledge & Kegan Paul, 1948) 78.

[9] This chapter is revised and adapted from a paper previously published in V Mitsilegas, P Alldridge and L Cheliotis (eds), *Globalisation, Criminal Law and Criminal Justice* (Oxford, Hart, 2015).

[10] For a somewhat parallel comparison, see Jan Terpstra, 'Two Theories on the Police: The Relevance of Max Weber and Emile Durkheim to the Study of the Police' (2011) 39 *International Journal of Law, Crime and Justice* 1–11.

it possesses and can deploy pragmatically. Central to these techniques is the relatively formal character of modern law which sustains the idea of both its autonomy as a rational system and its usefulness as an all-purpose regulatory device, available equally for private purposes and for the state to fulfil its administrative functions. If the modern state typically successfully claims a monopoly of legitimate violence,[11] much of its power, in Weber's view, is exercised through enunciated rules, and administration (rather than politics) typifies the everyday life of state and society.[12] His emphasis on rational administration easily morphs into more abstract contemporary social theories that envisage systems and networks as somehow taking on lives of their own, perhaps even ultimately unbounded by the jurisdictional reach of nation states.

One might imagine that as the administrative structures and tasks of the state extend and its law proliferates to frame these, the possibilities of criminalisation also expand, but into esoteric areas of regulation that reflect the sheer complexity of modern social and economic organisation – what can be called forms of *administrative* criminalisation. 'Crime' does not appear at all in the index of the English edition of Weber's magnum opus *Economy and Society*,[13] but we might imagine that, in his typical modern state, categories of *mala prohibita* proliferate. So if criminal law is, indeed, actually two fields – one highly visible in popular consciousness, the other largely unseen – perhaps the growth of the unseen part really typifies the progress of modernity and the flourishing of the state.

Can we then speculate that, as the state grows more ambitious (Weber's theory suggests no strong reasons why it should not), the contours of crime as a category change – the process of politicolegal criminalisation potentially embraces more and more wrongs that are distant from everyday popular conceptions of crime? And can it also be assumed that no particular problems arise from this divorce from popular conceptions?

Émile Durkheim provides a striking contrast to such an outlook.[14] He too sees the modern state's regulatory capacities and ambitions as vastly expanding; there is surely more and more law. But, unlike Weber, he pays careful attention to assessing how much of it is properly to be seen as penal. Whereas Weber's modern state seems to need no specific cultural authorisation for its criminalisation practices, Durkheim's does. Punishing crime has to be seen as a *special* focus of law, to be distinguished clearly from all the many other regulatory objectives that law and state must address.

As modern regulation expands, most of this expansion is aimed not at defining and punishing crime but at peacefully and non-violently coordinating and repairing

---

[11] Weber (n 8) 78. See also Max Weber, *Economy and Society: An Outline of Interpretive Sociology* [1968], transl E Fischoff et al (Berkeley, University of California Press, 1978) 314: 'Today legal coercion by violence is the monopoly of the state.'

[12] A striking illustration of this point is that a stable state may be able to continue administrative functions effectively even when political processes fail to produce a government: see eg Geert Bouckaert and Marleen Brans, 'Governing Without Government: Lessons from Belgium's Caretaker Government' (2012) 25 *Governance* 173–76; Carl Devos and Dave Sinardet, 'Governing Without a Government: The Belgian Experiment' (2012) 25 *Governance* 167–71.

[13] Weber (n 11).

[14] Emile Durkheim, *The Division of Labour in Society*, transl WD Halls (London, Macmillan, 1984).

social relations: for example, by guaranteeing compensation, rectifying arrangements turned sour, providing useful administrative structures, and facilitating cooperation and interdependence. Despite all the many new regulatory demands on the state in modern conditions, the idea of crime remains something that 'society', not the state, determines. So the state operates through what I earlier called cultural authority in criminalising and punishing.

There is something both powerful and unreal in this Durkheimian picture – a paradox that has long produced deeply polarised views in the criminological literature. Crucially, as regards Stuntz's postulated 'two fields' of criminal law, how does Durkheim analyse the 'unseen' field – the areas of *mala prohibita* largely unknown to most people; the realm of regulatory, technical, managerial, administrative, public health and other offences not necessarily seen as 'wrong in themselves'? Occasionally, Durkheim refers to examples of such offences but they are clearly not his concern and he mainly ignores them. When he writes of crime he means something *popularly condemned* generally in society – affronting the shared moral outlooks of average people. So he sees only part of what criminal law addresses.

On the other hand, a strength of Durkheim's view is that the idea of crime in it is something powerful, enduring (despite all regulatory changes) and stable. The political authority of the state (acting on behalf of society) in punishing crime meshes with the cultural authority that makes crime a readily intelligible concept. Crime is a distinct moral phenomenon (however varied the forms it takes). It consists of wrongdoing regarded generally by citizens as constituting such a serious threat to the moral security of society (not just particular interests of individuals) that it is to be repressed by collective action through the agency of the state. Crime, as Durkheim puts it, offends the collective consciousness (or conscience) of society.

From a Weberian perspective the main problem of transnational criminalisation must be to ensure adequate political authority to support appropriate regulation. The key question will be: what happens to the state's monopoly of legitimate violence? Can it be extended transnationally, shared with other states, or somehow conferred on transnational political authorities? In a Durkheimian perspective, however, as ideas of crime become transnational, cultural authority must be found for them if they are to be coherent and meaningful.[15]

The implications of this can, however, be pushed well beyond anything in Durkheim's writings. If the idea of crime were somehow to be loosened from the state's modern monopoly of criminalisation could it become a focus for potentially unlimited *struggle and dispute*? Does the power to fix the meaning of crime potentially become a political prize to be fought over? If the idea of crime has been used to identify threats to a social order and to justify the use of penal violence to repress these threats, what if *competing* claims are made to harness the idea of crime for such purposes? What if the nature of the threats and their sources are viewed in competing ways? Finally, what if those who could once be securely labelled by the state as criminals now invoke the idea of crime to *condemn the state* and its agents as criminal? The

---

[15] Salif Nimaga, *Émile Durkheim and International Criminal Law: A Sociological Exploration* (Saarbrücken, VDM Verlag Dr Müller, 2010).

ultimate scenario is that the idea of crime might become uncontrollably contested and unstable. So the issue of cultural authority returns to haunt insecure political authority in conceptualising crime and legitimising criminal punishment.

In the transnational development of criminal justice, debates around the meaning of crime assume increasing importance. For example, both extradition and extraterritorial law enforcement sometimes attract popular controversy as to whether 'crime' is being given the same meaning in all states involved, or whether one state is seeking to impose its own understanding of crime (and the way it should be dealt with) on another. As transnationalism advances, nationalistic views of crime find new prominence. 'Loose interpretation' of strict dual criminality requirements[16] for transnational criminal justice cooperation, or reliance on 'analogies' between offences in different jurisdictions, can be causes for concern.[17] Popular, nationalistic 'extradition fury'[18] fanned by media reports suggests that the idea of crime is not something to be entrusted entirely to the state to negotiate with other states; cultural resonances are important. This may be specially so where extradition offences are outside Stuntz's field of popularly 'known' crimes and so their wrongfulness may depend on technical definition.[19]

Aspects of cybercrime provide other illustrations. Hacking and cyber attacks are perpetrated not only by individuals or organised crime groups targeting state or other public facilities or private businesses, bank accounts and databases. They may also be acts of state agencies trying to crush opposition or attack other states.[20] So, transnational crime can destabilise distinctions between the state and the criminal, and between cybercrime, cyber terrorism and cyber warfare.[21] The idea of the *criminal state* (or its agents) arises as an aspect of the broader relocation of the state from a position of overall supervisor and controller of criminal justice processes to that of a participant or subject in these processes – sometimes as victim, agent, offender, or promoter or obstructer of criminal justice.

The state is said to be 'losing control over the monopoly of coercion hitherto under its aegis'[22] but it is unwise to generalise so broadly. Certainly, in some cases the state is subject to attacks (from terrorism, corruption and organised crime) that it

---

[16] Requirements that the act for which extradition is sought must amount to an offence in both the requested and requesting state. Cf John G Kester, 'Some Myths of United States Extradition Law' (1988) 76 *Georgetown Law Journal* 1441–1493, 1461 (claiming that in US practice 'the double criminality requirement often does not mean much'); Alison E Lardo, 'The 2003 Extradition Treaty Between the United States and United Kingdom: Towards a Solution to Transnational White Collar Crime Prosecution?' (2006) 20 *Emory International Law Review* 867–903, 890 (noting the 'liberal interpretation of dual criminality espoused by US prosecutors'). Under the European Arrest Warrant procedure, the requirement has been either weakened or removed.

[17] Lardo (n 16) 889–92, 898–902.

[18] Outcry against the handing over of fellow-citizens to another state for trial and potential punishment.

[19] Kester (n 16) 1492 (stressing that 'social norms and business ethics and duties vary considerably, and not improperly, even among the Western democracies'); and see Lardo (n 16) 898–99 on UK–US controversies.

[20] Charles Billo and Welton Chang, *Cyber Warfare: An Analysis of the Means and Motivations of Selected Nation States* (Hanover, NH, Institute for Security Technology Studies, Dartmouth College 2004) http://www.ists.dartmouth.edu/docs/cyberwarfare.pdf.

[21] Tom CW Lin, 'Financial Weapons of War' (2016) 100 *Minnesota Law Review* 1377–1440.

[22] James H Mittelman and Robert Johnston, 'The Globalization of Organized Crime, the Courtesan State and the Corruption of Civil Society' (1999) 5 *Global Governance* 103–26, 123.

struggles to criminalise in the face of weakening resources and authority.[23] Instead of being above the criminal fray, some states find themselves in the midst of it, battling to enforce their view of criminality in the face of disinterest or controversy – so that the crime label may seem to cease to matter (only the balance of coercive forces counts), or it is harnessed to the interests of those who wish to use it to condemn opposing interests. Otherwise criminalisation in practice is partially taken from the control of the state through privatisation initiatives, or by being entrusted to the care of transnational criminal justice agencies (such as international tribunals) or merely to stronger states with greater power to impose it.

3. THE CONCEPT OF CRIME AND INTERNATIONAL CRIMINAL LAW

The emergence of international criminal law (ICL), especially in the past half century, represents perhaps the most visible emergence of a transnational arena of criminalisation in which some states (at least, their agents) have become potentially subjects (rather than controllers) of criminal justice. It is necessary to say 'some' states because others surely dominate in practice in this transnational arena, lending their continuing monopolies of legitimate force within their territory to guarantee ICL in operation. Because this guarantee is limited, selective and uneven, so that it is presently hard to imagine some state authorities being subject to it, ICL is seen as both embryonic and insecure in its legitimacy.[24] And although it is called *international* law, it might be best described as transnational[25] because it is individuals rather than states that are addressed by it, in some cases irrespective of nationality or citizenship.

Like criminal law in national contexts, ICL can be rationalised juristically into a system of thought[26] but it displays no general idea of crime as a social phenomenon. Crime is primarily what the Statute of the ICC and the Court's interpretations declare as offences. The Statute lists specific crimes organised under headings of genocide, crimes against humanity and war crimes, the headings not themselves being defined apart from the specific offences they encompass.[27] The assumption seems to be that – in the light of ICL's history – these offences need only be stated in order to be accepted as instances

---

[23] eg David Garland, 'The Limits of the Sovereign State: Strategies of Crime Control in Contemporary Society' (1996) 36 *British Journal of Criminology* 445–71.

[24] The issues have long featured in public debate: eg James Copnall, 'Bashir Warrant: Chad Accuses ICC of Anti-African Bias', *BBC News Africa*, 22 July 2010, http://www.bbc.co.uk/news/world-africa-10723869 (focus of ICL only on African cases); and Seumas Milne, 'If There Were Global Justice, NATO Would Be in the Dock over Libya' *The Guardian*, 16 May 2012, http://www.guardian.co.uk/commentisfree/2012/may/15/global-justice-nato-libya#start-of-comments (effective impunity of NATO leaders in ICL). See generally Hans Köchler, 'Justice and Realpolitik: The Predicament of the International Criminal Court' (2017) 16 *Chinese Journal of International Law* 1–9; Ralph Henham, 'Some Reflections on the Legitimacy of International Trial Justice' (2007) 35 *International Journal of the Sociology of Law* 75–95.

[25] Eric K Leonard, *The Onset of Global Governance: International Relations Theory and the International Criminal Court* (Aldershot, Ashgate, 2005) 6.

[26] Kai Ambos, 'Toward a Universal System of Crime: Comments on George Fletcher's Grammar of Criminal Law' (2007) 28 *Cardozo Law Review* 2647–2673, 2667–2671.

[27] ICC Statute Arts 5–8. The statute does add requirements of context; for example, that crimes against humanity occur as part of a widespread or systematic attack on a civilian population. And a 2010 amendment to the statute now defines the crime of aggression, previously merely signalled in the text.

of crime: a reasonable assumption insofar as they include such matters as 'murder', 'extermination', 'enslavement', 'torture', 'rape', 'causing serious bodily or mental harm', 'enforced sterilization', wanton 'destruction and appropriation of property' and 'pillaging'. Central ideas of crime in ICL are clearly built out of categories of crime accepted in both juristic and popular understandings in all modern Western societies – that is, as transnational extensions of ideas of crime in the first of Stuntz's two fields of criminal law, the 'known' field that most obviously defines crime in popular understandings. Beyond these ideas of crime in ICL is, however, much else which invokes, for example, established categories of illegality enshrined in the 1949 Geneva Conventions or in other principles of international law, and includes acts aimed at destroying specific victim groups, wanton destruction of natural environments or cultural heritage, and a range of outlawed weapons and tactics for waging war.

Looked at in terms of possibilities for cultural legitimation, the category of crime in ICL seems a strange compendium – a packaging of disparate elements. They include:

- efforts to 'humanise' modern warfare (eg outlawing the use of certain kinds of weapons or tactics) – that is, rules about the way to conduct violence that surely find little or no presence in domestic (national) cultural understandings of crime;

- concerns to protect natural and cultural environments, which are present in many Western legal systems but often as civil rather than criminal matters; and, when criminal, perhaps popularly seen as *mala prohibita* as much as, if not more than, *mala in se*; and

- much that in popular perceptions is usually very obviously crime (eg deliberately inflicting serious harm to the person or to property without lawful excuse).

If some kind of popular legitimation is available for ICL it might be hard to spell it out in general terms. But could it be that this is not needed; that adequate politicolegal authority, relying on the combined monopolies of violence possessed by the treaty-supporting states, sustains the somewhat incoherent transnational concept of crime?

Politicolegal authority alone seems, however, an unstable basis for extending transnationally the concept of crime. The spectre of victors' justice that has hung over ICL since the Nuremburg trials is now transformed into the suspicion that ICL is a means by which some states try to impose a global criminal justice system on other (usually weaker) ones. So, the concept of crime appears as a mechanism of military-police control extended beyond the national arena to control foreign populations, perhaps by analogy with the 'dangerous classes' or 'underclasses' addressed by state criminal justice. It may be that the only way to avoid ICL being seen in this way is clearly to identify forms of cultural legitimation on which it can draw, but also to recognise that in present conditions there is no single global culture that can legitimise fully a transnational concept of crime. Instead, what may exist are important networks of community existing not only within nations but also transnationally that can support the extension of ideas of crime across national boundaries.

The serious violent acts that constitute crimes against humanity according to the legal definitions may seem to epitomise 'crime' so obviously that universal cultural authority for their recognition is undeniable – the cultural appeal is to a global idea of 'humanity'. But what one population sees as atrocities are sometimes dismissed as justified retaliation by another; wanton destruction can appear as collateral damage, targeted killings as suppressing terrorism, and terrorist violence as action against injustice and to achieve freedom. Where killing, rape, enslavement, appropriation of property, etc, are directed against people seen as enemies or as utterly alien, their criminal character is sometimes totally denied.

A popular understanding of crime presupposes a degree of *solidarity in a network of community*, whether that network is national or transnational. It is doubtful that 'humanity' designates such a communal network of solidarity today, except as an aspiration for the future.[28] But something less may exist – an evolving transnational arena in which some ideas of human rights and human dignity are acquiring relatively stable meanings and can thus inform criminalisation.

Without stable cultural understandings of crime its politicolegal designation risks ongoing challenge, especially because, being ultimately guaranteed by the authority of states, it cannot escape controversy about the extent of this state authority. Attitudes to war as an instrument of the state reveal this starkly. During the twentieth century the idea became established that criminal liability could arise from the mere pursuit of war by states (as distinct from anything occurring in the course of that pursuit).[29] So, to that extent, rights of nation states in international law were scaled down. Military historian Martin van Crefeld writes: 'Once the legal monopoly of armed force, long claimed by the state, is wrested out of its hands, existing distinctions between war and crime will break down.'[30]

One consequence could be that war (involving invasion, military intervention, imposed regime change), although distinguished legally in modern times from the idea of punishment, might come to be treated as a sanction against criminal activity by states. David Luban has suggested that the idea of war as punishment 'remains alive and well in the moral imaginations of modern societies, even if diplomats and lawyers carefully scrub it from official justifications for armed conflict'.[31] While he rejects this view of war he sees no reason why states, like corporations, should not be capable of assuming criminal responsibility.

The idea of criminal acts by states has been debated juristically, but it has been suggested that such acts should not be called crimes 'as they do not provoke punishment in a way analogous to that of domestic law'.[32] Punishability is surely a key issue. But various sanctions against states are possible including economic sanctions (which might be analogised to fines in domestic law); or isolation, boycott or exclusion as a 'pariah' from the international intercourse of states (which might be analogised to exclusion from 'the social' produced by imprisonment of an offender); or military

---

[28] cf Carol C Gould, 'Transnational Solidarities' (2007) 38 *Journal of Social Philosophy* 148–64.

[29] Gerhard Werle and Florian Jessberger, *Principles of International Criminal Law*, 4th edn (Oxford, Oxford University Press, 2020) ch 6.

[30] Quoted in Stanley Cohen, 'Crime and Politics: Spot the Difference' (1996) 47 *British Journal of Sociology* 1–21, 16.

[31] David Luban, 'War as Punishment' (2011) 39 *Philosophy & Public Affairs* 299–330, 300–01.

[32] Nimaga (n 15) 62.

action to effect regime change (which might even be imagined as 'capital punishment' of a state).

These speculations remain unreal if acts against an 'offender' state are seen only as serving the special interests of another state (or a limited coalition of states). Such acts could only be legitimised as punishment if they were aimed at addressing not the 'private' interests of particular aggrieved states,[33] but serious threats to the 'international community' of states as a whole; that is, action to protect the existence of a common transnational sociopolitical order which international criminal justice is seen to serve.

Generalising to current forms of transnational criminalisation, two basic requirements for a transnational concept of crime are highlighted by this discussion: first, the existence of *mechanisms to punish offenders*; and, second, *transnational communal networks* on behalf of which criminalisation and punishment is undertaken. Efforts to address the first of these requirements are being made through transnational cooperation between states. The streamlining of extradition and European Arrest Warrant procedures, on the one hand, and the willingness of coalitions of states to engage in humanitarian intervention, on the other, represent strongly contrasting examples (whatever controversies may surround them). But the nature of transnational social networks supporting criminalisation needs much more analysis. References to an 'international community' or 'community of humanity'[34] served by ICL remain for the most part purely rhetorical because ungrounded in any sociological inquiry about what 'community' might mean and what kind of existence it might have.

4. LOCATING IDEAS OF CRIME IN COMMUNAL NETWORKS

This chapter has referred to cultural (as contrasted with politicolegal) authority to conceptualise crime. That cultural authority can best be seen as arising in many different communal networks. Bonds of community of varying degrees of stability, fluidity, transience or permanence, can arise from (i) common or convergent interests, (ii) shared beliefs or ultimate values, (iii) coexistence in particular cultural or physical environments or (iv) emotional allegiances. In social life, these different types of bonds are combined (often with some types dominating) in social networks of varying size, complexity and stability: examples would be trading or financial networks; networks of religious believers; social or ideological movements; ethnic or kinship groups; or local or linguistic populations linked primarily by coexistence in the same territory or by common history or traditions. Membership in such networks overlaps; people move in and out of and are usually involved simultaneously in many of them. Crucially today, such communal networks can be not merely national in extent but also intranational or transnational – not limited in their extent by the boundaries of

---

[33] That war is usually a matter of such 'private' inter-state conflicts is a key reason why Luban (n 31) denies that it can be accepted as a form of punishment.

[34] See eg Massimo Renzo, 'Crimes against Humanity and the Limits of International Criminal Law' (2012) 31 *Law & Philosophy* 443–76, 454, claiming that accountability for crimes against humanity is 'to the members of the international community (rather than just to their fellow citizens)'.

nation states.[35] Just as emerging forms of transnational law find (or need) cultural bases of authority in such transnational networks, so do transnational ideas of crime.

Can anything be said in general terms about ideas of crime that emerge from such communal sources? It was noted earlier that, when scholars' efforts to replace politicolegal definitions of crime have gained a sympathetic hearing, this has been because, in various ways, they have reflected widespread popular ideas about crime. Three such broad approaches in criminological and penological literature are most prominent.

First is a *social harm conception* of crime. On this view the essence of crime (or perhaps the fundamental problem that legal ideas of crime only partly address) is serious social harm or injury,[36] or the creation of danger, significant risk or insecurity to individuals or society. A second approach views *crime as upsetting a 'moral balance'* in society, so that justice requires punishment of the offender to re-establish this – to proclaim society's condemnation, its recognition and its judgment of the gravity of the wrong done; in this perspective, law in practice might not always provide what criminal justice is thought to require.[37] A third approach is grounded in a *need to protect human rights and dignity* so that what the idea of crime recognises (or should recognise) are serious denials or attacks on basic conditions of life that humans are entitled to enjoy.[38]

In the context of discussion here, these approaches suggest possible broadenings of or amendments to politicolegal ideas of crime – ones that might reflect sentiments, interests, values or traditions not always seen as fully reflected in criminal law. Because these approaches tend to focus on what crime does, more than on the nature of the criminal, some criminologists extend them to embrace not only acts of individual offenders but also those of corporations, groups, states, state agents or international organisations[39] and even – at the extreme – to include wrongs (such as poverty, racism, sexism, imperialism, colonialism and exploitation) that are not necessarily seen as always having specific, identifiable agents.

On the other hand, doubts among critical criminologists themselves about such ideas as 'too woolly and polemical'[40] may suggest that they go beyond what most popular ideas of crime will encompass. Jeffrey Reiman, criticising such expansive concepts of crime, claims: 'Individuals think about their actions, they respond to arguments and moral considerations, and their actions are subject to their choices. None of this applies easily to groups or structures.'[41] Thus, he argues, the idea of

---

[35] See generally, on the concepts of community and communal networks in sociolegal theory, Roger Cotterrell, *Law, Culture and Society: Legal Ideas in the Mirror of Social Theory* (Abingdon and New York, Routledge, 2006); and in transnational context, Roger Cotterrell, *Sociological Jurisprudence: Juristic Thought and Social Inquiry* (Abingdon and New York, Routledge, 2018) 112–14.

[36] Kristian Lasslett, 'Crime or Social Harm? A Dialectical Perspective' (2010) 54 *Crime, Law & Social Change* 1–19.

[37] cf Robin L West, 'The Lawless Adjudicator' (2005) 26 *Cardozo Law Review* 2253–2261 on the 'criminal' judge.

[38] For discussion of these various orientations, see eg Henry and Lanier (n 6) 2001.

[39] David O Friedrichs and Jessica Friedrichs, 'The World Bank and Crimes of Globalization: A Case Study' (2002) 29 *Social Justice* 13–36.

[40] Cohen (n 30) 6.

[41] Jeffrey Reiman, 'Book Review' (2006) 46 *British Journal of Criminology* 362–64, 363.

individual responsibility is basic to most contemporary ideas of crime. Extensions outside it will need special justification.

To go beyond these limited suggestions about conceptualising crime it is necessary to return to the notion of networks of community. No meaningful concept of crime could encompass *all* kinds of popularly recognised harms, injustices or infringements of rights. What could distinguish those that are covered? Crime surely involves some harm, injustice or dehumanising right-infringement produced by the acts of others in *a common social environment* (embracing both victim and offender) that presupposes basic conditions for coexistence in it. Absence of such a common environment can, as noted earlier, make ideas of crime so controversial as to be practically unworkable.

So, popular ideas of crime in fact presuppose the context of some network of community. Even if it is individuals who are victims of crime, the seriousness of the crime has to be judged ultimately by its consequences for that network *as a whole*. If criminal punishment rather than individual redress is required it is because the wrong is viewed as sufficiently serious to threaten the order or security of the entire communal network, the general ideas of justice widely presumed within it, or the basic conditions of trust and interdependence (solidarity) that underpin it. People can be passionate about crime because they treat it as *a threat to the way that social life – that is, the communal networks in which they see themselves as involved – must be organised.*

This is a view of crime clearly much closer to Durkheimian than Weberian perspectives. Weber's image of powerful modern states extending their regulatory capacities suggests a growing scope of what I earlier called administrative criminalisation (focused on managing socioeconomic complexity) and it allows us easily to imagine its expansion transnationally through the cooperation of states. But it does not address issues of cultural authorisation of ideas of crime. So it is necessary to see, through some examples, how ideas of crime might be shaped and stabilised by transnational networks of community and what the limits of any transnational cultural legitimation of ideas of crime may be.

The international crime of piracy provides an interesting illustration since it seems, both historically and today, the perfect example of a globally recognised crime, long-established in international custom and supported by universal jurisdiction. The nationality or state allegiance of both offenders and victims is largely irrelevant, and the authorities of any state have authority in international law to prosecute piracy. The pirate is said to be the 'enemy of all humanity' (*hostis humani generis*) and criminally punishable on this basis.[42]

Is this then a rare example of criminalisation supported by a genuinely universal (global) network of community – a true community of humanity? Perhaps unfortunately, the answer has to be negative. What supports this idea of crime is not a global community of belief or ultimate values (perhaps focused on universal human rights and dignity) but rather the existence of common or convergent interests in transnational trade. The relevant transnational communal network is primarily economic

---

[42] eg Kenneth C Randall, 'Universal Jurisdiction under International Law' (1988) 66 *Texas Law Review* 785–841, 792–95.

in nature. States now address piracy to protect their nationals from physical harm, but more fundamental (certainly in establishing customary piracy jurisdiction) is the need to protect property and *economic interaction* via the high seas or air routes.[43] In this respect states act on behalf of transnational trading networks from whose welfare and success they benefit.

Much other transnational criminalisation is similarly grounded in the interests of transnational economic networks. Hence its cultural legitimacy comes from those networks – not from any wider constituency of global authorisation. Much administrative criminalisation[44] is concerned to facilitate effective instrumental relations on which the increasingly complex structures of productive economic interaction across national boundaries depend. Crimes of money-laundering, fraud, counterfeiting, insider-trading, corruption, price-fixing, racketeering, environmental pollution, etc, proliferate in this context.

But many of these crimes are poorly understood by most people; the exact nature of the criminality involved – the practical meaning of these crimes – is mainly given by understandings internal to the primarily economic networks of community (eg business and financial networks, and the networks of state and international enforcers policing them) that are involved. Hence what might be readily understood *inside* these networks as crime – as *mala in se* – might well be seen outside them as criminality only in some vague sense: as offences because designated as such – *mala prohibita*.[45]

In this light Durkheimian approaches to understanding crime in transnational contexts surely need substantial modification to be convincing. Transnational crime in general cannot be seen as an affront to some all-embracing transnational collective consciousness.[46] The idea of such a global consciousness as a basis of universal cultural authority for criminalisation is a myth, just as the idea of a global 'international community' is a mythical foundation of a universal politicolegal authority.

More plausible is the idea of limited transnational networks relying on different kinds of dominant relations of community. Many are networks of primarily instrumental (economic) community. Others are territorially based – regional networks dominated by traditional (eg historically evolved) relations of community based on coexistence in a single environment. Often there is overlap: so that the European Union's transnational criminal law can be seen as supported by the Union's nature as both a region of geographically and historically determined coexistence (a matter of common fate and common tradition) and as a relatively integrated economic network (a matter of increasing instrumental interaction in industry, commerce and finance). But it might also be seen as based in a Europe-wide community of belief – in 'European values' – lending it cultural authority; or even in an emotional allegiance to a presumed distinct European identity requiring protection.

---

[43] Piracy is defined as a crime committed for 'private' (ie typically economic not political) purposes; and under old customary international law it covered robbery but not murder: see eg Eugene Kontorovich, '"A Guantanamo on the Sea": The Difficulty of Prosecuting Pirates and Terrorists' (2010) 98 *California Law Review* 243–75, 252–53.

[44] The phrase, though not Weber's, surely reflects the outlook of his sociolegal theory.

[45] By contrast, attacks on the person and property (homicide, theft, etc) that threaten local environments of coexistence are easily and widely 'visible' as crime insofar as these environments are essential to life.

[46] Henham (n 24) 84–85.

Despite its difficulties, the Durkheimian understanding of crime as related to a collective consciousness – a set of beliefs and ultimate values held in common by people and uniting them in social relations of community – should not be discarded. Durkheim saw this collective consciousness as a reality in modern political societies, however limited the scope of universally shared beliefs and values might have become in complex, diverse modern life. He saw 'moral individualism' – the value system that defends the autonomy and dignity of every human being as of equal value – as not only possible but necessary as the overarching moral bond of complex modern societies. Only by treating every other person as of equal human worth with oneself would it be possible to relate constructively with people in conditions where their experiences, lifestyles, aspirations and understandings might differ radically. Durkheim thus saw moral individualism – which can be seen as the prototype of universal human rights discourse – as actually essential for basic solidarity in diverse, complex and fragmented modern societies.[47]

If the value system of moral individualism is very limited in scope (it leaves much to be filled in as to what dignity and autonomy entail) it is nevertheless powerful in its demands. As regards criminal law it mandates condemnation of fundamental human rights violations but also humane treatment of offenders and prisoners. It outlaws all cruel and unusual punishments, including capital punishment, and it marks out all serious physical and psychological harms deliberately inflicted on individuals (whether free citizens or prisoners in custody) as the most important crimes. Hence, one might think, this value system offers powerful moral authority to support international criminal law in many of its most central designations of offences.

Up to a point this is so. ICL can be seen as gaining cultural authority from a transnational network of community held together primarily by a common commitment to beliefs and ultimate values centred on human rights. Its authority not only derives politically from the acceptance by states of the Rome Statute and the jurisdiction of the ICC. It comes also from the fact that this law and its court reflect a widely held popular aspiration to the realisation of humanitarian values. However, it seems important to accept that this network of community is not worldwide. It coexists with other networks that may espouse different beliefs or values or not be characterised by any public agreement on ultimate values or beliefs. It is sometimes said, indeed, that the human rights constituency reflects a specifically European experience, with which non-European states and populations may or may not find reasons to link themselves. The idea of networks of community emphasises always the *relativity* of cultural authority: the diversity and contingency of its locations.

Although human rights embodying the values of an international community are often said to underpin ICL it is important to note that Durkheim's value system of moral individualism is justified not juristically or philosophically, but *sociologically as appropriate to complex, secular, highly diverse modern societies*. This value system is necessary (even if often violated in practice) to unite and underpin networks of interdependence in such societies. One could speculate that, insofar as more and

---

[47] For full discussion, see Cotterrell (n 35, 2018) 172–203; and, for analysis in a sentencing context, Ralph Henham, *Sentencing Policy and Social Justice* (Oxford, Oxford University Press, 2018).

more of the world takes on the characteristics of these societies, moral individualism will spread, extending a transnational network of community emphasising human rights understood in a Western European sense. But in a sociological view this extension might not be inevitable. Ideas of human rights remain the property of *certain* networks of community, not of a 'community of humanity'.

5. THE RELATIVITY OF THE CONCEPT OF CRIME

As argued earlier, crime, treated as a cultural rather than a purely politicolegal idea, is best seen as action threatening the very existence of a network of community – its basic conditions of order, underlying ideas of justice or fundamental supports of solidarity. Because there are innumerable networks of community reflecting different combinations of communal bonds – common interests, shared beliefs or ultimate values, emotional allegiances and rejections, or the mere fact of coexistence in a common environment – it follows that ideas about crime will vary. Crime is a relative idea, rooted in specific social settings. The idea of criminal responsibility presupposes not some irreducible characteristics of human beings, but a *social environment* that gives meaning to the concept of crime. Insofar as states retain the monopoly of legal violence in their territory, any cultural legitimacy comes from the national political society as a communal network. But as criminalisation increasingly crosses state boundaries or even ignores them, this social environment to give cultural legitimacy must itself become transnational.

So, criminalisation has to reflect transnational ideas of order, justice and solidarity. If it does not do so, the popular support it obtains for law enforcement may be inadequate. Like all transnational law, transnational criminal law has to find secure grounding in populations that can culturally 'own' this law. To ignore that requirement is to risk stretching the politicolegal authority of regulation beyond the point where its success can be assumed. The message is hardly new. It is one that Eugen Ehrlich taught a century ago: official state-created and state-supervised law, if it is to be strong, has to take account of the 'living law' of popular experience:[48] in this chapter's terms – politicolegal authority has to be grounded in cultural authority.

The relativity of the concept of crime as understood in networks of community is certainly troubling in important respects. Relations of community judged valuable by the members of such a network may sometimes be condemned as pathological and evil when viewed from outside it. And what is seen as criminal in one such network may be the opposite in another. Within Nazi networks of community shaped by a common purpose of organising genocide, any form of brutality could be justified for the larger shared aims. And such networks were also based, for some members at least, on bonds of shared belief. Individuals challenging such aims and beliefs in any way could be and often were judged as heinous criminals.[49]

---

[48] Eugen Ehrlich, *Fundamental Principles of the Sociology of Law* [1936] transl WL Moll (New Brunswick, NJ, Transaction, 2002).

[49] HW Koch, *In the Name of the Volk: Political Justice in Hitler's Germany* (London, IB Tauris, 1989).

Today, from the standpoint of some transnational networks of community united especially by shared beliefs, Western secular states can be condemned as criminal. At the same time, acts condemned in many networks of community as terrorist crimes can be hailed in others as heroic deeds. Again, economic networks of community (eg some business communities) may have different 'internal' conceptions of acceptable or expected behaviour, so that what might be seen in one communal context as corrupt or otherwise criminal could be seen in another as normal and necessary practice. And transnational networks of community may exist specifically to pursue enterprises that are seen as obviously and seriously wrongful (transnational organised crime) beyond them.

As transnational processes of criminalisation accelerate, the problem of different understandings of the nature of crime may be addressed partly by forceful repression of some understandings by others – as in the destruction of the Nazi regime in war and the criminalisation of its leaders. In such circumstances, the old Weberian claimed monopoly of legal violence by the nation state is transformed into organised repression by coalitions of international states, or by international agencies supported by adequate military power supplied by states. In other cases, forms of coercion, influence or persuasion not involving the use of military force may be available.

Broadly speaking, it is necessary to envisage the process of transnationalisation of the idea of crime on two planes. The first is that of the *political* relations between states, and the dynamics of international organisations supported by the politico-legal authority of states. The other is that of *intercultural* dialogue, involving the interaction, interpenetration and eventual coordination of networks of community. Both of these planes are ones on which juristic ideas have to be formed.

Durkheimian theory gives some grounds for predicting the ongoing spread of ideas of human rights, though not necessarily their global universalisation or the removal of major differences of interpretation of their meaning. On both the politicolegal and the cultural planes, however, it seems clear that the ongoing transnationalisation of the idea of crime will be pursued most effectively and enduringly through negotiation and compromise. This, in turn, will depend on an ongoing effort to translate, transnationally, innumerable communal understandings of what can be assumed as universal aspirations for order and justice within a framework of solidarity. The possibilities and limits of that process indicate the extent to which the concept of crime can acquire stable transnational content.

3

'The Mob Is Fickle, Brother': Bringing Public Morality into Sentencing Policy

MARK A. DRUMBL

WITH THESE DUPLICITOUSLY delivered words, Lucilla tries to calm her brother Commodus, the Emperor – who agonises over Maximus' favour with the Roman crowds – in the Hollywood blockbuster *Gladiator*. Notwithstanding the brutalist kitsch, an insight remains: the mob, and its assignations of mercy or revenge, has long endured as an audience for sentencers and as a source of what constitutes appropriate punishment.

What, then, to do with the mob and its values, however fickle, in the determination of sentencing policy?

In his 2014 book *Sentencing: Time for a Paradigm Shift*,[1] Ralph Henham explicitly advocates for a tighter relationship between social morality and penal ideology; in particular, one that is attuned to gender and racial inequities.[2] He calls for a sentencing policy that is socially inclusive: in other words, one that brings in the crowd.[3] He calls for sentencing to take the form of a social activity more responsive to pluralistic needs and values, notably to those of disempowered groups, and which pivots toward restorative justice.[4]

This chapter takes Henham's exhortation as a point of departure. But it then turns to tell a somewhat different story, to wit, the counternarrative that one of the dangers of sentencing policy as inclusive popular morality is that such morality may vacillate over and through time. Moreover, in terms of operational effects, popularly held values may depart from the *grand finale* that Henham envisions. In this regard, this chapter fits snugly within a core theme of this book, namely, the relationship between the social and the legal in terms of not only conceptualising the law (see, for example, Paul Behrens's chapter 14 on genocide) and administering the law (see Candace McCoy's chapter 7 on plea bargaining), but in this case in terms of sentencing through the law.

---

[1] Ralph Henham, *Sentencing: Time for a Paradigm Shift* (New York, Routledge 2014).
[2] See generally ibid.
[3] See ibid 111 (noting that 'the relationship between penal ideology and sentencing outcomes should be conceived as both socially inclusive and recursive').
[4] ibid.

This chapter picks up the life cycle of section 718.2(e) of the Canadian Criminal Code[5] as a case study of what it means to import public morality into sentencing. Statutorily introduced in 1996, this provision was intended to address the grievous over-incarceration of aboriginal persons in Canadian prisons. The then Canadian minister of justice, in pushing for this legislation, noted at the time that aboriginal persons represented about 2 percent of Canada's overall population but 10.6 percent of its prison population.[6] Section 718.2(e) explicitly obliges judges to consider aboriginality and circumstances of aboriginal oppression in sentencing an aboriginal convict.[7]

Section 718.2(e), regrettably, has not been effectual. Imprisonment rates for aboriginals have not declined since its enactment in 1996.[8] On the contrary, these rates have increased.[9] In 2015, the Canadian Parliament amended section 718.2(e) in a fashion that gutted its initial language.[10] The energy behind this amendment was at best cosmetically sourced in an objective assessment of section 718.2(e)'s operational effectiveness. The actual legislative motivations lurked in politics and law-and-order ideology. As part of a long-standing commitment to get tough on crime, a conservative government weakened section 718.2(e) within a much broader reform of the criminal justice system that pushed hard for victims' rights. Promoting an agenda of victims' rights, to be sure, may reflect democratic inclusion, civic participation and transparency. This agenda, often hued in retributivism, nonetheless evokes scant empathy for the perpetrator.

The denouement of section 718.2(e) can therefore be constructed as reflecting the unsure and unsteady grounding of sentencing policy when rooted in public morality.

Hence, perhaps a firmer footing for a restorative, empathetic and gracious sentencing policy lies elsewhere than the crowd? And if so, then, where? Perhaps instead of searching for social consensus through sentencing, we should embrace dissensus, to wit, the tension that emerges when sentencers act in ways that depart from the will of popular morality, however undemocratic or elitist such moves might be, or even abandon penal frameworks entirely in certain contexts. The result is a sentencing structure that incurs a democratic deficit – or punctures the demos – but in turn may come to shape, or alter, what the democratic values of tomorrow might be. Henham's goal of a sentencing policy that promotes restorative ends, up-ends social inequities, and knocks down gender- and race-based hierarchies may not be as readily obtained through welcoming existing public morality as it may be by challenging or shattering it.

*

---

[5] Criminal Code, RSC, 1985, s 718.2(e).

[6] Elizabeth Sheehy and Isabel Grant, 'A Tragic Tale of Two Gladues', *Toronto Star* (27 April 2015).

[7] Criminal Code, RSC, 1985, s 718.2(e).

[8] See Canada Department of Justice, 'Spotlight on *Gladue*: Challenges, Experiences, and Possibilities in Canada's Criminal Justice System' (4 April 2019) https://www.justice.gc.ca/eng/rp-pr/jr/gladue/p2.html.

[9] See ibid.

[10] Whereas the original wording of s 718.2(e) suggested that alternative sentencing be imposed so long as it proved 'reasonable in the circumstances', the amended language prioritises punishment 'consistent with the harm done to victims or the community'. See Criminal Code, RSC, 1985, s 718.2(e).

Henham begins his project with the observation that: 'Sentencing is the process through which the legitimacy of punishment is declared and justified.'[11] He then creatively argues that 'the future legitimacy of sentencing ... ultimately depends upon the strength of the relationship between social morality and penal ideology'.[12] Henham envisions the fulfilment of this legitimacy when sentencing 'become[s] more socially inclusive, so that it contributes to the maintenance of social harmony and promotes social cohesion'.[13] Henham contemplates this process as democratic, in that 'citizens should feel that their interests ... are recognized and respected by the penal system, thus promoting greater attachment and reinforcement of its values and outcomes'.[14] He sees this move as particularly germane for the viability of restorative and other alternative justice mechanisms.[15] On this note, Henham's work bears directly upon initiatives such as those contemplated by section 718.2(e) in light of its incorporation of alternative community-based sanctions rooted in the aboriginal experience.[16]

Henham clearly recognises, as many others have previously, that majority views have generated a sentencing policy in Western nations that may prove to be 'discriminatory and oppressive for particular citizens'.[17] He details at length how the will of the majority disturbingly reinforces the primacy of the powerful and subordinates those constituencies most in need of a thoughtful sentencing practice.[18] But Henham retains faith in the ability of a process of social inclusion to create a 'shared morality' that, ultimately, would serve the interests of serially disadvantaged groups.[19] The discursive process, then, conveys for Henham the possibility of meaningful engagement with the 'sensibilities, emotions and subjective understandings that citizens hold about criminal justice'.[20] He believes in the possibility of transcending 'penal policies that tend to increase social division and endorse the status quo towards those that engage with a broader moral constituency and so draw wider popular support'.[21] Henham equates dominant retributive (and intrinsically adversarial) frameworks with patriarchy and privilege.[22] He urges, for example, that we go further than 'parsimony in the use of imprisonment for women',[23] advocating instead for a reconceptualisation of penal ideology that 'better reflects the needs and aspirations of women' and integrates restorative mechanisms.[24]

---

[11] Henham (n 1) 3.
[12] ibid 1.
[13] ibid.
[14] ibid 2.
[15] ibid.
[16] ibid.
[17] ibid.
[18] See generally ibid.
[19] See ibid 100: 'Ultimately, the ability of judicial discretionary power to engage with social morality depends on the extent to which an identifiable common morality can be said to influence the exercise of discretion. Such a shared morality will only exist where the notion of inclusiveness has been adopted as a key element of penal ideology.'
[20] ibid 10.
[21] ibid 35.
[22] See generally ibid.
[23] ibid 66.
[24] ibid.

A tenet of Henham's work is its universalism. Although rooted in the English and Welsh experience, his scholarship is exportable. His retheorisation operates regardless of the locus of sentencing (a national, international or local court) and irrespective of the crime in question (genocide or shoplifting). He moves seamlessly and effortlessly among jurisdictions and levels of governance. Regardless of locus, however, Henham doggedly sees social inclusiveness as a portal through which sentencing policy can be diversified so as to invigorate restorative options that, in turn, will promote the interests of disadvantaged groups and, when aggregated, overall social equality.

Henham's optimism is admirable. It uplifts. Yet I remain somewhat more circumspect of the social justice possibilities of sentencing when appreciated as a political process. Considerable empirical evidence arises that, for example in the United States, 'African Americans and males receive longer sentences when local courts are embedded in conservative political environments where a law-and-order presidential candidate received more votes … [t]hese results support theoretical claims that punishment is an intensely political process.'[25] Politics seems to offer little in the way of antidote, or cure, to the ills that bedevil sentencing. The introduction of victims' rights, moreover, often is couched in the language of democratic inclusion, civic participation and transparency. Henham welcomes victim input: in fact, he envisions this input as supportive of restorative modalities insofar as these modalities focus on the repair – whether individual or community – for which victims often clamber.[26] Yet in my experience, the politics of victims' rights generally elicits precious little in the way of empathy for the perpetrator. Rather, these politics embed retributivism. They ensconce *othering* within the social fabric, leading to a painful situation in which the rotten social background of many perpetrators barely obtains any traction – whether that of a poor young inner-city youth in a local court or former child soldier Dominic Ongwen at the ICC (sentenced at trial in 2021 to a term of twenty-five years). The more the public is involved in selecting those who sentence, and what the terms of punishment ought to be, the harsher sentences seem to become.

Henham nonetheless remains unflaggingly inspired. He locates within the mob the opportunity to systematically relax the grip of the adversarial trial paradigm, predicated as it is on assessments of individual guilt and the restriction of dialogue about the broader social causes of criminality.[27] Provisions such as section 718.2(e) may therefore serve as probative examples of a sentencing policy, derivative of popular legislative efforts, that Henham would welcome. Hence, perhaps some practical insights can be gleaned from Canadian approaches to sentencing aboriginal offenders

---

[25] Ronald Helms and David Jacobs, 'The Political Context of Sentencing: An Analysis of Community and Individual Determinants' (2002) 81(2) *Social Forces* 577–604 at abstract. On the other hand, perhaps (in the United States, at least) now that sentences have become so harsh (particularly with mandatory minimum requirements), and the structural racism of the criminal justice system so evident in an era of iPhones and YouTube, it may be that public morality is becoming increasingly tepid when it comes to law-and-order discourse.
[26] See Henham (n 1) 112 n 2.
[27] ibid 4.

within Canada's routine criminal justice system. It is to these approaches, and their staccato trajectories, that this chapter now turns.

*

Aboriginal persons endure significantly disproportionate overrepresentation in the Canadian prison system.[28] The percentages are glaring.[29] Aboriginal citizens constituted about 3 percent of Canada's population in 2008 but comprised 18 percent of the male inmate population and 24 percent of the female inmate population.[30] Statistics from individual provinces are even more distressing. In Saskatchewan, for example, while aboriginal persons made up approximately 10 percent of the province's adult population, in the period from 1999 to 2004 they constituted 57 percent of the population under correctional supervision.[31]

In Canada, the administration of justice falls to the provinces whereas the substantive law of application – the Canadian Criminal Code – is a federal piece of legislation. In the mid-1990s, presented with incontrovertible evidence of persistent discrimination against First Nations persons throughout the criminal justice system,[32] federal lawmakers enacted a series of amendments to the Criminal Code. These amendments took the form of Bill C-41, which received Royal Assent in 1995 and was proclaimed into force in September 1996. While these amendments addressed the sentencing of all offenders, aboriginal carceral overrepresentation constituted a specific concern. Newly enacted section 718.2(e) was prominent among these amendments. It read as follows:

> (e) all available sanctions other than imprisonment that are reasonable in the circumstances should be considered for all offenders, with particular attention to the circumstances of aboriginal offenders.

This provision embedded itself in a list of other factors for courts to consider when sentencing offenders. It was felt at the time that aboriginal overimprisonment derived from inappropriate sentencing, derivative of the colonial experience, and that

---

[28] See Canada Department of Justice (n 8).

[29] See ibid.

[30] See Michelle O'Bonsawin, 'Introduction and Legal Foundation', *Gladue Principles and Their Applications in Criminal Justice and Mental Health Systems: A Symposium*, www.hsjcc.on.ca/ Resource%20Library/Mental%20Health%20and%20Justice/Gladue%20Principles%20and%20 Their%20Applications%20In%20Criminal%20Justice%20and%20Mental%20Health%20Systems%20-%202013.pdf.

[31] See Brian Pfefferle, '*Gladue* Sentencing: Uneasy Answers to the Hard Problem of Aboriginal Over-incarceration' (2008) 32(2) *Manitoba Law Journal* 113, 116, n 16 (citing Statistics Canada, 'Aboriginal People Over-represented in Saskatchewan's Prisons', http://www41.statcan.ca/2693/ceb2693_002_e.htm) (noting that the recidivism rate among aboriginal offenders in 1999–2000 was double that of non-Aboriginal offenders).

[32] The evidence is overwhelming. See eg *Report of the Commission on Systemic Racism in the Ontario Criminal Justice System* (Toronto, Queen's Printer, 1995); Julian Roberts and Ronald Melchers, 'Incarceration of Aboriginal Offenders: Trends from 1978 to 2001' (2003) *Canadian Journal of Criminology and Criminal Justice* 211; Canada, Royal Commission on Aboriginal Peoples, *Bridging the Cultural Divide: A Report on Aboriginal People and Criminal Justice in Canada* (Ottawa, Canadian Communication Group, 1996).

modifying sentencing practices to unleash more creative possibilities could deflate this miserable situation.[33] Hence, section 718.2(e) was intended to serve a remedial purpose.[34] According to Chartrand, it is the only provision in the Canadian Criminal Code to expressly identify aboriginal peoples for 'special positive treatment'.[35]

Section 718.2(e) did not emerge in a vacuum. For some time prior, 'at common law' in Canada, requirements arose for judges 'to take into account the Aboriginality of the offender'.[36] However, section 718.2(e) 'is more than a simple codification of existing sentencing provisions'.[37]

*

Section 718.2(e) quickly attracted judicial interpretation, which augmented the significance of the provision and also narrowed its ambit by emphasising its focus on aboriginal offenders.[38]

In 1999, in *R v Gladue*, the Supreme Court of Canada interpreted section 718.2(e) to yield an approach to sentencing aboriginal offenders that has since been referred to as the *Gladue* principles.[39] *Gladue* was quickly followed by the Supreme Court of Canada's judgment in *R v Wells*.[40] In 2012, the Supreme Court of Canada once again weighed in on section 718.2(e). In *R v Ipeelee*,[41] the Court underscored the provision's remedial nature 'to ameliorate the serious problem of overrepresentation of Aboriginal people in Canadian prisons'.[42] The Court noted that Parliament had concluded that 'nothing short of a specific direction to pay particular attention to the circumstances of Aboriginal offenders would suffice to ensure that judges undertook their duties properly'.[43] Central among these duties, to be sure, is for judges not to contribute to ongoing patterns of discrimination but, instead, to endeavour to stanch them. Insofar as Canadian courts associate indigenous traditions with values of restorative justice, practically speaking, what section 718.2(e) means is that consideration of community-based, non-carceral sanctions becomes required in the case of aboriginal offenders. Nevertheless, section 718.2(e) operates within the context of all other factors (including denunciation and deterrence) that remain germane to sentencing.

---

[33] Pfefferle (n 31) 116 n 14.

[34] For discussion of s 718.2(e) as part of a broader framework of reparative programming for aboriginal communities in Canada, see Larry Chartrand, 'The Aboriginal Sentencing Provision of the *Criminal Code* as a Protected "Other Right" Under Section 25 of the Charter' (2012) 57 *Supreme Court Law Review* (2d) 389; see also Carmela Murdocca, *To Right Historical Wrongs: Reparative Justice, Sentencing and the Production of Racial Difference* (Vancouver, University of British Columbia Press, 2012).

[35] Chartrand (n 34) 409 n 17.

[36] ibid 394–95, citing as specific examples *R v Fireman* [1971] 3 OR 380 (ONCA) and *R v Moses* [1992] 71 CCC (3d) 347 (YT Terr Ct).

[37] ibid 398 n 17.

[38] Chartrand queries whether the focus only on aboriginal offenders could constitute discrimination because other offenders are unable to benefit from this sentencing approach. He argues that such an argument would not be successful, however. See ibid at 398–99.

[39] *R v Gladue* [1999] SCC 679, [1999] 1 SCR 688.

[40] *R v Wells* [2000] SCC 10, [2000] 1 SCR 207.

[41] *R v Ipeelee* [2012] SCC 14, [2012] 1 SCR 433.

[42] ibid para 59.

[43] ibid para 68.

Jamie Gladue, a nineteen-year-old aboriginal woman, killed her common law husband.[44] She stabbed him twice in the chest following an argument.[45] Gladue pled guilty to manslaughter[46] and at trial was sentenced to three years in prison.[47] Because she was perceived as an 'urban-aboriginal person' at trial, she was found not to be within the aboriginal community; hence, the sentencing judge did not apply section 718.2(e).[48] The Supreme Court of Canada ultimately found this approach to be in error.[49] It held that section 718.2(e) applies to any class of aboriginal offender regardless of whether the offender is a status or non-status Indian, Métis or Inuit person; specifically to the case at hand, the Court ruled that the provision applies to an 'urban-Aboriginal person (even if the offender has been estranged from their culture) as it would to an on-reserve Aboriginal person'.[50] In this regard, the Court avoided cartoonish assessments of indigenousness or aboriginality and embarrassing forays into who (and what) 'counts' in this regard.[51] Importantly, the Court interpreted section 718.2(e) as requiring the differential treatment of aboriginal offenders in certain circumstances on the basis that aboriginal offenders are unique in comparison to non-aboriginal offenders.[52] Pursuant to *Gladue*, judges must first consider the unique systemic or background factors that may have played a part in bringing the aboriginal offender before the courts, and, secondly, the types of sentences that may be appropriate in the circumstances because of the offender's aboriginal heritage or connection.[53] When it came to the specific circumstances of Jamie Gladue, however, the Court did not alter the initially awarded three-year sentence.

Following this decision, the production of what is referred to as a '*Gladue* Report' became required in the case of sentencing any aboriginal offender.[54] A *Gladue* Report is a pre-sentence report concerned with the circumstances of an aboriginal offender. It may form part of a general pre-sentence report or take the place thereof.

Wells involved a sexual assault.[55] The sentencing judge accounted for the accused's aboriginal background but also determined that the gravity of the offence warranted more than a conditional community sentence.[56] The Supreme Court of Canada

---

[44] *Gladue* (n 39).
[45] ibid 689.
[46] ibid.
[47] ibid 698.
[48] Pfefferle (n 31) 117.
[49] ibid.
[50] ibid.
[51] That said (and notwithstanding this admonition), in subsequent cases provincial courts have emphasised that restorative sentencing outputs may be more evidently applicable to aboriginals who 'earn [their] sustenance in the traditional aboriginal way by hunting, trapping and fishing'. *R v Cappo* [2005] SKCA 134, [2005] 269 Sask R 311 at para 15.
[52] *Gladue* (n 39) paras 33, 36; see also ibid para 33 (holding that s 718.2(e) gives 'direction' to sentencing judges to 'undertake the process of sentencing aboriginal offenders differently, in order to endeavour to achieve a truly fit and proper sentence in the particular case').
[53] *Gladue* (n 39) para 66.
[54] See eg *R v Kakekagamick* [2006] ONCA 28549, [2006] 21 CCC (3d) 289 para 52.
[55] *R v Wells* (n 40).
[56] ibid 10, para 12 (determining that, given the violent nature of the crime, the necessary elements of deterrence and denunciation would be lacking if such a sentence were imposed).

upheld the trial judge's decision, emphasising the value of discretion and noting that methodologically he had applied section 718.2(e).[57]

In *Wells* and *Gladue*, the Supreme Court of Canada underscored the systemic roots of aboriginal disadvantage, patterns of dislocation, and the prevalence of racism and discrimination. The Court in *Gladue* observed the following as factors to be considered: 'low incomes, high unemployment, lack of opportunities and options, lack or irrelevance of education, substance abuse, loneliness and community fragmentation, ... overt racism, ... family or community breakdown'.[58] *Wells* was unequivocal, however, that while section 718.2(e) mandates a 'different methodology for assessing a fit sentence for an aboriginal offender', it does not necessarily flow that the ultimate 'result' (ie sentence) will also be different.[59] Section 718.2(e) is about appropriate methodology, not necessarily substantive outcomes. In the factual context in *Wells*, for example, the Court opined that denunciatory and deterrent goals militated against a conditional sentence.[60]

In the 2012 *Ipeelee* judgment, the Supreme Court of Canada unequivocally upheld the differential sentencing for aboriginals. It stated:

> To be clear, courts must take judicial notice of such matters as the history of colonialism, displacement, and residential schools and how that history continues to translate into lower educational attainment, lower incomes, higher unemployment, higher rates of substance abuse and suicide, and of course higher levels of incarceration for Aboriginal peoples. These matters, on their own, do not necessarily justify a different sentence for Aboriginal offenders. Rather, they provide the necessary context for understanding and evaluating the case-specific information presented by counsel.[61]

Differential sentencing is predicated upon the notion that the underlying causes of criminal conduct may drain some of the offender's moral blameworthiness.[62] As noted by Chartrand, this jurisprudence may be seen as compatible with the notion that an 'Aboriginal offender can be regarded simultaneously as an offender *vis-à-vis* the specifics of the criminal offence and as an indirect victim in the larger racialized societal context of Aboriginal-Crown cultural, political and social conflict.'[63]

Ipeelee involved two cases that concerned two separate aboriginal offenders. Both offenders were under long-term supervision orders. These orders constituted a form of conditional release and were intended to rehabilitate convicts and guide their resocialisation.[64] Both offenders, in any event, breached their orders, so the question arose as to the appropriate sanction for their breaches. The first appellant, Manasie Ipeelee, presented as a thirty-nine-year-old Inuk man and alcoholic, in jail or detention

---

[57] ibid 14, para 24.
[58] *Gladue* (n 39) paras 67, 80.
[59] *Wells* (n 40) 229–30, para 44.
[60] ibid.
[61] *Ipeelee* (n 41) 469, para 60.
[62] ibid 477, para 73; but see *R v Delorme* [2017] SKCA 3, [2017] 136 WCB (2d) 115 (citing *R v Chanalquay* [2015] SKCA 141, [2015] Sask R 110, para 52) ('However, a sentencing judge should not simply muster all of the Gladue-type considerations at play and automatically conclude these have had a substantial limiting effect on the offender's culpability. The required analysis is more demanding').
[63] Chartrand (n 34) 410.
[64] *Ipeelee* (n 41) 487, para 89.

since 1985. His mother died when he was five. Ipeelee had been sentenced to a six-year term on sexual assault charges and breached the long-term supervision order granted as part of this sentence. As a result, he was newly sentenced to a three-year custodial term. The second offender, Frank Ralph Ladue, aged forty-nine, had endured abuse in residential schools. He had a long criminal record and was also a substance abuser. He had been convicted of the sexual assault of an unconscious woman and jailed for several breaches of his long-term supervision order. The Supreme Court of Canada allowed Ipeelee's appeal but then dismissed Ladue's appeal. Ipeelee was sentenced to one year in prison, while Ladue's one-year sentence was not revisited.

*

Taken as a whole, this case law has helped clarify a number of interpretive questions. Who is an aboriginal for the purpose of section 718.2(e)? Does the individual in question need to reside on a reservation? *Gladue* broadly applied section 718.2(e),[65] and this approach has overall been consolidated in subsequent jurisprudence,[66] albeit not without exception depending on the province in question.[67] A lack of clarity also persists as to who bears the burden of proof of establishing aboriginality; this conversation remains poignant in light of the fact that past Canadian governments deliberately pursued policies to assimilate aboriginal communities. The creation of a protection for aboriginals then triggers a need to determine insiders and outsiders in complex identity assessments; a process itself tinged with the painful reality that aboriginal identity has been subject to systematic governmental deformation and manipulation. Although section 718.2(e) may be somewhat purposively applied in the case of aboriginal offenders, what about offenders from other disempowered groups? Here, the courts have been reticent. Murdocca, for instance, documents and critiques how courts have shied away from applying this provision to African Canadians.[68]

To what kinds of proceedings must a *Gladue* analysis apply? It has been held, in addition to criminal proceedings and violations of long-term supervision orders, that when a Review Board makes determinations regarding whether an offender presents a continuing threat to public safety, it is to obtain a *Gladue* report where such information would be pertinent and relevant to the reintegrative disposition it is being called upon to make.[69] To which offences does section 718.2(e) apply? It has been held that, methodologically, *Gladue* applies to all offences.[70] For instance, in *Ipeelee* the Court was clear that *Gladue* principles and the aspirations of rehabilitation and

---

[65] S 718.2(e) extends 'at least' to 'all who come within the scope of s 25 of the *Charter* and s 35 of the *Constitution Act*, 1982'. *Gladue* (n 39) para 90.

[66] See *R v Brizard* [2006] ONCA 5444 (explaining that *Gladue* principles apply to all aboriginal offenders, even offenders not connected to the aboriginal community).

[67] The Saskatchewan Court of Appeal has underscored the need for the offender, the offender's background, and the crime to be connected in order for *Gladue* and s 718.2(e) to apply to the proceedings. *See R v PC* [2004] 249 Sask R 143 (SKCA).

[68] See Murdocca (n 34) 113.

[69] See *R v Sim* [2005] 78 OR (3d) 183 (ONCA). This outcome was reached despite the finding that the Review Board was not a sentencing court and, hence, that s 718.2(e) did not formally apply.

[70] See *R v Jensen* [2005] 74 OR (3d) 561 (ONCA).

reintegration are to be weighed heavily even in cases of repeat offenders of grave crimes.[71] That said, as discussed in greater detail below, the case law tapers *Gladue*'s effects with the seriousness of the offence.

Other interpretive questions, however, have not been satisfactorily resolved (or even settled, however unsatisfactorily). What are the 'circumstances' of aboriginal offenders? In sentencing, the Court is to consider histories and realities of poverty, discrimination and insecurity in aboriginal communities.[72] Less clear is whether the offender's conduct should be placed within the context of ongoing criminality that may roil the community. The Saskatchewan Court of Appeal, for example, held in a fraud case that it was inappropriate to consider illicit conduct by other community members in a section 718.2(e) analysis: in other words, criminal acts within a context where such acts are prevalent would not serve to affect sentence.[73] Also under-analysed is the question as to the meaning of reasonable alternative sanctions. If the 'circumstances' of aboriginal offenders are understood to support restorative and reintegrative methodologies to sentencing, which is a definite thread in jurisprudence as early as *Wells*, then how does this impetus mesh with the other declared goals of sentencing, namely, denunciation and deterrence? Pursuant to the case law, it is far from the case that an aboriginal offender should be sentenced with priority towards restoration as opposed to priority to denunciatory or deterrent goals. This outcome may not be surprising in light of the fact that, textually, section 718.2(e) presents restorative approaches as an exception to an overall retributive framework, which in turn reinforces the subaltern status of restoration as a penological goal. Judges have issued explicit cautions in the case of particularly violent or serious offences.[74] In such situations, even if the offender's violence traces to factors germane to the *Gladue* principles, these factors shed their probative salience.[75] The judge must still consider *Gladue* factors, but in such cases, these will typically not impact the length or nature of the sentence. Hence, the distinct sentencing methodology for aboriginal offenders has limits. It remains unclear, however, whether it is theoretically justifiable – in light of the goals of section 718.2(e) – to view the provision's application as most robust in the case of lesser offences. Another vexing question is how to deploy restorative

---

[71] See *Ipeelee* (n 41) 464 (noting that 'to suggest ... that rehabilitation has been determined to be impossible to achieve in the long-term offender context is simply wrong').

[72] See *Gladue* (n 39) 730, para 80 (explaining that 'systemic or background forces' possibly contributing to the offence should be examined on a case-by-case basis).

[73] See *R v Gopher* [2006] SKCA 86, [2006] 285 Sask R 191, para 36 (warning of a 'self-reinforcing spiral' if 'the presence of criminal activity becomes a factor mitigating against strong sentences to punish that activity'). For a sharp critique of this decision, in particular of its ignoring of social circumstances when these may be criminal in nature, see Pfefferle (n 31) 124–25. Pfefferle notes that 'on-reserve crime rates in 2004 were about three times higher than rates in the rest of Canada', ibid 13. He also points to criminological research that examines the role 'one's region or territory may have on one's criminal activity', ibid 126 n 85.

[74] See eg *Ipeelee* (n 41) 439 (affirming the sentencing judge's determination that the only way to protect the community, given the particularly violent nature of the offender's crime, was to 'emphasize the objective of isolation' over rehabilitation or other forms of alternative sentencing).

[75] See eg *Chanalquay* (n 62) para 32 (increasing the sentence delivered by the trial judge and emphasising that the court had repeatedly imposed heavy custodial sentences for similarly violent offences, despite compelling *Gladue* factors). For a recent example, see *R v Ratt* [2021] SKCA 7, para 21 (finding that due to the offender's violent criminal record, 'the principle of restraint specific to Indigenous offenders ... should play a lesser role in determining a fit sentence').

justice mechanisms in cases of aboriginal offenders with only a thin connection to the community in which such mechanisms would be applied. To what extent should awarding a restorative sentence, and hence the *Gladue* principles, hinge upon the capacity of the community in question to actually provide such an option? It would seem inequitable to deny a sentencing alternative to an aboriginal offender on the basis that the receiving community lacks the capacity to deliver such an alternative.

Also unresolved is the question of whether restorative justice approaches resonate within aboriginal communities in the fashion that outsiders (perhaps stereotypically) presume. Many victims of crimes committed by aboriginal offenders themselves are aboriginal: does section 718.2(e) reflect their aspirations and sentiments? In *Wells*, it was noted that aboriginal communities value goals of denunciation and deterrence depending on the nature of the offence and the harm inflicted on the community.[76] How should section 718.2(e) apply in the case of criminal conduct that emerges from violent masculinities and, hence, reinforces sex- and gender-based inequities? The British Columbia Court of Appeal, for example, has ruled that in such instances, the goals of denunciation, isolation and deterrence trump 'the mitigating effects of the appellant's aboriginal background'.[77] Carmela Murdocca's careful analysis of the formulation of Bill C-41 reveals the opposition of aboriginal women's organisations to traditional alternatives to incarceration.[78] A final question that has arisen is whether violent acts by an aboriginal offender against a non-aboriginal victim should be subject to different scrutiny under *Gladue* than acts inflicted upon an aboriginal victim.[79]

Fragmentation on these questions among the provincial courts prompted the general observation that 'consistent application of the *Gladue* case and section 718.2(e) has yet to occur'.[80]

*

What about the actual effects of section 718.2(e)? Writing in 2005, Justice Harry LaForme of the Ontario Court of Appeal noted that while the 1996 amendments to the Criminal Code led to a 22 percent decline in the number of non-aboriginals admitted into custody, aboriginals experienced a 3 percent *increase*.[81] In 2012, in *Ipeelee*, the Supreme Court of Canada for its part explicitly noted that the crisis of

---

[76] *Wells* (n 40) para 42; see also *R v Kasakan*, [2006] SKCA, 8 WWR 23. In *Ipeelee*, the sole dissenting judge, Rothstein J, contended that 'Aboriginal communities are not in a separate category entitled to less protection because the offender is aboriginal.' *Ipeelee* (n 41) 439.

[77] *R v LDW*, [2005] 215 BCAC. 64 (British Columbia Court of Appeal) para 27. Custodial sentences are to be imposed in such situations.

[78] Murdocca (n 34) 65.

[79] Pfefferle observes in the case of violence against a non-Aboriginal victim that 'an attack that is racially motivated is demonstrative of community dislocation, class hatred, and perhaps even societal racism that may have been faced by the [Aboriginal] accused or members of the [well known Aboriginal] gang'. Pfefferle (n 31) 129.

[80] Pfefferle (n 31) 115.

[81] Harry S LaForme, 'The Justice System in Canada: Does it Work for Aboriginal People?' (Fall 2005) 4 *Indigenous Law Journal* 1, 15.

aboriginal overrepresentation that had prompted the adoption of section 718.2(e) in 1996 remained unabated and indeed had become worse.[82] The Court voiced frustration with *Gladue*'s limited effects:

> Over a decade has passed since this Court issued its judgment in *Gladue*. As the statistics indicate, section 718.2(e) of the Criminal Code has not had a discernible impact on the overrepresentation of Aboriginal people in the criminal justice system. … Granted, the *Gladue* principles were never expected to provide a panacea. There is some indication, however, from both the academic commentary and the jurisprudence, that the failure can be attributed to some extent to a fundamental misunderstanding and misapplication of both s 718.2(e) and this Court's decision in *Gladue*.[83]

Whether section 718.2(e)'s paltry deliverables could be augmented by superior judicial management remains an open-ended question. Even more opaque is the question of whether section 718.2(e) has contributed to the goal of supporting aboriginal cultural and social traditions.

*

The choppy history of a courageous provision – and one that Ralph Henham likely would have welcomed – was indelibly altered in 2014 when the Canadian Parliament amended section 718.2(e) in a manner that weakened its language. Parliament did so as part of the Victims' Bill of Rights Act (Bill C-32), a so-called 'war on crime' bill which was introduced to Parliament in April 2014. The protection of the public was explicitly added as an overall purpose of sentencing. The amended language to section 718.2(e) now requires a judge also to consider 'the harm done to victims or to the community'. The consolidated provision therefore reads as follows:

> (e) All available sanctions, other than imprisonment, that are reasonable in the circumstances and consistent with the harm done to victims or to the community should be considered for all offenders, with particular attention to the circumstances of Aboriginal offenders.[84]

On the one hand, it is possible that this amendment changes little in terms of the actual application of the differential sentencing regime for aboriginals. The details remain to be ironed out by the courts. On the other hand, however, elemental canons of statutory interpretation provide that, when Parliament amends a legislative provision, the courts are required to give effect to the intention that motivated the amendment. In this case, according to Sheehy and Grant, 'the intent is clearly to limit the ameliorative purpose of this provision'.[85] The Canadian Criminal Code had already required courts to consider the harm done to victims or the community when it comes to sentencing determinations; Canadian courts had consistently recognised this factor in *Gladue*

---

[82] *Ipeelee* (n 41) 470, para 62.
[83] ibid 471, para 63. See also Murdocca (n 34) (arguing compellingly that s 718.2(e) has not yielded substantive justice outcomes for Aboriginal people).
[84] Criminal Code, RSC, 1985, s 718.2(e).
[85] Sheehy and Grant (n 6).

deliberations. The amendments, therefore, appear clearly intended to gore an already ineffective provision.[86] Media reports suggested that the push to amend section 718.2(e) emanated from the office of then Canadian Prime Minister Stephen Harper, which 'was directing the Justice department to reword portions of the Criminal Code to "diminish" the effect of *Gladue* principles for Aboriginal offenders before the courts'.[87] Ironically, the effects of *Gladue* were certainly not to enhance restorative sentencing options for aboriginal offenders. Hence, the push to dismantle it appears to service only rhetorical and political goals. This push validates the concern, raised by Henham, that sentencing may be 'destined to remain a partisan political weapon of social control'.[88] Henham's goal of a sentencing policy that promotes restorative ends, up-ends social inequities, and knocks down gender- and race-based hierarchies may not be as readily obtained through welcoming public morality as it may be by challenging it. Now that the provision has been textually gutted, then, perhaps this is how Canadian judges might approach the subject-matter; that is, by resisting the intent of the legislator at the time of enactment, however anti-democratic.

*

So, what is the takeaway?

Section 718.2(e) of the Canadian Criminal Code, in sum, is a probative case study of the need for and also the limits to the paradigm shift that Henham exhorts. While introduced through popular efforts, section 718.2(e) has also suffered because of popular input. Its life-cycle underscores the fickleness of the crowd. Moreover, the anaemic effects of this provision suggest the shortcomings of restructuring sentencing policy through the injection of some specific oases of restorative modalities within a system that remains profoundly retributive in nature. Something more radical is required, perhaps, and the radical nature of this reform intimates that its provenance may have to lie beyond the mob. Possible avenues could be anti-democratic

---

[86] In its submissions regarding the amendment when proposed, in which it recommended that the amendments to s 718 be deleted, the Criminal Justice Section of the Canadian Bar Association noted that legislative repetition of harm to victims or the community as a principle of sentencing 'suggests to judges that greater weight must be attributed to the consideration of harm over other important considerations of sentencing, like proportionality, the circumstances of the offender and the offence, rehabilitation and reintegration, and others. The fine balance required could easily be skewed by the Bill'. See Canadian Bar Association, Criminal Justice Section, 'Submissions, Bill C-32' (November 2014), section V, 6, available at www.cba.org/CMSPages/GetFile.aspx?guid=3e5c81e7-c4ef-4418-b38c-ceb832678962 (noting also that: 'The cumulative impact of these proposed amendments, with the increased use of mandatory minimum penalties and the elimination of conditional sentence orders for many non-violent offenders, risks adding to Canada's over-reliance on incarceration').

[87] Kenneth Jackson, 'PMO Ordered Justice Department to Re-word Criminal Code to Weaken *Gladue* Principles for Aboriginal Offenders', *APTN National News* (25 March 2015) (noting also that 'the PMO is hoping the courts give more weight to the effect the crime has had on the victim or community rather than an offender's past and the Gladue principles'). Cf Kenneth Jackson, 'Senate Passes Victims Bill of Rights that Will "Dilute" Gladue Principles', *APTN National News* (22 April 2015) ('Aboriginal people before the courts may soon find applying Gladue principles more difficult after the Senate … passed the Harper government's Victims Bill of Rights. … The legislation adds 11 words to the pre-existing Gladue section that could have a devastating impact on Aboriginal offenders, according to expert testimony').

[88] Henham (n 1) 7.

interpretive initiatives by elitist judges; exercises of discretion by prosecutors that countervail public hunger for retribution; or the fragmentation of the body politic into contexts where members of disadvantaged groups are sentenced by peers within those groups, and are consequently fully removed from the ordinary criminal justice system whose coercive apparatus would thereby splinter. Rather that cohering communities – a methodology that may lead to subordination – consideration might be given to decoupling communities from the state system and thereby empowering their self-governance.

4

Ethics, Education and Employment: Criminal Defence Solicitors, Law Schools and the Legitimacy of the Criminal Justice System

KLEARCHOS A. KYRIAKIDES

1. INTRODUCTION

IN THE DECADES since the beginning of his academic career, Professor Ralph Henham has made substantial contributions to legal education, to legal research and to the literature on criminal justice. What underpins these contributions is a dedication to truth, to justice and to legitimacy. Allied to this is an acute concern for the ethical challenges facing practitioners within both the domestic and international criminal justice systems. This concern is reflected in a number of the works of Professor Henham. These include an article on the nexus between ethics, rights and sentencing policy[1] plus a separate article on the ethics of plea bargaining in international criminal trials.[2] For these reasons, it is appropriate that a book dedicated to Professor Henham should include a chapter focusing on how the legitimacy of the domestic criminal justice system is inextricably linked to the ethics of the solicitors' branch of the legal profession and the role of law schools in terms of fostering ethics among students.

Acknowledgments: The first draft of this chapter was written during the summer of 2015 at which time the author was still employed by the School of Law of the University of Hertfordshire. This chapter reproduces (i) Crown Copyright material or other public-sector information licensed under the Open Government Licence v3.0, details of which may be viewed on the website of the National Archives of the United Kingdom, Kew Gardens, Surrey, at www.nationalarchives.gov.uk/doc/open-government-licence/version/3/ (last accessed 28 July 2021) and (ii) British parliamentary copyright material or other parliamentary information licensed under the Open Parliament Licence, details of which may be viewed on the website of the Parliament of the United Kingdom at www.parliament.uk/site-information/copyright-parliament/ (last accessed 28 July 2021).

[1] Ralph Henham, 'Protective Sentences: Ethics, Rights and Sentencing Policy' (1997) 25 *International Journal of the Sociology of Law* 45–63.

[2] Ralph Henham, 'The Ethics of Plea Bargaining in International Criminal Trials' (2005) 26(3) *Liverpool Law Review* 209–24.

If this chapter has any overarching thesis, it is subdivided into three intertwined parts.

Firstly, the actual and perceived legitimacy of the criminal justice system hinges upon the actual and perceived legitimacy of the judiciary and of the legal profession that interfaces with it on so many levels. This proposition is a natural corollary of what the Judicial Committee of the Privy Council depicted in 2014 as 'the common law requirement that justice must not only be done, but clearly be seen to be done'.[3]

Secondly, the actual and perceived legitimacy of the criminal justice system hinges upon the high ethical standards maintained by members of the legal profession, including solicitors. Yet, the undergraduate legal education system of England and Wales has suffered from a serious yet systemic and sustained deficiency flowing from an alarming fact: the absence of ethics as a compulsory stand-alone module on the traditional LLB degree of many university law schools.[4] Indeed, the 'Joint Statement issued [in 2002] by the Law Society and the General Council of the Bar on the Completion of the Initial or Academic Stage of Training by Obtaining an Undergraduate Degree' does not list ethics among the various 'Foundations of Legal Knowledge' that must form part of 'a qualifying law degree'.[5] This deficiency has magnified the responsibilities of all tutors involved in the teaching of ethics on the Legal Practice Course (LPC), particularly but not solely within the compulsory Professional Conduct & Regulation (PCR) module. After all, as the Solicitors Regulation Authority (SRA) has made clear: 'Professional conduct and ethics are intended to be pervasive, impacting on all aspects' of the design, delivery and content of the course [ie the LPC].'[6] Time will tell whether any substantive change will arise as the 'qualifying law degree' is phased out from the traditional pathway towards qualification as a solicitor[7] and as ethics is 'tested throughout' the new Solicitors Qualification Examination (SQE)[8] that replaces the elements of assessment in the LPC.[9]

Thirdly, the actual and perceived legitimacy of the criminal justice system is inextricably bound up with the ethical literacy of new entrants to the solicitors' branch of the legal profession in England and Wales. In turn, this places an enormous responsibility upon university law schools in that jurisdiction. Despite the LLB-related deficiency referred to above, every university law school ought to play a

---

[3] *Yiacoub & Another v The Queen* [2014] UKPC 22 [1] (Lord Hughes, who delivered the judgment of the Judicial Committee of the Privy Council).

[4] See, for example, the results of a survey recorded in Phil Harris and Sarah Beinart, 'A Survey of Law Schools in the United Kingdom, 2004' (2005) 39(3) *Law Teacher* 299–366, 308 and 'Table 5. Was a course on lawyers' professional responsibilities offered as part of the syllabus?' (309); also see Maxine Evers and Lesley Townsley, 'The Importance of Ethics in the Law Curriculum: Essential or Incidental?' (2017) 51(1) *The Law Teacher* 17–39.

[5] 'Joint Statement on the Academic Stage of Training', SRA website, www.sra.org.uk/students/academic-stage/academic-stage-joint-statement-bsb-law-society/ (last accessed 28 July 2021).

[6] 'Legal Practice Course Information Pack', SRA website, 25 November 2019, www.sra.org.uk/students/resources/legal-practice-course-information-pack/ (last accessed 30 July 2021).

[7] 'Common Protocol on the Academic Stage of Training', SRA website, November 2020, www.sra.org.uk/students/academic-stage/common-protocol/ (last accessed 28 July 2021).

[8] 'SQE at a Glance', SRA website, 25 May 2021, www.sra.org.uk/students/sqe/sqe-visuals/ (last accessed 30 July 2021).

[9] For details on the SQE, see www.sra.org.uk/students/sqe/ (last accessed 30 July 2021).

much more pronounced role in fostering the ethical literacy[10] of their undergraduate and postgraduate students, some of whom will enter the legal profession, the ranks of solicitors specialising in criminal law and, possibly, the judiciary.

In advancing the three-part thesis articulated above, the author has drawn upon the works of the leading academic experts on legal ethics[11] and upon other works forming part of the existing literature on that subject. This literature includes books[12] as well as articles published in journals specialising in legal ethics.[13] No less importantly, the literature also includes various reports commissioned or published by inter alia the Centre for Ethics & Law at University College, London,[14] the Law Society of England and Wales[15] and the Legal Education and Training Review.[16]

Against this background, the chapter dwells on the meaning and significance of two interconnected topics that go to the essence of the legitimacy of the criminal justice system generally and the specific role of criminal defence solicitors. One is the requirement that every solicitor in England and Wales must act with integrity. The other is the status of each such solicitor as an officer of the court with potentially conflicting duties to both the court and the client.

It is hoped, therefore, that this chapter will be of interest to anybody directly or indirectly connected with the criminal justice system of any jurisdiction, be they academics, students, judges, members of the legal profession or others. That being said, subject to one caveat, the chapter is mainly addressed to those connected with the criminal justice system in England and Wales. The caveat is that the author cannot lay claim to any expertise in relation to Welsh affairs and to any relevant legislation specifically relating to Wales, whether made by the Welsh Assembly under the Government of Wales Act 2006 or otherwise.

---

[10] Ethical literacy is explored by Lynda Crowley-Cyr, 'Towards Ethical Literacy by Enhancing Reflexivity in Law Students' in Michael Robertson, Lillian Corbin, Kieran Tranter and Francesca Bartlett (eds), *The Ethics Project in Legal Education* (London, Routledge, 2010) 142–70.

[11] The leading academic experts on legal ethics include Andy Boon, Kim Economides, Julian Herring and Richard Moorhead. The biographies and publications of each one are at www.city.ac.uk/about/people/academics/andy-boon#profile=1, https://staffprofile.usq.edu.au/Profile/Kim-Economides, www.law.ox.ac.uk/people/jonathan-herring and www.ucl.ac.uk/laws/people/prof-richard-moorhead, respectively (last accessed 31 July 2021).

[12] These include the classic textbook by Julian Herring, *Legal Ethics*, 2nd edn (Oxford, Oxford University Press, 2017).

[13] In the common law world, the leading journals devoted to legal ethics include, but are not limited to, *Legal Ethics* (published by Taylor & Francis) at www.tandfonline.com/loi/rlet20#.VhobHflVikp, the *Georgetown Journal of Legal Ethics* (published by Georgetown University) at www.law.georgetown.edu/legal-ethics-journal/ and the *Notre Dame Journal of Law, Ethics and Public Policy* (published by the University of Notre Dame) at https://scholarship.law.nd.edu/ndjlepp/ (last accessed 31 July 2021).

[14] See the publications available on the website of the Centre for Ethics & Law at UCL at www.ucl.ac.uk/ethics-law/ (last accessed 28 July 2021).

[15] See eg Kim Economides and Justine Rogers, *Preparatory Ethics Training for Future Solicitors* (London, Law Society of England and Wales, March 2009). A copy has been made available by the University of Exeter at https://ore.exeter.ac.uk/repository/handle/10036/64973 and https://ore.exeter.ac.uk/repository/bitstream/handle/10036/64973/TLS%20Ethics%20Report.pdf?sequence=1&isAllowed=y (last accessed 28 July 2021).

[16] The Report and Papers published by the Legal Education and Training Review are available on its website at http://letr.org.uk/ (last accessed 28 July 2021).

2. THE BACKGROUND OF THE AUTHOR AND THE PRIMARY
PURPOSES OF THIS CHAPTER

The author of this article is a legal academic and non-practising solicitor who, when he was in private practice in London from 2003 until 2007, did not generally handle any cases directly involving criminal law. Somewhat ironically, it is largely away from private practice that the author has gained an insight into the gritty realities and ethical dilemmas associated with the criminal justice system.

To begin with, for twelve years from 2003 until 2015, the author served as a university lecturer of ethics on the LLB degree and of PCR on the LPC. In that academic role, the author had the privilege of teaching numerous students who went on to practise as criminal defence solicitors. Indeed, some have kept in touch with the author and, without breaching confidentiality or otherwise acting improperly, they have sometimes shared their experiences with the author.

Beyond the LLB and LPC, the author has become a seasoned tutor of continuing professional development courses; he has not only chaired but has also delivered or co-delivered many seminars to criminal defence solicitors, plus others, on their ethical and professional duties. Moreover, the author has been an executive committee member of two local law societies whose members have included several criminal defence solicitors and employees of the Crown Prosecution Service. Over the years, they have offered the author invaluable perspectives into how the criminal justice system operates in England and Wales.

As a combined consequence, this chapter is the product of years of learning the law, practising law, teaching at the coalface of the legal education system and conversing with many solicitors who specialise in criminal law.

3. THE WORK OF CRIMINAL DEFENCE SOLICITORS IN CONTEXT

Broadly speaking, solicitors practising in the field of criminal law are carved up into two camps, reflecting the adversarial nature of criminal litigation in England and Wales. In one camp one finds the solicitors who often act or work for the Crown Prosecution Service or for one of the other public bodies involved in criminal prosecutions. In the other camp one finds solicitors who are known as criminal defence solicitors. They are, for the most part, partners, executive members or employees of private firms of solicitors.

The salaries awarded to many criminal law solicitors are relatively meagre,[17] especially when compared to the salaries awarded to solicitors in some commercially focused firms such as those in the City of London. Yet, the relative smallness of their salary is not commensurate to the vastness of their responsibilities. What effectively hangs upon the collective shoulders of criminal law solicitors is the liberty, livelihood and reputation of thousands of people who have been rightly or wrongly accused of

---

[17] For evidence, one only needs to read the jobs advertised in each week's *Law Society Gazette*. These are also advertised by the *Gazette* online at http://jobs.lawgazette.co.uk/ (last accessed 28 July 2021).

committing one or more criminal offences. This represents an awesome responsibility. It is all the more awesome if one recalls the history of miscarriages of justice,[18] not to mention the acute challenges involved in acting for somebody who has been arrested or is under investigation or is facing a prosecution or is immersed in a trial, an appeal, a judicial review or other form of legal action stemming from the criminal justice system.

For the criminal defence solicitors involved in the criminal justice system, the challenges are even more awkward and the responsibilities all the more grave if, as is often the case, the client does not speak English, has learning difficulties, has mental health problems, is under duress, is frightened or is otherwise vulnerable for one reason or another.

In recent years, the anxieties faced by criminal defence solicitors have been aggravated by various reforms undertaken to the legal aid system and the consequential pressures placed on firms which handle criminal defence cases. For their part, ministers have tried to justify the reforms, for example, on the basis that 'resources are not limitless' and that '[w]hen reform began, we had one of the most expensive legal aid systems in the world, at about £2 billion a year'.[19] However, the reforms have provoked wave after wave of condemnatory words from several solicitors and other members of the legal profession. For instance, in a lecture given on 2 August 2015 to mark the 800th anniversary of Magna Carta, Jonathan Smithers, the then President of the Law Society of England and Wales, claimed that 'recent governments of all political colours have emaciated the provision of ... legal aid to the poorest in our society'.[20]

To cap it all, since March 2020, the COVID-19 pandemic has exacerbated the plight of criminal defence solicitors – by threatening their well-being,[21] by generating awkward professional problems[22] and by worsening the pre-existing financial predicaments of many firms specialising in criminal law.[23]

For all of the various problems faced by criminal defence solicitors, there can be little doubt that they are among the foremost linchpins of the rule of law, the proper

---

[18] See eg Sam Poyser, Angus Nurse and Rebecca Milne, *Miscarriages of Justice: Causes, Consequences and Remedies* (Bristol, Policy Press, University of Bristol, 2018).

[19] Statement on Legal Aid Funding by Chris Grayling MP, Secretary of State for Justice and Lord Chancellor, Hansard, *House of Commons Debates*, 3 February 2015, col 111.

[20] Jonathan Smithers, President of the Law Society of England and Wales, 'Magna Carta in 2015–800 Years of the Rule of Law' (transcript of a speech), 2 August 2015, Law Society of England and Wales, www.lawsociety.org.uk/news/speeches/magna-carta-in-2015-800-years-of-the-rule-of-law/ (last accessed 11 October 2015).

[21] Patrick Roche, Keir Monteith QC, Victoria Meads and Lucie Wibberly, 'COVID-19: A Protocol to Assist Solicitors Who Are Working Remotely and Advising Suspects in Relation to Police Interviews', Garden Court Chambers, 1 April 2020, www.gardencourtchambers.co.uk/news/covid-19-a-protocol-to-assist-solici-tors-who-are-working-remotely-and-advising-suspects-in-relation-to-police-interviews (last accessed 28 July 2021).

[22] Law Society of England and Wales, 'Coronavirus (COVID-19) Guidance and Best Practice for Member Safety in Court and Tribunal Buildings', 22 July 2021, www.lawsociety.org.uk/topics/coronavirus/coronavi-rus-covid-19-best-practice-for-member-safety-in-court-and-tribunal-buildings (last accessed 28 July 2021).

[23] Law Society of England and Wales, '120 Criminal Firms Have Collapsed with More to Follow – Law Society Demands More from Government Proposals', 17 June 2020, www.lawsociety.org.uk/contact-or-visit-us/press-office/press-releases/120-criminal-firms-have-collapsed-with-more-to-follow (last accessed 28 July 2021).

administration of justice, the prevention of miscarriages of justice and the reversal of any miscarriages that have already arisen. To appreciate the criticality of such solicitors, one may point to various sources. It suffices to cite two.

One is the speech of Lord Millett in a case decided in 2003 by the then Appellate Committee of the House of Lords. In the context of the right of access to legal advice of a person detained in Northern Ireland by the Royal Ulster Constabulary, the predecessor of the Police Service of Northern Ireland, Lord Millett observed that:

> Access to legal advice and the independence and integrity of the legal profession are cornerstones of a free society under the rule of law. They are guarantees against the practice of holding undesirables incommunicado, which is a hallmark of a totalitarian regime. Yet they are of little intrinsic value in themselves. For most people and for most of the time there is no need of them. What matters is that they should be there when needed. Their importance lies in the potential seriousness of the consequences if they are not.[24]

Another source is the judgment of the Supreme Court of the United Kingdom in a case decided in 2014. To quote from the judgment:

> Miscarriages of justice may occur, however full the disclosure at trial and however careful the trial process. A convicted defendant clearly has a legitimate interest, if continuing to assert his innocence, to such proper help as he can persuade others to give him .... Quite apart from the defendant's interest, the public interest is in such miscarriages, if they occur, being corrected. There is no doubt that there have been conspicuous examples of apparently secure convictions which have been demonstrated to be erroneous through the efforts of investigative journalists, or of solicitors acting on behalf of convicted persons or, sometimes, of other concerned persons.[25]

The Supreme Court of the United Kingdom was right to highlight the 'efforts' of solicitors in the context of miscarriages of justice. In turn, these 'efforts' underline the critical role performed by lecturers who teach law students, some of whom may one day become solicitors whose actions may determine whether or a not a miscarriage of justice is prevented or, if it has already arisen, overturned. The reason flows from a basic reality that must never be forgotten amid the multiple duties shoved onto legal academics and amid the multiple shockwaves generated by the radical reforms to the legal education in England and Wales introduced in 2021: the quality of each new entrant to the solicitors' branch of the legal profession will be determined, in large part, by the quality of that entrant's legal education.

4. THE MULTIDIMENSIONAL DUTIES OF CRIMINAL DEFENCE SOLICITORS

Labels or titles can sometimes be ambiguous or misleading. A good example is the term 'criminal defence solicitor'. The term is accurate in the sense that it is used to describe a solicitor who acts for a defendant in a case concerning criminal law. Even so, the simplicity of the term disguises the multidimensional role performed by each

---

[24] *Cullen v Chief Constable of the Royal Ulster Constabulary* [2003] UKHL 39 [50] (Lord Millett).
[25] *R (Nunn) v Chief Constable of Suffolk Constabulary & Anor* [2014] UKSC 37 [36] (Lord Hughes, with whom Lords Neuberger, Clarke, Reed and Carnwath agreed).

criminal defence solicitor: as an integral element of the architecture of the criminal justice system; as a cog in the machinery of a palpably underfunded legal aid system; as an officer of the court by virtue of section 50 of the Solicitors Act 1974; as the trusted adviser as well as representative of every client; and as a regulated person who must comply with the duties imposed by the SRA, by the specific legislation, common law principles and rules of equity applicable to solicitors and by the general law of the land.

In addition, as already indicated, each criminal defence solicitor is normally a partner, executive member or employee of a firm with concomitant duties to the firm, to colleagues and to others. These duties include the duty of the individual solicitor to earn enough money within the law to make ends meet. Bearing in mind the financial pressures faced by solicitors who are immersed in the legal aid system, that is far from easy.[26]

Meanwhile, away from the working environment, each criminal defence solicitor may owe a number of separate duties to others, such as a spouse, a partner, children or other family members, and to any mortgagee or other lender. In that latter respect, many members of the current generation of new entrants to the legal profession are almost certainly saddled with debts as a result of the student loan scheme.

It follows that, by dint of being a solicitor, every criminal defence solicitor owes multiple duties while being under relentless daily pressure, if not stress, arising from various sources. It also follows that every criminal defence solicitor is accountable for his or her actions or inactions. Such accountability will bite in the event of any alleged transgression of the law, any alleged breach of the SRA Codes of Conduct[27] or any other alleged form of misconduct.

Generally speaking, solicitors are accountable for their actions or inactions in different ways. Subject to the common law standards of procedural fairness and, in certain circumstances, Article 6 of the European Convention on Human Rights, a solicitor may be held to account: via the court exercising its inherent jurisdiction over the solicitor as an officer of the court; via the ordinary processes of criminal or civil justice; via an investigation carried out by the SRA resulting in a referral to or disciplinary prosecution brought before the Solicitors Disciplinary Tribunal (SDT); via the complaints mechanism overseen by the Legal Ombudsman; via the internal disciplinary procedures of the employer of the solicitor; or via any other legal means.

5. THE BAD APPLES IN THE BARREL

As a combined result of the above, a complex legal and regulatory framework already exists to protect the actual and perceived legitimacy of the solicitors' branch of the legal profession and, by extension, the criminal justice system. In addition to the court, this

---

[26] See eg Owen Bowcott, 'Fears for Legal Aid Justice as Lawyer Admits "I Can't Afford My Own Wig"', *Guardian* (online edition), 27 February 2014, www.theguardian.com/law/2014/feb/27/legal-aid-cuts-low-wages-solicitors-fears-criminal-justice (last accessed 31 July 2021).

[27] See Solicitors Regulation Authority, 'SRA Code of Conduct for Solicitors, RELS and RFLs', www.sra.org.uk/solicitors/standards-regulations/code-conduct-solicitors/ and Solicitors Regulation Authority, 'SRA Code of Conduct for Firms', www.sra.org.uk/solicitors/standards-regulations/code-conduct-firms/ (last accessed 28 July 2021).

framework encompasses other bodies, notably the SRA and the SDT. The latter rests on a statutory basis[28] and, to quote its official website, 'adjudicates upon alleged breaches of the rules and regulations applicable to solicitors and their firms', such rules and regulations having been 'specifically designed to protect the public, including consumers of legal services, and to maintain the public's confidence in the reputation of the solicitors' profession for honesty, probity, trustworthiness, independence and integrity'.[29]

To illustrate the types of cases handled by the SDT, one may turn to texts such as the *SDT Annual Report 2011/2012*, which was published at a time the author was still teaching PCR on the LPC and whose approach to teaching PCR was influenced by its contents. According to the *SDT Annual Report 2011/2012*, during the twelve calendar months from 1 May 2011 until April 2012: '18 Solicitors were suspended indefinitely'; '29 Solicitors were suspended for one year or more'; '13 Solicitors were suspended for less than one year'; and numerous others were reprimanded or fined. Meanwhile, 52 solicitors were struck off the Roll of Solicitors/Register of Foreign Lawyers.

Which types of misconduct resulted in so many solicitors becoming subject to striking off orders? To quote the *SDT Annual Report 2011/2012*:

> Examples of conduct leading to striking off were:
> - Respondents found dishonestly to have misappropriated clients' money
> - Respondents had a criminal conviction
> - Respondents charged success fees in circumstances where the Tribunal found it was improper to do so
> - Respondents grossly misled clients
> - Respondents failed to discharge their professional duties honestly and reliably ...[30]

Subsequent reports of the SDT have painted a broadly similar picture. For instance, the *The Solicitors Disciplinary Tribunal Annual Report 2019* reveals that, during the period from 1 January 2019 until 31 December 2019, '67 solicitors were struck off'.[31]

To be sure, the number of solicitors who are struck off each year pales by comparison with the sizeable number of practising solicitors in England and Wales; according to the SRA, in June 2021, there were 152,762 practising solicitors.[32] In other words, in 2010, Lord Neuberger of Abbotsbury MR was right to point out the following during his tenure as Master of the Rolls: 'The overwhelming majority of solicitors and barristers ... are principled individuals, who act in accordance with their professional obligations.'[33] Even so, the fact that, in 2019, 67 solicitors were struck off

---

[28] Solicitors Act 1974, ss 46–49.

[29] Solicitors Disciplinary Tribunal, 'About Us', www.solicitorstribunal.org.uk/about-us (last accessed 31 July 2021).

[30] Solicitors Disciplinary Tribunal, 'Annual Report 2011/2012' (1 April 2011–31 May 2012) 17, www.solicitorstribunal.org.uk/Content/documents/Annual%20Report%202011-2012%20final.pdf (last accessed 11 October 2015).

[31] Solicitors Disciplinary Tribunal, 'Annual Report 2019' (London, Solicitors Disciplinary Tribunal, 24 July 2020), 41, www.solicitorstribunal.org.uk/sites/default/files-sdt/SDT%20Annual%20Report%20for%202019_0.pdf and www.solicitorstribunal.org.uk/about-us/annual-reports (last accessed 28 July 2021).

[32] Solicitors Regulation Authority, 'Population of Solicitors in England and Wales', www.sra.org.uk/sra/how-we-work/reports/statistics/regulated-community-statistics/data/population_solicitors/ (last accessed 28 July 2021).

[33] Lord Neuberger of Abbotsbury MR, 'The Ethics of Professionalism in the 21st Century', Inner Temple Lecture, 22 February 2010, Judiciary of England and Wales, www.judiciary.gov.uk/NR/

is 67 too many for an honourable profession which prides itself on the individual and collective integrity of its members.

It should come as little surprise that the solicitors who have been struck off embrace persons from disparate fields of practice, including criminal justice.

A characteristic example is Ritesh Brahmbhatt. Before his fall from grace, Mr Brahmbhatt was a practising solicitor in the field of criminal law. However, at Blackfriars Crown Court on 12 March 2012, he was sentenced to 'a total period of 6 years imprisonment' after pleading guilty to three counts. In February 2014, Mr Brahmbhatt sought to persuade the Court of Appeal 'to have his plea of guilty set aside and his conviction quashed' on the grounds that 'his plea was entered under duress of circumstances'.[34] However, on 27 March 2014, for reasons outlined below, the Court of Appeal dismissed his appeal. The details relating to the conviction of Mr Brahmbhatt are especially useful in terms of illustrating how easily one or more unwise decisions on the part of a solicitor involved in the criminal justice system can spell disaster for such a solicitor – by means of the deprivation of his or her liberty, reputation and, indeed, status as a solicitor; such decisions may also deliver a blow to the collective reputation of the solicitors' branch of the legal profession.

The facts giving rise to the conviction of Mr Brahmbhatt are outlined in the judgment of the Court of Appeal at the conclusion of his unsuccessful appeal in 2014. To quote some of the salient passages of the judgment:

> On 22 July 2011 in the Crown Court at Blackfriars before His Honour Judge Pillay the appellant pleaded guilty to conspiring to convey a List A article into a prison (count 1) and two counts of conspiring to convey a List B article into a prison (counts 2 and 4). ... The appellant was a practising solicitor at the material time. ....[35]

When rejecting the unsuccessful attempt of Mr Brahmbhatt to have his conviction quashed, the Court of Appeal inflicted a further blow to his reputation. To quote from its judgment:

> We have no hesitation in finding that there was no basis whatsoever for the application to vacate the pleas of guilty. Unfortunately we found little in what the appellant said remotely credible. He gave us the clear impression of someone prepared to say or do anything to escape the consequences of his actions.[36]

Not surprisingly, the case of *R v Brahmbhatt* caught the attention of the media, not least because it began after Mr Brahmbhatt was stopped in his tracks while wearing shoes three sizes too big for him and after he was exposed by a sniffer dog at the entrance of a prison. Needless to say, he used these shoes to conceal prohibited items. Hence, the composition of crude media headlines such as 'Shoedunnit!'[37]

rdonlyres/E25B661A-7F64-43BD-8D37-DF0936A63465/0/mrinnertemplelecturefeb2010.pdf (accessed 17 August 2011).

[34] *R v Brahmbhatt* [2014] EWCA Crim 573 [1], [2], [3], [32] (Lady Justice Hallett).

[35] ibid [1], [4].

[36] ibid [26].

[37] See eg Martin Fricker, 'Shoedunnit! Lawyer Jailed for Smuggling Drugs and Phones into Jail in his Footwear', *Mirror* (online edition), 13 March 2012 and updated on 1 June 2012, www.mirror.co.uk/news/uk-news/lawyer-jailed-for-smuggling-drugs-and-phones-759597 (last accessed 31 July 2021).

In June 2014, a few months after the Court of Appeal had dismissed his appeal, Mr Brahmbhatt faced separate proceedings before the SDT. After a hearing held on 24 June 2014, the Tribunal decided to strike his name off the roll of solicitors and he was ordered to pay £2,149 in costs. Against this background, Gordon Ramsay, the then Director of Legal and Enforcement at the SRA, issued the following statement:

> It is worth echoing the words of the sentencing judge. Solicitors occupy positions of trust, and also have a duty to uphold the rule of law. Mr Brahmbhatt abused the trust placed in him and failed to uphold his professional obligations, so striking him off and ensuring he cannot work as a solicitor when he is released is a wholly appropriate punishment.[38]

Mr Brahmbhatt's spectacular fall from grace serves as a warning to law students, new entrants to the profession and solicitors alike. Compliance with the law and adherence to ethics are central to the work of solicitors generally and critical to public confidence in the criminal justice system as operated by criminal defence solicitors and others involved in that system.

6. ETHICS AND THE INDIVIDUAL AND COLLECTIVE INTEGRITY OF SOLICITORS

The English word 'ethics' is derived from the ancient Greek word ἠθικά (*ethika*). As a concept, it owes much to Aristotle's *Nicomachean Ethics*.[39] Both philosophically and linguistically, ethics amount to a set of moral principles, rules and standards governing the conduct, behaviour and mindset of a person or a group of persons, particularly those who are members of a profession. In the memorable words of Sir Gerard Brennan, as expressed in 1992 during his spell as a Justice of the High Court of Australia (and, thus, prior to his tenure as the Chief Justice of Australia from 1995 until 1998): 'Ethics are the hallmark of a profession … Ethics give practical expression to the purpose for which a profession exists, so a member who repudiates the ethical code in effect repudiates members of the profession.'[40]

In England and Wales, ethics are effectively woven into the regulatory framework of solicitors by means of the SRA Principles, under which every regulated person, including every criminal defence solicitor, must 'act':

1. in a way that upholds the constitutional principle of the rule of law, and the proper administration of justice.
2. in a way that upholds public trust and confidence in the solicitors' profession and in legal services provided by authorised persons.

---

[38] Solicitors Regulation Authority, 'Solicitor Struck Off for Smuggling Drugs to Inmates', 26 June 2014, www.sra.org.uk/sra/news/press/solicitor-struck-off-drugs-shoes.page (last accessed 11 October 2015). See also Solicitors Regulation Authority, 'Ritesh Brahmbhatt', www.sra.org.uk/consumers/solicitor-check/355256/ (last accessed 31 July 2021).

[39] Aristotle (trans David Ross, ed Lesley Brown), *The Nichomachean Ethics* (Oxford, Oxford University Press, 2009).

[40] The Hon Sir Gerard Brennan AC KBE, Justice of the High Court of Australia (and Chief Justice of Australia from 1995 until 1998), 'Ethics and the Advocate', transcript of a talk delivered on 3 May 1992, New South Wales Bar Association, http://archive.nswbar.asn.au/docs/professional/pcd/brenan.pdf (last accessed 11 October 2015).

3. with independence.
4. with honesty.
5. with integrity.
6. in a way that encourages equality, diversity and inclusion.
7. in the best interests of each client.[41]

Each of the SRA Principles directly injects integrity and indirectly injects ethics into the professional bloodstream of solicitors. At the same time, each Principle underpins the exacting standards of conduct that solicitors are obliged to live up to in accordance with legislation or the principles laid down by leading cases. The latter include *Wingate & Anor v The Solicitors Regulation Authority* in which Lord Justice Rupert Jackson (Jackson LJ) explored the legal meaning of integrity. To that end, Jackson LJ cited a string of earlier cases, such as *Hoodless v Financial Services Authority* [2003] UKFSM FSM007 in which the Financial Services and Markets Tribunal had concluded that: 'In our view "integrity" connotes moral soundness, rectitude and steady adherence to an ethical code. A person lacks integrity if unable to appreciate the distinction between what is honest or dishonest by ordinary standards.'[42]

Having reviewed several earlier cases, Jackson LJ decided that integrity and dishonesty are distinct concepts:

> … As a matter of common parlance and as a matter of law, integrity is a broader concept than honesty. …
>
> Integrity connotes adherence to the ethical standards of one's own profession. That involves more than mere honesty. To take one example, a solicitor conducting negotiations or a barrister making submissions to a judge or arbitrator will take particular care not to mislead. …
>
> The duty to act with integrity applies not only to what professional persons say, but also to what they do.[43]

Jackson LJ proceeded 'to give many illustrations of what constitutes acting without integrity'. An example is by acting '[r]ecklessly, but not dishonestly, [by] allowing a court to be misled'.[44]

The clarification provided by Jackson LJ builds upon the earlier observations of Sir Thomas Bingham MR (as the late Lord Bingham of Cornhill was then known) in *Bolton v The Law Society*, another leading case:

> It is required of lawyers practising in this country that they should discharge their professional duties with integrity, probity and complete trustworthiness. That requirement applies as much to barristers as it does to solicitors. … Any solicitor who is shown to have discharged his professional duties with anything less than complete integrity, probity and trustworthiness must expect severe sanctions to be imposed upon him by the Solicitors Disciplinary Tribunal.[45]

---

[41] Solicitors Regulation Authority, 'SRA Principles', www.sra.org.uk/solicitors/standards-regulations/principles/ (last accessed 28 July 2021).

[42] *Wingate & Anor v The Solicitors Regulation Authority* [2018] EWCA Civ 366 [66] (Jackson LJ).

[43] ibid [95], [100], [101] (Jackson LJ).

[44] ibid [101(ii)] (Jackson LJ).

[45] *Bolton v The Law Society* [1994] 1 WLR 512, 518–19 (Sir Thomas Bingham MR).

It is implicit in the SRA Principles, the clarification of Jackson LJ and the observations of Sir Thomas Bingham MR that all solicitors, including those handling criminal law, are required to have integrity, to be honest and to meet other exceptionally high standards of conduct. It follows that the solicitors of England and Wales form part of an honourable profession under a strict regulatory framework that effectively requires each and every one of its members to be ethical in the office, in court and, it would appear, in other settings. Depending upon the circumstances, such settings may even include the home or other places normally within the sphere of the private or family life of the solicitor. Hence the carefully worded warnings issued by Edward Nally, a Solicitor Member and the President of the SDT in his 'Introduction' to the *Solicitors Disciplinary Tribunal 2020 Annual Report*:

> It is noteworthy that this year we have seen examples of cases where the actions of solicitors in a private capacity have come under the microscope in terms of professional misconduct. Sexual misconduct and offensive social media activity are two obvious high-profile areas, but there will no doubt be many other areas where the delicate balance between personal and professional conduct arises. My personal perspective is that it is impossible for solicitors to leave their practising certificates at home completely and expect to act with total impunity in a personal capacity. It would be most odd if appalling behaviour in a personal capacity could completely be disregarded in terms of whether it also constitutes professional misconduct, or whether it calls into question the integrity of an individual.
>
> The Tribunal is being asked to adjudicate on these areas on occasions. The cases are fact specific, difficult and cutting edge at times. Our role is to consider where the regulatory reach of the Solicitors Regulation Authority starts and stops, and we must do that fearlessly in the public interest.
>
> The public and the profession should expect no less of us. What I will say is that the privilege of trust and confidence that the public endows upon the profession has to be maintained. I believe that if we keep that firmly in our minds as we deliberate, we should not go far astray.[46]

For the reasons pinpointed above, plus others, a solicitor must juggle several balls at the same time. These include acting in line with the SRA Principles, being competent and protecting the interests of the client but without breaking the law, without straying beyond the bounds of propriety and without breaching the overriding duty owed to the court. All of which is much easier said than done but it hopefully captures the essence of what it means to be a solicitor. Yet, it also captures what every lecturer in the legal education system ought to have in mind when teaching law students at any level. Aspiring solicitors must be left in no doubt as to the austere regulatory environment that awaits them should they enter that branch of the legal profession.

---

[46] Solicitors Disciplinary Tribunal, 'Annual Report 2020' (London, Solicitors Disciplinary Tribunal, 30 July 2021), 1, www.solicitorstribunal.org.uk/sites/default/files-sdt/2020%20ANNUAL%20REPORT_0. pdf (last accessed 30 July 2021).

7. THE STATUS OF EACH SOLICITOR AS AN OFFICER OF THE COURT WITH CORRESPONDING DUTIES TO THE COURT

Among the responsibilities foisted onto the shoulders of all solicitors, but particularly those immersed in criminal litigation, are those flowing from the status of each solicitor as an officer of the court – a status that ought to be highlighted throughout the legal education of every aspiring solicitor. In turn, this begs an obvious question in three parts. What is the history, what is the legal basis and what are the implications of the status of each solicitor as an officer of the court?

Let us begin with the history of solicitors as officers of the court. In 2021, this was helpfully outlined by the UK Supreme Court in *Harcus Sinclair LLP & Anor v Your Lawyers Ltd*. In the context of the 'supervisory jurisdiction' of the court 'to enforce solicitors' undertakings' as 'an aspect of its inherent jurisdiction over solicitors as officers of the court',[47] the Supreme Court explained:

> In around the 13th century the profession of attorney emerged. Attorneys managed the formal aspects of the litigation process, such as representing absent clients, taking out writs, gathering evidence, liaising with other court officials and, where necessary, instructing counsel. They were admitted to the legal profession by the court in which they intended to practise, in contrast to barristers who were admitted by the Inns of Court. On admission, an attorney's name was entered on the roll and he became an 'officer of the court'. This title reflected the fact that attorneys were appointed by the court, required to attend court at regular intervals, benefited from privileges attached to the office and worked closely alongside the clerical staff of the courts. Attorneys were 'sworn to good behaviour' on admission and were bound to adhere to strict professional standards, with the courts assuming an inherent jurisdiction to ensure that those standards were upheld – see generally Holdsworth, *A History of English Law*, vol 6, 2nd ed (1937), pp 432–434.[48]

The Supreme Court added that a barrister is not quite in the same boat as solicitors:

> A barrister is not subject to this jurisdiction, but only to the conceptually distinct inherent jurisdiction of the court to manage its processes and protect them from abuse. This is because a barrister is not an officer of the court. Conversely solicitors, simply because of their status as officers of the court, are subject to the jurisdiction in relation to the provision of conveyancing services, even though those services usually have nothing at all to do with the court's processes. The jurisdiction applies to one and not the other purely because of the difference of status between them.[49]

With regard to the legal basis of each solicitor as an officer of the court, this is the Solicitors Act 1974, under which: 'Any person duly admitted as a solicitor shall be an officer of the Senior Courts …'.[50] It does not matter whether or not an individual solicitor has ever appeared before the court, or whether his or her 'diet' of cases involves or does not involve civil or criminal litigation. Upon admission, a solicitor becomes

---

[47] *Harcus Sinclair LLP & Anor v Your Lawyers Ltd* [2021] UKSC 32 [94] (Lords Briggs, Hamblen and Burrows, with whom Lord Lloyd-Jones and Lady Arden agreed).
[48] ibid [95].
[49] ibid [135].
[50] Solicitors Act 1974, s 50(1).

an officer of the court and remains so for as long as he or she remains a solicitor. Put another way, every solicitor is an ex officio officer of the court, that is, a solicitor is automatically an officer of the court by virtue of his or her admission as a solicitor. This applies as much to solicitors involved in the criminal justice system as to all other solicitors. To quote from a Law Society Practice Note aimed at solicitors: 'You are an officer of the court and therefore always owe duties to the court.'[51]

The preceding points have been graphically expressed in the context of Australia. In a speech, the Hon Marilyn Warren AC, an Australian judge, reminded her audience that:

> A candidate presenting [himself or herself] for admission today may ... have aspirations to advise publicly listed Blue Chip clients ..., while another might wish to defend the criminally accused. Both will go on to perform very different duties as lawyers, however, both candidates will owe the same duty to the court.[52]

According to this Australian judge, the reason is straightforward: 'Being admitted means that a lawyer owes a paramount duty to the court in all of their future dealings.'[53]

What, then, are the implications of the status of each solicitor as an officer of the court? To begin with, as officers of the court, solicitors are subject to a unique regime overseen by the courts themselves. To quote Lord Neuberger of Abbotsbury MR, during his tenure as Master of the Rolls and Head of Civil Justice, a judicial office with historic ties to the solicitors' branch of the legal profession:

> Solicitors, as officers of the court, are subject to a special jurisdiction and are liable to punishment for any kind of contempt [of court]. A solicitor may be committed for contempt for breach of his undertakings, even if they were not given directly to the court. Similarly a solicitor may be held guilty of contempt for failing to obey an order of the court or for wrongfully withholding funds belonging to a client.[54]

As officers of the court, solicitors are confronted with a pair of professional duties that are not always easy to reconcile, particularly in criminal defence work. One is the duty of every solicitor to the court and the other is the separate duty of every solicitor to the client.

What should a solicitor do when confronted with an ethical dilemma arising from any conflict due to a clash between the duty to the court and the separate duty to the client? In addition to consulting the SRA Codes of Conduct, a solicitor should take account of what has been laid down in cases, including the two cited below.

---

[51] Law Society of England and Wales, 'Criminal Procedure Rules 2013', Practice Note, 3 October 2013, paragraph 2.1: www.lawsociety.org.uk/support-services/advice/practice-notes/criminal-procedure-rules-2011/ (last accessed 15 October 2015).

[52] Marilyn Warren AC, 'The Duty Owed to the Court – Sometimes Forgotten', transcript of a speech delivered at the Judicial Conference of Australia Colloquium, Melbourne, on 9 October 2009, published at: www.austlii.edu.au/au/journals/VicJSchol/2009/15.pdf (last accessed 13 October 2015).

[53] ibid.

[54] Lord Neuberger of Abbotsbury, 'The Tyranny of the Consumer or the Rule of Law', 25th Annual Bar Conference, 6 November 2010: www.judiciary.gov.uk/NR/rdonlyres/94B96FE7-2844-4603-BA86-A0E9D037E50D/0/morspeechbarconferencelecture.pdf (last accessed 17 August 2011).

In the first case, which was decided in 2014, Lord Thomas of Cwmgiedd, the then Lord Chief Justice of England and Wales, made 'two observations' which were clearly aimed at all practising lawyers.[55] Lord Thomas began by noting that: 'It has always been the duty of a barrister, solicitor, legal executive or any other professional representing a client in proceedings before any court to discharge not only the duties to his client but the duty to the court.'[56] Lord Thomas went on to warn that:

> Every lawyer must be alive to the fact that circumstances can arise during the course of any lawyer's professional practice when matters come to his knowledge (or are obvious to him) which may have the effect of making his duty to the court his paramount duty and to act in the interests of justice. In many cases it will be clear what course the lawyer must take, either through the way in which the case is presented or by withdrawing from acting for the client. In others it may be more difficult.[57]

Lord Thomas proceeded to offer guidance that every solicitor and law student should note. More to the point, for the purposes of this chapter which dwells on the legitimacy of the criminal justice system, Lord Thomas explained that 'the reputation of the system of the administration of justice in England and Wales and the standing of the profession depends particularly upon the discharge of the duties owed to the court'.[58] Lord Thomas went on to issue the sternest of warnings:

> Where an advocate or other representative or a litigator puts before the court matters which he knows not to be true or by omission leads the court to believe something he knows not to be true, then as an advocate knows of these duties, the inference will be inevitable that he has deceived the court, acted dishonestly and is not fit to be a member of any part of the legal profession.
>
> As conduct that is dishonest, such as misleading the court with such knowledge will inevitably be, is so serious, it is of the utmost importance that in difficult circumstances which can confront any advocate or litigator, that advocate or litigator has at the forefront of his mind his duty to the court, the necessity to avoid breach of that duty and, if he has any doubt as to how to discharge that duty, by taking independent advice.[59]

Although these 'observations' were made by the Lord Thomas LCJ in the context of a case concerning a 'Legal Manager' who was 'in effect', the 'in-house solicitor' of Times Newspapers Limited facing 'allegations of breach of the code of conduct concern[ing] litigation in the High Court of Justice, Queen's Bench Division',[60] they surely apply to all solicitors including those engaged in criminal litigation.

The second case was decided in 2015 via a judgment of Sir Brian Leveson, the then President of The Queen's Bench Division of the High Court of England and Wales. In the context of 'legal representatives acting for claimants in judicial review proceedings', the President affirmed that there exists a duty to act 'in a professional

---

[55] *Brett v The Solicitors Regulation Authority* [2014] EWHC 2974 (Admin) [105] (Lord Thomas of Cwmgiedd LCJ).
[56] ibid [106].
[57] ibid [110].
[58] ibid [111].
[59] ibid [112]–[113].
[60] ibid [4], [5].

manner both towards their clients but also towards the Court, bearing in mind that the paramount duty of all legal representatives acting in proceedings before courts is to the Court itself'.[61] The President immediately proceeded to underline the gravity of his warning in terms which seem to be applicable across the spectrum of civil and criminal litigation:

> The need for this warning to be taken seriously increases as the resources available to the Courts to act efficiently and fairly decreases. If the time of the Court and its resources are absorbed dealing with utterly hopeless and/or unprofessionally prepared cases, then other cases, that are properly advanced and properly prepared, risk not having devoted to them the resources that they deserve.[62]

What are the ramifications of all this for the legal education system and its role as the stepping stone enabling law students to leap into the criminal justice system?

Firstly, the legal education system ought to ensure that aspiring solicitors are made fully aware of a self-evident reality: practising as a solicitor equates to practising as an officer of the court in an austere regulatory environment, with all that entails, especially in the field of criminal justice. At the same time, every student ought to appreciate the parallel duties owed to the court and to the client.

Secondly, the legal education system ought to ensure that aspiring solicitors are as ethically literate as reasonably possible. The reasons are manifold. However, a major reason is that every solicitor must be intellectually capable of spotting, addressing and resolving any ethical dilemma that may arise, particularly as a consequence of the solicitor being an officer of the court subject to the parallel duties referred to above.

Thirdly, the legal education system ought to ensure that aspiring solicitors have as much moral courage as reasonably possible. This is particularly important vis-à-vis aspiring criminal defence solicitors. As some of their clients may operate in the criminal underworld and have few qualms about misbehaving, criminal defence solicitors are inherently vulnerable to potential bullying, intimidating, threatening, violent or otherwise inappropriate behaviour. Indeed, in 2018, the Law Society of Scotland reported that:

> One third of Scottish solicitors who took part in a recent survey have been victims of violence or threatening behaviour in connection with their work. ... The responses showed that:
>
> - Almost 40% of criminal defence solicitors, 25% of family lawyers and 19% of prosecutors have been victims of violence.
> - Around 70% of criminal defence solicitors, 54% of family lawyers and 61% of prosecutors have been victims of threatening behaviour ...[63]

---

[61] *R (Akram & Anor) v Secretary of State for the Home Department* [2015] EWHC 1359 (Admin) [2] (Sir Brian Leveson, President of the Queen;s Bench Division).

[62] ibid.

[63] Law Society of Scotland, 'Third of Solicitors Are Victims of Violence or Threats, According to Survey', 17 September 2021, www.lawscot.org.uk/news-and-events/law-society-news/employment-survey-violence-findings/ (last accessed 28 July 2021).

There is no reason to believe that the picture in Scotland is significantly out of kilter with the picture in England and Wales. On that basis, every law-related university course in England and Wales should seek to instil a sense of moral courage in every student, coupled with clear guidance as to what a solicitor should – and should not do – when faced with any form of improper pressure.

8. ETHICS, EDUCATION AND EMPLOYMENT

In view of the onerous consequences of the duty to act with integrity, the gravity of the consequences that might arise for any solicitor who is found to have breached this duty, the ethical problems inherent in the status of each solicitor as an officer of the court and the need to sustain the legitimacy of the criminal justice system, one is obliged to ask a key follow-up question relating to legal education. What more can university law schools do to nourish the ethical literacy of their students and to expose them to the ethical dilemmas associated with contemporary legal practice, particularly in the field of criminal defence work?

Based on his own experiences, the author of this chapter hereby identifies three achievable and relatively straightforward means by which law schools may help to nourish the ethical literacy of their students.

One straightforward way is by drawing upon the expertise of judges and members of the legal profession, as well as representatives of public bodies that engage with solicitors for one reason or another. Such persons may be invited to university law schools to talk about their own experiences of approaching ethical dilemmas, ensuring the centrality of ethics in their day-to-day work and abiding by the principles of professionalism. Police officers, too, may play an important role in describing their experiences of conducting investigations into solicitors suspected of infringing the criminal law.

Ideally, each visiting speaker should give a lecture before the student body as a whole and, with his or her consent, the lecture should be recorded and accompanied by a written transcript for the benefit of the students who attend and who are absent. If, during each academic year, each law school arranged a short series of lectures on ethics, this may help to foster a culture of ethics within the law school while imprinting ethics onto the conscience of students. Such a series would also supplement whatever is taught about ethics in the formal syllabus. Needless to say, all of this requires preparation and planning but the benefits should be incalculable.

A second way in which each law school may nourish the ethical literacy of their students is by encouraging students to attend events organised by the Law Society of England and Wales, by the Junior Lawyers Division of the Law Society, by local law societies and by other professional bodies. Each year, these bodies organise a host of continuing professional development lectures, seminars and other events, some of which are free and open to students. Irrespective of the subject-matter, these events normally attract members of the profession and their professionalism will inevitably rub onto any student who attends. Against this background, law schools have a choice. On the one hand, they may simply draw these events to the attention of their students and encourage them to attend after registering to attend in the prescribed manner. On the other hand, they can go further by striving to forge a relationship with their local law society or other professional bodies.

A third way in which each law school may nourish the ethical literacy of their students is by encouraging each student to plough their own furrow in search of greater knowledge and deeper understanding of the legal system and the ethical dilemmas that flow from it. From the standpoint of the individual student, this is best done by visiting various courts of law, undertaking a stint of marshalling by the side of a judge and rubbing shoulders with practising members of the legal profession via work-placement opportunities or other forms of work experience.

9. CONCLUSIONS

In this chapter, the author has argued that the actual and perceived legitimacy of the criminal justice system hinges upon the actual and perceived legitimacy of the judiciary and the legal profession with which the judiciary interfaces. He has also argued that such legitimacy not only hinges upon the high ethical standards maintained by solicitors but upon the ethical literacy of new entrants to the solicitors' branch of the legal profession in England and Wales. Moreover, the author has indicated that, if equipped with ethical literacy coupled with an understanding of key concepts, such as integrity, a solicitor may limit the risk of ever facing any complaint or any civil, criminal, disciplinary or other type of proceedings. If the author is correct, it is surprising if not absurd that, in recent decades, ethics has not constituted a compulsory element of every LLB degree in every law school in England and Wales. This deficient state of affairs must change.

In the meantime, all legal academics and law schools must do their utmost to encourage students to cultivate critical thinking skills, to become infused with the spirit of justice, to gain moral courage and to acquire the intellectual strength necessary to handle difficult situations, such as those presented by ethical dilemmas.

All in all, the author has advanced arguments that are broadly in line with the memorable words of the late Rev Dr Martin Luther King, Jr, the American civil rights activist, Baptist preacher and Nobel Peace Laureate. Dr King once submitted that education should not be limited to teaching students to 'to think intensively and to think critically'. An education should also be devoted to the cementing of 'intelligence' to 'character', for 'that is the goal of true education'.[64]

---

[64] Martin Luther King, 'The Purpose of Education', *Maroon Tiger* (Atlanta, GA), January–February 1947, reproduced online by the Martin Luther King, Jr, Research & Education Institute, Stanford University, https://kinginstitute.stanford.edu/king-papers/documents/purpose-education (accessed 31 July 2021).

Part 2

Domestic and Comparative Criminal Justice

5

Mainstreaming Redress in Criminal Justice

JONATHAN DOAK

1. INTRODUCTION

ONE OF THE most salient features of Ralph Henham's research over the past three decades has been his constant call for the radical reform of norms and structures of trial justice and sentencing to better reflect the needs and expectations of victims and communities.[1] In one of their widely acclaimed works, Findlay and Henham propose a new framework of trial justice that synthesises restorative and retributive approaches.[2] Building on this work, this chapter explores whether one of the core benchmarks of restorative approaches, namely redress, can realistically be implemented within the normative and structural framework of the English criminal justice system.

The notion of 'making amends' or 'righting wrongs' has come to feature prominently across a variety of criminal justice frameworks over the past two decades, and is something of a strange bedfellow to deeply embedded retributive objectives. Reparation, as the root of the term ('repair') suggests, is frequently used to describe a range of measures that aim to rectify the harm caused and to restore victims to their position before the act in question occurred, in so far as that is possible. Few areas of law have been untouched by the rise of reparatory justice. On the international platform, there has been increasing emphasis on reparations for historical wrongs, the search for remedies for abuses of human rights and humanitarian law, an upsurge in apologies being made by governments and heads of state, and on the need to facilitate systems of restitution and compensation within international courts

---

[1] Ralph Henham, 'Conceptualizing Access to Justice and Victims' Rights in International Sentencing' (2004) 13(1) *Social & Legal Studies* 27; Ralph Henham, 'Some Reflections on the Role of Victims in the International Criminal Trial Process' (2004) 11(2–3) *International Review of Victimology* 201; Ralph Henham, 'International Sentencing in the Context of Collective Violence' (2007) 7(2) *International Criminal Law Review* 449; Ralph Henham, *Sentencing and the Legitimacy of Trial Justice* (London, Routledge, 2013).

[2] Mark Findlay and Ralph Henham, *Beyond Punishment: Achieving International Criminal Justice* (London, Springer, 2007).

and tribunals. There is also recognition of a growing sense of disconnect between international policy interventions and the needs of victims and communities on the ground in the aftermath of civil conflict. As Roht-Arriaza puts it, the very idea of 'redress' is now widely seen as falling 'among the most venerable and most central of legal principles'.[3]

Domestic legal systems have not been immune from this trend; there has been significant research on the perceived growth of 'compensation culture' within the civil justice system,[4] whilst the entrenchment of human rights legislation has provided new bases for action which have not previously been open to parties before domestic courts.[5] Criminal justice has been no exception; following the rise of state compensation for criminal injuries during the 1960s and 1970s,[6] many jurisdictions also empowered their criminal courts to order offenders to pay compensation as part of a sentence for personal injury or loss incurred as the result of an offence. In more recent times, the exponential expansion of restorative justice programmes has elevated the concept of redress to a pivotal position in contemporary law and policy debates, with evidence of a corresponding decline in the state/offender dichotomy that has tended to dominate criminal justice discourse for the best part of forty years.[7] It might even be suggested that the system has reached a 'tipping' point, whereby the myriad of conflicting and conceptually incoherent aims and goals of criminal justice law and policy must finally be clarified and prioritised.

In spite of a near-universal assumption that the law should make provision for redress, considerable ambiguity pervades much of the contemporary scholarship over the more specific attributes of the concept. Indeed, its widespread usage – in both legal and non-legal contexts – often obfuscates the nature of the concept. It is not uncommon, for example, for the term 'reparation' to be used interchangeably with terms such as 'compensation', 'damages', 'restitution' or 'restoration'.[8] Such casual usage stems from a common misconception that 'reparation' equates to financial compensation. As illustrated below, redress may well *entail* some form of compensation and/or restitution of property, but the concepts should not be construed as being synonymous.

Against this backdrop, this chapter seeks to shed conceptual clarity on the proper place of redress within the criminal justice system and proposes a new 'assimilated sentencing model' (ASM) which seeks to synthesise redress alongside public censure. The chapter begins by providing a contextual account of the rebirth of redress within criminal justice discourse and traces the rise of the concept as a norm on

---

[3] N Roht-Arriaza, 'Punishment, Redress, and Pardon: Theoretical and Psychological Approaches' in N Roht-Arriaza (ed), *Impunity and Human Rights in International Law and Practice* (Oxford, Oxford University Press, 1995) 13–23, 17.

[4] See generally Kevin Williams, 'State of Fear: Britain's "Compensation Culture" Reviewed' (2005) 25(3) *Legal Studies* 499.

[5] See generally Jason N Varuhas, *Damages and Human Rights* (London, Bloomsbury, 2016).

[6] See generally David Miers, 'Offender and State Compensation for Victims of Crime: Two Decades of Development and Change' (2013) 6 *International Review of Victimology* 377–405.

[7] Jonathan Doak, *Victims' Rights, Human Rights and Criminal Justice: Reconceiving the Role of Third Parties* (Oxford, Hart 2008).

[8] ibid 307.

the international platform. It calls for a rethink of the standardised parameters of the criminal justice system, and a more holistic and non-adversarial approach to the resolution of criminal conflicts. Arguing that the practical and normative limitations on redress are inherently fallacious, the chapter proceeds to unpick some of the objections that are commonly raised to redress within the criminal justice system, before proffering the ASM as a potential solution to mainstream redress as a focal point of trial justice.

2. THE REBIRTH OF REPARATION

Most common law systems see loss or damage sustained through the actions of third parties as a private wrong, actionable through the civil courts.[9] There would appear to be an assumption that the interests of victims are inherently built into the central institutions of the system, alongside the public interest in denouncing and punishing unacceptable behaviour.[10] The criminal law, which began to break away from the law of tort following the Assize of Clarendon of 1166,[11] has since been concerned with those offences considered sufficiently injurious to the interests of the state, and has thus been conceptually orientated towards the punishment of offenders as opposed to any reparatory interests of the victim.[12] This distinction was clearly arbitrary from the outset; the decision as to which forms of harm to delineate as crimes rested with those who wielded power; in earlier times this was the monarch, whereas in later times it has rested with Parliament.

Until recently, the notion of redress for victims within the criminal justice system received relatively scant attention. As noted above, this stemmed mainly from the underlying normative conception that its proper function was to regulate trial and punishment of the offender in the name of the state. It is the civil justice system, rather than its criminal justice counterpart, that has been regarded as the proper channel for victims to pursue their reparatory interests. Ashworth describes the purpose of the criminal law as 'to penalise those forms of wrongdoing which … touch public rather than merely private interests'.[13] In his view, the proper approach in determining the role of the victim within the criminal justice system is on the basis of this distinction between criminal and civil proceedings, and the rights and the interests of the victim

---

[9] Andrew Ashworth, 'Punishment and Compensation: Victims, Offenders and the State' (1986) 6(1) *Oxford Journal of Legal Studies* 86.

[10] David B Moore and Terry O'Connell, 'Family Conferencing in Wagga Wagga: A Communitarian Model of Justice' in Christine Alder and Joy Wundersitz (eds), *Family Conferencing and Juvenile Justice: The Way Forward or Misplaced Optimism?* (Canberra, Australian Institute of Criminology 1994).

[11] See further Justine Greenberg, 'The Victim in Historical Perspective: Some Aspects of the English Experience' (1984) 40(1) *Journal of Social Issues* 77–101.

[12] Ashworth (n 9).

[13] Andrew Ashworth, 'What Victims of Crime Deserve', paper presented to the Fulbright Commission on Penal Theory and Penal Practice, University of Stirling, September 1992, cited by James Dignan and Mick Cavadino, 'Towards a Framework for Conceptualising and Evaluating Models of Criminal Justice from a Victim's Perspective' (1996) 4 *International Review of Victimology* 153.

should be pursued under the civil, as opposed to the criminal law.[14] However, civil actions are notoriously expensive and burdensome for victims with little prospect of much in the way of tangible compensation, and state criminal injuries compensation (introduced widely during the 1960s and 1970s) only provided for a minority of victims deemed 'worthy' under the law. As reparatory interests began to percolate into the criminal process itself, the rationale for the long-standing civil/criminal divide was also called into question.

One of the first critiques was advanced in a 1977 article by Randy Barnett, who called for the introduction of a 'new paradigm' which he labelled 'pure restitution'.[15] In effect, this would turn the historical orientation of the criminal law on its head, rendering the state's interests in the denunciation and punishment of crime secondary to the reparatory interests of the victim. Drawing on Epstein's theory of tort liability, Barnett called for an end to the distinction between public and private harms, and proposed 'a single system of corrective justice that looks to the conduct, broadly defined, of the parties to the case with a view toward the protection of individual liberty and private property'.[16] This approach, he contends, is a 'common sense view of crime'.[17]

The same year witnessed the publication of a second seminal article by the late Nils Christie, 'Conflicts as Property'.[18] The paper opens by recalling a practice in a rural village in Tanzania, whereby a dispute is settled through a deliberative process involving the victim, the offender, family members and community elders. In a damning critique of Western criminal justice that follows, Christie notes how conflicts between individuals have been appropriated by the state and legal professionals over the course of the centuries. Lawyers, he contends, have essentially stolen the disputes of the protagonists, a state of affairs that is reflected in the organisation of the criminal process, the legalistic manner in which the criminal law is framed, and the ways in which offenders and victims are routinely sidelined by lawyers in court. He proceeds to outline an alternative vision for a justice system that revolves around the victim and the community, with outcomes designed to provide redress for the victim as well as reintegrating the offender into society. Unlike Barnett, Christie maintains a role for a judicial officer to impose some form of additional punishment on the offender, which might exceed the reparation that might be required to rectify the harm caused to the victim.

Although they differ in the level of detail they propose, and the value they attach to the role of punishment within the criminal process, these accounts have much in common.[19] Both provide substantial critique of the conventional criminal justice

---

[14] See also Ashworth (n 9); Andrew Ashworth, *The Criminal Process: An Evaluative Study*, 2nd edn (Oxford, Oxford University Press, 1998).

[15] Randy E Barnett, 'Restitution: A New Paradigm of Criminal Justice' (1977) 87 *Ethics* 279–301.

[16] ibid 290, citing RA Epstein 'Intentional Harms' (1975) *Journal of Legal Studies* 391–442, 441.

[17] Barnett, ibid 288.

[18] Nils Christie, 'Conflicts as Property' (1977) 17 *British Journal of Criminology* 1–15.

[19] Other aAccounts making similar arguments emerged around the same time: see eg Gilbert Cantor, 'An End to Crime and Punishment' (1976) 39(4) *The Shingle* (Philadelphia Bar Association) 99–114; Richard L Abel, 'A Comparative Theory of Dispute Institutions in Society' (1973) 8 *Law and Society Review* 217; Charles F Abel and Frank H Marsh, *Punishment and Restitution: A Restitutionary Approach to Crime*

system on the grounds that it tends to prioritise punishment over redress and tends to exclude the victim and the community from the conflict resolution process. There is also a moral onus placed on the offender to provide this redress to those who have been harmed. Such calls for a 'paradigm shift' were both imaginative and ambitious at the time of publication, and there was undoubtedly a realisation at some level on the part of the authors that the prevailing paradigm was so readily entrenched within societal structures that reform of this nature was unlikely in the short to medium term.

3. INTERNATIONAL TRAILBLAZING

What neither Barnett nor Christie could have foreseen, however, is the extent to which victims' interests would be catapulted to the forefront of criminal justice discourse in decades ahead. The rapid growth of the victim movement in the United States, and subsequently throughout the Western world,[20] posed major new challenges for criminal justice on legal, policy and (consequently) normative platforms. The international rise of the victim was accompanied by a growing realisation that crime was not only a legalistic offence against the state, but also carried far-reaching social ramifications for victims and communities. Such an understanding is now reflected in a range of international instruments. Obligations on the state to put in place mechanisms that allow compensation or restitution to be payable by perpetrators directly to victims were contained in the (non-binding) 1985 UN Victims' Declaration,[21] and the 2005 Basic Principles and Guidelines on the Right to a Remedy and Reparation for Victims of Gross Violations of International Human Rights Law and Serious Violations of International Humanitarian Law,[22] and Council of Europe Recommendations 85(11) and 06(08). The European Union's 2012 Victims' Directive[23] provides victims with the right to obtain a decision on compensation by the offender within a reasonable time in the course of criminal proceedings and also encourages mechanisms to recover compensation awards from the offender.[24]

This increasing emphasis placed on the idea of reparation as a moral and legal norm has gone hand in hand with the expansion of instruments that promote restorative justice, or mediation-based processes as alternatives to orthodox criminal procedure. The UN Basic Principles on the Use of Restorative Justice Programmes in Criminal Matters, adopted in August 2002,[25] provide that restorative justice programmes should be generally accessible at all stages of the penal procedure; and the Eleventh UN Congress on the Prevention of Crime and the Treatment of Offenders

---

and the Criminal (Westport, CT, Greenwood Press, 1984); Abraham S Goldstein, 'Defining the Role of the Victim in Criminal Prosecution' (1982) 52 *Mississippi Law Journal* 515.

[20] See generally Sandra Walklate, *Imagining the Victim of Crime* (Maidenhead, McGraw-Hill Education, 2006) ch 1.

[21] Principle 8.

[22] Principles 17–19.

[23] Directive 2012/29/EU.

[24] Art 16.

[25] ECOSOC Res 2002/12 (24 July 2002).

(2005) encouraged Member States to acknowledge the importance of implementing restorative justice policies, procedures and programmes that include alternatives to prosecution. The following year the United Nations published the *Handbook of Restorative Justice Programmes*,[26] which surveyed and benchmarked a range of international best practices in the implementation of restorative schemes. The ascendancy of restorative justice has also been evident on the European Platform, with the 2001 EU Framework Decision on the Standing of Victims in Criminal Proceedings calling on Member States to promote mediation in criminal cases for offences it considers appropriate for this sort of measure[27] and to ensure that any subsequent agreements between victims and offenders are factored into the sentencing exercise.[28] Although a self-standing obligation to put in place restorative mechanisms was not contained within the 2012 Directive, it did provide that safeguards should be afforded to victims where the service is offered.[29]

Likewise, the centrality of reparation as an integral component of 'justice' is evidenced by its apparently pivotal position within the relatively nascent field of transitional justice. Such measures may assume widely different forms and extend far beyond the pecuniary or proprietary focus of many of the more traditional criminal justice instruments highlighted above. The UN Basic Principles and Guidelines on the Right to a Remedy and Reparation for Victims of Violations of International Human Rights and Humanitarian Law categorise reparations according to whether they are material or symbolic in nature. Examples of the former include proprietary and pecuniary measures, most notably restitution of rights and property and compensation for physical and mental harm or damage to property, whereas symbolic restitution is potentially much broader, including concepts such as 'rehabilitation', 'satisfaction' (including verification of facts, official apologies, judicial sanctions against violations, and acts of commemoration) and 'guarantees of non-repetition' (which may include entrenching international human rights standards and putting in place mechanisms to monitor conflict resolution). Of course, not all reparations programmes will be capable of realising all these objectives, but the instrument reflects the fact that victims have a complex range of needs which ought to be addressed using a diverse range of methods.

Indeed, on the international platform, the inclusion of reparatory mechanisms within the Rome Statute of the International Criminal Court underlines that redress need not be neatly (and arbitrarily) separated from punishment process. Article 75(1) stipulates that the Court shall 'establish principles relating to reparations to, or in respect of, victims'. It may then 'determine the scope and extent of any damage, loss and injury to, or in respect of, victims' and, under paragraph 2, 'make an order

---

[26] United Nations, *Handbook of Restorative Justice Programmes* (Vienna, United Nations, 2006).

[27] EU Framework Decision on the Standing of Victims in Criminal Proceedings. European Communities, Council Framework Decision (2001/220/JHA).

[28] The Framework Decision was superseded by Directive 2012/29/EU, otherwise known 'the Victims' Directive'. The Directive establishes minimum standards on the rights, support and protection of victims of crime. Although it does not oblige Member States to make restorative justice programmes available and lacks the promotional obligation contained in the 2001 Framework Decision, Art 12(2) does provide that 'Member States shall facilitate the referral of cases, as appropriate to restorative justice services'.

[29] EU Directive, Art 12.

directly against a convicted person specifying appropriate reparations to, or in respect of, victims, including restitution, compensation and rehabilitation'. Whilst this definition of reparation is much narrower than that provided by the United Nations in its 2006 Body of Principles, the conception is broad enough to embrace different modalities of rectifying harm.[30] From a legal perspective, this is the most straightforward means of awarding reparations, although, as an alternative, the Court may order that reparations be made available through the Trust Fund established under Article 79 of the Statute.[31] Although the inclusion of these provisions has been widely lauded,[32] doubts remain as to how effective they are in practice, not least because the sheer scale of international crimes would likely dwarf monetary resources of both individual perpetrators and the Court itself.[33] Notably, in the *Lubanga* case,[34] the Court denied a prosecution request for survivors of sexual violence to be factored into the decision-making on reparation, limiting them to child soldiers who were conscripted into his militia.[35]

Few would doubt the moral basis that an offender should make amends for wrongdoing to an injured party. Wrongs have been said to damage 'morally adequate relationships' including 'victims' ability to cope and their confidence and trust in moral standards and the receptivity of those standards'.[36] They also cause damage through 'insulting' the victim since they infer that they (or their rights) are inherently less worthy than those of the wrongdoer.[37] Whilst the concept of reparation is somewhat paradoxical in that redress is fundamentally incapable of undoing the effects of a serious or traumatic crime,[38] it nonetheless serves to restore the equilibrium that has been upset by the offender's actions and thereby validate the status of the victim as a citizen whose rights have been violated.[39] Yet the case for redress not only rests on moral principles; it should also assist victims in more practical terms by making

---

[30] Joanne M Wemmers, *Reparation and the International Criminal Court: Meeting the Needs of Victims* (International Centre for Comparative Criminology, University of Montreal, 2006).

[31] Victims can access the Trust Fund even if they do not appear before the Court.

[32] Jonathan Doak, Ralph Henham and Barry Mitchell, 'Victims and the Sentencing Process: Developing Participatory Rights?' (2009) 29(4) *Legal Studies* 651–77; DDN Nsereko, 'The Role of Victims in Criminal Proceedings – Lessons National Jurisdictions Can Learn from the ICC' (2010) 21 *Criminal Law Forum* 399–415; Wemmers (n 30).

[33] See further Conor McCarthy, *Reparations and Victim Support in the International Criminal Court* (Cambridge, Cambridge University Press, 2012). For a general critique, see Regina E Rauxloh, 'Good Intentions and Bad Consequences: The General Assistance Mandate of the Trust Fund for Victims of the ICC' (2021) 34(1) *Leiden Journal of International Law* 203.

[34] *Prosecutor v Lubanga*, Judgment on the Appeals against the 'Decision Establishing the Principles and Procedures to Be Applied to Reparations' of 7 August 2012, ICC-01/04-01/06-3129, 3 March 2015.

[35] See further Luke Moffett, 'Reparations for Victims at the International Criminal Court: A New Way Forward?' (2017) 21(9) *International Journal of Human Rights* 1204.

[36] Margaret U Walker, *Moral Repair: Reconstructing Moral Relations after Wrongdoing* (Cambridge, Cambridge University Press, 2006) 28.

[37] Linda Radzik, *Making Amends: Atonement in Morality, Law, and Politics* (Oxford, Oxford University Press, 2009).

[38] Naomi Roht-Arriaza, 'Reparations Decisions and Dilemmas' (2004) 27 *Hastings International and Comparative Law Review* 157–219. She asks: 'What could replace lost health and serenity; the loss of a loved one or of a whole extended family; a whole generation of friends; the destruction of home and culture and community and peace?' (159).

[39] Mick Cavadino and James Dignan, 'Reparation, Retribution and Rights' (1997) 4 *International Review of Victimology* 233.

the loss easier to bear. In this sense, it should help restore the dignity of victims.[40] In doing so, it may also help in bestowing a sense of trust between victims and state institutions thereby encouraging them to report crime in the future and cooperate with the criminal justice system.

Why, however, should the right to redress be located *within* the criminal justice process as opposed to outside it (ie through the use of civil justice system or mediation/restorative justice schemes that operate beyond its parameters)? As inferred above, there would seem to be an omnipresent concern that diffusing the objectives of the civil and criminal justice system would render the criminal process incoherent and incapable of carrying out its primary functions, namely the adjudication of guilt and the punishment of crime.

This need not be so. Redress within criminal justice is inextricably linked to the question around how society punishes offenders, and is not inherently incompatible with the various public interest justifications that are frequently cited as underpinning sentencing (which, in any case, often conflict with each other).[41] If punishment is regarded as 'anything that is unpleasant, a burden, or an imposition of some sort on an offender',[42] then it would seem that the criminal objective of punishing crime is capable of being met through reparation. Although the payment of a financial penalty has very obvious onerous connotations, it can also be noted that much of the restorative justice literature has highlighted that symbolic gestures, and even restorative processes themselves, are often very difficult and highly emotive experiences for the offender.[43] As Randy Barnett argues, the key difference in such a shift would be a change in the rationale for imposing punishment:

> The point is not that the offender deserves to suffer; it is rather that the offended party desires compensation. ... This represents the complete overthrow of the paradigm of punishment. No longer would the deterrence, reformation, disablement, or rehabilitation of the criminal be the guiding principle of the judicial system. The attainment of these goals would be incidental to, and as a result of, reparations paid to the victim.[44]

A similar perspective is proffered by Anthony Duff, who has argued that reparative measures ought to be viewed as penal measures because they involve the intentional infliction of a burden upon an offender for transgressing the criminal law.[45] Restoration, he argues, 'is not only compatible with retribution: it *requires* retribution'.[46] Thus, although according to common law theory, the criminal law may not specifically aim

[40] Cherif M Bassiouni, 'International Recognition of Victims' Rights' (2006) 6(2) *Human Rights Law Review* 203.
[41] Andrew Ashworth and Elaine Player, 'Criminal Justice Act 2003: The Sentencing Provisions' (2005) 68(5) MLR 822–38; Susan Easton and Christine Piper, *Sentencing and Punishment: The Quest for Justice* (Oxford, Oxford University Press, 2012).
[42] Kathleen Daly, 'Revisiting the Relationship between Retributive and Restorative Justice' in Heather Strang and Jon Braithwaite (eds), *Restorative Justice: Philosophy to Practice* (London, Ashgate, 1999) 10.
[43] Jon Braithwaite, *Crime, Shame and Reintegration* (Cambridge, Cambridge University Press, 1989); R Anthony Duff, *Punishment, Communication and Community* (Oxford, Oxford University Press, 2003) 47; Heather Strang, *Repair or Revenge: Victims and Restorative Justice* (Oxford, Clarendon Press, 2002).
[44] Barnett (n 15) 289.
[45] Duff (n 43).
[46] ibid 43 (emphasis retained).

to resolve private conflicts, its objective in regulating offending behaviour may be furthered if reparative measures assist in terms of either reductivism, deterrence or any of the other well-rehearsed arguments concerning the objectives of the penal system.[47] As Groenhuijsen puts it, the distinction between punishment and reparation is 'a dogmatic aberration' that derives from a conceptual misunderstanding concerning crime and punishment:

> For the offender, there is no difference in the imposition of a fine on the one hand and an obligation to pay (the same amount of) restitution on the other. The proceeds of the crime have usually been spent a long time before, so the financial burden is equal in both situations. For the offender, the hardship – the pain – is neither affected by the recipient of the financial offer he has to make (the state or the victim) nor by its legal origin (tort/civil law v crime/punishment).[48]

Yet from the victim's perspective, the difference is immense. One will result in tangible compensation whereas the other will not. It may be timely to pause for thought and re-examine whether it may be possible to express denunciation 'in a currency other than that of retributive-style punishments'.[49] The nature of this new 'currency', however, needs to be carefully unpicked. Traditionally, fines and monetary damages have accounted for the vast majority of legal sanctions within most Western legal systems by acting as the primary tool for punishing, deterring, compensating and regulating.[50] However, although there may be little problem in attaching a monetary value to stolen goods or damaged property, the task of measuring physical, psychological and emotional injuries against any sort of monetary scale is fraught with difficulty since the impact of the offence will vary significantly according to the experiences of individual victims. To make reparation effective and meaningful for victims, the task of repairing harm ought not to be construed in purely financial terms. A more flexible concept is needed which is better placed to realise the various non-pecuniary components. It could, for example, include some of the salient redress features of international human rights law and transitional justice, such as apologies, explanation, guarantees of non-repetition, and uncovering facts or access to truth.[51] In developing such a concept of reparation along these broader lines, the criminal justice system could distinguish itself from the stale and ingrained dichotomy of the civil and criminal law, towards a unitary system of justice that seeks to address the reparatory rights of the victim alongside the punitive function of the penal process.

The advantages of reconceiving redress in this way would not be limited to the victim, but may also contribute to the rehabilitation of the offender. If proper processes are put in place that facilitate deliberative interaction between the victim

---

[47] eg Goldstein (n 19) notes that 'potential offenders are likely to be deterred from wrongdoing by the civil courts and punitive damages may be awarded there' (531).

[48] Marc S Groenhuijsen, 'Victims' Rights and Restorative Justice: Piecemeal Reform of the Criminal Justice System or a Change of Paradigm?' in H Kaptein and M Malsch (eds), *Crime, Victims and Justice. Essays on Principles and Practice* (London, Routledge, 2004) 74.

[49] Cavadino and Dignan (n 39) 241.

[50] Pat O'Malley, *The Currency of Justice: Fines and Damages in Consumer Societies* (London, Routledge, 2009) 1.

[51] See Jonathan Doak, 'Enriching Trial Justice for Crime Victims in Common Law Systems: Lessons from Transitional Environments' (2015) 21 *International Review of Victimology* 139–60.

and the accused, the consequences of his or her actions may be more readily impressed upon the offender than a speech denouncing his conduct from the bench. Emotionally intelligent processes, which engage with complex but readily observed emotions such as guilt, fear, remorse and forgiveness, can assist in the alleviation of guilt and may encourage a feeling among both parties that amends have been made.[52] Although such terms may appear clichéd, there is significant evidence of the rehabilitative effect of reparatory processes. Recent restorative justice studies suggest that offenders may be able to gain a sense of empathy for the victim through engaging in conferencing which, in turn, can imprint a new 'co-narrative' that affirms legal norms, vindicates victims, and denounces the act of wrongdoing without labelling any person as a villain.[53] In turn, this can help to engineer a transformed sense of identity and self-responsibility which may help them to desist from future offending.[54] Just as labelling theory has long illustrated a link between labelling someone a criminal and their propensity to commit further offences, the reverse is also true. If the offender is exonerated (and thus notionally rehabilitated) by the victim and/or the state, their capacity to desist from future offending is increased.

Yet even if it is conceded that redress within criminal justice may contribute in some measure to fulfilling the objectives of sentencing, an objection may be that it nevertheless ought to be eschewed because of the risk it poses to the principle of proportionality, which broadly states that the burden imposed on the offender reflects the seriousness of the offence. Critics warn that proportionality may be compromised in restorative practices where the victim, whose desired levels of vengefulness or forgiveness will inevitably differ from case to case, has a say in what happens to the offender.[55] Victims have long been regarded as unpredictable and irrational actors whose enhanced participation in the criminal justice systems could effect a 'reversion to the retributive, repressive and vengeful punishment of an earlier age'[56] and may introduce a new and unpredictable variable into the penalty equation and would jeopardise core principles such as 'just-deserts', certainty and objectivity.

This objection can be countered on two grounds. First, the notion of the vengeful victim is something of a myth. Far from seeking vengeance, research seems to suggest that most victims prioritise reparation over retribution and many display a desire to help the offender.[57] There is no evidence to suggest that victims are more

---

[52] Lucia Zedner, 'Reparation and Retribution: Are They Reconcilable?' (1994) 57(2) *MLR* 228–50, 233.

[53] Jon Braithwaite, 'Narrative and "Compulsory Compassion"' (2006) 31 *Law and Social Inquiry* 425–46.

[54] Tom R Tyler et al, 'Reintegrative Shaming, Procedural Justice, and Recidivism: The Engagement of Offenders' Psychological Mechanisms in the Canberra RISE Drinking-and-Driving Experiment (2007) 41(3) *Law and Society Review* 553; M Rossner, *Just Emotions: Rituals of Restorative Justice* (Oxford, Oxford University Press, 2013). On restorative justice and desistance, see generally Bart Claes and Joanna Shapland, 'Desistance from Crime and Restorative Justice' (2016) 4(3) *Restorative Justice* 302.

[55] Andrew von Hirsch and Andrew Ashworth, *Proportionate Sentencing: Exploring the Principles* (Oxford, Oxford University Press, 2005).

[56] Edna Erez, L Roeger and F Morgan, 'Victim Harm, Impact Statements and Victim Satisfaction with Justice: An Australian Experience' (1997) 5(1) *International Review of Victimology* 37–60, 40.

[57] James Chalmers, Pete Duff and Fiona Leverick, 'Victim Impact Statements: Can Work, Do Work (for Those Who Bother to Make Them)' [May 2007] *Criminal Law Review* 360–79, 374; Jonathan Doak and

punitive and would want to impose a harsher burden on the offender than the public at large.[58]

Secondly, irrespective of the personal desires of victims, it is possible to envisage a model of criminal justice that is capable of delivering redress that also encapsulates the idea of proportionality. One of the most sophisticated proposals is set out by Cavadino and Dignan,[59] who propose an 'integrated restorative justice model', wherein reparation is effected through relatively flexible proportionality principles. The model gravitates around the idea of 'public tariff', which would effectively seek to transpose existing penal sanctions into a form of redress. In practical terms, this could mean, for example, include converting monies due by way of a fine payable into a compensation order, or community service into a period of time geared towards helping specific groups or victim communities. The form and extent of such reparation would ultimately be a decision for the court which, through clear guidelines, would aim to pass a sentence that reflected both the private interests of the victim alongside the public interests of wider society. Private or informal agreements between victims and offenders could also be taken into account by the sentencer, who would be obligated to ensure that 'retributive maximum' and 'retributive minimum' standards were applied. Where such agreements were not forthcoming, the principle of proportionality would provide a 'default setting' for determination of the final outcome.

Although innovative and carefully thought out, these ideas are not unproblematic. In critiquing a similar proposal by Braithwaite,[60] von Holderstein Holtermann cautions that trying to convert orthodox disposals into reparative ones amounts to 'entering the dubious business of comparing oranges and apples – or … of finding out how many oranges it takes to exceed, say, ten apples'.[61] While this objection may appear well grounded at first sight, it should be borne in mind that the business of determining orthodox penal sanctions is also rather haphazard and prone to a measure of guesswork. The sentencer's exercise – which usually consists of determining levels of culpability and harm – also involves an imprecise conversion exercise to calculate the form and quantum of the punishment to be imposed by the court. If harm and culpability can be used as concepts to determine the degree of punishment, then so too can they be used to determine the degree of reparation.

David O'Mahony, 'The Vengeful Victim? Assessing the Attitudes of Victims Participating in Restorative Youth Conferencing' (2006) 13(2) *International Review of Victimology* 157–77; Strang (n 43).

[58] Mike Hough and Alison Park, 'How Malleable Are Attitudes to Crime and Punishment? Findings from a British Deliberative Poll' in Julian Roberts and Mike Hough (eds), *Changing Attitudes to Punishment* (Cullompton, Willan, 2002); Pat Mayhew and John Van Kesteren, 'Cross-National Attitudes to Punishment' in Roberts and Hough (eds), ibid; Joanna Mattinson and Catriona Mirrlees-Black, *Attitudes to Crime and Criminal Justice: Findings from the 1998 British Crime Survey* Home Office Research Study (London, Home Office, 2002) 200.

[59] Cavadino and Dignan (n 39).

[60] Jon Braithwaite, *Restorative Justice and Responsive Regulation* (Oxford, Oxford University Press, 2002).

[61] Jakob von Holderstein Holtermann, 'Outlining the Shadow of the Axe – On Restorative Justice and the Use of Trial and Punishment' (2009) 3(2) *Criminal Law and Philosophy* 187, 200.

4. REALISING REDRESS WITHIN CRIMINAL JUSTICE

Although the normative arguments for accommodating reparation within the criminal justice system may appear persuasive, the question of realising it through praxis is more difficult to resolve. Since the 1970s, the preferred means of the criminal courts have been some form of compensation/restitution/reparatory order payable, by the offender to the victim for loss or injury sustained. These may either form a component of the sentence itself (as in England and Wales and New Zealand)[62] or stand-alone ancillary orders which carry little or no relevance to the sentencing equation (as in New South Wales and Victoria). Compensation orders have been shown to be problematic in a number of respects, generally being used on an inconsistent basis, and offering small (often derisory) amounts to victims that may only be payable over a long period of time.[63]

To some extent, such problems may stem from the possibility that such orders are perceived as being disproportionately severe by sentencers owing to the general lack of means of offenders to pay.[64] However, there may also be deeper, structural factors at work insofar as – for reasons above – many judges may be uncomfortable with the normative confusion that is inherent in mixing aspects of civil and criminal law and may be unsure how they ought to factor restitution into the penal system.[65] There is seemingly a fundamental tension stemming from the civil/criminal divide insofar as the victim's reparatory interest may interfere with the state's rationale for imposing a particular sentence. If, for example, a victim has suffered long-term debilitating injury, his or her entitlement to a relatively high level of compensation may impose a crushing financial burden on the defendant. This, in turn, might undermine any rehabilitatory objective of the sentence through undermining the defendant's capacity to desist from future offending because the imposition of an unrealistic burden may simply encourage them to resort to crime to obtain the necessary funds. As such, many jurisdictions impose an upper limit on the amount of compensation that can be ordered,[66] and the offender will usually be allowed to pay this over a period of time.

A further problem with compensation orders is that – like damages in the civil courts and state compensation for criminal injuries – the task of repairing harm is construed in purely financial terms. As argued above, this is likely to prove unsatisfactory for many victims and is, in any case, a poor means of appraising the nature of the harm sustained. Such an approximation exercise is exacerbated by the fact that the victim has no standing to influence this decision and must rely on the prosecutor to

---

[62] Originally contained in the Criminal Justice Act 1972, the power is now contained in the Powers of Criminal Courts (Sentencing) Act 2000, s 130.

[63] Brian Williams, *Victims of Crime and Community Justice* (London, Jessica Kingsley, 2005) 99.

[64] Basia Spalek, *Crime Victims: Theory. Policy and Practice* (London, Palgrave, 2006) 103.

[65] See Joanna Shapland, Jon Willmore and Peter Duff, *Victims in the Criminal Justice System* (Aldershot, Gower 1985) 134; Home Office, Compensation and Support for Victims of Crime: A Consultation Paper on Proposals to Amend the Criminal Injuries Compensation Scheme and Provide a Wide Range of Support for Victims (London, Home Office, 2004).

[66] In England and Wales, for example, the maximum amount is capped at £5,000 in magistrates' courts although it is uncapped for offences tried in crown courts. However, the court must take into account the means of the offenders: see ss 130–31 Powers of Criminal Courts (Sentencing) Act 2000.

request that an order be made in the first place. Moreover, some of the key symbolic forms of redress that matter most to victims (such as an explanation as to why they were victimised, or a simple apology) cannot be the subject of such a court order. It has been said that such symbolic acts may help to fulfil the needs of victims 'for telling the story, for justice, and for measures to avoid repetition'.[67]

Finally, it is questionable whether a compensation order amounts to any genuine form of accountability from the perspective of the offender. There is a real risk that they will be unable to distinguish between a compensation order and a fine because both impose financial burdens, and thus few offenders are likely to consider the impact of their actions and are unlikely to feel personally accountable given that the victim has neither applied to the court for the order nor had any significant input into determining its terms.[68] From the point of view of both victim and offender, the compensation order does little to empower either party, since neither has any control over its allocation.

5. OPTIONS FOR REFORM

Given that the compensation order is the only avenue for redress in most common law criminal justice jurisdictions, there is pressing need to consider more effective mechanisms. Perhaps the most obvious – and radical – option might be through some form of *partie civile* process, not dissimilar to that which currently operates in many continental jurisdictions.[69] The procedure basically facilitates victims seeking civil compensation orders against the offender, thereby avoiding the need for a separate legal action. Usually, victims (or their legal representatives) appear in court and will demonstrate their claim through documentary evidence. Unlike the proposal above which is confined to sentencing hearings, *parties civiles* can usually participate at any stage of the trial.[70] In a similar vein (and aside from the Trust Fund discussed above), victims before the ICC can seek reparation orders directly against the accused; the court is empowered to 'determine the scope and extent of any damage, loss or injury to, or in respect of, victims' and establish principles for reparation, restitution, compensation and rehabilitation.[71] However, given the deeply entrenched nature of the adversarial system, and the clear demarcation of the fact-finding and sentencing phases of trial, the wholesale adoption of a *partie civile* system could lead to an unwieldy and protracted trial process, and would also be likely to face significant

---

[67] Roht-Arriaza (n 38) 159.

[68] See Groenhuijsen (n 48) 74.

[69] See further Marion EI Brienen and Ernestine H Hoegen, *Victims of Crime in 22 European Criminal Justice Systems: The Implementation of Recommendation (85) 11 of the Council of Europe on the Position of the Victim in the Framework of Criminal Law and Procedure* (Nijmegen, Wolf Legal Productions, 2000).

[70] However, most continental trial proceedings do not differentiate between the adjudication of guilt and sentencing stage of the process.

[71] Art 75(1). In the *Lubanga* case (n 34), the Trial Chamber considered this issue and held that the Court would be able 'without difficulty, to separate out the evidence that relates to the charges from the evidence that solely relates to reparations, and to ignore the latter until the reparations stage (if the accused is convicted)' [121].

pushback on the grounds of perceived interference with fair trial rights (in particular, the principle of equality of arms in the fact-finding phase). As such, it is difficult to see how such a mechanism might operate successfully without more far-reaching reform to the legal system as a whole.

A slightly less radical approach, but perhaps equally controversial, would be through the adoption of what I term the ASM, a variation of the 'integrated restorative justice model' proposed by Cavadino and Dignan.[72] Essentially, the ASM would seek to capture the question of redress alongside that of public censure. In any sentencing hearing where a victim is identified and consents to be dealt with through the ASM, one of two mechanisms might be triggered: referral to an out-of-court restorative conferencing programme, or, where this is not feasible, the facilitation of a more emotionally intelligent and dialogical sentencing process that takes a holistic view of matters pertaining to both redress and punishment.

Under the ASM, it is suggested that courts be obliged to consider whether the case is suitable for referral to a restorative conference. Where both parties consented and the court was satisfied that the process stood a reasonable chance of success, the court would defer sentence pending the outcome of such referral. This would involve convening a conference involving the victim, offender and their respective family members or supporters, who would discuss the circumstances surrounding the offence guided by a trained facilitator. Where agreement was reached, this would return to the court for ratification, ensuring that it respected the rights of all parties and complied with maximum and minimum proportionality standards. Such a programme could either be overseen by a state agency or an approved third-party provider, although failure to reach agreement or to comply with the terms of the agreement would result in the offender being returned to court for a more conventional sentencing process. In Braithwaite's words, the scheme would thus operate 'in the shadow of the axe',[73] meaning that conventional court structures would be triggered where the referral had essentially failed.

A similar model already operates in respect of young offenders in Northern Ireland and New Zealand, whilst New South Wales has adopted a process known as 'forum sentencing', in which magistrates can refer cases to conferencing before passing sentence.[74] With appropriate safeguards, court-ordered mediation and conferencing could serve to complement existing sentence practice. Referrals to mediation are becoming increasingly commonplace within continental Europe; Austria and Finland both operate schemes whereby the law provides that certain cases may be diverted away from court at the prosecution stage.[75] Such a restorative intervention, however, can only work where the offender accepts responsibility for the harm and both parties agree to the process.

---

[72] Cavadino and Dignan (n 39).

[73] Braithwaite (n 53) 36. For a critique, see von Holderstein Holtermann (n 61), stating that 'the exact size and shape of [the shadow] remains blurry throughout' (139).

[74] Ineligible offences include those involving serious violence, murder, manslaughter, family violence and offences involving a weapon: Criminal Procedure Regulation 2010 (NSW) regs 63(2)–(4). A similar scheme, known as 'ustice Mediation' operates in Queensland.

[75] See further O'Mahony and Doak (n 57) 132–50.

For a number of reasons, restorative conferencing may not be suitable for the case in question (for example, the offender may not consent to the process or the risks of secondary victimisation may be assessed as unacceptable). Where the case is not deemed appropriate, the court itself might seek to resolve the question of redress alongside that of punishment. In a previous article, I suggested with Louise Taylor that criminal courts might strive to follow an 'emotionally intelligent' sentencing process to deliver a package that meets the needs of both victims and offenders.[76] The gist of this proposal would be that, where possible, sentencing proceedings would be stakeholder-led rather than lawyer-led. The sentencing hearing would thus gravitate around a dialogue-driven encounter, facilitated by the trial judge. Victims, if they should choose to participate, might read a statement to the court on the impact of the offence, and as part of this might include photographs, drawings or poems as is currently permitted in the Australian state of Victoria.[77]

Crucially, victims could also ask the offender the 'why me?' question, which research suggests tends to ruminate in the minds of many victims of serious crime.[78] For their part, offenders should have the opportunity to respond – and potentially challenge – victims' statements. Pleas in mitigation (which tend to be written and delivered solely by lawyers) might be either complemented or replaced by the opportunity for the offender to deliver an oral statement in person to the court. They would be free to recount aspects of their life stories and their emotions before, during and after the offence. Such emotions would not only cover the 'acceptable' feelings of shame and remorse but offenders would also be free to make protests of innocence or defiance. Just as offenders would have a right to challenge aspects of the victim's evidence, so too would victims be empowered to challenge any aspect of the offender's statement. It is, perhaps, self-evident that a risk exists that a dialogue of this nature could quite easily spiral into a freewheeling fracas, or indeed the victim narrative could become dominant, thereby drowning or pre-empting the account of the offender.[79] However, with careful formulated ground rules, close preparation with legal professionals and robust judicial oversight, this risk might be substantially reduced.

Like restorative conferencing, such an exercise would give the court a more nuanced and comprehensive understanding of the backgrounds of the victim and offender and the impact of the offence. This should enable the court to tailor a much more effective reparation package than the existing compensation order, which would speak more closely to the needs of victims and the individual circumstances of the offenders. It would also broaden the potential forms of reparation that might be made available. These would not be limited to pecuniary compensation, but might also include aspects such as an apology; an undertaking not to repeat the offence or commit any further act that would cause further distress to the victim; restitution or

---

[76] Jonathan Doak and Louise Taylor, 'Hearing the Voices of Victims and Offenders: The Role of Emotions in Criminal Sentencing' (2013) 64(1) *Northern Ireland Legal Quarterly* 25–46.

[77] ibid.

[78] Lawrence Sherman and Heather Strang, 'Repairing the Harm: Victims and Restorative Justice' (2003) 1 *Utah Law Review* 15.

[79] Susan Bandes, 'Empathy, Narrative, and Victim Impact Statements' (1996) 63 *University of Chicago Law Review* 361, 386.

repair of damaged or stolen property; or undertaking some form of work such as cleaning graffiti, picking up litter or giving time to assist with a similar charitable or community cause. As with the existing compensation order, such reparation might operate alongside other sentencing components, with the overall 'punitive tariff' being reduced for remorse, apology, forgiveness and any acts of contrition.[80] As with the restorative referral outlined above, the overall burden imposed on the offender would also be subject to the higher and lower proportionality limits. The ASM would ensure the delivery of a package of reparative measures which might go some way to meeting victims' needs and expectations of the justice system, which is also a proportionate and just response to the offending behaviour.

Whilst the ASM may be attractive on paper, it risks – like the compensation order – being undermined by the attitudinal barrier regarding the role of redress within criminal justice that would appear to be commonplace within certain quarters of the judiciary. To offset this risk, a (rebuttable) presumption should be introduced through legislation to ensure that either a referral to restorative conferencing or a reparation order (issued through the process outlined above) will be issued in all cases involving a direct victim where an injury or loss has occurred. Under New Zealand's Sentencing Act 2002, the court is under an obligation to adjourn sentencing in order to assess the suitability of all cases for referral to restorative justice where the offender has pleaded guilty and where the judge is aware that a programme is available. Likewise, a similar obligation applies under the Act requiring that a court 'must impose [a reparation order] unless it is satisfied that the sentence or order would result in undue hardship for the offender or the dependants of the offender, or that any other special circumstances would make it inappropriate'.[81]

6. CONCLUSIONS

Randy Barnett famously proposed that a similar procedure ought to be adopted in common law jurisdictions, whereby adjudication would concern itself with 'the conduct, broadly defined, of the parties to the case with a view toward the protection of individual liberty and private property'.[82] As proposed by the ASM, viewing conflicts through such a unitary lens would potentially address a much wider set of aims above and beyond either criminal justice or the private law of tort. Victims would not be the only beneficiaries of such an approach. The injection of the victim's private interest into the somewhat elusive concept of the 'public interest' could lend additional legitimacy to the outcome of the case, thereby benefiting the criminal justice system as a whole since the community is made up of 'victims, potential victims and the fellow citizens of victims'.[83] As Weisstub contends, the civil justice system could benefit from infusing itself with the symbolism of criminal sanctions, thereby

---

[80] See Stephanos Bibas, 'Forgiveness in Criminal Procedure' (2007) 4 *Ohio State Journal of Criminal Law* 329.
[81] Sentencing Act 2002 (NZ) s 12(1).
[82] Barnett (n 15) 290.
[83] Cavadino and Dignan (n 39) 237.

showing itself to be 'consonant with public morality and conscience'.[84] There are also various economic arguments that could be used in support of this view: reparative sentences significantly lessen the financial burden on the taxpayer and a corresponding reduction in separate civil claims could reduce litigation in the courts.[85]

However, the prevalence of the common law paradigm which draws a neat (though unconvincing) line between the private and public realms means that such a radical reconfiguration of the criminal trial remains an indeterminate prospect. Past failings of the compensation order, and institutional reluctance to integrate restorative justice programmes within the formal parameters of the criminal justice system, indicate that opposition to such reforms remains deeply entrenched. Although the normative case for redress has been widely advanced, and a considerable evidence base exists as to how reparative justice might be operationalised in practice, the challenge now is to explore concrete means to counter the cultural and attitudinal resistance to redress in order to move towards a more legitimate and holistic form of criminal procedure, which better encapsulates the range of harms that stem from criminal acts.

---

[84] N Weisstub, 'Victims of Crime in the Criminal Justice System' in E Fattah (ed), *From Crime Policy to Victim Policy* (London, Macmillan, 1986) 207.
[85] Zedner (n 52) 233.

6

Murder, the Mandatory Life Sentence and the Question of Perceived Legitimacy*

BARRY MITCHELL

1. INTRODUCTION

THIS CHAPTER IS essentially concerned with what has been referred to as the perceived legitimacy of the way in which the criminal justice system deals with a particular group of offenders – an issue on which Ralph Henham produced detailed analysis and close argument.[1] More specifically, the chapter addresses the question of perceived legitimacy in the context of the way in which the justice system deals with murder and the punishment of convicted offenders. 'Perceived legitimacy' here refers to the public perception of the legitimacy of the current arrangements. As Mark Drumbl reminds us in chapter 3 of this volume, for Henham the importance of this legitimacy lies in the extent to which it helps to uphold social harmony and promote social cohesion. Hitherto, discussions of legitimacy have tended to concentrate on the trial process and on sentencing, but it will be helpful to preface consideration of the mandatory life sentence with an examination of the substantive law relating to murder.

Following this brief introduction the chapter looks (in Part 2) at the relationship of the law and the legal system to public opinion. Part 3 sets out some of the main concerns about the legal definition of murder, identifying a number of aspects that may not sit altogether comfortably with public views and assumptions. The chapter then turns in Part 4 to examine the sentence for murder, and focuses on apparent shortcomings that have been revealed through either survey research or theoretical analysis. The implications to be drawn from this regarding the methodology that is used in public surveys are outlined in Part 5. Finally, in Part 6 the chapter looks at some immediate reforms that should be made to the existing law and then suggests

---

* The cut-off point for legal and factual developments for this chapter was 31 December 2016.
[1] See eg his 'Penal Ideology, Sentencing, and the Legitimacy of Trial Justice' (2012) 57 *Crime, Law and Social Change* 77; 'Exploring the Relationship between Sentencing and the Legitimacy of Trial Justice' (2009) 37 *International Journal of Law, Crime and Justice* 65; and 'Theorising Law and Legitimacy in International Criminal Justice' (2007) 3(3) *International Journal of Law in Context* 257.

the kind of further public opinion research that would underpin a much-needed fundamental review of the current arrangements.

2. LAW AND PUBLIC OPINION

From a purely theoretical perspective there is clearly a good case for arguing that public opinion ought to have some sort of influence on the criminal law and the criminal justice system. In a democracy such as that in England and Wales political parties seeking election to government set out their criminal and penal policies, so that the electorate have an opportunity to reflect their views on crime and punishment through the ballot box. Of course, the extent to which this enables the public to influence government criminal and penal policy should not be exaggerated. There are numerous other very important issues in the minds of the electorate when completing their ballot forms – the economy, the welfare system, education, the national health service, foreign policy, etc – which also, to varying degrees, play a part in the electoral process. But it would be foolish to ignore the opportunity given to the electorate to express their opinion on party policy on crime and criminal justice. At the same time, it should be acknowledged that even if penal policy was the dominant issue in the minds of the electorate, it does not follow that government policy will be supported by the majority of the public.

Quite apart from public influence through general elections, the development and evolution of the criminal law and criminal justice system may result, at least in part, from the activities of pressure groups and support groups, or through campaigns undertaken by the media. Again, there is no certainty that the views of such groups and organisations are shared by the majority of the public, but these avenues enable pressure to be brought to bear on governments and politicians to bring change – ie perceived improvements – to the legal system.

The relationship between the law and public opinion is one that is constantly evolving, and in recent years it seems that criminal justice policymakers have been keen to take account of popular sentiment. One obvious explanation for this is the desire to maintain public confidence in the administration of justice.[2] It is also true to say that the way in which the criminal justice system deals with offenders is influenced by cultural factors. The culture of any society is reflected in the way in which offenders are punished – the seriousness of sentences, and the factors that are regarded as aggravating or mitigating seriousness. Similarly, there is a social and cultural dimension to the allocation of moral blameworthiness, otherwise it would be impossible to communicate the appropriate degree of blame to the offender.

It is therefore understandable that there should be a relationship between sentencing practice and societal values. Moreover, concerns would rightly be expressed about the perceived legitimacy of the criminal justice system if public opinion and community values were simply ignored. From a purely pragmatic perspective, levels of compliance with the law are likely to be dependent on the extent to which people

---

[2] See eg Paul Robinson, *Distributive Principles of Criminal Law: Who Should be Punished How Much?* (Oxford, Oxford University Press, 2008).

regard the legal system as legitimate; threats of unpleasant sanctions are unlikely to suffice by themselves.[3] Thus, failure to provide a sufficient degree of correlation between the law and legal practice will damage popular perceptions of legitimacy and levels of compliance with the law.

Retributivism, an important objective of the criminal justice system, requires offences and offenders to incur society's condemnation, and that in turn suggests there must be some form of general agreement (or understanding) about the kinds of behaviour that merit condemnation and the degree of condemnation that is appropriate in each case. If no account was taken of public attitudes and opinion, there would be no condemnation of offences or offenders. In this respect, the perceived legitimacy of the sentencing process is based on its relationship with the values and opinion of society on whose behalf the process operates.

It is important to recognise that the need to take on board community values and opinions is not confined to the sentencing of convicted offenders. Our concerns about perceived legitimacy also relate to the substantive criminal law, especially from a retributive perspective. Assessment of the relative seriousness of different forms of criminality should not ignore public sentiment, not simply to maintain public confidence in the criminal justice system but also because public opinion is an inherent feature of that assessment. The moral wrongfulness and blameworthiness of criminal conduct is assessed by the extent to which it conflicts with the norms and values that society seeks to uphold. In chapter 2 Roger Cotterrell provides a valuable analysis of the relationship between legal and popular opinion on what should be regarded as 'criminal', and the implications of any variation between the two.

Thus, notwithstanding methodological difficulties in obtaining accurate and reliable data, and (as Mark Drumbl points out in chapter 3) the fact that social morality does not remain static over time, there are clear grounds for taking account of public opinion and values when evaluating the substantive criminal law and the punishment of convicted offenders. Arguably, nowhere is that more true than in relation to the conviction and punishment of the most serious forms of homicide.

3. MURDER

3.1. Murder under English Criminal Law

English criminal law has long recognised a distinction between the two crimes of murder (which is meant to encompass the more serious forms of criminal homicide) and manslaughter (which is aimed at the less serious cases).[4] This distinction continues to be maintained, in part at least, because of the assumption that it is supported by public opinion.[5] Failure to recognise the distinction would, it is said, cause people

---

[3] See eg Tom R Tyler, *Why People Obey the Law* (Princeton, Princeton University Press, 2006).

[4] See eg J M Kaye 'The Early History of Murder and Manslaughter' (1967) 83 *LQR* 365–95, 569–601.

[5] See eg Criminal Law Revision Committee, *Fourteenth Report: Offences against the Person* (London, HMSO 1980) paras 15, 23 and 28; and R Goff, 'The Mental Element in the Crime of Murder' (1988) 104 *LQR* 30–59.

to think that the law had been weakened. Indeed, it is not difficult to find instances of where the criminal law and legal practice is believed to be supported by public opinion. For example:

- A person who deliberately kills another in self-defence is entitled to an acquittal provided it was reasonable to use force in the circumstances and provided also that no more than reasonable (or proportionate) force was used.[6] In *Palmer* Lord Morris argued that: 'If a jury thought that in a moment of unexpected anguish a person attacked had only done what he honestly and instinctively thought was necessary that would be most potent evidence that only reasonable defensive action had been taken.'

- A person who deliberately kills another whilst acting under duress by threats (of death or serious harm) should nonetheless be convicted of murder. In justifying this Lord Hailsham commented: 'I have known in my own lifetime of too many acts of heroism by ordinary human beings of no more than ordinary fortitude to regard a law as either "just or humane" which withdraws the protection of the criminal law from the innocent victim and casts the cloak of its protection upon the coward and the poltroon in the name of a "concession to frailty".'[7]

- A person who carries out what would widely be regarded as a 'mercy killing' – the victim, with full mental capacity, freely expresses a desire to die, but is unable to kill himself, and the defendant kills the victim solely to give effect to the victim's desire and to alleviate suffering – should (according to the law in textbooks) be convicted of murder. The law does not formally recognise any sort of defence based on 'good' or 'compassionate motive'. But in practice, such a defendant may well be convicted of the lesser crime of manslaughter – the partial defence of diminished responsibility is stretched and made to apply on the basis that, as the Criminal Law Revision Committee remarked, 'no-one connected with [a mercy killing] case wants to see the defendant convicted of murder'.[8]

3.2. Concerns about the Law of Murder

Nevertheless, over the years there has been no shortage of criticism of the law relating to murder (and manslaughter) by commentators and experts in the subject. Whilst it must not be assumed that any such criticisms are widely shared by members of the public and that there is therefore a lack of public support from the law, the possibility remains that at least some of these criticisms do reflect discrepancies between legal

---

[6] *Palmer v R* [1971] AC 814. But if excessive force was used, the killer should be convicted of murder – the law adopts an 'all-or-nothing' approach here, and there should be no compromise verdict of manslaughter. One wonders, however, whether the courts – especially juries – adhere rigidly to this particular letter of the law.

[7] See *Howe et al* [1987] 2 WLR 568. Commentators have, however, been highly critical of this 'heroism argument': Professor JC Smith suggested that 'Even the most resolute and well-disposed citizen would be likely to comply [with the threat]': 'R v Howe and others: Commentary' (1987) *Crim LR* 480–85.

[8] Criminal Law Revision Committee (1980) (n 5) para 115.

and public opinion. It is therefore helpful to look – albeit briefly – at some of the major concerns that have been expressed.

In 2004, having conducted a review of the law of provocation, diminished responsibility, excessive force in self-defence, and abused women who kill, the Law Commission concluded that '[t]he present law of murder in England and Wales is a mess', and went on to say '[t]here is both a great need to review the law of murder and every reason to believe that a comprehensive consideration of the offence and the sentencing regime could yield rational and sensible conclusions about a number of issues'.[9] The Commission was then asked to carry out a more general review of the law of murder, but the punishment of offenders – including the mandatory life sentence for murder – was excluded. At the end of this review the Commission reported that '[t]he law governing homicide in England and Wales is a rickety structure set upon shaky foundations',[10] and '[t]he sentencing guidelines that parliament has recently issued for murder cases presupposes that murder has a rational structure that properly reflects degrees of fault and provides appropriate defences. Unfortunately, the law does not have, and never has had, such a structure.'[11]

3.2.1. The Definition of Murder is Stretched Too Far

On this latter issue the Law Commission thought that the existing two-offence structure – whereby the majority of criminal homicides are catered for by the crimes of murder and manslaughter – is 'not fit for purpose'.[12] Both murder and manslaughter are being stretched too far, so that they cover too broad a range of cases: the obvious concern here is that the crime of murder in particular fails to fulfil its function of encapsulating the most serious instances of criminal homicide. Senior members of the judiciary have expressed similar worries about the need to narrow the definition of murder. In *Hyam v DPP* Lord Kilbrandon asserted '[i]t is no longer true, if it was ever true, to say that murder as we now define it is necessarily the most heinous example of unlawful homicide'.[13] A few years later, in *Howe et al*, Lord Hailsham reiterated that:

> Murder, as every practitioner of the law knows, though often described as one of the utmost heinousness, is not in fact necessarily so, but consists in a whole bundle of offences of vastly differing degrees of culpability, ranging from brutal, cynical and repeated offences like the so-called Moors murders to the almost venial, if objectively immoral 'mercy killing' of a beloved partner.[14]

---

[9] Law Commission, *Partial Defences to Murder*, Law Com No 290, Cm 6301 (London, TSO, 2004) para 2.74.

[10] Law Commission, *Murder, Manslaughter and Infanticide*, Law Com No 304, HC 30 (London, TSO 2006) para 1.8.

[11] ibid para 1.9.

[12] ibid para 1.34. Apart from the Law Commission's review, relatively little serious consideration seems to have been given to the structure of the substantive homicide law. One issue that arguably merits further examination is the way in which the law deals with multiple-victim cases, and whether a separate offence should be created to distinguish them from single-victim murders; see Barry Mitchell, 'Multiple-Victim Murder, Multiple Murders and Schedule 21 to the Criminal Justice Act 2003' (2011) 75(2) *Journal of Criminal Law* 122–31.

[13] [1974] 2 WLR 607, 640.

[14] *Howe et al* (n 7) 581.

Similarly, manslaughter covers such a vast range of homicides, some of which seem more serious than some (of the lesser) murders, that it is impossible to get a clear perception of what the crime represents.

The comments of Lords Kilbrandon and Hailsham above were made thirty or forty years ago, but there have been no developments in the substantive law that diminish their relevance today. It is thus perhaps not surprising that verdicts in some homicide cases – resulting from contested trials or from guilty pleas – do not appear to reflect the theoretical distinctions between murder and manslaughter.[15] The apparent 'anomalies' in some cases did not seem to result from evidential issues but may have reflected the personal views of the individuals involved, including jurors. Not surprisingly, in 2006 the Law Commission made a recommendation that the status quo be replaced with three offences – murder in the first degree, murder in the second degree and manslaughter – but this has been ignored by the previous (New) Labour administration, the subsequent Coalition (Conservative and Liberal Democrat) government, and the current Conservative government.

3.2.2. The (In)adequacy of Intent to Cause Serious Harm

One fairly obvious explanation for this criticism that the definition of murder is too wide is that the prosecution only have to show that the defendant intended to cause serious injury, and even that need not be life-threatening.[16] The Law Commission thought this set the bar too low and recommended that liability for the most serious homicide should only be possible where the defendant was (also) aware that his or her conduct might cause death.[17] Moreover, research conducted for the Commission indicated – not surprisingly – that the public assume that murder requires an intent to kill or some sort of moral equivalent (such as showing a total disregard for the life of another). If serious but non-life-threatening harm was intended, then even if the victim died their death was regarded as 'accidental' because the defendant's act did not appear to put life at risk.[18]

3.2.3. The Law is Too Narrow

Paradoxically, whilst it may be said that the legal definition of murder is in one respect too broad, it is arguable that in another respect it is unduly narrow insofar as it fails to include some instances of criminal homicide that are amongst the most serious.

3.2.4. Indifference to Consequences – Disregard for Life

Effectively, the law's insistence on an intent either to kill or to cause serious injury means that cases where the defendant showed a complete disregard for the life of

---

[15] BJ Mitchell, 'Distinguishing Between Murder and Manslaughter' (1991) 141 *New Law Journal* 935–37, 969–71.

[16] See eg *Woollin* [1999] AC 82.

[17] Law Commission (n 10) paras 1.17–1.19.

[18] Law Commission, *A New Homicide Act for England and Wales? A Consultation Paper*, Consultation Paper No 177 (London, TSO 2005) Appendix A, paras A7 and A8.

another might well fall outside the definition of murder. This gives rise to the concern that the legal definition is unduly narrow. The concept of intent (to cause harm) does not seem to be an adequate means of distinguishing the most serious offences from the lesser cases, and the law should find a way to take account of the defendant's attitude towards the consequences of his behaviour.[19]

This problem is often illustrated by what might called a 'Russian roulette' killing: D has a gun with a cylinder that can accommodate up to six bullets. He puts one bullet in the cylinder and spins it, so that he does not know whether the bullet is in line with the barrel. He points the gun at V and fires it. At that moment D has no positive desire or purpose to kill or injure V, nor is he virtually certain that V will die or be seriously injured because he does not know whether the bullet is going to be fired or not – the gun may just 'click'. But let us further suppose that the jury take the view that even if told in advance that the bullet would be fired from the gun D would still have pulled the trigger. That kind of callous indifference as to the consequences of his action for V would lead us to regard D's conduct as extremely blameworthy, and if V did in fact die we would surely regard this as one of the more culpable homicides. Yet in law it cannot truly be said that D intended to kill or cause serious injury, and therefore D ought not to be convicted of murder.

3.2.5. *Killing in the Course of Another Serious Crime*

There is a second group of cases which arguably illustrate that the current legal definition of murder is unduly narrow. It has long been argued that killing someone in the course or furtherance of committing another serious crime should be treated as murder even though the defendant did not intend to kill or cause serious injury. (This is sometimes referred to in certain US states as 'felony[20] murder'.) Put simply, the argument is that the context in which the homicide is carried out – ie the commission of another serious offence – compensates for the lesser *mens rea* vis-à-vis causing the victim's death. Thus, taking a holistic approach, the case should be treated as murder.

There are, moreover, good reasons for thinking that the public might share this criticism of the law. In a public survey carried out in October 1995, in which respondents were asked to rank a group of hypothetical scenarios in order of gravity, the one that was frequently regarded as the most serious was: 'A burglar was disturbed by the owner of the house, a 25-year old woman. He panicked. He picked up an ashtray which was near at hand and hit her over the head with it. She died of her injuries.'[21] The fact that he panicked and just picked up the first thing that came to hand might well enable the burglar to argue that he did not intend to kill or cause serious injury. At most, he was reckless as to whether he would kill or cause serious injury.

---

[19] See eg William Wilson, 'Murder and the Structure of Homicide' in Andrew Ashworth and Barry Mitchell (eds), *Rethinking English Homicide Law* (Oxford, Oxford University Press, 2000) 29, 39–43.

[20] 'Felony', of course, is the traditional term for referring to serious offences.

[21] Barry Mitchell, 'Public Perceptions of Homicide and Criminal Justice' (1998) 38(3) *British Journal of Criminology* 453–72.

There is, of course, a counter-argument against allowing subjectively reckless killing in the course of another serious crime to constitute murder; that it is better to treat such cases as examples of manslaughter and reflect the combination of wrong-doing (manslaughter and the other serious crime) in the sentence. The essential justification for this is that whether a homicide should be murder or manslaughter ought to be determined according to the defendant's moral culpability for causing death – which is the argument in favour of regarding indifference to whether V lives or dies as warranting a murder conviction. Knowingly risking death obviously implies a high level of moral blame, but that should not suffice for the most serious forms of criminal homicide.

Whatever the merits of these particular arguments and counter-arguments, the possibility is that the public may well regard the current law as unsatisfactory and in need of reform.

3.2.6. *The Ongoing Problem of Mercy Killing*

'Mercy killing' is a term that commonly refers to cases where the defendant was motivated to kill by compassion. The victim was almost invariably terminally ill, suffering severe pain and has often expressed a wish to die (whilst retaining full mental capacity). According to the law as stated in texts and reference books, mercy killing constitutes murder – the defendant has caused the victim's death, he intended to kill and the law does not recognise any kind of defence – complete or partial – based on compassionate or 'good' motive. Yet in practice, precisely because '[n]o-one ... wants to see the defendant convicted of murder ... legal and medical consciences are stretched to bring about a verdict of manslaughter by reason of diminished responsibility'.[22] In this way the courts have traditionally been able to avoid convicting mercy killers of murder, but (a) whether this stretching is possible under the new law on diminished responsibility[23] remains to be seen, and (b) whether it is acceptable to put pressure on lawyers and psychiatrists to stretch the law in this way is obviously open to debate.

Mercy killing presents a real paradox. The defendant intends to kill and thus prima facie fulfils the requirements of murder. Yet at the same time he intends to prevent further pain and suffering to the same person whom he intends to kill. In 2006 the Law Commission proposed a public consultation 'on whether and, if so, to what extent the law should recognise either an offence of "mercy" killing or a partial defence of "mercy" killing'.[24] Sadly, no such consultation has been held, but one factor behind that proposal was survey evidence that indicated not inconsiderable public sympathy for those who commit a mercy killing, especially where the victim has expressed a desire to die.[25] Such cases are clearly not regarded as examples of the most serious forms of homicide, and this obviously implies that a murder conviction would be unwarranted.

---

[22] Criminal Law Revision Committee (n 5).
[23] See ss 52 and 53 Coroners and Justice Act 2009.
[24] Law Commission (n 10) para 7.49.
[25] Law Commission (n 18) para A13.

3.3. Summary

This brief review suggests there may well be a number of differences between what the law regards as murder and what the public think ought to be treated as the most serious forms of criminal homicide.

4. THE SENTENCE FOR MURDER

4.1. The Current Law

Since 1965 whenever a person is convicted of murder in England or Wales the judge is required to impose a sentence of life imprisonment[26] or equivalent. (Those under the age of 21 at the date of conviction must be sentenced to 'custody for life',[27] whereas offenders under 18 when the murder was committed must be 'detained at Her Majesty's pleasure'.[28]) Initially, the 1965 legislation replaced capital punishment for murder with life imprisonment for a period of four or five years, but the position was made indefinite by both Houses of Parliament in 1969. The abolition of the death penalty for murder in 1965 was the culmination of an extremely lengthy debate, and it was widely accepted that the debate had not ended there.

It was generally assumed that the mandatory sentence of life imprisonment (hereafter 'MLS') was effectively the political price that had to be paid in order to be rid of the death sentence – though there was, strictly, no wholly objective or scientific evidence to demonstrate this. More recently, surveys have been carried out which seek to identify public opinion about the sentencing of some murders, but one comprehensive and detailed survey conducted in May 2010 found no overwhelming public support for the MLS and reported instead that respondents often felt that a fixed period of imprisonment would have been a satisfactory punishment.[29]

One of the controversial features of the MLS is that most offenders serve a lengthy period in custody but are then released into the community under supervision. (Members of the public are generally aware that most convicted murderers do not literally spend the rest of their lives in prison, but seem largely unaware that when released they are placed under supervision.) The phrase 'life imprisonment' is to that extent misleading: the sentence remains in force until the end of the offender's lifetime, but immediate imprisonment is usually for a finite period. When passing a life sentence the judge must make either a 'minimum term order' or a 'whole life order'.[30] The former is the amount of time the offender must serve in prison before she/he can

---

[26] S 1(1) Murder (Abolition of Death Penalty) Act 1965.

[27] S 9 Powers of Criminal Courts (Sentencing) Act 2000. If and when s 61 Criminal Justice and Courts Services Act 2000 is brought into force the sentence of 'custody for life' would be abolished and replaced by life imprisonment.

[28] S 90 Powers of Criminal Courts (Sentencing) Act 2000.

[29] Barry Mitchell and Julian V Roberts, *Exploring the Mandatory Life Sentence for Murder* (Oxford, Hart, 2012).

[30] S 321(2) Sentencing Act 2020.

formally apply for release on licence. If the offender was aged at least 21 years when the offence was committed the judge may feel that the seriousness of the murder was such that it would be inappropriate to identify a minimum term and impose a whole life order instead:[31] those on whom a whole life order is imposed can expect to spend the rest of their lives in prison.

Whole life orders are relatively uncommon; minimum term orders are much more frequent and when deciding what order to make the judge should consider the provisions in Schedule 21 of the Sentencing Act 2020, paragraphs 2–6 of which identify 'starting points',[32] which the judge "must have regard to" but should not stick to slavishly.[33] According to paragraph 2(2), a whole life order would be an appropriate starting point where the offender was aged at least 21 years when he/she committed the offence and in any of the following:

- the murder of two or more persons, where each murder involves (i) a substantial degree of premeditation or planning, or (ii) the abduction of the victim, or (iii) sexual or sadistic conduct;
- the murder of a child if involving the abduction of the child or sexual or sadistic motivation;
- the murder of a police officer or prison officer in the course of his or her duty where the offence was committed on or after 13 April 2015;
- a murder done for the purpose of advancing a political, religious, racial or ideological cause; or
- a murder by an offender previously convicted of murder.

A 30-year starting point, according to paragraph 3(2) is indicated (in cases falling outside paragraph 2 above) in any of the following:

- where the offence was committed before 13 April 2015, the murder of a police officer or prison officer in the course of his or her duty;
- a murder involving the use of a firearm or explosive;
- a murder done for gain (such as murder in the course or furtherance of robbery or burglary, done for payment or done in the expectation of gain as a result of the death);
- a murder intended to obstruct or interfere with the course of justice;
- a murder involving sexual or sadistic conduct;
- the murder of two or more persons;
- a murder that is aggravated by racial or religious hostility or by hostility related to sexual orientation;

---

[31] S 321(3) Sentencing Act 2020.
[32] S 323(3)(b) Sentencing Act 2020. The judge should also give reasons for the choice of order made; s 323(4) Sentencing Act 2020.
[33] See eg *Sullivan and others* [2004] EWCA Crim 1762.

- a murder that is aggravated by hostility related to disability or transgender identity, where the offence was committed on or after 3rd December 2012 (or over a period, or at some time during a period, ending on or after that date); or

- a murder falling within paragraph 2(2) by an offender who was aged under 21 when the offence was committed.

By paragraph 4, a 25-year starting point is appropriate if the case does not fall within either of the previous paragraphs, if the offender was aged at least 18 years when the offence was committed, the offence was committed on or after 2 March 2010 and if the offender took a knife or other weapon to the scene intending either (a) to commit any offence, or (b) to have it available to use as a weapon, and used that knife or other weapon in committing the murder.

If the case does not fall within paragraphs 2, 3 or 4 and the offender was aged at least 18 years when the murder was committed, the starting point for the minimum term is 15 years (paragraph 5). But where the offender was aged less than 18 years, the starting point is 12 years (paragraph 6).

Having identified the starting point, the judge should take account of other aggravating[34] and mitigating[35] factors, examples of which are listed in paragraphs 9 and 10 respectively.

4.2. A Brief Critical Review of the Current Law in Operation, Especially Schedule 21

The current framework for sentencing convicted murderers was introduced by the Criminal Justice Act 2003 which came into force on 18 December 2003. This Act was recently amended by the Sentencing Act 2020 which largely reproduced, with some relatively minor alterations in the wording, the relevant provisions in the 2003 legislation.

In 2003 the average minimum term was 13.68 years. There was then a distinct increase and six years later, in 2009, the average minimum term was 17.54 years. In other words, an upturn of 28.22 percent in the first seven years under the new sentencing framework.

This increase in the minimum terms for murder was quite deliberate. When during the parliamentary debates of the Criminal Justice Bill the then Home Secretary was asked by Douglas Hogg MP to explain why they were 'being asked to approve a range

---

[34] Para 9 lists the following aggravating factors: significant planning or premeditation; victims who are vulnerable through age or disability; the infliction of mental or physical suffering before death; abuse of trust; the use of duress or threats to facilitate the murder; the fact that the victim was providing a public service or performing a public duty; and concealment, destruction or dismemberment of the body.

[35] Para 10 lists the following mitigating factors: an intent to cause serious harm rather than kill; lack of premeditation; the fact that the defendant was suffering from a mental disorder or disability (not amounting to diminished responsibility) which reduced his culpability; the fact that the defendant was provoked (eg by prolonged stress) but not sufficiently for a plea of (formerly provocation but now) loss of control; the fact that the defendant acted to any extent in self-defence; a belief by the defendant that the murder was an act of mercy; and the offender's age.

of life sentence tariffs which are greatly in excess of the range set out in the practice directions from the Lord Chief Justice of May 2002',[36] David Blunkett replied:

> Yes, I accept that entirely. I disagreed with the Lord Chief Justice's practice guidance. I happen to believe, and the House can take a contrary view if it wishes, that we should lay down a framework that will give the people of this country confidence in the system, for two reasons – first, that those who commit the most horrendous murders will get what used to be called, in old-fashioned language, their just deserts. Secondly, when people have confidence in the system and there is consistency in the treatment of the most difficult and dangerous crimes, they might be prepared to listen to a broader debate about sentencing policy, the sentencing framework and the work of the Sentencing Guidelines Council, and about how we stop lower-level repeat offenders reoffending. We can have, in the House and in the country, a much more rational debate if people believe that we have got it right at a level that they currently do not understand.[37]

So not only was the increase in minimum terms deliberate, but it was done on the basis that it would ensure public confidence in the way the criminal justice system deals with serious offenders. Yet no clear or convincing evidence was offered to substantiate the belief that public opinion favoured such an increase in the punishment of convicted murderers.

Furthermore, real concern was expressed by MPs that there was inadequate opportunity to discuss what was being proposed.[38] Thus, right from the outset there was good cause not to assume that what was subsequently enshrined in Schedule 21 of the Criminal Justice Act 2003 carried large swathes of public support.

Indeed, one leading authority echoed these concerns and identified what he described as 'major flaws' in Schedule 21:[39]

> The first is the width of the gap between what may ... be called murders of normal seriousness, for which the starting point for consideration of the minimum term is 15 years, and murders of particularly high seriousness, for which the starting point is 30 years. The second flaw is the width of the gap between the starting point for determining the minimum term for offenders under the age of 18 (12 years) and the starting point for murderers over 18. This can cause particular difficulty when two persons, one just under and one just over 18, are convicted of a murder which falls into the 'particularly high seriousness' category, with the result that the starting points for the two offenders are 12 years and 30 years respectively.[40]

---

[36] Douglas Hogg explained that in Lord Woolf's Practice Statement 'the suggested starting point was 12 years, rising to 15 and 16 years, then to 20 years, and only in exceptional cases, 30 years or whole life'.

[37] House of Commons, *Hansard*, Debates for 20 May 2003, cols 871, 872.

[38] Examples are given in Barry Mitchell, 'Sentencing Guidelines for Murder: From Political Schedule to Principled Guidelines' in Andrew Ashworth and Julian V Roberts (eds), *Sentencing Guidelines: Exploring the English Model* (Oxford, Oxford University Press, 2013) 58.

[39] 'Schedule 21 to the Criminal Justice Act 2003 was cobbled together at high speed as a result of the decision of the House of Lords in *R (on the application of Anderson) v Secretary of State* [2002] UKHL 46 ... that the previous system of determining the minimum term to be served by those convicted of murder did not comply with the European Convention on Human Rights. It was added at a late stage to the massive Bill which became the Criminal Justice Act 2003, which ... reached the statute book without any significant consideration in Parliament.' See David Thomas, '*R v Bonellie*: Commentary' (2008) *Crim LR* 904, 905.

[40] ibid.

In short, the presence of a single element of aggravation is meant to justify the doubling of the starting point. The obvious danger is that this leads to unwarranted differences in minimum terms unless judges try to bridge the gap by attaching great weight to other, individual elements of aggravation and mitigation (when considering the impact of paragraphs 9 and 10).

In addition, there is the ambiguity of some of the words and phrases in Schedule 21. Paragraph 2(2) refers to 'a *substantial* degree of planning or premeditation', but does this mean the planning or premeditation should simply be more than minimal, or does it mean something more than that?[41] And is there any difference between this and 'significant degree of planning or premeditation' in paragraph 9? This lack of clarity is not confined to Schedule 21, but there is an undoubted danger of inconsistency.

The failure to adequately discuss and debate the relevant clauses of what was the Criminal Justice Bill has almost certainly led to other apparent deficiencies in Schedule 21. For example, when dealing with the murder of two or more victims the trial judge might identify a starting point of either a whole life or 30 years. If each murder involved a substantial degree of planning or premeditation, or the abduction of the victim, or sexual or sadistic conduct, a whole life order would be indicated (by virtue of paragraph 2(2)). Without one of these additional aggravating factors, no more than 30 years is warranted under paragraph 3(2)). But the starting point would be a whole life if there was only one victim who was a child who had been abducted or the murder had been sexually or sadistically motivated, or if the murder was motivated by advancement of a political or religious or racial or ideological cause, or if the defendant had a previous conviction for murder.

Thus, Schedule 21 clearly states that the presence of the aggravating factors in paragraph 2(2) can justify the imposition of a higher starting point (a whole life) in a single-victim murder than would be appropriate in a multiple-victim murder where there are no additional aggravating factors (30 years). It is suggested that this is unsound and it is doubted whether it is supported by the majority of the public. Faced with, say, a five- or six-victim murder, a trial judge might, of course, set the starting point at a whole life, rather than at 30 years. But the fact that Schedule 21 is drafted as it is surely illustrates the need for a thorough re-evaluation of the status quo.

4.3. Public Attitudes Towards Sentencing for Murder

When the current law governing the sentencing of convicted murderers was enacted (through the Murder (Abolition of Death Penalty) Act 1965), it was assumed that the overwhelming majority of the public in England and Wales supported the MLS. At that time, no research evidence was available to indicate whether the assumption was

---

[41] This very problem has recently arisen in cases where defendants (charged with murder) plead diminished responsibility; see Barry Mitchell and Ronnie Mackay, 'The *Golds* Standard of Substantial Impairment' (2015) 4 *Archbold Review* 7–9.

well-founded. Now, however, the situation has changed; public opinion polls on the subject have been conducted, both in this country and elsewhere.

A review of previous polls on the punishment for murder points to certain general conclusions about the most appropriate methodology.[42]

- It is important to provide respondents with an explanation of what constitutes murder in law. The vast majority of respondents presumably have no knowledge of the substantive criminal law, and any assumptions they are effectively required to make for the purposes of participating in the poll may well be ill-founded. Asking them to consider (brief) factual scenarios of murder is a better strategy.

- It is important to provide respondents with a range of sentencing options from which they indicate their preference. Failure to do this may mean that they will overlook options that would have appealed to them.

There are good reasons to question whether the assumption of overwhelming public support in England and Wales for the mandatory life sentence is well-founded. First, there is some evidence that mandatory sentencing does not attract widespread support. Although the public frequently seem to feel that sentencing 'in general' is too lenient, they nonetheless favour judicial discretion when punishing offenders.[43] Second, two very small-scale studies (one based on 62 respondents; the other on 56) conducted as part of wider Law Commission projects found that the mandatory life sentence had about 50 percent support.[44] But these studies did not investigate the issue in any depth and respondents were not provided with a list of alternative sentences.

A much larger survey was conducted in England and Wales in May 2010, which found that four-fifths of respondents thought that in general sentencing in murder is too lenient.[45] More importantly, though, respondents were invited to choose from a list of sentencing options what they regarded as the most appropriate punishment for a series of nine scenarios. Each scenario was based on a real case that had resulted in conviction for murder. The scenario regarded as most serious by the largest number of respondents was one in which:

> Jim decided to rob a bank. He bought a shotgun and was prepared to kill anyone who tried to prevent him. He entered the bank, pointed the gun at the cashier and demanded money. When the cashier pushed the alarm bell Jim shot him dead and fled.

Just over half (52 percent) favoured imprisonment for his natural life.[46] In the other eight scenarios between 67 percent and 96 percent of respondents felt that a fixed term of imprisonment (after which the offender would then be released) was an appropriate punishment.

---

[42] A useful summary of these can be found in Mitchell and Roberts (n 29) 88, 89.

[43] See eg J V Roberts, M Hough, J Jacobson and N Moon, 'Public Attitudes to Sentencing Purposes and Sentencing Factors: An Empirical Analysis' (2009) 11 *Crim LR* 771–82.

[44] See Law Commission, *Partial Defences to Murder*, Law Com No 290 (London, TSO 2004) Appendix C; and Law Commission, Consultation Paper No 177, *A New Homicide Act for England and Wales? A Consultation Paper*, (London, TSO 2005) Appendix A.

[45] Mitchell and Roberts (n 29) 93.

[46] ibid Table 6.3, 96.

It is also worth noting that a second scenario included significant elements of mitigation, in that it might well be viewed as an instance of mercy killing:

> Graham was six years old and suffered from a series of untreatable extremely serious mental and physical disabilities. His mother Jane testified that she could not bear to see him suffer any more. One day she walked into a side ward in the hospital and disconnected the life-support machinery from Graham.

More than two-thirds of respondents would have imposed a sentence of four years' imprisonment or less on Jane, and four-fifths favoured a sentence of less than ten years. Obviously, the gap between these preferred punishments and that which the court would be obliged to impose is significant. Those who favour the current system might point out that the trial judge could identify a low (single-figure) minimum term, but Jane would still be kept under supervision and would remain at risk of recall to prison for the remainder of her natural life.

Further evidence of the lack of public support for the status quo was provided when respondents were invited to say whether they thought that a fixed term of imprisonment would be acceptable as an alternative to a life sentence for murder. Three scenarios were used for this purpose, and between 55 percent and 70 percent of respondents said that the fixed term would be 'definitely' or 'probably' acceptable.[47]

An important but not surprising finding of this research was the extent of public support for proportionality: they favoured harsher punishments for the more serious cases. The authors concluded:

> This represents another way in which the current murder sentencing arrangements are at odds with community views; while courts may vary the minimum terms imposed to reflect variation in seriousness, the imposition of the same mandatory life sentence undermines proportionality. Schedule 21 creates only a very crude statutory form of proportionality. Yet proportionality can only be accurately established if courts are free to vary the length of the sentence imposed, and not just the likely period of detention.[48]

Finally, the research found evidence that the public do not necessarily feel that offenders should be kept under supervision indefinitely.[49] Each case should be treated on its own merits, and where the offender has demonstrated that he/she has complied with the terms of the licence and has shown him/herself to be fully rehabilitated, the licence should be brought to an end. In addition, in what the judges regard as the 'least serious' cases offenders are released at the expiry of a relatively short minimum term – perhaps no more than six or seven years. They may then remain under supervision for 50 or 60 years even though they fully comply with the terms and conditions of the licence and are rightly regarded as law-abiding members of the community. The rigidity of the current law in such cases is likely to be viewed unfavourably by a significant proportion of the public.

---

[47] ibid Table 7.1, 113.
[48] ibid 105.
[49] ibid 113.

5. IMPLICATIONS FOR SURVEY METHODOLOGY AND PUBLIC EDUCATION

Apart from the apparent absence of evidence of overwhelming support for the MLS, the other striking result of the 2010 national survey was the extent to which the public have a very limited knowledge and understanding of the law and the criminal justice system. Given the likely importance that politicians will almost certainly continue to attach to public support and confidence, there is a real need to ensure that ignorance and misunderstanding is eradicated – or at least minimised – so that the results of public surveys can be relied upon.

Two related lessons can arguably be drawn from this. The first is the significance of the way in which questions are posed to respondents – the kinds of questions that are asked, the wording of the questions and the structure of the surveys. As was pointed out by the researchers in the 2010 survey, the second, and closely linked, lesson is the need for some form of public legal education.[50] Those conducting surveys must be careful to ensure that questions are drafted so as to eliminate the risk of misunderstanding or misinterpretation. The need to provide explanation – in succinct, non-legal language – whenever there is any doubt that the question will be accurately understood is paramount. If, for example, a question is asked about the crime of murder, respondents must be told how the law defines murder. Or if the people are asked for their opinion on sentences imposed by the courts, they should be given some explanation of that before they reply.

But the burden should not be placed exclusively on the shoulders of those conducting public surveys. More could be done to make people aware of some of the basic realities of the criminal law and the criminal justice system. Research demonstrating public misconception and ignorance in these matters has been in the public domain for some time,[51] but hitherto very little progress appears to have been made in redressing it. An obvious candidate to play a part in this is surely the Sentencing Council, one of whose functions is to promote public awareness of the realities of sentencing in the magistrates' and Crown Courts.[52]

There can be little doubt that the law relating to murder and the punishment of convicted murderers leaves much to be desired, in the minds of both legal experts and the public in general. Before the matter can be addressed, however, there is scope for much further investigation of public opinion so as to provide a more comprehensive and sound basis on which to make judgments about legitimacy. Those judgments can then be taken on board in an increasingly belated review of the substantial and sentencing law.

---

[50] See Mitchell and Roberts (n 29) 141; and Barry Mitchell and Julian V Roberts, 'Sentencing for Murder: Drawing Lessons from Research' in Julian V Roberts (eds), *Exploring Sentencing Practice in England and Wales* (Basingstoke, Palgrave Macmillan 2015) 246.

[51] See eg M Hough and JV Roberts, *Attitudes to punishment: Findings from the British Crime Survey*, Home Office Research Study No 179 (London, Home Office, 1998).

[52] S 129 Coroners and Justice Act 2009.

6. IMPLICATIONS FOR LAW REFORM AND FURTHER RESEARCH

Clearly, a strong case can be made for reviewing both the substantive law of murder (and manslaughter) and the punishment of offenders. No legal definition of an offence can be absolutely perfect – some degree of imperfection is inevitable – but to make allowance for such imperfections, and bearing in mind the public's apparent desire for proportionality, the current mandatory sentence should surely be abolished and replaced so that murder attracts a maximum punishment of life imprisonment. Not only would this give due recognition to the evidence of the 2010 national survey but more particularly it would reflect the views expressed in that survey supporting the need for judicial discretion – so that variations in seriousness can be better reflected in the sentence.[53] Respondents also felt that this should be balanced by limiting the discretion, so that the risk of unduly under- or oversentencing should be minimised. One obvious way in which this might be achieved would be through the setting of minimum and maximum punishments. But given that all offences consist of a cocktail of varying combinations and permutations of aggravating and mitigating factors, an element of leeway would have still to be permitted to avoid having to impose a manifestly disproportionate sentence.

Thus, a more successful approach might be to maintain the current practice of identifying starting points, as indicated by the presence of specified factors, and then increase or decrease the punishment by taking account of other features. However, Schedule 21 has been subjected to such criticism that further and more considered guidance is surely needed. Two obvious sources of such guidance are the Sentencing Council, which could be asked to produce general guidelines,[54] and the Court of Appeal, which can continue to provide clarification and assistance through its decisions in individual cases.

Before the Sentencing Council is asked to issue guidelines, and to inform the discussion of the reforms to be made to Schedule 21, further, more detailed research should be conducted to shed more light on public attitudes towards punishing convicted murderers. One of the many fairly obvious future surveys would test the level of support for the whole life, 30-year and 25-year starting points as set out in paragraphs 2, 3 and 4 of Schedule 21. It is important not to overlook the extent of the increase that these provisions seem to have intended in the lengths of minimum terms. Shortly before the Criminal Justice Act 2003 was passed, some of the most senior judges in the country provided guidance for judges when sentencing for murder.[55] For example, the then Lord Chief Justice, Lord Woolf explained that the 'normal starting point' should be 12 years: this would be appropriate in 'the killing of an adult victim, arising from a quarrel or loss of temper between two people known to each other'.[56] The presence of certain aggravating factors would then warrant an increase

---

[53] Mitchell and Roberts (n 29) 99, 100.
[54] See Mitchell (n 38).
[55] See *Practice Statement (Juveniles: Murder Tariff)* [2000] 4 All ER 831; *Practice Statement (CA (Crim Div): Life Sentences)* [2002] 3 All ER 412; and *Practice Statement: The Consolidated Criminal Practice Direction* [2002] 3 All ER 904.
[56] [2002] 3 All ER 412, para 10.

in the starting point to 15 or 16 years. What is particularly worth noting is that the majority of factors he then listed appear in paragraph 3(2) of Schedule 21 as indicating a 30-year starting point, and one or two of them might even correspond to what is listed in paragraph 2(2) as potentially justifying a whole life order.[57] In other words, Schedule 21 set out to double the period of imprisonment to be served in the more serious cases of murder, and it would be helpful to get some objective survey data to assess the level of public support.

At first sight it may be assumed that the majority of the public support the fact that those convicted of the most serious murders should expect to spend the rest of their natural lives in prison. Yet a brief consideration of the nature of such orders may cause many people to have second thoughts. When the order is made the sentence can only be quantified very loosely because the offender's lifespan is unknown, and in that respect it is impossible to make a confident comparison with cases where a very lengthy minimum term is imposed. The offender given a whole life order may have committed a relatively more serious offence than a man with (say) a 35-year minimum term, but it is impossible to make any meaningful judgment about proportionality between the sentences in the two cases.

There seems to have been a lack of detailed discussion about the way in which those convicted of the most serious murders should be punished. More specifically, there is no guidance – in Schedule 21 or elsewhere – about when to impose a whole life order as opposed to a very long minimum term. Whole life orders surely have a unique mental dimension to them. The 40-, 45- or 50-year minimum term prisoner knows he/she must spend a very long time in prison but, provided he/she lives long enough and is perceived not to pose an unacceptable risk to public safety, he/she will ultimately be released. But the whole lifer must expect to die in prison, however long his/her lifespan. Admittedly, the discretionary power of the Secretary of State for Justice to release a prisoner on compassionate grounds under section 30 of the Crime (Sentences) Act 1997 applies to someone serving a whole life order. In *Vinter et al v UK*[58] the Grand Chamber felt that all prisoners, regardless of the heinousness of their criminality, should retain some hope of release, especially if they were fully rehabilitated, and to that end criticised current English law for failing to provide what they regarded as an adequate process for reviewing the sentence. There has been no detailed examination of public attitudes towards sentencing in these extremely serious cases and it would be interesting to see what a well-constructed survey would reveal.

---

[57] ibid para 12. Horrendous though the murders are that contain the factors listed in paras 2(2) and 3(2) of Schedule 21, they leave relatively little room to reflect what might nonetheless be significant variations in seriousness. Many single-victim murders attract at least a thirty-year starting point or even a whole life order, so that there is very limited scope to differentiate such cases from those where, say, numerous victims have been murdered. In contrast, Lord Woolf's *Practice Statement* seems to make far better provision for proportionality. Having identified the higher starting-point as appropriate where 'the offender committed multiple murders' (para 12), he went on to suggest that in 'the most serious cases' such as those 'involving a substantial number of murders, or if there are several factors identified as attracting the higher starting point', a minimum term of thirty years might be warranted (para 18).

[58] Appl Nos 66069/09, 130/10 and 3896/10.

In addition to testing support for paragraphs 2 and 3 of Schedule 21, other aspects of public opinion should be examined. The 2010 survey found that attitudes tended to change according to the amount of information respondents were given,[59] and this might be pursued further to useful effect. For example, might public views be influenced if respondents were made aware of the financial costs of imprisonment and of supervision in the community? Precisely to what degree (if at all) such a consideration ought to play in the matter is open to debate, although it might be interesting to see how the public counterbalance the cost against their preferred form of punishment.

Another interesting question that is worth pursuing is whether people would be prepared to see shorter terms of imprisonment as long as the risk to their security was not compromised. Under current arrangements the law seeks to cater for the needs of both retribution (through the minimum term) and public safety (otherwise the prisoner will not be released on licence). But what if there is clear evidence that an offender is fully rehabilitated even though his/her minimum term is not about to expire? There are two specific reasons for raising this question. The first is that the longer a person spends in prison – especially someone such as a convicted murderer who is serving a lengthy sentence – the greater the problems he/she may encounter in adjusting when released into the community. So if D has a minimum term of 25 years and is regarded as fully rehabilitated at the 22-year point, would there be significant public support to release him even though he ought to stay in prison for another three years in order to 'do the time for the crime'?

The second reason is that, as was pointed out by the Grand Chamber in *Vinter and others v UK*,[60] it seems that rehabilitation is increasingly being regarded as the principal aim or consideration for the sentencing court in EU jurisdictions. Of course, it would be easy to dismiss the idea that the public would be content to give priority to the needs of rehabilitation over those of retribution as unduly naïve. But some surveys, such as that in 2010, suggest that even when considering the sentence for murder the public are not always as punitive as may have traditionally been assumed. In the more serious cases, and especially those that receive a high public profile, the quest for retribution may prove dominant. But in lesser cases the desire to allow the offender to take advantage of his/her rehabilitation and successfully rejoin the community where he/she can make a much more significant contribution to society may take precedence in the public mind. Furthermore, looking at the issue from a wider political perspective, it will be interesting to see how far English courts come under pressure to follow the trend identified by the Grand Chamber.

It is to be hoped, therefore, that a formal review will be instigated. It would be preferable to include reconsideration of the definition of murder and its relationship with manslaughter. But at the very least the review should involve a comprehensive re-examination of the sentence for murder in England and Wales, so that the issues raised in this chapter can be addressed and our knowledge of the relationship between the law and public opinion can be improved.

---

[59] Mitchell and Roberts (n 29) ch 7.
[60] See n 58.

7

Pleas Without Bargains: Guilty Plea Discount or Coercive Trial Penalty?

CANDACE McCOY

I s IT POSSIBLE to have pleas without bargains? Why would a person accused of a crime plead guilty without any investigation into the strength of the prosecution's case or negotiation over its impact on the charge of conviction and the expected sentence?

Plea bargaining in criminal courts is the process by which an accused defendant relinquishes the right to have a jury trial in return for the promise of a certain expected sentence, with the understanding that this punishment will be less than would be expected had the case proceeded to trial and ended in conviction. In short, the defendant pleads guilty in return for a lower sentence, whether achieved when the prosecutor agrees to drop some charges or agrees to recommend a lower sentence to the judge as a result of the guilty plea. The prosecutor and defender agree on this outcome after negotiation in which the strength of proof in the case is discussed and the effect of pieces of evidence on likely guilt – and corresponding expected sentence – is determined. Functionally, this negotiation substitutes for the evidentiary challenge that otherwise would occur in a trial. If the guilty plea procedure discourages or even explicitly penalises the defence for insisting on full investigation of the facts of the case and adversarial negotiation over them in a plea-bargaining session, serious concerns about lack of due process arise.

The guilty plea constitutes a confession and results in a criminal conviction. The trial penalty – or confession reward, depending on point of view – is the difference in sentencing severity imposed when a defendant pleads guilty versus that which would be imposed had the case instead gone through a trial and ended in conviction. If the penalty becomes so severe that no rational defendant would risk having a trial, and/or if the penalty for not pleading guilty early in the process prompts any rational defendant to forego demanding that the prosecution show proof of guilt beyond a reasonable doubt, the process could be said to have moved from 'bargaining' to 'coercion'. If that is so, the guilty plea procedure which first developed under assumptions of adversarial negotiation can be said to have devolved into a system for eliciting coerced confessions. Whether that happens, and if so, how it happens, is the concern of this chapter.

Almost all observers agree that such a sentencing differential indeed exists (see Brereton and Casper[1] and early US studies cited below, and most recently the debate between Abrams who denies that the penalty exists[2] and Kim who insists that it does and is steep[3]). In the United Kingdom, other scholars who have reviewed and studied the issue up to the present day, such as Henham[4] and Roberts and Bradford,[5] and most recently Tata and Gormley,[6] agree that the penalty exists and are concerned about whether sentencing guidelines which regulate its size are effective. But researchers over the decades have disagreed about what accounts for the sentencing differential; only if we know what factors influence it significantly can we determine how steep it is and whether that size is big enough to frighten defendants into confessing. Some say that most of the variance in sentencing severity can be explained by differing strength of evidence in each case,[7] but the strength of the prosecution's case is very rarely measured or reported in publicly available databases. Because researchers have to look into actual case files, which are confidential, there are extremely few studies of this issue based on actual data.

Jurisprudentially, 'strength of the evidence' is the most important factor in determining whether the sentence received after a guilty plea is just. A defendant should plead guilty only if he is in fact guilty and the state can prove it. A prosecutor concerned to do justice – as of course is the primary mission – has no qualms in demanding that a defendant caught red-handed and against whom the evidence is very clear should plead guilty and receive only a small sentencing discount for doing so. By contrast, if the state's case is weak, more investigation and more negotiation is expected. The prosecutor would not try to circumvent the wheels of justice, even though they are grinding exceedingly fine, by offering a deeper sentencing discount as incentive to the defendant to confess. But if after investigation the defendant is willing to admit to a level of wrongdoing everyone then understands to be actually provable, while the prosecutor drops charges relating to the acts that cannot be proven beyond a reasonable doubt, a guilty plea would occur. The question is: should the severity of the sentence received after the confession by guilty plea differ in these two cases?

Most people would say that it should, and that the current plea-bargaining system indeed operates this way, because charges are regularly dropped and sentences lowered when a defendant admits to some bad acts but not others which cannot be proven beyond a reasonable doubt. After all, the quality of the evidence against the

---

[1] See David Bereton and Jonathan Casper, 'Does it Pay to Plead Guilty? Differential Sentencing and the Functioning of Criminal Courts' (1981–82) 16 *Law & Society Review* 45.

[2] Andrew S Abrams, 'Putting the Trial Penalty on Trial' (2013) 51 *Duquesne Law Review* 777.

[3] Andrew Chongseh Kim, 'Underestimating the Trial Penalty: An Empirical Analysis of the Federal Trial Penalty and Critique of the Abrams Study' (2014) 84(5) *Mississippi Law Journal* 1195–1256.

[4] Ralph J Henham, 'Truth in Plea Bargaining: Anglo-American Approaches to the Use of Guilty Plea Discounts at the Sentencing Stage' (2000) 29(1) *Anglo-American Law Review* 1–38.

[5] Julian V Roberts and Ben Bradford, 'Sentence Reductions for a Guilty Plea in England and Wales: Exploring New Empirical Trends' (2015) 12(2) *Journal of Empirical Legal Studies* 187–210.

[6] Cyrus Tata and Jay M Gormley, 'Sentencing and Plea Bargaining: Guilty Pleas versus Trial Verdicts' (Oxford, Oxford University Press, 2015).

[7] James Eisenstein and Herbert Jacob, *Felony Justice* (Boston, Little Brown, 1977).

defendant was satisfactorily probed in both cases, they say. Charge bargaining and sentence bargaining are based on this dynamic; the second defendant against whom not all charges can be proven should get a lower sentence.

Yet sentencing guidelines governing guilty pleas are designed to do the exact opposite. The cases that needed investigation (and the time it takes) receive harsher sentences than those which end in early guilty pleas. From a due-process point of view, giving deeper discounts the earlier a defendant confesses would perversely encourage attorneys to avoid investigating the cases. That is, a person who pleads guilty imme-diately because the proof against him is incontrovertible and is willing to admit it should receive a higher sentence because he must confess to the charges 'straight up' without reduction. By contrast, the person who resists confessing and is then able to demonstrate weaknesses in the state's case should receive a lower sentence because not all the wrongdoing was proven and weak charges will be dropped. Thus, the case that takes longer to resolve should get the lower sentence. This is exactly the opposite of what guilty plea guidelines set out.

This is one reason that scholars and practitioners often refer to the sentencing differential between plea and trial as the 'trial penalty', because it encourages defend-ants to avoid putting the prosecution to its proof. Yet data about the strength of evidence during the prosecutorial process are very seldom collected systematically from all cases and are almost never publicly available. Nevertheless, a rough proxy of the quality of evidence available in a case is the time during the prosecutorial process in which it was resolved. Early guilty pleas are more likely to have been finalised before the attorneys investigated much, so the quality of evidence would be sketchy. The timing of guilty pleas is often reported in official statistics, and as Johnson's excellent literature review shows, its effect on sentences imposed is now a ripe topic for empirical exploration.[8]

1. WHAT ACCOUNTS FOR THE DIFFERENCES IN SENTENCES AFTER GUILTY PLEAS VERSUS TRIALS?

Researchers have examined other case-related factors to explain variation in sentenc-ing severity in cases that end in guilty pleas versus those that go to trial, looking for explanations other than mode of disposition that could account for it. The type of offence alleged, especially its severity, is often mentioned as important because defendants facing prison terms may think differently about whether to plead guilty than those facing short jail terms or probation and fines. Other case characteristics such as whether a co-defendant testified ('snitched'), the defendant's criminal record, and individual characteristics such as the defendant's gender, race or age may also be significantly related to whether the defendant agrees to plead guilty, such that the mode of disposition (guilty plea/trial) is not the only variable explaining the deep sentencing discounts.

---

[8] Brian D Johnson, 'Trials and Tribulations: The Trial Tax and the Process of Punishment' (2019) 48(1) *Crime and Justice* 313–63, 344–45.

Early studies used multiple regression techniques in which sentencing severity was the dependent variable and disposition type (ie plea or trial) along with other such case-related factors served as the independent variables.[9] These studies attempted to address the 'what accounts for the trial penalty other than disposition type?' question, and arrived at the answer: not much. Plea versus trial is statistically significant, and whether a co-defendant testifies is statistically significant, and not much else is. (Caveat: some studies have found that race of the defendant matters, but this is partly because black defendants in the jurisdictions studied were more likely to insist on jury trial than white defendants were, with the predictable result of receiving the heavier punishment correlated with jury trial.[10]) One study of the trial penalty across five US states that have sentencing guidelines simply compared the expected guidelines sentences to those imposed after trial within offence types, but was able to test a better 'mode of conviction' variable by adding 'bench trial' (ie a trial before a judge alone, acting as fact-finder, without a jury) as well as guilty plea/jury trial.[11] The study described wide divergence among the various states in the size of the trial penalty, which could be attributable to differing political culture in each state.

Some economists deny that the sentencing differential is real. Recently, a debate has emerged in the US legal literature about whether the likelihood of acquittal should be included as a factor in measuring the size of the trial penalty. Abrams has gone so far as to argue that in a great number of cases, the trial penalty does not exist at all (and in fact that there is a trial discount) if probability of acquittal is included in the measurement.[12] This argument assumes that prosecutors conduct vigorous evidentiary investigations and know what the likelihood of acquittal would be at trial, and that they offer to allow defendants to plead guilty and receive lower sentences based on that likelihood. The proper comparison, he argues, is not among cases all convicted by different modes of disposition, but among all cases including those dismissed and acquitted (which count as a sentence of 'zero' in sentencing severity) and all differing among themselves as to whether the prosecutor can prove all the elements of the crime charged. Abrams used 42,552 cases from Chicago to test his hypothesis, and he controlled for selection bias using an 'independent variable' technique. Controlling in this way for acquittal probability and including the value of 'zero' in the statistics for cases that were either dismissed pretrial or acquitted, he finds that the trial penalty shrinks and, he says, all but disappears. This is due to the fact that case seriousness results in a higher trial probability. Chicago cases resolved at trial had about 10 percent more charges than those resolved by guilty plea originally had, which he interprets as an indication that the seriousness of these cases separated them out to proceed to trial. In short, he believes other researchers observed a steep

---

[9] Eisenstein and Jacob (n 7); William M Rhodes, 'Plea Bargaining: Its Effect on Sentencing and Convictions in the District of Columbia' (1979) 70 *Journal of Criminal Law & Criminology* 360.

[10] Roger Hood, *Race and Sentencing* (Oxford, Oxford University Press, 1992); Marie Provine, 'Too Many Black Men: The Sentencing Judge's Dilemma' (1998) 23 *Law and Social Inquiry* 823–56.

[11] Nancy King, David A Soul and Sara Steen, 'When Process Affects Punishment: Differences in Sentences After Guilty Plea, Bench Trial, and Jury Trial in Five Guidelines States' (2005) 165 *Columbia Law Review* 943.

[12] David S Abrams, 'Is Pleading Guilty Really a Bargain?' (2011) 8 *Journal of Empirical Legal Studies* 200; Abrams (n 2).

trial penalty only due to poor methodology (ie researchers are comparing the wrong things; they should include cases that were not convicted in determining the size of the trial penalty) and seriousness of cases that go to trial explain why they have such long sentences.

There are two different ways to regard what prosecutors and defenders are thinking as they decide whether to agree to a sentence after a guilty plea, Abrams says. One is 'unconditional', which assumes they know the average punishments that have been imposed in the past and include in that calculus the likelihood based on past experience that the case will be dismissed or the defendant acquitted. They predict the likelihood that the sentence could thus be 'zero' or some higher punishment. The other scenario is 'conditional' on a finding of guilt at trial; the lawyers think ahead to predict the sentence that will be imposed after a full jury trial and conviction. Abrams compares the predictions of sentencing severity under these two assumptions and says that the trial penalty would be the difference in expected sentence between the two. He shows that the trial penalty under these conditions does not exist.

This is not the way legal scholars regard the trial penalty. They do not think about sentences at all if the case is dismissed, naturally, and therefore would not include any consideration of these cases in their thoughts about the likely outcome of cases that continue into the prosecutorial stream. But they *will* think about the likelihood of acquittal and whether the defendant would be willing to risk conviction at trial depending on the probable punishment. It is at this point that a possible trial penalty has an important impact on their thinking. The higher the possible sentence, the less they would be willing to take the risk even if the likelihood of acquittal is high. It is for this reason that legal scholars worry about the size of the trial penalty, as a possible violation of due process.

A year later, Kim published a hard-hitting rebuttal to Abrams.[13] Summing up the legal point of view in opposition to Abrams's economic modeling, Kim says that 'the non-zero average sentence' (ie what Abrams calls 'unconditional' predictions of sentence) 'is a metric with little relevance to criminal law debates'.[14] Kim says that Abrams assumes random distribution of the likelihood of acquittal and presence of evidentiary factors across all cases, but actual defendants assess their odds of acquittal based on the strength of evidence in their cases. These odds are not randomly distributed through the population of defendants. Furthermore, Kim says, the trial penalty is so high that average defendants who might consider challenging the state's case would be better off pleading guilty even after assessing their chances of acquittal. Although Kim does not say this, the reader wonders whether the penalty is set very high precisely to force them to plead. It would be important to know exactly how high it is, because if defendants are so frightened of a high penalty that they do not seriously entertain the possibility of going to trial and being acquitted, Abrams's 'unconditional' plea situation does not exist.

---

[13] Kim (n 3).
[14] ibid 1200.

2. HOW STEEP IS THE SENTENCING DIFFERENTIAL?

Kim uses data reported by the US Sentencing Commission for the years 2006–2008 to test whether the difference between sentence after guilty plea versus sentence after trial conviction is indeed so steep that few defendants would even consider not pleading guilty. Note that these data describe only cases that have been sentenced; therefore, there are no cases that were dismissed or acquitted. Within this very large number of cases, the typical trial penalty approach would be to compare sentences in the 97 percent of cases that end in guilty pleas to those from the 3 percent that went to trial and were convicted. But the structure of the federal sentencing guidelines allows a stronger method to be used, says Kim. In the federal system, after a case is convicted the probation officer will gather information from the lawyers and determine the presence of a wide variety of evidentiary factors, which themselves were subject to negotiation. Each factor has a point value and when they are added up, the guideline sentence corresponding to that point value is recommended to the judge. There are a few factors whose presence in the case could reduce points rather than add them, and the most commonly used by far is the 'acceptance of responsibility' (ie guilty plea) factor. Kim says that the way to determine the size of the federal trial penalty is simply to calculate what the sentence would have been had these defendants not 'accepted responsibility', and compare it to the actual sentence recommendation. (This method has the admirable effect of controlling for a host of evidentiary factors.) He used ordinary least-squares regression on logged sentence length to measure which portion of the sentence length was attributable to the guilty plea.[15] He performed these tests on several categories of offences, because the size of the trial penalty presumably varies among offences of different seriousness.

Kim found that the raw difference between sentences recommended after 'acceptance of responsibility' and what the point value and corresponding sentence would be without a guilty plea was 64 percent of the sentence. Defendants who also got credit for providing substantial assistance to the prosecution in convicting co-defendants received departures below even those recommended sentence lengths. A trial penalty of 64 percent is quite a lot higher than what the sentencing guidelines at face value seem to allow. Kim explains: 'Practitioners widely assume that acceptance of responsibility alone produces a 25–35% reduction to final sentences',[16] guesstimated by moving 2–4 points down the sentencing table, which means an average case with 7–8 points would get about that reduction. But this is not the average.

Kim's study has strength because it does not have a selection bias problem. (Abrams tried to control for selection bias in his study through the use of 'instrumental variables', but the results were inconclusive.) Because Kim is comparing cases to themselves – that is, comparing a case outcome with the counterfactual of the identical case without a guilty plea – all the cases are observed at the same time in the prosecutorial process. Most other studies of the trial penalty must address the major methodological problem of selection bias. Subtracting average sentences imposed after a guilty plea

---

[15] ibid 1237.
[16] ibid 1231.

from the average sentences imposed after conviction at trial produces a misleading statistic. Cases that end in guilty pleas are so different from those convicted after trial that their sentencing outcomes should not be compared. (We have already noted that defendants 'plead out' at different times, and that evidentiary factors continue to change as the case proceeds.) Social scientists call this 'selection bias' because those cases that seem exactly comparable to others are removed from the sample as the process moves forward; comparing them at the end of the process presents a classic 'apples and oranges' problem. In criminal procedure, since no individual defendant can be sentenced following a guilty plea and also be sentenced following a trial, there can be no clean comparison of punishments that would determine the existence and magnitude of the trial penalty. In criminology, a Heckman procedure has been used to analyse data, and it gives differing weights to various factors as they move through a system such that they have equal weights at final analysis. The procedure is weak.[17] In previous decades, researchers used a different methodology to correct for selection bias, using randomly generated variables in criminal case vignettes administered in questionnaires to prosecutors and defenders, asking these subjects to predict sentences in simulated cases. This method determines the effect of mode of disposition (ie guilty plea versus trial) on sentencing length controlling for the presence of various evidentiary factors assuming all factors had been proven. One such study determined that, in the federal system in the United States prior to implementation of the US Sentencing Guidelines, the trial penalty accounted for statistically significant differences in punishment net of other case factors.[18] Another study, this one more recent, used the same method and benefited from modern technological advances.[19] It reached approximately 1,500 prosecutors, defenders and judges to ask them to estimate the probability of conviction at trial in sixteen hypothetical cases each with randomly generated clusters of different case facts (exculpatory DNA, eyewitness identification, confession, criminal history). Next, respondents said what the expected punishment would be in the various cases if the defendants pled guilty, and then what the sentences would be after trial. This study was able to test what the strength of evidence was in each case and determine its effect on sentencing outcome controlling for case factors. The researchers found that the three different types of court professionals agreed quite closely as to strength of evidence and its impact on guilty pleas, but that judges were somewhat more concerned about efficiency and less with evidence. They also found that the 'shadow of the trial' is generally a good

---

[17] Shawn Bushway, Brian D Johnson and Lee Ann Slocum, 'Is the Magic Still There? The Use of the Heckman Two-Step Correction for Selection Bias in Criminology' (2007) 23(2) *Journal of Quantitative Criminology* 151–78.

[18] Candace McCoy, 'What We Say and What They Do: Prosecutors' and Judges' Sentencing Decisions at Guilty Plea versus Trial', paper presented at the Annual Meeting of the American Society of Criminology, New Orleans, LA, November 1994. This study was based on vignette data developed at the US Sentencing Commission and not released to outside researchers. However, these data and interviews with prosecutors and defenders before the Guidelines took effect, compared with data on plea bargaining after the Guidelines were fully implemented, are discussed in Ilene H Nagel and Stephen J Schulhofer, 'A Tale of Three Cities: An Empirical Study of Charging and Bargaining Practices under the Federal Sentencing Guidelines' (1992) 66 *Southern California Law Review* 501.

[19] Shawn D Bushway, Allison D Redlich and Robert J Norris, 'An Explicit Test of Plea Bargaining "in the Shadow of the Trial"' (2014) 52 *Criminology* 723–54.

metaphor for legal decision-making as a procedure moves forward, so that strength of various evidentiary factors was crucial in determining what the parties would accept for sentencing outcome:

> Compar[ing] the values [in the case] which has all three evidence conditions and the longer criminal history with the [case] which has none of the three evidence conditions and the shorter criminal history: average probability of conviction was 82 percent, the average sentence at trial was 12.56 years, and the acceptable plea was 8.68 years, [but in the case with weak prosecution evidence] the values plummet to 31 percent, 8.73 years, and 3.26 years, respectively.[20]

In short, the few studies that have been able to examine strength of evidentiary proof in affecting plea bargaining indicate that it significantly affects the prosecutors' offers based on guilty pleas and defendants' decisions to plead guilty or not, and if the defendant does not plead guilty and is convicted after trial, the sentence will be significantly longer.[21] Although the highest value of the sentence after trial would be lower in cases with weak evidence from the state's point of view, nevertheless the trial penalty was much steeper for these cases (8.73 years in prison after trial versus 3.26 after plea). From one perspective, it is good that cases in which the prosecution is unlikely to prove major elements of the crime will receive lower punishments. From another perspective, it appears that punishment over twice as severe if the defendant insists on a trial will force any rational defendant to plead guilty even when the state's case is weak. In other words, most defendants who are most likely to be factually innocent will nevertheless plead guilty if time in prison is important to them, and almost certainly will plead guilty in less serious cases in which they will be promised probation instead of prison.

This important study (and others from the 1980s that tested variations in strength of evidence) improves the accuracy in measuring the factors that actually matter to prosecutors and defenders as they decide what punishments are appropriate in return for guilty pleas. Another very important factor has not been tested in any of the literature reviewed for this chapter: the *timing* of the guilty plea. This factor interacts with the evidentiary factor as lawyers bargain 'in the shadow of the law'. It takes time to gather and assess the evidence. (For instance, in the case simulations of this study by Bushway, Redlich and Norris, the DNA testing might take months to come back from the laboratory. It takes time to interview witnesses who might contradict the prosecutor's eyewitness. And so forth.) If the defence does not have time to investigate and then determine how strong the proof is, but faces pressure to produce a guilty plea because the sentence gets heavier the longer the case proceeds, then the plea-bargaining system can devolve into machinery that is not concerned with evidence and proof beyond a reasonable doubt. Thus, the timing of guilty pleas and how they affect sentencing outcomes emerges as an important focus of research.

---

[20] ibid 741.

[21] For a recent study that did not control for evidence experimentally, but did utilise several evidence-related variables to determine how much they accounted for the size of an observed trial penalty, see Besiki Luka Kutadeladze, Victoria Z Lawson and Nancy Andiloro, 'Does Evidence Really Matter? An Exploratory Analysis of the Role of Evidence in Plea Bargaining in Felony Drug Cases' (2015) 39(5) *Law and Human Behavior* 431–42.

In sum: almost all of the well-designed studies conclude that the sentencing differential indeed exists and can be attributed primarily to the mode of conviction (guilty plea versus trial) controlling for other case factors including strength of proof. The next question is: 'how steep is this sentencing differential?' The most rigorous studies find that it is steep indeed (64 percent in Kim's federal sentencing study; over 100 percent for non-serious cases in Bushway et al). But perhaps harsher sentences are appropriate for defendants who will not admit their guilt although this is clear from the provable facts. Presumably, if the difference in punishment an offender receives after trial is only marginally more severe than what would have been received had she/he pled guilty, the defendant has received a 'confession reward' and not a grant of leniency (or, depending on point of view, another way of expressing this is that the defendant has not been coerced into confessing for fear that the possible sentence after trial would be extremely harsh). In the United States, the size of the trial penalty is not regulated, although sentencing guidelines provide that a guilty plea mitigates the sentence that would otherwise be imposed. How deep this mitigation may be will vary depending on the case and the jurisdiction. The federal US Sentencing Guidelines state that pleading guilty will reduce a sentence by two points, and pleading guilty quickly will reduce it by three points. Similarly, the sentencing laws of many US states regard a guilty plea as a 'mitigating factor' on severity of punishment, with similar measurable results.[22] The effect of these point reductions on final sentencing outcomes differs depending on the severity of the offence and, in the federal system at least, the other 'points' that were counted in the case due to evidentiary factors.

3. DOES SIZE MATTER?

Thus, the *size* of the sentencing differential, rather than its mere existence, became the subject of study and public policy debate. Because it is acknowledged and appears to be standardized due to its use in sentencing guidelines, the trial penalty is thought to be small enough that it does not amount to a blunderbuss almost forcing defendants to confess, even when their cases are still under investigation. This may be a mistaken assumption. Furthermore, there is scant research which measures the average size of the sentencing differential and its probable impact on defendants' decisions to plead guilty *at various procedural points*, in these sentencing guidelines jurisdictions. This could be a very important consideration because it explores the due process problem. Defendants who insist on their innocence will not plead guilty quickly, yet should not be penalised for doing so if due process is expected to run its course. There would not be a penalty for investigating and negotiating the case.

Nevertheless, the sentencing guidelines themselves appear to be keyed to regulate the size of the sentencing differential, and to do so at three different procedural points. In England and Wales, sentencing guidelines amended in the Criminal Justice Act of 1994 do not use a point system like the federal courts' guidelines in the United States,

---

[22] An overview is found in Henham 2000 (n 4).

but they do quantify the size of the trial penalty overall by comparing the sentence imposed after a guilty plea to the statutorily required sentence that would be imposed after trial. English and Welsh judges are instructed that the difference in sentencing severity imposed after trial must be no higher than 33 percent of the sentence offered for a guilty plea. Furthermore, as in the federal US Sentencing Guidelines, the law requires that sentencing discounts be granted depending on when the defendant agrees to plead guilty. A defendant who confesses early receives a 33 percent discount; a plea at an 'intermediate' point in the process receives a 25 percent reduction, and a guilty plea 'at the courthouse door' receives a 10 percent reduction.[23]

In his 1999 literature review on the research about timing of guilty pleas and its effect on sentencing outcomes, Henham noted that the size of the trial penalty apparently depends on two factors: the seriousness of the crime and the timing of the plea.[24] Well before the sentencing law changed to regulate the size of the trial penalty in England and Wales (as Henham described), McConville and Baldwin had conducted a study in British courts to determine the effect of guilty pleas on non-serious crimes for which non-custodial sentences were possible.[25] They found a very steep average sentencing discount (or penalty for going to trial) that ranged from 69.3 percent difference in punishment for accused persons who would plead guilty quickly to 50 percent for those who pled 'straight-up' later, but 42.6 percent for those who delayed their guilty pleas up to the day of trial. A sentencing differential of over two-thirds was apparently not regarded as forcing defendants to forego trials because their reward for pleading guilty was so advantageous: they would receive sentences of probation. In these circumstances, it seems that defendants who adamantly want to stay out of jail will plead guilty even if they believe in their actual innocence. In turn, the courts can dispose of a great glut of quotidian crimes that are not regarded as very serious. Perhaps the most important finding is seen in the fact that the size of the penalty *diminished* the longer the case remained in the system, indicating that evidentiary factors were exerting influence as investigations matured.

Two decades later, the Criminal Justice Act of 1994 aimed to reduce the guilty plea/trial differentials, such as McConville and Baldwin had observed, by regulating the size of the differences. Henham studied the trial penalty after the law passed. He noted that prosecutors will not offer such steep discounts to defendants charged with more serious crimes, and in turn a higher percentage of these defendants are likely to opt for trial. Presumably this is because they know they will go to prison either way – though for different lengths of term – whether they plead guilty or are convicted after trial. Many are willing to try to prove their innocence at trial under those circumstances. The state response might be to increase the expected sentence after trial very

---

[23] Roberts and Bradford (n 5).

[24] Ralph J Henham, 'Bargain Justice or Justice Denied? Sentence Discounts and the Criminal Process' (1999) 62(4) *MLR* 515, 535–38. Reprinted in Cyrus Tata and Neil Hutton (eds), *Sentencing and Society: International Perspectives* (Aldershot, Ashgate, 2002), under the title 'Sentencing Policy and Guilty Plea Discounts'.

[25] Michael McConville and John Baldwin, 'Courts, Prosecution and Conviction' (Oxford, Clarendon Press, 1981).

steeply to discourage this. Henham explored the phenomenon of 'cracked trials', in which defendants plead guilty on the very day that a trial is scheduled, which was one of the reasons that the Royal Commission on Criminal Justice promulgated the 'graduated sentence discount' scale described above. The same problem of penalising people for putting the state to its proof could apply to the Criminal Justice and Public Order Act of 1994 and its subsequent amendments: the more time spent in investigation and negotiation which underpin due process, the more the system punishes the defendant. Henham considered the problem and looked for mention of it in the various studies, but concluded 'the research results do not provide any evidence which would lead us to question the conclusion that the extent of any sentencing discount does not vary significantly according to the strength of the prosecution case'.[26] Rather, the later codification of the sentencing discount placed the timing of the plea, not the 'quality' of it, in the forefront of sentencing policy.

This sentencing law in section 144(1) of the Criminal Justice Act of 2003 in England and Wales required judges to take 'the stage of the proceedings' at which the guilty plea was entered into account, and in 2005 and 2007 it was updated to set out the exact size of the sentencing discounts that would result at each stage. The size of the trial penalty was mandated to shrink from that which McConville and Baldwin had observed in the late 1970s in non-serious cases. Twenty years later, for all cases serious or less so, judges are instructed to give defendants who plead guilty at the first opportunity 33 percent off the sentence expected otherwise, while those who plead at a later time get 25 percent discounted, and those who 'crack the trial' by pleading after a trial date is set receive only 10 percent off their sentences. Roberts and Bradford analysed court data about what actually happened under these guidelines and found that 86 percent of the criminally accused persons pled guilty. Of these, 63 percent received sentencing discounts of 33 percent off the expected trial sentence and 7 percent got an even steeper discount, for unexplained reasons. (There is no indication whether all actually pled guilty immediately or were given some leeway in timing by the judges. But it seems plausible that this group is so large – 70 percent of the total caseload – because defendants charged with non-serious crimes are pleading guilty quickly knowing this will keep them out of jail). Eleven percent received discounts from 20 to 32 percent, and 19 percent received less than 20 percent reduction in sentence.[27] Clearly, these judges are now following the guidelines which require them to calibrate punishment depending on timing of case disposition. The Act states that the reason that judges are instructed to do so is 'a need for effective administration of justice and not as an aspect of mitigation'.

The same policy decisions were made in the federal US Sentencing Guidelines. The original Sentencing Guidelines promulgated in 1986 set out a two-point reduction in the sentence that would otherwise be imposed if a defendant would 'accept responsibility'. Subsequently, in 1994, this guideline was amended to add another point for reduction if the guilty plea had been 'timely' made, 'thereby permitting the

---

[26] Henham (n 24) 528.
[27] Roberts and Bradford (n 5) Table 2.

government to avoid preparing for trial'.[28] An important difference between the UK and US guilty plea guidelines, however, is that the additional discount for a timely plea in the US guidelines applies only to those crimes at 'level 16 or greater', which means serious felonies. Less serious offenders can plead guilty to receive two points off their sentence scores, but cannot claim the extra discount for timely pleas. Apparently the federal law aims to exclude the glut of non-serious offenders from receiving the lowest discounts, as the English/Welsh guidelines permit. (Most would receive non-custodial sentences in any event, if they claim the two-point credit for pleading guilty and have no criminal record.)

Intuitively, the strength of proof would seem to be a very important factor in determining case outcome and probability of trial conviction, but almost all defendants plead guilty. Nevertheless, they should not be admitting to bad acts or aggravating factors that the prosecution is unlikely to be able to prove. The plea-bargaining system based on adversarial evidentiary proof would assume that the more likely the defendant is to be acquitted, the lower the offered sentence will be. The more likely the defendant is to be convicted, the higher the offered sentence will be, and the highest sentence would be imposed after conviction at trial. The problem with such a system from the defendant's perspective is that an accused who is likely to be acquitted is quite possibly innocent, but is expected to plead guilty anyway even though the offered sentence will be low. If she insists on a jury trial to prove her innocence, but is by a twist of fate convicted, she will receive the same high degree of punishment as the defendant who was probably guilty and also proceeded through trial.

If this is an accurate depiction of prosecutorial decision-making, the sentencing differential is low and in fact justifiable because prosecutors categorise cases according to evidentiary strength, after careful case investigation and extensive negotiations with the defence attorney. Cases that conclude early with low sentences would be those that the prosecutor thinks are unlikely to be proven at trial, so the parties agree to a guilty plea and low punishment (presumably the defendant has done *something* illegal even if acquittal is unlikely on the most serious charges; otherwise, innocent people will be pleading guilty). Probability of good proof seems an ethically defensible reason to regard cases differently. However, if this depiction of plea bargaining is not empirically accurate – in other words, if cases are not fully investigated so that prosecutors and defenders truly know the strength of the evidence and can thus determine the probability of acquittal – prosecutors instead are trying to get 'cheap pleas' by threatening defendants with ever-higher punishment the longer their cases continue into the criminal process. In such scenarios, serious questions of denial of due process would arise.

The next two sections of this chapter analyse these ideas in two ways. First, an overview of the policy debate and underlying jurisprudential principles raised by the trial penalty is presented. Second, building on Kim's study, a description of the effect of *timing* of guilty plea on sentencing outcomes under the US Sentencing Guidelines

---

[28] US Sentencing Guideline 3E1.1 (a)(2).

in the most recent year for which data were available at the time this chapter was written is presented. The implications for the due process/crime control policy debates will conclude this chapter.

4. DUE PROCESS VERSUS CRIME CONTROL DEBATES ON THE TRIAL PENALTY

The size of the trial penalty matters tremendously in its effect – perhaps its chilling effect – on due process and evidentiary investigation and proof. Debates about reform of plea bargaining have, in the past, tended to ask whether plea bargaining should be abolished altogether, presumably by allowing defendants to plead 'straight up' without any concessions, or in the alternative to go to trial. This approach has proven to be unrealistic in such places as the borough of the Bronx in New York City, where trial rates rose and clogged the courts after the district attorney refused to drop charges in return for guilty pleas (although it is important to note that most defendants nevertheless pled guilty 'straight up' and average sentence lengths did not rise). Today, people who are deeply concerned about the overall justice of the plea-bargaining system tend to focus their attention not on abolishing plea bargaining altogether in this way, but on whether the bargains are fair. If they are not, the sentencing differential should be regulated.

Theoretically, critics of both ideological stripes (due process advocates and crime controllers, under Herbert Packer's classic dichotomy) would be pleased to see the sentencing differential abolished. Due process advocates would be pleased that defendants would then have no threat associated with opting for trial. Factually innocent people and also those against whom the state cannot really prove a case would not be pressured to forego their right to a jury trial. For their part, crime control advocates would also be pleased that an almost-automatic deep mitigation of punishment in the great majority of cases would be ended. Realistically, however, both sides oppose any policy initiative that would permit guilty pleas only 'straight up', with no bargains or promises of sentencing outcome, which would be one way of abolishing the trial penalty. Due process advocates fear that the severity of punishment overall will increase if the discretion in decision-making permitted by the current plea-bargaining system were to be abolished. Crime control advocates fear that prosecution will bog down because all defendants would demand trials in the absence of the powerful disincentive to trial that the trial penalty represents – and they would be correct, if experience in the Bronx is a good indication.

Crime control advocates offer two reasons to support the trial penalty and oppose its abolition. The first is utilitarian: without the threat of a more serious penalty after trial, all defendants would decline to plead guilty and instead demand trials which the system cannot provide without massive spending of tax dollars for new judges, courtrooms, and personnel. The second argument rests on a deontological justification: that a defendant who pleads guilty is remorseful and thus less blameworthy than one who denies his/her guilt, and therefore deserves a lesser sentence.

The utilitarian argument dominates public discourse about the trial penalty, but it is unconvincing according to due process advocates who state that constitutional rights are fundamental to a constitutional democracy and worth paying for.[29] There is an uncomfortable misgiving that defendants who stand up for their constitutional right to trial are being punished for exercising that right if there will be a significantly more severe penalty than that which would attach to a guilty plea. The fact that they tend to be unattractive felons does little to diminish the discomfort in light of the fundamental nature of the right, which after all is the foundation upon which the entire adversarial system is said to rest. A suspicion arises: if the system becomes premised on guilty pleas (as it is, numerically at least) and defendants who ask to be tried in open court are told that their sentences will be much more severe if they are convicted, will innocent people plead guilty to avoid the uncertainty of trial conviction and the trial penalty? There is good evidence that they will, and have.[30] This is the heart of the due process advocates' coercion argument, and the size of the trial penalty matters because the higher it is, the more likely defendants will feel pressure to plead guilty in return for a certain low sentence.[31]

Economist Abrams's objection to claims that the trial penalty is so severe that defendants are coerced to plead guilty is that the probability of acquittal must be part of the calculus. In those cases in which prosecutors believe the chance of acquittal is high, they will offer the defendant a very low punishment, and a risk-averse defendant will accept it not only because the sentence after trial will be higher, but also because the sentence is justifiably proportionate to the degree of wrongdoing that can be proved. If due process proponents are willing to grant Abrams this point, they nevertheless are very concerned about that subset of defendants charged with serious crimes for which long prison sentences are possible and in which the evidence is strong for the prosecution, but who nevertheless may be innocent and want to prove it to a jury. Or, even if not innocent, they have the right to demand that the government actually *has* strong evidence; otherwise, how would any of us know what goes on between the lawyers as they bargain? Crime control advocates are impatient with this argument. How are we to regard a person who not only refuses to admit guilt in the face of overwhelming evidence, they ask, but even requires us to spend time and money on his case while he sits back waiting for us to make a mistake? Highfalutin appeals to constitutional principles pale in the face of such cold-hearted opportunism, they say, and such a person deserves to be punished in some extra measure for his failure to accept his responsibility for the crime; conversely, a person who pleads guilty deserves consideration for coming to terms with his crime and the harm it caused and showing remorse to the victims.

---

[29] Utilitarian arguments usually devolve to a cost–benefit calculus. Crime controllers prefer the benefits of speed, finality and low monetary outlay for trials to the costs of a small number of innocents being wrongfully convicted because the system pressures them to decide to confess. Due-process advocates making cost–benefit arguments claim that higher costs for trial courts are offset by the greater benefit of upholding constitutional rights, which in turn strengthens governmental accountability to the law and the citizens of the state. Innocent people should not be punished, and even people who in fact committed a crime (the degree of which is unknown) should not be punished if the government cannot prove that the person in fact did so. If they are, then there is no meaningful check on the power of law enforcement.

[30] Brandon L Garrett, *Convicting the Innocent: Where Criminal Prosecutions Go Wrong* (Cambridge, MA, Harvard University Press, 2011).

[31] Candace McCoy, 'Plea Bargaining as Coercion: The Trial Penalty and Plea Bargaining Reform' (2005) 50 *Criminal Law Quarterly* 67.

The due process retort is that, under the current guilty plea system, approximately 97 percent of all defendants plead guilty and receive lesser sentences than those who go to trial – do judges really believe all these defendants are remorseful? The remorse justification for the trial penalty appears disingenuous, they say. What is really at work is stark utilitarian coercion, the system shortcircuiting all the trials that would be necessary if the trial penalty did not force so many defendants into relinquishing their right to trial.

In the United States, the 'remorse' argument is often expressed as 'acceptance of responsibility', a phrase that has also found its way into penal codes. The way for a criminal defendant to demonstrate remorse is to 'accept responsibility' for the crime, and the way to accept responsibility is to plead guilty. In the previous century, the same argument was heard without the 'accept responsibility' language; rather, judges would say that a guilty plea indicated that a defendant was willing to reha-bilitate herself through criminal punishment. It is not surprising that the federal US Sentencing Guidelines, passed in 1986 (Sentencing Guidelines Act of 1986, United States Code title 28, section 994) do not mention the rehabilitation angle, since they were designed to do away with indeterminate sentencing based on defendant characteristics and amenability to reform. Further, remorse does not necessarily lead to rehabilitation. Many circumstances are likely to intervene.

Another rationale for imposing a steep trial penalty, somewhat analogous to the 'acceptance of responsibility' argument, is that a 'deadbang guilty' defendant who nevertheless goes to trial is committing perjury in maintaining his innocence, and upon conviction should be punished for this. Still another rationale is that the judge does not understand the depth of victim injury and heinous circumstances of the crime until the evidence at trial demonstrates them 'in living colour', thus prompting the judge to sentence more harshly after trial than after a sterile guilty plea.

The perjury rationale is certainly cogent – if in fact the defendant committed perjury. If so, perjury charges should be brought. If not, it is a denial of due process to punish a person for a crime that has not been charged and proven. The federal sentencing data are incapable of testing this rationale, since there is no way to know how many perjury charges emerge from typical prosecutions of defendants regarded as 'deadbang guilty' but who nevertheless demand trials. (The author is willing to bet that there are exceedingly few such cases.) Regarding the 'living colour' rationale, the suspicion is that experienced judges, who have surely seen the aftermaths of heinous crimes and understood the sad injuries of numerous victims, are casting about for a reason to justify to themselves their use of the trial penalty.

Measuring the size of the sentencing differential is possible using the type of data and experiments that were reviewed in the previous section. Measuring coercion, however, is impossible. How high does the difference in sentence have to be before we can say that any rational defendant would plead guilty rather than face the possibil-ity, even if slim, of conviction after trial and imposition of the highest punishment? That is a matter for each reader to judge (and a matter for real defendants to ponder deeply.) In the US federal system, Kim has determined that the overall trial penalty is 64 percent, which varies among different offence types. If you were a criminal defend-ant, would this induce you to plead guilty even though you are innocent, or at least even though you believe the prosecution cannot prove all the evidence necessary to convict you of the charges? Would it make any difference to you that the penalty would start off comparatively low but become steeper the longer you took to plead guilty?

5. A QUICK GLIMPSE AT THE EFFECT OF TIMING ON GUILTY PLEAS IN FEDERAL COURT

The sentencing differential has been of concern to federal policymakers for several decades. A 'Supplementary Report on the Initial Sentencing Guidelines and Policy Statements' from the US Sentencing Commission (18 June 1987: 48) said that prior to passage of the sentencing guidelines, defendants in the federal system 'who pled guilty received a sentence that averaged between thirty to forty percent lower than the sentence which would have been imposed had the defendant pled not guilty and been subsequently convicted'. The new Guidelines, which had been passed in 1986 and went into effect in 1988, were designed to maintain homeostasis; previous practices and sentences were expected to continue, but under a structure that was much more controlled and transparent. However, since that time much research about the trial penalty has shown that the methods to measure it must be very carefully chosen, that the factors which account for it must be statistically controlled so that the fact of disposition method alone can be determined, it must be studied not only in the aggregate but specifically in offence types of different levels of severity, and its actual impact on the decision-making of defendants cannot be simply assumed but should be studied empirically. To these concerns, this chapter adds another: the timing of the penalty, and how it may increase at different stages of criminal procedure, may affect defendants' choices and in the worst-case scenarios may prevent them from exercising their due process rights. If this is so, it is possible that these guilty pleas would be, in their practical effect, coerced confessions.

Quite probably, timing matters when the law specifically says it must. For instance, the courts in England and Wales operate under a Sentencing Act (described in the previous section) which sets out three procedural stages in guilty pleading and prescribes higher sentences the longer a case takes to reach a guilty plea. Henham has quoted a 1998 study from Her Majesty's Sentencing Office, Table 6.7, which states that 'the percentage of defendants pleading guilty on the trial date was 64.9% in 1997'.[32] After the new Sentencing Act went into effect, placing an explicit higher sentence on these cases, guilty pleas migrated to the early stage described as 'at the first opportunity', so that by 2005 approximately two-thirds of all cases were concluded at the earliest possible stage in the procedure rather than at the latest. This was the intent of the Act. The US Sentencing Guidelines used in federal courts were passed before the British Act was, but it was not until 1992 that they were amended to give an additional point of sentencing credit to early guilty pleaders. The effect of this extra point on timing of guilty pleas and subsequent sentencing severity is explored here, in a preliminary cut at federal sentencing data.

---

[32] Henham (n 24) 395, n 10.

Since implementation of the Sentencing Act of 1986, US federal criminal courts have operated under sentencing guidelines that record in remarkable detail all the factors that influence the final sentence, including several related to guilty pleas and a defendant's 'acceptance of responsibility'. Indeed, they institutionalise the sentencing differential by determining a defendant's sentence based on a host of factors related to the crime and the defendant's criminal history, and then by deducting two to three 'levels', or points, for 'acceptance of responsibility' if the judge determines the defendant did in fact do so. The 'acceptance' argument is captured in the data gathered by the US Sentencing Commission, which collects and records information on every sentence imposed in the federal system and the detailed circumstances of each case, but whether the judge truly believes the defendant is remorseful in 'accepting responsibility' is not capable of being discerned in these data. (You'd have to ask the judges.) During deliberations when writing the guidelines in 1985, the Commission's chairman cautioned that to provide 'an automatic fixed discount would reward every defendant who pled guilty regardless of the circumstances of the offence or the defendant's post-offence conduct. While it would continue the practice of encouraging guilty pleas, it would result in unjustified windfalls in many cases.'[33] A starker statement of crime control ideology would be harder to find, and perhaps it is not surprising that this is an explanation from the then-Chair of the US Sentencing Commission of the reasons that the Commission did not simply 'award a fixed and automatic "discount" for entering a plea of guilty',[34] as some commentators[35] had urged. Instead, the sentencing judge would have to be convinced that the defendant truly accepted responsibility, and only then would the federal judge bestow a 'confession reward'. Subsequent experience has been that almost all defendants who plead guilty receive points credit, while a tiny number do indeed plead guilty but the judge then refuses to lower the sentence because of accepting responsibility.

In fact, the federal sentencing database – called the 'Monitoring' database and available electronically from the ICPSR[36] – contains many variables that reflect the reasons that judges give sentencing discounts for pleading guilty. The ACCTRESP variable (for 'acceptance of responsibility') since 1992 has included not only a two-level reduction for 'acceptance' available to any defendant but also, under Guideline section 3E1.1 as amended in 1992 another point reduction if the defendant made 'timely' notification to 'the authorities of his intention to enter a plea of guilty, thereby permitting the government to avoid preparing for trial and permitting the court to allocate its resources efficiently'.[37] This language is very similar to that of

---

[33] William Wilkins, Jr, 'Plea Negotiations, Acceptance of Responsibility, Role of the Offender, and Departures: Policy Decisions in the Promulgation of the Federal Sentencing Guidelines' (1988) 23 *Wake Forest Law Review* 181.

[34] ibid 190.

[35] Notably Stephen J Schulhofer in hearings before the Commission on 23 September 1986. See transcript available at www.ussc.gov/policymaking/meetings-hearings/public-hearing-september-23-1986.

[36] Inter-University Consortium on Polical and Social Research, at the University of Michigan.

[37] Guideline 3E1.1 reads:

Acceptance of Responsibility.

(a) [If] the defendant clearly demonstrates acceptance of responsibility for his offense, decrease the offense level by two levels,

the Sentencing Act effective in England and Wales, which was passed at roughly the same time. The first part of the Guideline appears to be a prime example of giving a defendant credit for remorse and acceptance of personal responsibility for the crime, but the amendment is purely utilitarian – explicitly requiring that the defendant plead guilty in time for the government to avoid the time and expense of preparing for trial.

Furthermore, the concept of helping the prosecution – which could be interpreted either as an act of remorse or as a rational decision by the defendant to do what powerful prosecutors want, or both – is codified in a separate guidelines provision called 'Substantial Assistance to Authorities'[38] which is also recorded in the Monitoring database. If a defendant cooperates with the government in providing evidence or testifying against co-defendants, thus enabling the prosecution to convict more people, the prosecution will reward the defendant by making a motion asking the judge to 'depart' from the established guidelines sentence. Such departures can reduce sentences significantly. For example, after the new Guidelines had been fully implemented, researchers assessed how often a co-defendant helped the prosecution to convict another and received lower punishment for it. From 1 October 1993 to 30 September 1994, there were 7,012 departures for 'substantial assistance' in the federal system, 4,791 of them for drug trafficking.[39] For drug traffickers, the mean sentence reduction given in return for their 'substantial assistance' to the government was 63.9 months, ie over five years off a typical prison sentence. After the US Supreme Court held in the case of *United States v Booker*[40] that the Guidelines were advisory rather than mandatory, judges began to depart more often from the expected Guidelines ranges. When they do, they must state the reasons for the departures. One important reason would be that the defendant cooperated with law enforcement authorities, providing information or testifying against a co-defendant or even in extreme cases 'wearing a wire' to gather more information in ongoing investigations.

The data describing the facts of each case and the sentences imposed in the federal system include a variable called DISPOSIT which offers five ways that a case disposition may be achieved: (1) guilty plea, (2) *nolo contendere*, (3) trial by jury, (4) bench trial before a judge, or (5) both guilty plea and trial.[41] There are exceedingly

---

(b) if the defendant qualifies for a decrease under subsection (a), the offense level determined prior to the operation of subsection (a) is level 16 or greater, and the defendant assisted authorities in the investigation or prosecution of his own misconduct by taking one or more of the following steps

  (1) timely providing complete information to the government concerning his own involvement, or

  (2) timely notifying the authorities of his intention to enter a plea of guilty, thereby permitting the government to avoid preparing for trial and permitting the court to allocate its resources efficiently, decrease the offense level by one additional level.

  Source: 1995 Guidelines Manual, Chapter Three, 'Adjustments', amended 1992.

[38] US Sentencing Guidelines, s 5K1.1.

[39] Linda Drazga Maxfield and John H Kramer, 'Substantial Assistance: An Empirical Yardstick Gauging Equity in Current Federal Policy and Practice', report issued by US Sentencing Commission (January 1998) exhibit 11, 32.

[40] *United States v Booker*, 543 US 220 (2005).

[41] This seems logically inconsistent. But since the monitoring data count *sentences imposed*, and not convictions, theoretically it is possible for a defendant to plead guilty to one charge in the case but proceed

few pleas *nolo contendere*, so for purposes of counting guilty pleas in this study, they are merged with category (1). Perhaps the reason that there are few defendants who plead 'no contest' is that this is different from admitting guilt, which indicates low remorse and therefore the judge might not give credit for 'acceptance of responsibility'. Furthermore, in 2014, the data indicate that only 0.01 percent of the cases ended in bench trials. This is another indication that evidentiary challenge is discouraged in the federal system. Many scholars[42] have recommended bench trials as an excellent policy alternative to both plea bargaining and bloated, time-wasting jury trials, since such trials before a judge usually concentrate only on the particular evidence on which the parties disagree. It is an ominous sign for due process that only 0.01 percent of federal cases in 2014 utilised the device. As for 'both plea and trial', these cases are those in which the defendant pled guilty to some charges but went to trial on others. The case is counted as the most serious charge for statistical purposes.

In 1984, before the Sentencing Guidelines went into effect, the percentage of cases that went to trial in the federal system was about 15 percent. By 2014, the most recent data show, the trial rate has fallen to 3 percent. Put another way, today 97 percent of federal cases conclude through pleas of guilty or *nolo contendere*.

To explore the dynamics of the trial penalty, observing caseloads is often a first step. It is assumed that high caseloads create pressure to make more defendants plead guilty, although commentators have also said that the causation may work conversely – that is, if the courtroom workgroup becomes accustomed to guilty pleas, it will be capable of handling higher volumes of cases because of earlier pleas and disappearing trials.[43] From June 1991 to May 1992, federal judges sentenced a total of 36,376 defendants (when two points for 'acceptance of responsibility' could be deducted from the point count corresponding to expected sentence). In 1994, after amendment of the 'acceptance' guideline to add one more point if the defendant pled guilty immediately, that number rose to 38,614 cases. (No causation is implied. There are multiple reasons that caseloads may increase.) Ten years later in 2014, the number of people convicted and sentenced numbered 53,598 in US federal courts,[44] excluding immigration cases.

---

to trial on another. The case is then counted as having been disposed of through both plea and trial, because the data count as a 'case'; all charges are adjudicated, with the most serious registered as the offence of record.

[42] Steven Shulhofer, 'Is Plea Bargaining Inevitable?' (1984) 97 *Harvard Law Review* 1037, 1037–1107; King et al (n 11).

[43] McCoy (n 31).

[44] Note that these are federal cases, quite different from state criminal prosecutions. Street crimes are generally prosecuted in state courts, not federal courts. Federal courts handle only criminal offences that involve inter-state violations, or that were committed in federal protectorates such as Indian reservations or the capitol city of the District of Columbia. Federal courts handle economic crimes because the criminals operate nationwide using communications that cross state lines, or drug smuggling across state lines, for example. The District of Columbia has criminal justice agencies like those of other large US cities, and because the District is not a state but is the nation's capitol, there is a federal court there which handles street crimes, though this is unusual in the federal courts.

Did the percentage of cases pleading guilty at the earliest point in the procedure increase over time, as it did in England and Wales, after the guideline encouraging early pleas to save the court time and money was implemented? Recall Henham found that two-thirds of cases there would end in guilty pleas on or about the day of trial, but after the Criminal Justice Act of 2003 went into effect, giving extra discount for early plea, two-thirds were concluded instead 'at the earliest opportunity' to plead. We have no equivalent statistics from the US federal system because the timing of guilty pleas was not recorded prior to the change in 1994. We only knew how many defendants received two points discount for their 'acceptance of responsibility'. We can describe those, however, and also the subsequent three-point reductions, from the most recent data (2014).

Because the existing research about the trial penalty has found that its dynamics and size differ depending on the severity of the case – more severe cases exhibit a much steeper sentencing differential measured in length of prison term, while less serious cases exhibit a qualitative difference because defendants plead guilty so as to avoid prison altogether – the timing of guilty pleas and the effect this has on sentence are described here in three different sample offence categories: drug possession (personal use), drug dealing (trafficking) and fraud. These were chosen to illustrate guilty plea dynamics in a non-serious offence category, then to an offence of medium seriousness, then to an offence that is very serious indeed (inter-state drug trafficking). Drug possession is primarily prosecuted in the city of the District of Columbia and carries a possible sentence of from zero to six months jail time for a first offence and even a second offence unless the drug was heroin. (The 'zero' sentence indicates 'probation' often coupled with fines.) Fraud is a crime of medium severity. It is possible to receive a sentence of probation for committing fraud, but only if the amount stolen was less than US$6,500. Most federal fraud cases involve large amounts of money stolen, and the offence levels increase the more money involved. A median example would be offence level 20 for stealing $95,000; the expected guidelines sentence for level 20 is 33–41 months in prison. The severity of drug trafficking also depends on the quantity of drugs smuggled and/or sold and the offence level can range from a base level of 10 (4–10 months in prison) to 38 (235–283 months). We would expect defendants' guilty plea behaviour to vary depending on how serious the offence was. Less serious cases will plead out quickly to receive probation, while cases of medium seriousness would plead later because negotiation over the strength of evidence (and corresponding prison term) will delay the eventual plea. In very serious cases, we would expect a higher trial rate and a longer time to plead. Defendants would take time to try to challenge the evidence in their cases (for instance, in drug trafficking cases, to contest the amounts of drugs alleged, their purity, and whether the defendant or someone else actually controlled them, so that 'role in the offence' factors might lessen the sentence.) In very serious cases, the defendant might be expected to take time to challenge the evidence because the potential prison sentence is so long and a guilty plea would not lower that length significantly. (Compare the English/Welsh standard here: the trial penalty is expected to be 10 percent in such cases, if the defendant goes to trial and is convicted versus taking 10% off the expected sentence at trial in return for the guilty plea.)

Table 7.1 The results from 2014

	Drug possession	Fraud	Drug trafficking
0 (no credit for plea)	92.5%	2.7%	1.7%
−2 points (later plea)	6.9%	34.3%	7%
−3 points (quick plea)	0%	55.9%	90.9%
N	2,344	7,614	21,323

Where percentages do not add to 100%, there were missing values for the variable recorded in the case. For context, note that the overall guilty plea rate in these three offence categories was 99.09% for drug possession (there was only one trial in 2014), 94% in fraud cases and 97% in drug trafficking cases.

Source: US Sentencing Commission.

Surprisingly at first glance, defendants in the least-serious case category (drug possession) generally received no credit at all for 'acceptance of responsibility', despite pleading guilty! However, because probation is possible for first- and second-time offenders, all that is necessary is a plea 'straight up' without negotiation, and the judges in the District of Columbia would grant probation and require the offender to pay a fine. These rote cases do not even raise issues of remorse or responsibility; they are mechanical and the courts churn through them efficiently. A trial would be almost unthinkable because a poor defendant (and almost all defendants charged with drug possession in the District of Columbia are poor) would probably be jailed without bail to wait for trial. Better to plead guilty even without explicit promises and receive a fine and probation. The expectations about the trial penalty working very efficiently in crimes of low seriousness is supported by these statistics.

The fraud cases are much more interesting from the point of view of 'acceptance of responsibility' and timing of the plea. Quick guilty pleas were offered in over half, but in about a third 'accepting responsibility' occurred later in the process. Here is an example of the problems of due process. Inter-state frauds are complex crimes, often involving co-defendants, and because the guidelines severity depends on how much money the defendant stole, problems of proof of exact amounts and individual bad acts must be resolved. If over half these cases are concluding in guilty pleas at the first opportunity, have the defendants had a meaningful defence? This can take time, and the 34.3 percent of guilty pleas entered at later stages of prosecution is probably an indication of it. One point lower will not make much difference on the eventual sentence; at higher levels of amount stolen, one point deducted lowers the sentence by about 10 percent; the defendant may be inclined to continue to negotiate in this situation. However, at the lower levels of amount stolen, one point reduction of the offence level could mark the difference between prison and probation. Whether defendants at lower levels of crime severity forego the time necessary to defend these cases because probation or even only a couple of months in jail is exponentially more desirable than simply reducing a number of months from an otherwise lengthy prison term is not known, but it is clear that the three-point reduction encourages it.

Contrary to prediction, over 90 percent of the defendants in the most serious case category (drug trafficking) gave their guilty pleas immediately and claimed the extra point reduction on their offence score. Because the prison terms in these cases are very high and potentially involve mandatory sentences, the prediction would be that trials would be more likely because defendants will be imprisoned for long terms either after guilty plea or after conviction at trial – a defendant could try to roll the dice and go to trial and get acquitted. Even a three-point reduction for pleading guilty immediately will make little difference on a prison term over five years. Yet these offenders pled guilty quickly and took what minor reductions they could get. Apparently there is little point in challenging the prosecution's case in a drug-trafficking charge.

This finding contradicted expectations. But a twist in the guidelines sentencing provisions may explain why some of these defendants pled guilty quickly with little fuss. The judge can entertain a motion from the prosecution that the defendant 'substantially assisted' in obtaining the conviction of co-defendants, and should therefore receive a significant sentencing benefit. The defendant must demonstrate willingness to assist the prosecution, and to do so immediately. In conspiracies to smuggle and sell drugs, co-defendants who 'snitch' on their colleagues usually receive significantly lower sentences, to the point of significant downward departures from the sentence established under the offence point scores. This 'assistance to government authorities' in drug-trafficking cases renders the drug trafficking offence type a bit different from the typical prosecution profile, and may partly explain why over 90 percent of these defendants plead guilty quickly – by doing so, and then making a motion for downward departure due to 'substantial assistance', they can lower their sentencing severity quite significantly even beyond what the 'acceptance' guideline would produce. Demonstrating willingness to help the prosecution must be done congruent with an immediate guilty plea.

Recall that Maxfield and Kramer reported that in 1993–1994 there were 4,791 'substantial assistance' departures in cases of drug trafficking.[45] In 2014, 17.6 percent of all federal cases received sentencing discounts based on substantial assistance given to government authorities. In the specific offence category of drug trafficking, over a quarter of the defendants who pled guilty (26.2 percent of the 21,323 total number of cases) received credit for 'substantial assistance'. Clearly, an early guilty plea which has the effect of reducing a lengthy prison term only by a few months is not the only way to incentivise these defendants to plead guilty. If they will agree to give the prosecution all the information they have, the state will sort out issues of culpability and do so in negotiation with defence attorneys. However, the defendant must first confess and turn over all the evidence before negotiation over possible deep sentencing discount can begin. An old adage from prosecutors describes the situation: 'first through the door gets the best deal'. The deal will lower the sentence below what could be achieved from an early guilty plea alone, and it does so in 26.2 percent of the cases.

---

[45] Maxfield and Kramer (n 39).

6. CONCLUSION

Surely these data describe a criminal justice system in which the conventional wisdom about the trial penalty is supported – judges mitigate sentences in return for guilty pleas because the system is predicated on moving huge numbers of defendants into swift convictions without the cost of trials. This brute utilitarianism is further reinforced by the practice of giving mitigation credits for – in effect – assisting in one's own conviction and being sure to plead guilty before the government prepares for trial. To say that judges are giving lower sentences in this great bulk of cases because the defendants are remorseful is truly disingenuous. If policymakers wished to eliminate the trial penalty because it coerces defendants into surrendering their constitutional rights, in the federal system they could simply eliminate the 'acceptance of responsibility' credit from the sentencing guidelines altogether. Defendants who were truly remorseful would continue to plead guilty whether they received credit or not. It is extremely unlikely that such an amendment to the Guidelines would be approved. Clearly, the 'no remorse' justification for imposing after-trial sentences that are much steeper than those achieved after guilty plea in similar cases is unconvincing. Rather, efficiency arguments are consistent with the findings. The problem is that efficiency may eventually morph into cavalier refusal to investigate the facts of the crimes alleged. If defendants perceive that the benefits to be obtained through a guilty plea 'without a bargain', and the costs of unsuccessfully challenging that evidence are too high, they will acquiesce to this system. If they feel they have no other meaningful choice, the system could be said to have morphed into institutionalised coercion.

8

OFAC's Strict Liability Regime: Blackstone and Holmes were Right

STUART WEINSTEIN

Strict liability implies that it is sufficient to demonstrate that an event occurred, and not necessary to demonstrate that the person responsible caused it.[1]

THE US OFFICE of Foreign Asset Control (OFAC) is a strict liability regime. US sanctions violators are subject to penalty without regard to whether they acted with negligence or without fault. Failure to comply with US sanctions regulations can result in serious penalties, both civil and criminal. In determining a penalty assessment or settlement amount, OFAC generally weighs various mitigating and aggravating factors present in the administrative record. OFAC retains discretion concerning the importance it places on various factors, and it may also depart from historical practices in weighing these factors. This chapter suggests that the OFAC strict liability regime has the negative effect of criminalising non-blameworthy conduct for regulatory purposes.

Early and Peterson argue that the penalties imposed against sanctions violators by OFAC affect US firms' trade with target states and work to ensure that US trade with sanctioned states will be lower in the aftermath of OFAC enforcement actions.[2] Van Genugten suggests that OFACs co-opting of large financial institutions (LFIs) to the cause of sanctions enforcement through the imposition of large penalties against these LFIs incentivises the private policing capabilities at LFIs as a force multiplier in the battle against bad players worldwide.[3]

Arguing that this 'overcriminalisation' unwittingly traps banks, other financial entities and individuals who fall afoul of OFAC sanction without any criminal intent, the chapter concludes that a mistake-of-law defence should be available that would

---

[1] John Kay, *Other People's Money: Masters of the Universe or Servants of the People* (London, Profile Books, 2015) 295.

[2] BR Early and TM Peterson, 'Does Punishing Sanctions Busters Work? Sanctions Enforcement and US Trade with Sanctioned States' (2021) *Political Research Quarterly* doi: 10.1177/10659129211025620.

[3] Jesse Van Genugten, 'Conscripting the Global Banking Sector: Assessing the Importance and Impact of Private Policing in the Enforcement of US Economic Sanctions' (2021) 18 *Berkeley Business Law Journal* 136.

require OFAC to prove that the party it seeks to prosecute knowingly violated the law. In examining the history of OFAC sanctions imposed on banks and other financial entities, the research concludes that in certain cases these sanctions have led to the conviction of entities who are, morally speaking, not culpable. A mistake-of-law defence would have the effect of enhancing the sanctions regime to ensure that only those who are truly culpable are prosecuted and that entities found to be in violation of a 'regulatory crime' with no intent are not trapped unwarily.

Despite the passion of US jurisdictions, eg federal, state and local, to increasingly impose strict liability for regulatory crimes where criminal prohibitions apply, the author argues that to impose such sanctions without regard to the defendant's moral culpability is an absurdism that has outlived its usefulness. Blackstone traces the origin of these regulatory crimes to crimes *mala prohibita* which 'enjoin only positive duties, and forbid only such things as are not mala in se ... without any intermixture of moral guilt':

> Illustrative of this type of crime are 'exercising trades without serving an apprenticeship thereto, for not burying the dead in woollen, for not performing the statutework on the public roads, and for innumerable other positive misdemeanors. Now these prohibitory laws do not make the transgression a moral offense, or sin: the only obligation in conscience is to submit to the penalty, if levied.' and his conscience will be clear, whichever side of the alternative he thinks proper to embrace.[4]

In dicta, the Court in *Lambert v California*, 355 US 225, 228 (1957) noted: 'We do not go with Blackstone in saying that "a vicious will" is necessary to constitute a crime ... for conduct alone without regard to the intent of the doer is often sufficient.' Where the emphasis in a regulatory measure is the exercise of police power for the achievement of some social betterment rather than the punishment of the crimes as in cases of *mala in se*, there is no violation of due process when imposing a penalty for a violation made in good faith.[5]

Justice Frankfurter in his dissent in *Lambert* engages in critical opprobrium at the majority's comfort with what he sees as the idea of harshly punishing someone under a statute that does not impose some requirement of a certain mental element – some consciousness of wrongdoing and knowledge of the law's command – as a matter of statutory construction.[6] In support of his position, Frankfurter quotes what Justice Oliver Wendell Holmes wrote in *The Common Law* about 'blameworthiness':

> It is not intended to deny that criminal liability, as well as civil, is founded on blameworthiness. Such a denial would shock the moral sense of any civilized community; or, to put it another way, a law which punished conduct which would not be blameworthy in the average member of the community would be too severe for that community to bear.[7]

Moiseienko points out when states resort to non-judicial targeted sanctions a due process or natural justice question is raised by how the rights of sanctioned

---

[4] *Jordan v De George* (1951) 341 US 223, 237 n 10, quoting *Cooley's Blackstone* vol I, 54, 58 (4th edn).
[5] *United States v Balint* (1922) 258 US 250, 252, citing *Shevlin-Carpenter Co v Minnesota* (1910) 218 US 57, 65.
[6] *Lambert v California* 355 US 225, 232 (1957).
[7] Oliver Wendell Holmes, Jr, *The Common Law* (Abingdon, Routledge, 2004) §§49–50.

persons – individuals or organisations – should be protected as they can entail signifi-cant adverse effects on persons concerned.[8]

This chapter makes the argument that both Blackstone and Holmes got it right and that is time for the creation of a good faith defence to OFAC's strict liability regime which would be available where those facing civil monetary penalties (only) could establish beyond reasonable doubt that they operated under an honest and reasonable mistake of fact so long as they operated a rigorous sanctions compliance programme at the time the incidents occurred and their affirmative steps to comply were mistaken in their efforts.[9] Breen argues that while many would certainly agree that complying with the law is generally advisable, one may be more hesitant when it comes to complying 'too much'.[10]

In other words, when is too much of a good thing not healthy for an organisation? For instance, the extraterritorial effects of US sanctions constitute a geopolitical chal-lenge for the European Union as demonstrated with Iran and Russia.[11] This point is addressed further by noted European policymakers who have argued that the European Union should act against US extraterritorial sanctions affecting it and that in light of recent development related to COVID-19, Nord Stream 2, etc, the problem remains even though the Biden administration is seen as more cooperative than the Trump administration.[12]

1. AN OVERVIEW OF OFAC

OFAC is the part of the US Department of the Treasury charged with administering and enforcing economic and trade sanctions based on US foreign policy and national security objectives targeting foreign countries and regimes, terrorists, international narcotics traffickers, individuals engaged in activities related to the proliferation of weapons of mass destruction, and other threats to the national security, foreign policy or economy of the United States. OFAC acts under national emergency powers granted to the president of the United States, as well as authority granted by specific legislation, to place controls on transactions and freeze assets under US jurisdiction. Many of the sanctions are based on UN and other international mandates, are multi-lateral in scope and involve close cooperation with foreign governments.

---

[8] A Moiseienko, 'Due Process and Unilateral Targeted Sanctions' in Charlotte Beaucillon (ed), *Research Handbook on Unilateral and Extraterritorial Sanctions* (Cheltenham, Edward Elgar, 2021) https://doi.org/10.4337/9781839107856.00033 (accessed 12 November 2021).

[9] See Laurie L Levenson, 'Good Faith Defenses: Reshaping Strict Liability Crimes' (1993) 78 *Cornell Law Review* 401, 405, available at: http://scholarship.law.cornell.edu/clr/vol78/iss3/2 (accessed 10 November 2021).

[10] E Breen, 'Corporations and US Economic Sanctions: The Dangers of Overcompliance' in Beaucillon (n 8).

[11] C Portela, 'Creativity Wanted: Countering the Extraterritorial Effects of US Sanctions', European Union Institute for Security Studies Brief 22 (October 2021) available at: www.iss.europa.eu/sites/default/files/EUISSFiles/Brief_22_2021_0.pdf (accessed 12 November 2021).

[12] P Lamy et al, 'American Extraterritorial Sanctions. Did Someone Say European Strategic Autonomy?', Policy Paper, Hertie School, Jacques Delors Centre (22 March 2021), at www.delorscentre.eu/en/publications/detail/publication/american-extraterritorial-sanctions-did-someone-say-european-strategic-autonomy.

1.1. History of OFAC

The first use of sanctions arose with the Embargo Act of 1807 where the United States made exports from the US illegal in an attempt to pressure Britain and France to respect American interests during the Napoleonic Wars. This effort failed miserably, resulting in President Jefferson repealing the Embargo Act in March 1809.

During the US Civil War, Congress approved a 'trading with the enemy' law which prohibited transactions with the Confederacy, called for the forfeiture of goods involved in such transactions, and provided a licensing regime under rules and regulations administered by Treasury.[13] This theme, that all conduct is proscribed except when the US government 'gets a slice of the action' – is a recurrent modus operandi in sanctions enforcement.

At the start of World War II in response to the Nazi invasion of Norway in 1940, the United States created the Office of Foreign Funds Control (FFC).[14] Pursuant to executive order, the FFC was tasked with the responsibility 'to prevent the use of property, in which an Axis interest existed, in a manner inimical to the interests of the US, and to safeguard the property of citizens of Axis-occupied countries'.[15] Once the United States entered World War II, the FFC played a leading role in economic warfare against the Axis powers by blocking enemy assets and prohibiting foreign trade and financial transactions.[16] Following World War II, President Harry Truman formally established OFAC in December 1950 in response to the entry of China into the Korean War. President Truman blocked all Chinese and North Korean assets subject to US jurisdiction.[17]

1.2. Prohibited Transactions

At the heart of the OFAC regime are 'prohibited transactions', which are trade or financial transactions and other dealings in which US persons may not engage unless

---

[13] Phil Leigh, 'Disunion – Trading With the Enemy', *New York Times*, The Opinion Pages, 28 October 2012, available at: http://opinionator.blogs.nytimes.com/2012/10/28/trading-with-the-enemy/?_r=0 (accessed 4 February 2016).

[14] See US National Archives, 'Administrative History of the Records of the Office of Foreign Assets Control', available at: www.archives.gov/research/guide-fed-records/groups/265.html (accessed 4 February 2016).

[15] 86 Cong Rec 5180 (1940); Sen Rep No 911, 77th Cong, 1st Sess (1941) 2; HR Rep No 1507, 77th Cong, 1st Sess (1941) 3, quoted in Kenneth S Carlston, 'Foreign Funds Control and the Alien Property Custodian' (1945) 31 *Cornell Law Review* 1, available at: http://scholarship.law.cornell.edu/cgi/viewcontent.cgi?article=1499&context=clr (accessed 31 January 2016).

[16] Simon J Nusbaum, 'The Enemy Alien as Defendant' (1943) 43(7) *Columbia Law Review* 1050–1065, available at: http://doi.org/10.2307/1117716 (accessed 31 January 2016).

[17] US Department of the Treasury, About OFAC, available at: www.treasury.gov/about/organizational-structure/offices/Pages/Office-of-Foreign-Assets-Control.aspx (accessed 31 January 2016). See also Ronald A Brand, *Fundamentals of International Business Transactions* (The Hague, Kluwer Law International, 2000) 308, available at: https://books.google.co.uk/books?id=RHRs4ioXkNAC&dq=korean+emergency+1950+foreign+assets+control&source=gbs_navlinks_s (accessed 4 February 2016).

authorised by OFAC or expressly exempted by statute.[18] As each OFAC programme is based on different foreign policy and national security objectives, what may be prohibited in one programme may be permitted elsewhere. OFAC regulations allow also for the issuance of general licences which allow the performance of certain categories of transactions. These individual licences are issued pursuant to specific guidelines on a case-by-case basis. OFAC usually has the authority by means of a specific licence to permit a person or entity to engage in a transaction that otherwise would be prohibited. In some cases, however, legislation may restrict that authority. In some situations, authority to engage in certain transactions is provided by means of a general licence.

The use of general or specific licences where under certain circumstances OFAC 'will look the other way' at what would otherwise be a strict liability offence is an example that proves Blackstone's point. You can violate this law and your conscience will be clear so long as you negotiate a licence deal with OFAC. Where is the moral authority behind such a prohibitive law if you can negotiate your way out of its clutches ex ante as opposed to ex post facto?

1.3. Targeting Specific Governments and Individuals

OFAC runs several US economic sanction programmes and embargoes aiming to target geographic regions and governments. Whereas some of these programmes are comprehensive in nature and block the government through broad-based trade restrictions, others target specific individuals and entities. Named individuals and entities are listed in OFAC's list of Specially Designated Nationals and Blocked Persons (SDN list). In addition to the SDN list, there are other sanction lists. US persons may not deal with SDNs whose assets in the United States will be blocked. Entities that a person on the SDN List owns (defined as a direct or indirect ownership interest of 50 per cent or more) are also blocked, regardless of whether that entity is separately named on the SDN List.

Although title to blocked property remains with the target, the exercise of powers and privileges normally associated with ownership are 'frozen' and nothing may be done with the property absent the permission of OFAC including an across-the-board prohibition against transfer or disposition of such property.

1.4. US Citizens

US persons must comply with OFAC regulations, including all US citizens and permanent resident aliens regardless of where they are located, all persons and entities within the United States, all US incorporated entities and their foreign branches. In the case of certain programmes, foreign subsidiaries owned or controlled by US companies also must comply. Certain programmes also require foreign persons in possession of US-origin goods to comply.

---

[18] See 'Acts Prohibited' in Trading With the Enemy Act (TWEA) 50 USC (Ch 53) §4303(a) et seq.

1.5. Maximum Civil Monetary Penalties (MCMP) and Criminal Punishments

The MCMP[19] for violations and criminal punishments are as follows:

Trading with the Enemy Act[20]	Up to US $105,083 for each violation
International Emergency Economic Powers Act[21]	Up to US$ 356,579 or twice the amount of the underlying transaction for each violation
Foreign Narcotics Kingpin Designation Act[22]	Up to US$ 1,771,754 for each violation
Depending on[23] the programme	The maximum criminal fine for violations of most U.S. sanctions programmes is $1 million or 20 years in prison for each violation but certain narcotics-related sanctions violations can trigger criminal fines of up to $5 million or 30 years in prison per violation. Funds related to sanctions violations can also be subject to criminal forfeiture. There is no statutory ceiling on the size of the total penalty or forfeiture that could be imposed, and there have been several recent criminal sanctions enforcement actions that resulted in penalties and/or forfeitures of hundreds of millions and even billions of dollars.

Gowin et al examine the valuation effects of OFAC sanction violations on US LFI and conclude that a civil money penalty (CMP) adversely affects a bank's value in the next quarter without regard to the magnitude or type of OFAC violation, and the bank's ability to deal with an enforcement action cannot moderate the adverse effect of the CMP.[24]

1.6. Self-disclosure

A company can and is encouraged to voluntarily disclose a past violation. Self-disclosure is considered a mitigating factor by OFAC in civil penalty proceedings.[25] OFAC does not have an 'amnesty' programme.[26] OFAC's regulations are broader than the specific laws that deal with the terrorists and persons who support them.

---

[19] Federal Register, 'Office of Foreign Assets Control, Treasury, Final Rule, Inflation Adjustment of Civil Monetary Penalties' Federal Register / Vol. 88, No. 9 / Friday, January 13, 2023 / Rules and Regulations 2229 available at: www.govinfo.gov/content/pkg/FR-2023-01-13/pdf/2023-00593.pdf (accessed 2 July 2023).

[20] 50 USC §16.

[21] 50 USC §1705.

[22] CFR, Title 31, §598.701.

[23] International Comparative Legal Guides, Sanctions 2020, First Edition, US Section 4.4., p, 154 available at: www.paulweiss.com/media/3979073/iclg_sanctions2020.pdf (accessed 2 July 2023).

[24] KD Gowin et al, 'Impact on the Firm Value of Financial Institutions from Penalties for Violating Anti-Money Laundering and Economic Sanctions Regulations' (2021) 40 *Finance Research Letters*, 101675.

[25] US Department of the Treasury, 57593 Federal Register, vol 74, no 215 (9 November, 2009), Rules and Regulations, OFAC, 31 CFR Part 501, 'Economic Sanctions Enforcement Guideline', available at: www.treasury.gov/resource-center/sanctions/Documents/fr74_57593.pdf (accessed 6 February 2016).

[26] US Department of the Treasury, OFAC, 'Frequently Asked Questions', available at: www.treasury.gov/resource-center/faqs/Sanctions/Pages/faq_general.aspx (accessed 6 February 2016).

All individuals and entities that fall under US jurisdiction should use OFAC's SDN List. It is important to note that some OFAC sanctions, such as those pertaining to Iran, Sudan and Cuba, apply to persons acting on behalf of those targeted governments even if those persons do not appear on the SDN list. It is also important to note that OFAC's Cuba sanctions prohibit most transactions with Cuban nationals, wherever located. US persons are expected to exercise due diligence in determining whether any such persons are involved in a proposed transaction.

1.7. Triple-tier Structure of Sanctions

Sanctions are normally divided into three tiers with the first being primary sanctions that apply to US persons or entities which identify entities (persons, organisations or companies) and freeze their assets in the United States and prohibit US persons from engaging in dealings with them. Several sanctions programmes have a secondary measures component to them that implicate non-US persons in their dealings with target states and threaten non-US persons' access to the US financial system. Secondary sanctions provide non-US actors a Hobson's choice: they can continue dealing with the targeted country and targeted companies or they can continue having access to the US financial system.[27] The third category of sanctions are 'sectoral' sanctions which apply in addition to primary and secondary sanctions. These target specific transactions made by specific entities in selected economic sectors. To date, they have been applied only in the case of sanctions against Russia for its incursion into Ukraine and they specifically limit the ability of select Russian financial institutions to access the US debt and equity markets to raise funds.[28] The economic sanctions against Russia

> have developed into one of the most complex sanctions programmes, consisting of a complicated web of trade controls that includes blocking sanctions, geographical restrictions on the Crimea Region, sanctions targeting specific sectors, export controls and the potential for sanctions on non-US Persons conducting transactions with US nexuses and even sometimes with non-US nexus, contrary to US foreign policy objectives.[29]

2. NON-CULPABLE CONDUCT SHOULD NOT BE PUNISHED

2.1. Safe Harbour for Mistake of Law

It is the thesis of this chapter that OFAC should specifically create a 'safe harbour' to exempt those individuals and entities from prosecution for violating its various

---

[27] Kristin Casler, 'Sanctions Against Cuba, Iran Russia and More', Corporate Law Advisory, available at: www.lexisnexis.com/communities/corporatecounselnewsletter/b/newsletter/archive/2015/03/02/sanctions-against-cuba-iran-and-russia-and-more.aspx (accessed 10 February 2016).

[28] ibid.

[29] C Stinebower, D Jabaji and M Pendás-Fernandez, 'Russia Sanctions and Considerations in Building a Sanctions Compliance Programme' (2021) 4(4) *Journal of Financial Compliance* 298–312.

sanctions programmes in those cases where both the defendant involved, and no reasonable person, would have known or have reason to know that the actions involved constituted a violation of the OFAC sanctions programmes. The concern that such a prosecution is wrong 'because it leads to the conviction of persons who are, morally speaking, innocent' should guide thinking in this area.[30]

A mistake-of-law defence here can only succeed if the defendant can prove that (1) no reasonable person would have believed that his/her conduct was unlawful and (2) he/she did not hold that belief.[31] If there is any variety of circumstantial evidence, such as course of dealing, general knowledge of the industry or customer preferences, working relationships between the parties or other criteria that would prove the defendant knew or had reason to know that the conduct was proscribed in those circumstances, the mistake-of-law defence would be inapplicable. Additionally, the mistake-of-law defence would not apply where after learning that its conduct was culpable a defendant did not voluntarily disclose this matter to OFAC.

2.2. Quasi-criminal Regulations

A.P. Simester has suggested that where strict liability leads to conviction of the blameless, its use in stigmatic crimes is always unjustified.[32] However, it does not follow that all types of strict liability offences are wrong. Professor Simester suggests that there are reasons for thinking that strict liability may be legitimate in non-stigmatic offences (called quasi-criminal regulations). Here the very fact that OFAC will issue a licence to authorise an individual or entity to engage in a transaction that otherwise would be prohibited is indicative of the fact that the very wrongs OFAC wishes to prevent are non-stigmatic in nature. Kenneth Mann suggests that such licensing procedure is in line with the shrinking of the criminal law to fit it into its proper role in the law of sanctions, next to an expanding arena of punitive civil sanctions.[33] In fact, Mann goes further to argue that nowadays administrative agencies such as OFAC not only regulate action, but they also prosecute and that this new paradigm raises US constitutional due process concerns.[34]

2.3. Remedial Cases – Strict Liability

The author here agrees with Mann in arguing for the need for distinctive constitutional protections for defendants in harsh punitive civil proceedings such as the ones

---

[30] AP Simester, 'Is Strict Liability Always Wrong?' in AP Simester (ed), *Appraising Strict Liability* (Oxford, Oxford University Press, 2005) 21.

[31] Paul J Larkin, Jr, 'Regulatory Crimes and the Mistake of Law Defense', The Heritage Foundation Legal Memorandum #157 on Legal Issues, available at: www.heritage.org/research/reports/2015/07/regulatory-crimes-and-the-mistake-of-law-defense (accessed 15 February 2016).

[32] Simester (29).

[33] Kenneth Mann, 'Punitive Civil Sanctions: The Middleground Between Criminal and Civil Law' (1992) 101 *Yale Law Journal* 1795, 1802.

[34] ibid 1870.

most undertaken by OFAC. However, here, the author argues that there is an equally significant need for constitutional fairness to be followed when an administrative agency such as OFAC goes after individuals or entities in strictly remedial cases as these cases are most likely to impact disproportionately those least likely to bear the financial cost and burden of fines of any sort. For the US Constitution to work, the speed camera prosecution must be as scrupulous as the death penalty proceeding. The concern here for the author is that in the case of OFAC it is important that the remedial cases not get subsumed by the fulcrum of strict liability in order that justice may be seen to be done. There is little benefit to society to use a sledgehammer to crack a walnut and this appears to be the case in respect of prosecuting mistakes of law in non-egregious circumstances under a strict liability standard. Professor Coffee, however, disagrees: if a civil penalty equal to the social cost of the behaviour can be described as non-punitive, then arguably the full constitutional safeguards applicable to criminal prosecutions need not apply.[35]

2.4. The Unintentional Violation and the Middle Ground

One of the concerns raised by the OFAC sanctions region is that unintentional violations are more likely to result from the use of the criminal law as a backstop to enforce technical rules and regulations. Does the threat induced by the possibility of criminal sanctions create so much fear in individuals such that overdeterrence and consequent efficiency losses result? Probably not. Civil penalties for violations of the Trading with the Enemy Act range up to US$105,083 for each violation; civil penalties for violations of the International Emergency Economic Powers Act range up to US$ 356,579 or twice the amount of the underlying transaction for each violation; and, finally, civil penalties for violations of the Foreign Narcotics Kingpin Designation Act can range up to US$ 1,771,754 for each violation.

Given these draconian civil fines, the fact that criminal penalties for wilful violations can include fines ranging up to US$20 million and imprisonment of up to thirty years does not suggest that the deterrence of criminal penalties is particularly stronger than for the civil penalties identified already. The criminal penalties are serious, and the civil penalties are also severe. There is no 'middle ground' in OFAC's mind or a continuum of remedial penalties, punitive civil penalties and punitive criminal penalties as Professor Mann would advocate in his 'middle ground' approach; instead, any non-compliance is 'all bad'. This is not surprising as Professor Coffee notes: 'no agency believes that violations of its rules are simply regulatory offenses that lack inherent moral culpability … whatever the agency … it is a safe bet that its staffers believe that their agency's rules protect vital public interests'.[36] The OFAC website bears out Professor Coffee's views: 'The ramifications of non-compliance, inadvertent or otherwise, can jeopardize critical foreign policy and national security

---

[35] John C Coffee, Jr, 'Paradigms Lost: The Blurring of the Criminal and Civil Law Models – And What Can Be Done About It' (1992) 101 *Yale Law Journal* 1875, 1883.

[36] ibid 1889.

goals.'[37] However, at the same time, OFAC adds a 'moral culpability' standard on top of its strict liability regime to ensure accountability: 'OFAC does, however, review the totality of the circumstances surrounding any violation, including the quality of a company's OFAC compliance program.'[38]

3. REVIEW OF THE TOTALITY OF THE CIRCUMSTANCES

To blunt the 'Kafkaesque' nature of strict liability standards for small oversights, OFAC provides a general framework for the enforcement of all economic sanctions programmes it administers. The fulcrum of its analysis is that the greater a subject person's actual knowledge of, or reason to know about, the conduct constituting an apparent violation, the stronger the OFAC enforcement response will be:

1. *Actual Knowledge.* Did the subject person have actual knowledge that the conduct giving rise to an apparent violation took place?
2. *Reason to Know.* If the subject person did not have actual knowledge that the conduct took place, did the subject person have reason to know, or should the subject person reasonably have known, based on all readily available information and with the exercise of reasonable due diligence, that the conduct would or might take place?[39]

In short, OFAC may make concessions for the individual characteristics of the violator in the sense that a relatively unsophisticated player may fare better than a sophisticated corporate entity. Moreover, in the case of a corporation, awareness will focus on supervisory or managerial level staff in the business unit at issue, as well as other senior officers and managers. In its guidelines, OFAC will consider the volume of violations, the quality of the compliance programme and whether there was cooperation by self-disclosing or an agreement in place tolling any statute of limitations. Does the OFAC framework provide what Professor Mann would characterise as an appropriate procedural setting designed to permit substantial growth in the size and effectiveness of money sanction that corrects the excessive reach of the criminal law while reducing the proportion of cases that escape punitive sanctions altogether?[40]

4. OFAC STRICT LIABILITY AND THE MODERN BANKING SYSTEM

4.1. At Odds with the Way Money Moves Internationally

Professor Peter Fitzgerald makes the point that the strict liability regime is at odds with the reality of how money is moved through the banking system. Money is moved largely through automated transfers, and messages related to these interbank transactions lack sufficient individual account/customer identification information to screen

---

[37] OFAC (n 17).
[38] ibid.
[39] 31 CFR Part 501, Appendix A to Part 501 – Economic Sanctions Enforcement Guidelines, available at: www.law.cornell.edu/cfr/text/31/part-501/appendix-A (accessed 2 July 2023).
[40] Mann (n 32) 1872.

against the blacklists implemented by various sanctions. As such, it may only be at the very last stage when a bank is being directed to debit/pay a particular party that the transaction may be matched to the blacklist entries. Fitzgerald suggests that 'in such a complex multinational system, under the strict liability standard, it is unclear where the liability for a violation stops – where the institutional involvement becomes so remote from the improper action that liability for non-compliance ceases'.[41] In this author's view, the OFAC strict liability regime operates in certain circumstances like a game of musical chairs – the party being forced to pay civil fines did not commit the wrong but got caught out short when the music stopped playing.

4.2. A Perfect Compliance Standard?

From a policy perspective, the practical implications for US financial institutions are that OFAC expects 'near-perfect' compliance with OFAC's regulations according to John Reynolds and Cari Stinebower. This strict liability largely arises from OFAC's position that a voluntary disclosure will only result in penalty mitigation if OFAC has not received the information from another source or no other institution had an obligation to report.[42] This is not likely to happen in almost every circumstance because OFAC has agreements with US banking regulators to mine the data they have on all US-dollar-denominated banking transactions that banks engage in. This information allows OFAC to undertake forensic analysis of transactions to see if a bank failed to disclose to OFAC a transaction that they were required to do so to avoid strict liability.

A memorandum of understanding (MOU) entered into on 12 April 2006 between OFAC and the Board of Governors of the Federal Reserve System, the Federal Deposit Insurance Corporation, the National Credit Union Administration, the Office of the Comptroller of the Currency and the Office of Thrift Supervision (collectively, the 'Federal Banking Agencies') allows for the Federal Banking Agencies to share these data on banking transactions with OFAC.[43] When the MOU is read along with OFAC clarifying the definition of 'voluntary disclosures'[44] in its economic sanctions enforcement procedures for banking institution, it becomes clear that there is an expectation of a near-perfect compliance standard for banks operating in the United States.[45] A legitimate question must be asked whether low penalties for self-disclosures will result in more voluntary compliance and timely provision of useful

---

[41] Peter Fitzgerald, Written Memorandum Published by the House of Lords Economic Affairs Committee, 24 April 2007 available at: www.publications.parliament.uk/pa/ld200607/ldselect/ldeconaf/96/96we01.htm (accessed 21 February 2016).

[42] John B Reynolds, III and Cari N Stinebower, 'Implications of the Memorandum of Understanding Between Bank Regulators and OFAC: Strict Liability Has Gotten More Strict' (2006) 123 *Banking Law Journal* 637, 637.

[43] US Department of the Treasury, 'Memorandum of Understanding, 12 April 2006, between OFAC and the Federal Banking Agencies', available at: www.treasury.gov/resource-center/sanctions/Documents/mou_final.pdf (accessed 21 February 2016).

[44] See n 24 above.

[45] Reynolds and Stinebower (n 41) 639.

information – thereby advancing OFAC's fundamental role as a national security and foreign policy instrument of the president – as opposed to the present punitive approach taken by OFAC.[46]

5. HOW A MISTAKE-OF-LAW DEFENCE WOULD WORK WITH OFAC SANCTIONS

5.1. US Law does not Recognise a Mistake-of-Law Defence

Under US law, it is clear law that a mistake of law will not excuse criminally culpable conduct. The Supreme Court has held in 1998 that 'to act "knowingly" is to act with "knowledge of the facts that constitute the offense" but not necessarily with knowledge that the facts amount to illegal conduct, unless the statute indicates otherwise'.[47] More than a century earlier (1878) the Supreme Court ruled that 'ignorance of a fact may sometimes be taken as evidence of a want of criminal intent, but not ignorance of the law'.[48] This view confirms the 1833 dicta of the Supreme Court that 'it is a common maxim, familiar to all minds, that ignorance of the law will not excuse any person, either civilly or criminally'.[49]

5.2. Mistake of Law is Needed to Address the Imbalance

Paul J. Larkin, Jr suggests that a mistake-of-law defence should 'focus on situations in which the criminal code forms such a dense thicket that no "person of ordinary intelligence" could readily understand what the law forbids without the assistance of counsel'.[50] In the case of OFAC, the rules are so complex that it is very likely that an individual operating a small enterprise could unknowingly fall afoul of the various sanction programmes without intent and be subject to stiff civil penalties simply by being ignorant of the law.[51] In these circumstances, the same argument cannot be made by a sophisticated organisation or business person. However, the law should in essence protect those individuals from liability for conduct that no reasonable person would have thought had been outlawed. Professor Kass rightly argues that 'only a small kernel of logic lies inside this large and illogical doctrine, and if deprived of the unquestioning adherence to which it owes its presence form, *ignorantia legis* might pass away without harm to law enforcement and considerable benefit to the harmony of the criminal law'.[52]

---

[46] ibid.
[47] *Bryan v United States*, 524 US 184, 193, 118 SCt 1939, 141 LEd2d 197 (1998).
[48] *Reynolds v United States*, 98 US 145, 167 (1878).
[49] *Barlow v United States*, 32 US (7 Pet) 404, 411 (1833).
[50] Larkin (n 30) 5.
[51] See *Cortez v TransUnion, LLC*, 617 F3d 688 (3d Cir 2010) which arose from a credit reporting service's misreporting of consumer information known as 'OFAC alert' on an individual's credit reports, available at: www2.ca3.uscourts.gov/opinarch/082465p.pdf (accessed 21 February 2016).
[52] Ronald A Cass, 'Ignorance of the Law: A Maxim Reexamined' (1976) 17 *William & Mary Law Review* 671, 672, available at: http://scholarship.law.wm.edu/cgi/viewcontent.cgi?article=2493&context=wmlr (accessed 21 February 2016).

5.3. Accountability: A Key Issue

As much as individuals need to account to the authorities when they do wrong, the authorities must also be held to account in those circumstance where their actions produce unforeseen effects. Former US Attorney General Michael B. Mukasey and John Malcolm suggest that the proliferation of regulatory offences undercuts the moral force of criminal legislation:

> First, some of the regulations are vague and overbroad. Second, many of these regulations are so abstruse that they may require a technical or doctoral degree in the discipline covered by the regulations to understand them. Third, there are so many regulations located in so many places that laypeople and small companies subject to these regulations would be unable to locate them, much less understand them, even if they had the resources to do so. Fourth, the regulations often criminalise behaviour that is not obviously morally wrong, so even the most intelligent among the population cannot by reason or common sense determine what behaviours are criminalised.[53]

While these views refer to some 300,000 regulatory offences that Mukasey and Malcolm suggest are on the books of the federal government, it is the third point above that is most applicable in the circumstances here.

5.4. Too Many Regulations in So Many Places

The OFAC regulations are varied and numerous in nature. In some cases, multiple sanctions will apply to a single transaction. For instance, first, an organisation must examine the Consolidated Sanctions List which is a combined list of the following: the Foreign Sanctions Evaders (FSE) List; the Sectoral Sanctions Identifications (SSI) List; the Palestinian Legislative Council (NS-PLC) list; the List of Foreign Financial Institutions Subject to Part 561 (the Part 561 List); the Non-SDN (specially designated nationals) Iranian Sanctions Act (NS-ISA) List; and then finally the List of Persons Identified as Blocked Solely Pursuant to Executive Order 13599 (the 13599 List).[54] To check whether someone or some entity might be on the FSE, SSI, NS-PLC, the Part 561 List, the NS-ISA or the 13599 List, one must also develop a sophisticated level of expertise in understanding SDN Alias Screening Expectations.[55] For instance, if the name of the SDN is a common name such as Muhammad Ali, Juan Rodriguez or John Smith, one cannot be sure that the individual listed on the SDN is not the same individual that one is involved with in a transaction.

---

[53] Michael B Mukasey and John Malcolm, 'Criminal Law and Administrative State: How the Proliferation of Regulatory Offences Undermines the Moral Authority of Our Criminal Laws' in Dean Reuter and John Yoo (eds), *Liberty's Nemesis: The Unchecked Expansion of the State* (New York, Encounter Books, 2016) 283, 285.

[54] US Department of the Treasury, OFAC, 'Consolidated Sanctions List', available at: www.treasury.gov/resource-center/sanctions/SDN-List/Pages/consolidated.aspx (accessed 22 February 2016).

[55] US Department of the Treasury, OFAC, 'Recent OFAC Actions – SDN Alias Screening Expectations', available at: www.treasury.gov/resource-center/sanctions/OFAC-Enforcement/Pages/weak_strong_alias. aspx (accessed 22 February 2016). See also generally *Cortez* (n 50).

5.5. The Sanctions Rules are Vague and Unclear in Application

To access the information contained on the Consolidated Sanctions List, one must be able to understand the programme codes or 'tags' following each sanctions list entry to understand which sanctions programme pursuant to which the person has been blocked, designated or identified. A glimpse of the programme codes reveals eighty different pieces of legislation, regulation or executive order ranging from the Patriot Act,[56] a 342-page statute, to complex regulations such as the Terrorism Sanctions Regulations (TSR).[57] Most ominously, the first proviso of the TSR contains a warning not all that dissimilar to that found in the entry to Dante's inferno – 'abandon hope all ye who enter here' – in that it specifically states that what applies in the TSR only applies to it and not the other seventy-nine other pieces of law related to sanctions. Moreover, even within the TSR only, it is noted that 'differing foreign policy and national security contexts may result in differing interpretations of similar language among the parts of this chapter'.

5.6. The Sanctions Programmes are Too Abstruse

Once someone has consulted the Consolidated Sanctions List, they must then double-check the information they have against the SDN List.[58] The SDN List is a list of individuals and companies owned or controlled by, or acting for or on behalf of, targeted countries. The list also contains individuals, groups and entities, such as terrorists and narcotics traffickers designated under programmes that are not country specific. Moreover, entities that a person on the SDN List owns (defined as a direct or indirect ownership interest of 50 percent or more) are also blocked, regardless of whether that entity is separately named on the SDN List! In this regard, a person seeking to comply scrupulously with the OFAC sanctions regime may fall afoul of them simply because they could not keep one step ahead of the wrongdoers and their never-ending capacity to use shell companies and clever holding structures to avoid the effect of the sanctions regulations. Even OFAC itself was caught out in this regard when it was caught unawares by the ability of several Russian sanctioned entities to quickly transfer ownership and control in these entities to below 50 percent to evade sanctions.[59] In short, it is nigh but impossible to navigate all these regulations without the assistance of someone who is expert in them or the interpretation of same.

---

[56] USA Patriot Act of 2001, 115 STAT. 272, Public Law 107-56 (26 October 2001), available at: www.treasury.gov/resource-center/sanctions/Documents/hr3162.pdf (accessed 22 February 2016).

[57] Terrorism Sanctions Regulations, Title 31, Subtitle B, Chapter V, Part 595, CFR §595.101 et seq (available at: www.ecfr.gov/cgi-bin/text-idx?SID=48196552e0aad55ad643351f9e3d6055&mc=true&node=pt31 .3.595&rgn=div5#se31.3.595_1101 (accessed 22 February 2016).

[58] US Department of the Treasury, OFAC, 'SDN List', available at: www.treasury.gov/resource-center/sanctions/SDN-List/Pages/default.aspx (accessed 22 February 2016).

[59] 'Sanctions Against Russia – Fancy Footwork: How Businesses Linked to Blacklisted Oligarchs Avoid Western Sanctions', *The Economist*, 14 February 2015, available at: www.economist.com/news/business/21643122-how-businesses-linked-blacklisted-oligarchs-avoid-western-sanctions-fancy-footwork (accessed 22 February 2016).

6. IN DEFENCE OF OFAC

In fairness to OFAC, there is a clear recognition on its part that the strict liability regime should not be used to seek out and punish those who mistakenly violate the sanctions regime. According to Adam Szubin, a former director of OFAC and Acting Secretary of Treasury during the first days of the Trump administration, 'wilfulness' is a key issue when considering cases: 'Was this an example of benign or innocent neglect, or much worse, gross negligence or recklessness? All of those questions are the mostly intensely debated when we are sitting around at OFAC.'[60] It is the underpinning of the strict liability regime with discretion not to prosecute that assures proportionality in the application of civil penalties. In every case in which a civil penalty was assessed, the facts as stipulated in the OFAC Civil Penalties and Enforcement Information[61] indicate a level of culpability on the party being fined that goes beyond the element of strict liability. In all these circumstances, the party fined had either (a) known their conduct was wrong, (b) should have known their conduct was wrong or (c) failed to voluntarily disclose their transaction and come forward after the fact.

6.1. Does Failure to Disclose Rise to a 'Moral' Crime Justifying a Civil Penalty?

Whilst the first two scenarios (a) and (b) above address the scienter, a significant number of cases impose fines where the party's only failure was one of disclosure after the fact. In these cases, the party that receives the civil penalty engaged in a transaction prohibited under OFAC rules, failed to get a licence and then did not disclose such transaction afterwards.[62] It is often not clear from the facts alleged in the cases whether the party was aware of their legal obligation to get a licence prior to engaging in the transaction that took place. In this regard, a question exists as to whether these parties had the requisite scienter when they entered these prohibited transactions. Did the party know or should have known that they were violating the OFAC sanctions requirements?

6.2. Greater Guidance from OFAC

OFAC has worked hard to provide greater clarity of expectations in respect of enforcement actions.[63] In December 2018, Undersecretary of Treasury Sigal Mandelker

---

[60] Adam Szubin, Director, Office of Foreign Asset Control, US Department of the Treasury, 'Remarks' (30 September 2014), SIBOS Compliance Forum, reported in Sibos Issues, 1 October 2014, www.sibos.com/sites/default/files/Sibos_Issues_2014_Wednesday3.pdf (accessed 19 April 2015).

[61] US Department of the Treasury, OFAC, 'Civil Penalties and Enforcement Information', available at: www.treasury.gov/resource-center/sanctions/CivPen/Pages/civpen-index2.aspx (accessed 22 February 2016).

[62] See US Department of the Treasury, OFAC, 'Enforcement Actions for 6 April 2007', for examples, available at: www.treasury.gov/resource-center/sanctions/OFAC-Enforcement/Documents/04042007.pdf (accessed 22 February 2016).

[63] US Department of the Treasury, OFAC (Press Releases), 'Under Secretary Sigal Mandelker Remarks ABA/ABA Financial Crimes Enforcement Conference' (3 December 2018), available at: https://home.treasury.gov/news/press-releases/sm563 (accessed 12 November 2021).

offered some guidance to aid the compliance community in strengthening defences against sanctions violations by outlining the hallmarks of an effective sanctions-compliance programme which include:

- Ensuring senior management commitment to compliance.
- Conducting frequent risk assessments to identify and mitigate sanctions-specific risks within an institution and its products, services, and customers.
- Developing and deploying internal controls, including policies and procedures, to identify, interdict, escalate, report, and maintain records pertaining to activity prohibited by OFAC's regulations.
- Engaging in testing and auditing, both on specific elements of a sanctions compliance program and across the organisation, to identify and correct weaknesses and deficiencies; and
- Ensuring all relevant personnel, particularly those in high-risk areas or business units, are provided tailored training on OFAC obligation and authorities in general and the compliance program.[64]

Mandelker indicated that the compliance commitments would become an essential element in settlement agreements between OFAC and apparent violators.

This became the case in May 2019 when OFAC issued *A Framework for OFAC Compliance Commitments*.[65] The Framework is designed to provide organisations subject to US jurisdiction, as well as foreign entities that conduct business in or with the United States or US persons, or that use US-origin goods or services, with OFAC's understanding on the essential components of a sanctions' compliance program. The Framework offers sanctions compliance best practices, including essential components of a sanctions-compliance programme, describes how OFAC may evaluate these components in resolving investigations and determining the amount of any penalties, and includes analysis of some frequent violations of US economic and trade sanctions laws. These guidelines go a long way to reduce the likelihood of a complete innocent being caught up unwittingly in non-blameworthy but liable conduct. It is as if Mandelker channelled her 'inner' Blackstone or Holmes and thought up a practical solution to lessen the likelihood of an 'innocent abroad' falling into the sanctions web of OFAC. Now, it can be claimed that it takes more effort to fall within the ambit of OFAC than to stay clear of the net. Mandelker speaks of the importance of the compliance work of the private sector as being the partner of the US government in 'stopping the flow of funds to weapons proliferations such as North Korea and Iran, terrorist organizations like Isis and Hezbollah, countering Russia's continued aggressive behaviour, targeting human rights violators and corrupt actors, and disrupting drug traffickers such as the Sinaloa Cartel'.[66]

OFAC has pointed out that its sanctions-compliance obligations apply equally to transactions involving virtual currencies and those involving traditional fiat currencies

---

[64] ibid.

[65] US Department of the Treasury, OFAC, 'A Framework for OFAC Compliance Commitments', at https://home.treasury.gov/system/files/126/framework_ofac_cc.pdf.

[66] Sigel Mandelker, 'Forward to Global Investigations Review' in R Barnes et al (eds), *The Guide to Sanctions*, 2nd edn (London, Law Business Research, June 2021), available at: https://globalinvestigationsreview.com/guide/the-guide-sanctions/second-edition (accessed 12 November 2021).

and it has published for members of the virtual currency industry guidance to ensure that this industry does not engage, directly or indirectly, in transactions prohibited by OFAC sanctions, such as dealings with blocked persons or property, or engaging in prohibited trade- or investment-related transactions.[67]

7. MISTAKE OF LAW AS COUNTERBALANCE TO OFAC'S UNFETTERED PROSECUTORIAL DISCRETION

The creation of a mistake-of-law defence to an OFAC civil penalty assessment would better balance the critical policy need of the United States to prevent its citizens from engaging in transactions with those it deems to be off-limits, eg terrorists, narcotics traffickers and those countries that engage in conduct inimical to the United States with the important jurisprudential need for avoiding the harming of those who can reasonably and honestly believe their conduct was not in violation of the law. This defence would be available in civil penalty cases only and would be available only in cases where the individuals accused could satisfy the burden of proof that (1) no reasonable person would have believed that his/her conduct was unlawful and (2) he/she did not hold that belief.

8. CONCLUSION

This chapter has reviewed the case for a mistake-of-law defence to civil penalty prosecutions by OFAC for violations of its various sanctions' programmes. The current strict liability regime combined with the duty to disclose when one engages in a sanctioned transaction is tantamount to a 'stacked deck' against the unwary who might be unsophisticated in understanding all the complexities and nuances of the rather complicated OFAC sanctions regime. A mistake-of-law defence would serve to make for a fairer and more transparent playing field and avoid trapping those who through no fault of their own find themselves unwittingly caught in the spider's web that is OFAC compliance. Although OFAC has taken steps to proscribe more clearly what it is expected of LFIs with sophisticated compliance programmes to do to ensure that they do no run afoul of sanctions regime, less concern is addressed to the problem of the 'little guy' who might unwittingly be ensnared in the net of OFAC. Blackstone and Holmes were right – these individuals need protection against an unwieldy all-powerful state. A mistake-of-law defence might just even out the playing field for these folk.

---

[67] US Department of the Treasury, OFAC, 'Sanctions Compliance for the Virtual Currency Industry' (October 2021). Available at: https://home.treasury.gov/system/files/126/virtual_currency_guidance_brochure.pdf (accessed 12 November 2021).

9

Understanding (and Reforming) Criminal Justice in the Former Soviet Union

DAVID NELKEN

C AN WE FIND global, or at least regional solutions, to crime problems that transcend national boundaries? What forms do they take? What forms should they take? What can, and what should be, the goals of international criminal justice? What happens on the ground (and to some extent even what should happen), however, will also be affected by current international, national and local patterns of legal culture.[1] My chapter will first say something about the challenges posed by globalisation to the comparative study of criminal justice and then comment on a recent example of the work being done to enlarge criminology's gaze to the former Soviet Union.

1. GLOBALISATION AND COMPARATIVE CRIMINAL JUSTICE

The choice between different traditions of criminal procedure, the role of the victim and the place of the community are all key problems that Ralph Henham has explored in his work.[2] To find satisfactory answers also requires us to consider, as he noted, how far it still makes sense to think in terms of separable national jurisdictions at a time of global links between crime threats and criminal justice responses.[3] To what extent is a global 'gaze' on crime threats possible and desirable?[4] Do and should the nation-state or other more locally based justice practices shape or resist 'global'

---

[1] See eg David Nelken (ed), *Adapting Legal Cultures* (Oxford, Hart, 2001), and David Nelken (ed), *Using Legal Culture* (London, Wildy, Simmonds and Hill, 2012).

[2] See eg Mark J Findlay and Ralph Henham, *Transforming International Criminal Justice* (Culhompton, Willan, 2005).

[3] This section draws on David Nelken, 'Globalisation and the Challenge to Comparative Criminology' in Francis Pakes (ed), *Globalisation and the Challenge to Criminology* (Abingdon, Routledge, 2014) 9–26 and David Nelken (ed), *Comparative Criminal Justice and Globalization* (Farnham, Ashgate, 2011).

[4] See Cotterrell (ch 2 in this volume).

trends? How can we avoid both the risks of ethnocentrism and of relativism and avoid treating as global what is in fact local?[5]

Many studies of comparative criminal justice still devote themselves principally to explaining differences in national laws, ideas and practices across different juris- dictions. See, for example, the descriptive comparisons of juvenile justice in different jurisdictions in Muncie and Goldson's collection of country studies,[6] or the cross- national collaborative efforts to test hypotheses on the organisational variables that affect police integrity and corruption found in the Klockars et al's more synthetic type of comparison.[7] Conversely, most studies of the best ways to respond to supposed transnational threats or to spread human rights pay little attention to the difficulties of comparative enquiries, except perhaps to lament the obstacles created by differ- ences between places. These endeavours, to some extent, have different aims and audiences. But trying to keep comparative and globalisation issues strictly apart has little to recommend it other than to allow for the continuation of 'business as usual', and it risks, as will be seen, missing a variety of interesting interconnections.

Certainly, there are still remarkable differences in the types of conduct for which people are punished in, say, the United States, China, Thailand or Saudi Arabia, as well as in the type of penalties used. Local conditions also have a lot to do with explaining the differing involvement of immigrants in crime in different European countries and the response to this.[8] But decisions made by criminal justice actors here and elsewhere increasingly (have to) relate to their understandings about crimi- nal justice elsewhere and the desire to be similar or be different to them. Finland's successful efforts to reduce its incarceration rates have been linked to its desire to come into line with published evidence of the rates in other Scandinavian countries.[9] Conversely, the introduction of international crime victimisation surveys had an influence on policymakers and (to a lesser extent) public opinion in the Netherlands where it produced 'a wholesale change in the philosophy of criminal justice policy'.[10] This does not mean of course that those doing the comparison have got it 'right'. Typically, actors construct ideas and practices in other societies in terms that reflect their own concerns and assumptions – even when they are seeking to collaborate with them. As scholars come to study these 'second-order' problems they will increasingly need to move from 'methodological nationalism' to more cosmopolitan approaches.[11]

Comparative criminal justice textbooks and readers reveal considerable uncertainty about how best to integrate the effects of globalisation into traditional classificatory and descriptive schemes. Material that fits awkwardly into the normal comparative

---

[5] David Nelken, 'Comparative Criminal Justice: Beyond Ethnocentrism and Relativism' (2009) 6(4) *European Journal of Criminology* 291–311.

[6] John Muncie and Barry Goldson, *Comparative Youth Justice: Critical Issues* (London, Sage, 2006).

[7] Carl Klockars, Sonja, Ivkovich and Maria Haberfeld (eds), *The Contours of Police Integrity* (London, Sage, 2004).

[8] Luigi Solivetti, *Immigration, Integration and Crime: A Cross-National Approach* (London, Routledge, 2010).

[9] T Lappi-Seppälä, 'Penal Policy in Scandinavia' in Michael Tonry (ed), 'Crime, Punishment, and Politics in Comparative Perspective' (2007) 36 *Crime and Justice* 217–95.

[10] David Downes, 'Comparative Criminology, Globalization and the "Punitive Turn"' in Nelken (n 3, 2011) 24–48.

[11] Ulrich Beck and Natan Sznaider, 'Unpacking Cosmopolitanism for the Social Sciences: A Research Agenda' (2006) 57(1) *British Journal of Sociology* 1–23.

paradigm is sometimes relegated to a separate book,[12] to an early chapter[13] or a closing one.[14] Titles such as Winterdyk and Cao's *Lessons from International/ Comparative Criminology/Criminal Justice* also signal that a variety of related topics are being dealt with – but do not say how, if at all, they may be connected.[15]

Sheptycki and Wardak distinguish 'area studies', 'transnational crime issues' and 'transnational control responses'.[16] But they themselves admit that more needs to be said about when our account of a country's criminal justice system should focus more on internal factors or on external influences. It may be plausible that the account of criminal justice in Saudi Arabia in their book treats the country as autonomous (though more could have been said about its pan-Islamic mission). But it is less obvious why the chapter on South Africa focuses mainly on internal developments whereas the chapter on West Africa is all about its vulnerability to the outside world.

Some authors emphasise the limits of comparative criminal justice. Katja Aas, in her superb introduction to 'crime and globalisation', argues that 'one can no longer study, for example, Italy by simply looking at what happens inside its territory, but rather one needs to acknowledge the effects that distant conflicts and developments have on national crime and security concerns and vice versa'.[17] Not surprisingly, therefore, she devotes little energy in her textbook to the problems of comparing individual countries and instead seeks to show us the complex processes by which the 'global' and the 'local' are intertwined.

Nick Larsen and Russell Smandych likewise explain that the

> cross-cultural study of crime and justice has evolved from a 'comparative' or 'international' approach to what is now increasingly referred to as a 'transnational' or 'global' approach to crime and justice … the effects of rapid globalisation have changed social, political, and legal realities in such a way that comparative and international approaches to crime and justice are inadequate to capture the full complexity of these issues on a global scale.

In particular, they draw attention to 'global trends in policing and security, convergence and divergence in criminal justice and penal policy, and international criminal justice, war crimes and the global protection of human rights'.[18]

Interestingly, however, Piers Beirne, an experienced comparative researcher, in his preface to the Larsen and Smandych collection, warns against going too far down this road. He concedes that 'globalisation and transnational crime do indeed tend to

[12] Philip Reichel, *Handbook of Transnational Crime and Justice*, 4th edn (New York, Sage, 2007).

[13] Philip Reichel, *Comparative Criminal Justice Systems*, 5th edn (Upper Saddle River, NJ, Prentice Hall, 2008).

[14] Harry Dammer, Eric Fairchild and Jay S Albanese, *Comparative Criminal Justice* (Belmont, CA, Thomson, 2006).

[15] John Winterdyk and Lin Cao, *Lessons from International/Comparative Criminology/Criminal Justice* (Toronto, De Sitter, 2004).

[16] James Sheptycki and Ali Wardak (eds), *Transnational and Comparative Criminology* (London, Glasshouse Press, 2005).

[17] Katja Aas, *Crime and Globalization* (London, Sage 2007) 286; see also Katja Aas, 'Victimhood of the National? Denationalizing Sovereignty in Crime Control' in Adam Crawford (ed), *International and Comparative Criminal Justice and Urban Governance* (Cambridge, Cambridge University Press, 2011) 389–412.

[18] Nick Larsen and Russell Smandych, *Global Criminology and Criminal Justice: Current Issues and Perspectives* (Buffalo, NY, Broadview Press, 2008) ix.

blur the relatively distinct boundaries and mobilities that exist between nations and between sovereign territories ... it is thus increasingly moot whether it makes sense to talk of crime in "Russia" or in "India" or in "Northern Ireland" or in the "USA"'.[19] But he insists that

> comparative criminology still has a vital role to play, both in its own terms and also adjacent to global criminology and as one of its key constituents ... the question of how globalisation and transnational crime affect different societies – similarly or differently, both similarly or differently at the same time, or somewhere in between – is first and foremost a comparative one.[20]

For example, he sees a valuable role for comparative criminology in identifying which (failed) states are more vulnerable to the penetration of transnational organised crime – which he identifies as places where there are corrupt politicians, weak controls, lengthy borders and so on.

Francis Pakes too worries whether comparative criminal justice is now passé. The subject, he argues,

> is in the process of losing its relevance. Simply put, the reasoning is that the world has changed and comparative criminology has insufficiently changed with it. The charge against comparative criminology is that it tends to compare and contrast phenomena in distinct cultures or jurisdictions and that, by doing so, diffuse interrelations and complications brought about by globalisation are ignored or understated.

He asks whether global criminology will supersede the field of what we currently think of as 'classic' comparative criminology so that before comparative criminology gets its act together we will have moved on to doing international and transnational criminology, and replies that we should not embrace a 'vision of comparative criminology being abandoned as if it were a ghost town after the gold rush'. The comparative method will remain an influential tool in inquiries involving transnationalisation, globalisation, crime and control.[21]

Pakes suggests that the comparative approach could be seen as only a matter of methodology, whereas globalisation is an 'object of study'. Globalisation, he says, concerns the 'what' not the 'how', describing something taking place in the world such as the trafficking of illegal goods – or people. Hence there cannot really be any contradiction. But he also concedes that the term 'globalising criminology' can be used as if it related to methodology. He therefore draws a further distinction between two senses of global criminology, that are 'subject to conceptual confusion'. '"Strong" global criminology', he claims, 'should probably take the world as its unit of analysis.' It might address questions such as the relation between climate change and civil unrest, transgressions and control. Here, 'global' denotes object. In contrast, globalised criminology frequently refers to relations: those who advocate it frequently argue that we need to take the interconnectedness of the world into account.[22]

---

[19] Piers Beirne, 'Preface' in Larsen and Smandych (n 18) xi.
[20] ibid.
[21] Francis Pakes, 'The Comparative Method in Globalised Criminology' (2010) 43 *Australian and New Zealand Journal of Criminology* 17–34, 17ff.
[22] ibid 18–19.

In explaining his view of comparative criminology and global criminology as 'complementary projects' David Friedrichs agrees that there needs to be a careful division of intellectual labour.[23] 'A comparative criminology', he says,

> addresses the nature of the crime problem and the form and character of criminal justice systems in countries around the world; a transnational criminology is focused principally upon transnational or cross-border forms of crime, and endeavours on various levels to control and respond effectively to such crime; an international criminology focuses on international crime – or crime that is specifically recognized widely across nations as crime against humanity – and international law, as well as the institutions of international law; and a global criminology is best applied to the study of the evolving context within which crime and criminal justice now exists.[24]

Along the same lines, René Van Swaaningen argues that transnational comparative enquiry requires criminologists to be 'broadly interdisciplinary, catholic in taste and open to new insights in the pursuit of justice and humanity'. He distinguishes topics in terms of branches of knowledge (cultural anthropology, green criminology, etc) that need to be called on if we are to answer questions such as: how do we compare the experience of crime and victimisation across diasporic cultures and communities? How do we map the relationships between intra-group and inter-group crime and violence in multicultural contexts? How do we measure the social harm caused by different categories of crime (as various as hate crime; environmental crime; terrorist, political or state crime; or financial and economic crime) and evaluate its impact on different types of individual, community or population? Approaches can be brought together, he suggests, in terms of 'levels of analysis'. Thus his 'fourth level of analysis', for example, examines 'global flows' and relates them to 'global power-relations, the North–South divide and basic capitalist economic laws'. Here, neither the local consequences of globalisation nor the global implications of local developments are the central object of study, but the interconnectedness of nodal societies and global cities.[25]

2. EXTENDING OUR GENERALISATIONS TO INCLUDE CRIME AND CRIMINAL JUSTICE IN THE FORMER SOVIET UNION[26]

As globalisation breaks down barriers to crime and increases the spread of different blueprints[27] for dealing with it, criminologists who specialise in different areas of the world rightly show some impatience with a discipline that too often

---

[23] See also Paul Roberts, 'Comparative Law for International Criminal Justice' in Esin Orucu and David Nelken (eds), *Comparative Law: A Handbook* (Oxford, Hart, 2007) 339–70.

[24] David Friedrichs, 'Comparative Criminology and Global Criminology as Complementary Projects' in Nelken (n 3, 2011) 163–82.

[25] Rene Van Swaaningen, 'Critical Cosmopolitanism and Global Criminology' in Nelken (n 3, 2011) 125–44.

[26] This section draws on David Nelken, 'Post-Soviet Criminal Justice and Comparative Criminology' (2015) 19(2) *Theoretical Criminology* 289–95.

[27] Dario Melossi, Maximo Sozzo and Richard Sparks (eds), *Travels of the Criminal Question,* (Oxford, Hart, 2011).

incorporates Anglo-American assumptions about the nature of criminal behaviour and the best way to respond to it. It is undoubtedly true, for example, that the 'world map' of criminological knowledge is overwhelmingly skewed away from countries in Asia and the Global South. In line with the debate about globalisation just summarized, some think the way forward is to make the discipline itself more cosmopolitan, concerned also with transnational developments that cannot be grasped via 'methodological nationalism'. Others think (at least for the medium future) that what is needed is a better focus on topics that are relevant for regions that have so far been neglected (see, for example, the recently founded *Asian Journal of Criminology*. More generally, there is increasing talk of 'southernising' or 'decolonising criminology').

What seems beyond question is that if the field is to advance beyond this alleged ethnocentrism it will need to interrogate the strengths and limitations of current generalisations about crime and criminal justice. I was offered an opportunity to think about how best to do this when asked to comment on papers in a recent special issue of the journal *Theoretical Criminology* dealing with what is distinctive about crime and justice in former Soviet Union countries (as well as in some countries used for comparison.) The special issue included papers discussing efforts to reform criminal justice procedures,[28] worrying levels of ethnic and hate crime,[29] the deliberate underestimate of murder rate,[30] state manipulation of self-governance by prisoners,[31] the relationship between repressive and abusive policing,[32] and different forms of 'equilibrium' between state malfeasance and organised crime.[33]

The goal of bringing the papers together was to help bring research about this important region of the world into the mainstream of criminological thinking (as well as to enrich indigenous criminology in the countries being considered). But, as with so many examples of 'area studies' in the social sciences, it is not always easy to get the balance right between giving sufficient in-depth analysis to make case studies sufficiently convincing, whilst also showing the wider general relevance of the findings. To show this I shall offer a critical overview of the contributions in terms of what may be considered four possible goals of comparative criminology and criminal justice: description, explanation, interpretation and reform.[34] I will also illustrate how these goals overlap – and perhaps even get in each other's way.

---

[28] Peter H Solomon, Jr, 'Post-Soviet Criminal Justice: The Persistence of Distorted Neo-Inquisitorialism' (2015) 19 *Theoretical Criminology* 159–78.

[29] Richard Arnold, 'Systematic Racist Violence in Russia between "Hate Crime" and "Ethnic Conflict"' (May 2015) 19 *Theoretical Criminology* 239–56.

[30] Alexandra Lysova and Nikolay Shchitov, 'What Is Russia's Real Homicide Rate? Statistical Reconstruction and the "Decivilizing Process"' (2015) 19 *Theoretical Criminology* 257–77.

[31] Gavin Slade, 'Architecture and Attachment: Carceral Collectivism and the Problem of Prison Reform in Russia and Georgia' (2015) 19 *Theoretical Criminology* 179–97.

[32] Matthew Light, Mariana Mota Prado and Yuhua Wang, 'Policing Following Political and Social Transitions: Russia, Brazil, and China Compared' (2015) 19 *Theoretical Criminology* 216–38.

[33] Leonid Kosals and Anastasia Maksimova, 'Informality, Crime and Corruption in Russia: A Review of Recent Literature' (2015) 19 *Theoretical Criminology* 278–88.

[34] David Nelken, *Comparative Criminal Justice: Making Sense of Difference* (London, Sage, 2010).

3. DESCRIBING

The different papers about crime and criminal justice in the former Soviet Union give us much-needed information about what is going on in this part of the world. Richard Arnold, for example, teaches us about commonalities and differences in hate crime here and in other places (and we are told it is worse there).[35] A well-designed study by Light, Prado and Wang brings out key contrasts between the way police organisation has been affected by the transition from communism in Russia as compared to the transformations (or lack of them) in China and Brazil.[36] There is a valuable paper by Gavin Slade of the obstacles to changing prisons structure in Russia and Georgia which illustrates the cultural embeddedness of carceral collectivism (or what the author calls 'polyopticon' – the many watching the many).[37] The author describes this as a system of penal governance based on mutual peer surveillance, the dispersal of authority and governance to prisoners themselves, and communal living engendered by the spatial and temporal structuring of prison life. We learn about the 'law in books', discovering that Russia still retains many elements of an 'investigative' model of criminal justice where judges are subordinate to the prosecution,[38] but also about 'law in action' – as in the way homicide rates are massaged.[39] As this suggests, in this region there may be special difficulties in getting and trusting evidence about crime and criminal justice.

Looking through a comparative lens we get to see both the specificities about crime and the response to it – as well as the various ways they may be connected. We can follow efforts to reform police, judges and prisons, and understand how these fit into larger political and economic and cultural contexts. Finding similarities can be interesting where differences would be expected, and differences can be 'telling' where they arise from a similar starting point, as in the move from communism and totalitarianism towards democracy. But, in the desire to gain attention, comparative researchers sometimes exaggerate the differences they find. It is not only in Russia that criminal statistics are manipulated by politicians or police organisations, and prisons in many places are run by senior inmates. The devil, of course, is in the details.

The papers set out to tell us about similarities and differences between countries in this region, as well as differences between them and elsewhere. But the choice of comparator is not a simple one or without consequence. Would it not have been more constructive to use other ex-communist countries, especially those that have now joined the European Union?[40] 'The West' to which these countries are being compared is not always well defined. Is it the United States, Europe or Scandinavia? Arguably, there are as many differences between the United States and Finland as

---

[35] Arnold (n 26).
[36] Light, Prado and Wang (n 32).
[37] Slade (n 31).
[38] Solomon (n 28).
[39] Lysova and Shchitov (n 30).
[40] This would, for example, complicate the assumption that political control over judges is exerted through the prosecutors. In Poland the reverse is true, see Paolina Polak and David Nelken, 'Polish Prosecutors, Corruption and Legal Culture' in Alberto Febbrajo and Woijech Sadurski (eds), *East-Central Europe After Transition: Towards a New Socio-Legal Semantics* (Farnham, Ashgate, 2010) 21954.

there are between them and former Soviet Union countries. Is it really surprising that in the former Soviet region politicians do not 'govern through crime'? Perhaps this is because that is a distinctive feature of Anglo-American legal cultures – one much less true of many continental European jurisdictions and Scandinavia. It is not by chance that little is said in these papers about 'ordinary' property crime; this too would not be strange in continental Europe.

What is involved in comparing 'like with like' is therefore complicated. Certainly, it can be misleading to compare either principles and ideals, or 'law in the books', in one setting, with less edifying facts about the 'law in action', in another. It is some-times not easy to tell how far differences lie more at the level of social construction than underlying reality. The editors tell us that we are dealing with countries that have not developed strict divisions between formal, informal, licit and illicit, public and private, political power and economic wealth. Boundaries are blurred.[41] But we can ask how far these divisions are really that clear cut even in 'the West' or whether they often exist mainly as ideological mystifications.

Nor is it always easy to circumscribe the task of describing. In seeking to distin-guish the roots of corruption, countries from the former Soviet Union are classified in terms of three so-called equilibria, involving non-competitive and centralised, competitive and centralised, or chaotic and decentralised kinds of relationships between organised crime and politics. But it is not always obvious whether these categories are intended to function as 'ideal types', actual descriptions, or elements to be used in explaining why a given society is likely to develop in one direction or another. What does it mean to call a description paradoxical? Is it really so strange that in China 'changes in policing counteract a major social transformation rather than track it', in the way that police continue to serve their political masters despite the move to state'managed capitalism? This begs the question whether capitalism 'naturally' leads to political freedom or the connection belongs (belonged) only to the early modern history of the West.

4. EXPLAINING

Placing crime in the context of unfamiliar countries has the advantage of moving criminology's agenda away from its current 'geographically biased' obsession with the interesting (but over-debated) question of why prison use is going up when crime is declining.[42] But it does not have to lead to a ghettoisation of explanations linked to this specific region. Indeed, these authors draw on and advance explanations of crime or criminal justice that are, or could be, more widely relevant. We learn that

---

[41] Gavin Slade and Matthew Light, 'Crime and Criminal Justice after Communism: Why Study the Post-Soviet Region?' (2015) 19 *Theoretical Criminology* 147–58.

[42] In obeisance to the mainstream literature, commentators in other regions still feel the need to discuss the local applicability of the thesis of neoliberal 'culture of control' leading to greater punitiveness (Michael Cavadino and John Dignan, *Penal Systems: A Comparative Approach* (London, Sage, 2006)). See, for example, the extensive debate over recent criminal justice reforms in Japan, or, for China, see eg Li Enshen, 'The Neoliberal Penality Thesis in China: When Western Theory Meets Chinese Reality' (2014) 25(3) *Current Issues in Criminal Justice* 803–17.

vigilantes who engaged in ethnic violence often think of themselves as on the side of punishment.[43] They also tell us that the rise of homicide and violent crime in Russia is linked to the idea of de-civilising processes.

The articles discuss a wide range of thought-provoking explanatory variables, both legal and non-legal, including those found within the countries under consideration and those resulting from pressures from outside. We discover that proximity to drugs and arms routes – as well as having borders within reach of EU countries – makes a difference both for crime and criminal justice for reform. Although 'evil causes evil' accounts of the causes of high crime and poor criminal justice predominate, some links are more surprising. People in Russia were happier in the immediate aftermath of the collapse of communism despite the disruption (because they had hope of better things?); more police autonomy in Russia leads to more abuse but more judicial autonomy (in Estonia, and, to lesser extent, the Ukraine) leads to greater impartiality. Some findings directly challenge criminological common sense. As Kazakhstan or Belorussia have become more autocratic, their leaders have *cut back* on their prison populations.

Considerable explanatory effort is devoted to exploring the effects of the 'transition' from communism (which is of course also the subject of large political science and international relations literatures). For some authors, the units for comparison are thus identified less in space than by time – as in the paper contrasting Russia, China and Brazil. Transition is seen as providing the key to why something happens (or should happen) in producing, obstructing and directing change (the latter sometimes referred to as 'path dependency'). Long-standing features of culture – and legal culture – are used to explain the outcomes of reforms. But more short-term adaptive moves are also significant, as in the role that the police took on in Russia in the economic jungle that followed the collapse of communism. We are also invited to think about the effects of 'planned transition' (is transition still the right word?) – in the role played by the Chinese police in accompanying the move to state capitalism.

Crucially, however, not everything changes in a transition. The past persists in the form of 'legacies' embedded in mental, social or physical structures. Brazilian police get away with killings of the underclass because they are still covered by the military.[44] The older 'overseer system' was adapted rather than destroyed by Russian prison reforms; in general, 'carceral collectivism places limits on penal modernization'. But trajectories also depend on 'pull' factors, such as meeting the requirements entailed by belonging to the European Council or being subject to the European Court of Human Rights. The desire to join the European Union may be a necessary but not a sufficient factor to produce an impartial judiciary. Criminal justice systems may or may not evolve towards the European model; caution must be exercised not to assume that this is inevitable. Sometimes it is success rather than failure that needs more explanation.

---

[43] Although this insight applies more generally also to others accused of crimes. See Donald Black, 'Crime as Social Control' (1983) 48 *American Sociological Review* 34–45.

[44] See 'Brazil Police "Killed Hundreds" in Rio – Amnesty', *BBC News*, 3 August 2015, https://www.bbc.co.uk/news/world-latin-america-33757212.

5. INTERPRETING

The editors of the collection rightly suggest that these papers could and should stimulate debate about the assumptions behind Western criminology.[45] They warn that conceptual frames and theories developed in Western industrialised democracies may not be applicable to the study of criminal justice phenomena elsewhere. But this can even be true, more fundamentally, in talking about the sphere of 'criminal justice' (a term far from universal). It can lead us to focus too narrowly on the legal system, assuming an artificial autonomy from the outside. What good can impartial judges do if organised crime has a hold over politics? It can also lead us to take too much for granted. We need to put in question whether societies share the same conception of what is appropriate in responding to crime. It can be misleading to assume that places face 'the same' problems rather than investigating how what are seen as threats are themselves the products of given types of reaction.

Faithfully translating meaning is of the essence in all cross-cultural research (as is noting missing or absent categories). If comparison is to be done well, places have to be shown to be in some way commensurable. But how far can (and should) the search for neutral terms be taken? Does talking about 'political malfeasance' take us too far from the language actually used in the fight over what counts as good politics? Care must be taken in linking the observer's categories to those used locally. What is meant by claiming that, in Russia, the 'dictatorship of law' has not been achieved? How was that phrase, as announced by Putin, understood locally? How are we to interpret the meaning of 'low acquittal rates' – as this relates to confidence in the earlier stages of the criminal process? How do *they* do so (and who are 'they')? Words such as corruption and abuse are used both internationally and locally, but not necessarily in ways that are shared by all insiders. Do these terms 'travel well' – or are they too emotively evaluative?[46] We are told that the category of hate crime is inapplicable to former Soviet Russia because sexual minorities there are not included as subjects of protection. But, apart from variation over this point among Western jurisdictions, this argument treats the idea of hate crime as an ontologically universal rather than as a folk product of the West.

How far can we compare levels of 'repression' cross-culturally and over time?[47] One of the boldest suggestions in this special issue is of an inverse relation between police repression (defined as attacking regime opponents), on the one hand, and police abuse (defined as violation of citizen rights for police benefit) on the other. Support

---

[45] This issue often receives too little attention – a pseudo-scienticity prevails. As Vincenzo Ruggiero has pointed out, is there really an ontological difference between 'white-collar' and 'organised crime' or does this mainly reflect the (USA-shaped) ethnic stereotypes behind organised crime? (Vincenzo Ruggiero, *Organized and Corporate Crime in Europe: Offers That Can't Be Refused* (Farnham, Dartmouth Publishing, 1996)).

[46] William Twining, 'Have Concepts, Will Travel: Analytical Jurisprudence in a Global Context' (2005) 1(1) *International Journal of Law in Context* 5.

[47] When I visited Moscow in 1985, in the dying years of communism, I accompanied an arrested dissident to the police station, and was relieved when he was released quickly under the requirements of procedural law. When I returned to Saint Petersburg in 2011 to give some lectures I witnessed the violent breaking up of monthly protests organised for the right to protest – choosing the last day of the month so as to coincide with the relevant (but disregarded) Art 31 of the constitution.

for this comes from the counterintuitive finding that most Chinese citizens feel safe from their police, whereas most people in Brazil are convinced that police stations are places where abuse takes place. But much depends on who is thought likely to be punished (and therefore ends up in the police station). Do repressive regimes (always) require legitimacy from the public? From which publics? Are soft and more brutal types of repression on a continuum or different routes to the same end? Even the authors tell us that, in the Russian situation, 'repression and abuse are blurred'.

6. REFORMING

Many of the contributions combine explanatory and evaluative enquiries – as when seeking both to understand and to criticise mistreatment of vulnerable prisoners or ethnic minorities, or asking whether countries have made a 'successful' transition from communism.[48] From the perspective of the scholars represented in the collection (who also include scholars coming from the countries concerned), the working of criminal justice in much of the former Soviet region is assumed to fall well below acceptable standards and to be in need of wholesale reform. The problem is not just how to get police to respect the accused's rights even whilst achieving 'crime control', but how to avoid them crushing political opponents and preying on the population. The question is not how to reduce prison populations, but whether ways can be found to unwind the role of prison as part of the capillary network of political social control. The challenge is not merely overcoming racial bias in the judiciary but how to end its compliant subservience to prosecutors' *faits accomplis*. The message we are left with is that such concerns do not merely reflect the selective diet of news fed to us by Western media (in which the use of criminal law for political ends features so prominently); they are warranted by well-documented analyses from careful observers.

But, as the editors of the special issue rightly point out, comparative criminology is also supposed to increase reflexivity about different approaches to crime. Does such a uniformly critical stance help overcome or only reinforce what the editors call a 'geographically biased' perspective and the attendant risk of ethnocentrism? It would not be difficult to point to the many defects of Western criminal justice, above all in the case of the United States with its massive prison numbers, continuing use of capital punishment and racially skewed law enforcement. Should those who argue for the greater protection of individual rights offered by the accusatorial system, as compared to the (hybrid) inquisitorial alternatives, not also acknowledge that, in societies that (increasingly) produce economic and social inequity, this kind of process has also led to increasing numbers of people in prison? Doubts could also be raised about the success of the model of multicultural integration that stands behind hate crime but is looking politically increasing shaky. Western states too are guilty of political malfeasance – both at home and abroad (not least in the fight against terrorism or

---

[48] The contributors do not discuss whether a different kind or level of rule of law could be consistent with – and even justified by – a given stage of transition. China is sometimes described as having moved some way from autocracy without a concomitant rise in rule of law. The example of Singapore, on the other hand, is often used to raise the question of whether the rule of law presupposes democracy.

the exaggerations of data surveillance) and Western businesses and international organisations benefit from impunity for their serious violations of human rights.[49]

The issue of perspective is side-stepped when scholars consider themselves as primarily engaging in a (positivist) explanatory search for causal factors that produce given outcomes (an approach that rests on 'a view from nowhere'?) Alternatively, more prescriptive analyses of political corruption or judicial impartiality are written as if they merely endorse global and modern standards – 'a view from everywhere'? More tellingly, the contributors point out that many actors within the societies concerned have in fact signed on to European ideals of criminal justice, as shown by the decision to join the European Council or the Convention on Human Rights. European-style requirements are already part of their systems, with some real success stories such as the case of Estonia. In any case, transplanting what are perceived to be best practices from elsewhere is common across all jurisdictions, even if too often this is done without taking the 'law in action' fully into account.

But facing up to 'the politics of comparison' is important, especially in a period that sees the resurgence of something like a cold war (and sometimes more) between much of the West and Putin's Russia, involving some of the countries being discussed here. Although some contributors to the special issue recognise that 'penal reform is contested in this part of the world', we learn little about whether there could ever be *good* grounds for contestation. Both scholars (and activists) would find it useful to know more about the various stands taken by political and economic groups, as well as the elusive question of what the public really wants (not just what it should want). Speaking of 'long-standing legal nihilism' in Russia may be too glib an explanation, and more needs to be appreciated about continuing public attachment to highly formalist rule systems accompanied by active recourse to informal channels. 'Civilisational nationalism' or the 'Russian special path' may indeed be potent politically manipulated myths. But it would be 'Orientalist' to assume that aspirations for democracy and human rights (and systems of criminal justice that embrace these) are only found in the West. At the same time care needs to be taken lest unmitigated criticism of criminal justice arrangements in this part of the world are seen as no more than an effort 'to slander the past, exploit the present, and tout the future'.[50]

[49] Dawn Rothe and David Friedrichs, *Crimes of Globalization* (Abindgon, Routledge, 2014).
[50] Joseph Roth, *The Collected Stories of Joseph Roth* [1935], trans and ed Michael Hoffmann) (New York, WW Norton, 2002).

Part 3

International Criminal Justice

10

Victors' Justice? Selecting Targets for Prosecution

WILLIAM SCHABAS

IN HIS OPENING address at the Nuremberg trials, the US Prosecutor Robert Jackson said: 'That four great nations, flushed with victory and stung with injury stay the hand of vengeance and voluntarily submit their captive enemies to the judgment of the law is one of the most significant tributes that Power has ever paid to Reason.'[1] Jackson's colleague on the US Supreme Court, Harlan Fiske Stone, was less enthusiastic. He called the International Military Tribunal a 'high grade lynching party'.[2] Nuremberg has its enthusiasts, including the present author, but it also has its detractors. One of the most persistent charges is that the Nuremberg trials constituted 'victors' justice'. Far from 'stay the hand of vengeance', say critics, the Nuremberg trials were a vindictive exercise with little resemblance to a fair trial.

The victors' justice complaint can actually be divided into three somewhat distinct issues. The first concerns the legal norms being applied, particularly the crimes of which the Nazis were accused. Although war crimes had some pedigree, the other two categories, crimes against humanity and crimes against peace, were being prosecuted for the first time. This opened up the allegation that the trials amounted to ex post facto justice. The second issue concerns the overall fairness of the proceedings. There is a lingering sense that due process rights generally recognised as minimum guarantees were not fully respected. A very early ruling of the International Criminal Tribunal for the former Yugoslavia said that in devising their Rules of Procedure and Evidence, 'the Judges were conscious of the need to avoid some of the flaws noted in the Nuremberg and Tokyo proceedings'.[3] But this is like modern-day architects criticising the Parthenon because it doesn't have ramps for the disabled and proper emergency exits. It is wrong to assess trials in 1945 and 1946 by human rights standards that prevail five or six decades later. On balance, the proceedings certainly met the standards of the time.

---

[1] (1947) 2 IMT 99.

[2] Jeffrey D Hockett, 'Justice Robert H Jackson, the Supreme Court, and the Nuremberg Trial' (1990) 8 *Supreme Court Review* 257, 258.

[3] *Tadić* (IT-94-1-T), Decision on the Prosecutor's Motion Requesting Protective Measures for Victims and Witnesses, 10 August 1995, para 21.

The third issue concerns the selectivity of the Tribunal. It was directed at Nazi perpetrators alone, despite the fact that there was much evidence that some of the crimes over which the Tribunal exercised jurisdiction had also been perpetrated by those who had established the institution. War crimes and other atrocities perpetrated by the victors, ranging from the Katyń massacre to the dreadful bombings of cities in Germany and Japan, including the nuclear destruction of Hiroshima and Nagasaki, and the more quotidian breaches of international law associated with brutal armed combat such as murdering prisoners or the issuance of orders not to take them, were not addressed as part of postwar accountability and they remain unpunished to this day. At the Tokyo Tribunal the Indian judge, Radhabinod Pal, openly challenged the one-sided nature of the proceedings in his lengthy dissenting opinion. For Judge Pal, the European allies in the Pacific conflict were just as egregious as the Japanese. He voted to acquit.[4]

At Nuremberg, the judges were not immune to these concerns. For example, answering charges that two German admirals, Dönitz and Raeder, had ordered that unrestricted submarine warfare be conducted, defence lawyers produced evidence that the American admiral in the Pacific theatre had ordered the same thing, and that similar instructions had been given by the British Admiralty. What amounted to indiscriminate attacks on merchant ships was a violation of the Washington Naval Protocol of 1936. The Nuremberg judgment treated it as a war crime. But in light of the evidence that the Allies had done the same thing, the judges refused to impose a sentence upon the Nazi admirals for this particular crime. It is often reported that the Nazi admirals were acquitted on the submarine warfare count.[5] Careful reading of the judgment of the International Miltiary Tribunal suggests this is not the case. After noting an order of the British Admiralty to sink all vessels at night combined with testimony by US Admiral Nimitz stating that the United States conducted unrestricted submarine warfare, the judgment said the 'the sentence of Dönitz is not assessed on the ground of his breaches of the international law of submarine warfare'.[6] In other words, Dönitz had indeed violated international law but this would not aggravate his sentence given the conduct of the navies of Britain and the United States.

There can be little doubt that when the Nuremberg Charter was being crafted, the four powers (the United Kingdom, France, the United States and the Soviet Union) understood that they were establishing an international legal regime that would, in the future, apply to themselves as well. 'If certain acts and violations of treaties are crimes, they are crimes whether the United States does them or whether Germany does them. We are not prepared to lay down a rule of criminal conduct against others which we would not be willing to have invoked against us', said Robert Jackson, the US Prosecutor. For this reason, the founders of the Nuremberg Tribunal carefully limited the scope of crimes against humanity to acts associated with aggressive war. This is the so-called nexus by which peacetime acts were not subject to prosecution as

---

[4] Neil Boister and Robert Cryer (eds), *Documents on the Tokyo International Military Tribunal* (Oxford, Oxford University Press, 2008) 811–930.

[5] eg David Luban, 'The Legacies of Nuremberg' in Guénaël Mettraux (ed), *Perspectives on the Nuremberg Trial* (Oxford, Oxford University Press, 2008) 638–72, 660.

[6] *Göring et al v France et al*, (1947) 1 IMT 171, 313; also, with respect to Raeder, 317.

crimes against humanity. It was a careful, cynical choice intended to insulate the four 'great powers' from criminal liability for the racist, colonialist and repressive policies of their own regimes. But the orientation of the Court was also ensured by other more structural measures.

The jurisdiction of the Nuremberg trials was defined in such a way to make prosecution of any military or political leaders of the Allies a legal impossibility. Article 1 of the Charter of the International Military Tribunal confirmed that the institution's mandate was 'the just and prompt trial and punishment of the major war criminals of the European Axis'. The wording of the Charter of the Tokyo Tribunal was slightly different, referring to 'the major war criminals in the Far East' but without specifying which side they were on. In any event, those who created the two tribunals could also count on the cooperation of the prosecutors, who were their employees. Not only did they appoint them, they could also dismiss them. There seemed to be no particular unease with the idea that the prosecutors would consult with the governments that named them about important decisions during the trial. For added certainty, the Americans named General William J. Donovan as Deputy Prosecutor. Donovan was then the head of the Office of Strategic Services, the principal US intelligence agency and forerunner of the Central Intelligence Agency. One of the reasons he was there was to ensure that indictments were not issued against senior Nazis with whom the Americans had made deals in the final months of the war. The Soviets had a Special Government Commission for Directing the Nuremberg Trials, chaired by Andrey Vyshinsky. It gave instructions to their Prosecutor on matters such as the handling of the Katyń forest massacre issue.[7] It seems likely that the British and French prosecutors received political instructions as well. The extent to which the four Nuremberg prosecutors were controlled by the governments for whom they worked is not fully known. It makes a fascinating subject for future archival research by legal historians.[8]

When the modern generation of international criminal tribunals was established in the 1990s, it was often said that the alleged distortion in prosecutorial policy by which only one side would be brought to justice, believed to be an unavoidable consequence of political involvement in the international judicial process, was being addressed and corrected. The International Criminal Tribunal for the former Yugoslavia, created in May 1993, was held out as a progressive development over Nuremberg because it was spawned by the Security Council, acting in the name of the 'international community', rather than by one or more of the victors? At the time, in any event, there were no victors in the Balkan wars.

There were certainly important structural improvements. The Statutes of the ad hoc Tribunals contain provisions specifying that the Prosecutor is to act independently, and is to take instructions from no government. The Statutes vary slightly in mode of appointment. Prosecutors are elected by the UN Security Council or appointed by the Secretary-General to a three- or four-year term. Nothing indicates

---

[7] For some of the documents, see Anne M Cienciala, Natalia S Lebedeva and Wojciech Materski (eds), *Katyn, A Crime without Punishment* (New Haven, CT and London, Yale University Press, 2007) 326–29.

[8] William A. Schabas, 'The Katyn Forest Massacre and the Nuremberg Trial' in Morten Bergsmo, Cheah Wui Ling, Song Tianying and Yi Ping (eds), *Historical Origins of International Criminal Law*, vol 3 (Brussels, Torkel Opsahl Academic Publishers, 2015) 249–97.

the grounds for which the Prosecutor is subject to dismissal, perhaps only an oversight but more likely a discrete message that in fact he or she may be removed at any time at the pleasure of the Security Council or the Secretary-General. The method of appointment of the judges is also an improvement on Nuremberg and Tokyo. At the Yugoslavia and Rwanda tribunals they are elected from a list proposed by the Security Council. The actual process is not pretty, with much political horse-trading among Member States that is not always properly focused on the competence and integrity of the candidates. Nevertheless there is an acceptable degree of transparency, something that was lacking in the 1940s when the judges were simply appointed by the four powers that established the Tribunal.

An early decision of the Yugoslavia Tribunal stated that:

> The Nuremberg and Tokyo trials have been characterized as 'victor's justice' because only the vanquished were charged with violations of international humanitarian law and the defendants were prosecuted and punished for crimes expressly defined in an instrument adopted by the victors at the conclusion of the war. Therefore, the International Tribunal is distinct from its closest precedents.[9]

This was true, but only up to a point. As at Nuremberg, the jurisdiction of the ad hoc Tribunal was carefully delineated by those who had created it. The Tribunal could only prosecute serious international crimes 'committed on the territory of the former Yugoslavia since 1991'. The jurisdiction of the other three ad hoc tribunals, for Rwanda, Sierra Leone and Lebanon, is limited in a similar manner. It may be worth recalling that those who effectively control the establishment of the UN tribunals, namely the permanent members of the Security Council, are essentially the same countries (with the addition of China) that set up the Nuremberg court. In 1945 they were called the 'great powers', whereas today they are the 'permanent five'. Same product, different packaging. In 1945 they claimed to act on behalf of 'civilized nations'; today, they prefer a more modern and politically palatable term, the 'international community'. The essence remains largely equivalent. Targets for prosecution are chosen on the basis of a number of complex political calculations, premised as much on strategic national interests as on an abstract fidelity to principles of justice. To be sure, any one of the five can always veto the establishment of an international justice mechanism that comes too close to home. For this reason, criminal tribunals for Israel or Myanmar, for example, have never been seriously entertained.

1. TAKING SIDES AT THE AD HOC TRIBUNALS

When the International Criminal Tribunal for the former Yugoslavia was created, in 1993, significant military intervention by armies of the major powers was not contemplated. To some US senators, it came as a surprise that the 1999 Kosovo bombing undertaken by NATO forces, mainly by US bombers, was technically within the jurisdiction of the court. These were acts perpetrated on the territory of the former

---

[9] *Tadić* (IT-94-1-T), Decision on the Prosecutor's Motion Requesting Protective Measures for Victims and Witnesses, 10 August 1995, para 21.

Yugoslavia since 1991 and therefore were comprised within the Tribunal's jurisdictional framework set out in Article 1 of the Statute. Responding to pressure from civil society organisations, Prosecutor Carla Del Ponte opened an investigation and, unusually, published a report of the findings. Her office concluded that acts attributed to the NATO forces were not sufficiently prohibited by international law as to provide a reliable basis for launching a formal prosecution. The explanation was unconvincing, mainly because the Prosecutor's report only responded to specific allegations and did not, on its own initiative, propose that further investigations be carried out. Privately, many at the Tribunal said the Prosecutor had little choice because the Security Council would have shut down the entire operation if even serious consideration was given to prosecuting Americans, or other NATO nationals. In the Security Council, the permanent representative of Russia, Sergei Lavrov, complained:

> When it comes to reports of violations committed by the Federal Republic of Yugoslavia, the Tribunal immediately issues indictments and gets down to work, as, for example, in the case of the situation in Kosovo. However, if questions arise – for instance, concerning the actions of the North Atlantic Treaty Organization (NATO) – the Tribunal, even in the face of such obvious facts as the deaths of innocent civilians, the destruction by air strike of civilian targets, finds no grounds for launching an investigation. We are appalled by the Tribunal's failure to act in response to ongoing ethnic cleansing against Serbs and other national minorities in Kosovo.[10]

To be sure, in theory the ad hoc Tribunals have been authorised to prosecute all of the warring parties in the various conflicts, perhaps with the exception of Lebanon, where the remit is narrowest. The Special Tribunal for Lebanon is only authorised to deal with a handful of discrete incidents relating to a political assassination, one that figures as a small piece in a far greater and much protracted conflict. The International Criminal Tribunal for the former Yugoslavia held trials of Croats, Bosniacs, and Kosovars, as well as the Serbs against whom it was largely focused, albeit unofficially. Nobody was happy. The Serbs complained that they were bearing the brunt of the prosecutions, while the others grumbled that they were victims of a misguided attempt to make the institution look balanced. The Special Court for Sierra Leone probably manifests the best effort at addressing atrocities committed on all sides. Rather than reflecting a different philosophical perspective, its attempt to address perpetrators from the various combatant factions may well have been due to the difficulty in distinguishing the conduct of various participants. It was easy to be even-handed in Sierra Leone because all parties to the conflict behaved so badly.

The problem has presented itself most acutely at the International Criminal Tribunal for Rwanda. The Statute of the Tribunal, and the documents associated with its establishment, make clear that its purpose is to address the genocide of 1994, rather than the panoply of atrocity crimes perpetrated in Rwanda and in the subregion both before and after that tragic three-month period. In 1999 a judge of the Tribunal refused to confirm a genocide charge against an accused who had murdered the prime minister and several Belgian soldiers. He would only authorise counts of war crimes and crimes against humanity. The Prosecutor, Louise Arbour, chose to withdraw the

---

[10] UN Doc S/PV.4161, paras 7–8.

case. It seemed that she considered prosecuting charges other than genocide was a distraction from the Tribunal's mission. Her application to withdraw stated that:

> [T]he judicial proceedings instituted by the Prosecutor should be within the framework of a global policy aimed at shedding light on the events that occurred in Rwanda in 1994 and highlighting the complete landscape of the criminal acts perpetrated at the time, and that such objective would not be achieved through the prosecution of a single count indictment the factual elements of which relate solely to the murders of the former Prime Minister and ten UNAMIR Belgian soldiers.[11]

Later, the Prosecutor agreed to accept a few plea bargains whereby genocide charges were dropped in exchange for an acknowledgement of responsibility for crimes against humanity. But this was really an expedient enabling some quick convictions to be registered, freeing up the resources of the Office of the Prosecutor for other cases.

For many years, the Prosecutor of the International Criminal Tribunal for Rwanda was urged to deal with the 'flip-side' crimes perpetrated by the largely Tutsi forces who vanquished the *génocidaires* and who have held power in Kigali since 1994. There is much evidence to suggest their responsibility for serious international crimes, although not for genocide. Prosecutor Carla Del Ponte, who held office from 1999 to 2003, was keen on pursuing this, but her successor, Hassan Jallow, showed much less interest. Critics charge that his reluctance manifests a complacent relationship with the current Rwandan authorities, with whom cooperation is essential for the Tribunal to conduct its activities. But it may well reflect a genuine and sincere belief that the mission of the Tribunal is to address the 1994 genocide. Moreover, Prosecutor Jallow may feel that the pressure to prosecute the Tutsi military leaders is itself driven by a political constituency rather than some well-meant and altruistic vision of a court that deals with all sides in a conflict. He has been harshly criticised, notably by the NGO Human Rights Watch, on this account. In a letter from the organisation to Prosecutor Jallow, Human Rights Watch said: 'It would be a failure of justice – not merely victor's justice – if you do not vigorously investigate and prosecute senior RPF officials because they are currently senior officials or military leaders in Rwanda.' Moreover, '[f]ailure to do so will taint perceptions of the Tribunal's impartiality and undermine its legitimacy for years to come'.[12]

Over the years, advocates for one conflict or another have come to the United Nations and argued: 'You set up a tribunal for Yugoslavia and Rwanda, why don't you do it for our conflict?' The answer was rarely more than a diplomatic shrug of the shoulders. There was no rhyme or reason to the intervention of the Security Council. It operated when there was consensus among its permanent members. That meant, in particular, that it was inactive when the strategic interests of a permanent member or, for that matter, the behaviour of the permanent member itself, were threatened in some way. The Special Tribunal for Lebanon provides a striking example here.

---

[11] *Ntuyahaga* (ICTR-98-40-T), Decision on the Prosecutor's Motion to Withdraw the Indictment, 18 March 1999.

[12] 'Kenneth Roth to Hassan Jallow', 14 August 2009. See also: Human Rights Watch, 'Rwanda: Tribunal Risks Supporting "Victor's Justice": Tribunal Should Vigorously Pursue Crimes of Rwandan Patriotic Front', 1 June 2009.

The Security Council directed the establishment of an international court to prosecute the assassins of Rafiq Hariri, a former prime minister of the country and friend of presidents Bush and Chirac, but did nothing the following year when brutal armed conflict between Israel and Hezbollah devastated much of the country. In 1990, the United States and the United Kingdom launched an initiative to establish a tribunal aimed at Saddam Hussein for the invasion of Kuwait. But nobody seriously entertained the idea of a Security Council-created tribunal when the United States and the United Kingdom invaded Iraq in 2003, contrary to the very prohibition of aggression that they had invoked against the Iraqi president thirteen years earlier. When the permanent members feel threatened, the best hope of international justice still remains an unofficial initiative like the toothless 'tribunal' set up in the late 1960s by two of the world's great philosophers, Bertrand Russell and Jean-Paul Sartre, to deal with US atrocities in Vietnam.

2. SELECTING 'SITUATIONS' AT THE INTERNATIONAL CRIMINAL COURT

The International Criminal Court is not created by the Security Council and is, to some extent, immunised against control by the five permanent members. It is a treaty-based institution governed by its States Parties, all of whom are equal in principle. The most important manifestation of this independence from the Security Council is the so-called *proprio motu* Prosecutor. In contrast with all of the predecessors, the Prosecutor of the International Criminal Court has the authority to designate what are called 'situations'. A situation is distinct from a 'case', the term used to describe the stage in the proceedings when an individual defendant has been identified. At the earlier tribunals, the 'situation' was really the definition of the institution's jurisdiction. World War II, the conflicts associated with the break-up of Yugoslavia, the Rwandan genocide, terrorism in Lebanon and the civil war in Sierra Leone are all 'situations'. The prosecutors of these ad hoc institutions were generally free to select individual accused persons or 'cases' as long as they remained within the 'situation'. But they could not stray outside this perimeter. Any attempt to do so would have resulted in dismissal of a case by the judges on jurisdictional grounds. Besides, such a 'runaway prosecutor' would quickly have been replaced with one prepared to respect the terms of his or her engagement.

The Rome Statute of the International Criminal Court contemplates three ways of identifying a situation for prosecution. The first two are broadly similar to what has prevailed in previous models of international justice: referral by a State Party or by the Security Council. But the Prosecutor of the International Criminal Court is also empowered to designate a 'situation' even when States Parties and the Security Council are silent. To date, the two Prosecutors of the International Criminal Court have been rather deferential to States and to the Security Council. With respect to State Party referrals pursuant to Article 14 of the Rome Statute, this is explained in large part by the fact that the Prosecutor had actually encouraged the State to apply to the Court. Only in one case has the Prosecutor declined to proceed. In the *Gaza Flotilla situation*, submitted by Comoros, she invoked 'insufficient gravity' as a justification. The State Party appealed her ruling to the Pre-Trial Chamber in accordance with Article 53. The judges granted the application but, in accordance with the Statute, could do no more than ask the Prosecutor to 'reconsider' before making a final decision.[13]

Similarly, the Prosecutor has not questioned the validity of the two Security Council referrals adopted pursuant to Article 13(b), although the resolutions included clauses that are incompatible with the Statute.[14] Nevertheless, as the Prosecutor demonstrated in the *Gaza Flotilla situation*, even when a State Party or the Security Council refers a situation, she has the power to refuse to proceed. After years of persistent complaints about its failure to assist in implementing the Court's arrest warrants directed against Sudanese officials, including the president, in December 2014 the Prosecutor told the Security Council that she was

> left with no choice but to put investigative activities in Darfur on hold as I shift resources to other urgent cases, especially those where trial is approaching. It should thus be clear to the Council that unless there is a change of attitude and approach to Darfur in the near future, there will continue to be little or nothing to report to it for the foreseeable future.[15]

There is little that the State Party or the Security Council can do, given the relatively tame authority of the Pre-Trial Chamber to request reconsideration. Only if the Prosecutor bases her decision on the 'interests of justice' is the authority of the Pre-Trial Chamber more robust. But the Prosecutor takes long enough to deal with cases even when she is enthusiastic. When she is not, the wheels of justice are likely to turn very slowly.

The Prosecutor's power to proceed is limited only by the jurisdictional provisions of the Statute, which confine the Court's scope to the territory of States Parties and to their nationals, and to acts perpetrated subsequent to 1 July 2002 when the Statute entered into force. Thus, the Prosecutor has the authority to investigate and prosecute war crimes attributable to British troops in Iraq, because Britain is a State Party to the Rome Statute. He or she may also proceed with respect to war crimes committed by US troops in Afghanistan, which is a State Party to the Rome Statute. She has reported on 'preliminary examinations' concerning British forces in Iraq and US forces in Afghanistan without any apparent objection based upon jurisdiction. But the Prosecutor cannot initiate investigations of Sri Lankan generals in relation to the destruction of the Tamil Tigers in 2009 because Sri Lanka has not joined the Court. Exceptionally, the Prosecutor can also act where a State that has not joined the Court but has acknowledged its jurisdiction in accordance with Article 12(3) of the Statute.

If the independent Prosecutor of the International Criminal Court is not subject to the political whims of the five permanent members of the Security Council, or the States that created the Court, on what does she base decisions about the selection of 'situations' and the refusal to proceed upon 'complaints' from States Parties or the Security Council? One view might be that the Prosecutor should investigate and

---

[13] *Situation on Registered Vessels of the Comoros, the Hellenic Republic of Greece and the Kingdom of Cambodia* (ICC-01/13), Decision on the request of the Union of the Comoros to review the Prosecutor's decision not to initiate an investigation, 16 July 2015.

[14] UN Doc S/RES/1593 (2005); UN Doc S/RES/1970 (2011).

[15] UN Doc S/PV.7337, 2.

prosecute *all* situations in which crimes subject to the jurisdiction of the Court have been perpetrated where national justice systems have failed to act effectively. This would certainly be the logic of a victim-oriented approach. Why should one victim of a crime against humanity be less or more entitled to international justice than another? Some observers have seriously entertained such an interpretation, pointing to the requirement, in Article 15(3) of the Rome Statute, that the Prosecutor 'shall' proceed with an investigation if, acting upon a complaint, he or she determines that there is a reasonable basis a crime within the jurisdiction of the Court has been committed.

In a national justice system, this would assuredly be the expectation. Thinking in this respect is often coloured by analogies with domestic courts, where the idea of a politicised prosecutor is quite repulsive. At the national level in a functional justice system displaying the attributes of the rule of law all serious crimes against the person will be prosecuted. Case law of international human rights tribunals has established this as an entitlement of victims that flows from treaty norms.[16] Yet a mechanistic extrapolation based upon the model of national prosecution to the context of international criminal tribunals is fundamentally defective because there can be no serious prospect that all perpetrators of serious international crimes will be brought to justice by such institutions. The tribunals, and their budgets, were never conceived to deal with *all* crimes within their jurisdiction. By nature, they are selective.

Indeed, this selectivity also manifests itself at the national level when international crimes are concerned. States may recognise an obligation to prosecute the totality of serious crimes against the person, including war crimes and other international crimes, but only to the extent that they are perpetrated on their territory. They show no inclination to extrapolate this general principle when such crimes are committed elsewhere, even if the suspect is within their grasp. Under universal jurisdiction, where an international crime is concerned States are free to prosecute perpetrators in their custody despite the fact that the act was committed abroad. But in practice, they rarely do this. Prosecutions under universal jurisdiction generally focus on crimes committed in areas where the State has historically had national interests, often in its former colonies. Furthermore, States that actually exercise universal jurisdiction often require a form of internal political authorisation before a prosecution may be undertaken for such crimes. They do not generally entrust to an independent prosecutor the decision about whom to prosecute for international crimes committed outside their own territory.

3. THE LAW OF GRAVITY

Since the Rome Statute entered into force in July 2002, the International Criminal Court has been in a position to exercise jurisdiction over many tens of thousands of cases. Yet after more than a decade of activity, it has only actually proceeded with trials against a small number of individuals, all of them nationals of a handful of

---

[16] eg *MC v Bulgaria*, no 39272/98, Judgment, 4 December 2003, paras 102–07.

States in central Africa. Partly, this is a resource issue. With an annual budget of about €140 million, the number of major trials that the Court can undertake is seriously constrained. Perhaps the International Criminal Court has underperformed by comparison with the other international criminal tribunals. But even the most efficient and expeditious of them, the International Military Tribunal at Nuremberg, only managed to judge twenty-two individuals in a trial that lasted nearly a year. International justice, and especially the International Criminal Court, can only aspire to deal with a handful of the crimes that are committed. Choices must be made. But on what basis?

The Rome Statute provides little if any guidance here. Probably it would have been impossible for the Diplomatic Conference to reach agreement on the criteria to be employed. A subsequent instrument, the Rules of Procedure and Evidence, which was negotiated by the States Parties, did nothing to fill the void. Even before Luis Moreno-Ocampo took office as first Prosecutor of the International Criminal Court, lawyers in his Office had prepared draft Regulations that attempted to codify the process by which 'situations' would be selected among the many deserving possibilities. These draft regulations naïvely approached the matter of selection of situations in a manner that suggested the Prosecutor would proceed with everything that was admissible. There was to be a complex procedure, involving 'evaluation teams' and a 'draft investigation plan', leading to a decision by the Prosecutor. Nevertheless, nothing indicated the grounds on which the Prosecutor would make the determination. There was an intriguing reference to his or her 'inherent powers'. But the Prosecutor did not adopt the draft. Years later, he proclaimed a new and much streamlined version of the Regulations that vaguely referred to the 'seriousness of the information', 'jurisdiction, admissibility (including gravity), as well as the interests of justice'. These were the factors to be assessed in identifying the 'situations' that the Prosecutor would target. The Regulations said that in assessing gravity, 'various factors including their scale, nature, manner of commission, and impact' were to be taken into account.[17] They might just as well have said, like the US judge who was famously asked to define pornography: 'The Prosecutor, in his wisdom, will know an appropriate situation when he sees it.' Since adopting the Regulations, the Prosecutor has produced 'policy papers' to explain the way her discretion is exercised.[18] These cliché-ridden documents do nothing to clarify things. Above all, they obscure the discretionary nature of the exercise and suggest that the choices of targets for prosecution is devoid of subjectivity.

The word 'gravity' was used only once in the 2003 draft regulations. Presumably at the time, nobody in the Office of the Prosecutor thought that the concept of 'gravity' was very significant in the selection of situations or of cases. The term 'gravity', which appears in the Statute in two places relevant to the selection of cases and situations, did not figure in any significant manner in the early pronouncements of the Office of the Prosecutor. Up to that time, academic writers on the Rome Statute had

[17] Regulations of the Office of the Prosecutor, ICC-BD/05-01-09, Regulation 29.
[18] Office of the Prosecutor, Policy Paper on Preliminary Examinations, 1 November 2013; Office of the Prosecutor, Draft Policy Paper on Case Selection and Prioritisation, 29 February 2016.

generally failed to view the concept of 'gravity' as being particularly relevant to the exercise of prosecutorial discretion. The two major Commentaries published in the years following adoption of the Rome Statute virtually ignored the concept.

That changed in late 2005. The Prosecutor invoked the gravity criterion to explain his decision to proceed against the leaders of the Lord's Resistance Army in Uganda rather than against those of the government forces. When the first arrest warrants were issued by the Court, the Prosecutor found himself criticised by human rights NGOs, notably Human Rights Watch and Amnesty International, for only charging suspects on one side of the Ugandan civil war. In reply, the Prosecutor referred to 'gravity' and said that the Lord's Resistance Army had killed many more people than the soldiers of the Ugandan People's Defence Forces. In this context, he seemed to be talking about the selection of cases, rather than of situations. Or was he saying that the 'situation' of the Lord's Resistance Army was more serious than the 'situation' of the Ugandan People's Defence Forces, in effect relating the 'situation' to the identification of opposing combatant groups in a civil war? It was not really clear.

Within a few months the Prosecutor used the same gravity argument to resist entreaties that he investigate the conduct of British troops in Iraq. Probably many of the complainants felt strongly that the war was unlawful. They would not have understood or appreciated the distinction between the legality of the initiation of the war (*jus ad bellum*) and the conduct within it (*jus in bello*). At the time, the Court could not prosecute the crime of aggression. But there was no shortage of evidence that British soldiers had been engaged in various atrocities, including murder of civilians, and these were war crimes in the classic sense. Because the United Kingdom was a State Party to the Rome Statute, the Court had jurisdiction over war crimes perpetrated by British nationals. Furthermore, the allies of the United Kingdom, the Americans, were also suspected of important violations. However, neither the United States nor Iraq were States Parties to the Rome Statute. The Prosecutor could not investigate or proceed with charges against Americans for acts perpetrated on the territory of a non-party State. Some complaints suggested that the British could also be prosecuted as accomplices for war crimes committed by the Americans because they were part of a joint criminal enterprise.

In February 2006 the Prosecutor announced his decision not to proceed with an investigation into war crimes committed in Iraq by nationals of States Parties to the Rome Statute. He acknowledged that there was a reasonable basis to believe that crimes within the jurisdiction of the Court had been perpetrated. The Prosecutor referred to evidence that there had been four to twelve victims of wilful killing and a limited number of victims of inhuman treatment, totalling in all less than twenty persons. The sum of these violations, he reasoned, was 'of a different order' than the number of victims in other situations being investigated or analysed by the Office of the Prosecutor, notably Northern Uganda, the Democratic Republic of the Congo, and Darfur. He said each of the latter situations involved thousands of wilful killings as well as intentional and large-scale sexual violence and abductions. The explanation was unconvincing, because any reasonable observer knows that since the invasion by the United Kingdom and the United States in 2003, and largely as a consequence, Iraq has been the scene of massive human rights violations. At a minimum tens of thousands of innocent civilians have been killed and perhaps millions have been displaced.

By setting specific acts attributable to British troops of which he had evidence, rather than the war as a whole, alongside general reports of victimisation in other conflicts in central Africa, the Prosecutor was comparing apples and oranges. Or rather, he was comparing cases to situations.

The fallacy of the comparison between Iraq and central Africa became clear within a matter of days, when Moreno-Ocampo announced the arrest of the Court's first prisoner, Thomas Lubanga. A Congolese warlord, Lubanga was not charged with the massive murders, abductions and sexual violence that the Prosecutor had cited in his comparison with the British conduct in Iraq. Lubanga was accused only of the recruitment of child soldiers within the context of a civil war. Was that more serious than the murder and ill-treatment of civilians by British soldiers engaged in a war of aggression? Lubanga was eventually convicted and sentenced to a fourteen-year term of imprisonment, something that was itself an interesting indicator of the modest degree of gravity of the crimes he committed.

Many suspected that Moreno-Ocampo was actually trying to steer clear of a confrontation with one or two major powers. Sometimes, people around the Court would mutter such excuses under their breath, as if it was an embarrassing secret. Perhaps they hadn't suspected that much of the world is familiar with the double-standards by which the South is judged differently than the North. All that the Prosecutor's decision did was confirm suspicions that the Court was not the politically neutral body its proponents had bragged about. In addition to being an influential member of the Court, the United Kingdom is also a permanent member of the Security Council. In contrast, Uganda and the Democratic Republic of the Congo were soft targets for the Court's activities. And they were compliant ones, in a sense, to the extent that the Prosecutor appeared to be interested only in rebel groups rather than government forces.

The contrived reasoning about gravity also kept the Prosecutor sweet with the Americans, who would not have been keen on prosecutions relating to the behaviour of their principal military ally in the Iraq invasion. Indeed, it was about this time that the United States began to warm to the International Criminal Court. Years later, the Wikileaks website published a revealing confidential document, written in July 2003, from a US diplomat assessing the Prosecutor's attitude towards Iraq. 'Ocampo has said that he was looking at the actions of British forces in Iraq – which … led a British ICTY prosecutor nearly to fall off his chair', said the dispatch. 'Privately, Ocampo has said that he wishes to dispose of Iraq issues (ie Not to investigate them.)'[19]

The *proprio motu* authority to launch investigations on the Prosecutor's own initiative was held out as the crown jewel in the Rome Statute. It was this power that distinguished the Court from its predecessors, and promised to shelter it from the stigma of 'victors' justice'. Surprisingly, then, the Prosecutor did not in fact select a situation in the formal sense of exercising his own authority pursuant to Article 15 of the Statute until late 2009, more than six years after taking office. He applied to the Pre-Trial Chamber for authorisation to open an investigation into the post-electoral

[19] Afua Hirsch, 'WikiLeaks Cables Lay Bare US Hostility to International Criminal Court', *The Guardian*, 17 December 2010.

violence in Kenya. By then, there were four active situations, in Northern Uganda, the Democratic Republic of the Congo, the Central African Republic and the Sudanese province of Darfur. The first three had been referred to the Court by States Parties in accordance with Article 14. The fourth resulted from a Security Council resolution, pursuant to Article 13(b) of the Rome Statute. In other words, the initial situations before the Court largely resembled the Nuremberg approach and that of the ad hoc tribunals, in that they had been designated by governments, or by an intergovernmental body, the Security Council.

4. THE 'INTERESTS OF JUSTICE'

Even if the Security Council or a State Party refers a situation to the Court, the Prosecutor is not required to proceed. If this occurs, he or she may be called upon to justify the decision before a Pre-Trial Chamber in accordance with Article 53 of the Statute. Nothing of the sort has happened as yet. One of the grounds that the Prosecutor may invoke for refusal is that investigation or prosecution would be contrary to the 'interests of justice'. There have been attempts to parse the meaning of these words, including a rather prolix position paper issued at the instigation of human rights NGOs. The latter wanted the Prosecutor to rule out the possibility of resisting prosecution in the event of a political settlement involving amnesty.

The claim that the 'interests of justice' do not provide a basis for declining to prosecute when amnesties have been granted as part of a peace process is surely reading too much into the text of Article 53. The purpose of the reference to 'interests of justice' is to endow the Prosecutor with discretion. Given the range of views of States on such issues as amnesties, about which the Rome Statute is silent, it would have been impossible to devise a formula to guide such discretion. The words 'interests of justice' are often used in legal texts when it proves impossible to provide more definitive guidance in the exercise of a particular power or right. It is a way that lawmakers say 'we can't do any more here than trust that a wise person will know to do the right thing'. That is also the function of 'interests of justice' in Article 53 of the Rome Statute.

Thus, the Prosecutor of the International Criminal Court has been given extraordinary and largely unfettered powers that hitherto were the prerogative of bodies such as the four-power conference that created the Nuremberg Tribunal and the UN Security Council responsible for establishing the various ad hoc tribunals. She can decide where to prosecute and where not to prosecute, when to turn on the tap of international justice and when to turn it off. Currently, the 'gravity' criterion remains central to the Prosecutor's explanation for decisions about the selection of situations. But the Prosecutor's career at the Court is confined to a single nine-year term. Future prosecutors may view this differently, and dwell upon other criteria to account for their own subjectivity.

By way of example, in 1997 a conference on transitional justice in the former Yugoslavia held in Strasbourg considered the advisability of establishing a truth and reconciliation commission. The various experts and stakeholders at the meeting largely agreed that this was to be desired. A few days later, the Prosecutor of

the International Criminal Tribunal for the former Yugoslavia, who had been represented at the Strasbourg meeting, issued a statement that was harshly critical of the
initiative. Louise Arbour could not see the feasibility of a truth commission working
in parallel with the International Tribunal. Shortly thereafter, Arbour's predecessor
as Prosecutor, Richard Goldstone, published an op-ed in the *International Herald
Tribune* praising the proposed commission. The only point here is that reasonable
people such as Louise Arbour and Richard Goldstone may reach radically different
conclusions on important issues concerning the operation of international justice.
It will be no different if successive prosecutors at the International Criminal Court
choose to act in the 'interests of justice'.

The 'interests of justice' is a nebulous and intangible notion, ideally suited to
camouflage the real reasons behind choices about whether or not to proceed in
situations. The results are ultimately the product of the Prosecutor's own personal
determinations. This is not to suggest that the Prosecutor's selection of situations is
purely arbitrary or capricious. All of the situations that have been prosecuted by the
Court to date are certainly 'serious'. But this can also be said of other situations where
the Prosecutor is inactive and, seemingly, uninterested. In one sense or another, these
choices reflect the political judgments, prejudices, predispositions and leanings of the
individual to whom they are entrusted. Furthermore, the prosecutorial choices are
not simply about some triage between situations that are serious and those that are
not. The Prosecutor of the Court also conducts a ranking among situations already
deemed 'serious'. In 2006, he appeared to decide that murder and torture of civilians
by a foreign army following an illegal invasion was not as serious as the recruitment
of child soldiers by a rebel militia. Others might be inclined to reverse the order.

As an experiment, ask every individual in a room full of people to write the single
'situation' that they think is most deserving of international justice on a slip of
paper. Inevitably, the responses will vary greatly. If victims of atrocities are present,
they will almost invariably select the situations that concern them. Understandably,
victims cannot easily make such choices with objectivity. But even those who are more
detached will probably indicate the countries, regions and types of crime that, for
one reason or another, often related to their personal interests and experiences, are
closest to their hearts: Syria, Iraq, Gaza, Sri Lanka, Yemen, Colombia, North Korea,
child soldiers, sexual violence, cluster munitions, hate propaganda. Each situation
has its merits, each manifests gravity, and each has a legitimate claim to be at the top
of the list. But why is the individual determination made by the Prosecutor of the
International Criminal Court any more legitimate than that of one of the individuals
in this casual survey?

5. AN INCOMPLETE DEBATE ABOUT POLITICAL DIRECTION

The first eight 'situations' investigated by the Prosecutor concern countries in central
Africa: Uganda, Sudan, Central African Republic, Democratic Republic of the
Congo, Kenya, Libya, Côte d'Ivoire and Mali. Is it really conceivable that an objective
application of the gravity criterion, as proposed in materials from the Office of the
Prosecutor, leads inexorably to this result? Is it simply a coincidence, the unintended

conjuncture of the objective application of selection criteria built around an inchoate notion of 'gravity'? Can this be explained reasonably as a purely judicial determination flowing from application of the Rome Statute and the Regulations of the Office of the Prosecutor? There must surely be a strong presumption that some sort of policy determination is involved, absent any convincing explanation to the contrary.

Certainly, many States, especially States Parties in the Global North, and particularly the non-party State that had become one of the keener supporters of the Court under the Obama administration, the United States of America, seem very comfortable with the Prosecutor's focus on central Africa. There has been much interest in the apparent warming of the United States to the Court, which many attribute to the more enlightened orientation of the administration that replaced George W. Bush. Actually, the process was underway well before the 2008 election. It seems to be as much related to the fact that the Court's priorities correspond to the strategic interests of the United States as it is to the more progressive multilateralism of President Obama and Secretary of State Clinton.

The Court's first two Prosecutors have regularly insisted that their actions and decisions are based on judicial and not political factors. But if this is really the case, then a better explanation for the choice of situations for prosecution must be advanced. The 'gravity' language strikes the observer as little more than obfuscation, a laboured attempt to make the determinations look more judicial than they really are. The seriousness of the situations in central Africa is unquestioned. Yet there are many serious situations over which the Court can exercise jurisdiction elsewhere in the world. Nor are these observations meant to cast aspersions on the good faith of those involved in these determinations. They have undoubtedly convinced themselves that they have found a legalistic formula enabling themselves to do the impossible, namely, to take a political decision while making it look judicial.

Quietly, and despite the rhetoric about the absence of political considerations in the selection of situations, the Prosecutor does in fact draw upon a coterie of advisers based in what is called the Jurisdiction, Complementarity and Cooperation Unit. Possibly external experts are also consulted from time to time. It is an entirely opaque process, shrouded in the language of denial and the myth of the irrelevance of political factors. The problem here is not only transparency but also accountability. By contrast, the Security Council, which is responsible for the political triggering and guidance of the ad hoc tribunals, operates somewhat in the open. Its members are responsible for their choices not only to the international community as a whole but also to their national political constituencies.

The enormous discretion of the Prosecutor is restrained by the Rome Statute in a couple of ways. First, decisions to initiate prosecutions and to block them are subject to review by a three-judge Pre-Trial Chamber. The legal parameters to be followed by the judges are as oracular as those of the Prosecutor. In practice, it appears unlikely that judges will second-guess the exercise of the discretion of the Prosecutor, as long as it remains within reasonable bounds. After all, they are not asked to make assessments of prosecutorial priorities, merely to confirm that they have been made appropriately and are not entirely arbitrary. The judges are not charged with making the best determination of the selection policy of the Court, only with endorsing the validity of those situations that are chosen by the Prosecutor.

Second, a decision to prosecute, in either a 'situation' or a 'case', may be blocked by resolution of the UN Security Council, pursuant to Article 16 of the Statute. Here, we return to nakedly political considerations. But the Security Council's authority is itself closely circumscribed. It must act by resolution, and this means one of the permanent five can obstruct the process by means of the veto. The Security Council must renew any resolution on an annual basis. The United States has already shown itself to be remarkably adept at manipulating the Article 16 procedure, invoking it in 2002 and 2003 on spurious grounds, and then threatening to veto its use where it provided a solution to a genuine problem facing the Court in 2008.

The provisions in the Rome Statute concerning the relationship between the Prosecutor and the Security Council were probably the most contentious of the entire negotiations. The UN International Law Commission initially prepared the working draft statute that formed the basis of discussions. Finalised in 1994, its conception was of a court that was similar to the existing models – the Nuremberg Tribunal and the International Criminal Tribunal for the former Yugoslavia – in the sense that the selection of situations was entirely subject to the control of the political body responsible for the establishment of the institution. The proposed court would only be able to operate in situations that had been designated by the Security Council or by a Member State. But even if a Member State were to assign a situation to the court, this could not go ahead if the matter was already being considered by the Security Council. Given that virtually every potential situation that might merit prosecution would be a crisis of sufficient proportions to have already engaged the Security Council, in practice this meant that the Council was the gatekeeper of the proposed court.

When the debate about the draft statute shifted from the conservative International Law Commission to the more intoxicating atmosphere of the General Assembly, ideas began to circulate whose consequence was to weaken the control over the court by the Security Council in terms of the designation of situations. Some of this was nurtured by post-cold war euphoria and the political opportunities generated by the new unipolar world order. Important countries that were excluded from the inner circle of the United Nations, such as Germany, Canada, South Africa and Argentina, exploited the chance to attempt indirectly the long-awaited reform of the Security Council that had been unattainable directly through amendment of the Charter of the United Nations. This became merged with a very seductive discourse about establishing a purely judicial institution at the international level, one whose prosecutorial policy would be based upon objective criteria rather than political interests. From this alchemy, the independent prosecutor was born.

6. THE INDEPENDENT PROSECUTOR AND THE ROME STATUTE

Over the four years of negotiations that culminated in the Rome Conference at which the Statute of the International Criminal Court was adopted the concept of the independent prosecutor gained purchase. It was enshrined as one of the central policy planks of the 'like-minded caucus' that was so influential in the process. Over the course of this evolving debate, the theory of the independent prosecutor operated as a kind of Trojan horse for the campaign to weaken the grip of the Security Council. The principle of prosecutorial independence was consistent with general views on the mission of impartial criminal justice, although there was little serious reflection about the distinctions between the way this worked at the domestic level and the added complexities on the international plane. Nevertheless, it operated very effectively to challenge the vision of a court whose prosecutor would be subject to direction from the Security Council. It seems that no alternative to the Security Council was considered as a source of policy orientation for the Prosecutor in the determination of appropriate 'situations'. Many States wanted to remove the Security Council from the picture, and the most effective way to do so was chanting the mantra about political control being incompatible with a judicial institution. A more subtle and refined approach, which would acknowledge the imperative of some type of direction to the Prosecutor but from a source other than the Security Council, never emerged.

The challenge of political guidance may be one factor that explains the lacklustre performance of the Court in its first decade of activity. The ad hoc tribunals, and Nuremberg and Tokyo before them, succeeded not only because of the political forces that established them but also because of the political consensus that supported their work. The most famous of the cases directed against former heads of state, Milošević and Taylor, were only able to proceed because of widespread political backing in the regions affected by the conflicts for the idea that international justice be done. In the most celebrated case to come before the International Criminal Court, of Sudanese president Omar Al-Bashir, such support has been weak in the part of the world where it is most needed.

7. WHO'S AFRAID OF VICTORS' JUSTICE?

What does all of this have to do with 'victors' justice'? It has been the label attached to international trials allegedly tainted with the politics of those who established them. The critique suggests that matters improved somewhat at the ad hoc tribunals, compared with Nuremberg and Tokyo. Only with the International Criminal Court, and its *proprio motu* Prosecutor, has the problem been solved, goes the explanation. But has it? In reality, what we have at the International Criminal Court is a political determination, only with less transparency, not more. This is not to suggest that the Prosecutor receives instructions from some clandestine committee of political advisors and foreign intelligence agencies. But she is certainly compelled to select situations where objective, judicial criteria alone do not suffice as guidance. The discretion of the Prosecutor of the International Criminal Court in selecting situations on her own initiative (Article 15), and in accepting or rejecting selections that have already been referred by the Security Council or by States Parties (in accordance with Article 53), has an inherently political dimension.

The quest for the judicial international prosecutor – one who is above politics, and who is modelled on domestic prosecutors where all serious crimes against the person are addressed regardless of political considerations – is as elusive as the search for the end of the rainbow. For this reason, the Rome Statute is incomplete.

The Prosecutor does, in fact, make political choices. He or she does not seriously consider for prosecution all admissible situations that fall within the jurisdiction of the Court. Some, like Iraq, were set aside because the Prosecutor did not want to disturb powerful States, although the justification for this was dressed up in unconvincing language about comparative 'gravity'. Others have been selected where they seem to represent a consensus of some States, but not all. Prosperous States in the Global North have seemed pleased enough that prosecutorial energy is devoted to central Africa. When Palestine suggested that it was considering accession to the Rome Statute, many States in the Global North, many of them States Parties, tried to discourage this. To the complaints of African States they are being unfairly targeted comes the answer that the determinations are based upon 'gravity' and that they respond to objective criteria. This is about as persuasive as the suggestion that the UN Human Rights Council focuses on all serious country situations involving human rights violations, or that the UN Security Council deals in an even-handed manner with all threats to international peace and security. The only difference is that the Councils of the United Nations are avowedly political bodies and they make no pretence to the contrary.

Many war crimes committed by the Allied forces during the World War II went unpunished. Decades before World War II, international law had attempted to outlaw aerial warfare altogether. Probably the turning point was the infamous attack on the Basque city, Guernica, immortalised in the great mural by Picasso that hangs today in Madrid's Reina Sophia gallery. Thus began a gradual descent into violations of the laws and customs of war, sometimes rationalised in the name of reprisal. It eventually led to use of the atomic bomb at Hiroshima and Nagasaki, and the fire-storms that cremated uncounted civilian inhabitants of Dresden, Hamburg and Tokyo.

There are also many reports that Allied soldiers summarily executed German prisoners, something that, then as now, is a violation of the laws of war. Following the Malmédy massacre in December 1944, when eighty-four American soldiers were murdered by German forces during the Battle of the Bulge, an order was issued that SS troops and paratroopers were not to be taken prisoner and were to be shot on sight. In the *Abbaye Ardenne* case, the commander of an SS armoured unit, Kurt Mayer, was charged with killing Canadian prisoners. He led evidence showing that during the invasion of Normandy the Allied forces, including the Canadians, had issued written orders not to take prisoners. The Canadian force commander commuted Meyer's sentence from execution to life imprisonment because he was certain that his own soldiers had perpetrated similar acts.

The Katyń forest massacre is only one of the many examples of atrocities perpetrated by the Soviets as they fought the Nazis for survival. With the war ending, and victory virtually assured, Soviet soldiers committed large-scale rapes of German civilians, a war crime by any definition and one apparently perpetrated with official consent or indifference. After the political changes in eastern and central Europe associated with the end of the Cold War, a few prosecutions were attempted against anti-Nazi fighters for their behaviour during the war. Probably more are still to come in the Baltic States, Slovenia, and elsewhere, although the temporal window for prosecution of the ageing men and women suspected of such crimes is quickly closing. But there is no question of holding leaders and senior officials accountable. In any event, few if any remain alive. In a European Court of Human Rights case arising from the war crimes trial of a Latvian partisan, *Kononov v Latvia*, Russia intervened in the proceedings to argue, essentially, that only Nazis could commit war crimes. Its claim that anything else amounted to retroactive prosecution was dismissed by the Grand Chamber of the Court.[20]

Lawyers for the Nazi defendants raised the matter of Allied war crimes on behalf of SS *Einsatzgruppen* leaders in one of the subsequent proceedings held by the Americans in the Nuremberg courtroom after the big trial had finished. They argued that it was not a war crime to murder civilians, because the Allies had done the same when they indiscriminately bombed German population centres. The judges responded:

> Thus, as grave a military action as is an air bombardment, whether with the usual bombs or by atomic bomb, the one and only purpose of the bombing is to effect the surrender of the bombed nation. The people of that nation, through their representatives, may surrender and, with the surrender, the bombing ceases, the killing is ended. Furthermore, a city is assured of not being bombed by the law-abiding belligerent if it is declared an open city. With the Jews it was entirely different. Even if the nation surrendered they still were killed as individuals.[21]

Actually, the purpose of the bombing might better be described as terrorising the civilian population. There can be no doubt that today such massacres of civilians would be viewed as a war crime. What the judges were really doing was resisting the argument of moral equivalence.

All serious crimes ought to be addressed by courts of criminal justice, and these World War II atrocities perpetrated by the victors are no exception. That they have been left virtually unpunished is much to be regretted. But lamenting the impunity of Allied war crimes during World War II does not inexorably lead to the conclusion that the Nuremberg and Tokyo tribunals were distorted because they did not punish both sides. One can, as did the judges in the *Einsatzgruppen* case, argue that the Allied crimes were not comparable to those of the Nazis. In particular, to the extent that the core crime of the prosecutions was aggression, it seems obvious enough that it is the aggressor and not the victim of aggression who will be the focus of international justice. But that is not really the heart of the argument by the judges in *Einsatzgruppen*. Their logic is one of relative gravity. They obviously disagree with the modern-day Nazi supporters in Germany and elsewhere who claim: Auschwitz + Dresden = 0. But while courts are free to make assessments of relative gravity, as did the *Einsatzgruppen* judges, this is a decision that may be better left to other forums. Such determinations require the wisdom that comes from political rather than judicial assessments.

---

[20] *Kononov v Latvia* [GC], no 36376/04, ECHR 2010.
[21] *United States of America v Ohlendorf et al* ('Einsatzgruppen case'), (1948) 4 TWC 411 (United States Military Tribunal) 467.

8. THE INTRACTABLE CHALLENGE OF BALANCED PROSECUTIONS

Those who espouse the victors' justice critique of Nuremberg and Tokyo might turn their attention to describing what balanced justice at the end of World War II ought to have looked like. Would the victors' justice stigma be removed if there had been a trial of twenty-four American leaders, and twenty-four British leaders, and twenty-four Soviet leaders, along with the twenty-four Nazi defendants? If not twenty-four, how many? How big a sample, how much symbolism, is required to beat back the charge of victors' justice? This is not a question that lawyers or judges can answer. It is a matter for determination at the political level.

The Prosecutor of the International Criminal Tribunal for Rwanda has been frequently taken to task for his apparent refusal to launch trials for atrocities perpetrated by the Rwandese Patriotic Army forces during and after the 1994 genocide. Different arguments are advanced. One contention is that the Tribunal will not fulfil its mission of transitional justice, including reconciliation between the two ethnic groups of the Rwanda conflict, until both sides are brought to justice. Another holds that the alleged massacres committed by Tutsi troops as they fought for power against the genocidal regime in Rwanda are just as evil and deserving of prosecution as the crimes the Tutsi were fighting to stop. The first theory earns support among well-meaning but somewhat naïve enthusiasts for transitional justice. They seem to operate more on the basis of the personal intuitions of Western intellectuals and activists than hard, empirical evidence. The second finds its constituency among revisionists and deniers with their own political agenda, be it in Rwanda or Germany.

That even-handed prosecution of both sides – whatever that might look like – is important or necessary for reconciliation is an interesting hypothesis but no more than that. Do the wounds left by massive crimes such as the genocides in Nazi-occupied Europe or Rwanda heal better if the victims or those who liberate them acknowledge a part in the wrongdoing? It does not seem verifiable that where both sides are not prosecuted, justice cannot be done, or that its purported benefits in terms of reconciliation are diminished. The Nuremberg trials probably contributed to a shared narrative, one common to victor and vanquished alike, that enhanced the building of a democratic, pluralist and largely peaceful modern Europe. A Nuremberg-like trial of the victors might well have done more harm than good in terms of reconciliation, acknowledgement of the truth, and justice for the victims.

The debates continue. Such challenges are inherent in international prosecution, which is both selective and political by nature. There is no solution that relies exclusively on judicial standards. For these reasons, justice in such areas cannot be the preserve of the courts, the way it is at the domestic level. Inevitably, it is a mixture of the judicial and the political. The challenge for those involved in the judicial wing of this process is to ensure the greatest legitimacy without at the same time encouraging the myth that what they are doing is devoid of a political dimension.

11

Mr Seferovic's Pigeons: A Brief Encounter with International Criminal Justice

PAUL ROBERTS

1. INSTITUTIONAL AND DISCIPLINARY CONTEXT

RALPH HENHAM'S SCHOLARSHIP has consistently been animated by a desire to contextualise law and legal process and his published work has advocated a particular style of 'contextual modelling'.[1] Henham insists on '[t]he evaluation of legal process in its socio-political and historical context demand[ing] ... the development of a comparative contextual model to facilitate this task'.[2] His approach 'emphasises the broader social context in which information is attributed the status of fact and "truth" for the purposes of sentence'.[3] Further, '[t]he phenomenological context of any proposed analysis must also be evaluated'.[4] Contextualisation is the midwife of methodological reflection,[5] encouraging exploration of the various *methods* through which legal institutions (among other things) may be placed in context. This orientation tends to produce a healthy disregard for conventional disciplinary boundaries coupled with a pragmatic preference for methodological pluralism: follow the research problem wherever it leads, using whatever intellectual tools and methodological protocols may be best suited to the task! Interdisciplinarity is an almost obligatory implication of this way of thinking;[6]

---

[1] See eg Ralph Henham, *Sentencing and the Legitimacy of Trial Justice* (London, Routledge, 2012); Ralph Henham, 'Theorizing the Penality of Sentencing in International Criminal Trials' (2004) 8 *Theoretical Criminology* 429; Ralph Henham, 'Theory and Contextual Analysis in Sentencing' (2001) 29 *International Journal of the Sociology of Law* 253.

[2] Henham (2004) (n 1) 435.

[3] Ralph Henham, 'Penal Ideology, Sentencing and the Legitimacy of Trial Justice' (2012) 57 *Crime, Law and Social Change* 77, 78.

[4] Ralph Henham, 'Human Rights, Due Process and Sentencing' (1998) 38 *British Journal of Criminology* 592, 601.

[5] cf Mark Findlay and Ralph Henham, 'Integrating Theory and Method in the Comparative Contextual Analysis of Trial Process' in Mike McConville and Wing Hong Chui (eds), *Research Methods for Law*, 2nd edn (Edinburgh, Edinburgh University Press, 2017).

[6] For theoretical elucidation and practical applications, see Paul Roberts, 'Interdisciplinarity in Legal Research' in McConville and Chui (n 5); Paul Roberts, 'Renegotiating Forensic Cultures: Between Law,

a rejection, not of doctrinal scholarship, but of doctrinalism: the false idea that close textual analysis of primary legal authorities is the only valid or worthwhile form of jurisprudence.[7]

Contextualisation, sophisticated methodological pluralism and intelligent interdisciplinarity together constitute a powerful compound lens through which to examine novel institutional developments and disciplinary formations, such as the unprecedented expansion and reconfiguration of international criminal law that took flight in the final decade of the twentieth century. Dreamers have always dreamed,[8] and there were significant if disparate historical precedents,[9] but a living, breathing, censuring and sanctioning system of international criminal trials and punishments was something entirely new and – for many seasoned observers – somewhat unexpected.[10] This was intellectually energising, if head-scratchingly unfamiliar and potentially disorientating, terrain for those of us schooled primarily in domestic criminal law and penality[11] but equipped with the methodological nous to pay attention and ponder wider theoretical, institutional and disciplinary implications.[12]

Science and Criminal Justice' (2013) 44 *Studies in the History and Philosophy of Biological and Biomedical Sciences* 47; Paul Roberts, 'Penal Offence in Question: Some Reference Points for Interdisciplinary Conversation' in Andrew Simester and Andrew von Hirsch (eds), *Incivilities: Regulating Offensive Behaviour* (Oxford, Hart, 2006).

[7] For a powerful antidote, see William Twining, *General Jurisprudence* (Cambridge, Cambridge University Press, 2012).

[8] For a sense of enduring idealism, see eg Richard J. Goldstone, *For Humanity: Reflections of a War Crimes Investigator* (New Haven, CT, Yale University Press, 2000); Kofi Annan, 'Advocating for an International Criminal Court' (1997) 21 *Fordham International Law Journal* 363; Henry T King, Jr, 'The Meaning of Nuremberg' (1998) 30 *Case Western Reserve Journal of International Law* 143; M Cherif Bassiouni, 'Searching for Peace and Achieving Justice: The Need for Accountability' (1996) 59 *Law and Contemporary Problems* 9.

[9] Robert Cryer, *Prosecuting International Crimes: Selectivity and the International Criminal Law Regime* (Cambridge, Cambridge University Press, 2005); Gary Jonathan Bass, *Stay the Hand of Vengeance: The Politics of War Crimes Tribunals* (Princeton, NJ, Princeton University Press, 2002); Timothy LH McCormack, 'From Sun Tzu to the Sixth Committee: The Evolution of an International Criminal Law Regime', in McCormack and Simpson (eds), *The Law of War Crimes: National and International Approaches* (Dordrecht, Kluwer 1997); Telford Taylor, *The Anatomy of the Nuremberg Trial* (Boston, MA, Little, Brown, 1993); Matthew Lippman, 'The Other Nuremberg: American Prosecutions of Nazi War Criminals in Occupied Germany' (1992) 3 *Indiana International and Comparative Law Review* 1.

[10] Creating a trial court empowered to adjudicate individual criminal responsibility was an unprecedented application of the UN Security Council's Chapter VII enforcement powers, and the successful outcome of the Rome Conference to establish a permanent International Criminal Court was by no means assured: see John Hooper and Ian Black, 'Self-Interest Brings Court into Contempt', *The Guardian*, 15 July 1998; David J Harris, 'Progress and Problems in Creating an International Criminal Court' (1998) 3 *Journal of Armed Conflict Law* 1; Immi Tallgren, 'We Did It? The Vertigo of Law and Everyday Life at the Diplomatic Conference on the Establishment of an International Criminal Court' (1999) 12 *Leiden Journal of International Law* 683.

[11] David Garland's handy neologism encapsulating 'the whole of the penal complex, including its laws, sanctions, institutions, and practices and its discourses, symbols, rituals, and performances': David Garland, 'Penality and the Penal State' (2013) 51 *Criminology* 475.

[12] For embryonic thoughts, see Paul Roberts, 'Comparative Law for International Criminal Justice' in Esin Örücü and David Nelken (eds), *Comparative Law: A Handbook* (Oxford, Hart, 2007); Paul Roberts and Nesam McMillan, 'For Criminology in International Criminal Justice' (2003) 1 *Journal of International Criminal Justice* 315 and reprinted in Ruth Jamieson (ed), *The Criminology of War* (Ashgate, 2014); Paul Roberts, 'Restoration and Retribution in International Criminal Justice: An Exploratory Analysis' in Andrew von Hirsch et al (eds), *Restorative Justice and Criminal Justice* (Oxford, Hart, 2003).

Ralph Henham was in the first cohort of disciplinary scouts and outriders mapping a penologically informed approach to international criminal justice.[13]

My contribution to this celebratory volume combines my own, more granular interest in evidentiary questions with broader themes in international criminal trial procedure extensively canvassed in Ralph's trailblazing publications.[14] More specifically, this chapter employs a detailed case study as a vehicle for advancing a general proposition: that scholars of evidence, proof and procedure could learn a great deal from experiences of international criminal adjudication accumulated over the last three decades. This endeavour forms part of a programmatic agenda to supplement and contextualise primarily expository studies of the Law of Evidence[15] by 'taking facts seriously',[16] exploiting interdisciplinary resources,[17] and reimagining disciplinary frameworks in terms of Evidence and Proof or 'forensic science' in the literal, juristic sense.[18] The following discussion examines just one fragment of a single case, the trial of Duško Tadić for war crimes and crimes against humanity before the UN's' International Criminal Tribunal for the Former Yugoslavia (ICTY), which was conducted in The Hague in 1996–1997.

Tadić was, in fact, the first decision handed down by the ICTY.[19] In pronouncing the first truly international criminal conviction since the post-World War II military tribunals held in Nuremberg and Tokyo in 1945–1948, this new contender for 'trial of the century'[20] predictably, and quite properly, attracted international media

---

[13] See, in particular, Ralph Henham, 'Theorising Law and Legitimacy in International Criminal Justice' (2007) 3 *International Journal of Law in Context* 257 (engaging with me on issues of the intrinsic or instrumental value of criminal adjudication that I am still chewing over!); Ralph Henham, 'The Philosophical Foundations of International Sentencing' (2003) 1 *Journal of International Criminal Justice* 64.

[14] Ralph Henham and Mark Findlay (eds), *Exploring the Boundaries of International Criminal Justice* (Farnham, Ashgate, 2011); Mark Findlay and Ralph Henham, *Transforming International Criminal Justice* (London, Routledge, 2011).

[15] cf Paul Roberts, 'Adrian Zuckerman's New Evidence Scholarship' in Rabeea Assy and Andrew Higgins (eds), *Principles, Procedure, and Justice: Essays in Honour of Adrian Zuckerman* (Oxford, Oxford University Press, 2020).

[16] William Twining, 'Taking Facts Seriously' in N Gold (ed), *Essays on Legal Education* (Toronto, Butterworths, 1982); Paul Roberts, 'Rethinking the Law of Evidence: A Twenty-First Century Agenda for Teaching and Research' (2002) 55 *Current Legal Problems* 297; William Twining, 'Taking Facts Seriously – Again' in Paul Roberts and Mike Redmayne (eds), *Innovations in Evidence and Proof* (Oxford, Hart, 2007).

[17] William Twining, 'Evidence as a Multi-disciplinary Subject' (2003) 2 *Law, Probability and Risk* 91; Paul Roberts, 'Groundwork for a Jurisprudence of Criminal Procedure' in RA Duff and Stuart Green (eds), *Philosophical Foundations of Criminal Law* (Oxford, Oxford University Press, 2011).

[18] John Jackson and Paul Roberts, 'Beyond Common Law Evidence: Reimagining, and Reinvigorating, Evidence Law as Forensic Science' in Darryl K Brown, Jenia Iontcheva Turner and Bettina Weisser (eds), *The Oxford Handbook of Criminal Process* (Oxford, Oxford University Press, 2019); David Schum, 'Classifying Forms and Combinations of Evidence: Necessary in a Science of Evidence' in Philip Dawid, William Twining and Mimi Vasilaki (eds), *Evidence, Inference and Enquiry* (Oxford, Oxford University Press, 2011).

[19] *Prosecutor v Tadić*, IT-94-1 ('Prijedor'), Trial Chamber Judgment, 7 May 1997.

[20] MS Zaid, 'Trial of the Century? Assessing the Case of Dusko Tadic before the International Criminal Tribunal for the Former Yugoslavia' (1997) 2 *ILSA Journal of International and Comparative Law* 589. Cf Patricia M Wald, 'Running the Trial of the Century: The Nuremberg Legacy' (2006) 27 *Cardozo Law Review* 1559.

coverage[21] and extensive academic analysis.[22] Most of this commentary was, however, initially skewed towards examining the status of the ICTY in international law, the extent of its legal jurisdiction, broader political questions about the Tribunal's legitimacy, and the likely impact and consequences of its ongoing work – including the Tribunal's major contributions to the normative development of international humanitarian law, as a precursor to what would become, within another decade or so, the evolved jurisdiction of a permanent International Criminal Court (ICC).[23] The judgment in *Tadić* was, in short, primarily of interest to international lawyers, who understandably viewed it through Public International Law (PIL) – and subsequently, international criminal law – lenses. As a US judge at the ICTY observed, one implication of this spontaneous division of disciplinary curation or colonisation was that 'scholars and commentators on the Tribunals appear to pay much more attention to substantive law developments than to procedure and process'.[24]

In discussing some of *Tadić*'s evidentiary dimensions, and more generally in bringing international criminal adjudication to the attention of predominantly domestically orientated Evidence law scholars and teachers, this chapter provides a modest corrective to these lopsided tendencies in the scholarly literature on international criminal adjudication. As a contribution to a nascent scholarship developing international criminal procedure,[25] in which Ralph Henham was a prescient pioneer,[26] it might even encourage proceduralists to venture into the theoretical and policy debates surrounding, and to some extent still shaping, international criminal proceedings.

2. WITNESS TO COLD-BLOODED MURDER

In civilian life, Duško – aka 'Dule' – Tadić was a café owner and part-time policeman. During the vicious civil wars that tore through the Balkan region in the early 1990s, he served as a mid-ranking commander of a Serb paramilitary unit. Tadić was subsequently indicted by the ICTY for various war crimes and crimes against humanity,

---

[21] eg Christopher Bellamy, 'Bosnian Serb Found Guilty of War Crimes', *The Guardian*, 8 May 1997; Reuters, 'A Bosnian Serb Gets 20 Years for War Crimes', *New York Times*, 15 July 1997.

[22] A vast literature rapidly accumulated. For nuanced analysis, see José E. Alvarez, 'Rush to Closure: Lessons of the *Tadic* Judgment' (1998) 96 *Michigan Law Review* 2031.

[23] Antonio Cassese, Paola Gaeta and John RWD Jones (eds), *The Rome Statute of the International Criminal Court: A Commentary* (Oxford, Oxford University Press, 2002); Dominic McGoldrick, 'A Permanent International Criminal Court: An End to a Culture of Impunity' [1999] *Criminal Law Review* 627.

[24] PM Wald, 'Rules of Evidence in the Yugoslav War Tribunal' (2003) 21 *Quinnipiac Law Review* 761, 763.

[25] Early contributions include JRWD Jones, *The Practice of the International Criminal Tribunals for the Former Yugoslavia and Rwanda* (Irvington-on-Hudson, NY, Transnational, 1998); PM Wald, 'Rules of Evidence in the Yugoslav War Tribunal' (2003) 21 *Quinnipiac Law Review* 761; MP Scharf, 'Trial and Error: An Assessment of the First Judgment of the Yugoslavia War Crimes Tribunal' (1997–98) 30 *New York University Journal of International Law and Politics* 167; PL Robinson, 'Ensuring Fair and Expeditious Trials at the International Criminal Tribunal for the Former Yugoslavia' (2000) 11 *European Journal of International Law* 569; KL Fabian, 'Proof and Consequences: an Analysis of the *Tadic* & *Akayesu* Trials' (2000) 49 *DePaul Law Review* 981.

[26] Ralph Henham, *Punishment and Process in International Criminal Trials* (Farnham, Ashgate, 2005).

including torture and murder of civilians, forced expulsions of non-Serb populations from the Prijedor region of Bosnia ('ethnic cleansing') and appalling mistreatment of prisoners of war. Amongst this grisly catalogue of indicted offences featured the cold-blooded murder of two Bosnian Muslim police officers, Edin Besic and Osman Didovic, who were allegedly pulled out of a line-up of surrendered prisoners standing with their hands behind their heads and stabbed to death by the accused. Although this was far from being the worst of Tadić's behaviour in these dark days of civil war and sectarian occupation, these particular murders were significant because the prosecution could produce an apparently impressive eyewitness claiming to have seen the victims die at Tadić's own hand, rather than as part of a common enterprise (potentially diluting criminal responsibility amongst several co-accused) or unwitnessed murders of the 'disappeared'.

Nihad Seferovic had been at school with Duško Tadić. Indeed, their families lived within ten houses of each other on the same street where Tadić and Seferovic both grew up in a town called Kozarac in the Prijedor region of the former Yugoslavia. However, Seferovic was a Muslim, not a Serb like Tadić, and when the order came for Bosnian Muslims to report to Serb army collection points Seferovic fled to the hills, periodically thereafter venturing back down into the town on various errands. It was on one of these sorties that, whilst hiding in tall grass and concealed by overhanging plum trees, Seferovic caught sight of Tadić standing in a group of fifteen or so Serb paramilitaries in front of the Serb Orthodox church. The Serbs were apparently harassing a line of Muslim prisoners. Hiding less than thirty metres away, Seferovic was adamant that he recognised Tadić and saw him murder the two defenceless, already-detained policemen.

3. TRIAL AND APPEAL BEFORE THE ICTY

The Judgment of the ICTY Trial Chamber briefly rehearsed the testimony of witness Seferovic:

> Nihad Seferovic testified that on the afternoon of 26 May 1992, on his way back home from the hills in Besici, he stopped at the orchard of a house across from the Serbian Orthodox church. In front of the church he saw approximately six Muslim policemen from Kozarac, including Edin Besic, Ekrem Besic, Emir Karabasic and one Osman with their hands behind their necks standing in line. In front of them were the accused, Goran Borovnica, 'Dule' and about 15 other Serb paramilitaries who had weapons pointed at the Muslim policemen. He saw the accused pull two of the policemen, Osman and Edin Besic, out of the line and kill them by slitting their throats and stabbing each one several times.[27]

It was also recalled that '[t]he Defence challenged the witness's ability to view clearly the events occurring in the churchyard'.[28] Nonetheless, basing itself almost entirely on Seferovic's testimony, the Trial Chamber found 'beyond reasonable doubt that

---

[27] *Prosecutor v Tadić*, IT-94-1 ('Prijedor'), Trial Chamber Judgment, 7 May 1997, [393].
[28] ibid.

the accused ... killed two policemen, Osman [Didovic] and Edin Besic, in front of the Serbian Orthodox church in Kozarac'.[29] Tadić was accordingly convicted of murdering Besic and Didovic, amongst other atrocities, and sentenced to a term of twenty-five years' imprisonment.

On appeal, the defence took exception to Seferovic's evidence on several grounds, including the possibility that Seferovic was a Bosnian government 'plant' who had lied to the ICTY in order to exact revenge on Serbs.[30] Another argument, of particular interest to Evidence scholars, was that Seferovic's account was inherently implausible, for the reason later summarised by the ICTY Appeals Chamber:

> The Defence argues that the Trial Chamber erred in relying on the evidence of Mr Seferovic because it is implausible. Mr Seferovic, a Muslim who lived in an area under bombardment by Serbian paramilitary forces, fled to the mountains for safety. He testified at trial that he was so concerned about the welfare of his pet pigeons that he returned to town to feed them while the Serbian paramilitaries were still there. On his return to town, he saw Mr Tadic kill two policemen. Defence counsel contended at trial that the witness was never in town at the time of the killings.[31]

Indeed, this contention was advanced with some force in defence counsel's submissions to the ICTY Appeals Chamber. Appellate counsel called into question the Trial Chamber's willingness to conclude, beyond reasonable doubt, that Tadić had murdered Besic and Didovic solely in reliance on one eyewitness's testimony:

> That decision depended solely on the evidence of one witness, Nihad Seferovic. In our submission, the evidence of that witness was implausible when analysed. ... The background to his evidence is that he was a Muslim living in the area that had been under attack by Serb paramilitary forces. There had been a bombardment of the town where he lived, and he had fled to some nearby hills or mountains for safety. The cornerstone of his evidence was that before the bombardment, he had kept tame pigeons, and he was so concerned about their welfare that when the Serb paramilitaries were still in the town, he decided to return to the town in order to feed his pet birds. As a rational decision, that is, on any view, curious, because he was placing himself in the gravest of jeopardy in order to do no more than feed some pet birds who would have been most unlikely to have survived the bombardment of the town in any event; but that was the only explanation for him being in the town at the moment that these two men were killed, the evidence that he gave being that he approached the killing in an orchard to the distance of some 30 metres and, at that distance, was able to identify the defendant as the man who took two men out of a line of five and killed them in the area immediately in front of the Orthodox church. The evidence was identified in the judgement of the Trial Chamber at paragraph 393, and it merely recounts there the evidence that the witness gave. ... It was not, with respect to the

---

[29] ibid [397].

[30] This is not, alas, a completely fanciful accusation. Another witness who testified against Tadić was exposed as a perjurer seeking revenge on Serbs: see *Decision on Prosecution Motion to Withdraw Protective Measures for Witness L*, 5 December 1996, where the Trial Chamber observed that '[W]itness L had admitted ... that he had lied about the death of his father while under oath. Witness L asserted that he had done this at the behest of the Bosnian government authorities who had allegedly "trained" him to give evidence against the accused, Dusko Tadić. ... Consequently, the Prosecution advised the Trial Chamber that it could no longer support witness L as a witness of truth and invited the Trial Chamber to disregard his evidence entirely.' Also see Nancy Combs, *Fact-Finding Without Facts: The Uncertain Evidentiary Foundations of International Criminal Convictions* (Cambridge, Cambridge University Press, 2010) ch 5.

[31] *Prosecutor v Tadić*, IT-94-1-A (Appeals Chamber), 15 July 1999; (2002) 9 IHRR 1051, [58].

Trial Chamber, the most critical analysis of the evidence of the witness Seferovic; it was, in truth, no more than a recitation of the effect of what he said. ... And the unlikelihood is obviously a reflection of the inherent improbability of anybody with any regard to their own safety willingly entering a town currently occupied by Serb paramilitaries when they were in the process of actively deporting the Muslims to concentration camps in order to feed a pet bird. It is, we would submit, such an unlikely and improbable story that any Tribunal would want to reflect on whether it could possibly be true.[32]

Expressed in such stark terms, the proposition that a person would risk enemy bombardment and possible capture and internment in a concentration camp 'in order to feed a pet bird' does seem rather unlikely. Yet the ICTY Appeals Chamber remained unimpressed:

The Appeals Chamber does not accept as inherently implausible the witness' claim that the reason why he returned to the town where the Serbian paramilitary forces had been attacking, and from which he had escaped, was to feed his pet pigeons. It is conceivable that a person may do such a thing, even though one might think such action to be an irrational risk. The Trial Chamber, after seeing the witness, hearing his testimony, and observing him under cross-examination, chose to accept his testimony as reliable evidence. There is no basis for the Appeals Chamber to consider that the Trial Chamber acted unreasonably in relying on that evidence for its finding that the Appellant killed the two men.[33]

Tadić's appeal against his convictions of these two murders was accordingly dismissed, although his overall sentence was subsequently reduced to twenty years (including time served).[34] Having obtained Serbian citizenship whilst still in custody, Tadić was granted provisional release after serving two-thirds of his sentence, and deported to Serbia in 2008, where he resumed civilian life.

4. ANALYSIS[35]

The tale of Mr Seferovic's pigeons is worthy of extended commentary and analysis for the valuable light it sheds on issues of evidence, proof, legal process and adjudication. In the first instance, this memorable vignette constitutes an instructive study in fact-finding by international criminal tribunals. However, the resonances of this case study extend far beyond its peculiar institutional context. Indeed, the brief cameo appearance of Mr Seferovic's pigeons in the litigation histories of the ICTY would repay close study by any legal scholar with an interest in questions of evidence and proof, in domestic as much as international proceedings.

A first striking feature of this aspect of Tadić's case is the extent to which the facts discussed on appeal are at variance with the testimony actually given by witness Seferovic at trial. For although Seferovic was asked several questions about feeding his pigeons under cross-examination, bird-feeding did not feature in his testimony-in-chief as Seferovic's overriding motivation for venturing back into Kozarac during the

---

[32] *Prosecutor v Tadić*, IT-94-1-A (Appeals Chamber), Transcript of Proceedings, 385-389 (20 April 1999).
[33] *Prosecutor v Tadić*, IT-94-1-A (Appeals Chamber), 15 July 1999, [66].
[34] Richard Norton-Taylor, 'War Crimes Court Sentence Slashed', *The Guardian*, 27 January 2000.
[35] For methodological tools and context, see T Anderson, D Schum and W Twining, *Analysis of Evidence*, 2nd edn (Cambridge, Cambridge University Press 2005).

bombardment. In this exchange, for example, prosecution counsel tries to establish the day of the week when Seferovic came back into town:[36]

> A [Seferovic].No, I do not remember at all what day it was.
>
> Q. Was it within a -----
>
> A. I know that it was a very nice day in the morning.
>
> Q. Was it within approximately three days after the shelling began?
>
> A. I think so. I do not remember because I went through a terrible catastrophe myself.
>
> Q. In any event, whatever day of the week it was or whatever the date was, did you go into Kozarac? Did you leave Besici and go into Kozarac on the first day that people began to surrender?
>
> A. Yes, I did. I was looking for my brother, for my family members, friends, relatives.

And in the following two passages prosecution counsel is trying to establish witness Seferovic's precise location at the material time:

> Q. Can you point out on this map where your brother's house was?
>
> A. (Indicated) Here, somewhere here, yes.
>
> Q. That would be the street between the hospital and the church?
>
> A. Yes.
>
> Q. Was your brother at his home when you got there?
>
> A. No, I did not find anyone at home.
>
> Q. After that, did you move to a point a little bit closer to the Prijedor/Banja Luka highway?
>
> A. Yes, yes. I saw what was happening around the church ...
>
> Q. Mr. Seferovic, can you show us on this map where your brother's house was and the position you moved to after leaving your brother's house?
>
> A. (Indicated) I think here. This is where my brother's house, and I then went through the gardens, through the back yards and then I came to this house, the last house here.
>
> Q. What is across the street from that spot?
>
> A. There is a church yard and a church.

Having established his position just across from the churchyard, Seferovic then gave a graphic account of the murders:

> A. I could see clearly everything ...
>
> Q. Did you continue to observe this scene for some period of time?
>
> A. Yes, yes. Those paramilitaries provoked the civilians no end. At a certain point, Dule Tadic came, dragged Osman from the group, shouted, 'Follow me', got him by his neck, and cut his throat and then stabbed him below that several times ... and then he proceeded to Edin Besic, and with the same – and he hit him in the same way as he did Osman; and this was followed by incredible fire, and I then ran away. I followed the same path and I cut through and ran to Besici.

---

[36] Passages of verbatim witness examination reproduced in this chapter are excerpted from ICTY Case No IT-94-1-T, Transcript of Hearing, 2651-2706 (14 June 1996).

The first reference to birdlife in Seferovic's examination-in-chief is by way of volunteered incidental detail, in answer to a question about why he needed to return to town to recover some possessions:

Q. What did you do when the attack [ie the shelling of Kozarac] started?

A. I ran out into the road ... and then I went into the hills, into Besici.

Q. Did you stop to change your clothes or to pack any belongings?

A. No, no. No, I just left ...

Q. Did you go back to Kozarac at any point to retrieve some belongings?

A. Yes, yes. I did go back later. In the evening I went back home. I had a lot of birds and I fed the birds. I took my backpack and I went back into the hills.

It is only *after* Seferovic has already testified to witnessing the murders that we hear anything about pigeons being a motivating factor in his return to the scene:

Q. Within a few days did you return to Kozarac?

A. Yes, I kept coming back to Kozarac because I had many birds, I felt the need to feed them. The last time, unfortunately, I was hit in the leg by a bullet, I do not know where from, was it a stray bullet or whether it was on purpose but I was fired at all the time, non-stop around the clock.

Q. After you were struck by that bullet did you manage to make your way back to Besici?

A. Yes, yes. I did manage to get back to Besici with the help of a stick, on a stick, yes.

For a time, Seferovic hid in a natural hollow by a stream and tried to dress his wound with plum brandy. He was later apprehended by Serb militias on the road back to Kozarac and sent to Omarska concentration camp, but by this time he seems to have had much more on his mind than feeding pigeons:

Q. Did you finally leave the hole and attempt to go back to Kozarac in an effort to find your family or friends?

A. Yes, I do not remember how many days I spent in the hole, but the pain was excruciating. I fainted several times and when the swelling receded I stood up. I somehow found superhuman strength to stand up, to pull myself up, with the help of that stick, and move and go and try to find my brother because I knew he had stayed in Kozarac ...

Seferovic's sorties into Kozarac were also explored in cross-examination. Again, plausible reasons were stated with no initial mention of avian mercy missions:

Q. Did you stay in that basement, the first night, the Sunday, that the shelling started?

A. No, I did not. I went back to Kozarac. I took some personal belongings that I needed the most, my underwear, my shirts – and I really needed them when I was wounded because I used that to tie my leg. I did not have any bandages or anything like that.

Q. So, although the shelling was taking place on Kozarac on the Sunday night, you went back into Kozarac to get some of your personal belongings, is that right?

A. Yes, yes, the mortars were falling and I went to get my personal belongings.

When pigeon-feeding crops up again, it seems to be – at most – a secondary consideration in risking the shelling in Kozarac in order to retrieve essential provisions:

> Q. The next day, which would be the Tuesday, after you had spent the night in the basement, did you remain in Besici?
>
> A. No, in the morning I came home. I fed my birds. That was at dawn. I do not remember what hour exactly, but it was dawn. I fed my birds. I poured a lot of water for them, gave them a lot of seeds because I realised that I could not come back every day to feed the birds. Then I went back to Besici again, naturally with bread and blankets and other necessities because the houses were just filled with things. ...
>
> Q. So, having fed your birds at dawn, you left Kozarac and you went back up into the hills and again gave out some of the blankets and supplies that you had been able to take?
>
> A. Yes.

There then appears the following passage of cross-examination, which does place greater stress on Seferovic's concern for his pigeons' welfare:

> Q. So when you fed your birds in the early hours of Tuesday morning, presumably, you had fed them so that they would have enough for a few days, would that be right?
>
> A. Yes.
>
> Q. Did you return to those birds again to see that they were fed and watered?
>
> A. No, but I did go back constantly to the house to see the birds. Even after Kozarac surrendered, I did that and afterwards. I always went back home and paid attention to the birds, not just mine alone, but also my neighbour's.

It should be stressed, however, that in these exchanges defence counsel was not trying to suggest that Seferovic was fabricating his evidence because nobody would be so idiotic as to enter a town under bombardment in order to feed pet birds. Rather, counsel was trying to demonstrate that Seferovic was confused about the relevant dates, in an attempt to provide some substantiation for Tadić's alibi. This strategy proved largely fruitless, however. Seferovic just kept repeating that he could not really be sure what day it was, it might have been a Tuesday or possibly another day, but in any case he was absolutely certain that he had watched his old classmate Duško Tadić murder two unarmed Bosnian policemen in front of the Orthodox church on one of the days when the town of Kozarac surrendered to the Serbs:

> [Defence counsel]: So when you say you went back into Kozarac to your brother's house which was near the hospital, was that on the Wednesday, the day after you had fed your birds in the morning, or was it on the same day that you had fed them at dawn on Tuesday?
>
> A. No, I do not remember what day it was when Kozarac surrendered, but when Kozarac surrendered I went to see my brother.
>
> Q. When you went to your brother's house, did you go alone or were you with anyone else?
>
> A. No, I was alone. ... I just do not remember what day it was because, as I said, Kozarac could not have surrendered in one day. It took several days for it to surrender. I do not remember how many days because I was wounded and I do not remember.

On a close reading of the trial transcripts, therefore, it is apparent that Seferovic's desire to find food and additional clothes and to locate his brother were mentioned as significant – and on their face, much more plausible – reasons for forsaking the comparative safety of his hillside bolthole for the perils of a town under hostile occupation than any supposed preoccupation with pigeon-feeding.

Not only does the witness's evidence-in-chief deflate defence counsel's ridicule of the notion that Seferovic would have risked death or capture 'to feed a pet bird' (a tendentious, if forensically unremarkable, adversarial distortion); it also significantly qualifies the Appeals Chamber's bald assertion that '*the* reason why he returned to the town where the Serbian paramilitary forces had been attacking, and from which he had escaped, was to feed his pet pigeons'.[37] The welfare of his pigeons was, at most, only one factor amongst several prompting Seferovic to steal back through the streets of Kozarac, where he would become witness to a double murder. Taking advantage of this – for an Evidence scholar – unusual opportunity to compare trial transcripts against the facts recited on appeal, and uncovering such material discrepancies between them, inevitably prompts the uncomfortable speculation that similar factual distortions might be creeping into domestic criminal appeals in England and Wales, and with very little prospect of detection after the event. Similar distortions may arise in judicial fact-finding in other adjudicative fora, including the European Court of Human Rights.[38] Socio-legal scholars have for many decades explored the institutional dynamics of 'case construction'[39] and we are familiar with the ways in which police interview technique[40] or incomplete prosecution disclosure,[41] for example, can distort the factual narratives presented at trial. Less attention has been devoted to potential discrepancies between trial proceedings and factual claims or assumptions on appeal.[42]

A second intriguing dimension of forensic analysis concerns the nature of the prosecution's response to the defence argument challenging Seferovic's evidence on appeal. Ms Brenda Hollis, appearing for the prosecution, adopted what might be termed a 'confession and avoidance' strategy. She conceded that Seferovic's actions might not appear very rational by normal standards, but insisted that people often do irrational things – especially where pet animals are concerned:

> The appellant seemed to argue that because this witness, Nihad Seferovic, would say that he would go into a town where the Serbs were taking it over to feed his birds, that his testimony is inherently incredible. Now, is this a decision many people would think is rational?

---

[37] *Prosecutor v Tadić*, IT-94-1-A (Appeals Chamber), 15 July 1999, [66] (emphasis supplied).

[38] Compare the ECtHR Chamber's factual analysis in *Al-Khawaja and Tahery v United Kingdom* (2009) 49 EHRR 1 with the Grand Chamber's subsequent treatment (of ostensibly the same facts and evidence) in *Al-Khawaja and Tahery v United Kingdom* (2012) 54 EHRR 23.

[39] Mike McConville, Andrew Sanders, and Roger Leng, *The Case for the Prosecution: Police Suspects and the Construction of Criminality* (London, Routledge, 1991).

[40] Saul M Kassin et al, 'Police-Induced Confessions: Risk Factors and Recommendations' (2010) 34 *Law and Human Behavior* 3; David Dixon, 'Integrity, Interrogation and Criminal Injustice' in Jill Hunter, Paul Roberts, Simon NM Young and David Dixon (eds), *The Integrity of Criminal Process* (Oxford, Hart, 2016).

[41] Tom Smith, 'The "Near Miss" of Liam Allan: Critical Problems in Police Disclosure, Investigation Culture and the Resourcing of Criminal Justice' [2018] *Criminal Law Review* 711.

[42] Note that the point at issue here is *what facts were actually found* at first instance rather than appeal judges consciously second-guessing trial court determinations (which common law appellate courts are generally reluctant to do, especially regarding jury verdicts).

Of course, it is not. But how many times have we heard stories of people going into burning buildings to rescue pets, of doing other things that subject them to a very real and immediate threat of death to save a pet? Are these rational acts? No, they're not. Are these acts that people do engage in? Yes, they are.[43]

There is nothing inherently wrong with the prosecution's strategy of locking horns with the defence on the issue of contextual rationality and its implications for witness credibility. It is difficult to argue with the general proposition that people sometimes behave irrationally, or that one person's rational errand is another person's folly. A more culturally sensitive analysis might nonetheless have provided greater assistance to the Court. On the one hand, Western perceptions of animals are notoriously sentimental. In a culture where every deer calf is Bambi and even ants and fish can become CGI-conjured stars of Hollywood, small wonder that people anthropomorphise their pets! The story of Mr Seferovic's pigeons is almost inevitably viewed through these popular cultural filters by Western English-speakers, but I wonder just how much of this urban sentimentality can legitimately be projected onto the still predominantly agrarian Balkans of the early 1990s. Is it possible, in other words, that the prosecutor's burning-building pet rescue analogy sounds more plausible to *us* than it would do to the average Bosnian as a rationalisation of Mr Seferovic's return to Kozarac at such a dangerous – and, as it turned out, evidentially vital – moment in time?

Then again, it does not take much imagination to appreciate that attitudes towards animals are highly culturally divergent. Vivid examples immediately spring to mind, in the reverence for cattle displayed by Hindus and the Jewish disdain for pork,[44] to say nothing of some Buddhists' aversion to crushing insects underfoot. As a Yorkshireman, I know from personal observation that pigeon-fanciers derive long hours of enjoyment and entirely unsentimentalised peer-group status and prestige from breeding champion racing birds. 'My pigeons are my life', or similar extravagant sentiments, would not astonish hardcore members of the pigeon-fancying fraternity.[45] Pigeons may well have originated from the Middle East,[46] and seem to have a special place in regional history and cultural life. It is claimed that keeping and training homing pigeons dates back to the Egyptian pharaohs. The Sultan of Baghdad set up a pigeon-post system in 1150, but in Beirut, Damascus and Cairo today, 'it is a working-class pastime'.[47] Enthusiasts in Yemen reportedly continue to organise races in the midst of brutal civil war, whilst a particularly prized Iraqi specimen sold for

---

[43] Submissions of Prosecuting Counsel to the Appeals Chamber, Transcript, 20 April 1999, 419.

[44] cf David Fraser, *Anti-Shechita Prosecutions in the Anglo-American World, 1855–1913* (Brighton, MA, Academic Studies Press, 2018).

[45] If you doubt my testimonial credibility, consider this corroboration: Dave Higgens, 'Return of Pigeon Racing "Like Putting Oxygen" Back into Communities', *PA Yorks and Humber*, 1 June 2020: 'Retired miner Mr Greenshield, 72, said … "This is a very strong ex-mining area … So many people have lost people in the mines or are living with illnesses. The whole current situation has got people down and there are a lot of mental problems. The racing is something for people to get out of bed for. People are really looking forward to it. I think it would have killed some off if there hadn't been racing until next year. It's like putting oxygen back into the area."'

[46] Michael D Shapiro et al, 'Genomic Diversity and Evolution of the Head Crest in the Rock Pigeon' (2013) 339 *Science* 1063.

[47] Hugh Levinson, 'In Jordan, The Gentle Art of Keeping Pigeons Is Seen as Dangerously Sexy', *The Independent*, 17 December 2000.

US$180,000.[48] Do any of these cultural traditions and practices resonate with Mr Seferovic's situation,[49] and by extension help to illuminate the issue of his credibility as a witness? Since nobody took it upon themselves during the course of these lengthy proceedings to explore the local cultural context of Seferovic's wartime pigeon-feeding, we will presumably never really know.

A third noteworthy feature of the treatment of Seferovic's evidence concerns defence counsel's attempt to invoke academic commentary in order to attack Seferovic's testimonial credibility before the ICTY Appeals Chamber. In a case-note on *Tadić* published in the *American Journal of International Law*, Michael Scharf described Tadić's convictions of the murders of Besic and Didovic as 'curious', and characterised Nihad Seferovic as 'a Muslim who told the Tribunal the unlikely story that he had witnessed the murders when he returned to Kozarac to feed his pet pigeons after the Serb takeover of the town'.[50] This remark – almost a throwaway line in a Note mainly devoted to discussing the Trial Chamber's ruling on the (non) applicability of the Geneva Conventions to the conflict in Bosnia after 19 May 1992 (the date on which the Yugoslav National Army formally withdrew from hostilities) – was seized on by appellate counsel:[51]

> In our submission, the evidence of that witness [Seferovic] was implausible when analysed and has been described by distinguished commentators as 'curious'. … The evidence has been the subject of consideration and analysis by commentators, and if I could draw the Court's attention to just one, and it is … commentary on International Decisions by Michael Scharf of the New England School of Law, who says – the article beginning on page 718 – at page 719: 'The most important Prosecution victory was the trial chamber's determination that Tadic had stabbed and cut the throats of two Muslim policemen outside a church after they were taken into custody by a group of Serb paramilitary forces. This is the only killing for which Tadic was found guilty by the trial chamber and was the key reason he received a twenty-year sentence. The finding is curious for two reasons'. I underline the word 'curious'. 'First, the only evidence to support it was the testimony of a single witness Nihad Seferovic, a Muslim who told the Tribunal the unlikely story that he had witnessed the murders when he had turned to Kozarac to feed his pet pigeons after the Serb take-over of the town. Second, nowhere in the indictment, which was amended twice by the prosecutor before trial, is there any reference to this murder'. … I take no point on the drafting criticism. It is the evidential position that we say should exercise the minds of this Tribunal.

---

[48] France 24, 'Passion for Pigeons Persists in Arab World', 10 March 2021; BBC News, 'Turkey Lockdown: Pigeon-keeping in Istanbul on the Rise', 31 August 2021, www.bbc.co.uk/news/av/world-europe-58344157.

[49] cf Ed Vulliamy, 'Bosnia Allies Fight Out New War', *The Guardian*, 24 October 1992 (reporting '[a]n old man lies dead, shot on the way to feed his pigeons. Another day in Sarajevo'). More hopefully, see Nick Hawton, 'Army Chiefs Look to a Secure Future as Former Foes Unite', *The Times*, 6 October 2003: 'Ten years ago, Hamza Visca was involved in hand-to-hand fighting in the blown out suburbs of Sarajevo. These days he sits behind his desk in the grand army cultural centre in the Bosnian capital and talks happily about his hobbies of pigeon-fancying … "Well, I guess I've always liked pigeons," the 44-year-old brigadier said, smiling under his brown-tinted John Lennon-style glasses. "Whenever I go abroad, I take photographs of them. So far, I've taken pictures of pigeons in 37 capitals. Since the war, it's had a greater significance for me. They remind me of doves, of symbols of peace."'

[50] MP Scharf, 'Prosecutor v Tadić, Case No IT-94-1-T' (1997) 91 *American Journal of International Law* 718, 719.

[51] These passages are excerpted from ICTY Case No IT-94-1-A, Transcript of Appellant's Submissions, 385–389 (20 April 1999).

At this point Judge Shahabuddeen interrupted defence counsel's flow with the following perceptive and plain-speaking interrogatory:

> Why did Mr Scharf say that the witness told an 'unlikely story'? Did he give any reasons to make out that proposition, that the witness told an 'unlikely story'? Perhaps he did. I don't know.

The paucity and faltering tone of counsel's response unintentionally speak volumes:

> The words 'unlikely story' are followed by the assertion that the witness had returned to Kozarac to feed his pet pigeons after the Serb take-over, and I think that, as I read the commentary of Mr Scharf, is what he was saying was unlikely. ... And the unlikelihood is obviously a reflection of the inherent improbability of anybody with any regard to their own safety willingly entering a town currently occupied by Serb paramilitaries when they were in the process of actively deporting the Muslims to concentration camps in order to feed a pet bird. It is, we would submit, such an unlikely and improbable story that any Tribunal would want to reflect on whether it could possibly be true.

To which Judge Shahabuddeen indulgently replied: 'I understand. Thank you'.

What should be understood from this passage of argument? Michael Scharf has been one of the most well-informed and – as this passage intimates – influential commentators writing in English on the ICTY.[52] However, Scharf's offhand dismissal of Seferovic's evidence must have been based on the summary reproduced by the ICTY Trial Chamber which – as we have seen – bears only passing relation to the testimony Seferovic actually gave.[53] Thus, defence counsel on appeal was effectively invoking the authority of Scharf's academic commentary to dignify the appellant's submissions, but Scharf's opinion does not appear to have been particularly considered or supported by the trial record. Here, then, is a nice illustration of counsel's strategic attempt to rely upon expert (academic) authority for drawing factual inferences which (i) on the defence's own argument were supposedly self-evident, and thus presumably not in need of expert authority anyway; and (ii) rested upon no more than the Tribunal's own evidentiary analysis at first instance.

One does not need to be an adherent of autopoesis[54] to detect a (viciously) circular self-referentiality in the sequence of inferences underpinning counsel's argument. Reducing Seferovic's motivation to an avian mercy mission is the very definition of an institutionally constructed fact, which was then deployed forensically to suggest the inherent implausibility of his eyewitness account. Inherent implausibility is a familiar basis for impeaching the credibility of a witness,[55] but its epistemic legitimacy is predicated on the witness actually having made the claims attributed to them.

---

[52] Michael P Scharf, *Balkan Justice* (Durham, NC, Carolina Academic Press, 1997).

[53] Scharf, ibid, 143 and 211, repeats his summary dismissal of Seferovic's testimony in his book-length account of the Tadić trial: 'When the attack began on Kozarac in May 1992, Seferovic said that he fled to the hills seeking safety. Two days later, he ... snuck back into town to feed his pet pigeons, he said ... The ... witness was Nihad Seferovic who had ... told the unlikely story that he had seen the defendant slit the throats of two Muslim policemen when he snuck back into Kozarac after the Serb takeover to feed his pigeons.'

[54] cf Richard Nobles and David Schiff, *Understanding Miscarriages of Justice* (Oxford, Oxford University Press, 2000).

[55] For empirical elucidation, see Paul Roberts and Candida Saunders, 'Piloting PTWI – A Socio-Legal Window on Prosecutors' Assessments of Evidence and Witness Credibility' (2010) 30 *OJLS* 101, 116–20.

A fair reading of the trial record would not make pigeon-feeding the predominant, still less the exclusive, explanation for Seferovic's presence at the scene. Moreover, common law courts would generally exclude expert testimony of witness credibility (falling short of a clinical diagnosis) as an impermissible incursion on the trier of fact's primary institutional responsibility for resolving contested issues of fact.[56] Although there is no need to worry about protecting the lay jury in international criminal trials, which are always staffed by professional adjudicators, expert opinion of witness credibility is usually irrelevant and sometimes prejudicial. Scharf's editorialising opinion that Seferovic told an 'unlikely story' would appear to be both.[57]

5. LEVERAGING THE CRITICAL RESOURCES OF INTERNATIONAL CRIMINAL TRIALS

Beyond its intrinsic narrative appeal and vital role in securing two murder convictions, the tale of Mr Seferovic's pigeons was recounted in this chapter to exemplify the range and richness of the critical resources that international criminal adjudication offers to the student of evidence and proof. These resources are both material and intellectual. The following five exemplars and illustrations are by no means intended to be exhaustive.

(1) The websites of the UN's two ad hoc Tribunals, the ICTY[58] and ICTR,[59] house the most extensive collection of primary documents and ancillary information about contemporary international criminal trials currently available to the public. Although these Tribunals had ceased operation by 2017,[60] all the Courts' records and databases have been preserved 'as a monument to th[eir] accomplishments, and provid[ing] access to the wealth of resources that the Tribunal[s] produced over the years'.[61] The ICC has followed their lead, and currently has some thirty cases on foot. These unique, and for the ICC still accumulating, archives contain not merely appellate decisions, but full transcripts of first-instance trial proceedings, rulings and judgments – materials of a type that cannot be obtained easily, if at all, for domestic criminal trials. Running to millions of pages,[62] keyword-searchable transcripts of hearings and trials involving

---

[56] See eg *R v B* [2019] 1 WLR 2550, [2018] EWCA Crim 2733, [14]; *R v S; R v W* [2006] EWCA Crim 1404, [26]. For contextual discussion, see Paul Roberts and Tony Ward, 'Expert Evidence in Trials of Sexual Offences' in Pamela Radcliffe, Gisli Gudjonsson, Anthony Heaton-Armstrong and David Wolchover (eds), *Witness Testimony in Sexual Cases: Evidential, Investigative and Scientific Perspectives* (Oxford, Oxford University Press, 2016).

[57] Might it be said that invoking Scharf's assessment was strictly argument rather than evidence? This looks like a distinction without a difference in this forensic context, but if one were forced to choose for the sake of conceptual purity, the inherent credibility of Seferovic's story was surely a question of fact rather than a proposition of law.

[58] www.icty.org/.

[59] https://unictr.irmct.org/.

[60] Legacy functions are discharged by the UN's International Residual Mechanism for Criminal Tribunals: see www.irmct.org/.

[61] ICTY homepage, www.icty.org/.

[62] The ICTY's own estimate is 2.5 million pages of transcripts. The ultimately abortive four-year trial of former Yugoslav president Slobodan Milošević alone filled almost 50,000 pages of transcript: *Prosecutor v Slobodan Milošević* (IT-02-54).

more than 250 accused offer a fascinating window into the world of international criminal adjudication. It is a vantage point which Evidence scholars and teachers might readily exploit, not least as a partial corrective to the disproportionate influence of appellate judgments on the pedagogic emphasis and popular conceptions of our subject.

Even if transcripts of English criminal trials could be obtained more easily, they would not necessarily provide much indication of how the jury arrived at its peremptory general verdict of 'guilty' or 'not guilty'. Case analysis, for us, largely equates to dissecting what appellate courts have said about evidentiary norms or aspects of trial procedure, rather than having the opportunity to scrutinise evidence-taking and fact-finding processes. The proceedings and judgments of the ICTY, ICTR and ICC therefore contribute a source of valuable insights which are generally absent from English criminal jurisprudence; and also, it might be added, from the judgments of the ECtHR, which tend to adopt formulaic language and rarely explain how any factual conclusion has been proven or inferred.

(2) The transcripts of Seferovic's testimony allow us to study the microdynamics of the evidential narratives 'constructed' through counsel's examination-in-chief and cross-examination at trial. Here we can trace the intersection between the applicable normative framework for presenting and testing witnesses' evidence and strategies for developing one's case in an adversarial trial setting. Seferovic's testimony presented Tadić's defence with several acute difficulties. Most obviously, Seferovic claimed to have witnessed the entire crime with no room for errors of interpretation. It was not as if (on Seferovic's account) Besic or Didovic had provoked Tadić, or been killed in a fight in circumstances where Tadić might plausibly claim self-defence or lack of mens rea. Moreover, Seferovic and Tadic had known each other all their lives: this was a 'recognition', rather than the more common identification of a stranger, eyewitness scenario and there was consequently little room for suggesting that Tadić had been misidentified as the cold-blooded assassin. Well-rehearsed forensic scripts for emphasising the weaknesses of eyewitness identification evidence[63] and playing up its role in producing miscarriages of justice[64] were consequently largely redundant. Prosecution counsel had concluded Seferovic's examination-in-chief with the classic dock-identification routine:

> [Counsel] You have told us about knowing Dule Tadic since you were a child and he was a child. Can you look around the courtroom, please, and tell us if Mr. Tadic is here?
>
> A. Yes.
>
> Q. Can you point him out, please?
>
> A. Yes, the gentleman up there. (Indicated).
>
> Q. Is that the man with the dark hair wearing the blue jacket and tie?
>
> A. Yes, that is it.

---

[63] Richard A Wise, Clifford S Fishman and Martin A Safer, 'How to Analyze the Accuracy of Eyewitness Testimony in a Criminal Case' (2009) 42 *Connecticut Law Review* 435.

[64] Criminal trial judges in England and Wales are instructed to tell juries that 'there is a need for caution to avoid the risk of injustice' and that even witnesses who are honest, convinced and convincing may still misidentify perpetrators: Judicial College, *The Crown Court Compendium Part 1: Jury and Trial Management and Summing Up* (2020), 15-1.

Q. Mr. Seferovic, are you absolutely certain that this is the man you saw at the church slaughtering Osman and Edin?

A. Yes, I am certain. Yes, I am certain that this is the man.[65]

Defence cross-examination of Seferovic was therefore largely confined to whittling away at his account of the precise location and sight-lines of his hiding place, with the implication that either (1) Seferovic had been further away from the incident than he had led the court to believe when examined in-chief, so that he cannot have had a completely unobscured view of the murders as he claimed; or (2) – defence counsel's principal line of attack – that Seferovic had made the whole thing up: he was never in Kozorac at the material time, or at any rate never witnessed any murders:

Q. When you were going through the back yards and gardens down to the orchard after you had been to your brother's house, you said that you could see the church clearly from where you were in the orchard?

A. Yes, yes. I could see the church clearly, all too clearly, because there were leaves all over. The grass was a metre, a metre-and-a-half, tall. The hedge around the ground, the branches of plum trees, bending down to the ground. So that I could move as I liked and nobody, nobody could really see me.

Q. Those things would also stop you seeing clearly if you have to look through grass or trees, branches, hedges?

A. No, no. No, I was not moving then. I had found a spot and I had a good view. Nobody was paying attention to me, but to the police.

Q. How long did you remain then in this position in the orchard?

A. Not long, the incident happened perhaps a few minutes after I arrived. I did not have a watch so ...

Q. After the incident happened did you leave straightaway?

A. Yes, straightaway because there was very intensive fire and bullets were whistling by.

Q. Bullets were whistling by where you were in the orchard?

A. Yes, yes, when this incredible fire started, then I beat a retreat. ...

Q. Did you say that your brother's house was about 100 metres from the Serbian orthodox church in the centre of Kozarac?

A. I may have and maybe it is that far. I said I never measured the distance; it could be.

Q. Did you say that you only moved some 30 metres from your brother's house to a small orchard?

A. No, I said that the house, that is, was about 30 metres or more from the orchard to the church. That is what I said.

Q. Did you say that you were walking closer to a collection point?

A. No, no, I did not.

---

[65] This passage and following excerpted from ICTY Case No IT-94-1-T, Transcript of Hearing, 2651–2706 (14 June 1996).

Q. Because what I am suggesting to you is that you have made up this story about seeing this incident in the afternoon in Kozarac in front of the Serbian orthodox church?

A. No, I did not invent it. I saw it with my own eyes ...

Q. Again so it is clear, what I suggest to you is that you have made this up; you did not see this at all?

A. No, I did not make this up. I saw this with my own eyes and this is what I claim.

As may be inferred from these passages of cross-examination, Seferovic was a model witness from the prosecution's point of view. He stuck tenaciously to the basic outline of his story, provided considerable contextual detail, rarely appeared to contradict himself even on peripheral matters, and readily admitted that he could not remember certain significant facts, such as the day of the week on which the murders had occurred or precisely how far the church was from his brother's house in Kozarac.

We can further compare this trial record against findings of fact made at first instance, and the subsequent handling of disputed points of evidence on appeal. In this instance, striking discrepancies emerged between what the prosecution's star witness actually said at trial, and what counsel and the ICTY Appeals Chamber later assumed he had said. One can only speculate as to the frequency with which similar discrepancies might occur during the course of litigation generally. It is right to say that international criminal trials are atypical in many important respects: proceedings akin to those in *Tadić* are far more complex, lengthy and controversial than garden-variety domestic criminal prosecutions. On the other hand, we frequently read anecdotal reports that testifying in court is a frustrating and often distressing experience for lay witnesses.[66] They do not get to tell their story in their own words, and they sometimes leave with the impression that the court has not really heard what they came to say. Set in this institutional context, it does not seem fanciful to suggest that the corruption of testimony on appeal may be another way in which 'lay truth' is (mis)translated into 'lawyers' truth'[67] through further layers of reinterpretation. This is not to relativise the concept of truth,[68] but only an attempt to elucidate more fully the epistemological conditions and complexities of institutionally mediated truths (facts).[69]

(3) Seferovic's testimony also demonstrates how examining trials and appeals conducted by international tribunals can bring into sharper focus the extent to which justice depends on a shared cultural background of norms, assumptions

[66] See eg Owen Boycott, 'Courtrooms to Beef Up Protective Measures for Witnesses and Victims – Witnesses and Victims to be Better Protected after Survey Uncovers Widespread Dissatisfaction with Courtroom Experience', *The Guardian*, 11 September 2015.

[67] JD Jackson, 'Law's Truth, Lay Truth and Lawyers' Truth: The Representation of Evidence in Adversary Trials' (1992) III *Law and Critique* 29.

[68] For a concise conceptual primer, see Susan Haack, 'Truth, Truths, "Truth", and "Truths" in the Law' (2003) 17 *Harvard Journal of Law and Public Policy* 17. Note, in particular, Haack's elementary caution that, 'scare quotes ... turn an expression meaning "X" into an expression meaning "so-called 'X'". So scare-quotes "truth," as distinct from truth, is what is taken to be truth; and scare-quotes "truths," as distinct from truths, are claims, propositions, or beliefs, which are taken to be truths – many of which are not really truths at all', ibid 18.

[69] See further, Susan Haack, 'Of Truth, in Science and in Law' (2008) 73 *Brooklyn Law Review* 985; Robert S Summers, 'Formal Legal Truth and Substantive Truth in Judicial Fact-Finding – Their Justified Divergence in Some Particular Cases' (1999) 18 *Law and Philosophy* 497.

and expectations. We might think of this style of inquiry as a form of comparative institutional anthropology.[70] Wittgenstein memorably declared that 'if a lion could talk, we could not understand him.'[71] This was a striking way of expressing the thought that communication is rooted in a shared 'life-world' of meaning, not in the sounds we utter in speech or the abstract symbols we use to commit our experience to writing. Criminal trials of animals are, literally speaking, a thing of the past.[72] However, if international criminal adjudication figuratively exemplifies Wittgenstein's conundrum of communicating with 'lions', its study might also reasonably be expected to illuminate the dynamics of domestic trials, in which the beguiling familiarity of a common language may serve to conceal the divisions of cultural experience. In this way, international criminal proceedings may help to make explicit what is often relatively opaque at the domestic level.

The cultural conditioning of experience can hardly be ignored when trial participants do not even speak the same language (a situation also sometimes encountered in domestic criminal trials in England and Wales,[73] and an increasingly likely scenario in multicultural societies).[74] In extreme cases, international criminal proceedings involve participants, as accused, victims and witnesses, whose cultural experience and world-view are so divergent that their nations, tribes, parties or factions have recently resorted to genocidal violence and 'ethnic cleansing'. In these desperate circumstances, the capacity of any model of criminal procedure to deliver justice founded on secure inferences of fact is truly tested to the limit.

(4) The use of Scharf's article by appellate counsel in *Tadić* might be regarded by scholars as a mixed blessing. It is encouraging to know that academic literature is read by practitioners, and may even be cited in court and influence adjudicative outcomes. The law and practice of international criminal tribunals developed at an extraordinary pace, but relatively few scholars – especially during the first decades – commented on 'nuts-and-bolts' procedural issues, or even on major points of evidentiary principle. In this evolutionary institutional environment there is plenty of opportunity for scholars to make their mark and to contribute, in very tangible ways, to promoting the goals and serving the ideals of international criminal justice. But this kind of power carries with it a measure of responsibility. I do not know what basis Scharf had for branding Seferovic's testimony an 'unlikely story' leading to 'curious' convictions, but the tendentious use of these remarks by appellate counsel in *Tadić* might stand as a cautionary tale for commentators. In international criminal adjudication, the old cliché rings true: loose talk can cost lives.

(5) Tadić's convictions for the murders of Besic and Didovic shed interesting light on the question of sufficiency of proof and the related issue of the scope of appellate

---

[70] Robert Burns, Marianne Constable, Justin Richland and Winnifred Sullivan, 'Analysing the Trial: Interdisciplinary Methods' (2008) 31 *Political and Legal Anthropology Review* 303.

[71] L Wittgenstein, *Philosophical Investigations*, 3rd edn (Oxford, Blackwell, 1967 [1953]) 223: for elucidation, see M McGinn, *Wittgenstein and the Philosophical Investigations* (London, Routledge, 1997) 51–60.

[72] W Ewald, 'Comparative Jurisprudence (I): What Was it Like to Try a Rat?' (1995) 143 *University of Pennsylvania Law Review* 1889, part I; EP Evans, *The Criminal Prosecution and Capital Punishment of Animals: The Lost History of Europe's Animal Trials* [1906] (London, Faber & Faber, 1987).

[73] cf RG Parry, 'The Language of Evidence' [2004] *Criminal Law Review* 1015.

[74] See eg *Erlam v Rahman* [2015] EWHC 1215 (QB); *Bielecki v DPP* [2011] EWHC 2245 (Admin), [2012] Crim LR 785; *R v B* [2007] EWCA Crim 374.

review of findings of fact by first-instance tribunals. On appeal, defence counsel complained:

> The evidence [given by Seferovic] was identified in the judgement of the Trial Chamber at paragraph 393, and it merely recounts there the evidence that the witness gave; and at 394, it sets out the case for the Defence, that he was not in the town at the time those two people were killed. It was not, with respect to the Trial Chamber, the most critical analysis of the evidence of the witness Seferovic; it was, in truth, no more than a recitation of the effect of what he said.[75]

Read strictly in terms of the reasons actually stated in the Trial Chamber's judgment for finding Tadić guilty on these counts, this complaint has some merit and plausibility. The conclusion that Seferovic's testimony was sufficiently compelling to prove the charges against Tadić beyond reasonable doubt is delivered ex cathedra without context or explicit rationalisation. The ICTY Appeals Chamber nonetheless concluded that: 'There is no basis for the Appeals Chamber to consider that the Trial Chamber acted unreasonably in relying on that evidence for its finding that the Appellant killed the two men.'[76]

Common lawyers will not be surprised to find an appellate court refusing to overturn first-instance findings of fact, especially where assessments of witness credibility are crucial to the factual determination and the original fact-finder had the advantage of observing the witness testify and undergo cross-examination. Recall, however, that there are no lay juries at the ICTY: fact-finding is undertaken by professional judges, who must then, in the continental juristic fashion,[77] write authoritative judgments justifying their factual conclusions as well as setting out the law they have applied to the facts thus found.[78] The example of witness Seferovic's testimony is revealing on this score in at least two respects. First, even with professional fact-finders, appellate tribunals are likely to be reluctant to intervene for as long as demeanour and live cross-examination are felt to be significant in judging witness credibility. Put another way, introducing more non-jury trials in domestic criminal proceedings would not necessarily open up appellate review to the extent that might be imagined.

Secondly, this aspect of the *Tadić* judgment shows that the discipline of requiring reasons for verdicts may not amount to a very great deal in practice. The prosaic challenges of encapsulating the inferential processes of factfinding in a reasonably concise yet still appropriately informative summary deserve more careful consideration when critics of unreasoned jury verdicts extol the virtues of the continental model of

---

[75] ICTY Case No IT-94-1-A, Transcript of Appellant's Submissions, 386–87 (20 April 1999).

[76] ICTY Case No IT-94-1-A, Appeals Chamber Judgment, 15 July 1999, [66].

[77] Of course, common law judges in non-jury trials write such judgments, too. Also see John Jackson and Sean Doran, *Judge Without Jury: Diplock Trials in the Adversary System* (Oxford, Oxford University Press, 1995).

[78] See eg Stephen Ross Levitt, 'The Life and Times of a Local Court Judge in Berlin' (2009) 10 *German Law Journal* 169; Antoinette Perrodet and Elena Ricci, 'The Italian System' in Mireille Delmas-Marty and JR Spencer (eds), *European Criminal Procedures* (Cambridge, Cambridge University Press, 2002) 370 ('the judge must set out in a reasoned judgment the elements of the facts and of the law which form the basis of his judgment, stating the evidence he has accepted and the reasons for rejecting evidence to the contrary').

reasoned judgment-giving.[79] In this particular instance, however, much of the apparent mystery surrounding the evidentiary significance of Mr Seferovic's pigeons in the judgments of the ICTY Trial and Appeals Chambers can easily be dispelled, simply by reading the transcripts of Seferovic's testimony which directly and quite unequivocally implicated Duško Tadić in the murders of Edin Besic and Osman Didovic.

6. INCONCLUSIVE THOUGHTS ON METHODOLOGICAL WORK IN PROGRESS

Much has changed over the two decades since I started thinking, teaching and writing about evidence and proof in the context of international criminal adjudication.[80] The trial practice and appellate jurisprudence of the ICTY and ICTR, interpreting serial iterations of the tribunals' Rules of Procedure and Evidence,[81] have been reinforced by the ICC and the 'internationalised' tribunals,[82] producing rapid normative development in both substantive and procedural international criminal law.[83] This has, in turn, generated a critical secondary literature, spanning technical procedural and doctrinal issues,[84] broader theorisation of evidentiary norms,[85] synthetic comparisons of procedural models,[86] and even some exploration of the epistemological

---

[79] For discussion, see John D Jackson, 'Unbecoming Jurors and Unreasoned Verdicts: Realising Integrity in the Jury Room' in J Hunter, P Roberts, SNM Young and D Dixon (eds), *The Integrity of Criminal Process* (Oxford, Hart, 2016); Paul Roberts, 'Does Article 6 of the European Convention on Human Rights Require Reasoned Verdicts in Criminal Trials?' (2011) 11 *Human Rights Law Review* 213.

[80] P Roberts, 'Why International Criminal Evidence?' in P Roberts and M Redmayne (eds), *Innovations in Evidence and Proof* (Oxford, Hart, 2007).

[81] Between the original 1994 draft and the final 2015 iteration the ICTY's RPE underwent fifty published revisions.

[82] Cesare PR Romano, André Nollkaemper and Jann K Kleffner (eds), *Internationalized Criminal Courts: Sierra Leone, East Timor, Kosovo and Cambodia* (Oxford, Oxford University Press, 2004).

[83] For overviews, see Robert Cryer, Darryl Robinson and Sergey Vasiliev, *An Introduction to International Criminal Law and Procedure*, 4th edn (Cambridge, Cambridge University Press, 2019); Antonio Cassese and Paola Gaeta, *International Criminal Law*, 3rd edn (Oxford, Oxford University Press, 2013).

[84] See eg John D Jackson and Yassin M Brunger, 'Witness Preparation in the ICC: An Opportunity for Principled Pragmatism' (2015) 13 *Journal of International Criminal Justice* 601; R Cryer, 'A Message From Elsewhere: Witnesses Before International Criminal Tribunals' in P Roberts and M Redmayne (eds), *Innovations in Evidence and Proof* (Oxford, Hart, 2007); Richard May, David Tolbert, John Hocking, Ken Roberts, Bing Bing Jia, Daryl Mundis and Gabriël Oosthuizen (eds), *Essays on ICTY Procedure and Evidence in Honour of Gabrielle Kirk McDonald* (Dordrecht, Kluwer, 2001); Rod Dixon, 'Developing International Rules of Evidence for the Yugoslav and Rwanda Tribunals' (1997) 7 *Transnational Law and Contemporary Problems* 81.

[85] Michael Bohlander, 'Paradise Postponed? For a Judge-Led Generic Model of International Criminal Procedure and an End to "Draft-as-You-Go"', in M Ambrus and RA Wessel (eds), *Netherlands Yearbook of International Law 2014* (The Hague, TMC Asser Press, 2015); John D Jackson and Yassin M Brunger, 'Fragmentation and Harmonisation in the Development of Evidentiary Practices in International Criminal Tribunals' in Elies van Sliedregt and Sergey Vasiliev (eds), *Pluralism in International Criminal Law* (Oxford, Oxford University Press, 2014); Peter Murphy, 'No Free Lunch, No Free Proof: The Indiscriminate Admission of Evidence is a Serious Flaw in International Criminal Trials' (2010) 8 *Journal of International Criminal Justice* 539; Richard May and Marieke Wierda, 'Trends in International Criminal Evidence: Nuremberg, Tokyo, The Hague, and Arusha' (1999) 37 *Columbia Journal of Transnational Law* 725.

[86] Kai Ambos, *Treatise on International Criminal Law*, vol III: *International Criminal Procedure* (Oxford, Oxford University Press, 2016); Mireille Delmas-Marty, 'Reflections on the "Hybridisation" of Criminal Procedure' in John Jackson, Maximo Langer and Peter Tillers (eds), *Crime, Procedure and Evidence in a Comparative and International Context* (Oxford, Hart, 2008); Christoph JM Safferling, *Towards an International Criminal Procedure* (Oxford, Oxford University Press, 2001).

practices[87] and inferential logic of fact-finding in international criminal trials[88] – exemplars of the interdisciplinary scholarship advocated in this chapter. But one thing that has not changed much, on my reading, is the comparative neglect of evidence and procedure[89] relative to the oceans of ink devoted to commentary on other aspects of international criminal justice such as the politics of international prosecutions and trials (will any more 'great powers' ever sign up to the ICC Statute? Is the Court an unwitting instrument of neocolonialism?), questions of jurisdiction and institutional dynamics (eg the contested roles of the ICC Prosecutor and UN Security Council), theoretical tensions between retributive and restorative ideals (notably implicating victims' rights), and major developments in substantive criminal law. Besides, compared with domestic systems of criminal procedure and evidence evolved over centuries, international criminal procedure is still in its formative youth.

The story of Mr Seferovic's pigeons struck a chord and has stayed with me down the years. Although merely one tiny droplet in an ocean of pain and suffering and unspeakable atrocities prosecuted before the ICTY, Nihad Seferovic evidently cared about these small details – for him, pivotal life-events – and Duško Tadić was made to care.[90] Beyond the fact that human beings are hard-wired to love a good story,[91] perhaps it is the capacity of witness testimonies to render justice on a human scale that makes such narratives so memorable and compelling – the more so when the 'bigger picture' presents an invidious choice between abstracted summaries and generalisations or an accumulation of details too awful to contemplate and almost, literally, beyond comprehension.[92] Now, it is notoriously perilous to generalise from a single case; or more accurately regarding the case study presented in this chapter, from a single testimonial strand of one part of one case. But I think this standard objection to non-statistical inference misfires when targeted at methodological inquiries of the kind undertaken in much of Ralph Henham's published work. A method is not a theory, just as a tool is not a blueprint and a brick is not a house. If methodological

---

[87] Yvonne McDermott, 'Strengthening the Evaluation of Evidence in International Criminal Trials' (2017) 17 *International Criminal Law Review* 1; Nancy Combs, *Fact-Finding Without Facts: The Uncertain Evidentiary Foundations of International Criminal Convictions* (Cambridge, Cambridge University Press, 2010).

[88] Yvonne McDermott and Colin Aitken, 'Analysis of Evidence in International Criminal Trials using Bayesian Belief Networks' (2017) 16 *Law, Probability & Risk* 111; Yvonne McDermott, 'Inferential Reasoning and Proof in International Criminal Trials' (2015) 13 *Journal of International Criminal Justice* 507.

[89] Paul Roberts, 'The Priority of Procedure and the Neglect of Evidence and Proof: Facing Facts in International Criminal Law' (2015) 13 *Journal of International Criminal Justice* 479.

[90] At least according to a thin conception of 'made to care': Tadić was forced to listen to Seferovic's testimony, and was condemned and punished for the crimes that testimony established. Confession, remorse, repentance, apology – these are more ambitious, and elusive, goals, that may be beyond the institutional competence of public trials to deliver: cf RA Duff, *Punishment, Communication and Community* (Oxford, Oxford University Press, 2001); Alan Norrie, 'Albert Speer, Guilt, and "The Space Between"' in Matt Matravers (ed), *Punishment and Political Theory* (Oxford, Hart, 1999).

[91] Christopher Brooker, *The Seven Basic Plots: Why We Tell Stories* (London, Continuum, 2004); William Twining, *Rethinking Evidence: Exploratory Essays*, 2nd edn (Cambridge, Cambridge University Press, 2006) chs 9–13; Nancy Pennington and Reid Hastie, 'A Cognitive Theory of Juror Decision Making: The Story Model' (1991) 13 *Cardozo Law Review* 519.

[92] cf Lawrence Douglas, *The Memory of Judgment: Making Law and History in the Trials of the Holocaust* (Yale University Press, 2001); Hannah Arendt, *Eichmann in Jerusalem: A Report on the Banality of Evil* (London, Penguin, 1994 [1963]).

inquiries are always in this (methodological) sense work in progress, and may seem unsatisfactorily preliminary and incomplete (even to those undertaking them!), they are also essential precursors to robust theory construction, well-grounded substantive analyses, effective policy-making and responsible curation of the disciplines. Since ideas, concepts and research methods never retire, the intellectual and practical legacies of methodological scholarship are both unknown and potentially unlimited.

This chapter employed the case study of Mr Seferovic's pigeons to illustrate numerous ways in which the critical resources of international criminal adjudication might be leveraged to enrich scholarship on evidence, proof and procedure. In broader disciplinary contemplation, much of the potential value of these materials for Evidence scholars and teachers is encapsulated in a distinctive brand of comparativism. International criminal tribunals are an object lesson in sui generis comparative institutional design and procedural transplants. The ICTY, ICTR and ICC have all combined characteristic features of adversarial and inquisitorial process in novel and imaginative ways.[93] In an era of expanding and deepening legal cosmopolitanism, international criminal proceedings might be looked upon as laboratories of juridical innovation and potential models for domestic legal reform. Moreover, on a broad view of 'international criminal evidence' – one that embraces relevant aspects of international human rights law, in particular – it might be said that the old rigid distinction between 'domestic' and 'international' legal proceedings is already breaking down and heading for obsolescence. Supranational and foreign legal norms are increasingly applicable in national legal process – as persuasive authority or examples of state practice, if not technically as legal precedents.[94]

The notion of the 'domestic' Evidence lawyer is starting to seem anachronistic. For some years now, I have been advising my Criminal Evidence students that in order to get to grips with criminal procedure in England and Wales they need to become proficient in human rights jurisprudence and argumentation alongside mastering the intricacies of traditional common law evidence.[95] The right to a fair trial in international human rights law supplies a flexible normative framework for a new generation of evidentiary studies seamlessly integrating domestic criminal jurisprudence, comparative criminal procedure and international criminal law.[96] International criminal trials, and

---

[93] Kai Ambos, 'International Criminal Procedure: "Adversarial," "Inquisitorial" or "Mixed"?' (2003) 3 *International Criminal Law Review* 1. For theoretical challenges and complexities, see Máximo Langer, 'The Long Shadow of the Adversarial and Inquisitorial Categories' in Markus D Dubber and Tatjana Hörnle (eds), *The Oxford Handbook of Criminal Law* (Oxford, Oxford University Press, 2014); Paul Roberts, 'Faces of Justice Adrift? Damaska's Comparative Method and the Future of Common Law Evidence' in John Jackson, Maximo Langer and Peter Tillers (eds), *Crime, Procedure and Evidence in A Comparative and International Context* (Oxford, Hart, 2008).

[94] See further, Paul Roberts, 'Normative Evolution in Evidentiary Exclusion: Coercion, Deception and the Right to a Fair Trial' in Paul Roberts and Jill Hunter (eds), *Criminal Evidence and Human Rights* (Oxford, Hart, 2012); Anne-Marie Slaughter 'A Global Community of Courts' (2003) 44 *Harvard International Law Journal* 191; Elaine Mak, *Judicial Decision-Making in a Globalised World: A Comparative Analysis of the Changing Practices of Western Highest Courts* (Oxford, Hart, 2013).

[95] To similar effect, see John D Jackson, 'Common Law Evidence and the Common Law of Human Rights: Towards a Harmonic Convergence?' (2019) 27 *William & Mary Bill of Rights Journal* 689.

[96] Exemplars include Dimitrios Giannoulopoulos, *Improperly Obtained Evidence in Anglo-American and Continental Law* (Oxford, Hart, 2019); Kelly Pitcher, *Judicial Responses to Pre-Trial Procedural Violations in International Criminal Proceedings* (Berlin, Springer, 2018); Yvonne McDermott, *Fairness in International Criminal Trials* (Oxford, Oxford University Press, 2016); Alexander Heinze, *International*

in particular the permanent ICC, were invested with such high hopes and – to some extent contradictory – expectations that they were almost bound to disappoint their supporters and allow their critics to claim vindication. It is said that the honeymoon is over for international criminal justice as a project of global accountability for the worst of humanity's crimes.[97] From the institutional and disciplinary perspectives of cosmopolitan criminal jurisprudence, however, proceduralists' brief encounters with international criminal adjudication intimate the promise of a lasting affair.

Criminal Procedure and Disclosure (Berlin, Dunker & Humblot, 2014); John D Jackson and Sarah J Summers, *The Internationalisation of Criminal Evidence* (Cambridge, Cambridge University Press, 2012).
    [97] David Luban, 'After the Honeymoon: Reflections on the Current State of International Criminal Justice' (2013) 11 *Journal of International Criminal Justice* 505.

12

Defining 'Senior Leaders' and 'Most Responsible' for Prosecution at the Extraordinary Chambers in the Courts of Cambodia: A Jurisdictional Conundrum or a Policy-Driven Discretionary Diktat

MICHAEL G. KARNAVAS, TANYA PETTAY AND NOAH AL-MALT

1. INTRODUCTION

I would like to emphasize strongly that the laws to bring to trial those Khmer Rouge leaders are only having the jurisdiction to try these two categories of people – the senior leaders of Democratic Kampuchea. So who were the senior leaders of Democratic Kampuchea? And if they are identified then the Co-Prosecutors should have prosecuted them all. And the other category of those who are to be on trial were those who were most responsible for the crimes. So those who were most responsible for the crimes have to be punished. Otherwise the office of Co-Prosecutor has to terminate the criminal action. But so far the Office of Co-Prosecutor has failed to fulfil its mission and on top of that it even fails to list even one single individual who is classified as the most senior leaders of the Khmer Rouge regime or the most responsible people.[1]

A BELATED REFRAIN by Kar Savuth, the National Co-Lawyer for Kaing Guek Eav (alias 'Duch'), in the first case before the Extraordinary Chambers in the Courts of Cambodia (ECCC), known as Case 001. For the first time in his trial, Duch, through his National Co-Lawyer, argued during his closing argument that he should be acquitted because he was neither a senior leader nor one of those most responsible, and therefore fell outside the ECCC's personal jurisdiction.[2]

---

[1] *Case of KAING Guek Eav*, 001/18-07-2007-ECCC/TC, Transcript, 25 November 2009, E1/80.1, 84–85.
[2] ibid 85–117. See also ibid 117: 'So I request that Duch is now free from being prosecuted.'

This was contrary to what was argued by Duch's International Co-Lawyer, François Roux, who sought a lenient sentence for Duch for his substantial cooperation.[3]

The Trial Chamber made short shrift of Duch's argument, finding that he failed to object in timely fashion to the ECCC's jurisdiction by way of a preliminary objection.[4] On appeal, Duch again sought an acquittal on the basis that he was not a senior leader or one of those most responsible, and therefore fell outside the ECCC's personal jurisdiction.[5] The Supreme Court Chamber found otherwise. It found that the ECCC's personal jurisdiction was indeed limited to 'senior leaders of the Khmer Rouge who are among the most responsible and non-senior leaders of the Khmer Rouge who are also among the most responsible',[6] but then held that whether someone is considered a 'senior leader' or 'most responsible' is not a justiciable jurisdictional issue but a matter of prosecutorial and investigatorial discretion for the Office of the Co-Prosecutors (OCP) and the Office of the Co-Investigating Judges (OCIJ).[7] Notably, the Supreme Court Chamber failed to define the terms 'senior leaders' or 'most responsible'.

The ECCC was an extraordinary chamber established within the existing court structure of Cambodia to bring to trial 'senior leaders of Democratic Kampuchea and those who were most responsible for the crimes and serious violations of Cambodian penal law, international humanitarian law and custom, and the international conventions recognised by Cambodia, that were committed during the period from 17 April 1975 to 6 January 1979'.[8] The ECCC was established by an agreement between the Royal Government of Cambodia (RGC) and the United Nations reached on 6 June 2003.[9] Under Article 2(1) of the Agreement, the ECCC has 'personal jurisdiction over senior leaders of Democratic Kampuchea and those who were most responsible for the crimes referred to in Article 1 of the Agreement'.

The ECCC's subject matter and temporal jurisdictions were precisely defined and non-contentious. This was not so with personal jurisdiction. The meaning of the terms 'senior leaders' and 'most responsible' were not defined in the ECCC's founding documents. While the term 'senior leader' is less contentious and more readily discernible, the term 'most responsible' is elusive and malleable – susceptible to contorted interpretations so that 'it means just what [the Co-Prosecutors and Co-Investigating

---

[3] See *Case of KAING Guek Eav*, 001/18-07-2007-ECCC/TC, Transcript, 26 November 2009, E1/81.1, 9.

[4] *Case of KAING Guek Eav*, 001/18-07-2007-ECCC/TC, Judgment 26 July 2010, E188 ('*Case 001* Trial Judgment') paras 14–15.

[5] *Case of KAING Guek Eav*, 001/18-07-2007-ECCC/SC, Appeal Brief by the Co-Lawyers for Kaing Guek Eav Alias 'Duch' Against the Trial Chamber Judgment of 26 July 2010, 18 November 2010, F14, paras 1–65.

[6] *Case of KAING Guek Eav*, 001/18-07-2007-ECCC/SC, Appeal Judgment, 3 February 2012, F28 ('*Case 001* Appeal Judgment') para 81.

[7] ibid paras 62–79.

[8] Law on the Establishment of the Extraordinary Chambers in the Courts of Cambodia for the Prosecution of Crimes Committed during the Period of Democratic Kampuchea ('Establishment Law'), 27 October 2004, Art 1.

[9] Agreement between the United Nations and the Royal Government of Cambodia Concerning the Prosecution under Cambodian Law of Crimes Committed During the Period of Democratic Kampuchea, 6 June 2003 ('Agreement').

Judges] choose it to mean, neither more nor less'.[10] Invariably, the language selected in articulating who may be prosecuted at the ECCC leads to the question of whether '[o]n the one hand, the language may describe the personal jurisdiction of the ECCC; on the other hand, it may simply act as a guide to the prosecutors in exercising their discretion'.[11] As one commentator presciently predicted: 'The defense will argue the former while the prosecution argues the latter.'[12]

No international criminal tribunal has been set up to prosecute all those who may have been guilty of international crimes. A select group has always been targeted for prosecution. The International Military Tribunal (IMT) at Nuremberg was set up 'for the trial and punishment of the major war criminals of the European Axis countries'.[13] This did not mean others went unpunished. Prosecution of 'other war criminals and other offenders' was left to national military tribunals under Control Council Law No 10.[14] The International Criminal Tribunal for the Former Yugoslavia (ICTY) and the International Criminal Tribunal for Rwanda (ICTR) were set up with a broader jurisdiction to prosecute '*persons responsible*'.[15] Who would be targeted for prosecution at the ICTY and ICTR was left up to the prosecution.[16] Yet, certain procedures were introduced to restrict who would be prosecuted to reflect logistical and financial realities. Ten years after the ICTY's establishment, Rule 11*bis* – which allows the Prosecutor to request transfer of cases to national tribunals – was introduced to give effect to the Security Council's completion strategy.[17] In 2004, the ICTY introduced language into Rule 28 that required the Bureau[18] to determine whether an indictment concentrates on '*one or more of the most senior leaders suspected of being responsible* for crimes within the jurisdiction of the Tribunal'.[19] The ICTR also adopted a referral mechanism.[20] The Special Court for Sierra Leone (SCSL) had the power to prosecute '*persons who bear the greatest responsibility*'.[21]

At the ECCC, there were extensive and protracted negotiations about who would be prosecuted. Both the United Nations and RGC were careful not to explicitly name individuals in the Agreement or Establishment Law. Understandable. To have done so

---

[10] A line from *Through the Looking Glass, and What Alice Found There*, by Lewis Carroll, quoted by ICTY Appeals Chamber Judge Hunt in a dissenting opinion, noting that the majority had failed to provide any support for its interpretation of one of the ICTY Rules of Procedure and Evidence. *Prosecutor v Slobodan Milošević*, IT-02-54-AR73.4, Dissenting Opinion of Judge David Hunt on Admissibility of Evidence in Chief in the Form of Written Statements, 21 October 2003, para 19.

[11] Sean Morrison, 'Extraordinary Language in the Courts of Cambodia: Interpreting the Limiting Language and Personal Jurisdiction of the Cambodian Tribunal' (2009) 37 *Capitol University Law Review* 583, 588.

[12] ibid.

[13] Constitution of the International Military Tribunal (IMT), 8 August 1945, Art 6.

[14] Control Council Law No 10, 20 December 1945, Preamble.

[15] Statute of the International Criminal Tribunal for the former Yugoslavia ('ICTY Statute'), Art 1 (emphasis added); Statute of the International Criminal Tribunal for Rwanda ('ICTR Statute'), Art 1 (emphasis added).

[16] ICTY Statute, Art 16.

[17] See Security Council Resolution 1503, UN Doc No S/Res/1503, 28 August 2003.

[18] The Bureau, according to Rule 2 of the ICTY Rules of Procedure and Evidence, is a body composed of the President, the Vice-President and the Presiding Judges of the Trial Chambers.

[19] ICTY Rules of Procedure and Evidence, Rule 28. Emphasis added.

[20] See ICTR Rules of Procedure and Evidence, Rule 11*bis*.

[21] Statute of the Special Court for Sierra Leone ('SCSL Statute'), Art 1. Emphasis added.

would have violated the presumption of innocence[22] of any named suspect or charged person who would appear before the tribunal. But as Kar Savuth questioned, just who are the 'senior leaders' and 'most responsible'? Do these terms express jurisdictional elements or discretionary policy for the OCP and OCIJ? How satisfying is the Supreme Court Chamber's analysis and is it consistent with what was negotiated? Just what did the contracting parties in establishing the ECCC negotiate and just how did the RGC and the United Nations define these terms? Does it really matter what was negotiated?

In answering these questions, this chapter will explore the negotiations leading up to the establishment of the ECCC. It will also explore the Supreme Court Chamber's Judgment in Case 001, attempting to determine whether the terms 'senior leaders' and 'most responsible' constitute limitations on the ECCC's jurisdiction, or whether they were intended to be prosecutorial or investigatorial policy for the OCP and OCIJ. In doing so, an attempt will be made to define these terms.

This analysis is relevant not only when considering the jurisdiction of future tribunals, but because the issue of personal jurisdiction was particularly contentious in the ECCC's controversial Cases 003 and 004, in which – with public statements made by Cambodian officials[23] and others[24] – accusations of political interference abounded.

Some understanding of the ECCC procedure and context may be of assistance in appreciating the controversy of who was or should be considered 'most responsible'. The ECCC had two Co-Prosecutors, one National and one International, who enjoyed equal status and worked jointly.[25] If the Co-Prosecutors had 'reason to believe' that crimes within the ECCC's jurisdiction were committed, they opened an investigation by sending an Introductory Submission to the Co-Investigating Judges.[26] The two Co-Investigating Judges – one National and one International – were jointly responsible for conducting judicial investigations.[27] After concluding the investigations, the Co-Investigating Judges would issue a Closing Order 'either indicting the Charged Person and sending him or her to trial, or dismissing the case'.[28] A Pre-Trial Chamber

---

[22] International Covenant on Civil and Political Rights, adopted and opened for signature, ratification and accession by General Assembly Resolution 2200A (XXI) of 16 December 1966, entry into force 23 March 1976 ('ICCPR') in accordance with Article 49, Art 4(2).

[23] For example, on 27 October 2010, the *Phnom Penh Post* reported that Prime Minister Hun Sen told UN Secretary-General Ban Ki-moon 'Case 003 will not be allowed. … The court will try the four senior leaders successfully and then finish with Case 002.' *Phnom Penh Post*, 'Hun Sen to Ban Ki-moon: Case 002 Last Trial at ECCC', 27 October 2010. On 10 May 2011, the Cambodian Minister of Information reportedly stated: 'If they want to go into Case 003 and 004, they should just pack their bags and leave.' OCIJ Press Release, *Press Release by the International Co-Investigating Judge*, 10 October 2011.

[24] For example, on 5 May 2011, historian Stephen Heder, a former OCIJ employee (who had previously helped the OCP investigate and draft the Introductory Submission despite the obvious conflict of interest), alleged in a letter to the OCIJ that the closure of the Case 003 investigation was politically motivated. See *Safeguarding Judicial Independence in Mixed Tribunals: Lessons from the ECCC and Best Practices for the Future*, International Bar Association Report, September 2011.

[25] Establishment Law, Arts 16–22 new.

[26] ECCC Internal Rules, Rule 53.

[27] Establishment Law, Arts 23 new–28.

[28] ECCC Internal Rules, Rule 67.

composed of three National judges and two International judges decided disputes between the Co-Prosecutors or between the Co-Investigating Judges.[29] Voting in the Pre-Trial Chamber (and in the Trial and Supreme Court Chambers) required a super-majority of four votes.[30]

Initially, the Co-Prosecutors disagreed about whether to open investigations into Cases 003 and 004, because they disagreed as to whether the suspects were 'most responsible'.[31] The Pre-Trial Chamber was unable to reach a supermajority in adjudicating the Co-Prosecutors' disagreement, resulting in judicial investigations being opened in both cases.[32] In April 2011, International Co-Investigating Judge Siegfried Blunk and National Co-Investigating Judge You Bunleng closed the judicial investigation in Case 003 without charging any suspects.[33] Resigning prior to the issuance of a Closing Order, Judge Blunk stated that although he would not allow himself to be influenced by government pressure, he did not want allegations to call into doubt the integrity of the proceedings in Cases 003 and 004.[34]

Reserve International Co-Investigating Judge Laurent Kasper-Ansermet replaced Judge Blunk in November 2011[35] and unilaterally reopened the judicial investigation in Case 003.[36] However, the Cambodian Supreme Council of Magistracy refused to approve his nomination.[37] After Judge Kasper-Ansermet resigned, feeling unable to perform his work,[38] former ICTY senior prosecution trial lawyer Mark Harmon was sworn in as the new International Co-Investigating Judge[39] and continued investigating Cases 003 and 004.[40] Judge Harmon eventually charged three suspects in Cases

---

[29] Establishment Law, Arts 20 new, 23 new.

[30] Ibid, Arts 14 new, 20 new, 23 new.

[31] Press release, 'Statement of the Acting International Co-Prosecutor: Submission of Two New Introductory Submissions', 8 September 2009, available at www.eccc.gov.kh/sites/default/files/media/ECCC_Act_Int_Co_Prosecutor_8_Sep_2009_(Eng).pdf.

[32] See ECCC Internal Rules, Rule 71(4)(c): 'A decision of the Chamber requires the affirmative vote of at least four judges. This decision is not subject to appeal. If the required majority is not achieved before the Chamber, in accordance with Article 20 new of the Establishment Law, the default decision shall be that the action or decision done by one Co-Prosecutor shall stand, or that the action or decision proposed to be done by one Co-Prosecutor shall be executed.'

[33] *Case of MEAS Muth*, 003/07-09-2009-ECCC/OCIJ, Notice of Conclusion of Judicial Investigation, 29 April 2011, D13.

[34] Press release, 'Statement by the International Co-Investigating Judge', 10 October 2011, available at www.eccc.gov.kh/sites/default/files/media/correctedECCC-INT-CIJ%2010%20Oct%202011%20(Eng).pdf.

[35] Press release, 'Statement from the International Co-Investigating Judge', 19 March 2012, available at www.eccc.gov.kh/en/articles/press-release-international-reserve-co-investigating-judge.

[36] *Case of MEAS Muth*, 003/07-09-2009-ECCC/OCIJ, Order on Resuming the Judicial Investigation, 2 December 2011, D28.

[37] See UN Spokesperson for the Secretary-General on Cambodia, 'Press Statement', 20 January 2012, availableatwww.un.org/sg/en/content/sg/statement/2012-01-20/statement-attributable-spokesperson-secretary-general-cambodia.

[38] ECCC, 'Statement from the International Co-Investigating Judge', press release, 19 March 2012, www.eccc.gov.kh/en/articles/press-release-international-reserve-co-investigating-judge.

[39] ECCC, 'Mark Harmon Sworn in as International Co-Investigating Judge', press release, 19 November 2012, www.eccc.gov.kh/en/articles/mark-harmon-sworn-international-co-investigating-judge.

[40] ECCC, 'Statement by the Co-Investigating Judges Regarding Case 003', press release, 28 February 2013, www.eccc.gov.kh/sites/default/files/media/ECCC%20OCIJ%2028%20Feb%202013%20En.pdf.

003 and 004 – Meas Muth,[41] Im Chaem[42] and Ao An[43] – before resigning for 'strictly personal reasons'.[44] Michael Bohlander was sworn in as the next International Co-Investigating Judge on 31 July 2015.[45] Like his predecessor, he familiarised himself with the case file before investigating and gathering evidence, charging Yim Tith as a suspect in Case 004,[46] and charging Ao An[47] and Meas Muth[48] with additional crimes.

In July 2015, both Co-Investigating Judges requested submissions on whether Im Chaem should be considered a 'senior leader' or among 'those most responsible'.[49] Four months later, they notified the parties that they considered the investigation against Im Chaem to be concluded and that they were inclined to dismiss her case for lack of personal jurisdiction.[50] Im Chaem's case was then severed into Case 004/1,[51] while Ao An's case would later be severed into Case 004/2.[52]

After receiving separate Final Submissions from the International Co-Prosecutor (seeking indictment) and the National Co-Prosecutor (seeking dismissal),[53] the Co-Investigating Judges rendered the disposition of their Closing Order with full reasons to follow.[54] Finding that 'the ECCC has no personal jurisdiction over Im Chaem', the Co-Investigating Judges dismissed the charges against her and informed 'that more specific reasons will be provided at a later date'.[55] They explained that they did so in 'in the interest of the charged person's right to have the outcome of the proceedings against her determined as soon as possible' and in light of the 'logistical and budgetary restrictions', which 'would have delayed the issuance of the closing order without necessity'.[56] Full reasoning was provided on 10 July 2017.[57] On appeal,

---

[41] *Case of MEAS Muth*, 003/07-09-2009-ECCC-OCIJ, Decision to Charge MEAS Muth In Absentia, 3 March 2015; *Case of MEAS Muth*, 003/07-09-2009-ECCC-OCIJ, Notification of Charges against MEAS Muth, 3 March 2015, D128.1.

[42] *Case of IM Chaem*, 004/07-09-2009-ECCC/OCIJ (PTC19), Considerations on IM Chaem's Appeal Against the International Co-Investigating Judge's Decision to Charge Her In Absentia, 1 March 2016, D239/1/8.

[43] See *Case of AO An*, 004/2/07-09-2009-ECCC-OCIJ Closing Order (Indictment), 16 August 2018, D360 ('*Case 004/2* Indictment') para 4.

[44] ECCC, 'Judge Harmon Announces his Resignation', press release, 7 July 2015, www.eccc.gov.kh/en/articles/judge-harmon-announces-his-resignation.

[45] ECCC, 'Michael Bohlander Appointed as New Co-Investigating Judge', press release, 24 August 2015, https://www.eccc.gov.kh/node/34050.

[46] *Case of YIM Tith*, 004/07-09-2009-ECCC-OCIJ, Closing Order, 28 June 2019, para 4.

[47] *Case 004/2* Indictment, para 4.

[48] *Case of MEAS Muth*, 003/07-09-2009-ECCC-OCIJ, Closing Order, 28 November 2018, D267 ('*Case 003* Indictment') para 1.

[49] See *Case of IM Chaem*, 004/1/07-09-2009-ECCC/OCIJ (PTC50), Considerations on the International Co-Prosecutors Appeal of Closing Orders (Reasons), 28 June 2018, D308/3/1/20 ('*Case 004/1* Considerations') para 7.

[50] *Case 004/1* Considerations, para 8.

[51] *Case of IM Chaem*, 004/07-09-2009-ECCC-OCIJ, Order for Severance of IM Chaem from Case 004, 5 February 2016, D286/7.

[52] ibid.

[53] *Case 004/1* Considerations, para 11.

[54] *Case of IM Chaem*, 004/07-09-2009-ECCC-OCIJ, Closing Order (Disposition), 22 February 2017, D308.

[55] ibid para 14.

[56] ibid para 12.

[57] *Case of IM Chaem*, 004/07-09-2009-ECCC-OCIJ, Closing Order (Reasons), 10 July 2017, D308/3.

the Pre-Trial Chamber failed to reach the requisite supermajority for a decision, meaning that the Closing Order dismissing the case against Im Chaem stood.[58]

In Cases 004/2, 003, and 004, the Co-Investigating Judges disagreed over personal jurisdiction based on the results of their respective investigations. In September 2017, the Co-Investigating Judges notified the parties that 'they considered separate and opposing closing orders based on a disagreement between them as permissible under the law applicable before the ECCC, and of the likely consequences of the appellate process',[59] ie that '[i]f there were to be no supermajority in the [Pre-Trial Chamber] for upholding one of the closing orders, both would appear to stand'.[60] In all three cases, the National Co-Investigating Judge issued his Dismissal Orders[61] simultaneously with the International Co-Investigating Judge's Indictments.[62]

On appeals of the Closing Orders in Case 004/2, the National and International Pre-Trial Chamber Judges also disagreed on personal jurisdiction, with the National Judges upholding the Dismissal Order and the International Judges upholding the Indictment.[63] Despite unanimously declaring that the Co-Investigating Judges acted illegally in issuing two Closing Orders, the National Pre-Trial Chamber Judges upheld the Dismissal Order while the International Pre-Trial Chamber Judges upheld the Indictment,[64] leaving no clear determination as to which Closing Order, if any, stood.

Eventually, Case 004/2 progressed to the Supreme Court Chamber.[65] Finding that 'it flowed' from the Pre-Trial Chamber's considerations in Case 004/2 that 'neither Closing Order was valid', the Supreme Court Chamber concluded that 'in the absence of a definitive and enforceable indictment against AO An, Case 004/2 against him should be terminated before the ECCC'.[66] As instructed by the Supreme Court Chamber, the Co-Investigating Judges archived Case 004/2 on 14 August 2020.[67]

---

[58] ECCC Internal Rules, Rule 77(13). If the Pre-Trial Chamber could reach a supermajority of four votes, Rule 77(13) provides two 'default decisions': under Rule 77(13)(a), the 'order or investigative action other than an indictment ... shall stand', while under Rule 77(13)(b), the Trial Chamber is seized 'on the basis of the Closing Order of the Co-Investigating Judges'.

[59] *Case 004/2* Indictment, para 14. *Case of AO An*, 004/2/07-09-2009-ECCC-OCIJ, Decision on AO An's Urgent Request for Disclosure of Documents Relating to Disagreements, 18 September 2017, D262.2, para 15.

[60] *Case of AO An*, 004/2/07-09-2009-ECCC-OCIJ, Decision on AO An's Urgent Request for Disclosure of Documents Relating to Disagreements, 18 September 2017, D262.2, para 16.

[61] *Case of AO An*, 004/2/07-09-2009-ECCC/OCIJ, Order Dismissing the Case Against AO An, 16 August 2018, D359; *Case of MEAS Muth*, 003/07-09-2009-ECCC/OCIJ, Order Dismissing the Case Against MEAS Muth, D266; *Case of YIM Tith*, Order Dismissing the Case Against YIM Tith, 28 June 2019, D381.

[62] *Case 004/2* Indictment; *Case 003* Indictment; *Case of YIM Tith*, 004/07-09-2009-ECCC-OCIJ, Closing Order, 29 June 2019, D382.

[63] *Case 004/1* Considerations; *Case of AO An*, 004/2/07-09-2009-ECCC/OCIJ (PTC60), Considerations on Appeals Against Closing Orders, 19 December 2019, D359/24 and D360/33 ('*Case 004/2* Considerations'); *Case of MEAS Muth*, 003/07-09-2009-ECCC/OCIJ (PTC35), Considerations on Appeals Against Closing Orders, 7 April 2021, D266/27 & D267/35 ('*Case 003* Considerations').

[64] *Case 004/2* Considerations, 61, paras 273–302, 304–687.

[65] *Case of AO An*, 004/2/07-09-2009-ECCC/TC/SC, Decision on International Co-Prosecutor's Immediate Appeal of the Trial Chamber's Effective Termination of Case 004/2, 10 August 2020, E004/2/1/2.

[66] ibid para 69.

[67] *Case of AO An*, 004/2/07-09-2009-ECCC-OCIJ, Order Sealing and Archiving Case File 004/2, 14 August 2020, D363.3.

In Case 003, the Pre-Trial Chamber Judges again split along national and international lines.[68] While the National Pre-Trial Chamber Judges considered that Case File 003 'should be held at the ECCC archives', the International Judges considered that Case 003 must progress to trial,[69] again leaving the disposition unclear.[70] After the Co-Investigating Judges rejected the International Co-Prosecutor's request to forward Case File 003 to the Trial Chamber,[71] the International Co-Prosecutor and the Defence seized the Pre-Trial Chamber with cross-requests, respectively, to forward the Case File and to terminate, seal and archive the case.[72] After the Pre-Trial Chamber considered itself no longer seized of the case, the Supreme Court Chamber decided – as it had in Case 004/2 – that absent a valid indictment, Case 003 could not proceed to trial and must be archived.[73]

It is beyond the scope of this chapter to opine on the motives behind the Co-Prosecutors' and Judges' disagreements as to whether the charged persons are most responsible, though suffice it to say, barring any concrete evidence, it is imprudent to suggest that they have extraneous reasons for their disagreements. Since reasonable minds can reasonably disagree in interpreting the law and assessing the facts, more profit can be gained by reviewing what the founding parties of the ECCC had in mind, what was negotiated, and what was agreed. Only within this historical context can the Supreme Court Chamber's findings in Duch be critically analysed.

2. OVERVIEW OF THE NEGOTIATIONS

This section of the chapter will discuss the negotiation history leading up to the establishment of the ECCC. This analysis is based on available sources gathered from the Supreme Court Chamber, party submissions, materials in the UN archives, timelines[74] and materials relied upon by various authors who have participated in the negotiations, and/or have argued what the terms 'senior leaders' and 'most responsible' mean.[75]

---

[68] *Case 003* Considerations, 40, paras 111–18, 119–358.

[69] ibid para 259.

[70] ibid paras 111–18, 119–358.

[71] *Case of MEAS Muth*, 003/07-09-2009-ECCC-OCIJ, Decision on International Co-Prosecutor's Request to Forward Case File 003 to the Trial Chamber, 20 May 2021, D270/7.

[72] *Case of MEAS Muth*, 003/07-09-2009-ECCC/OCIJ (PTC37), International Co-Prosecutor's Request for Conclusion of the Pre-Trial Stage of the Case 003 Proceedings, 21 June 2021, D271/1; *Case of MEAS Muth*, 003/07-09-2009-ECCC/OCIJ (PTC38), MEAS Muth's Request to Terminate, Seal, and Archive Case 003, 22 June 2021, D272.

[73] *Case of MEAS Muth*, 003 08 10 2021 ECCC SC(05), Decision on International Co-Prosecutor's Appeal of the Pre-Trial Chamber's Failure to Send Case 003 to Trial as Required by the ECCC Legal Framework, 17 December 2021, 3/1/1/1.

[74] 'Composite Chronology of the Evolution and Operation of the ECCC prepared by the Center for International Human Rights', Northwestern University School of Law, *Cambodia Tribunal Monitor*, available at www.cambodiatribunal.org/wp-content/uploads/2013/08/history_composite-chronology_english.pdf.

[75] Stephen Heder, *The Personal Jurisdiction of the Extraordinary Chambers in the Courts of Cambodia as Regards Khmer Rouge 'Senior Leaders' and Others 'Most Responsible' for Khmer Rouge Crimes. A History and Recent Developments*, 26 April 2012 ('Heder, *Personal Jurisdiction*'), available at www.cambodiatribunal.org/assets/pdf/reports/Final%20Revised%20Heder%20Personal%20 Jurisdiction%20Review.120426.pdf (much of the source material Heder cites in this article is unavailable

A diligent attempt was made to gather all available source material in order to scrutinise all claims and assertions. Unfortunately, not all relevant documents are publicly available. Some negotiation materials leading up to the establishment of the ECCC are available in the UN archives, listed online;[76] however, only limited material is downloadable. The remainder must be requested and purchased from the United Nations. Curiously, the material that appears most relevant to the negotiations has a classification level of 'confidential' or 'strictly confidential'.[77]

2.1. Early Efforts by UN Special Representative Thomas Hammarberg and the RGC's Request for International Assistance

The ECCC was established after protracted negotiations between the RGC and the United Nations, which began[78] in June 1996 when the Special Representative of the UN Secretary-General for Human Rights in Cambodia, Thomas Hammarberg, went on his first mission to Cambodia.[79] Observing that 'the Khmer Rouge crimes in the 1970s still cast a paralyzing shadow over Cambodian society', Hammarberg suggested during the April 1997 session of the UN Commission on Human Rights

---

or inaccessible, and thus some of his claims may be inaccurate); David Scheffer, *All the Missing Souls: A Personal History of the War Crimes Tribunals* (Princeton, NJ, Princeton University Press, 2012) 343 ('Scheffer, *All the Missing Souls*'); Stephen Heder, 'Politics, Diplomacy, and Accountability in Cambodia' in Manfred Berg and Bernd Schaefer (eds), *Historical Justice in International Perspective: How Societies Are Trying to Right the Wrongs of the Past* (Cambridge, Cambridge University Press, 2009); David Scheffer, 'The Negotiation History of the ECCC's Personal Jurisdiction', *Cambodia Tribunal Monitor*, 22 May 2011; David Scheffer, 'The Extraordinary Chambers in the Courts of Cambodia' in M Cherif Bassiouni (ed), *International Criminal Law*, 3rd edn (Leiden, Martinus Nijhoff, 2008); Morrison (n 11) 583, 599. Thomas Hammarberg, 'How the Khmer Rouge Tribunal was Agreed: Discussions Between the Cambodian Government and the UN', *Searching for the Truth* (Documentation Center of Cambodia, 2001), available at http://d.dccam.org/Tribunal/Analysis/How_Khmer_Rouge_Tribunal.htm; Randle DeFalco, 'Cases 003 and 004 at the Khmer Rouge Tribunal: The Definition of "Most Responsible" Individuals According to International Law' (2014) 8 *Genocide Studies and Prevention: An International Journal* 45, 58.

[76] Available at United Nations, Archives and Records Management Section, https://archives.un.org. See also Heder, *Personal Jurisdiction* (n 75). Heder notes that 'it should be possible for the UN to take a discretionary decision to make all relevant records of the negotiations officially available to the ECCC along with certification of their authenticity, pursuant to Article 21 of the 1946 Convention on the Privileges and Immunities of the United Nations', a position shared by Corel. See Luc Reydams et al (eds), *International Prosecutors* (Oxford, Oxford University Press, 2012).

[77] See UN Executive Office of the Secretary-General, *Cambodia Tribunal*, 26 December 2001–1 June 2001, sub-files 'S-1914-0001-0007' (marked strictly confidential) at United Nations, Archives and Records Management Section, https://archives.un.org; UN Executive Office of the Secretary-General, *Cambodia, International Trial of Pol Pot et al*, 9 February 1997–23 June 1997, 'S-0291-0020-0007' (marked strictly confidential); UN Executive Office of the Secretary-General, *Executive Assistant to the Secretary-General – Shashi Tharoor – Cambodia – Human Rights issues and Khmer Rouge Tribunal*, 21 June 1997–8 March 2000, 'S-1914-0001-0007' (marked strictly confidential).

[78] The Cambodian government's intention to conduct prosecutions for the crimes committed from 1975 to 1979 existed much earlier, when the new government, the People's Republic of Kampuchea (PRK), regained control of Phnom Penh in 1979. In 1979, the PRK established the People's Revolutionary Tribunal to try the 'Pol Pot–Ieng Sary clique' for 'acts of genocide'. See Decree Law No 1, 15 July 1979, Art 1, reproduced in Howard J De Nike et al (eds), *Genocide in Cambodia* (Philadelphia, PA, University of Pennsylvania Press 2000) 43–44. Pol Pot and Ieng Sary were convicted in absentia by the People's Revolutionary Tribunal. See Judgment of the People's Revolutionary Tribunal, 19 August 1979, De Nike, ibid, 549.

[79] See Hammarberg (n 75).

that a paragraph be included in the Cambodian resolution.[80] Hammarberg suggested that the paragraph 'mention the possibility of international assistance to enable Cambodia to address past serious violations of human rights'.[81] On 11 April 1997, the UN Commission on Human Rights passed Resolution 1997/49, which requested the Secretary-General to examine any 'request by Cambodia for assistance in responding to past serious violations of Cambodian and international laws as a means of bringing about national reconciliation, strengthening democracy and addressing the issue of individual accountability'.[82]

In June 1997, Hammarberg discussed the implications of Resolution 1997/49 with the two RGC Co-Prime Ministers, Hun Sen and Prince Norodom Ranariddh, and pointed out that the United Nations would probably respond positively to a request for assistance in order to address Khmer Rouge crimes.[83] According to Hammarberg, Prince Ranariddh appeared hesitant about the effects of the tribunal on the possibility of coaxing Khmer Rouge cadre to defect to the RGC.[84] Nonetheless, Prince Ranariddh agreed to sign such a request if Hammarberg did the drafting.[85] When presented with the draft request, Hun Sen reportedly 'said that he of course would sign, that to defeat the Khmer Rouge had for him been a lifelong battle'.[86]

On 21 June 1997, the Co-Prime Ministers sent a letter to the UN Secretary-General, Kofi Annan, seeking the United Nations' assistance 'in bringing to justice those persons responsible for the genocide and crimes against humanity during the rule of the Khmer Rouge from 1975 to 1979'.[87] The letter noted similar efforts to respond to atrocities in Rwanda and Yugoslavia, and 'ask[ed] that similar assistance be given to Cambodia'.[88]

Following this request for assistance, in December 1997, the UN General Assembly adopted a resolution 'not[ing] with concern that no Khmer Rouge leader has been brought to account for ... crimes' and requesting Annan to examine the request and consider the possibility of appointing a group of experts to evaluate the existing evidence and propose measures to bring about national reconciliation, strengthen democracy and address the issue of individual accountability.[89]

On 31 July 1998, Annan appointed a three-member Group of Experts with the following mandate:

(a) To evaluate the existing evidence with a view to determining the nature of the crimes committed by Khmer Rouge leaders in the years 1975–1979;

---

[80] ibid.
[81] ibid.
[82] UN Commission on Human Rights, Resolution 1997/49, UN Doc E/CN.4/1997/49 (1997).
[83] Hammarberg (n 75).
[84] ibid.
[85] ibid.
[86] ibid.
[87] Identical letters dated 15 March 1999 from the Secretary-General to the President of the General Assembly and the President of the Security Council, 53rd Sess, Agenda Item 110(b), UN Doc A/53/850-S/1999/231 (16 March 1999), 3.
[88] ibid.
[89] Resolution Adopted by the General Assembly 52/135, Situation of Human Rights in Cambodia, UN Doc No A/RES/52/135, 27 February 1998, paras 15–16.

(b) To assess, after consultation with the Governments concerned, the feasibility of bringing Khmer Rouge leaders to justice, their apprehension, detention and extradition or
surrender to the criminal jurisdiction established;
(c) To explore options for bringing to justice Khmer Rouge leaders before an international
or national tribunal.[90]

Annan appointed Judges Sir Ninian Stephen (Australia) and Rajsoomer Lallah
(Mauritius) and Professor Steven Ratner (United States) to the Group of Experts.[91]
At a press conference at the conclusion of the visit to Cambodia in November 1998,
Group Chairman Sir Ninian Stephen indicated that only 'top leaders' would be
prosecuted.[92]

Shortly thereafter, in December 1998, Nuon Chea (alleged to be 'Brother Number 2'
after Pol Pot and Pol Pot's 'right-hand man'[93]) and Democratic Kampuchea (DK) head
of state Khieu Samphan[94] surrendered to the Cambodian government.[95] Following
Nuon Chea's and Khieu Samphan's defection,[96] Hun Sen presented an aide-memoire
to Hammarberg to deliver to the Secretary-General, explaining that the 'RGC is now
controlling all corners of the country. ... The threats of return of the genocidal
regime that was in existence within the past 20 years had come to an end.'[97] Hun Sen
questioned the temporal limits of any potential tribunal's jurisdiction, stating that
'[it] is ... necessary to conduct investigations on crimes and offenders of each stage':
from 1970 to 1975, 1975 to 1979, and 1979 to 1998.[98]

Why was 1975–1979 chosen by the Secretary-General as the temporal limit for the
Group of Expert's mandate? These dates coincide with the fall of Phnom Penh: in
1975 to the Khmer Rouge and in 1979 to the Cambodian rebels backed by Vietnamese
troops.[99] This time period would focus any investigations 'on crimes committed
by Khmer Rouge'[100] – and exclude the conduct of any foreign nation during the

---

[90] Letter dated 31 July 1991 from the Secretary-General addressed to the President of the General
Assembly, A/52/1007, 7 August 1998, 1.

[91] ibid 2.

[92] See Heder, *Personal Jurisdiction* (n 75) 21, citing UNCOHCHR [*sic*], Cambodia Office, Press
Conference by the United Nations Group of Experts, 17 November 1998, 11am–12.30pm, Hotel Le Royal,
Phnom Penh.

[93] See *Case of NUON Chea et al*, 002/19-09-2007-ECCC-OCIJ, Closing Order, 15 September 2010,
D427, para 870.

[94] ibid, para 1135.

[95] See Kay Johnson and Khuy Sokhoeun, 'Khieu Samphan, Nuon Chea Join Government at Pailin',
Cambodia Daily, 28 December 1998, available at www.cambodiadaily.com/archives/khieu-samphan-nuon-
chea-join-government-at-pailin-12598/; BBC News, 'World: Asia-Pacific Letters of Surrender – Full Text',
26 December 1998, available at http://news.bbc.co.uk/2/hi/asia-pacific/242670.stm; US Department of
State, Office of the Spokesman, press statement, 'Surrender of Top Khmer Rouge Leaders Nuon Chea
and Khieu Samphan', 27 December 1998, available at http://1997-2001.state.gov/www/briefings/state-
ments/1998/ps981227.html.

[96] See Johnson and Sokhoeun (n 95).

[97] Hun Sen, 'Aide Memoire: An Analysis on Seeking a Formula for Bringing Top KR Leaders to Trial'
(January 1999) 14 *Cambodia New Vision* 1.

[98] ibid 2.

[99] See *Case 001* Trial Judgment, paras 59–65.

[100] Letter dated 31 July 1991 from the Secretary-General addressed to the President of the General
Assembly, A/52/1007, 7 August 1998, 1, para (c).

Pol Pot regime.[101] In mid-January 1998, David Scheffer, US Ambassador-at-Large for War Crimes, claims to have discussed with Wang Yi, Assistant Chinese Foreign Minister, that a possible UN tribunal under Chapter VI or VII of the UN Charter should limit the scope of the tribunal's jurisdiction to actions committed from March 1975 to January 1979, and that the tribunal should not 'examine the conduct of any foreign country during the Pol Pot regime'.[102] Scheffer warned Wang Yi that

> it was in the interests of the permanent members of the Security Council, which includes China, to ensure that the council supervised the tribunal-building process. Otherwise, the process could spin out of control with negative consequences for both China and the United States.[103]

Serendipitously, Scheffer would serve as UN Special Expert to advise on the UN Assistance to the Khmer Rouge Trials from January 2012 to June 2017, and again from March to October 2018. The United Nations, too, had reasons to keep the ECCC's temporal jurisdiction circumscribed to the period between 17 April 1975 and 6 January 1979.[104]

2.2. The Group of Experts' Report

In February 1999, the Group of Experts issued its report, recommending that the Security Council establish an ad hoc international criminal tribunal 'to try Khmer Rouge officials for crimes against humanity and genocide committed from 17 April 1975 to 7 January 1979'.[105] It specifically pointed to the ad hoc tribunals created under Chapter VII of the UN Charter: the ICTY and the ICTR.[106] As an alternative, it recommended an international criminal tribunal established by the UN General Assembly.[107]

Concerning personal jurisdiction, the Group of Experts did not 'believe that prosecutions should attempt to bring to justice all or even most people who committed violations of international or Cambodian law during the relevant time period',[108]

---

[101] See Christopher Hitchens, *The Trial of Henry Kissinger* (London, Verso, 2001) 48–49. Hitchens estimates that as many as 600,000 civilians in Cambodia lost their lives during the secret programme of heavy bombardment carried out by the US government in Cambodia in the late 1960s and early 1970s. See also Tom Fawthrop and Helen Jarvis, *Getting Away with Genocide?* (London, Pluto Press, 2004) 24–39, 53–55, 87–88. Fawthrop and Jarvis detail the conduct of nations such as the United States, China, and ASEAN nations such as Thailand in supporting the Khmer Rouge post-1979.

[102] Scheffer, *All the Missing Souls* (n 75) 377.

[103] ibid.

[104] The UN continued to recognise the DK as the legitimate representative of Cambodia until 1990. See eg Suellen Ratlif, 'UN Representation Disputes: A Case Study of Cambodia and a New Accreditation Proposal for the Twenty-First Century' (1999) 87 *California Law Review* 1207.

[105] Identical letters dated 15 March 1999 from the Secretary-General to the President of the General Assembly and the President of the Security Council, 53rd Sess, Agenda Item 110(b), UN Doc A/53/850-S/1999/231 (16 March 1999), Annex ('Group of Experts Report'), para 219(1).

[106] ibid para 140.

[107] ibid paras 140–48.

[108] ibid para 106.

recognising that it is 'logistically and financially impossible for any sort of tribunal that respects the due process rights of the defendants'.[109] The Group of Experts recommended that:

(a) '[A]ny tribunal focus upon those persons most responsible for the most serious violations of human rights during the reign of Democratic Kampuchea. This would include senior leaders with responsibility over the abuses as well as those at lower levels who are directly implicated in the most serious atrocities.'[110]

(b) The scope of investigations 'should be no more than a guide for prosecutors and not form an element of the jurisdiction of any tribunal'.[111]

(c) The potential tribunal's founding documents 'should give it personal jurisdiction over any persons whose acts fall within its subject matter jurisdiction, and the decision on whom to indict should rest solely with the prosecutor, bearing the above guidance in mind'.[112]

The Group of Experts also noted that the available documentary evidence 'appears quite extensive for some atrocities, most notably the operation of the interrogation centre at Tuol Sleng [S-21]'.[113] For other atrocities, however, the Group of Experts noted that such evidence directly implicating other individuals, whether at the senior or lower levels, 'is currently not available and may never be found'.[114]

In March 1999, the Secretary-General forwarded the Group of Expert's Report to the UN General Assembly and Security Council.[115] In his introduction to the Report, the Secretary-General claimed that the Group of Experts concluded that there was sufficient evidence to 'justify proceedings against Khmer Rouge *leaders*'.[116] The Secretary-General did not use the term 'most responsible' anywhere in his introduction and only spoke of 'crimes committed by Khmer Rouge *leaders*'.[117] The Commission on Human Rights endorsed a variation of the Group of Experts' formula.[118] Hammarberg stated that there was a need 'to find a legal formulation which would limit the number of prosecutions without giving an implicit amnesty to those outside that limited group', and that the Group of Experts had attempted to resolve this issue by concluding that it should be a matter of 'prosecutorial policy'.[119]

---

[109] ibid para 106.
[110] ibid para 110.
[111] ibid para 111.
[112] ibid.
[113] ibid para 55.
[114] ibid.
[115] See identical letters dated 15 March 1999 from the Secretary-General to the President of the General Assembly and the President of the Security Council, UN Doc No A/53/850 and S/1999/231, 16 March 1999, available at https://undocs.org/A/53/850.
[116] ibid 1 (emphasis added).
[117] ibid (emphasis added).
[118] Commission on Human Rights, Report of the 55th Session, Resolution 1999/76, UN Doc E/1999/23, 28 April 1999, 237, para 14.
[119] Thomas Hammarberg, 'Efforts to Establish a Tribunal against KR Leaders', *Phnom Penh Post*, 14 September 1999, available at www.phnompenhpost.com/national/special-insert-efforts-establish-tribunal-against-kr-leaders.

2.3. RGC Reaction to the Group of Experts' Report

The RGC expressly rejected the Group of Experts' recommendations that an ad hoc international tribunal similar to the ICTY/ICTR be constituted and the formula for who should be brought to trial. On 3 March 1999, Hun Sen wrote to Annan, directing him back to his January 1999 aide-memoire, and explaining that 'if improperly and heedlessly conducted, the trials of Khmer Rouge leaders would panic other former Khmer Rouge officers and rank and file, who have already surrendered'.[120] While not rejecting 'the accountability of Khmer Rouge leaders for the crimes of genocide in Cambodia', Hun Sen explained that the RGC was contemplating the South African model for truth and reconciliation,[121] rather than trials.[122]

On 12 March 1999, RGC Foreign Minister Hor Nam Hong presented Annan with an aide-memoire, explaining that 'two former top leaders ... Khieu Samphan and Nuon Chea' had defected to the RGC,[123] and that Ta Mok (Secretary of the Southwest Zone and member of the DK Standing Committee)[124] had been recently arrested.[125] Hor Nam Hong stated that the RGC intended to try Ta Mok before a Cambodian court under Cambodian law.[126] He also explained that while the RGC would not restrict itself to a trial of only Ta Mok, a trial of all Khmer Rouge leaders would cause political instability.[127]

Hammarberg considered that the RGC's apparent shift in position was because its purpose behind establishing a tribunal was to defeat the Khmer Rouge.[128] Hammarberg theorised that after Nuon Chea and Khieu Samphan surrendered, and the last remaining holdout, Ta Mok, was arrested in March 1999, the government no longer felt the need for an international tribunal to be established.[129]

---

[120] Letter dated 3 March 1999 from the Prime Minister of Cambodia addressed to the Secretary-General, UN Doc A/53/581 and S/1999/230, 3 March 1999.

[121] The South African Truth and Reconciliation Commission (TRC) was set up by the Government of National Unity for 'the investigation and the establishment of as complete a picture as possible of the nature, causes and extent of gross violations of human rights committed during the period from 1 March 1960 to the cut-off date contemplated in the Constitution ... the granting of amnesty to persons who make full disclosure ... taking of measures aimed at the granting of reparation ... reporting to the Nation about such violations and victims ... [and] the making of recommendations aimed at the prevention of the commission of gross violations of human rights'. Preamble to the South African Promotion of National Unity and Reconciliation Act 34 of 1995.

[122] Letter dated 3 March 1999 from the Prime Minister of Cambodia addressed to the Secretary-General, UN Doc A/53/581 and S/1999/230, 3 March 1999.

[123] Hor Nam Hong, 'Aide-Memoire on Report of the UN Group of Experts for Cambodia of 18 February 1999' (12 March 1999) 2.

[124] *Case of NUON Chea et al*, 002/19-09-2007/ECCC/TC, *Case 002/01* Judgment, 7 August 2014, E313, para 219.

[125] Hor Nam Hong (n 123) 2–3.

[126] ibid.

[127] Elizabeth Becker, 'Cambodia Spurns UN Plan for Khmer Rouge Tribunal', *New York Times*, 13 March 1999.

[128] See Hammarberg (n 75): 'Hun Sen has obviously seen the international tribunal as an instrument to defeat the Khmer Rouge more than as a means of establishing justice.'

[129] ibid.

Annan relayed Hun Sen's and Hor Nam Hong's statements to the President of the General Assembly, stating that he 'remain[ed] concerned about the credibility of any trial process'.[130] Annan said that the decision to establish an international tribunal under Chapters VI or VII of the UN Charter would be 'for the Security Council or General Assembly to make',[131] but that in his view 'Khmer Rouge leaders responsible for the most serious of crimes should be brought to justice and tried before a tribunal which meets the international standards of justice, fairness and due process of law'.[132] Annan's concern was that 'the trial of a single Khmer Rouge military leader [Ta Mok] which would leave the entire leadership unpunished would not serve the cause of justice and accountability'.[133] Annan concluded that the tribunal 'must be international in character',[134] but not necessarily modelled after the existing ad hoc tribunals; other options could be explored.[135] He cautioned that the success of any international tribunal 'presupposes the cooperation of the Government of Cambodia and its readiness to apprehend Khmer Rouge leaders'.[136] Annan reiterated his concerns in a letter to the Group of Experts.[137]

On 24 March 1999, Hun Sen presented Annan with a letter explaining that Cambodia would welcome international assistance 'in terms of legal experts from foreign countries' to ensure that the existing national tribunal of Cambodia meets international standards.[138] Hun Sen stated: 'The issue of whether to try Ta Mok alone or any other Khmer Rouge leaders depends entirely on the competence of the tribunal.'[139] He assured that the RGC would not exert influence on the proceedings.[140] Hun Sen repeated these assurances to US Senator John Kerry on 6 April 1999.[141] In a subsequent letter to Annan dated 28 April 1999, Hun Sen stated that the trial of Ta Mok would be conducted in a national court, with the possibility that foreign judges and prosecutors would be allowed to fully participate in the proceedings.[142] Hun Sen reiterated: 'The possibility of further indictment and prosecution of other Khmer Rouge leaders is rested in the sole competence of the court to decide.'[143]

---

[130] Letter from Kofi Annan to Didier Opertti, President of the General Assembly, 15 March 1999, 4, available at www.eccc.gov.kh/en/document/court/letter-dated-15-march-1999-secretary-general-annan-addressed-president-general.

[131] ibid.

[132] ibid.

[133] ibid.

[134] ibid 5.

[135] ibid.

[136] ibid.

[137] Letters from Kofi Annan to Judge Rajsoomer Lallah, Ninian Stephen and Steven Ratner, 17 March 1999, available at www.eccc.gov.kh/en/document/court/letter-secretary-general-sir-ninian-stephen.

[138] Hun Sen's Letter on 24 March 1999 to HE Kofi A Annan, Secretary-General of the United Nations, *Cambodia New Vision* (March 1999), 4.

[139] ibid.

[140] ibid.

[141] Statement made on 18 April 1999 by the Cabinet of Samdech Hun Sen, Prime Minister of the Royal Government of Cambodia, UN Doc S/1999/443, 19 April 1999, Annex.

[142] Letter of Samdech Prime Minister Hun Sen to the Secretary-General of the United Nations Kofi Annan on 28 April 1999, in *Cambodia New Vision*, issue 17 (April–May 1999).

[143] ibid.

2.4. The Arrest of Duch and Emergence of 'Most Responsible'

In April 1999, S-21 Chairman Duch emerged from obscurity in western Cambodia where he was working as a volunteer aid-worker after becoming a born-again Christian.[144] Duch spoke to Western journalists, fully admitting to his role as Chairman of S-21.[145] He described the gruesome details of the executions performed at S-21 and implicated other Khmer Rouge cadres such as Nuon Chea, Khieu Samphan, Ieng Sary, Kè Pork and Ta Mok.[146] Duch would soon be arrested in May 1999.[147] Historian Stephen Heder claims that Hun Sen was compelled to place Duch in detention 'to shut him up' after Duch gave interviews and implicated others.[148]

From the summer of 1999 forward, the United Nations attempted to craft a new formula that reflected the updated circumstances. In a note to Annan dated 19 July 1999, UN Assistant Secretary-General for Legal Affairs, Ralph Zacklin put forward the following formula:

> The personal jurisdiction of the tribunal shall be defined to reach the major political and military leaders of the Khmer Rouge and those most responsible for the most serious violations of human rights. Thus, all Khmer Rouge leaders presently in Cambodia shall be included – as their responsibility for the crimes committed flows from their position as leaders and the principle of 'command responsibility' – and other persons most responsible for the most serious violations of human rights shall not be excluded. While the political and military leadership is a well defined group of probably less than a dozen, other persons responsible for the most serious of crimes is a much larger, less defined group.[149]

According to Scheffer, on 30 July 1999, UN Assistant Secretary-Generals Alvaro de Soto (political affairs) and Zacklin (legal affairs), briefed members of the Security Council that the tribunal should have personal jurisdiction 'reaching the major political and military leaders of the Khmer Rouge and those most responsible for the most serious violations of human rights'.[150] According to Heder, during negotiations, the UN Office of Legal Affairs

> suggested several forms of words that might be appended to the basic limitation on 'senior leaders' to cover Duch, such as those 'who, because of their special functions or duties,

---

[144] See Anthony C Lobiado, 'Pol Pot's Nazi-Style Experiments', *World Net Daily*, 7 June 1999, available at www.wnd.com/1999/06/3715/; Nic Dunlop and Nate Thayer, 'Duch Confesses', *Far Eastern Economic Review*, 6 May 1999, available at http://natethayer.typepad.com/blog/2011/11/duch-confesses-he-was-the-chief-executioner-in-one-of-historys-most-murderous-regimes-now-hes-a-born.html.

[145] See Christophe Pechoux, 'Interview with Kaing Guek Eav, also Known as Duch, Chairman of S-21, 28–29 April 1999 Ta Sanh village, 4–6 May 1999, Battambang', available at https://repository.monash.edu/items/show/1304#?c=0&m=0&s=0&cv=0; Nic Dunlop and Nate Thayer, 'Duch Confesses', *Far Eastern Economic Review*, 6 May 1999, available at http://natethayer.typepad.com/blog/2011/11/duch-confesses-he-was-the-chief-executioner-in-one-of-historys-most-murderous-regimes-now-hes-a-born.html.

[146] Pechoux (n 145) 10–15, 21–24.

[147] *Case of KAING Guek Eav*, 001/18-07-2007/ECCC-OCIJ, Closing Order, 8 August 2008, D99, paras 3, 166.

[148] Stephen Heder, *Cambodia, Nazi Germany and the Stalinist Soviet Union: Intentionality, Totalitarianism, Functionalism and the Politics of Accountability* (Draft for Presentation at the German Historical Institute, Washington, DC, 29 March 2003) 51–52.

[149] Heder, *Personal Jurisdiction* (n 75) 27, quoting Ralph Zacklin, 'Note to the Secretary-General: A Mixed Tribunal for Cambodia', 19 July 1999.

[150] Scheffer, *All the Missing Souls* (n 75) 385.

were most responsible for crimes and serious violations;' or were 'most notorious perpetrators of crimes serious violations;' [*sic*] or – as it had originally suggested – who were 'most responsible for crimes and serious violations.' In communications to UN member states, [the UN Office of Legal Affairs] now talked in terms of a trial of 'senior leaders of the Khmer Rouge et al,' while Hun Sen reminded Special Representative Hammarberg that the 'et al' must not include anyone who – like Chea Sim [President of the Cambodian People's Party and President of the RGC Senate], Heng Samrin [First Vice-President of the RGC National Assembly] and himself – could be credited with having 'helped to overthrow the genocide'.[151]

On 16 September 1999, Hun Sen presented another aide-memoire to Annan stating that he did not want the issue to go forward before the Security Council or General Assembly.[152] Hun Sen stated that he did not want a 'mixed tribunal' or 'special court', but would allow for foreign judges and prosecutors to participate in a domestic trial.[153] Hun Sen then presented three options for the Secretary-General to consider concerning the United Nations' participation: (1) provide UN legal experts to work with Cambodian lawyers to draft an additional law, and for international judges and prosecutors to participate in hearings in an existing Cambodian tribunal; (2) provide legal experts, without their involvement in the proceedings, and without the presence of foreign judges or prosecutors; or (3) cease involvement in the proceedings.[154]

In December 1999, Hun Sen reported to the media that: 'Four to five (Khmer Rouge leaders) will be tried.'[155] However, he appeared to back away from this statement in January 2000, when he was reported to have said: 'anyone who specifies the number of leaders to be tried "is wrong, and that includes UN legal experts who mentioned 20 or 30 people"'.[156]

2.5. Finalising Jurisdiction

On 18 January 2000, Ouch Borith, Permanent Representative of the RGC to the United Nations, forwarded a copy of the draft Establishment Law to the Secretary-General. Article 1 of the draft Establishment Law stated that the purpose of the law was 'to bring to trial *senior leaders of Democratic Kampuchea and those who were responsible* for crimes … committed during the period from April 17, 1975 to

---

[151] Heder (n 148) 53, citing, inter alia, Hans Corell, 'Note to Interested Member States: Establishment of a National Court in Cambodia to Try Senior Leaders of Khmer Rouge et al', 12 July 2000; Hun Sen, 'Khmer Rouge Leaders Will Not Escape the Law', *AFP*, New York, 11 September 2000.

[152] 'Aide Memoire for the UN Secretary General HE Kofi annan [*sic*]', *Cambodia New Vision*, issue 21 (September 1999) 1, 6.

[153] ibid.

[154] ibid, 6.

[155] *Kyodo News*, 'Hun Sen Says Five Khmer Rouge Leaders May Be Tried', 22 December 1999, available at www.thefreelibrary.com/Hun+Sen+says+five+Khmer+Rouge+leaders+may+be+tried.-a058533640.

[156] *Kyodo News*, 'Hun Sen Regrets Stating Number of K Rouge Leaders to be Tried', 7 January 2000, available at www.thefreelibrary.com/Hun+Sen+regrets+stating+number+of+K.+Rouge+leaders+to+be+tried.-a058677590.

January 6, 1979'.[157] Article 2 ('competence') stated that the ECCC 'shall be established in the existing court structure, namely the trial court, the appeals court, and the supreme court to bring to trial *senior leaders of Democratic Kampuchea and those who were responsible*'.[158]

The United Nations did not find the draft law acceptable. Although not explicitly taking an issue with the RGC's formulation on personal jurisdiction, Annan urged the RGC to reconsider its position on several issues in the draft Establishment Law including: the guarantees for the arrest and surrender of indictees, the issue of amnesty and pardon, the independence of the Prosecutor and Investigating Judge, and the United Nations' wish to have a majority of international judges on the bench and the manner of their appointment.[159] Annan maintained that

> a national law cannot serve as the sole legal basis for the United Nations cooperation activities in the territories of member States. The engagement of the United Nations in the process in establishing a tribunal for Khmer Rouge leaders will, therefore, necessitate an international agreement between the United Nations and the Government of Cambodia.[160]

Hun Sen replied that the RGC was 'surprised by the gap between the position raised in [Annan's] letter and ours which has already been supported by a number of distinguished UN member states. This gap cannot be welcomed as it is unfair to Cambodia and does not reflect the achievements of our efforts made so far.'[161]

In March 2000, Sok An, RGC Senior Minister and Minister in Charge of the Council of Ministers, exchanged a series of letters with Hans Corell, UN Under-Secretary-General and Head of the UN Office of Legal Affairs, regarding the draft Articles of Cooperation between the United Nations and the RGC,[162] later to become known as the 'Agreement'. Corell emphasised that the United Nations' formula for the composition of the chambers, selection of judges and prosecutors, and decision-making, constituted a 'package'; and that unless the RGC would accept the United Nations' formula for the investigating judges and prosecutors, the UN was not willing to accept the RGC's formula for the composition of the chambers and decision-making rules.[163] On 21 March 2000, the Secretary-General relayed the United

---

[157] Draft Law on the Establishment of Extraordinary Chambers in the Courts of Cambodia for the Prosecution of Crimes Committed During the Period of Democratic Kampuchea, UN Doc RC/MP/0008/00, 18 January 2000, Art 1 (emphasis added).

[158] ibid Art 2 (emphasis added).

[159] See United Nations, Archives and Records Management Section, 'Letter from Kofi Annan to Hun Sen' (8 February 2000) 2–3, item S-1096-0225-05-00024, https://archives.un.org.

[160] ibid 4.

[161] See United Nations, Archives and Records Management Section, 'Letter from Hun Sen to Kofi Annan' (10 February 2000), item S-1096-0225-05-00023, https://archives.un.org.

[162] See United Nations, Archives and Records Management Section, 'Letter from Hans Corell to Sok An, 20 March 2000' (21 March 2000), item S-1096-0225-05-00021, https://archives.un.org; 'Letter from Hans Corell to Sok An' (21 March 2000); 'Letter from Sok An to Hans Corell' (21 March 2000); 'Letter from the Secretary-General to Prime Minister Hun Sen' (21 March 2000) (Annex: Articles of Cooperation between the United Nations and the Royal Government of Cambodia in the Prosecution under Cambodian Law of Crimes Committed during the period of Democratic Kampuchea), item S-1096-0225-05-00021, https://archives.un.org.

[163] See United Nations, Archives and Records Management Section, 'Letter from Hans Corell to Sok An' (21 March 2000), item S-1096-0225-05-00021, https://archives.un.org.

Nations' draft Articles of Cooperation, proposing to Hun Sen that if the terms were agreeable to the RGC, then the Articles of Cooperation could constitute an agreement between the United Nations and the RGC, which would enter into force upon signature.[164] Article 4 of the United Nations' draft Articles of Cooperation states: 'The investigating judges shall be independent in the performance of their functions and shall not accept or seek instructions from any Government or any other source. *It is understood, however, that the scope of investigations is limited to senior leaders of Democratic Kampuchea and those who were most responsible.*'[165] This language is repeated in Article 5 concerning the Prosecutors.[166]

On 19 April 2000, Corell phoned Sok An to discuss a 'new formula' where '[i]f there were a difference of opinion between investigating judges/prosecutors, one would need a super majority to proceed with the investigation or prosecution'.[167] On the same day, Annan wrote to Hun Sen, noting 'the close connection between [the proposed provisions regarding the settlement of disputes between the Co-Investigating Judges and the Co-Prosecutors] and the question of the scope of jurisdiction of the special chambers. … The more precise this latter provision, the less risk for disagreements between the Co-Investigating Judges or Co-Prosecutors.'[168] Hun Sen wrote back to Annan that the RGC would revise the tribunal's jurisdiction to cover crimes committed from 1970 to 1979, and to cover 'all those involved' in crimes.[169]

The United Nations continued to develop a formula for personal jurisdiction, taking issue with the language in Article 1 of the RGC draft Establishment Law submitted by Ouch Borith. In one set of comments in March 2000, the United Nations commented that the definition in Article 1 of the draft Establishment Law (senior leaders of DK and those who were responsible) was 'so broad that it encompasses almost anyone who was involved. We doubt this was intentional. Some qualifications are necessary.'[170] In another set of comments provided on 5 July 2000, the UN delegation stated that the scope of jurisdiction in the draft Establishment Law before the National Assembly 'is too broad; it practically covers everyone who had any part in the criminal activities of the Khmer Rouge. Such a result is obviously not intended by the government, and it would be impossible for the Extraordinary Chamber to deal with such a magnitude of cases.'[171] The UN delegation explained that it 'has therefore added the word "most" as an illustration of *how one could limit the scope*

---

[164] See United Nations, Archives and Records Management Section, 'Letter from the Secretary-General to Prime Minister Hun Sen' (21 March 2000) and Annex (n 162).

[165] ibid Art 4 (emphasis added).

[166] ibid Art 5.

[167] See United Nations, Archives and Records Management Section, 'Letter from Hans Corell to Kofi Annan, Urgent Call from Cambodia – Options to Settle Differences Between the Investigating Judges/ Prosecutors' (19 April 2000), item S-1096-0225-05-00006, https://archives.un.org.

[168] See United Nations, Archives and Records Management Section, 'Letter from Kofi Annan to Hun Sen' (19 April 2000), 2, item S-1096-0225-05-00006, https://archives.un.org.

[169] See United Nations, Archives and Records Management Section, 'Letter from Hun Sen to Kofi Annan' (22 April 2000), item S-1096-0225-05-00004, https://archives.un.org.

[170] Heder, *Personal Jurisdiction* (n 75) 33, quoting Amendments Required to the Draft Cambodian Law, 28 March 2000.

[171] Heder, *Personal Jurisdiction* (n 75) 35, quoting UN Delegation, Phnom Penh, 7 July 2000: Law on the Establishment of Extraordinary Chambers in the Courts of Cambodia for the Prosecution of Crimes Committed During the Period of Democratic Kampuchea.

of personal jurisdiction in a reasonable way'.[172] The United Nations also provided an alternative formula: 'and the most notorious perpetrators of the crimes and serious violations, etc'.[173]

On 10 July 2000, Corell wrote to Sok An: 'I think that it is an extremely sensitive issue of policy: how to limit the scope of personal jurisdiction in such a way that the Extraordinary Chambers can manage to deal with the caseload.'[174] He explained:

> It is important to note in this context that those suspects who would fall outside the competence of these Chambers do not thereby escape responsibility. How this matter will be dealt with – prosecution before the national court or no prosecution but eg a Truth and Conciliation Commission – is a separate matter for the Royal Government of Cambodia to decide upon.[175]

A few days later, on 14 July 2000, Corell explained the use of the word 'most' in the United Nations' formulation 'most responsible':

> Upon further examination, we have come to the conclusion that the word 'notorious' could cause problems. When I expressed concern about a possible violation of the principle of presumption of innocence, it was because among the synonyms you find words like 'undeniable' and [']unquestionable'. ...

> Another problem is that the persons most responsible may, after all, not have been 'notorious' or 'well-known'. The prosecution should not be limited in this respect.

> Therefore, upon further reflection, we think that by adding the word 'most' to the text of the 18 January draft would provide sufficient guidance for the Co-Investigating Judges and the Co-Prosecutors to formulate a strategy. Ultimately, this is of course for the Legislature to decide upon.[176]

The RGC then adopted the 'most responsible' formula in its revised draft of the Establishment Law.[177] In October 2000, the *Phnom Penh Post* reported that Article 1 of the revised draft Establishment Law contained the following language:

> The purpose of this law is to bring to trial senior leaders of Democratic Kampuchea and those who were most responsible for crimes and serious violations of Cambodian penal law, international humanitarian law and custom, and international conventions recognized by Cambodia, that were committed during the period from 17 April 1975 to 6 January 1979.[178]

On 29 December 2000, Sok An spoke before the Cambodian National Assembly and diplomatic representatives explaining the content of the draft Establishment Law.[179] He began his speech by giving an overview of the various international criminal tribunals

---

[172] ibid (emphasis added).

[173] ibid.

[174] Heder, *Personal Jurisdiction* (n 75) 36, quoting Hans Corell, 'Letter to Sok An' (10 July 2000).

[175] ibid.

[176] Heder, *Personal Jurisdiction* (n 75) 36–37, quoting Hans Corell, 'Letter to Sok An' (14 July 2000).

[177] *Phnom Penh Post*, 'UN Accepts Flawed Tribunal for KR', 13–26 October 2000.

[178] ibid.

[179] 'Presentation and Comments on the Draft Law on the Establishment of the Extraordinary Chambers in the Courts of Cambodia for the Prosecution of Crimes Committed During the Period of Democratic Kampuchea', 5th Session of the 2nd Legislature, National Assembly, 29 December 2000, reprinted in (December 2000) 35 *Cambodia New Vision* 8–9.

created after World War II, such as the IMT, the International Military Tribunal for the Far East, ICTY, ICTR, and the International Criminal Court (ICC).[180] While Sok An detailed the number of 'leaders'[181] brought before other international tribunals, he emphasised that:

> These tribunals, however, are different than what we are doing. The ones we described above … were imposed from without to bring to justice people or leaders of one country, while what we are creating has new characteristics, no precedent in the world and the international level, because it is a tribunal organized with agreements from the country concerned – Cambodia – and the outsiders – the United Nations.[182]

On 2 January 2001, the Cambodian National Assembly unanimously passed forty-seven of forty-eight articles of the Establishment Law.[183] Articles 1 and 2 of the January draft law contain the same language as the draft leaked by the press in October 2000.[184] After the passing of this text, Hun Sen and other RGC ministers made comments in the media about who would be covered by these terms. Heng Samrin, First Vice-President of the Cambodian National Assembly, stated to former Khmer Rouge who defected: 'Please don't worry, we will only [prosecute] the leaders and the people who were responsible for the [Khmer Rouge] regime.'[185] When asked by the media how far the tribunal should go in prosecuting those most responsible, Hun Sen replied: 'It's up to the court of law. But as a citizen of Cambodia, I don't think it should cover more than 10 people. … If we prosecute all the lower-level [cadres], it will mean war.'[186]

---

[180] ibid.

[181] ibid, 8.

[182] ibid, 9.

[183] *Phnom Penh Post*, 'Trial Law Sails Through National Assembly', 5 January 2001.

[184] Law on the Establishment of Extraordinary Chambers in the Courts of Cambodia for the Prosecution of Crimes Committed During the Period of Democratic Kampuchea, HJ/1/3/01, Art 1 (ed Helen Jarvis on 29 December 2000):

> Article 1
>
> The purpose of this law is to bring to trial senior leaders of Democratic Kampuchea and those who were most responsible for the crimes and serious violations of Cambodian penal law, international humanitarian law and custom, and international conventions recognized by Cambodia, that were committed during the period from 17 April 1975 to 6 January 1979.
>
> Article 2
>
> Extraordinary Chambers shall be established in the existing court structure, namely the trial court, the appeals court and the supreme court to bring to trial senior leaders of Democratic Kampuchea and those who were most responsible for the crimes and serious violations of Cambodian laws related to crimes, international humanitarian law and custom, and international conventions recognized by Cambodia, that were committed during the period from 17 April 1975 to 6 January 1979.
>
> Senior leaders of Democratic Kampuchea and those who were most responsible for the above acts are hereinafter designated as 'Suspects'.

Helen Jarvis is an advisor to the Royal Government of Cambodia and former head of the ECCC Public Affairs Section from the inception of the ECCC until 1 June 2009. See ECCC, *Dr Helen Jarvis*, www.eccc. gov.kh/en/persons/dr-helen-jarvis.

[185] *Phnom Penh Post*, 'Trial Law Sails Through National Assembly', 5 January 2001.

[186] PR *Newswire Association*, 'Cover: "Return to the Killing Fields"', 5 August 2001, available at www.thefreelibrary.com/Cover%3A+'Return+to+the+Killing+Fields'.-a076982607.

The Establishment Law was passed by the Cambodian National Assembly on 11 July 2001 and was approved by the Senate and the Constitutional Council on 11 July and 7 August 2001, respectively.[187] It was promulgated on 10 August 2001.

In October 2001, Corell sent a letter to Sok An, insisting that a future Agreement between the United Nations and the Cambodian government take precedence over the Establishment Law.[188] In November 2001, Sok An sent a letter to Corell stating that the agreement would not take precedence over the Establishment Law.[189] In February 2002, the United Nations announced that it would no longer negotiate with the RGC on the establishment of the ECCC, mainly because of Cambodia's insistence that the Establishment Law would prevail over an agreement between the United Nations and the RGC.[190] After encouragement from many states to resume negotiations, on 13 November 2002, the Third Committee of the General Assembly adopted a draft resolution calling for a resumption of negotiations. Concerning personal jurisdiction, it recommended: 'that the Extraordinary Chambers should have personal jurisdiction over senior leaders of Democratic Kampuchea and those who were most responsible for the crimes'.[191] In December 2002, the General Assembly adopted a resolution approving the Third Committee's resolution.[192] Negotiations resumed and, in March 2003, a draft Agreement between the United Nations and the Cambodian government was prepared.[193]

Upon the conclusion of the negotiations, and his departure from Phnom Penh, Corell stated:

> Who would be investigated and prosecuted? This would be for the co-investigating judges and the co-prosecutors to decide independently. But it is clear from the text of the agreement that the Extraordinary Chambers would have jurisdiction only over senior leaders of Democratic Kampuchea and those who were most responsible for the crimes and serious violations of Cambodian penal law, international humanitarian law and custom, and international conventions recognized by Cambodia. There would also be a temporal limitation. This would mean that only crimes committed during the period from 17 April 1975 to 6 January 1979 would fall under the jurisdiction of the Chambers.[194]

On 31 March 2003, Annan announced that: 'The jurisdiction of the Extraordinary Chambers would be limited to crimes committed by senior leaders of Democratic

---

[187] See ECCC, *Establishment of the ECCC – Chronology*, available at www.eccc.gov.kh/en/about-eccc/chronologies. This law was later amended in 2004, but these amendments are unrelated to the status of the ECCC as a domestic court, or to the personal jurisdiction of the ECCC.

[188] See Composite Chronology (n 74) 17.

[189] ibid.

[190] Statement by UN Legal Counsel Hans Corell at a press briefing at UN Headquarters in New York, 8 February 2002, available at www.un.org/news/dh/infocus/cambodia/corell-brief.htm.

[191] *Human Rights Questions: Human Rights Questions, Including Alternative Approaches for Improving the Effective Enjoyment of Human Rights and Fundamental Freedoms, France and Japan*, Draft Resolution, Khmer Rouge Trials, UN Doc No A/C.3/57/L.70, 13 November 2002, para 3, available at https://digital-library.un.org/record/478603?ln=en.

[192] Resolution adopted by the General Assembly 57/228. Khmer Rouge Trials, UN Doc No A/RES/57/228, 27 February 2003, available at https://undocs.org/A/RES/57/228.

[193] See Composite Chronology (n 74) 21.

[194] See United Nations, Archives and Records Management Section, 'Statement by Under-Secretary General Hans Corell Upon Leaving Phnom Penh on 17 March 2003', 2 (emphasis in original), item S-1096-0114-10-00011, https://archives.un.org.

Kampuchea and those who were most responsible for crimes falling within the subject-matter and temporal jurisdiction of the Chambers.'[195] On 22 May 2003, the General Assembly passed a resolution noting the Secretary-General's report and approving the draft Agreement.[196] On 6 June 2003, the Agreement was signed by Sok An and Corell.[197] In August 2004, Cambodia ratified the Agreement,[198] giving it the status of law in Cambodia.[199]

In October 2004, some members of the Cambodian National Assembly opposed to the Cambodian People's Party questioned the tribunal's personal jurisdiction.[200] Sok An explained that:

> [T]here are two types of targets: senior leaders who are most important targets of the EC and some others who might not be senior leaders but their actions were much more serious, and there is enough evidence to prove that they really did much more seriously than others. However, we have already considered that there would not be too many, as is also the case in Sierra Leone's tribunal. According to the information, Sierra Leone's court has prosecuted 9 criminals. In the case I have mentioned, there was joint agreement when we determined the targets to be written down in article 2.[201]

Sok An explained that the government could not simply list names to be indicted: 'Considering senior leaders, we refer to no more than 10 people, but we don't clearly state that they are the members of the Standing Committee. This is the task of the Co-Prosecutors to decide who are the senior leaders.'[202] As for who would be considered 'most responsible', he is less clear: 'There is no specific amount of people in the second group to be indicted. Those committing odd and atrocious crimes shall be possibly indicted.'[203] He then explained that 'if there is no agreement between the Cambodian judges and Co-Prosecutor and the foreign judges and Co-Prosecutor, there is no indictment and prosecution'.[204]

In his 2004 report on the Khmer Rouge trials, Annan stated that 'for the purpose of workload planning and resource-needs estimation, a range from 5 to 10 indictees had been assumed' and that 'it will be the prerogative of the co-prosecutors and co-investigating judges, within the parameters laid down in the Agreement, to decide who exactly is to be investigated and prosecuted'.[205] According to a UN news report, for the purpose of drafting a budget proposal, a range of five to ten indictees was

---

[195] Report of the Secretary-General on Khmer Rouge Trials, UN Doc A/57/769, 31 March 2003, para 47.
[196] General Assembly Resolution 57/228B, UN Doc A/Res/57/228B, 22 May 2003.
[197] See Composite Chronology (n 74) 22.
[198] ibid 24.
[199] Art 31 of the Agreement states: 'The present Agreement shall apply as law within the Kingdom of Cambodia following its ratification in accordance with the relevant provisions of the internal law of the Kingdom of Cambodia regarding competence to conclude treaties.'
[200] First Session of the Third Term of the Cambodian National Assembly, Debate and Approval of Amendments to the Law on Trying Khmer Rouge Leaders, 4–5 October 2004.
[201] ibid 16.
[202] ibid 30.
[203] ibid.
[204] ibid 17.
[205] Report of the Secretary-General on the Khmer Rouge Trials, UN Doc A/59/432, 12 October 2004, para 16.

assumed by both parties, 'but this figure could change depending on the investigative and prosecutorial strategy that the future court may wish to adopt'.[206]

3. PERSONAL JURISDICTION IN CASE 001

Duch was the first accused to stand trial at the ECCC. He was the chairman of the S-21 detention facility in Phnom Penh (also known as Tuol Sleng), where more than 12,000 prisoners are estimated to have been tortured and executed.[207] In the Closing Order indicting Duch, the Co-Investigating Judges found that 'while Duch was not a senior leader of Democratic Kampuchea, he may be in the category of the most responsible ... due both to his formal and effective hierarchical authority and his personal participation as Deputy Secretary then Secretary of S21'.[208]

Although the Trial Chamber held that Duch failed to object in timely fashion to the ECCC's jurisdiction, it nonetheless considered whether the ECCC had jurisdiction over him.[209] It held: 'Personal jurisdiction is confined either to "senior leaders of DK" or "those who were most responsible for the crimes and serious violations of Cambodian penal law, international humanitarian law and custom, and international conventions recognized by Cambodia"'.[210] It noted: 'Neither the ECCC Agreement nor the ECCC Law expressly defines "senior leaders of DK" or "those who were most responsible".'[211]

To determine the meaning of 'most responsible', the Trial Chamber considered the Group of Experts' recommendations as well as language from the UN Secretary-General and the Commission on Human Rights.[212] The Trial Chamber then turned to the ICTY and the ICC, noting that both examine the gravity of the crimes charged and the level of responsibility of the accused.[213] Using the ICTY and ICC criteria, the Trial Chamber concluded that Duch fell within the ECCC's personal jurisdiction 'as one of those most responsible for crimes committed during the period from 17 April 1975 to 6 January 1979'.[214] It found no need to consider whether he was also a senior leader.[215]

On appeal, the parties did not challenge whether the term was jurisdictional or a discretionary matter of investigative and prosecutorial policy. Duch argued only that

---

[206] 'UN Team, Cambodia Agree on Issues Related to the Establishment of Khmer Rouge Court', UN News Center (17 December 2003), available at www.un.org/apps/news/story.asp?NewsID=9252&Cr=cambodia&Cr1=.

[207] See *Case 001* Trial Judgment, para 23.

[208] *Case of KAING Guek Eav*, 001/18-07-2007-ECCC-OCIJ, Closing Order Indicting Kaing Guek Eav alias Duch, 8 August 2008, D99, para 129.

[209] *Case 001* Trial Judgment, paras 14–15.

[210] ibid para 17.

[211] Ibid, para 19.

[212] *Case 001* Trial Judgment, paras 19–21, citing Commission on Human Rights resolution 1999/76, 28 April 1999, para 14.

[213] *Case 001* Trial Judgment, para 22.

[214] ibid para 25.

[215] ibid.

he was neither a *senior leader* nor one of the *most responsible*.[216] The OCP and Civil Party Group Three[217] argued that Duch's challenge was untimely but did not challenge the assumption that the terms *senior leaders* and *most responsible* limited the ECCC's personal jurisdiction.[218]

The Supreme Court Chamber invited the parties to make oral submissions on the question of whether the term 'senior leaders of Democratic Kampuchea and those who were most responsible' 'constitutes a jurisdictional requirement that is subject to judicial review, or is a guide to the discretion of the Co-Prosecutors and Co-Investigating Judges that is not subject to judicial review'.[219] At the appeal hearing, Duch made no specific submissions on this question, arguing instead that the ECCC did not have personal jurisdiction over him.[220] The National Co-Prosecutor stated without any elaboration, in response to a direct question by Judge Noguchi: 'I think the issue is not related to the jurisdiction, rather it is related to the competence and the prosecutorial discretion.'[221] The International Co-Prosecutor remained silent. The international lawyer representing Civil Party Group Three stated that the terms *senior leaders* and *most responsible* are 'jurisdictional requirement[s]'.[222]

The Supreme Court Chamber held that whether someone is considered a 'senior leader' or 'most responsible' was not a justiciable jurisdictional issue, but rather a matter of prosecutorial and investigatorial policy for the OCP and OCIJ.[223] It held that a decision to prosecute or investigate was subject to narrow appellate review for abuse of discretion.[224]

The Supreme Court Chamber determined that the Vienna Convention on the Law of Treaties (VCLT)[225] was applicable.[226] Under the VCLT, the Supreme Court Chamber had to consider the ordinary meaning of the terms of the Agreement in light of its object, purpose and context and could turn to supplementary means of interpretation, including preparatory work of the treaty, where it believed the meaning to be unclear.[227] The Supreme Court Chamber also considered that it could 'seek

---

[216] *Case of KAING Guek Eav*, 001/18-07-2007-ECCC/SC, Appeal Brief by the Co-Lawyers for Kaing Guek Eav Alias 'Duch' Against the Trial Chamber Judgment of 26 July 2010, 18 November 2010, F14, paras 1–65.

[217] Civil Party Group Three is one of the groups of civil parties that participated in *Case 001*.

[218] *Case of KAING Guek Eav*, 001/18-07-2007-ECCC/SC, Co-Prosecutors' Response to the Appeal Brief by the Co-Lawyers for Kaing Guek Eav Alias 'Duch' Against the Trial Chamber Judgment of 26 July 2010, 20 December 2010, F14/4; *Case of KAING Guek Eav*, 001/18-07-2007-ECCC/SC, Response of the Lawyers for the Group 3 Civil Parties, to the Appeal of the Co-Lawyers for Duch against the Judgment of 26 July 2010, 3 December 2010, F14/2.

[219] *Case of KAING Guek Eav*, 001/18-07-2007-ECCC/SC, Order Scheduling Appeal Hearing, 4 March 2011, F20, 3.

[220] See eg *Case of KAING Guek Eav*, 001/18-07-2007-ECCC/SC, Transcript of Appeal Proceedings, 29 March 2011, F1/3.2, 28–29.

[221] *Case of KAING Guek Eav*, 001/18-07-2007-ECCC/SC, Transcript of Appeal Proceedings, 28 March 2011, F1/2.1, 91.

[222] ibid 104 (emphasis added).

[223] *Case 001* Appeal Judgment, paras 62–79.

[224] ibid para 80. See also ibid paras 44–57.

[225] Vienna Convention on the Law of Treaties, 23 May 1969, 1155 UNTS 331 (VCLT).

[226] *Case 001* Appeal Judgment, para 59.

[227] VCLT, Arts 31–32.

guidance in international jurisprudence on comparable provisions in other jurisdictions' in accordance with Article 12(1) of the Agreement.[228]

The Supreme Court Chamber noted that the words 'personal jurisdiction' in Article 2(1) of the Agreement indicated that the terms operated as a legal requirement of the Trial Chamber's jurisdiction,[229] thus requiring it to consider whether this interpretation was consistent with the object and purpose of the Agreement and whether it would lead to an absurd result.[230] This led the Supreme Court Chamber to consider three categories: 'Khmer Rouge official', 'senior leader' and 'most responsible'. The Supreme Court Chamber held that the category of 'Khmer Rouge official' constituted a jurisdictional limitation, with the Trial Chamber being well suited to decide this factual issue.[231] However, the Supreme Court Chamber held that an absurd result would occur if the terms 'senior leader' and 'most responsible' were interpreted as jurisdictional limits, which would frustrate the object and purpose of the Agreement. The Supreme Court Chamber reasoned:

- '[T]here is no objective method for the Trial Chamber to decide on, compare, and then rank the criminal responsibility of all Khmer Rouge officials.'[232]

- The notion of comparative criminal responsibility wasinconsistent with Article 29 of the Establishment Law, which says that the position or rank of any Suspect shall not relieve that person of criminal responsibility or mitigate punishment. Determining a person's relative criminal liability would indirectly amount to permitting a defence of superior orders and frustrate the purpose of Article 29.[233]

- The determination of whether someone was 'most responsible' requires a large amount of discretion.[234]

The Supreme Court Chamber considered the competence afforded to the Co-Investigating Judges and Co-Prosecutors to be the 'chief' indicator among 'many' that the term 'most responsible' should be interpreted as a non-justiciable matter of prosecutorial and investigatorial policy.[235] Turning to the drafting history of the Agreement, the Supreme Court Chamber noted that the Group of Experts recommended interpreting 'most responsible' as a policy guideline.[236] The Supreme Court Chamber also turned to international jurisprudence, observing that a comparison of the ECCC with the ICTY and ICTR indicated the term was a policy guideline rather than a jurisdictional limitation.[237] It held that the ICTY's referral mechanism suggested that the term is not a jurisdictional requirement but rather reflects

---

[228] *Case 001* Appeal Judgment, para 59.
[229] It is unclear why the Supreme Court Chamber referred specifically to the Trial Chamber's jurisdiction here, rather than that of the ECCC as a whole.
[230] *Case 001* Appeal Judgment, para 60.
[231] ibid para 61.
[232] ibid para 62.
[233] ibid.
[234] ibid.
[235] ibid paras 63–64. Arts 5(3) and 6(3) of the Agreement vested the Co-Investigating Judges and Co-Prosecutors, respectively, with authority to determine whether a particular investigation or prosecution fell within the scope of the term 'most responsible'.
[236] *Case 001* Appeal Judgment, paras 66–68.
[237] ibid para 69.

prosecutorial policy,[238] and noted that the SCSL *Brima et al* Appeals Chamber held that the term 'greatest responsibility' in the SCSL Statute was not jurisdictional.[239]

Finally, the Supreme Court Chamber explained that it did not consider the term 'senior leaders' to operate as a jurisdictional limit because the term was 'sufficiently flexible' that it might not be limited to Central or Standing Committee members.[240] It noted that debates in the Cambodian National Assembly confirmed that the definition of the term was not fixed.[241]

4. UNPEELING THE ONION: AN ANALYSIS OF CASE 001 APPEAL JUDGMENT

Analysing the Supreme Court Chamber's Judgment in Case 001 on the issue of the ECCC's personal jurisdiction requires a knowledge and appreciation of the context of the negotiations leading up to the establishment of the ECCC. Now that this context has been set out, this section will analyse the judgment, going point by point through the Supreme Court Chamber's analysis. First, however, to consider whether the Supreme Court Chamber properly interpreted the terms 'senior leaders' and 'most responsible', one must understand the proper methods by which the ECCC's founding documents – the Agreement and Establishment Law – should be interpreted.[242]

The Agreement is a treaty between the United Nations and the RGC. Interpretation of its terms is governed by the VCLT as stated in Article 2(2) of the Agreement.[243] Under Article 31 of the VCLT, '[a] treaty shall be interpreted in good faith in accordance with the ordinary meaning to be given to the terms of the treaty in their context and in the light of its object and purpose'. Under Article 31(2), context, in addition to the text of the treaty, may comprise agreements made in connection with the conclusion of the treaty, or instruments made by one or more parties in connection with the conclusion with the treaty and accepted by the other parties as an instrument related to the treaty. Under Article 31(3), along with context, the following are also taken into account:

(a) Any subsequent agreement between the parties regarding the interpretation of the treaty or the application of its provisions;

---

[238] ibid para 71.

[239] ibid paras 72–73.

[240] In *Case 002/01*, the Trial Chamber found that the Central Committee was intended by statute to be the 'highest level of operational authority' in the Khmer Rouge regime. See *Case of NUON Chea et al*, 002/19-09-2007-ECCC-TC, *Case 002/01* Judgment, 7 August 2014, para 202. The Standing Committee was a smaller committee within the Central Committee that ultimately exercised effective control over the regime (ibid para 203).

[241] *Case 001* Appeal Judgment, paras 75–76.

[242] The following section and much of the analysis in section 3 was argued by the *MEAS Muth (Case 003)* Defence in a motion filed to the Co-Investigating Judges on 10 November 2015, which is currently classified as confidential.

[243] Cambodia is not a party to the VCLT. See the UN Treaty Collection website, available at https://treaties.un.org/Pages/ViewDetailsIII.aspx?src=TREATY&mtdsg_no=XXIII-1&chapter=23&Temp=mtdsg3&clang=_en. However, this does not affect the VCLT's application to interpretation of the Agreement, due to the express agreement between the parties that it may be applied.

(b) Any subsequent practice in the application of the treaty which establishes the agreement of the parties regarding its interpretation;
(c) Any relevant rules of international law applicable in the relations between the parties.

To confirm the meaning resulting from the application of Article 31, or where the interpretation under Article 31 leaves the meaning ambiguous or obscure, or leads to a result that is manifestly absurd or unreasonable, Article 32 of the VCLT permits recourse to supplementary means of interpretation, 'including the preparatory work of the treaty and the circumstances of its conclusion'.

The Establishment Law is not a treaty; it is a Cambodian law. National methods of statutory interpretation apply. Cambodian law does not have stated rules governing statutory interpretation. Since the Cambodian legal system is based on the French system, the French method of interpretation may be of assistance.[244] Under this method, if the text of the legislation is unclear, courts will attempt to discern the will of the legislature.

4.1. The Plain Language of the Agreement and Establishment Law

According to both the VCLT[245] and general provisions on statutory interpretation,[246] consideration of the plain language of a provision is the starting point to determine its meaning. The plain language of both the Agreement and Establishment Law indicates that the phrase 'senior leaders and those who were most responsible' was a jurisdictional limitation on the ECCC.[247]

Article 2(1) of the Agreement explicitly states: 'The present Agreement further recognizes that the Extraordinary Chambers have *personal jurisdiction* over senior leaders of Democratic Kampuchea and those who were most responsible for the crimes referred to in Article 1 of the Agreement.'[248] In the Establishment Law, the phrase appears in the 'General Provisions' section and is repeated in Article 2 new in the section titled 'Competence'.

The Agreement and Establishment Law also set out the ECCC's subject matter jurisdiction and its temporal jurisdiction. There was never any suggestion that the subject matter and temporal jurisdiction were mere policy guides for the Co-Prosecutors and Co-Investigating Judges. One queries, then, whether it was logical to suggest that only the provision on personal jurisdiction should be interpreted in this way. Even the ECCC's website refers to the phrase 'senior leaders and those who were most responsible' as defining the ECCC's personal jurisdiction[249] – although obviously this is not a source of legal authority to be considered.

---

[244] See Claire M Germain, 'Approaches to Statutory Interpretation and Legislative History in France' (2003) 13 *Duke Journal of Comparative and International Law* 195, 201–02.

[245] VCLT, Art 31(1).

[246] This is the 'golden rule' of statutory interpretation. See *Black's Law Dictionary*, 9th edn (2009) 761.

[247] This is a different matter than the interpretation of the meaning of the terms 'senior leaders' and 'most responsible'. The plain language does not assist in determining to whom 'senior leaders' or 'most responsible' refers.

[248] Emphasis added.

[249] See ECCC, 'Personal Jurisdiction', available at https://www.eccc.gov.kh/en/tags/personal-jurisdiction.

The Supreme Court Chamber correctly found that the phrase 'senior leaders and those who were most responsible' by its plain meaning when placed in context was clearly a jurisdictional limitation on the ECCC.[250] Where the Supreme Court Chamber went astray was in finding that this interpretation would lead to an absurd result. Its reasoning is as lacking as its disregard for the intent of the parties in establishing the ECCC. According to *Black's Law Dictionary*, an 'absurdity' is '[t]he state or quality of being grossly unreasonable; esp., an interpretation that would lead to an unconscionable result, esp. one that the parties or (esp. for a statute) the drafters could not have intended and probably never considered'.[251] Having pronounced that the interpretation of 'senior leaders and those who were most responsible' as jurisdictional limits leads to an absurd result, the Supreme Court Chamber failed to demonstrate that such a result would occur if the phrase were interpreted to limit the ECCC's personal jurisdiction.

4.2. An Absurd Result?

The Supreme Court Chamber found that the terms 'senior leaders' and 'most responsible' could not be jurisdictional limitations because the notion of comparative criminal responsibility was inconsistent with Article 29[252] of the Establishment Law.[253] However, Article 29 new only applied to those who fell within the ECCC's jurisdiction. It was *those* people whose position or rank would not relieve them of responsibility or mitigate punishment. Article 29 new says nothing about others who did not fall within the ECCC's jurisdiction. A person who was found to be within the category of *most responsible* but had a relatively low rank could not, according to Article 29 new, rely on his low rank to mitigate his punishment. Such a person could not rely on a defence of superior orders. Similarly, the ICTY's Statute states: 'The fact that an accused person acted pursuant to an order of a Government or of a superior shall not relieve him of criminal responsibility.'[254] Yet, the ICTY still considered whether someone acted pursuant to orders when determining whether that person met the criteria for referral to national courts under ICTY Rule 11*bis*.[255] There is no inconsistency between determining whether someone fell within the ECCC's jurisdiction and applying Article 29 new. No absurd result would follow, and to suggest otherwise is absurd.

Conversely, an argument could be made that an absurd result would occur if the terms were considered a mere guideline in exercising prosecutorial and investigatorial discretion. If the Supreme Court Chamber's holding that 'there is no *objective*

---

[250] *Case 001* Appeal Judgment, para 60.

[251] *Black's Law Dictionary* (n 246) 10.

[252] The Supreme Court Chamber referred to 'Article 29' rather than 'Article 29 new' (the Article in force in the current version of the Establishment Law); however, this appears to be an oversight.

[253] The Supreme Court Chamber reasons that this would indirectly amount to permitting a defence of superior orders and frustrate the purpose of Art 29 new. See *Case 001* Appeal Judgment, para 62.

[254] ICTY Statute, Art 7(4).

[255] See *Prosecutor v Lukić & Lukić*, IT-98-32/1-AR11*bis*.1, Decision on Milan Lukić's Appeal Regarding Referral, 11 July 2007, paras 21–22.

method for the Trial Chamber to decide on, compare, and then rank the criminal responsibility of all Khmer Rouge officials'[256] were correct, one queries whether such categories of persons should have been prosecuted at the ECCC. The UN Human Rights Committee has indicated: 'If ... exceptional criminal procedures or specially constituted courts or tribunals apply in the determination of certain categories of cases, *objective and reasonable grounds must be provided to justify the distinction.*'[257] If, as the Supreme Court Chamber held,[258] a 'large amount of discretion' is involved in a decision whether a person would be prosecuted or investigated at the ECCC and 'there is no *objective method*' for the Trial Chamber to make this determination, then the right to equality before the courts[259] would be violated because similar cases might not be dealt with in similar ways. Without an objective method of determining who may be prosecuted, decisions to prosecute would be arbitrary and open to allegations of political interference.[260]

4.3. The Drafters' Intent

Having found that an absurd result would occur if 'senior leaders and those who were most responsible' were interpreted as a jurisdictional limitation, under Article 32 of the VCLT, the Supreme Court Chamber should have considered supplementary means of interpretation, including the preparatory work of the Agreement and the circumstances of its conclusion. The negotiation history indicates that *both parties* to the Agreement intended that the phrase 'senior leaders of Democratic Kampuchea and those who were most responsible' be a limit on the ECCC's jurisdiction as opposed to a guideline for prosecutorial or investigatorial policy.

For example, in the draft of the March 2000 Articles of Cooperation, the language *'senior leaders ... and those who were most responsible'* was placed in the provisions concerning the Co-Investigating Judges and Co-Prosecutors.[261] In the final draft of the Agreement, this language was ultimately removed from the provisions concerning the Co-Investigating Judges and Co-Prosecutors. Article 2 of the Agreement states: 'The present Agreement further recognizes that the Extraordinary Chambers have

---

[256] *Case 001* Appeal Judgment, para 62 (emphasis added).

[257] Human Rights Committee, CCPR/C/GC/32, 'General Comment No 32, Article 14: Right to Equality before Courts and Tribunals and to a Fair Trial;, 23 August 2007, para 14 (emphasis added).

[258] *Case 001* Appeal Judgment, para 62.

[259] Constitution of the Kingdom of Cambodia dated 24 September 1993, modified by Kram dated 8 March 1999, promulgating the amendments to Articles 11, 12, 13, 18, 22, 24, 26, 28, 30, 34, 51, 90, 91, 93 and other Articles from Chapter 8 through Chapter 14 of the Constitution of the Kingdom of Cambodia which was adopted by the National Assembly on 4 March 1999, Art 31; Universal Declaration of Human Rights, GA Res 217A (III), UN Doc A/810 at 71 (1948), Art 7; ICCPR Arts 14(1), 26.

[260] See Sergey Vasiliev, 'ECCC Appeals, Appraising the Supreme Court Chamber's Interventions' (2020) 18 *Journal of International Criminal Justice* 723, 740–41. Professor Vasiliev argues that by adopting a laissez faire attitude to the Co-Prosecutors' and Co-Investigating Judges' discretionary decisions on the selection of suspects – circumventing 'an essentially *legal*, albeit politically charged, issue of whether someone is among the "most responsible"' – the Supreme Court Chamber 'opened itself to the criticism of abdicating judicial control and succumbing to *Realpolitik*'.

[261] See United Nations, Archives and Records Management Section, 'Letter from the Secretary-General to Prime Minister Hun Sen' (21 March 2000) and Annex (n 162) (emphasis added).

personal jurisdiction over the senior leaders of Democratic Kampuchea and those who were most responsible.' It thus appears that the Co-Investigating Judges and Co-Prosecutors would have to exercise their discretion concerning whom to prosecute within that jurisdictional limitation.

Had the parties intended the terms to be prosecutorial or investigatorial guidelines for the OCP or OCIJ, presumably such an intention would have been more clearly articulated throughout the negotiations – especially when considering the painstaking process as shown above. Quite the contrary, the negotiations and end result of the Agreement and Establishment Law demonstrate that the parties intended the terms to be jurisdictional limits.

The *only* piece of drafting history pointing to a contrary interpretation is the Group of Experts' report, which curiously, was the only piece of negotiation history considered by the Supreme Court Chamber. The Group of Experts recommended an international tribunal modelled on the ICTY and ICTR, which had jurisdiction over *all* persons who committed certain crimes.[262] To ensure that hundreds or thousands of people were not prosecuted at the envisaged Khmer Rouge tribunal, the Group of Experts proposed that the Prosecutor be given the discretion to limit prosecutions. Since the ICTY/ICTR model was *not* the model ultimately chosen in establishing the ECCC, the Group of Experts' recommendation concerning prosecutorial discretion is largely irrelevant. The RGC expressly rejected the Group of Experts' recommendations, as was made clear in Hun Sen's and RGC Foreign Minister Hor Nam Hong's exchanges with the Secretary-General.[263]

4.4. Use of Other International Jurisprudence

Rather than thoroughly considering the intent of the drafters, the Supreme Court Chamber sought guidance from international jurisprudence on comparable provisions to determine whether the phrase 'senior leaders and those who were most responsible' was jurisdictional. Because the intent of the drafters is clear, it was inappropriate to look to international jurisprudence for guidance. Article 12(1) of the Agreement provides that:

> The procedure shall be in accordance with Cambodian law. Where Cambodian law does not deal with a particular matter, or where there is uncertainty regarding the interpretation or application of a relevant rule of Cambodian law, or where there is a question regarding the consistency of such a rule with international standards, guidance may also be sought in procedural rules established at the international level.[264]

---

[262] ICTY Statute, Art 1; ICTR Statute, Art 1.

[263] Letter dated 3 March 1999 from the Prime Minister of Cambodia addressed to the Secretary-General, UN Doc A/53/581 and S/1999/230, 3 March 1999; Hor Nam Hong, 'Aide-Memoire on Report of the UN Group of Experts for Cambodia of 18 February 1999' (12 March 1999); 'Aide Memoire for the UN Secretary General HE Kofi annan [sic]', in (September 1999) 21 *Cambodia New Vision* 1, 6.

[264] Similar guidance is set out in the Establishment Law, but only for the Co-Prosecutors, Co-Investigating Judges, and Trial Chamber (eg 'the Co-Prosecutors may seek guidance in procedural rules established at the international level …'). See Establishment Law, Arts 20 new, 23 new, 33 new.

The ECCC's personal jurisdiction was not a mere procedural matter. Nor was it a matter that international jurisprudence could resolve. Consideration should have been given to the different procedural systems at the various international tribunals and the different motivations behind their establishment.

4.4.1. ICTY and ICTR Procedure and Jurisprudence

Even if it were appropriate to consider international jurisprudence to resolve the question of whether the phrase 'most responsible' limited the ECCC's jurisdiction, the Supreme Court Chamber incorrectly found that a comparison of ICTY and ICTR practice supported its interpretation that the phrase was not jurisdictional at the ECCC.[265] Those tribunals had an entirely different mandate and procedural system.

The Supreme Court Chamber pointed to Rule 28(A) of the ICTY and ICTR Rules of Procedure and Evidence; however, Rule 28(A), titled 'Reviewing and Duty Judges', was not intended to be a jurisdictional limitation on either Tribunal. It states that: 'The President shall refer the matter to the Bureau which shall determine whether the indictment, prima facie, concentrates on one or more of the most senior leaders suspected of being most responsible for crimes within the jurisdiction of the Tribunal.' Rule 28(A) is a *Rule* and is not part of the ICTY's Statute. Further, Rule 28(A) was not amended to include this language until 6 April 2004.[266] Language limiting the personal jurisdiction of the Tribunal is not found in the ICTY Statute, which states that the ICTY had jurisdiction over 'persons responsible'.[267] The ICTR's Rule 28 is not comparable to ICTY Rule 28(A), and it is unclear why the Supreme Court Chamber referred to it at all.[268]

The Supreme Court Chamber also considered the Rule 11*bis* referral mechanism at the ICTY, but this does not relate to the ICTY's jurisdiction, or even the Prosecutor's discretion. Instead, this procedure allows a Referral Bench to refer a case from the ICTY to a national court *proprio motu* or at the request of the Prosecutor.

> The major purpose of the rule is to enable the Referral Bench, where it is in the interests of justice to do so, to give effect to the policy of the Security Council, as reflected in Resolution 1534, that the efforts of the Tribunal should be concentrated on trying the most senior leaders suspected of being most responsible for crimes within the Tribunal's jurisdiction.[269]

It did not limit the ICTY's jurisdiction to try any cases, but instead allowed cases to be referred so that the ICTY could more expeditiously wrap up its work.

---

[265] Note too that while the SCSL had an obligation to be guided by the Appeals Chambers decisions of the ICTY and ICTR (pursuant to Art 20(3) SCSL Statute), the ECCC had no such obligation. See SCSL Statute, Art 20(3); *Prosecutor v Norman et al*, SCSL-04-14-T, Decision on Interlocutory Appeals against Trial Chamber Decision Refusing to Subpoena the President of Sierra Leone, 11 September 2006, para 13.

[266] ICTY Rules of Procedure and Evidence, IT/32/Rev 30, Rule 28(A).

[267] ICTY Statute, Art 1.

[268] Rule 28 of the ICTR Rules of Procedure and Evidence.

[269] *Prosecutor v Trbić*, IT-05-88/1-PT, Decision on Referral of Case under Rule 11*bis* with Confidential Annex, 27 April 2007, para 18. See also Security Council Resolution 1503, UN Doc No S/Res/1503, 28 August 2003.

4.4.2. SCSL Procedure and Jurisprudence

The Supreme Court Chamber also found that its interpretation of the phrase 'most responsible' was consistent with SCSL jurisprudence.[270] At the SCSL, the *Brima et al* Appeals Chamber determined that the phrase 'persons bearing greatest responsibility' was a prosecutorial guideline rather than a jurisdictional limitation. Reliance on *Brima et al* is misplaced. Several differences between the SCSL and the ECCC warrant a different outcome.

The *Brima et al* Appeals Chamber decision was issued after two Trial Chambers (*Norman* and *Brima et al*) reached different conclusions on whether the phrase 'persons who bear the greatest responsibility' in the SCSL Statute was a jurisdictional limitation.[271] The *Brima et al* Appeals Chamber gave two reasons that the phrase was not jurisdictional.

First, Article 1 of the SCSL Statute states that: 'The Special Court shall ... have the power to prosecute persons who bear the greatest responsibility.' Article 15 states that: 'The Prosecutor shall be responsible for the investigation and prosecution of persons who bear the greatest responsibility.' The *Brima et al* Appeals Chamber decided that the phrase was not jurisdictional because these Articles refer to the Prosecutor's competence.[272] The *Brima et al* Appeals Chamber rationale is likely the basis for the Supreme Court Chamber's conclusion that Articles 5(3) and 6(3) of the Agreement were the 'chief' indication that the phrase is discretionary and not jurisdictional. Second, the *Brima et al* Appeals Chamber considered that it would be inconceivable to conclude after a lengthy and expensive trial that the Court had no jurisdiction over the accused, if it had determined beyond reasonable doubt that the crimes were committed.[273] Neither rationale applied at the ECCC.

Concerning the first rationale, the Establishment Law differs from the SCSL Statute. While the SCSL Statute's wording can be taken to indicate that it was the Prosecutor who had the competence to determine whether individuals bore the greatest responsibility for the crimes, the Establishment Law simply states in Article 16 (concerning the role of the Co-Prosecutors) that '[a]ll indictments in the Extraordinary Chambers shall be the responsibility of two prosecutors ... who shall work together to prepare indictments against the Suspects in the Extraordinary Chambers'. If the terms 'senior leader' or 'most responsible' were intended to be a mere guide for prosecutorial discretion, they would have been included in *this* provision, rather than in the 'competence' Article with the other jurisdictional requirements.[274]

Further, limiting the ECCC's personal jurisdiction did not limit the OCP's or OCIJ's independence any more than limiting the ECCC's subject matter jurisdiction

---

[270] *Case 001* Appeal Judgment, paras 72–73.

[271] *Prosecutor v Norman et al*, SCSL-04-14-PT, Decision on the Preliminary Defence Motion on the Lack of Personal Jurisdiction Filed on Behalf of Accused Fofana, 3 March 2004; *Prosecutor v Brima et al*, SCSL-2004-16-T, Judgment, 20 July 2007, paras 636–59. See also Charles Chernor Jalloh, 'Prosecuting Those Bearing "Greatest Responsibility": The Lessons of the Special Court for Sierra Leone' (2013) 96 *Marquette Law Review* 863.

[272] *Prosecutor v Brima et al*, SCSL-2004-16-A, Judgment, 22 February 2008, paras 277–82.

[273] ibid para 283.

[274] Establishment Law, Art 2 new.

did. As the International Pre-Trial Chamber Judges held, the Co-Prosecutors had no discretion to determine who will be prosecuted:

> [T]here is no discretion to be exercised by the Co-Prosecutors under Internal Rule 53(1). ... Once the conclusion is drawn that there is 'reason to believe that crimes within the jurisdiction of the ECCC have been committed', then the Co-Prosecutors are obliged to open a judicial investigation by sending an Introductory Submission.[275]

Concerning the second rationale, the Pre-Trial Chamber also had jurisdiction to determine whether the charged persons fit within the ECCC's personal jurisdiction based on the Closing Order, prior to any trial ever taking place.[276] The Pre-Trial Chamber had jurisdiction to hear challenges to the ECCC's jurisdiction,[277] which arose as appeals against indictments (Closing Order). The Pre-Trial Chamber would have the Closing Order with the available supporting evidence to enable it to decide this jurisdictional challenge. In contrast, at the SCSL, there was no judicial investigation and no Pre-Trial Chamber with the jurisdiction to settle jurisdictional challenges. There, a determination on personal jurisdiction could not realistically be made until the conclusion of a lengthy and expensive trial.

Finally, nothing concerning the Court's personal jurisdiction was stated clearly in the agreement between the United Nations and Sierra Leone to establish the SCSL. The term 'persons who bear greatest responsibility' was mentioned only in the SCSL Statute. The opposite is true at the ECCC, where the Agreement explicitly states that 'the Extraordinary Chambers have *personal jurisdiction* over senior leaders of Democratic Kampuchea and those who were most responsible'.[278] According to one commentator, this is 'perhaps the strongest evidence' that the ECCC's language is jurisdictional.[279]

4.5. The Meaning of the Terms 'Senior Leaders' and 'Most Responsible'

While the plain language is clear, and the negotiations confirm that the terms 'senior leaders' and 'most responsible' are meant to be jurisdictional limits – rather than a mere guideline for prosecutorial or investigatorial policy – the parties did not concretely articulate who would be considered a 'senior leader' or 'most responsible'. Understandable. This is an issue in setting up any international criminal tribunal: 'how one could limit the scope of personal jurisdiction in a reasonable way'.[280] Courts have finite and limited resources and cannot handle excessive caseloads. On the other

---

[275] Considerations of the Pre-Trial Chamber Regarding the Disagreement between the Co-Prosecutors Pursuant to Internal Rule 71, Opinion of Judges Lahuis and Downing, 18 August 2009, para 23.

[276] See *Case 001* Appeal Judgment, para 28. The Supreme Court Chamber held that the Pre-Trial Chamber's role in settling disagreements does not alter its conclusion that the phrase is not jurisdictional, but this ignores the Pre-Trial Chamber's role in determining challenges to the ECCC's jurisdiction.

[277] ECCC Internal Rules, Rule 74(3)(a).

[278] Agreement, Art 2 (emphasis added).

[279] Morrison (n 11) 583, 599.

[280] Heder, *Personal Jurisdiction* (n 75) 35, quoting UN Delegation, Phnom Penh, 7 July 2000 at 3:00 pm: Law on the Establishment of Extraordinary Chambers in the Courts of Cambodia for the Prosecution of Crimes Committed During the Period of Democratic Kampuchea.

hand, to have explicitly named people would have violated the right to presumption of innocence.[281]

Going through each provision of Article 31 of the VCLT in turn, it becomes clear that the Article 31 interpretative approach does not provide assistance with determining the meaning of the terms 'senior leaders' and 'most responsible':

- Article 31(1): it is impossible to determine the ordinary meaning of 'senior leaders' and 'most responsible' in light of the Agreement's object and purpose, because bringing to trial these groups of individuals *is* the Agreement's object and purpose; accordingly, the Agreement does not define what these terms mean.

- Article 31(2)(a): no agreement relating to the treaty (the Agreement) has been made between the RGC and the United Nations in connection with the conclusion of the treaty.

- Article 31(2)(b): the Establishment Law *could* be considered an instrument made by one of the parties in connection with the treaty; however, since the Establishment Law contains the same language concerning personal jurisdiction as the Agreement, this provision does not assist in interpreting the Agreement.

- Article 31(3)(a): there has been no subsequent agreement between the parties concerning the interpretation of the treaty.

- Article 31(3)(b): there has been no subsequent practice by the RGC or the United Nations in the application of the treaty that would establish the agreement of the parties.

- Article 31(3)(c): there are no relevant rules of international law applicable in the relations between the RGC and the United Nations.

The terms 'senior leaders' and 'most responsible' are ambiguous because they are relative terms.[282] Because Article 31 of the VCLT does not assist in interpreting the meaning of the terms 'senior leaders' and 'most responsible', Article 32 of the VCLT, 'Supplementary Means of Interpretation', including the preparatory work of the Agreement and the circumstances of its conclusion, must be considered.

Unlike 'most responsible', 'senior leader' is less contentious and more readily discernible. Several hints from the negotiation history and context imply (although they do not expressly state) that the intent was to try members of the Standing Committee (Pol Pot, Ieng Sary, Nuon Chea, Son Sen, Ta Mok), important/high-level members of the Central Committee (Khieu Samphan, Kè Pork), and possibly high-level government ministers (Ieng Thirith) ('senior leaders'):

- The Cambodian government consistently identified Pol Pot and Ieng Sary as 'senior leaders' since 1979. The Cambodian government in 1979 (then the People's Republic of Kampuchea) established the People's Revolutionary Tribunal to try

---

[281] ICCPR Art 4(2) states: 'Everyone charged with a criminal offence shall have the right to be presumed innocent until proved guilty according to law.'

[282] As the Supreme Court Chamber explained concerning the term 'most responsible': 'neither a suspect nor the ECCC can verify whether a suspect is "most responsible" pursuant to sharp-contoured, abstract and autonomous criteria'. *Case 001* Appeal Judgment, para 62.

the 'Pol Pot–Ieng Sary clique' for 'acts of genocide'[283] and convicted Pol Pot and Ieng Sary of genocide in absentia.[284]

- In 1998, prior to Pol Pot's death, the US State Department also offered 'support bringing to justice Pol Pot and other senior Khmer Rouge leaders responsible for crimes against humanity'.[285] US Ambassador Kent Weideman indicated that the 'top leader' category included Nuon Chea, Ta Mok, Ieng Sary, Ieng Thirith, Khieu Samphan and Kè Pork.[286]

- RGC Foreign Minister Hor Nam Hong's 12 March 1999 aide-memoire explained that 'two former top leaders … Khieu Samphan and Nuon Chea' defected to the RGC, and that Ta Mok – a 'top Khmer Rouge hard-liner' – was recently arrested.[287]

- In 1999, UN Assistant Secretary-General for Legal Affairs Ralph Zacklin wrote to Annan stating that 'the political and military leadership is a well defined group of probably less than a dozen'.[288]

- In December 1999, Hun Sen reported to the media that: 'Four to five (Khmer Rouge leaders) will be tried.'[289]

While someone's senior leadership position is more readily discernible, the term 'most responsible' is more malleable and elusive. Once Duch came into the public eye in April 1999 and was placed into the custody of the military tribunal in May 1999, it appears that the phrase 'most responsible' was added to discussions of the ECCC's jurisdiction to ensure that he could be prosecuted by any future tribunal even though he was not considered to be a senior leader.[290] Comparatively, Duch was a small fish. He was head of S-21, approximately one of 200 security centres in Cambodia during the DK period.[291] He was not a member of the Standing or Central Committees, or otherwise involved in the upper or middle levels of government.[292] Why was he targeted for prosecution? Likely because he had confessed to crimes at S-21,[293] a site specifically focused on by the Group of Experts,[294] and was readily available for trial.

---

[283] See Decree Law No 1, 15 July 1979, reproduced in De Nike (n 78) 43–44, Art 1.

[284] Judgment of the People's Revolutionary Tribunal, 19 August 1979, reproduced in De Nike (n 78) 549.

[285] Stanley O Roth, Assistant Secretary for East Asian and Pacific Affairs, 'Statement Before the House International Relations Committee, Subcommittee on Asia and the Pacific', 26 February 1998, available at https://1997-2001.state.gov/policy_remarks/1998/980226_roth_cambodia.html.

[286] See Heder, *Personal Jurisdiction* (n 75) 37, quoting email posting by US Ambassador Kent Wiedeman, 16 October 2000.

[287] Hor Nam Hong, 'Aide-Memoire on Report of the UN Group of Experts for Cambodia of 18 February 1999', 12 March 1999, 2–3, available at https://digitallibrary.un.org/record/1492649?ln=en.

[288] See Heder, *Personal Jurisdiction* (n 75) 27, quoting Ralph Zacklin, 'Note to the Secretary-General: A Mixed Tribunal for Cambodia', 19 July 1999.

[289] *Kyodo News*, 'Hun Sen Says Five Khmer Rouge Leaders May Be Tried', 22 December 1999, available at www.thefreelibrary.com/Hun+Sen+says+five+Khmer+Rouge+leaders+may+be+tried.-a058533640.

[290] See Heder, *Personal Jurisdiction* (n 75) 27, quoting Thomas Hammarberg to Ralph Zacklin, 2 July 1999.

[291] *Case of KAING Guek Eav*, 001/18-07-2007/ECCC/SCC, Appeal Brief by the Co-Lawyers for Kaing Guek Eav alias 'Duch' against the Trial Chamber Judgment of 26 July 2010, 18 November 2010, para 23.

[292] *Case of KAING Guek Eav*, 001/18-07-2007-ECCC-OCIJ, Closing Order Indicting Kaing Guek Eav alias Duch, 8 August 2008, D99.

[293] See Pechoux (n 145).

[294] See Group of Experts Report, para 55.

Hammarberg remarked: '[Duch] had no leading position in the party but is regarded as highly responsible for the mass killing. If he were not indicted, there would definitely be questions.'[295]

Based on the negotiations, it seems that Duch, as head of S-21, was considered to fall under the category of 'most responsible' – without the parties actually declaring or finding him 'most responsible'.[296] However, it is not clear who else would fall into this category. Nor were there any criteria indicated in the negotiations as to how a Chamber would decide if someone is 'most responsible'.

In their Closing Order in Case 004/1, the Co-Investigating Judges disagreed with the Supreme Court Chamber's 'classification of "personal jurisdiction" as a non-jurisdictional criterion', but felt 'bound, by reason of practical judicial defence' to follow the Supreme Court Chamber's case law 'unless there are exceptional reasons for a disagreement'.[297] They explained that although the Pre-Trial Chamber was the only direct appellate panel above the OCIJ and there was no doctrine of *stare decisis* in a civil law system such as Cambodia's, it would be undesirable for clarity and uniformity to disregard Supreme Court Chamber case law.[298] Nonetheless, the Co-Investigating Judges considered that 'whether one calls the criterion a jurisdictional requirement or a policy guideline' became 'a secondary question of terminology'.[299]

The Co-Investigating Judges held that determining personal jurisdiction 'entails a wide but not entirely non-justiciable margin of appreciation for the OCP and OCIJ'.[300] They considered that the Supreme Court Chamber 'cannot have had in mind an entirely free-wheeling selection policy approach by the OCP or OCIJ'.[301]

> [T]he very reference to an abuse of discretion based on bad faith or unsound professional judgement presupposes that there are parameters against which the exercise of discretion can and must be measured, ie what constitutes the boundaries of good faith and sound professional judgment before the decision moves into the field of arbitrariness.[302]

The Co-Investigating Judges also disagreed 'with the argument that comparisons to other persons are not appropriate or feasible.'[303]

By applying the 'substance' of the Supreme Court Chamber's appeal judgment in Case 001, the Co-Investigating Judges noted that: '[T]here is no merit in any historical-political contention that the negotiations around the establishment of the ECCC led to a joint and binding understanding that only a certain finite number of (named) individuals were to be considered under the Court's jurisdiction.'[304] Based

---

[295] See Heder, *Personal Jurisdiction* (n 75) 27, quoting Thomas Hammarberg to Ralph Zacklin, 2 July 1999.
[296] See Group of Experts Report, para 109.
[297] *Case 004/1* Closing Order (Reasons), para 10.
[298] ibid para 10.
[299] ibid para 9.
[300] ibid.
[301] ibid.
[302] ibid.
[303] ibid. See also *Case 001* Appeal Judgment, para 62. The OCIJ 'quer[ied] the correctness' of the Supreme Court Chamber's reference to Art 29 of the Establishment Law in this context. *Case 004/1* Closing Order (Reasons), n 7.
[304] *Case 004/1* Closing Order (Reasons) para 37.

on their independent analysis of the negotiation history and ECCC jurisprudence, they articulated four factors to assess in determining whether a charged person is among those 'most responsible':

(a) the intent of the drafters of the ECCC Agreement to restrict the ECCC's personal jurisdiction to those with the greatest responsibility in the DK period;[305]
(b) the principles of *in dubio pro reo* and strict construction of criminal law;[306]
(c) the charged person's formal role in the hierarchy and the degree to which he or she was able to determine Communist Party of Kampuchea (CPK) policies and/or their implementation;[307] and
(d) the relative gravity of the charged person's acts and their effects, subject to the understanding of the drafters of the ECCC Agreement that there were a large number of potential perpetrators 'who each alone could have been responsible for hundreds or thousands of deaths'.[308]

At the outset of their analysis, the Co-Investigating Judges disagreed with a theoretical argument that they should exercise their discretion as broadly as possible in favour of finding personal jurisdiction in order to avoid 'a massive impunity gap for crimes committed during the DK era'.[309] While acknowledging that limiting the ECCC's personal jurisdiction would axiomatically cause such an impunity gap, the Co-Investigating Judges considered that 'this finding must have no policy impact on [their] exercise of discretion'.[310] Finding that the drafters of the Agreement 'wanted to restrict personal jurisdiction to those with the greatest responsibility under the DK, fully aware [of] the death toll',[311] they concluded that the ECCC was a court of 'selective justice' because 'only a certain small group of people will ever be prosecuted'.[312] Since the 'negotiated context in the case of the ECCC was knowingly different' than that of other international tribunals, the Co-Investigating Judges determined that '[a]n unqualified comparison to the [ICTY]'s referral bench's case law' to gauge comparable levels of seriousness and responsibility is 'ultimately not helpful'.[313] They considered that the sheer scale of casualties during the Khmer Rouge era, the negotiating history and the evidence made applying the ICTY's criteria 'impossible', since this would make ordinary soldiers who performed mass executions, or their direct superiors who ordered them, into most responsible persons.[314]

Also among the factors the Co-Investigating Judges took into account are the principles of *in dubio pro reo* and strict construction of criminal law, which they considered to be essential 'because of the pressure exerted by the public's

---

[305] ibid paras 11–25.
[306] ibid paras 26–36.
[307] ibid para 39.
[308] ibid para 38.
[309] ibid para 25.
[310] ibid.
[311] ibid para 18.
[312] ibid para 31.
[313] ibid para 18 (emphasis in original).
[314] ibid paras 18–19, citing *Prosecutor v Lukić and Lukić*, ICTY-98-32/1-AR11bis.1, Decision on Milan Lukić's appeal regarding referral, 11 July 2007 ('*Lukić & Lukić* Referral Decision') para 25.

expectations and the media on the grounds of concerns around the concept of impunity for mass atrocities, political agendas, as well as previous historical research into the underlying events'.[315] Disavowing Benedict Carpzov's odious statement that '[i]t is well-known that in the cases of the most serious offences the boundaries of the law may be disregarded because of the enormity of the crime',[316] the Co-Investigating Judges considered that the 'ultimate principle' is to 'put no man on trial under the forms of judicial proceedings if you are not willing to see him freed if not proven guilty'.[317]

Another 'important, but not conclusive or exclusive' factor the Co-Investigating Judges considered was the degree to which the charged person was able to contribute to or determine CPK policies and/or their implementation.[318] The Co-Investigating Judges found that 'decision-making in the Khmer Rouge hierarchy was not a formal democratic process with the possibility for egalitarian input from functionaries at any level',[319] as vertical lines of communication in the chain of command and the accompanying secrecy did not permit free exchange of information below the top leadership.[320] 'Indeed, openly discussing instructions from *Angkar* ... could easily have been considered by the superior levels as the first step to insubordination, and no-one could be safe in the assumption that such conversations would not be reported in interested quarters with adverse effect upon themselves.'[321]

Lastly, the Co-Investigating Judges determined that the charged person's position in the CPK hierarchy and the relative gravity of the alleged acts and their effects were relevant in their assessment of personal jurisdiction, subject to the drafters' intent to limit the scope of the ECCC's jurisdiction.[322] While the Co-Investigating Judges considered that the 'obvious initial filtering' was the charged person's formal position, they also considered that determining whether the charged person was among those 'most responsible' required taking into account whether he or she was able to contribute to or determine CPK policies and/or their implementation.[323] They also considered that a valid point of reference for assessing gravity would not be 'entirely dissimilar to those [considerations] one would use for sentencing purposes'[324] – subject to the drafters' intent to limit the ECCC's jurisdiction to those with the greatest responsibility under the DK, despite the large death toll and number of potential perpetrators.[325]

---

[315] *Case 004/1* Closing Order (Reasons) para 28.

[316] ibid para 30, quoting Benedict Caprzov, *Practica nova imperalis Saxonica rerum criminalium, Paras III, Quaestio C II* (1652) (translated in text by the OCIJ). 'Notissimum est, quod in delictis atrocissimis propter criminis enormitatem jura transgredi liceat.'

[317] ibid para 29, quoting Justice Robert H Jackson's remarks at the American Society of International Law on 13 April 1945 cited in Christoph Safferling, 'Nürnberg und die Zukunft des Völkerstrafrechts' (2015) 70 *Juristenzeitung* 1063, n 34.

[318] *Case 004/1* Closing Order (Reasons) para 40.

[319] ibid.

[320] ibid.

[321] ibid para 41.

[322] ibid paras 38–39.

[323] ibid para 39.

[324] ibid para 38.

[325] ibid para 38.

Selective prosecution in an already selective jurisdiction presented 'wider moral issues' to the Co-Investigating Judges, which they considered only 'enhances the need for … a rigorous and robust evaluation of the evidence against those few who are being investigated'.[326] Finding themselves bound to respect the political decisions of the drafters, they opined that there should not be 'an automatic presumption of senior responsibility for those few who *are* brought before the court by the allegations of the OCP'.[327] Signing the ECCC Agreement in the absence of a residual jurisdiction clause was a 'conscious political choice', balancing 'the call for integration of the remaining Khmer Rouge into society against the desire for some form of judicial closure for the horrendous suffering of the victims'.[328]

In Cases 004/1, 004/2 and 003, the Pre-Trial Chamber unanimously held that it must be able to review the Co-Investigating Judge's findings and conclusions on personal jurisdiction.[329] Finding that the terms 'senior leaders' and 'those who were most responsible' represented the limits of the ECCC's personal jurisdiction, the Pre-Trial Chamber considered that the determination of whether someone fell into these categories 'is a judicial one and does not permit arbitrary action' and 'should … be exercised in accordance with well-settled principles'.[330] While the Pre-Trial Chamber found that the 'flexibility of these terms inherently required some margin of appreciation on the part of the Co-Investigating Judges',[331] and that their decision was reviewable under the standard of review for discretionary decisions,[332] it did not define the terms 'senior leaders' or 'most responsible' or set out factors for their assessment. In these three cases, the Pre-Trial Chamber Judges reached different opinions on the law of personal jurisdiction, with the National Pre-Trial Chamber Judges reasoning inconsistently.

In Case 004/1, the National Pre-Trial Chamber Judges issued a three-page separate opinion restating their agreement with the National Co-Prosecutor that the Introductory Submissions in Cases 003 and 004 should never have been issued and finding that the International Co-Prosecutor 'does not have a clear principle for selecting suspects for prosecution'.[333] In Case 004/2, the National Pre-Trial Chamber Judges issued a thirty-five-page opinion explaining their view of the negotiation history in establishing the ECCC,[334] concluding that there was 'no agreement on the

---

[326] ibid para 33.

[327] ibid para 35 (emphasis in original).

[328] ibid para 32.

[329] *Case 004/1* Considerations, para 20; *Case 004/2* Considerations, para 28. See also *Case 003* Considerations, para 41.

[330] *Case 004/1* Considerations, para 20; *Case 004/2* Considerations, para 28; *Case 003* Considerations, para 45.

[331] *Case 004/1* Considerations, para 20; *Case 004/2* Considerations, para 28.

[332] *Case 004/1* Considerations, para 21; *Case 004/2* Considerations, para 29: 'A discretionary decision may be reversed where it was: (i) based on an incorrect application of the governing law (*ie* an error of law) invalidating the decision; (ii) based on a patently incorrect conclusion of fact (*ie* an error of fact) occasioning a miscarriage of justice; and/or (iii) so unfair or unreasonable as to constitute an abuse of the Co-Investigating Judges' discretion and to force the conclusion that they failed to exercise their discretion judiciously.' See also *Case 003* Considerations, para 47.

[333] *Case 004/1* Considerations, paras 88, 91.

[334] ibid paras 186–203.

number of persons to be prosecuted'.[335] They went on to find that the 'senior leaders are the Standing Committee members of the CPK Central Committee', including Pol Pot, Nuon Chea, Ieng Sary, Sao Phim, Ta Mok, Von Vet and Son Sen,[336] and that although Duch was not a senior leader, he 'definitely falls within the category of those most responsible'.[337] No reasoning was offered for this finding. After again restating their view that the preliminary investigation in Cases 003 and 004 by the International Co-Prosecutor was illegal,[338] the National Pre-Trial Chamber Judges in Case 004/2 found that Judge Bohlander should not have carried out an investigation,[339] concluding that the indictment 'is also contrary to the ideas of the law drafters, the administrative structure of Democratic Kampuchea, international jurisprudence and his previous assertions'.[340] By contrast in Case 003, the National Pre-Trial Chamber Judges did not assess personal jurisdiction at all, limiting their analysis to Rule 72 governing disagreements between the Co-Investigating Judges and Rule 77(13) concerning appeals of Closing Orders.[341]

In all three cases, the International Pre-Trial Chamber Judges in their separate opinions considered that 'the identification of those who were amongst the "most responsible" entailed the assessment of both the gravity of the crimes alleged or charged and the level of responsibility of the suspect'.[342] In their view, 'this assessment must be done from both a quantitative and qualitative perspective', with no exhaustive list of factors to consider or 'filtering standard in terms of positions in the hierarchy', when assessing level of responsibility.[343] To determine whether the charged persons were 'most responsible', the International Pre-Trial Chamber used the following factors articulated in ECCC jurisprudence, which, in turn were gleaned from ICTY jurisprudence:

1.   The gravity of the crimes charged, which includes consideration of:

   (a) the number of victims;[344]

   (b) the geographic and temporal scope of the crimes;[345]

---

[335] *Case 004/2* Considerations, para 202.

[336] ibid para 224.

[337] ibid para 223.

[338] ibid para 260.

[339] ibid, para 271.

[340] Ibid para 293.

[341] *Case 003* Considerations, paras 113–18.

[342] *Case 004/1* Considerations, para 321; *Case 004/2* Considerations, para 352; *Case 003* Considerations, para 286.

[343] *Case 004/1* Considerations, para 321; *Case 004/2* Considerations, para 352; *Case 003* Considerations, para 286.

[344] *Case 004/1* Considerations, para 327; *Case 003* Considerations, para 287; *Case of MEAS Muth*, 003/07-09-2009-ECCC-OCIJ, Decision on Personal Jurisdiction and Investigative Policy Regarding Suspect, 2 May 2012, D48 ('RICIJ Personal Jurisdiction Decision') para 16; *Lukić & Lukić* Referral Decision, para 25; *Prosecutor v Kovačević*, IT-01-42/2-I, Decision on Referral of Case Pursuant to Rule 11*bis*, 17 November 2006 ('*Kovačević* Referral Decision') para 20; *Prosecutor v Trbić*, IT-05-88/1-PT, Decision on Referral of Case under Rule 11*bis* with Confidential Annex, 27 April 2007, para 19 ('*Trbić* Referral Decision'); *Prosecutor v Janković*, IT-96-23/2-PT, Decision on Referral of Case under Rule 11*bis*, 22 July 2005 ('*Janković* Referral Decision') para 19.

[345] *Case 004/1* Considerations, para 327; *Case 003* Considerations, para 287; RICIJ Personal Jurisdiction Decision, para 16; *Case 001* Trial Judgment, para 22; *Kovačević* Referral Decision, para 22; *Prosecutor v Ljubičić*, IT-00-41-PT, Decision to Refer the Case to Bosnia and Herzegovina Pursuant to Rule 11*bis*,

(c) manner in which crimes were allegedly committed;[346] and

(d) the number of separate incidents;[347] and

2. The level of responsibility of suspect/charged person, which includes consideration of:

(a) the level of participation in the crimes (including function within a larger Joint Criminal Enterprise);[348]

(b) the de jure and de facto hierarchical rank or position;[349]

(c) the number of subordinates and hierarchical echelons above him or her;[350]

(d) the permanence of his position/period of time in authority.[351]

Notably, the International Pre-Trial Chamber Judges did not consider the following factors gleaned by the Reserve International Co-Investigating Judge from ICTY jurisprudence, which, at a minimum, would appear to give a more precise indication of the charged person's de facto level of authority:

(a) function in the hierarchy;[352]

(b) capacity to issue orders;[353]

(c) whether the orders were in fact followed by his subordinates;[354]

(d) procedure followed for appointment into position;[355]

---

12 April 2006 ('*Ljubičić* Referral Decision') para 18; *Trbić* Referral Decision, para 19; *Prosecutor v Ademi & Norac*, IT-04-78-PT, Decision for Referral to the Authorities of the Republic of Croatia Pursuant to Rule 11*bis*, 14 September 2005 ('*Ademi & Norac* Referral Decision') para 20; *Prosecutor v Mejakić et al*, IT-02-65-PT, Decision on Prosecutor's Motion for Referral of Case Pursuant to Rule 11*bis*, 20 July 2005 ('*Mejakić* Referral Decision') para 21; *Janković* Referral Decision, para 19.

[346] *Case 004/1* Considerations, para 327; *Case 003* Considerations, para 287; RICIJ Personal Jurisdiction Decision, para 16; *Case 001* Trial Judgment, para 22; *Trbić* Referral Decision, para 19.

[347] *Case 004/1* Considerations, para 327; *Case 003* Considerations, para 287; RICIJ Personal Jurisdiction Decision, para 16; *Case 001* Trial Judgment, para 22; *Trbić* Referral Decision, para 19.

[348] *Case 004/1* Considerations, para 332; *Case 003* Considerations, para 300; *Case 001* Trial Judgment, para 18, quoting *Case of KAING Guek Eav alias Duch*, 001/18-07-2007-ECCC-OCIJ, Closing Order, para 129; *Case 001* Trial Judgment, para 22; *Case of NUON Chea et al.*, 002/19-09-2007-ECCC-OCIJ, Closing Order, 15 September 2010, D427, para 1328; *Lukić & Lukić* Referral Decision, para 21; *Trbić* Referral Decision, para 20; *Mejakić* Referral Decision, para 23.

[349] *Case 004/1* Considerations, paras 332, 335–36; *Case 003* Considerations, para 300; *Case 001* Trial Judgment, para 18, *quoting Case of KAING Guek Eav*, 001/18-07-2007-ECCC-OCIJ, Closing Order, para 129; RICIJ Personal Jurisdiction Decision, para 24; *Case 001* Trial Judgment, para 22; *Lukić & Lukić* Referral Decision, para 25; *Kovačević* Referral Decision, para 20; *Trbić* Referral Decision, para 20; *Ademi & Norac* Referral Decision, para 30; *Mejakić* Referral Decision, para 24; *Prosecutor v Rašević & Todović*, IT-97-25/1-PT, Decision on Referral of Case under Rule 11*bis*, 8 July 2005, para 23; *Janković* Referral Decision, para 19.

[350] *Case 004/1* Considerations, para 332; *Case 003* Considerations, para 300; RICIJ Personal Jurisdiction Decision, para 24; *Case 001* Trial Judgment, para 22; *Lukić & Lukić* Referral Decision, para 22; *Trbić* Referral Decision, para 22; *Prosecutor v Dragan Milošević*, IT-98-29/1-PT, Decision on Referral of Case Pursuant to Rule 11*bis*, 8 July 2005, para 23.

[351] *Case 004/1* Considerations, para 332; *Case 003* Considerations, para 300; RICIJ Personal Jurisdiction Decision, para 24; *Case 001* Trial Judgment, para 22; *Prosecutor v Dragan Milošević*, IT-98-29/1-PT, Decision on Referral of Case Pursuant to Rule 11*bis*, 8 July 2005, para 23.

[352] RICIJ Personal Jurisdiction Decision, para 21.

[353] ibid; *Trbić* Referral Decision, para 20.

[354] RICIJ Personal Jurisdiction Decision, para 24.

[355] ibid.

(e) the degree of authority including authority to negotiate, sign or implement agreements;[356]
(f) actual knowledge that his subordinates were committing crimes, including knowledge on the number, type and scope of the crimes, the time during which they were committed, their geographic location, as well as the eventual widespread nature of the acts;[357]
(g) control of access to territory;[358] and
(h) whether those more senior in rank than the suspect/accused have already been convicted (if so, this makes it less likely that the suspect/accused is one of the most responsible).[359]

Assessing gravity and level of responsibility as a yardstick is one thing, drawing conclusions based on who may or may not have been prosecuted by the ad hoc tribunals is entirely different, and unhelpful. No themes emerge or can be drawn, suggesting, as tempting as it may be because of the nature of the crimes charged before these tribunals, that in case of doubt as to whether a suspect is a senior leader or most responsible there is a preference for prosecution. The ICTY declined to prosecute suspects based on findings that they were not among those 'most responsible',[360] resulting in the suspects' prosecution in domestic courts. On the other hand, the SCSL did not decline to prosecute any suspects charged by the prosecution because they did not fit in the category of having the 'greatest responsibility'. The fact that the SCSL did not find any suspects or accused to fall outside the meaning of 'greatest responsibility' says nothing about whether the suspects in Cases 003 and 004 should be prosecuted or investigated at the ECCC. Furthermore, the ICTY's decisions to refer cases to national courts were not made based on any 'preference for prosecution' but because of the UN Security Council's completion strategy for the ICTY.[361] Had the cases not been referred to national courts, they would have been prosecuted at the ICTY because the ICTY did not have a limited personal jurisdiction.[362]

It is equally unpersuasive to argue that prosecution waspreferred at the ECCC if a suspect is targeted by the Co-Prosecutors because, unlike cases at the ICTY which were referred to national courts through the Rule 11*bis* procedure, the charged persons in Cases 003 and 004 would avoid prosecution altogether if they are not prosecuted at the ECCC.[363] Simply because someone is suspected of a crime, there is no principle of international criminal law that this person *must* be prosecuted, *regardless*

---

[356] ibid; *Prosecutor v Dragan Milošević*, IT-98-29/1-PT, Decision on Referral of Case Pursuant to Rule 11*bis*, 8 July 2005 ('*Milošević* Referral Decision') para 23.
[357] RICIJ Personal Jurisdiction Decision, para 24.
[358] ibid; *Milošević* Referral Decision, para 23.
[359] RICIJ Personal Jurisdiction Decision, para 24; *Kovačević* Referral Decision, para 20; *Ljubičić* Referral Decision, para 19.
[360] See eg *Trbić* Referral Decision, paras 22–24; *Ljubičić* Referral Decision, para 19; *Prosecutor v Rašević & Todović*, IT-97-25/1-PT, Decision on Referral of Case under Rule 11*bis*, 8 July 2005, para 23.
[361] See Security Council Resolution 1503, UN Doc No S/Res/1503, 28 August 2003.
[362] ICTY Statute, Art 1; Security Council Resolution 1534, UN Doc No S/Res/1534, 26 March 2004.
[363] Randle DeFalco makes such an argument. See DeFalco (n 75) 55.

of any jurisdictional limitations on the courts.[364] There is no legal authority justifying such a notion, irrespective of the emotive and didactic rhetoric understandably attendant to a perceived miscarriage of justice resulting from a technicality – such as forgoing prosecution of a suspect because he or she does not fit within the definition of 'most responsible'. This is a policy-driven argument grounded in situational ethics and based on emotional reasoning masquerading for rational legal analysis.

Just because many thousands of Cambodians allegedly bear some responsibility for the crimes that occurred during the Khmer Rouge period, limiting the ECCC's personal jurisdiction violates no principle in international criminal law. As Corell indicated during the negotiations,[365] nothing prevents the Cambodian government from conducting domestic prosecutions or using alternative means to deal with those believed to have committed crimes during the DK period. But this is an entirely different issue and should not be factored in when determining the definition of 'most responsible' and whether it was a jurisdictional issue or a matter of prosecutorial and investigatorial discretion not subject to judicial review. Had the RGC and the United Nations intended to ensure that no person would avoid criminal prosecution, they would not have restricted the ECCC's jurisdiction to senior leaders and those most responsible. A review of the negotiations demonstrates that this was not the intention of either party.

Judges are not politicians in robes. They have no remit to decide where the RGC and the United Nations *should* have set the jurisdictional contours on who is to be prosecuted at the ECCC. The objective to hold individuals accountable for crimes must not be confused with the criteria set by the applicable law to do so. Given the agreed objectives and criteria by the RGC and United Nations in setting the jurisdictional contours of the ECCC, judicial restraint in interpreting who or what constitutes 'most responsible' was salutary. The allegations made in the Introductory Submissions were mere allegations made after preliminary investigations. The International Co-Prosecutor was required to determine, after only a preliminary investigation, that the suspects were 'most responsible' before he could file Introductory Submissions naming them.[366] The point of the judicial investigation was to determine whether there was sufficient evidence to support the allegations made in the Introductory Submissions. The Co-Investigating Judges would have abdicated their judicial functions if they failed to conduct a full investigation and to reach *their own* conclusion as to whether any suspect can be considered 'most responsible'.[367] But the enquiry does not stop there: because it is a jurisdictional issue, any decision made by the Co-Investigating Judges was subject to judicial review by the Pre-Trial Chamber.

---

[364] For example, in the Australian case *Nulyarimma v Thompson*, the Federal Court of Australia heard together two joined cases where the appellants, Aboriginal Australians, argued that the prime minister and other members of government were guilty of genocide for conduct contributing to the destruction of the Aboriginal people as an ethnic or racial group. Australia had ratified the Genocide Convention but had not enacted implementing legislation. The Court held that the crime of genocide did not exist in domestic Australian law and so the government officials could not be tried for genocide. The fact that Australian criminal law did not include the crime of genocide was found to be a bar to prosecution. *Nulyarimma v Thompson* [1999] FCA 1192 (Federal Court of Australia).

[365] See Heder, *Personal Jurisdiction* (n 75) 36, quoting Hans Corell, 'Letter to Sok An' (10 July 2000).

[366] ECCC Internal Rules, Rule 53.

[367] ECCC Code of Judicial Ethics, 5 February 2007, Arts 5(3), 5(4).

Also, it was unsound to compare the allegations in Cases 003 and 004 to the ICTY cases that were not referred to national courts by the ICTY because the accused in those cases were considered to be 'most responsible' (*Lukić*, *Milošević* and *Delić*), or to make comparisons with SCSL cases, as one author suggests.[368] As the ICTY, SCSL and ECCC deal with completely different factual scenarios, no meaningful comparison may be made between cases at the different tribunals. For example, Milan Lukić may have been considered 'most responsible' for certain crimes that occurred in the Former Yugoslavia and perhaps these crimes were less grave than those that allegedly occurred in Cambodia. This tells us nothing about whether the suspects in Cases 003 and 004 were 'most responsible' for their alleged crimes. Perhaps there were twelve people who bore greatest responsibility for crimes that occurred in Sierra Leone. This also tells us absolutely nothing about how many people may have been 'most responsible' for crimes that occurred in Cambodia.

Contextually, the only legitimate comparison to determine whether the suspects in Cases 003 and 004 are 'most responsible' may be to compare the gravity of their alleged crimes and their alleged level of responsibility to that of those who were convicted in Cases 001 and 002. Even so, making such comparisons may not necessarily be helpful. When tribunals have applied the gravity of the crimes and level of responsibility formula, the results have shown that these criteria do not necessarily reflect how cases are handled in reality.

For example, the ICTY Prosecution frequently argued that the accused should be referred to national courts even though the crimes charged were serious.[369] In the ICTY *Lukić* case (in which former International Co-Investigating Judge Mark Harmon was the senior prosecuting lawyer), the Prosecution argued that the case should be referred to a state court '[d]espite the obvious gravity of the crimes'.[370] Lukić, who preferred to be tried by the ICTY rather than at the Bosnia and Herzegovina State Court (and serve his sentence in a Bosnia and Herzegovina prison), argued that 'the level of responsibility of the accused and the gravity of the crimes charged are incompatible with transfer'.[371] Similarly, many indicted at other tribunals were neither senior leaders nor most responsible based on the gravity of the crimes and level of responsibility. One famous example is Duško Tadić, the first accused to go to trial before the ICTY.[372] Tadić was accused of crimes committed at Omarska camp in Prijedor in northwest Bosnia.[373] Tadić had no official position at Omarska, was not one of the leaders of the Republika Srpska (the Serb forces in Bosnia and Herzegovina) and was not one of the primary actors in the conflict between the Serbs

---

[368] DeFalco (n 75) 45, 58.

[369] See eg *Prosecutor v Ademi & Norac*, IT-04-78-PT, Request by the Prosecutor under Rule 11*bis*, paras 18–19. *Prosecutor v Mejakić et al.*, IT-02-65-PT, Request by the Prosecutor under Rule 11*bis*, 2 September 2004, paras 20–23. *Prosecutor v Trbić*, IT-05-88-PT, Request by the Prosecutor under Rule 11*bis* for Referral of the Indictment to Another Court, 4 May 2006, para 18. *Prosecutor v Lukić & Lukić*, IT-98-32/1-PT, Prosecutor's Submissions Pursuant to Order of 30 June 2006, 28 July 2006, para 3.

[370] *Prosecutor v Lukić & Lukić*, IT-98-32-I, Request by the Prosecutor under Rule 11*bis*, 1 February 2005, para 25. See also para 15.

[371] *Prosecutor v Lukić & Lukić*, IT-98-32-I, Submission of Defence Counsel for Milan Lukić Pursuant to Order of 30 June 2006, 4 September 2006, opening para.

[372] *Prosecutor v Tadić*, IT-94-1-T, Judgment, 7 May 1999.

[373] *Prosecutor v Tadić*, IT-94-1-I, Amended Indictment, 1 September 1995.

and Muslims in Bosnia and Herzegovina.[374] As one author recalls: "'the big fish–little fish" issue has permeated the discussion about the *Tadić* case from its earliest stages. By now, of course, there is certainly no question that the Tribunal's mandate and its limited resources require it to focus on the persons most responsible for violations of international law.'[375]

5. CONCLUSION

No international criminal tribunal has ever been of general jurisdiction – intended to prosecute all who may be guilty of certain crimes. Each tribunal identifies only a select group of individuals to prosecute. No meaningful comparisons concerning jurisdiction can be drawn across the various tribunals as each was created for different sets of circumstances with different objectives in mind. One must look carefully into what was negotiated and the intent of the drafters.

Contrary to what was held by the ECCC's Supreme Court Chamber, the plain language of the Agreement and Establishment Law indicates that the terms 'senior leaders' and 'most responsible' operated as jurisdictional limits, rather than prosecutorial or investigatorial policy for the OCP and OCIJ. No absurd result followed by interpreting the terms according to their plain-language meaning. On the contrary, an absurd result could arguably ensue when considering the terms as mere guidelines in exercising prosecutorial and investigatorial discretion. Without an objective method of determining who may be prosecuted, decisions to prosecute would be arbitrary and open to allegations of political interference. A review of the negotiation history reveals that this was not what the parties intended.

Admittedly, defining the jurisdictional limitation – 'senior leaders' and those 'most responsible' – is not as straightforward as these simple terms may seem. During the negotiations leading up to the establishment of the ECCC, unfortunately, the parties did not clearly articulate or provide concrete criteria to determine who would fall into these categories. While it is understandable that to name the individuals in these categories to be prosecuted would have violated the right to be presumed innocent, by failing to articulate precise criteria, the parties effectively (and not necessarily unintentionally) embraced constructive ambiguity. Whether someone was a 'senior leader' is more readily discernible, particularly when considering that, as in any government structure, there are defined hierarchical lines that can readily guide an individual's de jure authority and de facto authority. Conversely, determining who may fit within the category of 'most responsible', is malleable and thus subject to manipulation. To paraphrase from *Through the Looking Glass*, it means whatever the Co-Prosecutors and Co-Investigating Judges chose it to mean, 'neither more nor less'.[376] While some

---

[374] See *Prosecutor v Tadić*, IT-94-1-T, Judgment, 7 May 1999. The Trial Chamber never established that Tadić had any official role at Omarska, or any level of responsibility within Republika Srbska. See ibid paras 180–92. See also eg ibid paras 154–79, 379.

[375] Kitty Felde et al, 'The Prosecutor v Dusko Tadic' (1998) 13(6) *American University International Law Review* 1441, 1445.

[376] See above, n 10.

criteria can be gleaned from international jurisprudence, any comparisons made must be within the context of the particular conflict and the intent of the drafters.

In defining these terms and in determining the personal jurisdictional contours at future tribunals or courts, a thorough and in-context review of what was negotiated and the facts of the particular case is warranted. There are lessons to be drawn from the ECCC's experience by those who may in the future be responsible for establishing similar ad hoc, internationalised, or national tribunals with international assistance. The founding documents must clearly articulate the criteria of the categories of those who are the targets for prosecution, and must clearly and unequivocally identify whether these categories are a matter of personal jurisdiction subject to judicial review or a matter of prosecutorial and investigatorial discretionary policy.

13

Standing the Test of Time: The Dynamic Interpretation of the Genocide Convention

CAROLINE FOURNET

1. INTRODUCTION

THE 1948 UNITED Nations Convention on the Prevention and Punishment of the Crime of Genocide (Genocide Convention)[1] 'was the first *human rights treaty* adopted by the General Assembly of the United Nations. ... Its adoption marked a crucial step towards the development of international human rights and international criminal law as we know it today.'[2]

The definition of the crime of genocide contained in this human rights treaty permeated international criminal law, where it is reproduced verbatim.[3] All the relevant international instruments thus define genocide as a series of specific acts, perpetrated against specific groups with the specific intent to bring about the destruction of the given group in whole or in part:

[genocide] means any of the following acts committed with intent to destroy, in whole or in part, a national, ethnical, racial or religious group, as such:

(a) Killing members of the group;
(b) Causing serious bodily or mental harm to members of the group;
(c) Deliberately inflicting on the group conditions of life calculated to bring about its physical destruction in whole or in part;
(d) Imposing measures intended to prevent births within the group;
(e) Forcibly transferring children of the group to another group.[4]

---

[1] Convention for the Prevention and Punishment of the Crime of Genocide, United Nations, 1948. Approved and proposed for signature, ratification or accession by the General Assembly of the United Nations, Resolution 260 A (III) of 9 December 1948 (entered into force 12 January 1951).

[2] United Nations, Office on Genocide Prevention and the Responsibility to Protect, 'The Genocide Convention', www.un.org/en/genocideprevention/genocide-convention.shtml, accessed 31 July 2021. Emphasis added.

[3] See Art 4 of the Statute of the International Criminal Tribunal for the former Yugoslavia (ICTY); Art 2 of the Statute of the International Criminal Tribunal for Rwanda (ICTR); Art 6 of the Statute of the International Criminal Court (ICC).

[4] Art 4 ICTY Statute; Art 2 ICTR Statute; Art 6 ICC Statute.

Noticeably, the Genocide Convention – just like subsequent international criminal law instruments[5] – fails to define the terms it employs, thus generating legal uncertainty and arguably paving the way for judicial activism. Faced with the silence of the conventional text, the ad hoc international criminal tribunals were left with no other choice than to resort to judicial interpretation, a role that remains typically within the confines of their mandates and thus beyond criticism. Yet, because these judicial constructions are based on hardly any textual indication, besides of course when they resort to the *travaux préparatoires*, the creativity of the international criminal tribunals has sometimes dangerously grazed legislative action. As the following contribution proposes to explore, the lack of conventional precision has indeed prompted the ICTY and the ICTR to elaborate on the terms used in the definition of the crime of genocide, notably with respect to the acts proscribed, the groups protected and the intent of the genocider to destroy the group in whole or in part.

In interpreting the Genocide Convention, it appears that, rather than freeze the meaning of the crime of genocide to when it was defined back in 1948, the ad hoc international criminal tribunals have implicitly made use of dynamic methods of interpretation, possibly borrowed from the European Court of Human Rights (ECtHR)[6] – a claim that finds some credential in the origins of the Convention as a human rights instrument. Two particular constructions here seem to stand out: the 'living instrument' doctrine – as applied to the genocidal *actus reus*; and the teleological doctrine – as adapted to the groups protected. This dynamism notwithstanding, the ad hoc tribunals have generally refrained from overstretching the concept of genocide and, when it comes to their understanding of the genocidal *mens rea*, conservatism seems to have been their overarching principle.

2. A MODERN UNDERSTANDING OF THE GENOCIDAL *ACTUS REUS* 'IN THE LIGHT OF PRESENT-DAY CONDITIONS'

The 'living instrument' doctrine was first elaborated and explicited by the ECtHR in the 1978 *Tyrer* case: 'The [European Convention on Human Rights (ECHR)] is a living instrument which ... must be interpreted in the light of present-day conditions.'[7] Put differently, rather early on, the ECtHR opted for an interpretation of the ECHR that is made not in the light of past events or of the circumstances at the time of the drafting but rather in the light of contemporary conditions.

---

[5] Note, however, that the ICC 'Elements of Crimes' do offer some clarification. See Art 6, Elements of Crimes, *Official Records of the Assembly of States Parties to the Rome Statute of the International Criminal Court*, First Session, New York, 3–10 September 2002 (UN publication, Sales No E.03.V.2 and corrigendum) part II.B.

[6] Note that the Tribunals were not bound by human rights law. Art 21(3) ICC Statute, by expressly providing that '[t]he application and interpretation of law pursuant to this article must be consistent with internationally recognized human rights', constitutes an innovation in the text of international criminal law.

[7] ECtHR, *Tyrer v The United Kingdom*, Appl No 5856/72, Judgment, 25 April 1978, para 31.

The Genocide Convention proceeds to an exhaustive list of prohibited acts. In so doing, it limits itself to a strict catalogue of proscribed acts, without, however, defining them. It is precisely this interplay between the restrictive list and the lack of definition of the proscribed acts that prompted the ad hoc international criminal tribunals to define these acts and to ultimately include within the original enumeration acts that had not been initially contemplated, thus going beyond the intention of the drafters, admittedly to the detriment of the principle of legal certainty but in favour of a contemporary reading of the text. To this end, the tribunals seem to have – implicitly – resorted to the established human rights law 'living instrument' doctrine. As it will be discussed, they embarked on an interpretation of genocidal acts that mirrors present-day conditions rather than the conditions at the time of the drafting of the Convention.

2.1. A 'No-Nonsense' Approach

Even before they had to face definitional issues, the international criminal tribunals had to overcome obstacles generated by a slightly incoherent choice of vocabulary on the part of the drafters of the Genocide Convention. As noted by Quigley, the genocidal act of 'killing members of the group' 'reads oddly in this context. "Killing" is not a term ordinarily used to define crime in English-speaking countries, since it implies no culpability. A killing can be accidental, or in self-defense.'[8] In light of the fact that this oddity is further enhanced by the reference in the French version of the text to 'meurtre' – a penal qualification that requires intent and implies culpability – the ICTR had to resolve this linguistic discrepancy and, in all sovereignty, decided to concur with the French version of the conventional text:

> The Trial Chamber is of the opinion that the term 'killing' used in the English version is too general, since it could very well include both intentional and unintentional homicides, whereas the term '*meurtre*', used in the French version, is more precise. It is accepted that there is murder when death has been caused with the intention to do so, as provided for, incidentally, in the Penal Code of Rwanda which stipulates in its Article 311 that 'Homicide committed with intent to cause death shall be treated as murder'.[9]

Elaborating on its decision, Trial Chamber I defined the act of 'killing' in the following terms:

> In order to be held criminally liable for genocide by killing members of a group, in addition to showing that an accused possessed an intent to destroy the group as such, in whole or

---

[8] John Quigley, *The Genocide Convention: An International Law Analysis* (Aldershot, Ashgate, 2007) 94.

[9] *Prosecutor v Akayesu*, ICTR-96-4-T, Judgment, Trial Chamber I, 2 September 1998, para 500. See also *Prosecutor v Kayishema and Ruzindana*, ICTR-95-1-T, Judgment, 21 May 1999, paras 101–04; *Prosecutor v Rutaganda*, Judgement and Sentence 6 December 1999, ICTR-96-3, para 50; *Prosecutor v Musema*, ICTR-96-13-A, Trial Chamber I, Judgment and Sentence, 27 January 2000, para 155; *Prosecutor v Bagilishema*, ICTR-95-1A-T, Judgment, Trial Chamber I, 7 June 2001, paras 57–58.

in part, the Prosecutor must show the following elements: (1) the perpetrator intention-ally killed one or more members of the group, without the necessity of premeditation; and (2) such victim or victims belonged to the targeted ethnical, racial, national, or religious group.[10]

Subsequent definitional efforts shine by their brevity, 'killing' being merely defined as 'homicide committed with intent to cause death';[11] a brevity judicially justified by the fact that '"Killing" in sub-paragraph (a) needs no further explanation. As regards the underlying acts, the word "killing" is understood to refer to intentional but not neces-sarily premeditated acts.'[12] This 'no-nonsense' approach was also accompanied with a common-sense approach that reflected, within the law of genocide, general trends in international criminal law and notably the explicit recognition of acts of sexual violence as international crimes.

2.2. The Interpretation of Genocidal Acts in the Light of the Criminalisation of Sexual Violence

Although regrettably late, the law of war crimes and the law of crimes against humanity have been amended to include crimes of sexual violence.[13] This evolution, however, had no impact on the textual definition of the crime of genocide, which has remained untouched since 1948. Yet, in a progressist fashion, the ad hoc international criminal tribunals – perhaps inspired by the more general and contemporary trend to criminalise sexual violence – have interpreted genocidal acts so as to include within their scope sexual crimes.

In interpreting the act of 'causing serious bodily or mental harm to members of the group', the ICTR specified that 'to a large extent, "causing serious bodily harm" is self-explanatory. This phrase could be construed to mean harm that seriously injures the health, causes disfigurement or causes any serious injury to the external, internal organs or senses.'[14] This judicial contentment as to the clarity of the notion notwithstanding, the ICTR was nonetheless prompt in finding that 'serious bodily or mental harm' is to be 'determined on a case-by-case basis, *using a common sense approach*',[15] a finding which, if it could be seen as contravening the principle of legal

---

[10] *Bagilishema* (n 9) para 58 (footnotes omitted). See also *Prosecutor v Semanza*, ICTR-97-20-T, Judgment and Sentence, 15 May 2003, para 319. See also *Prosecutor v Kajelijeli*, ICTR-98-44A-T, Trial Chamber II, 1 December 2003, Judgment and Sentence, para 813.

[11] *Musema* (n 9) para 155. See also *Prosecutor v Seromba*, ICTR-2001-66-I, Judgment, Trial Chamber, 13 December 2006, para 317.

[12] See *Prosecutor v Stakić*, IT-97-24-T, Judgment, Trial Chamber II, 31 July 2003, para 515. See also *Prosecutor v Kamuhanda*, ICTR-95-54A-T, Trial Chamber II, Judgment, 22 January 2004, para 632; *Prosecutor v Ntagerura, Bagambiki, Imanishimwe*, ICTR-99-46-T, Judgment and Sentence, Trial Chamber III, 25 February 2004, para 664.

[13] For war crimes, see Art 4(e) ICTR Statute; Art 8(2)(b)(xxii) and Art 8(2)(e)(vi) ICC Statute. For crimes against humanity, see Art 3(g) ICTR Statute; Art 5(g) ICTY Statute; Art 7(1)(g) ICC Statute.

[14] *Kayishema and Ruzindana* (n 9) para 109. See also *Prosecutor v Krstić*, IT-98-33, Judgment, Trial Chamber I, 2 August 2001, para 483; *Semanza* (n 10) para 320 and 322; *Stakić* (n 12) para 516; *Ntagerura, Bagambiki, Imanishimwe* (n 12) para 664; *Seromba* (n 11) para 317.

[15] *Kayishema and Ruzindana* (n 9) para 108. Emphasis added. For the case-by-case assessment of mental harm, see ibid paras 110 and 113.

certainty and predictability, is admittedly reasonable. In a similar vein, Trial Chamber I of the ICTY stated that:

> The gravity of the suffering must be assessed on a case by case basis and with due regard for the particular circumstances. In line with the *Akayesu* Judgement, the Trial Chamber states that serious harm need not cause permanent and irremediable harm, but it must involve harm that goes beyond temporary unhappiness, embarrassment or humiliation. It must be harm that results in a grave and long-term disadvantage to a person's ability to lead a normal and constructive life.[16]

The international criminal tribunals used the textual uncertainty to expressly include within the realm of 'causing serious bodily or mental harm' acts which are not conventionally mentioned, while simultaneously refraining from proceeding to an exhaustive enumeration, thus leaving the door open for further acts to be included within the – initially strictly limitative – list of genocidal acts. It has thus been judicially found that 'serious bodily and mental harm does not necessarily mean harm that is permanent or irremediable'[17] and notably encompasses '*acts of sexual violence, rape*,[18] mutilations and interrogations combined with beatings, and/or threats of death',[19] acts of bodily or mental torture, inhumane or degrading treatment, persecution,[20] 'cruel treatment, torture, *rape* and deportation'.[21] In *Seromba*, the ICTR Appeals Chamber referred to 'torture, *rape*, and non-fatal physical violence that causes disfigurement or serious injury to the external or internal organs'[22] as '*quintessential examples* of serious bodily harm'. This express inclusion of acts of sexual violence within the ambit of genocide notwithstanding, the *Akayesu* Trial Chamber adopted an ever more straightforward approach by emancipating crimes of a sexual nature from the pre-existing categories of genocidal acts:

> [T]he Chamber wishes to underscore the fact that in its opinion, [rape and sexual violence] *constitute genocide in the same way as any other act* as long as they were committed with the specific intent to destroy, in whole or in part, a particular group, targeted as such. Indeed, rape and sexual violence certainly constitute infliction of serious bodily and mental harm on the victims and are even, according to the Chamber, *one of the worst ways of inflicting harm on the victim* as he or she suffers both bodily and mental harm. In light of all the evidence before it, the Chamber is satisfied that the acts of rape and sexual violence described above, were committed solely against Tutsi women, many of whom

---

[16] *Krstić* (n 14) para 486. Footnote omitted.

[17] *Kayishema and Ruzindana* (n 9) para 108. Footnotes omitted. See also *Akayesu* (n 9) para 502. *Rutaganda* (n 9) para 51. *Musema* (n 9) para 156; *Semanza* (n 10) paras 320–21.

[18] See eg *Akayesu* (n 9) paras 706–07. Emphasis added; *Kayishema and Ruzindana* (n 9) para 110; *Rutaganda* (n 9) para 51. *Musema* (n 9) para 156; *Semanza* (n 10) paras 320–21.

[19] *Kayishema and Ruzindana* (n 9) para 108. Footnotes omitted. See also *Akayesu* (n 9) para 502; *Rutaganda* (n 9) para 51; *Musema* (n 9) para 156; *Semanza* (n 10) paras 320–21.

[20] *Akayesu* (n 9) para 504; *Rutaganda* (n 9) para 51.

[21] *Krstić* (n 14) paras 482–86. Footnotes omitted. Emphasis added. It is also interesting to note that the Preparatory Commission for the ICC indicated that serious bodily and mental harm 'may include, *but is not necessarily restricted to*, acts of torture, rape, sexual violence or inhuman or degrading treatment'. Cited in ibid (emphasis added).

[22] *Prosecutor v Seromba*, ICTR-2001-66-A, Judgment, Appeals Chamber, 12 March 2008, para 46.

were subjected to the worst public humiliation, mutilated, and raped several times, often in public, in the Bureau Communal premises or in other public places, and often by more than one assailant. These rapes resulted in physical and psychological destruction of Tutsi women, their families and their communities. *Sexual violence was an integral part of the process of destruction*, specifically targeting Tutsi women and specifically contributing to their destruction and to the destruction of the Tutsi group as a whole.[23]

Although rape and sexual violence have not explicitly been included in the Rome Statute's definition of the crime of genocide, the Preparatory Commission for the ICC still confirmed the Tribunals' earlier case law and indicated that serious bodily and mental harm 'may include, but is not necessarily restricted to, acts of torture, *rape, sexual violence* or inhuman or degrading treatment'.[24] Although it may be regretted that crimes of sexual violence have not made it into the text of the law, their judicial inclusion is to be welcomed. There is no doubt such crimes constitute 'serious bodily [and] mental harm', and that – if perpetrated with the intent to destroy one of the protected groups – they constitute genocide. Had the international criminal tribunals perpetuated the conventional omission of sexual violence from the ambit of the crime of genocide, they would have problematically frozen the prohibition of genocide in time and completely overlooked the fact that sexual violence is, more often than not, part of the genocidal process.[25]

This evolutive judicial approach to genocidal acts is thus necessary to allow for the adjudication of acts that are essentially genocidal and cause 'serious bodily or mental harm'. The same conclusion could be reached with respect to the genocidal act constituted by 'imposing measures intended to prevent births within the group'. As per the *Akayesu* Trial Chamber:

> [T]he measures intended to prevent births within the group, should be construed as sexual mutilation, the practice of sterilization, forced birth control, separation of the sexes and prohibition of marriages. In patriarchal societies, where membership of a group is determined by the identity of the father, an example of a measure intended to prevent births within a group is the case where, during rape, a woman of the said group is deliberately impregnated by a man of another group, with the intent to have her give birth to a child who will consequently not belong to its mother's group. ... Furthermore, the Chamber notes that measures intended to prevent births within the group may be physical, but can also be mental. For instance, rape can be a measure intended to prevent births when the person raped refuses subsequently to procreate, in the same way that members of a group can be led, through threats or trauma, not to procreate.[26]

This judicial interpretation, by expressly including acts of sexual violence within the realm of measures imposed to prevent births within the group, here also mirrors the evolution of international criminal law, which – although slowly – has gradually and increasingly recognised sexual crimes as international core crimes.

---

[23] *Akayesu* (n 9) para 731. Emphasis added.
[24] See Elements of Crimes (n 5), Art 6(b)(1), fn 3. Emphasis added.
[25] See eg *Akayesu* (n 9).
[26] *Akayesu* (n 9) paras 507–08. See also *Kayishema and Ruzindana* (n 9) para 117; *Rutaganda* (n 9) para 53; *Musema* (n 9) para 158.

2.3. A 'Common-Sense' Approach

A similar evolutive approach was adopted with respect to the scope of the genocidal act of 'serious mental harm', which has been found to 'be construed as some type of impairment of mental faculties, or harm that causes serious injury to the mental state of the victim'[27] and to 'mean more than minor or temporary impairment of mental faculties'.[28] According to Bryant, mental harm includes 'anything from racial or ethnic slurs by individuals directed at members of a group, to an overt pattern of governmental discrimination or harassment of a group, to deliberate debilitation and demoralization of a group through the use of addictive narcotic drugs'.[29] This rather wide understanding of the notion of 'mental harm' seems a far cry from the original intention of the drafters of the Genocide Convention for whom it was 'absolutely clear that "mental harm", within the meaning of the Convention, can be caused *only* by the use of narcotics'.[30] Here also, the approach of the international criminal tribunals has brought the evasive notion of 'serious mental harm' into the twenty-first century – undoubtedly departing from its original meaning to transform it into a more modern concept, fit to be adjudicated before contemporary international criminal courts and tribunals.

Likewise resorting to a realistic, case-by-case approach to define the act of 'deliberately inflicting on the group conditions of life calculated to bring about its physical destruction in whole or in part', the ICTR justified it by the fact that

> it is impossible to enumerate in advance the 'conditions of life' that would come within the prohibition of Article II; … Instances of genocide that could come under subparagraph (c) are such as placing a group of people on a subsistence diet, reducing medical services below a minimum, withholding sufficient living accommodations, etc., provided that these restrictions are imposed with intent to destroy the group in whole or in part.[31]

This 'impossibility' explains why judicial findings have remained rather elusive and merely gave illustrations of which acts could potentially constitute a deliberate infliction on the group of conditions of life calculated to bring about its physical destruction:

> [T]he expression deliberately inflicting on the group conditions of life calculated to bring about its physical destruction in whole or in part, should be construed as the methods of destruction by which the perpetrator does not immediately kill the members of the group, but which, ultimately, seek their physical destruction. [They] include, *inter alia*, subjecting a group of people to a subsistence diet, systematic expulsion from homes and the reduction of essential medical services below minimum requirement.[32]

---

[27] *Prosecutor v Gacumbitsi*, ICTR-2001-64-T, Trial Chamber III, Judgment, 17 June 2004, para 291. Footnote omitted.

[28] *Semanza* (n 10) para. 321. Footnote omitted. See also *Kajelijeli* (n 10) para 815; *Kamuhanda* (n 12) para 634; *Ntagerura, Bagambiki, Imanishimwe* (n 12) para 664; *Seromba* (n 11) para 317.

[29] Bunyan Bryant, 'Substantive Scope of the Convention' (1975) 16 *Harvard International Law Journal* 686–96, 693.

[30] Nehemiah Robinson, *The Genocide Convention – A Commentary* (New York, Institute of Jewish Affairs, 1960) ix. Emphasis added.

[31] ibid 64.

[32] *Akayesu* (n 9) paras 505–06.

Providing what is admittedly a common-sense and reasonable definition of the 'conditions of life calculated to bring about its physical destruction in whole or in part', the ad hoc international criminal tribunals have also included therein the concept of 'slow death genocide', that is, 'circumstances which will lead to a slow death, for example, lack of proper housing, clothing, hygiene and medical care or excessive work or physical exertion'.[33] They specified that

> the conditions of life envisaged include rape, the starving of a group of people, reducing required medical services below a minimum, and withholding sufficient living accommodation for a reasonable period, provided the above would lead to the destruction of the group in whole or in part.[34]

A comparable dynamic reading was also applied to the act of 'forcibly transferring children of the group to another group':

> With respect to forcibly transferring children of the group to another group, the Chamber is of the opinion that, as in the case of measures intended to prevent births, the objective is not only to sanction a direct act of forcible physical transfer, but also to sanction acts of threats or trauma which would lead to the forcible transfer of children from one group to another.[35]

This act, which undoubtedly puts at risk the cultural identity of the group, is generally considered as the last remain of 'cultural genocide' within the conventional ambit. The initial draft of the Genocide Convention included cultural genocide among acts of genocide and defined it as the destruction of the specific characteristics of the persecuted groups by various means, such as forced exile, prohibition of the use of the national language, destruction of books, and similar acts.[36] If cultural genocide was subsequently abandoned in the final version of the Convention, a look at the case law reveals that the international criminal tribunals have not been reluctant to take into account the cultural aspects of the crime. Although recalling the legality principle, the ICTY still found that the proof of attacks directed against cultural institutions and monuments, committed in association with killing, may prove important in establishing the existence of a genocidal intent:

> The Trial Chamber is aware that it must interpret the Convention with due regard for the principle *nullum crimen sine lege*. It therefore recognises that, despite recent developments, customary international law limits the definition of genocide to those acts seeking the physical or biological destruction of all or part of the group. ... The Trial Chamber

---

[33] *Kayishema and Ruzindana* (n 9) para 115. Footnote omitted. See also *Rutaganda* (n 9) para 52; *Musema* (n 9) para 157; *Stakić* (n 12) para 517.

[34] *Kayishema and Ruzindana* (n 9) para 116.

[35] *Akayesu* (n 9) para 509. See also *Kayishema and Ruzindana* (n 9) para 118; *Rutaganda* (n 9) para 54; *Musema* (n 9) para 159.

[36] UN Doc A/AC.10/41 and UN Doc A/362 (Appendix II). See also Lemkin's definition of 'genocide in the cultural field' which consisted of 'the prohibition or the destruction of cultural institutions and cultural activities, of the substitution of education in the liberal arts for vocational education, in order to prevent humanistic thinking, which the occupant considers dangerous because it promotes national thinking': Raphaël Lemkin, *Axis Rule in Occupied Europe – Laws of Occupation, Analysis of Government, Proposals for Redress* (Washington, DC, Carnegie Endowment for International Peace, Division of International Law, 1944) xi–xii.

however points out that where there is physical or biological destruction there are often simultaneous attacks on the cultural and religious property and symbols of the targeted group as well, attacks which may legitimately be considered as evidence of an intent to physically destroy the group. In this case, the Trial Chamber will thus take into account as evidence of intent to destroy the group the deliberate destruction of mosques and houses belonging to members of the group.[37]

While it maintained that 'an enterprise attacking only the cultural or sociological characteristics of a human group ... would not fall under the definition of genocide',[38] the Trial Chamber implicitly applied the 'living instrument' doctrine when it recognised the existence of 'recent developments' towards the recognition of the crime of cultural genocide. One such development may be found in the case law of the Federal Constitutional Court of Germany:

[T]he statutory definition of genocide defends a supra-individual object of legal protection, ie, the *social* existence of the group ... the intent to destroy the group ... extends beyond physical and biological extermination. ... The text of the law does not therefore compel the interpretation that the culprit's intent must be to exterminate physically at least a substantial number of the members of the group.[39]

Reflecting on the attitude of the international criminal judge, Schabas pointed to the role of 'a contemporary interpreter of the definition of genocide', noting that

it can be argued that a contemporary interpreter of the definition of genocide should not be bound by the intent of the drafters back in 1948. The words 'to destroy' can readily bear the concept of cultural as well as physical and biological genocide, and bold judges might be tempted to adopt such progressive construction.[40]

This 'contemporary interpretation' did not solely involve an implicit resort to the 'living instrument' doctrine developed in human rights law, and notably by the ECtHR. The judicial interpretation of the groups protected by the Genocide Convention also appears to have turned to another Strasbourg-elaborated construction, that of safeguarding rights that are both 'practical and effective'.

3. A TELEOLOGICAL APPROACH TO THE GROUPS PROTECTED: SAFEGUARDING RIGHTS THAT ARE 'PRACTICAL AND EFFECTIVE'

Aside from the 'living instrument' doctrine, the Strasbourg Court has also developed a teleological interpretation, asserting that the ECHR is 'intended to guarantee not rights that are theoretical or illusory but rights that are practical and effective'.[41] When looking at their judicial construction of the groups protected under the

---

[37] *Krstić* (n 14) para 580. Emphasis added.

[38] ibid.

[39] Federal Constitutional Court, 2 BvR 1290/99, 12 December 2000, para (III)(4)(a)(aa). Emphasis added. Cited in *Krstić* (n 14) para 579.

[40] William A. Schabas, *An Introduction to the International Criminal Court*, 3rd edn (Cambridge, Cambridge University Press, 2007) 94.

[41] ECtHR, *Airey v Ireland*, Appl No 6289/73, Judgment, 9 October 1979, para 24.

definition of genocide, the international criminal tribunals seem to have adopted a similar purposeful approach, interpreting the definition so as to guarantee its effective use and application in practice.

Just like it fails to define the acts it proscribes, the Genocide Convention also falls short of precisely clarifying the groups it aims at protecting – leaving here again the door open for judicial interpretation. Article II merely refers to 'national, ethnical, racial [and] religious' groups, without providing for any form of indication as to what these categories of groups cover in reality. The confusing aspect of this group classification had already emerged during the drafting of the conventional text, when it had been argued that 'ethnic' was equivalent to both 'racial' and 'national'[42] and when the distinction between religious groups and national groups proved controversial.[43] Notwithstanding the fact that the reference to 'racial' groups is highly problematic, if not altogether literally racist, it also appears that, from its very inception, the categorisation drawn by the conventional text, by ignoring the interweaving of the different groups, proved artificial and hardly a workable tool. In the words of Drost:

> [A] convention on genocide cannot effectively contribute to the protection of certain described minorities when it is limited to particular defined groups … it serves no purpose to restrict international legal protection to some groups; firstly, because the protected members always belong at the same time to other unprotected groups.[44]

In this context, it is unsurprising that the ad hoc international criminal tribunals had to define the groups protected, sometimes forcing an improbable interpretation of the conventional text but – here also – using common sense and filling the gaps of a defective text. The limits of the conventional group characterisation became particularly clear when, so as to qualify the acts perpetrated in Rwanda as genocide, the *Akayesu* Trial Chamber was left with little other choice than to interpret in an extensive fashion the conventional scope of protection. As Tutsi did not fit in any of the conventionally listed groups,[45] the Trial Chamber proactively decided to turn to the *travaux préparatoires* and recalled that the conventional text was meant to

---

[42] See 3 UN GAOR C.6 (75th meeting) 115–16, UN Doc A/633 (1948). Cited in Lawrence J LeBlanc, 'The United Nations Genocide Convention and Political Groups: Should the United States Propose an Amendment?' (1988) 13 *Yale Journal of International Law* 271.

[43] See Report of the Ad Hoc Committee on Genocide, 3 UN ESCOR Supp 6, UN Doc E/794 (1948) 6.

[44] Pieter N Drost, *The Crime of State – Penal Protection for Fundamental Freedoms of Persons and Peoples, Book II: Genocide* (UN Legislation on International Criminal Law, Leyden, AW Sythoff, 1959) 122–23.

[45] The Tutsi did not fit in any of the groups described as they were not really a different ethnic group compared to the Hutu: they shared the same language, and probably the same culture: 'The Hutu and the Tutsi cannot even correctly be described as ethnic groups for they both speak the same language and respect the same traditions and taboos. It would be extremely difficult to find any kind of cultural or folk-loric custom that was specifically Hutu or Tutsi. … [There] were certainly distinguishable *social categories* in existence before the arrival of the colonisers, but the differences between them were not based on ethnic or racial divisions. [The colonisers reinforced the antagonism between Hutus and Tutsis which] has since become absorbed by the people themselves': Alain Destexhe, *Rwanda and Genocide in the Twentieth Century* (London, Pluto Press, 1995) 36. Emphasis added.

cover 'permanent and stable' groups,[46] an argument that thankfully allowed for the recognition that Tutsi were victims of genocide but whose grounds can be debated.[47]

More specifically, the *Akayesu* Trial Chamber also individually defined the different groups conventionally protected, holding that 'a national group is defined as a collection of people who are perceived to share a legal bond based on common citizenship, coupled with reciprocity of rights and duties';[48] 'an ethnic group is generally defined as a group whose members share a common language or culture';[49] a 'racial group is based on the hereditary physical traits often identified with a geographical region, irrespective of linguistic, cultural, national or religious factors';[50] and a 'religious group is one whose members share the same religion, denomination or mode of worship'.[51] In subsequent case law, the ICTR further defined the groups as protected by the Genocide Convention. In the *Kayishema and Ruzindana* case, Trial Chamber II gave a rather wide definition of 'ethnic group' as a group 'whose members share a common language and culture; or, a group which distinguishes itself as such (self identification); or, a group identified as such by others, including perpetrators of the crimes (identification by others)'.[52]

This definitional effort notwithstanding, the artificiality of the distinction between the different groups was subsequently acknowledged by the international criminal tribunals, and notably by the ICTY when the *Krstić* Trial Chamber found that:

> To attempt to differentiate each of the named groups on the basis of scientifically objective criteria would thus be inconsistent with the object and purpose of the Convention. ... A group's cultural, religious, ethnical or national characteristics must be identified within the socio-historic context which it inhabits. As in the *Nikolic* and *Jelisic* cases, the Chamber identifies the relevant group by using as a criterion the stigmatisation of the group, notably by the perpetrators of the crime, on the basis of its perceived national, ethnical, racial or religious characteristics.[53]

Put differently, the Trial Chamber here decided to proceed to both an objective and a subjective understanding of the notion of group – an arguably reasonable decision that allows for the concept of genocide to be meaningful and applicable in practice.

---

[46] *Akayesu* (n 9) paras 511–16, 701.

[47] Only one day after the adoption of the Genocide Convention, the General Assembly adopted the Universal Declaration of Human Rights (UDHR) whose Arts 15(2) and 18 expressly recognise the rights to change nationality as well as religion respectively. Art 15(2) provides that 'No one shall be ... denied the right to change his nationality' and Art 18 that 'Everyone has the right to ... freedom to change his religion.' In the words of the UK representative, the Genocide Convention 'should also provide protection to groups the members of which were as free to leave them as they were to join them. National or religious groups were obvious instances of that kind.' UN GAOR, 6th Committee, 3rd session, 69th Meeting (1948) para 60.

[48] *Akayesu* (n 9) para 512.

[49] ibid para 513.

[50] ibid para 514.

[51] ibid para 515. See also *Kayishema and Ruzindana* (n 9) para 98.

[52] ibid.

[53] *Krstić* (n 14) paras 556–57. Footnotes omitted.

With the Genocide Convention, 'determining the meaning of the groups protected by the Convention seems to dictate a degree of subjectivity. It is the offender who defines the individual victim's status as a member of a group protected by the Convention.'[54] The judicial acknowledgement of the importance of subjective elements in determining the perpetration of genocide is thus to be welcomed insofar as it reflects the specificity of the crime of genocide. As explained by the *Bagilishema* Trial Chamber, 'the perpetrators of genocide may characterize the targeted group in ways that do not fully correspond to conceptions of the group shared generally, or by other segments of society'.[55] Although expressing the view that 'a subjective definition alone is not enough to determine victim groups',[56] the same Trial Chamber simultaneously noted that 'for the purposes of applying the Genocide Convention, membership of a group is, in essence, a subjective rather than an objective concept. The victim is perceived by the perpetrator of genocide as belonging to a group slated for destruction.'[57] The necessity to adopt a semi-subjective approach also justifies judicial recourse to a case-by-case assessment of the facts:

> The determination of whether a group comes within the sphere of protection created by Article 2 of the Statute ought to be assessed on a case-by-case basis by reference to the *objective* particulars of a given social or historical context, and by the *subjective* perceptions of the perpetrators.[58]

Adopting a similar view, Trial Chamber I of the ICTY found that the qualification of the group could be achieved 'by using as a criterion the stigmatisation of the group, notably by the perpetrators of the crime, on the basis of its perceived national, ethnical, racial or religious characteristics'[59] and further held that 'the correct determination of the relevant protected group has to be made on a case-by-case basis, consulting both objective and subjective criteria'.[60] This 'correct determination' constitutes a means of guaranteeing the effectiveness of the group protection as envisaged in the Genocide Convention. Short of this semi-subjective approach it is conceivable that the concept of groups would have remained too rigid to be effectively used in court.

The teleological approach was admittedly further used – albeit implicitly – to solve interpretational discrepancies, such as the one that arose at the ICTY with respect to the determination of genocidal intent in an instance where only military-aged men had been targeted. Turning to the judicially created concept of the group 'as a distinct entity',[61] Trial Chamber I in the *Krstić* case qualified the crimes as genocide and found that:

> The Bosnian Serb forces could not have failed to know, by the time they decided to kill all the men, that this selective destruction of the group would have a lasting impact upon the

---

[54] William A Schabas, *Genocide in International Law – The Crimes of Crimes* (Cambridge, Cambridge University Press, 2000) 109.

[55] *Bagilishema* (n 9) para 65.

[56] *Rutaganda* (n 9) para 57. See also *Musema* (n 9) para 162.

[57] *Rutaganda* (n 9) para 56. See also *Musema* (n 9) para 161; *Kajelijeli* (n 10) para 811; *Gacumbitsi* (n 27) para 254.

[58] *Semanza* (n 10) para 317. Emphasis in original. See also *Musema* (n 9) para 163; *Kajelijeli* (n 10) para 811; *Seromba* (n 11) para 318.

[59] *Krstić* (n 14) para 557.

[60] *Prosecutor v Blagojević and Jokić*, IT-02-60-T, Judgment, Trial Chamber I, 17 January 2005, para 667.

[61] ibid para 590. Emphasis added.

entire group. … By killing all the military aged men, the Bosnian Serb forces effectively destroyed the community of the Bosnian Muslims in Srebrenica as such and eliminated all likelihood that it could ever re-establish itself on that territory.[62]

Yet, only one month after the *Krstić* judgment, Trial Chamber III of the ICTY reached an opposite conclusion in the *Sikirica* case,[63] and, while this divergence was ultimately settled by the Appeals Chamber when it concurred with the *Krstić* Trial Chamber,[64] it still remains that the judicial uncertainty caused by the conventional vagueness could seriously endanger the applicability of the law of genocide.

The dynamic interpretation of the international criminal tribunals, which do point to a certain degree of flexibility,[65] did not, however, dilute or trivialise the concept of genocide. Nor did it contravene the initial understanding of the drafters of the Convention. For instance, when the *Jelisić* Trial Chamber added a 'negative approach' to the subjective understanding of the victim group,[66] it was rapidly contradicted by the *Stakić* Trial Chamber which argued that in 'cases where more than one group is targeted, it is not appropriate to define the group in general terms, as, for example, "non-Serbs"'.[67] The Appeals Chamber subsequently concurred with the *Stakić* Trial Chamber,[68] recalling that 'genocide was *originally conceived* of as the destruction of a race, tribe, nation, or other group with a particular positive identity – not as the destruction of various people lacking a distinct identity'.[69] Thus, 'a group, for the purpose of the law of genocide, can only be defined *positively*, ie, as encompassing individuals who share certain characteristic features relevant to the law of genocide'.[70] Ultimately, '[u]nder the law of genocide, subjective considerations can have evidential relevance, but a protected group must have an *objective* existence'[71] – an interpretation that is both dynamic and respectful of the object and purpose of the original definition of the crime.

Where this 'flexibility' could be seen as more problematic is in the fact that the lack of detailed definitions in the conventional provisions left states parties with significant discretion as to the groups which are to be protected. As 'defining the groups more precisely was presumably left to the implementing legislation which parties to the Convention are to adopt in accordance with Article V', 'different states have varying definitions of protected groups and problems could arise in interpreting and applying the Convention'.[72] It is, for instance, striking that, while the Convention famously excludes political and social groups from its protective ambit,

---

[62] ibid paras 595–97.

[63] See *Prosecutor v Sikirica*, IT-95-8-T, Judgment on Defence Motions to Acquit, Trial Chamber III, 3 September 2001, paras 55–97.

[64] *Prosecutor v Krstić*, IT-98-33-A, Judgment, Appeals Chamber, 19 April 2004, para 23.

[65] The term is borrowed from Schabas who wrote: 'the label "group" is flexible'. William A Schabas, *Genocide in International Law: The Crimes of Crimes*, 2nd edn (Cambridge, Cambridge University Press, 2009) 123.

[66] *Prosecutor v Jelisić*, IT-95-10-T, Judgment, Trial Chamber I, 14 December 1999, para 71.

[67] *Stakić* (n 12) para 512.

[68] *Prosecutor v Stakić*, IT-97-24-A, Appeals Chamber, Judgment, 22 March 2006, para 28.

[69] ibid para 21. Emphasis added.

[70] Guénaël Mettraux, *International Crimes: Law and Practice*, vol II: *Crimes Against Humanity* (Oxford, Oxford University Press, 2020) 580. Footnote omitted.

[71] ibid.

[72] LeBlanc (n 42) 271–72.

some domestic provisions chose to depart from the conventional sphere, thereby raising questions as to possible interpretations of the Convention in the future.[73]

4. THE JUDICIAL UNDERSTANDING OF THE GENOCIDAL *MENS REA*: AN OVERLY CONSERVATIVE APPROACH?

The definition of the crime of genocide requires an extremely high standard of proof regarding the mental element in the sense that a very specific 'intent to destroy in whole or in part, a national, ethnical, racial, or religious groups, as such'[74] must exist in order to qualify the act as genocide. While this requirement of a specific intent, construed as the distinctive element of the crime,[75] is a key safeguard against any abuse and trivialisation of the crime of genocide, it nonetheless remains that this extremely strict understanding of the *mens rea* requirement holds the risk of turning genocide into an unprovable crime and of thus resulting in acquittals for the charge of genocide in cases of actual genocide.[76] Far from being purely theoretical, this is argu-ably the scenario that unfolded at the ICTY as the Tribunal has limited its finding of genocide to Srebrenica and has consistently refuted the qualification of genocide for crimes perpetrated in other municipalities, even if it recognised that the perpetrators had genocidal intent.

Elaborating on the conventionally undefined notion of genocide 'in part', the ICTY read in a new requirement: substantiality. In other words, the genociders needed to have the intent to destroy a group not 'in part' but in 'substantial part'. Relying on previous ICTY case law,[77] the *Mladić* Trial Chamber recalled

> that in determining the *substantiality* of the group, the numerical size of the targeted part of the protected group in absolute terms is one factor among many. Other factors

---

[73] See notably Art 281 of the Ethiopian Penal Code (1957); Art 373 of the Costa Rican Penal Code and Art 127 of the Costa Rican Penal Code Project (1998), which offer an extremely wide protection as the definition of genocide covers gender, age, political, sexual, social, economic and civil groups; Art 319 of the Peruvian Penal Code (1998); Art 211-1 of the French New Penal Code; Art 356 of the Romanian Socialist Republic Penal Code (1976). It may be recalled here that, in its Resolution 96 (I) on the crime of genocide, the UN General Assembly expressly included political groups within the definitional scope of the crime of genocide. See GA Resolution 96 (I), UN Doc A/231 (11 December 1946). It is also noteworthy that, in his Report, Special Rapporteur Whitaker proposed to include genocide against social and political groups in an additional optional protocol to the Genocide Convention. See *Review of Further Developments in Fields with which the Sub-Commission Has Been Concerned, Revised and Updated Report on the Question of the Prevention and Punishment of the Crime of Genocide Prepared by Mr B Whitaker, United Nations Economic and Social Council, Commission on Human Rights, Sub-Commission on Prevention of Discrimination and Protection of Minorities*, Thirty-eighth session, E/CN.4/Sub.2/1985/6, 2 July 1985 (herein after referred to as the Whitaker Report) 19, para 37.

[74] Art II of the Genocide Convention. Emphasis added.

[75] 3 UN GAOR, Sixth Committee, 89–97 (1948). Cited in Bryant (n 29) 692.

[76] In this respect, see the concerns raised by the French and Soviet delegates during the drafting of the conventional text. UN Doc A/C.6/SR.73 (Chaumont, France; Morozov, Soviet Union).

[77] See *Jelisić* (n 66) para 82. Emphasis added. A 'targeted part of a group would be classed as *substantial* either because the intent sought to harm a large majority of the group in question or the most representa-tive members of the targeted community'. See also *Sikirica* (n 63) paras 76–77: the 'important element here is the targeting of a selective number of persons who, by reason of their special qualities of leadership within the group as a whole, are of such importance that their victimisation within the terms of Article 4(2) (a), (b) and (c) would impact upon the survival of the group, as such.' See *Krstić* (Appeal) (n 64) para 8.

include: numerical size of the part in relation to the overall size of the group; the prominence of the part of the group within the larger whole and whether it is emblematic of the overall group or essential to its survival; the area of the perpetrators' activity and control; and the perpetrators' potential reach.[78]

This added requirement of substantiality is not new. In his early commentary of the Genocide Convention, Robinson explained that the characterisation of genocide requires a substantial number of victims, even if it is left to the courts to decide in each case whether 'the number was *sufficiently large*'.[79] Likewise, in his report on the Genocide Convention, Whitaker had pointed out that the term 'in part' implied 'a reasonably significant number, relative to the total of the group as a whole, or else a significant section of a group such as its leadership'.[80] On the judicial front, the ICTR had found that there must be a '*considerable number*' of victims for the crime to qualify as genocide,[81] while the ICTY referred to a '*substantial*' part, although not necessarily a '*very important part*'.[82] By contrast, the 'Elements of Crimes' adopted by the Preparatory Commission for the ICC specify that '*one or more* persons' may be the victim of the crime of genocide,[83] a specification that finds some support in academic writings. As Drost had explained,

> both as a question of theory and as a matter of principle nothing in the present [Genocide] Convention prohibits its provisions to be interpreted and applied to *individual cases* of murder by reason of the national, racial, ethnical or religious qualities of the *single victim* if the murderous attack was done with the intent to commit similar acts in the future and in connection with the first crime.[84]

If the above citations seem to refer to the actual result of the crime of genocide, that is, the number of victims, it is arguable that substantiality has in fact been envisaged as directly linked to genocidal intent as an intent to destroy a protected group not 'in part' but in *substantial* part.[85] This is exactly what the *Mladić* Trial Chamber found when it concluded – Judge Orie dissenting – that 'the physical perpetrators of the prohibited acts in Sanski Most, Vlasenica, and Foča Municipalities, and certain named perpetrators in Kotor Varoš and Prijedor Municipalities, *intended to destroy the Bosnian Muslims in those Count 1 Municipalities* as a part of the protected group',[86] but that, in these municipalities, the perpetrators had not perpetrated their

---

[78] *Prosecutor v Mladić*, IT-09-92-T, Judgment, Trial Chamber I, 22 November 2017, para 3528. Emphasis added. See also ibid para 3437.

[79] Robinson (n 30) 58. Emphasis added.

[80] Whitaker Report (n 73) 16, para 29.

[81] *Kayishema and Ruzindana* (n 9) para 97. Emphasis added.

[82] *Jelisić* (n 66) para 82. Emphasis added.

[83] See Art 6(a)(1), Elements of Crimes (n 5). Emphasis added.

[84] Drost (n 44) 85.

[85] This is in line with most academic opinions and case law. See eg Robinson (n 30) 58; Whitaker Report (n 73) 16, para 29. Contra, Drost (n 44) 85. For case law, see eg *Kayishema and Ruzindana* (n 9) para 97; *Bagilishema* (n 9) para 64; *Jelisić* (n 66) paras 81–82. At the domestic level, it seems only the US legislation requires that the acts be committed 'with the specific intent to destroy, in whole or in *substantial* part' a protected group. See T Hoffmann, 'The Crime of Genocide in Its (Nearly) Infinite Domestic Variety' in M Odello and P Łubiński (eds), *The Concept of Genocide in International Criminal Law: Developments after Lemkin* (Abingdon, Routledge, 2020) 67–97, 74. Emphasis added.

[86] *Prosecutor v Mladić* (n 78) para 3526. Emphasis added.

acts with the intent to destroy the Bosnian Muslims and Bosnian Croats as a '*substantial* part' of the protected groups in Bosnia-Herzegovina.[87] The crimes were thus not qualified as genocide but as crimes against humanity. Following the *Mladić* appeals judgment,[88] which confirmed the trial judgment, this reading of genocidal intent is admittedly one of the – regrettable – legacies of the ICTY.[89] It impedes the qualification of genocide to cases of genocide.

5. CONCLUDING REMARKS

The definition of the crime of genocide, as encapsulated in the Genocide Convention, that is, in a text adopted in 1948, has remained untouched in spite of the fact that it admittedly lacks precision. As the first international criminal tribunal to apply it fifty years later in the *Akayesu* case, the ICTR thus had no other choice than to embark on an interpretation exercise to specify the contours of this definition and the scope of the crime. The ICTY quickly followed suit and, as has been discussed, the international tribunals took their definitional role seriously and conscientiously, but not without a pinch of creativity and activism. In doing so, they seem to have borrowed certain methods of interpretation elaborated by the ECtHR, resorting to the 'living instrument' doctrine to elucidate the genocidal *actus reus* and to a teleological construction to specify the groups protected. If these dynamic approaches have at times gone beyond the notion of genocide as originally conceived by the drafters of the Genocide Convention, they have undoubtedly allowed the definition of the crime to conform to contemporary international criminal law and to be practical and effective. Departing from the text of the law can, however, be a two-way street and, at other times, the interpretation of the tribunals – notably with respect to the concept of destruction 'in part' – has questionably shown more conservatism, reading in requirements and arguably misreading the text of the law.[90] This mixed legacy notwithstanding, one thing seems certain: in applying the Genocide Convention, the ad hoc international criminal tribunals have enabled the 1948 definition of the crime to stand the test of time.

---

[87] ibid para 3536. Emphasis added.

[88] See *Prosecutor v Mladić*, MICT-13-56-A, Judgment, Appeals Chamber, 8 June 2021.

[89] See Caroline Fournet, 'The (Expected) Guilty Verdict against Ratko Mladić', *International Law Under Construction, Blog of the Groningen Journal of International Law* (2017) https://grojil.org/2017/12/27/the-expected-guilty-verdict-against-ratko-mladic/, accessed 31 July 2021. See also Caroline Fournet, '"Face to Face with Horror": The Tomašica Mass Grave and the Trial of Ratko Mladić' (2020) 6(2) *Human Remains and Violence* 23–41, www.manchesteropenhive.com/view/journals/hrv/6/2/article-p23.xml, accessed 31 July 2021.

[90] Fournet (ibid, 2017) and Fournet (ibid, 2020).

14

'A Matter of Utmost Gravity': Approaching the Magnitude of Genocide

PAUL BEHRENS

1. GENOCIDE AND THE PROBLEM OF MAGNITUDE: AN OVERVIEW

W HEN, IN DECEMBER 2019, counsels of The Gambia and Myanmar were heard before the International Court of Justice (ICJ) in its most recent case concerning the application of the Genocide Convention,[1] the magnitude of the crimes committed against the Rohingya – the Muslim group in Myanmar whose protection The Gambia sought[2] – formed an important aspect for both sides.

As counsel for Myanmar, Schabas observed that '10,000 deaths out of a population of well over one million might suggest something other than an intent to physically destroy the group'.[3] Counsel for The Gambia (Sands), on the other hand, noted that genocide was 'not just a numbers game', and that intention to destroy a group 'in part' was sufficient.[4] It is a controversy which goes to the very core of the contemporary understanding of the crime.

The interpretation of genocide takes place in a context determined by two objectives which tend to generate polarising effects. They are aims identifiable in the Genocide Convention itself:[5] on the one hand, the protective purpose which obliges Contracting Parties 'to prevent and punish' genocide (Article II);[6] on the other hand,

---

[1] International Court of Justice, *Application of the Convention on the Prevention and Punishment of the Crime of Genocide (The Gambia v Myanmar)*, *Application Instituting Proceedings and Request for Provisional Measures*, 11 November 2019 ('Gambia Application').

[2] Gambia Application, para 2.

[3] International Court of Justice, *Application of the Convention on the Prevention and Punishment of the Crime of Genocide (The Gambia v Myanmar)*, Public Sitting, 11 December 2019, Verbatim Record, Schabas, para 48 ('Myanmar Hearing 11 December 2019'). The 'killing of up to 10,000 Rohingya' had been mentioned by the Prosecutor of the International Criminal Court (ICC), Office of the Prosecutor, *Request for Authorisation of an Investigation Pursuant to Article 15* (ICC-01/19), 4 July 2019, para 68; referred to in Myanmar Hearing 11 December 2019, para 68.

[4] *The Gambia v Myanmar*, Public Sitting, 12 December 2019, Verbatim Record, Sands, para 17 ('Myanmar Hearing 12 December 2019').

[5] Convention on the Prevention and Punishment of the Crime of Genocide, 9 December 1948, 78 UNTS 277 ('Genocide Convention').

[6] Art II Genocide Convention. See also ibid Art VIII.

the need to assess the crime as bearing a particular stigma that sets it apart from other offences and possibly even other international crimes.[7]

At the time of the conclusion of the Genocide Convention, these two aspects may well have been considered as complementary parts, even as conducive to one another. Today, interpretive efforts move more uneasily between them, and often enough, the tension exercised by the different directions they indicate in the application of the Convention and the subsequent instruments[8] is all too clear.

The stigmatic principle appears to support an interpretation that considers genocide a crime of a certain magnitude: where genocidal intent is concerned, it would thus lend support to a restrictive reading, to enable a distinction between genocide and other crimes involving the loss of human life. Yet taken to its extremes, a reading along these lines would result in a limitation of the scope of the Convention to such a degree that it could only ever apply to a few scenarios.

The protective principle, on the other hand, appears to favour a broader interpretation: one in which the intended destruction even of a comparably small part of a group would be sufficient. That, however, risks depriving the concept of its characteristics: if 'genocide' applies to a wide range of situations, there is no need for the negotiation of a particular threshold, and at that stage, its specific stigma disappears.

The element of magnitude is certainly seen as an important feature in the understanding of genocide that underlies general usage,[9] but also in that adopted by several social scientists.[10] There, it retains its place on the objective side: from that perspective, its heinousness is at least in part to be seen in the large actual victim numbers it generates.[11]

---

[7] The preamble thus refers to genocide as an 'odious scourge' from which mankind must be 'liberate[d]', and as a crime 'condemned by the civilized world', ibid, Preamble, operative paras 1 and 2. See also below at n 14. On the need to preserve the stigma of the crime, see also Paul Behrens, 'The Need for a Genocide Law' in Paul Behrens and Ralph Henham (eds), *Elements of Genocide* (Abingdon, Routledge 2012) 237–53.

[8] The definition of genocide in Art 4 Statute of the International Criminal Tribunal for the Former Yugoslavia (25 May 1993, SC Res 827); Art 2 Statute of the International Criminal Tribunal for Rwanda (8 November 1994, SC Res 955); Art 6 Rome Statute of the International Criminal Court, 17 July 1998, 2187 UNTS 90 is based on that of Art II Genocide Convention.

[9] The definition for genocide provided by the *Oxford English Dictionary*, for instance, includes an element of objective magnitude ('[t]he deliberate and systematic extermination of an ethnic or national group', *Oxford English Dictionary*, 'genocide, n.' 2nd edn 1989). Several media have adopted a similar definition, including the BBC: 'the mass extermination of a whole group of people, an attempt to wipe them out of existence', 'How Do You Define Genocide?', *BBC Online*, 17 March 2016, https://www.bbc.co.uk/news/world-11108059. The Truth and Reconciliation Commission of Canada defined 'physical genocide' as the 'mass killing of the members of a targeted group', and 'biological genocide' as the 'destruction of the group's reproductive capacity', Truth and Reconciliation Commission of Canada, *Honouring the Truth, Reconciling for the Future. Summary of the Final Report of the Truth and Reconciliation Commission of Canada* (2015) Introduction.

[10] See Frank Chalk and Kurt Jonassohn, *The History and Sociology of Genocide: Analyses and Case Studies* (New Haven, CT, Yale University Press, 1990) 23 ('one-sided mass killing'); Israel Charny, 'Toward a Generic Definition of Genocide' in George Andreopoulos (ed), *Genocide: Conceptual and Historical Dimensions* (Pittsburgh, PA, University of Pennsylvania Press 1994) 75 ('mass killing of substantive numbers of human beings'); Irving Horowitz, *Taking Lives: Genocide and State Power* (New Brunswick, NJ, Transaction Books, 1980) 85 ('physical dismemberment and liquidation of people on a large scale').

[11] See, for instance, the numerical distinction made by Kuper and Charney between 'genocide' and 'genocidal massacres', Charny (n 10) 64.

If a similar approach were adopted in international law, there would be reason to consider it a crime capable of overcoming the apparent disassociation of international criminal justice from popular understanding to which Cotterrell refers in Chapter 2.[12] The word 'genocide' certainly has wide currency even outside international law;[13] it seems to be the archetypal *malum prohibitum in se* and a phenomenon whose destructive character is commonly recognised. The General Assembly, too, referred to it in 1946 as conduct which 'shocks the conscience of mankind';[14] the drafters of the Genocide Convention thus appeared to respond to a need which could claim, as its basis, a foundation in cultural authority around the world.[15]

And yet, there is reason to believe that the legal concept of the crime differs in crucial aspects from its common understanding; and it is the question of substantiality that highlights the divide more than any other of its features (with the possible exception of its restrictive group element).[16]

Under the law, substantiality is not expressly mentioned as part of the objective elements – indeed, the Elements of Crimes make clear that it is sufficient that one member of a protected group had been a victim.[17] It is tempting to consider the introduction of a contextual element in the same instrument as an attempt to introduce objective substantiality: the perpetrator's conduct must have taken place 'in the context of a manifest pattern of similar conduct directed against that group' or must have been conduct 'that could itself effect such destruction'.[18] However, quite apart from the debate about the validity of this element,[19] the Elements make clear that the phrase 'in the context of' includes 'initial acts in an emerging pattern'[20] – at the very stage, therefore, when objective substantiality cannot be expected.

In the framework of the legal concept of genocide, therefore, any notion of magnitude must be seen on the subjective side: in particular, in the destructive intent. The identification of substantiality there constitutes an area of controversy, and

---

[12] Roger Cotterrell, 'The Concept of Crime in Transnational Perspective' (ch 2 in this volume) after n 7.

[13] Stefan Kirsch, 'The Two Notions of Genocide: Distinguishing Macro Phenomena and Individual Misconduct' (2009) 42 *Creighton Law Review* 347.

[14] General Assembly Resolution 96(I), The Crime of Genocide, 11 December 1946, para 1 ('GA Res 96/I').

[15] The fact that the crime is still committed, does not militate against the existence of 'cultural authority' supporting the criminalisation of the relevant conduct (but see Cotterrell's reference to justification attempts by 'Nazi networks of community': Cotterrell (n 12) after n 48). It might, in fact, be difficult to find a community of substance which does not recognise genocide as conduct worthy of criminalisation – including perpetrator communities which would rather claim that their acts did not qualify as 'genocide'.

[16] On that element, see David L Nersessian, 'The Razor's Edge: Defining and Protecting Human Groups under the Genocide Convention' (2003) 36(2) *Cornell International Law Journal* 293.

[17] Elements of Crimes of the International Criminal Court, PCNICC/2000/1/Add.2 (2000) ('Elements of Crimes') Art 6, the first two elements to each alternative. But see Kai Ambos, *Internationales Strafrecht* (Munich, CH Beck, 2008) 205 for a critical view.

[18] Elements of Crimes, Art 6(a)–(e), the last element of each alternative.

[19] See Otto Triffterer, 'Genocide, Its Particular Intent to Destroy in Whole or in Part the Group as Such' (2001) 14 *Leiden Journal of International Law* 399, 407; but also International Criminal Court (ICC), Pre-Trial Chamber, *The Prosecutor v Omar Hassan Ahmad Al Bashir*, ICC-02/05-01/09, Decision on the Prosecution's Application for a Warrant of Arrest of 4 March 2009, paras 128 and 132.

[20] Elements of Crimes, Art 6, Introduction.

the methods of establishing it have caused consternation even among international judges. Bhandari, in a Separate Opinion in the 2015 ICJ case of *Croatia v Serbia*, expressed surprise about the method of finding substantiality which the International Criminal Tribunal for the Former Yugoslavia (ICTY) had employed in a case where 'only three killings [had been] proven'.[21]

Yet if ICJ judges are taken aback by that, it is a fair assumption that the average user of the term 'genocide' would be astonished to learn that, legally, genocide is not a concept requiring the existence of objective magnitude. And if that is the case, the claim that the crime finds a strong base in cultural authority is weakened. The link between the act as it is commonly understood and the crime 'as it is' would then seem tenuous: it would consist in little more than the fact that the same term is employed by general users of language and international lawyers alike, while both communities attach entirely different meanings to it.

The critique which Cotterrell applied to international criminal law in general applies with equal force here: the regulation of genocide may appear to be divorced from a concept that could claim ground in a population that can 'culturally "own" this law';[22] genocide, rather, would emerge as an example for crimes which are quite removed from 'everyday popular conceptions of crime'.[23]

The following sections analyse the concept of subjective substantiality as a crucial point at which different understandings of the crime of genocide emerge. In so doing, they explore the genesis of the substantiality requirement and the particular approaches which have been advanced to establish its existence. They reflect on the criticism which these methods have faced, in particular in view of the subjectivity inherent to their application in practice and in view of the difficulty of aligning the relevant approaches with fundamental principles of international criminal law. A particular approach, the 'individualised approach', will be discussed as a potential way to address the relevant criticism. The conclusion returns to the question raised at the outset and discusses whether a divergence between the legal concept of genocide and its cultural understanding exists, but also whether it is desirable to overcome the potential divide, since societal 'ownership' may not be the only aspect that has to play a role in its interpretation.

The title is taken from an observation made by Aung San Suu Kyi, Agent for Myanmar, referring to the invocation of the Genocide Convention as 'a matter of utmost gravity'[24] – an understanding on which counsel for The Gambia found himself in agreement.[25] It is, in fact, not uncommon to find broad agreement on the need to preserve the stigma of the crime. The difficulty lies in establishing an interpretation that protects the particular threshold that a finding of genocide has to negotiate.

---

[21] ICJ, *Application of the Convention on the Prevention and Punishment of the Crime of Genocide* (*Croatia v Serbia*), Judgment of 3 February 2015, Separate Opinion of Judge Bhandari, para 20 ('*Bhandari Opinion*'). On the relevant ICTY case, see below at n 72.

[22] Cotterrell (n 12) section 5.

[23] ibid after n 13.

[24] Myanmar Hearing 11 December 2019, Aung San Suu Kyi, para 2.

[25] Myanmar Hearing 12 December 2019, Sands, para 10.

2. DIFFICULTIES INHERENT IN THE TRIAL CHAMBER'S APPROACHES TO DESTRUCTION 'IN PART'

Under the legal concept of genocide, the importance of its subjective part, and in particular of 'specific intent', is well recognised. It is this element which, in the words of the international criminal tribunals, 'characterises' and 'distinguishes' the crime.[26]

Yet genocidal intent in its codified form – that is, 'intent to destroy, in whole or in part, a national, ethnical, racial or religious group, as such'[27] – does not expressly carry a substantiality requirement: mathematically, even the intended destruction of one group member would qualify as intent to destroy the group 'in part'.

If that were the appropriate reading, the particular stigma of genocide[28] would disappear from the objective and the subjective side alike. It is in that context interesting that the problem of lowering the threshold had been appreciated even at codification stage. The Ad Hoc Committee, which the UN Economic and Social Council (ECOSOC) had convened to debate the draft of the future convention, decided not to include a reference to the possibility of partial destruction, after concerns had been voiced that the resulting threshold for genocide might be too low.[29] It was only when the text was debated in the (General Assembly's) Sixth Committee that the phrase 'in whole or in part' was included.[30] But it was not to be the end of the debate: in 1996, the International Law Commission (ILC) noted that the crime, 'by its very nature' required an intention to destroy 'at least a substantial part of a particular group';[31] a point supported by the international criminal tribunals.[32] However, the determination of the parameters of substantiality continues to cause interpretive problems for tribunals and commentators alike.

An early method for the evaluation of substantiality was provided in the 1985 Whitaker report whose author referred to a 'reasonably significant number, relative to the total of the group as a whole, or else a significant section of a group such as

---

[26] See ICTR, Trial Chamber, *The Prosecutor v Jean-Paul Akayesu*, ICTR-96-4-T, Judgment, 2 September 1998 ('*Akayesu* (Trial Chamber)'), para 517; ICTY, Trial Chamber, *The Prosecutor v Radoslav Brđanin*, IT-99-36-T, Judgment, 1 September 2004 ('*Brđanin* (Trial Chamber)'), para 695; ICTY, Trial Chamber, *The Prosecutor v Milomir Stakić*, IT-97-24-T, Judgment, 31 July 2003 ('*Stakić* (Trial Chamber)'), para 520; ICTR, Trial Chamber, *The Prosecutor v Clément Kayishema and Obed Ruzindana*, ICTR-95-1-T, Judgment, 21 May 1999 ('*Kayishema* (Trial Chamber)'), para 91.

[27] Art II Genocide Convention; Art 4 ICTY Statute; Art 2 ICTR Statute; Art 6 ICC Statute.

[28] See above at n 7.

[29] See on this William Schabas, *Genocide in International Law* (Cambridge, Cambridge University Press 2009) 274.

[30] The Sixth Committee followed a suggestion by Norway in this regard. UN GAOR, 3rd session, 6th Committee, 73rd meeting, 92, 97.

[31] International Law Commission, Report on the Work of its 48th Session, *Yearbook of the International Law Commission* 1996, Vol II, Part 2 ('(1996) II/2 YILC') 45, para 8.

[32] ICTY, Appeals Chamber, *Prosecutor v Radislav Krstić*, IT-98-33-A, Judgment, 19 April 2004 ('*Krstić* (Appeals Chamber)'), para 12; ICTY, Trial Chamber, *Prosecutor v Radislav Krstić*, IT-98-33-T, Judgment, 2 August 2001 ('*Krstić* (Trial Chamber)'), para 586; ICTY, Trial Chamber, *The Prosecutor v Vujadin Popović, Ljubisa Beara, Drago Nikolić, Ljubomir Borovčanin, Radivoje Miletić, Milan Gvero, Vinko Pandurević*, IT-05-88-T, Judgment, 10 June 2010 ('*Popović et al* (Trial Chamber)'), para 831; *Brđanin* (Trial Chamber), para 701; see also ICJ, *Case Concerning the Application of the Convention on the Prevention and Punishment of the Crime of Genocide (Bosnia and Herzegovina v Serbia and Montenegro)* ('*Bosnia v Serbia*'), ICJ Reports 2007, 126, para 198.

its leadership'.[33] These considerations form the basis for two principal methods which will be discussed below: the numerical and the functional approaches to substantiality. In the deliberations of the tribunals, they are joined by a third – the geographical approach – which overlaps the other two.

2.1. A Matter of Quantity? The Problem of the 'Numbers Game'

The numerical (or quantitative) approach has at times received strong support in the Trial Chambers: the International Criminal Tribunal for Rwanda (ICTR) in *Kayishema* thus noted that 'in part' required 'intention to destroy a considerable number of individuals who are part of the group'.[34]

Later case law of the international criminal tribunals was more cautious – in *Jelisić*, for instance, the judges saw the numerical approach as only one possible method;[35] and the *Krstić* Appeals Chamber spoke of it as a 'necessary' starting point, but 'not in all cases the ending point of the inquiry'.[36] In any event, the assessment of numerical significance is not exhausted by an examination of actual numbers, but needs to involve an assessment of the part in relation to the group itself.[37]

The numerical approach is not free from controversy. In the 1980s, LeBlanc noted the difficulty of establishing substantiality on the basis of this method: 'Is a part or a substantial part of a group 1 out of 5, ... 1,001 out of 2,000, 100,001 out of 200,000, etc?' and expressed the view that the discussion had 'often degenerated into a numbers game'[38] – the very phrase used by Counsel for The Gambia in 2019.[39] Yet the method has traditionally played an important role: the ICTY thus went to some extent to compare the number of Bosnian Muslims in Srebrenica[40] and in municipalities of the Autonomous Region of Krajina, respectively,[41] to the overall group size. In *Sikirica*, the Chamber noted that the victims in the Keraterm camp amounted to approximately 1,000–1,400 persons, stating that this 'would represent between 2% and 2.8% of the Muslims in the Prijedor municipality and would hardly qualify as a "reasonably substantial" part of the Bosnian Muslim group in Prijedor'.[42] In *Bosnia v Serbia*, it was the ICJ which, having discussed

---

[33] UN Economic and Social Council (ECOSOC), Whitaker Report, UN Doc. E/CN.4/Sub.2/1985/6 (1985), para 29 ('Whitaker Report').

[34] *Kayishema* (Trial Chamber), para 97.

[35] ICTY, Trial Chamber, *The Prosecutor v Goran Jelisić*, IT-95-10-T, Judgment of 14 December 1999 ('*Jelisić* (Trial Chamber)'), para 82.

[36] *Krstić* (Appeals Chamber), para 12. See also *Popović et al* (Trial Chamber), para 832.

[37] See *Brđanin* (Trial Chamber), para 702 and *Krstić* (Appeals Chamber), para 12.

[38] Lawrence J LeBlanc, 'The Intent to Destroy Groups in the Genocide Convention: The Proposed US Understanding' (1984) 78 *American Journal of International Law* 380, in the context of the discussion on substantiality then taking place in the United States.

[39] See above at n 4.

[40] *Krstić* (Appeals Chamber), paras 25–27.

[41] *Brđanin* (Trial Chamber), para 967.

[42] ICTY, Trial Chamber, *Prosecutor v Sikirica, Došen, Kolundžija*, IT-95-8-T, Judgment on Defence Motions to Acquit, 3 September 2001 ('*Sikirica* Defence Motions'), paras 69–72. It appears that the number of 1,000–1,400 persons would have included non-Muslim detainees at Keraterm.

methods of establishing subjective substantiality, gave clear preference to the 'quantitative' approach.[43]

Yet making the protection of the Genocide Convention dependent on arithmetic mechanisms is a questionable procedure. Its potential of depriving victims once more of their individuality is particularly apparent when a Chamber resorts to the term 'negligible' in its reference to the number of victims in a camp.[44]

There is a further consideration which attaches to the adoption of the numerical approach and casts doubt on its suitability for the evaluation of substantiality.

LeBlanc notes that the establishment of substantiality cannot be expected to proceed on the basis of 'some rigid mathematical formula', but that, 'in the final analysis, the matter calls for a judicial construction'.[45] It is a seductive approach; and yet, the very acceptance of a judicial decision in lieu of objective parameters causes difficulties.

The ICTY's observations in *Sikirica* is an illustration. If it dismissed the figure of 'between 2% and 2.8%' as sufficient for the requirements of a 'reasonably substantial' part of a protected group,[46] the question may be asked on what basis this finding had been reached. In this context, Alonzo-Maizlish refers to the example of the Muslim group in India, in whose case 2% would amount to three million people.[47] It is understandable that some observers would consider numbers in this region to fulfil substantiality requirements[48] and there is evidence that some Trial Chambers would agree.[49] The fact remains that the numerical approach provides courts with considerable discretion, and what may, at first, seem the application of a mathematical mechanism,[50] and therefore objective parameters, is in fact a method that invites significant arbitrariness into the establishment of substantiality.[51] It is, as will be seen, not the only approach which carries this difficulty.

2.2. More Equal than Others? The Problem of 'Functionality'

The second method which the Whitaker Report had outlined is most appropriately termed the 'functional approach'.[52] The perpetrator in that scenario does not

---

[43] *Bosnia v Serbia*, para 200. See also below n 95 and accompanying text.

[44] *Sikirica* Defence Motions, para 74.

[45] LeBlanc (n 38) 380.

[46] See above at n 42.

[47] David Alonzo-Maizlish, 'In Whole or in Part: Group Rights, the Intent Element of Genocide, and the "Quantitative Criterion"' (2002) 77 *New York University Law Review* 1386, 1398.

[48] cf eg Whitaker Report, para 29.

[49] In *Brđanin*, for instance, the Chamber considered the numerical approach to rely on two factors: 'absolute terms' and the relation of the part 'to the overall size of the entire group': *Brđanin* (Trial Chamber), para 702.

[50] Thus Angela Paul, *Kritische Analyse und Reformvorschlag zu Art II Genozidkonvention* (Berlin, Springer, 2008) 314.

[51] See also Alonzo-Maizlish (n 47) 1398.

[52] See above at n 33. On the phrase of the 'qualitative' criterion, which is not used here, see below (at n 88).

necessarily select a numerically significant part of the group, but targets a section which has significance for the group because of particular functions associated with it.[53]

This approach, too, has been embraced by the international criminal tribunals: in *Jelisić*, for example, the Trial Chamber referred to the 'desired destruction of a more limited number of persons selected for the impact that their disappearance would have upon the survival of the group as such'.[54] Academic literature has likewise voiced support for this approach,[55] sometimes based on the view that campaigns against a group have often begun by targeting specific members (its leadership, intellectuals, etc).[56]

Yet there is still a considerable amount of variation regarding the determination of the targeted part – so much so that the functional approach has to be seen as the most complex of the three 'traditional' methods of assessing substantiality. The *Brđanin* Trial Chamber referred to the 'prominence' of the part within the group; to the *Jelisić* judges, the selection 'of the most representative figures' mattered,[57] and the *Krstić* Appeals Chamber expressed the view that the targeted Bosnian Muslims of Srebrenica were 'emblematic of the Bosnian Muslims in general'.[58]

A section of the targeted victims which features with some regularity is the group leadership,[59] with some Chambers relying heavily on that factor.[60] Other sections which have received prominent consideration include men of military age,[61] but also law enforcement or security personnel.[62]

For the functional approach, too, the assessment of substantiality requires not only that a part of the group has been identified but also involves an evaluation of the effect that the targeting of this part has on the group as a whole.[63] In *Krstić*, the ICTY thus went to some length to elaborate on the impact which the disappearance of the military-aged men would have had on the community of the Bosnian Muslims in Srebrenica 'as such'.[64] But it was in the context of this particular case that difficulties in the application of the functional approach emerged which have not lost their significance. According to the Defence, the Trial Chamber had concluded that Krstić

---

[53] See Whitaker Report, para 29.

[54] *Jelisić* (Trial Chamber), para 82.

[55] cf Kriangsak Kittichaisaree, *International Criminal Law* (Oxford, Oxford University Press, 2001) 73.

[56] Paul (n 50) 314.

[57] The Trial Chamber found that it was not possible to conclude beyond reasonable doubt that the defendant had performed such a selection; *Jelisić* (Trial Chamber), para 93.

[58] *Krstić* (Appeals Chamber), para 37 and see ibid, para 16; *The Prosecutor v Radovan Karadžić*, IT-95-5/18-T, Judgment, 24 March 2016 ('*Karadžić* (Trial Chamber)'), para 5672; and cf *The Prosecutor v Ratko Mladić*, IT-09-92-T, Judgment, 22 November 2017 ('*Mladić* (Trial Chamber)'), para 3535, as opposed to ibid, paras 3553, 3554.

[59] Whitaker Report, para 29; UN Security Council, Final Report of the Commission of Experts Established Pursuant to Security Council Resolution 780 (1992), UN Doc S/1994/674 (1994) Annex ('Commission of Experts'), para 94. See also Florian Jessberger, 'The Definition and the Elements of the Crime of Genocide' in Paola Gaeta (ed), *The UN Genocide Convention: A Commentary* (Oxford, Oxford University Press, 2009) 109.

[60] cf *Sikirica* Defence Motions, paras 77 and 81.

[61] *Krstić* (Trial Chamber), para 579.

[62] Commission of Experts, para 94.

[63] See *Jelisić* (Trial Chamber), para 82.

[64] *Krstić* (Trial Chamber), para 597. See also *Krstić* (Appeals Chamber), para 28.

had targeted the Bosnian Muslim men of military age of Srebrenica. These formed part of the Bosnian Muslims of Srebrenica, which in turn were part of the actual protected group – the Bosnian Muslims.[65] Following that view, the Trial Chamber had therefore identified 'part of a part' of a group.[66] By comparison to the protected group as a whole (the Bosnian Muslims), it would not have been acceptable to see the Bosnian Muslim men of Srebrenica as fulfilling the requirements of a 'substantial' part.[67]

In this particular case, the Defence argument was rejected, with the Appeals Chamber finding that the military-aged men had been considered not as 'part of a part', but that their killing had been used as evidence for the fact that the perpetrator had intent to destroy a (substantial) part of the group (the Bosnian Muslims of Srebrenica).[68] But the case highlights difficulties inherent to the functional approach. It is its very purpose to allow consideration of a 'more limited number' for the assessment of the 'part of the group',[69] and there is a realistic concern that such considerations can considerably lower the threshold which substantiality was supposed to establish.

More recently, the *Tolimir* case underlined the problem. Zdravko Tolimir, a high-ranking Bosnian Serb military commander, stood accused of genocide committed in eastern Bosnia. The Prosecution supported its findings, inter alia, with a reference to the seizing and killing of three Bosnian Muslim leaders from the town of Žepa.[70]

It is this case which led Judge Bhandari in the ICJ case of *Croatia v Serbia* to comment that the Trial Chamber had entered a finding of genocide 'where only three killings [had been] proven',[71] and it is true that the majority of the judges in the Trial Chamber found that 'the acts of murder against these three men constitute[d] genocide'.[72] It cited with approval the *Jelisić* conclusions on the functional approach[73] – as did the Appeals Chamber when, in 2015, it reviewed the judgment.[74] And yet, it is questionable whether the functional approach had, in this case, been appropriately applied.

The protected group, as the Trial Chamber affirmed, consisted of the Bosnian Muslims.[75] If the 'substantial' part consisted of the three community leaders, the *Jelisić* formula would demand that they had been selected for the impact that their disappearance would have had on the Bosnian Muslims as a whole. Not even the Prosecution went as far as to claim that.

---

[65] *Krstić* (Appeals Chamber), para 18.
[66] *Krstić* (Appeals Chamber), Partial Dissenting Opinion of Judge Shahabuddeen, para 43.
[67] *Krstić* (Appeals Chamber), para 18.
[68] ibid.
[69] See *Jelisić* (Trial Chamber), para 82.
[70] ICTY, Prosecution, *The Prosecutor v Zdravko Tolimir*, IT-05-88/2-PT, Third Amended Indictment, 4 November 2009, para 23.1.
[71] *Bhandari* Opinion, para 20.
[72] ICTY, Trial Chamber, *Prosecutor v Zdravko Tolimir*, IT-05-88/2-T, Judgment, 12 December 2012 ('*Tolimir* (Trial Chamber)'), para 780.
[73] ibid, para 777, and see above at n 54.
[74] ICTY, Appeals Chamber, *Prosecutor v Zdravko Tolimir*, IT-05-88/2-A, Judgment, 8 April 2015 ('*Tolimir* (Appeals Chamber)'), para 261.
[75] *Tolimir* (Trial Chamber), para 750.

If, on the other hand, the substantial part of the group had been the Bosnian Muslims of eastern Bosnia (as the Trial Chamber at one point accepted),[76] the *Krstić* problem would manifest itself again: the community leaders would be 'part of a part' of the protected group,[77] and their substantiality would be subject to doubt. And the Appeals Chamber in *Tolimir* was less clear than in *Krstić* on the position which the killing of the military-aged men occupied in the judges' evaluation:[78] it stated, in fact, that there was no error in finding that the selective targeting of community leaders 'may amount to genocide and may be indicative of genocidal intent'.[79] It is a curious statement which leaves open the question whether the Chamber was referring to the selection of the leadership as evidence for intent or as a constitutive element of the crime.

What is clear is the fact that the Appeals Chamber gave its approval to the functional approach. In the actual case, it was not convinced that the disappearance of the community leaders had a destructive impact on the group as such[80] and therefore reversed Tolimir's conviction in that regard.[81] But it supported the underlying methodology and the possibility of finding that 'genocide may be committed through the killings of only certain prominent members of the group', provided always that they were selected with a view to the impact which their disappearance would have on the survival of the group.[82] On that basis, it would appear possible to establish substantiality when three members of a group had been selected – or indeed, even fewer members. If the fate of the group is closely tied up with the fate of its leaders, this might even be a consistent approach. But it also raises questions about the rationale for the stigma of the crime. If a perpetrator who killed one influential community leader may be guilty of the same crime as a perpetrator who killed thousands of group members, one may wonder whether the degree of the criminal energy which either perpetrator expends is truly on the same level.

The focus on the political leadership also causes problems with regard to the group element. Political groups had been mentioned among the victims of genocide in General Assembly Resolution 96/I,[83] but after considerable debate in the codification process, the decision was made not to include them in the Convention.[84] The reasons included the view that they did not constitute stable groups;[85] and the reference to 'stable and permanent' groups to which the Convention supposedly intended

---

[76] ibid, para 774.

[77] See above at n 66.

[78] See above at n 68.

[79] *Tolimir* (Appeals Chamber), para 263.

[80] ibid, para 267.

[81] ibid, para 272.

[82] ibid, para 263 and see also ibid, paras 261–62. This criterion has indeed been understood as applying to all approaches which the tribunals have supported, Jessberger (n 59 above); Lars Berster, 'Article II' in Christian Tams, Lars Berster and Björn Schiffbauer (eds), *Convention on the Prevention and Punishment of the Crime of Genocide: A Commentary* (Munich, CH Beck 2014) 149.

[83] GA Res 96/I, para 2.

[84] See, on the debate, Patrick Thornberry, *International Law and the Rights of Minorities* (Oxford, Oxford University Press, 1991) 68.

[85] ibid 69 and Sonali Shah, 'The Oversight of the Last Great International Institution of the Twentieth Century: The International Criminal Court's Definition of Genocide' (2002) 16 *Emory International Law Review* 351, 357.

to grant protection did survive into the age of the international criminal tribunals.[86] Yet if this opinion were followed, the emphasis placed on the political leadership as a substantial part appears strange. Political groups as such would then not be stable enough to warrant the Convention's protection, yet sufficiently stable to represent national, racial, ethnic and religious groups. The impression would be hard to dispel that certain political groups had thus been brought into the protective remit of the Convention through the back door.

The preference which this method allocates to certain group members at the expense of others also became apparent in *Sikirica*, when the Trial Chamber, in discussing persons interned at Keraterm camp, dismissed the suggestion that they were considered leaders of their communities and pointed to evidence that 'among those detained were taxi-drivers, schoolteachers, lawyers, pilots, butchers and café owners'.[87] Some voices in the literature, and indeed in international courts, go further and refer to a 'qualitative group' which the perpetrator targeted, or a 'qualitative criterion' that had been applied.[88] These are unfortunate phrases: they invite the interpretation that the commentators follow the thinking which the perpetrators had laid down and accept that a differentiation among group members according to their 'quality' is possible.

It is true that the *Tolimir* Appeals Chamber emphasised that the focus on the leadership of the group was justified by the fact that they had been selected for the impact that their disappearance would have on the group as a whole.[89] This, indeed, is a mechanism which imposes a cap on a judicial discretion which would otherwise know few bounds.

At the same time, it is questionable whether these parameters have always been appropriately applied. A categorical emphasis on group leadership[90] can yield fundamentally different results, depending on the status which this section enjoys within the group itself. Some groups may harbour a cynical attitude towards their political leaders and their disappearance may therefore have limited effect on the survival of the group. Some groups may find it impossible to survive in a hostile climate without the spiritual guidance offered by their teachers rather than their administrative elite; a categorical rejection of teachers in considerations of substantiality[91] may thus not always be an adequate reflection of the importance which that section carries.

Particular questions arise when the part of the group has been selected for the 'strategic importance' of the location it inhabits.[92] On its own, the position a territory plays in the military planning of the perpetrators does little to answer the question whether a 'substantial' part has been targeted. In theory, it is conceivable that the survival of the group can be guaranteed in spite of attempts to conquer the region in which it resides. Similar problems arise when the targeted part of the group is seen as

---

[86] *Akayesu* (Trial Chamber), para 516.
[87] *Sikirica* Defence Motions, para 80.
[88] Paul (n 50) 314; *Krstić* (Trial Chamber), para 634; *Bosnia v Serbia*, para 200.
[89] *Tolimir* (Appeals Chamber), para 263.
[90] See *Stakić* (Trial Chamber), para 525.
[91] See above at n 87.
[92] *Karadžić* (Trial Chamber), para 5672. *Mladić* (Trial Chamber), para 3554.

'emblematic' for the group as a whole:[93] the identification of the qualifying part of the group is not, after all, a quest for its most representative image, but for a part that carries substantiality.

At the same time, it is possible to discern a certain caution among the tribunals at least with regard to an autonomous application of this approach: the *Krstić* Appeals Chamber noted that it was 'only one of several' methods to assess substantiality,[94] while the numerical approach, on the other hand, had been considered the 'necessary and important starting point' of any such assessment.[95] *Tolimir*, however, may have heralded a change: in Judge Bhandari's words, the Trial Chamber's decision constituted 'a departure from the Bosnia formula's dogged insistence that the numerosity of the victims of predicate acts under Article II of the Genocide Convention be considered a pre-eminent factor in the substantiality equation'.[96]

2.3. A Matter of Regional Restrictions? The Weight of Geographical Considerations

When the ILC issued its 1996 Draft Code of Crimes against the Peace and Security of Mankind, it pointed out that the intended destruction of a protected group 'from every corner of the globe' was not a necessary requirement of the crime of genocide.[97] That opens the possibility of a third way of assessing substantiality: the 'geographical approach'. From that perspective, the destruction of the relevant part of the group would have to be assessed in the geographical context in which the crime had taken place. The Trial Chambers have indeed embraced the view that the relevant part of the group might be limited to a particular geographical zone,[98] a view which is also reflected in the case law of some domestic courts[99] and which finds support in the literature.[100]

In that regard, the view has been expressed that the relevant part might be limited to a single region or community.[101] In its Review of Indictment in the *Nikolić* case, the Trial Chamber focused only on the Vlasenica region when discussing the possibility that genocide might have been committed.[102] The *Krstić* Trial Chamber outlined the possibility that genocide might be committed even in a municipality.[103] Having

---

[93] *Popović et al* (Trial Chamber), para 832; *Krstić* (Appeals Chamber), para 37.

[94] *Krstić* (Appeals Chamber), para 12, fn 22.

[95] ibid, para 12. See also *Bosnia v Serbia*, para 200, 201. See also n 43 above and accompanying text.

[96] *Bhandari* Opinion, para 20.

[97] (1996) II/2 *YILC* (n 31) 45, Art 17, para 8.

[98] See *Brđanin* (Trial Chamber), para 703; *Krstić* (Trial Chamber), para 590.

[99] Federal Court of Justice (Bundesgerichtshof) (BGH), Judgment 30 April 1999, 3 StR 215/98, III.2; Federal Constitutional Court (Bundesverfassungsgericht), Decision of 12 December 2000 (2001) 28 *Europäische Grundrechte-Zeitschrift* 76, 79.

[100] Nehemia Robinson, *The Genocide Convention* (New York, World Jewish Congress, 1960) 63; *Jessberger* (n 59) 108.

[101] *Sikirica* Defence Motions, para 68; ICTY, Trial Chamber, *Prosecutor v Dragan Nikolić*, IT-94-2-R61, Review of Indictment Pursuant to Rule 61 of the Rules of Procedure and Evidence, 20 October 1995 ('*Nikolić* Review'), para 34.

[102] *Nikolić* Review, para 34.

[103] *Krstić* (Trial Chamber), para 589.

considered the *Nikolić* Review, the *Jelisić* Trial Chamber found that the 'object and goal' of the Convention as well as its subsequent interpretation militated in favour of including genocidal intent which was limited to a particular geographical zone.[104]

Opposition to the geographical approach tends not to concern the underlying principle, but to raise questions about the qualifying area. The *Sikirica* Trial Chamber would not have allowed a perspective that focused on Bosnian Muslims and Bosnian Croats who had been victims of acts of genocide 'while detained in the Keraterm camp'.[105] In the literature, Paul objects to the inclusion of single municipalities (*Ortschaften*) as delineating the extent of the part of a group.[106] Such concerns highlight a problem which the geographical approach shares with the functional approach: here too, the substantiality threshold might be lowered considerably. It is a difficulty which has been recognised by several Trial Chambers in the past.[107]

A further difficulty arises from the need to establish an intent which still targets the group 'as such'. The smaller the accepted geographical region, the more likely is it that intent encompasses factors which lie outside the objective to eliminate the group as such – especially if the perpetrator's control extended beyond a particular zone. In some cases, perpetrators may have deliberately limited their intent to a specific region and could therefore not necessarily be said to have targeted the group 'as such'. Situations of this kind arise when group members in a particular zone are selected as objects of a punitive expedition – acts which will usually be covered by crimes against humanity, but might, because of their limited nature, not be prompted by genocidal intent. This is more than a question of evidence: motives which diverge from genocidal intent may occupy such a dominant position in the mindset of a perpetrator that they induce relative incompatibility with the required *dolus specialis*.[108]

Most of all, however, the danger of arbitrary decisions forms as much part of the geographical as of the numerical approach.[109] For one, terms like 'municipality' are only on a superficial level objective: some municipalities have thousands of inhabitants, the population of others counts in double digits.[110] More fundamentally, the question might still be asked on what basis the employment of a geographical unit for the establishment of substantiality is performed. Why would it be acceptable to consider genocidal intent as limited to a region but not a municipality?[111] Why a municipality and not a detainment camp[112] (especially given the fact that the population of some camps exceeds that of some municipalities)? Would the population of individual houses be 'substantial'? The question is not entirely theoretical. In *Croatia v Serbia*, the applicant referred to an incident in which the Serbian paramilitary

---

[104] *Jelisić* (Trial Chamber), para 83.

[105] *Sikirica* Defence Motions, para 68.

[106] Paul (n 50) 317.

[107] See *Brđanin* (Trial Chamber), para 966 and *Stakić* (Trial Chamber), para 523.

[108] See on this Paul Behrens, 'Genocide and the Question of Motives' (2012) 10 *Journal of International Criminal Justice* 501, 519–22.

[109] See above at n 51.

[110] In 2016, it was reported that the Swiss municipality Corippo had thirteen inhabitants. Anon, 'Bewährungsprobe für Lega bei Tessiner Gemeindewahlen', *SDA Basisdienst Deutsch*, 31 March 2016.

[111] cf Sikirica Defence Motions, para 68 and Paul (n 50) 371.

[112] See above at n 105.

leader Željko Ražnatović ('Arkan') had reportedly told his troops to take care not to kill Serbs and that, 'since Serbs were in the basements of buildings and the Croats were upstairs, rocket launchers should be used to "neutralize the first floor"'.[113] The ICJ found that this constituted only 'one isolated phase in the very lengthy siege of Vukovar', and the judges noted that it was 'difficult to infer anything from one isolated instance'.[114] But if the geographical approach seeks to avoid an unrealistically restrictive concept of genocidal intent – one where the perpetrator would be required to pursue the elimination of the group in the entire world[115] – there is no reason why substantiality could not be established on the basis of a municipality, a detainment camp or indeed individual houses.

Yet what the divergent interpretations of the geographical approach show is that this method, too, is dependent on the decisions of individual chambers; and what may at first sight have appeared an application of objective parameters reveals itself ultimately as an arbitrary choice by the relevant judges.

For all its faults, the geographical approach must be credited with recognising one of the key characteristics of the concept. Genocide, even when carried out in the context of a larger campaign, is committed by individuals; and individuals are endowed with different degrees of authority. Each individual's range of action is limited by a variety of factors – of which geography is one – and the limitations of each individual need to be assessed when genocide has been charged.

This consideration leads to the formulation of yet another approach: one whose focal point is the personality of the perpetrator itself. It shall in the context of this chapter be termed the 'individualised approach', and it is suggested that it has a decisive role to play in any attempt to assess the substantiality of specific genocidal intent.

3. WAYS OUT OF THE QUAGMIRE? UNDERSTANDING THE ROLE OF THE INDIVIDUAL

Neither the Genocide Convention nor the subsequent instruments indicate that the perpetrators must hold positions of leadership. But if genocide can be committed by persons of any rank and none, then the assessment of subjective substantiality on the basis of parameters that are the same for everyone appears questionable. Considerations of this kind militate in favour of an approach that acknowledges that substantiality is inseparable from the perpetrators and the circumstances in which they find themselves.

This method – the 'individualised approach' – does feature in the consideration of the ad hoc tribunals. Yet where it is discussed, the close connection to the geographical approach from which the chambers derive it is typically still apparent. In *Krstić*, the Appeals Chamber noted that the perpetrators of genocide in Rwanda in 1994 'did not seriously contemplate the elimination of the Tutsi population beyond the

---

[113] ICJ, *Application of the Convention on the Prevention and Punishment of the Crime of Genocide (Croatia v Serbia)*, Judgment, 3 February 2015 ('*Croatia v Serbia*'), para 438.

[114] ibid.

[115] See above at n 97.

country's borders'[116] and argued on this basis that intent to destroy 'will always be limited by the opportunity' presented to the perpetrator; the area of his activity 'as well as the possible extent of [his] reach, should be considered'.[117] In subsequent cases, the *Krstić* finding, linking 'area of activity' and 'possible extent of their reach', was usually taken aboard with no or only minimal changes,[118] and the analysis of this 'extent of the reach' has, in the absence of geographical factors, not been given adequate weight. In *Croatia v Serbia*, the ICJ mentioned the geographical approach, the functional approach and the 'quantitative element', but did not refer to the perpetrator's personal reach as a separate factor.[119] In *Bosnia v Serbia*, the same court expressed a certain hesitancy towards the individualised method, but confused its approaches: it acknowledged that 'the opportunity available to the perpetrators [was] significant', but then found that the opportunity 'might be so limited that the substantiality criterion is not met' and claimed that the ICTY had underlined the need for caution, 'lest this approach might distort the definition of genocide'.[120] That, however, is a misinterpretation of the *Stakić* judgment on which the court sought to rely. There, the ICTY had expressly referred only to the difficulties which the establishment of substantiality through the identification of specific geographical units carried and had shown reluctance in following that approach.[121]

Ignoring the individualised approach is more than a missed opportunity. If specific intent is indeed the element which 'characterises' genocide,[122] then genocide is predicated on elements highly personal to the individual perpetrator. Intent varies from situation to situation and from perpetrator to perpetrator: it is thus not helpful to work with an immutable formula under which destructive intent exists whenever 'more than 3%' of a population are affected or 'more than a municipality' has been targeted. The perpetrator's reach and control is an inescapable consideration: the authority of a footsoldier is different from that of the commander of an army, and the relevant substantiality differs accordingly. A hundred victims may mean that a footsoldier has done all he could have done to achieve the destruction of the group within his reach. The same number killed pursuant to orders of a general controlling the fates of thousands may raise the question why he limited his actions to that particular part of the group.

It is for that reason that the evaluation by the ICJ in *Croatia v Serbia* of certain instances with which the parties sought to substantiate a finding of genocide is to be regretted. Reference has already been made to the situation involving a paramilitary leader who had specified parts of buildings at which rocket launchers should be aimed, so that Croats, and not Serbs, would be targeted.[123] It is certainly true that this speech, by itself, would not be conclusive for a finding on the matters with which the Court was concerned. Further inquiries would have been indicated: including an

---

[116] *Krstić* (Appeals Chamber), para 13.
[117] ibid.
[118] See *Brđanin* (Trial Chamber), para 702; *Karadžić* (Trial Chamber), para 555.
[119] *Croatia v Serbia*, para 142.
[120] *Bosnia v Serbia*, para 199.
[121] *Stakić* (Trial Chamber), para 523.
[122] See above at n 26.
[123] See above at n 113.

examination of Arkan's general scope of control in the siege of Vukovar.[124] However, to simply dismiss the incident as an 'isolated instance'[125] hardly amounts to an investigation which dealt with the matter in appropriate depth. It is, at the very least, possible that these instructions gave some of his troops the opportunity to do all they could have done to achieve the destruction of the group and that, therefore, from an individualised perspective, substantiality did exist.

In her memorial in this case, Croatia had also referred to cases of sexual mistreatment and to ethnically derogatory utterances which were made during the infliction of violence of this kind – a consideration which appears in the list of factors on whose basis she advanced her claim that genocidal intent had existed.[126] The fate of a male victim in Bapska may be seen as carrying particular significance for the establishment of intent: according to his statement, he had been told, during severe mistreatment of his genitals, that he would not 'make any more little Croats'.[127]

The ICJ found these statements credible and gave them 'evidential weight'.[128] It concluded that members of a protected group had been subjected to ill-treatment,[129] and that the *actus reus* of genocide had been fulfilled.[130] However, where genocidal intent was concerned, the Court contented itself with a generalised approach: it referred to the 'overall context' of the act and supported the view that it had not been 'committed with intent to destroy the Croats, but rather with that of forcing them to leave the regions concerned'; the context, in the ICJ's eyes, did not allow the conclusion that genocidal intent was 'the only reasonable inference to be drawn'.[131] With specific reference to the list of factors which Croatia had supplied to support a finding of genocidal intent, the ICJ simply stated that these aspects did not 'lead to the conclusion that there was an intent to destroy, in whole or in part, the Croats in the regions concerned'.[132]

In light of that, it appears that the above mentioned incident of sexual mistreatment, with the accompanying remarks, did not have a significant effect on the Court's determination of genocidal intent. The ICJ here seems to have applied broad brushstrokes to the establishment of that element – a method which is inappropriate for a crime whose assessment depends on personalised factors.[133] That is true even for a court dealing with genocide in the context of State responsibility: there, too, the

---

[124] The identification of the responsibility of Serbia would have involved additional questions, including those pertaining to attribution. See *Croatia v Serbia*, para 438.

[125] See above at n 114.

[126] See *Croatia v Serbia*, para 408. The ICJ interprets the list as factors which Croatia invited the court to consider for a finding that a 'systematic policy of targeting Croats with a view to their elimination from the regions concerned' existed. The nearly identical list in Croatia's memorial, however, makes reference to 'genocidal intent' which the State felt had been evidenced, *Croatia v Serbia*, Memorial of the Republic of Croatia (vol 1), 1 March 2001 ('Croatia Memorial'), para 8.16.

[127] Croatia Memorial, para 4.91.

[128] *Croatia v Serbia*, para 314.

[129] ibid, para 315.

[130] ibid, para 360.

[131] ibid, para 428.

[132] ibid, para 439.

[133] See, on the whole, the discussion in Paul Behrens, 'Between Abstract Event and Individualised Crime: Genocidal Intent in the Case of Croatia' (2015) 28 *Leiden Journal of International Law* 923, 925–32.

investigation has to begin with the acts of individual perpetrators (whose conduct is attributable to the State) – and indeed with their specific mindset.[134]

The lack of attention dedicated to the perpetrator's statements in particular is surprising: derogatory utterances have been accepted by international criminal tribunals in the past as aspects on which a finding of genocidal intent can be based.[135] For the individualised approach, their significance reaches beyond the level of evidentiary value: situations of this kind may well confirm that a low-ranking individual perpetrator had fulfilled his personal aim to destroy a substantial part of the group.[136]

A decisive advantage of the individualised approach lies in the coherence which it brings to the assessment of substantiality and in its capacity to overcome the spectre of arbitrariness that haunts the other methods. The individualised approach employs a verifiable and consistent standard in every case, the decisive question concerns the substantiality that the relevant perpetrator, within his particular reach and authority, could have achieved. This is an element which can be positively established and which, where the Trial Chamber reached an assessment which no reasonable trier would have reached, can be subject to review on appeal.[137]

A further consideration, closely linked to the matter of coherence, arises from the application of fundamental principles of international criminal justice – in particular, to the rule *nullum crimen sine lege*, which is enshrined in the major human rights treaties[138] as well as the statute of the International Criminal Court (ICC).[139] Its main emanations, including the requirement of a foreseeable and accessible law, have also been accepted by the international criminal tribunals.[140] In that regard, the *Stakić* Trial Chamber found that a law which did not possess 'sufficient clarity, precision and definiteness' could constitute a violation of the principle of *nullum crimen sine lege certa*.[141] That does not mean that criminal law cannot be advanced through judicial interpretation, but, as the ECtHR outlined in human rights law, the 'resultant

---

[134] See on this, International Law Commission, *Commentaries to the ILC Draft Articles on the Responsibility of States for Internationally Wrongful Acts*, GAOR, 56th Sess, Suppl 10, 59, Art 2, comm, para 3.

[135] See eg *Kayishema* (Trial Chamber), para 538.

[136] It is true that the evaluation of the mindset of the individual perpetrators carries difficulties for a body which, like the ICJ, has no criminal jurisdiction. See on this, *Croatia v Serbia*, Separate Opinion of *Judge Skotnikov*, para 12 ('ill-equipped to resolve') and Behrens (n 133) n 2.

[137] In these situations, the ad hoc tribunals as well as the International Criminal Court accept that appeal against a Trial Chamber judgment is possible. ICC (Appeals Chamber), *The Prosecutor v Thomas Lubanga Dyilo*, ICC-01/04-01/06 A 5, Judgment of 1 December 2014, paras 24–27, with further references.

[138] Art 15(1) International Covenant on Civil and Political Rights, 16 December 1966, 999 UNTS 171; Art 7(1) European Convention for the Protection of Human Rights and Fundamental Freedoms, 4 April 1950, 213 UNTS 221; Art 9 American Convention on Human Rights (21 November 1969) 1144 UNTS 123.

[139] Art 22(1) ICC St.

[140] ICTY, Appeals Chamber, *Prosecutor v Milorad Krnojelac*, IT-97-25-A, Judgment, 17 September 2003, para 220.

[141] *Stakić* (Trial Chamber), para 719. The Appeals Chamber did not disturb the Trial Chamber's definition of the principle and its requirements, but disagreed on its application in the particular instance. See ICTY, Appeals Chamber, *Prosecutor v Milomir Stakić*, IT-97-24-A, Judgment, 22 March 2006 ('*Stakić* (Appeals Chamber)'), paras 313–14. See also ECCC (Appeals Chamber), *Co-Prosecutors v Nuon Chea and Khieu Samphan*, 002/19-09-2007-ECCC/SC, Judgment, 23 November 2016, para 577.

development' must be 'consistent with the essence of the offence', and it must have been reasonably possible to foresee it.[142]

That, however, presupposes a reasoning by the courts which is based on coherent and verifiable factors: arbitrary considerations do not offer legal certainty. It is here that the individualised approach demonstrates particular strength. Under this method, the perpetrator is not asked to reach an understanding of substantiality on the basis of static parameters – he is not required to know whether a municipality or a detention camp qualifies or whether 2 or 3% constitute a sufficiently substantial proportion of the population. The question is simpler than that: the task of the international criminal tribunals is to evaluate whether, in the context of his own field of control and field of vision, the targeted part had been substantial. That is a consistent standard; and once this element is established, it is difficult for any perpetrator to claim that the foreseeability of this aspect had not been in existence.

4. CONCLUDING THOUGHTS

An assessment of subjective substantiality which complies with the main purposes of the Genocide Convention[143] is not an easy task; and the work is not facilitated if the Trial Chambers proceed on the basis of approaches which employ static parameters. A threshold which is set too high – say, at the targeted destruction of the group from nearly 'every corner of the world' – risks the inapplicability of the Convention to the great majority of situations and thus defeating its protective purpose. A threshold set too low no longer conveys the particular stigma of the crime and dilutes the deterrent effect which is meant to inhabit prosecution under this category.

It is also at that stage that the danger of a disconnect between the codified international crime and its popular understanding – the disassociation to which Cotterrell made reference in Chapter 2[144] – manifests itself. The application of various approaches which have been discussed above is certainly capable of resulting in a concept of genocide that is far removed from the common understanding of the term. It is more than questionable whether, for the ordinary user of the concept, the targeting of just one municipality would be seen as sufficient – or indeed, the intended killing of three leaders of a community. That is a point that merits serious reflection, not least in view of Cotterrell's observation that criminal law which does not find a basis 'in populations that can culturally "own" this law' risks stretching its authority 'beyond the point where its success can be assumed'.[145]

Has such 'ownership' truly been lost in the case of genocide? The insistence on subjective substantiality does not mean that destructive acts resulting in large actual victim numbers have been withdrawn from the scope of the crime. In fact, at least where international criminal tribunals were concerned, such acts were typically at

---

[142] See ECtHR, *SW v The United Kingdom*, Appl No 20166/92, Judgment of 22 November 1995, para 36; ECtHR, *Radio France and Others v France*, Appl No 53984/00, Judgment of 30 March 2004, para 20.

[143] See above, at nn 5–7.

[144] See above at n 12.

[145] Cotterrell (n 12), Section 5.

the core of genocide charges; and the limitation of the jurisdiction of the ICC to 'the most serious crimes of concern to the international community as a whole'[146] makes it likely that acts whose consequences carry magnitude on both the subjective and the objective side will be at the centre of genocide trials before that court as well.

Yet on the level of the substantive law, the identification of substantiality in the subjective part of the crime is certainly a development which may not have been expected by those who approach genocide from the perspective of its 'cultural understanding'. If this difficulty is seen together with other particularities that apply to the legal understanding of genocide – such as its restrictive group element and the fact that large victim numbers are not required on the objective side – it appears understandable why some authors postulate that it would be more appropriate to speak of two different concepts of the crime that are in use. '[S]ocial scientists, journalists, and historians', writes Kirsch, 'do not refer to the legal concept when talking about genocide', and he terms the concept that prevails outside legal consideration the 'social concept' of the crime.[147]

There may be good reasons to follow that view and to acknowledge that the law works with different parameters – which, at the same time, invokes the difficulties Cotterrell outlined in this study.[148]

At the same time, the question may be asked whether alignment with the 'social concept' is the only aspect which informs (and should inform) the understanding of instruments of international criminal law. It lies in the nature of international criminal justice that it calls additional factors into consideration, and these may be of such significance that the aim of reaching absolute alignment with the social concept with regard to every element of genocide might not be the decisive objective in the assessment of the crime.

An important consideration in that regard is the need to protect the certainty of the law, whose essential position in international criminal law has been outlined above.[149] Legal certainty requires a minimum degree of consistency in the interpretation of the law; and it is with regard to that requirement that the employment of various approaches towards substantiality and the use of static parameters puts the application of that principle at risk.

It may well be that the international criminal tribunals appreciate the danger inherent in methods which so strongly rely on the preferences of individual benches. An understanding of this kind would explain efforts by the Appeals Chamber to play down the significance of the various approaches by referring to them as 'useful guidelines' and stating that their applicability and weight will 'vary depending on the circumstances of a particular case'.[150] That, however, only compounds the problem. If the assessment is ultimately left to the discretion of the Trial Chambers,[151] it is entirely possible that a perpetrator who intended to kill thousands of group members

---

[146] Art 5 ICCSt; see also Art 17(1)(d) ICCSt.
[147] Kirsch (n 13) 348.
[148] See above at n 145.
[149] See above at n 141.
[150] *Krstić* (Appeals Chamber), para 14.
[151] *Krstić* (Trial Chamber), para 590.

is acquitted of genocide under a strict numerical approach, whereas his fellow in crime, whose destructive intent was limited to a much smaller municipality, is convicted by a Chamber that placed greater emphasis on the geographical approach. The problem does not lie in the fact that in some cases a (comparatively) low numerical victim count may suffice for a conviction – after all, the perpetrator who targeted a small municipality may have achieved all he could have done to destroy a substantial part of the group. The problem lies in the fact that the current position encourages arbitrariness – as Fournet notes in Chapter 13 in a related context, the existing 'judicial uncertainty [...] could seriously endanger the applicability of the law of genocide'.[152]

It is for that reason that it is suggested that the individualised approach must be an inevitable part of any assessment of a situation in which subjective substantiality is at issue. Unlike the other methods, it allows for a consistent evaluation and leads to the application of verifiable parameters, resulting in conclusions capable of review by a higher instance.

It is, at the same time, in line with the understanding of genocide as a crime whose characteristic lies in destructive intent. If the particular blameworthiness of genocide rests on the subjective side, then the interpretation of subjective substantiality has to be seen in the same context: the relevant part is substantial because it is substantial to the perpetrator. At the same time, the individualised approach does not remove the threshold of genocide: a perpetrator still has to take a high psychological hurdle if he is to direct his intent at the destruction of a protected group and to formulate a resolve to eliminate the part, which, from his perspective, is substantial.

There is another factor which justifies a degree of deviation between the legal and the social concept of the crime of genocide.

If the drafters of the Convention had so wished, they could easily have conferred on the crime an understanding that closely resembled its social concept: in particular, by stipulating that the existence of large actual victim numbers form an indispensable aspect of genocide.[153] The legal concept, however, owes its position not least to its incorporation in a treaty which stipulates a clear protective purpose,[154] and it is doubtful if that purpose would have been fulfilled if the drafters had chosen that way. On the contrary: actual victim numbers which reach that level of substantiality are a certain sign that preventative measures have failed.

If prevention is to be achieved at all through the threat of criminal sanctions, it has to start at an earlier stage. From that perspective, there is good reason to pay attention to the mindset of the perpetrator and to appreciate that the threshold for the commission of genocide has been crossed when substantiality has been established on the subjective side. It is an uncomfortable, yet inescapable, fact that genocide can be committed by ordinary persons, that the footsoldier, the journalist, the priest, are quite capable of forming subjective substantiality. What makes genocide heinous is that its perpetrators pursued destructive intent to such an extent that they were

---

[152] Caroline Fournet, 'Standing the Test of Time: The Dynamic Interpretation of the Genocide Convention' (ch 13 in this volume) at n 64.

[153] Such formulations, after all, were adopted for other crimes. See eg *Elements of Crimes*, Art 7(1)(b), 2nd element.

[154] See above at n 6.

willing to surmount their own personal threshold of substantiality. From the point of view of protection, this means that the international community has an opportunity to intervene at a point when intervention still has the potential of changing the course of events – there is no need to wait until the first mass executions have taken place or the first death camps are operational.

The price for this may well be that the legal concept of genocide and its 'cultural understanding' are not perfectly aligned. Yet if this is an approach which carries the chance of preventing mass atrocities, it may be a price worth paying.

And it may indeed be an advantage which even users of the social concept may come to appreciate. The development of a concept of a crime raises legitimate questions if it means that the conscience of mankind is shocked only when the 'denial of the right of existence of entire human groups'[155] is manifested across society as a whole. In that sense, genocide is indeed not a 'numbers game'; it is a crime that begins and is manifested in the mind and the deeds of the individual *génocidaire*.

---

[155] See on this GA Res 96/I, preamble, 1st operative para.

Part 4

Transnational Criminal Justice

15

The Offence of Incitement to Terrorism

STEN IDRIS VERHOEVEN AND YI ZHANG

1. INTRODUCTION

THE CRIME OF incitement to terrorism is a recent addition to the arsenal of counterterrorism measures. Incitement to terrorism came into focus after the London bombing of 7 July 2005. In the unanimously adopted Security Council Resolution 1624 (2005), for the first time, the Security Council called upon Member States of the United Nations to prohibit in their laws incitement of terrorism.[1] The resolution was sponsored by the United Kingdom and influenced by the Council of Europe Convention on the Prevention of Terrorism, which was adopted a few months earlier.[2] Article 5 of the Convention requires state parties to make 'public provocation to commit a terrorist offence' a criminal offence in itself. The criminalisation of incitement to terrorism is regarded as a quintessential tool for the prevention of terrorist attacks, in particular attacks carried out by 'home-grown' terrorists. In order to persuade persons to commit terrorist acts against their fellow citizens a long process of indoctrination will often have to take place through propaganda, glorification or direct appeals to commit terrorist acts.[3] Furthermore, the combating and prevention of incitement to terrorism is equally quintessential in cases of foreign terrorist fighters who are incited to travel abroad to fight on behalf of terrorist groups.[4] Of all media, the internet has proved to be a particularly useful tool for the spreading of terrorist propaganda, recruitment and other information on how

---

[1] Security Council Resolution 1624, §1(a), UN Doc S/RES/1624 (2005).

[2] D Barak-Erez and D Scharia, 'Freedom of Speech, Support for Terrorism, and the Challenge of Global Constitutional Law' (2011) 2 *Harvard National Security Journal* 20; B Saul, 'Speaking of Terror: Criminalising Incitement to Violence' (2005) 28 *University of New South Wales Law Journal* 870; B van Ginkel, 'Incitement to Terrorism: A Matter of Prevention or Repression', ICCT Research Paper (2011) 18, available at: www.icct.nl/download/file/ICCT-Van-Ginkel-Incitement-To-Terrorism-August-2011.pdf.

[3] Saul (n 2) 868; Y Ronen, 'Incitement to Terrorist Acts and International Law' (2010) 23 *Leiden Journal of International Law* 655; A Spataro, 'Why Do People Become Terrorists? A Prosecutor's Experiences' (2008) 6 *Journal of International Criminal Justice* 509.

[4] Security Council Resolution 2178, §§24–25, UN Doc S/RES/2178 (2014); Counter-terrorism Committee Executive Directorate, 'Global Survey of the Implementation of Security Council Resolution 1624 (2005) by Member States', UN Doc S/2016/50 (2016) §3.

to commit terrorist acts.[5] Due to its global reach, ease of access, relative anonymity and the possibility to hide traces, the internet is the choice of means by terrorist groups to easily reach those susceptible to ideological or religious radicalisation.[6]

Despite the necessity to prohibit incitement to terrorism to prevent future attacks, the offence is barely regulated at the international level. What precisely constitutes incitement to terrorism remains unclear since its definition and what constitute the elements of this crime have rarely been crystallised in international documents. Security Council Resolution 1624 (2005) provides no definition of incitement to terrorism. To be effective, Security Council resolutions need to be incorporated in the national legal system of the Member States, and hence it may be expected that in the absence of a clear definition UN Member States will adopt different definitions. In the European context the situation is fortunately different since a definition is provided in the Council of Europe Convention on the Prevention of Terrorism, which was also adopted in Council Framework Decision 2008/919/JHA of the European Union and elaborated upon by Directive (EU) 2017/541.[7] This definition has been considered a model to criminalise incitement to terrorism internationally.[8]

With regard to the offence of incitement to terrorism, the main point of contention is whether indirect incitement is covered by the offence. Indirect incitement is characterised by the lack of a call to violence, but instead publicly justifies acts of terrorism or glorifies terrorists and their acts.[9] Such statements may shock or offend, especially the victims of terrorist crimes, but do not necessarily amount to a criminal offence.[10] Furthermore, indirect incitement may be problematic from a human rights perspective because it necessarily limits freedom of expression. Even if it is clear what encompasses

---

[5] UN Office on Drugs and Crime, 'The Use of the Internet for Terrorist Purposes' (2015) 3ff, available at: www.unodc.org/documents/frontpage/Use_of_Internet_for_Terrorist_Purposes.pdf. On the other hand, the internet is also used to seek people with similar ideas, which entails that persons already had radical ideas before they are further influenced by propaganda: International Peace Institute, 'Combating Incitement of Terrorism and Promoting Intercultural Dialogue' (October 2010) 3, available at: www.ipinst.org/wp-content/uploads/publications/combating_incitement_meetingnote_oct2010.pdf. Moreover, publication of violent materials may actually cause supporters to distance themselves from the terrorist group: Counter-Terrorism Implementation Task Force, 'Countering the Use of the Internet for Terrorist Purposes', CTITF Report (2009) §86, available at: www.un.org/en/terrorism/ctitf/pdfs/ctitf_internet_wg_2009_report.pdf.

[6] UN Office on Drugs and Crime (n 5) 4 and 6; P Cornish, 'Cyber Security and Politically, Socially, and Religiously Motivated Violence', European Parliament, Foreign Affairs Committee (Chatham House 2009) 11–13, available at: www.europarl.europa.eu/RegData/etudes/etudes/join/2009/406997/EXPO-AFET_ET(2009)406997_EN.pdf; Global Survey on the Implementation by Member States of Security Council Resolution 1624 (2005), UN Doc S/2012/16 (2012) §96; European Commission, 'Terrorist Recruitment: Addressing the Factors Contributing to Violent Radicalisation (2005) 4, available at: http://eur-lex.europa.eu/legal-content/EN/TXT/PDF/?uri=CELEX:52005DC0313&from=EN.

[7] Art 5 Council of Europe Convention on the Prevention of Terrorism (2005) CETS No 196; Art (1)(1) Council Framework Decision 2008/919/JHA, [9 December 2008] OJ L330/21; Art 5 Directive 2017/541 [31 March 2017] OJ L88/6.

[8] Report of the Special Rapporteur on the Promotion and Protection of Human Rights and Fundamental Freedoms While Countering Terrorism ('Special Rapporteur on Counter-Terrorism and Human Rights'), UN Doc A/HRC/16/51 (2010) §§29–32.

[9] Committee of Experts on Terrorism, 'Apologie du terrorism and Incitement to Terrorism, Analytical Report', 3rd Meeting, Strasbourg, 6-8 July 2004, CODEXTER (2004) 5.

[10] UN Office on Drugs and Crime (n 5) 3–4 and 6; UN Secretary-General, 'The Protection of Human Rights and Fundamental Freedoms While Countering Terrorism', UN Doc A/63/337 (2008) §61.

incitement, there is no internationally accepted definition of terrorism. Instead, states will introduce national definitions of terrorism, some of which may be broad. The inclusion of indirect incitement together with an unclear or broad definition of terrorism may extend the crime to a wide variety of statements that have no terrorist purpose and may thereby violate the principle of legality or undermine free speech.[11] Other contentious issues involve whether the incitement should be public, and if so, when a statement can be regarded as made in public, whether causation between the incitement and the terrorist acts is needed, and what is the required *mens rea*.

This chapter aims to clarify the scope of incitement to terrorism and argues that the adoption of a clear definition of the crime of incitement to terrorism at the international level would be desirable. It will examine similar crimes at the international level, such as incitement to genocide, which has been discussed and applied by the International Criminal Tribunal for Rwanda (ICTR). In addition, the chapter will draw inspiration on how national jurisdictions have implemented the crime of incitement to terrorism. The chapter will not, however, dwell upon a definition of terrorism, which in itself would deserve a separate discussion. Regardless, the problem of definition of terrorism may be circumvented by defining terrorist offences as offences within the scope of a number of conventions on terrorism.[12]

Section 2 will set out the relevant legal framework of the offence of incitement of terrorism by examining existing international and regional legal acts and by looking into human rights law. Section 3 will subsequently look into how different states have tried to integrate incitement to terrorism in their legal system. Section 4 will then turn to an analysis of the elements of a possible international crime of incitement to terrorism. In this regard, the section will examine whether the international crime of incitement to genocide can serve as a blueprint for the offence of incitement to terrorism.

2. THE INTERNATIONAL LEGAL FRAMEWORK OF INCITEMENT TO TERRORISM

The offence of incitement to terrorism is governed by two areas of law, which frequently are in tension with one another: international law on terrorism and international

---

[11] UN Office on Drugs and Crime (n 5) 6; UN Secretary-General (n 10) §53; Report of the Special Rapporteur on Counter-Terrorism and Human Rights, UN Doc A/65/258 (2010) §46; Human Rights Committee, General Comment No 34, Art 19 ('HRC General Comment 34'): Freedom of Opinion and Expression, UN Doc CCPR/C/GC/34 (2011) §46; OSCE, ODIHR, 'Countering the Incitement and Recruitment of Foreign Terrorist Fighters: The Human Dimension' (2015), 4, available at www.osce.org/odihr/166646?download=true; Joint Declaration by the UN Special Rapporteur on Freedom of Opinion and Expression, OSCE Representative on Freedom of the Media and the OAS Special Rapporteur on Freedom of Expression (2005), available at: www.oas.org/en/iachr/expression/showarticle.asp?artID=650&lID=1; International Commission of Jurists, 'Response to the European Commission Consultation on Inciting, Aiding or Abetting Terrorist Offences' (2007) 4, available at: www.un.org/en/sc/ctc/specialmeetings/2011/docs/icj/icj-2007-ec-questionnaire.pdf.

[12] Which was the option selected by the drafters of the Council of Europe Convention on the Prevention of Terrorism: Annex to the Council of Europe Convention on the Prevention of Terrorism (2005), CETS No 196.

human rights law. After focusing primarily on acts of international terrorism itself, states have more recently started to focus on acts that facilitate terrorism by aiding or abetting or creating the terrorist mindset. In this regard, incitement to terrorism has been described as 'an insidious activity contributing to the spread of the scourge of terrorism'.[13] In light of this statement a proactive approach to incitement to terrorism would require that incitement to terrorism has to be prohibited as a separate crime, even if acts of terrorism would not flow from the incitement.[14] Nevertheless, the prohibition of certain forms of speech inherently limits the internationally recognised freedom of expression and therefore equally becomes a matter of human rights law. The two fields of law can be reconciled since freedom of expression is not absolute and may be restricted under certain conditions.

2.1. The Criminalisation of Incitement to Terrorism

2.1.1. *The United Nations and Incitement to Terrorism*

The United Nations has condemned incitement of terrorism in General Assembly and Security Council resolutions. Initially, UN General Assembly resolutions focused on the obligation of states not to support or tolerate acts of terrorism against other states, by inter alia the instigation of acts of terrorism.[15] In addition, UN General Assembly resolutions have condemned incitement to terrorism in general, regardless of state involvement.[16] Moreover, the UN Global Counter-Terrorism Strategy includes the adoption of measures that prohibit incitement to terrorism.[17] Despite the activities of the General Assembly, the Security Council has taken centre stage in the fight against terrorism. Security Council Resolution 1373 (2001) already provided that inciting terrorism is contrary to the purposes of the Charter of the United Nations.[18] With regard to the offence of incitement of terrorism, Security Council Resolution 1624 (2005) is, however, the linchpin. This resolution condemns and repudiates in its preamble the incitement of terrorist acts and attempts at the justification or glorification of terrorist acts. Furthermore, operative paragraph 1 calls upon states to prohibit by law incitement to commit terrorist acts. The resolution does not, however, create an obligation to prohibit incitement to terrorism in domestic

---

[13] Report of the Security Council Working Group Established Pursuant to Security Council Resolution 1566 (2004), UN Doc S/2005/789 (2005), §29.

[14] A Conte, *Human Rights in the Prevention and Punishment of Terrorism* (Heidelberg, Springer, 2010) 451.

[15] Declaration on Principles of International Law concerning Friendly Relations and Co-operation among States, in Accordance with the Charter of the United Nations, Annex to General Assembly Resolution 2625 (XXV), UN Doc A/RES/25/2625 (1970); General Assembly Resolution 40/61, §6, UN Doc A/RES/40/61 (1985); Declaration on Measures to Eliminate International Terrorism, Annex to General Assembly Resolution 49/60, §5(a) UN Doc A/RES/49/60 (1994).

[16] General Assembly Resolution 59/195, §12, UN Doc A/RES/59/195 (2005); Declaration to Supplement the 1994 Declaration on Measures to Eliminate Terrorism, Annex to General Assembly Resolution 59/210, §2, UN Doc A/RES/51/210 (1995).

[17] Plan of Action, Measures to Address the Conditions Conductive to the Spread of Terrorism, §4, Annex to Resolution 60/228, United Nations Global Counter-terrorism Strategy, UN Doc A/RES/60/228 (2006).

[18] Security Council Resolution 1373 (2001) §5, UN Doc S/RES/1373 (2001).

law. To determine whether Member States have an obligation pursuant to Article 25 Charter of the United Nations to carry out a particular resolution, the mandatory language of the resolution is the determining factor.[19] The wording used in Security Council Resolution 1624 – to call upon – is exhortatory and therefore does not create a binding obligation.[20] Nevertheless, the Counter-Terrorism Committee monitors the implementation of the resolution,[21] which has in practice exerted a compliance pull on the Member States.[22]

Security Council Resolution 1624 (2005) unfortunately does not define incitement. Therefore, it remains unclear whether incitement also covers indirect incitement. On the one hand, incitement may include direct and indirect incitement. On the other hand, the clear distinction drawn in the preamble between incitement and *apologie* of terrorism indicates that the Security Council does not equate both concepts.[23] Whereas the resolution calls upon UN Member States to adopt legislation that prohibits incitement to terrorism, the resolution's preamble does not require penalisation, but repudiates 'attempts at the justification or glorification (apologie) of terrorist acts that may incite further terrorist acts'. Furthermore, the ordinary meaning of incitement in international criminal law requires direct and explicit encouragement to commit a crime.[24] The UN Secretary-General's non-binding definition of incitement adopts this approach: incitement involves 'a direct call to engage in terrorism, with the intention that this will promote terrorism, and in a context in which the call is directly causally responsible for increasing the actual likelihood of a terrorist act occurring'.[25] Therefore, Security Council Resolution 1624 (2005) does not require the criminalisation of glorification of terrorism.[26] In any event, incitement is considered to be speech directed at an unspecified audience and therefore public.[27]

Security Council Resolution 1624 (2005) does not seem to require a causal link between the incitement and the actual commission of terrorist acts, which means that incitement to terrorism is regarded as an inchoate offence.[28] Nevertheless, although this may be justified for direct calls to commit terrorist offences, it is more questionable for indirect incitement since otherwise all statements which are somewhat supportive of terrorists and their acts risk being criminal, even if there is no likelihood that they will increase the probability of terrorist offences.[29] In this regard, the UN Secretary-General and Special Rapporteurs require that incitement to terrorism

---

[19] *Legal Consequences for States of the Continued Presence of South Africa in Namibia (South West Africa) notwithstanding Security Council Resolution 276*, Advisory Opinion, ICJ Rep 1971, §114.

[20] Conte (n 14) 451; Ronen (n 3) 650. See also Saul (n 2) 870; van Ginkel (n 2) 18.

[21] Security Council Resolution 1624, §5, UN Doc S/RES/1624 (2005); Security Council Resolution 1963, UN Doc S/RES/1963 (2010).

[22] Ronen (n 3) 650; on the disciplinary function of the Counter-Terrorism Committee: I Roele, 'Disciplinary Power and the UN Security Council Counter Terrorism Committee' (2014) 19 *Journal of Conflict and Security Law* 49ff.

[23] Ronen (n 3) 663.

[24] A Cassese, *International Criminal Law* (Oxford, Oxford University Press, 2003) 218.

[25] UN Secretary-General (n 10) §61.

[26] Barak-Erez and Scharia (n 2) 21.

[27] ibid 19; Ronen (n 3) 666.

[28] Ronen (n 3) 667.

[29] Van Ginkel (n 2) 19.

causes a danger that the advocated acts would be committed.[30] Finally, Security Council Resolution 1624 (2005) is silent on the required *mens rea*. Hence, Security Council Resolution 1624 (2005) by its indeterminacy gives UN Member States considerable discretion in implementing the resolution, which in practice has led to a divergent implementation.[31]

2.1.2. Europe and the European Union

Incitement to terrorism was first addressed at the European level. Article 5(2) of the Convention on the Prevention of Terrorism obliges states to criminalise the public provocation of a terrorist offence. Article 5(1) of the Convention helpfully provides a definition of public provocation, namely 'the distribution, or otherwise making available, of a message to the public, with the intent to incite the commission of a terrorist offence, where such conduct, whether or not directly advocating terrorist offences, causes a danger that one or more such offences may be committed'. The definition of incitement is based on Article 3 of the Additional Protocol to the Convention on Cybercrime. In addition, spurred by the Council of Europe Convention and Security Council Resolution 1624 (2005), the European Union adopted Council Framework Decision 2008/919/JHA, which contained a virtually identical definition of what constitutes incitement.[32] This definition served as blueprint for the improved definition of public provocation to terrorism in Article 5 of Directive (EU) 2017/541, which obliges Member States to criminalise

> the distribution, or otherwise making available by any means, whether online or offline, of a message to the public, with the intent to incite the commission of [a terrorist offence], where such conduct, directly or indirectly, such as by the glorification of terrorist acts, advocates the commission of terrorist offences, thereby causing a danger that one or more such offences may be committed.

The Convention and Directive (EU) 2017/541 do not limit incitement to direct incitement, but include indirect incitement, such as justification and glorification, under incitement to terrorism.[33] This is limited by the requirement of causality and the requirement of a specific intent. The direct or indirect advocating of terrorist offences must cause a danger that one or more such offences may be committed. Nonetheless, it is not clear how direct the danger has to be. In this regard, the wording of Article 5 of Directive (EU) 2017/541 diverges from Article 5(1) of the Convention (and Article 1(1) of Council Framework Decision 2008/919/JHA). Article 5 of the Directive requires that the conduct 'thereby caus[es] a danger', which implies more a

---

[30] UN Secretary-General (n 10) §61; Special Rapporteur on Counter-Terrorism and Human Rights (n 8), 16; Report of the Special Rapporteur on the Promotion and Protection of the Right to Freedom of Opinion and Expression, UN Doc A/66/290 (2011) §34.

[31] See Global Survey on the Implementation by Member States of Security Council Resolution 1624 (2005) UN Doc S/2012/16 (2012); the country reports are available at: www.un.org/en/sc/ctc/resources/1624. html.

[32] Art 1(1) Council Framework Decision 2008/919/JHA.

[33] Council of Europe, *Explanatory Report to the Council of Europe Convention on the Prevention of Terrorism* (2005) §§94–96, available at: https://rm.coe.int/16800d3811 ('CoE Explanatory Report'); Recital (10) and Art 5 Directive (EU) 2017/541.

consequence than a requirement. A literal reading of this provision therefore seems to imply that the direct or indirect public incitement of terrorist offences automatically causes a danger.[34] Article 5(1) of the Convention requires that the conduct creates a danger; in other words, direct or indirect incitement in public that does not create a danger is not an offence. It remains unclear whether the rephrasing of the causality element in Article 5 of the Directive had this purpose, since the preamble still refers to the previous 'causes' a danger test.[35]

In any event, whether the incitement causes a danger is determined by the wording used, the nature of the speaker and addressee, and the context; in addition, the significance and credibility of the danger has to be taken into consideration.[36] However, it is not required that a terrorist offence is committed: incitement is an inchoate offence under the Convention and the Directive.[37] The definition explicitly provides that the offence of incitement to terrorism has to be made in public, so that private incitement is not covered by the definition.[38] Finally, the definition in the Convention and Directive specifies that the subjective element requires that the incitement is done willingly and knowingly, but the person making the incitement must equally have the specific purpose to provoke others to commit a terrorist offence,[39] which entails that he or she must also have the special intent required for terrorism.[40]

2.2. Incitement to Terrorism and Human Rights

2.2.1. Incitement to Terrorism and Limitations to the Right of Freedom of Expression

States are constantly reminded that their legitimate fight against terrorism must respect their commitments under human rights law.[41] Human rights law is therefore an indelible part of the international legal framework on incitement to terrorism. In this respect, the prohibition, criminal or otherwise, of incitement to terrorism necessarily implies a limitation to the right of freedom of expression, protected in international

---

[34] S De Coensel, 'Incitement to Terrorism: The Nexus between Causality and Intent and the Question of Legitimacy, A Case Study of the European Union, Belgium and the United Kingdom' in C Paulussen and M Scheinin (eds), *Human Dignity and Human Security in Times of Terrorism* (The Hague, TMC Asser Press, 2020) 279–81.

[35] ibid 281.

[36] CoE Explanatory Report §100; Consideration (10) Directive (EU) 2017/541.

[37] Art 8 Convention on the Prevention of Terrorism; CoE Explanatory Report §78; Art 13 Directive (EU) 2017/541.

[38] Private incitement may amount to a mode of criminal liability, eg instigation: J-P Laborde and M DeFeo, 'Problems and Prospects of Implementing UN Action against Terrorism' (2006) 4 *Journal of International Criminal Justice* 1097; Ronen (n 3) 666; van Ginkel (n 2) 14. Instigation requires that the instigated act occurs: van Ginkel (n 2) 14.

[39] Art 5 Convention on the Prevention of Terrorism: 'with the intent to incite the commission of a terrorist offence'; European Commission, 'Proposal for a Directive of the European Parliament and the Council on Combating Terrorism and Replacing Council Framework Decision 2002/475/JHA on Combating Terrorism', COM(2015) 625 final, 16.

[40] Ronen (n 3) 669; van Ginkel (n 2) 14; De Coensel (n 35) 281.

[41] Preamble §2 Security Council Resolution 1624 (2005); Preamble §§8–9 Convention on the Prevention of Terrorism; Consideration (35) Directive (EU) 2017/541.

and regional human rights conventions.[42] The freedom of expression is of the utmost importance in a democratic society since it allows minority voices to be heard against the political majority who at a certain point in time control the legislative and executive power. It is therefore important for the advancement of a democratic society and, in addition, for an individual's self-fulfilment.[43] Freedom of expression is therefore not limited to speech which is widely accepted in or by society, but equally includes speech deemed offensive, shocking or disturbing.[44] Consequently, the voicing of opinions sympathetic to terrorists or terrorist acts may be morally questionable, shock society or be offensive to the victims, but may be protected by the right to freedom of opinion and expression.

Nonetheless, states, groups and individuals cannot invoke human rights to deny the human rights of others or excessively restrict human rights.[45] In general, if an organisation promotes changes through illegal and undemocratic means or when it proposes changes, even if advocated legally, which would undermine democracy and its values, it may not benefit from the protection offered by human rights law.[46] In this regard, Article 20(2) of the International Covenant on Civil and Political Rights (ICCPR) states that: 'Any advocacy of national, racial or religious hatred that constitutes incitement to discrimination, hostility or violence shall be prohibited by law.' The prohibition has to respect the general requirements of any limitation of the freedom of expression: legality, legitimate purpose and necessity.[47] In addition, Article 20 requires three elements to be satisfied: (1) advocacy of hatred; (2) advocacy which constitutes incitement; and (3) incitement likely to result in discrimination, hostility or violence. Crucially, advocacy of hatred on the basis of national, racial or religious grounds is not prohibited as such. The advocacy needs to constitute an incitement to discrimination, hostility or violence.[48] 'Advocacy' requires 'explicit, intentional, public and active support and promotion of hatred towards a targeted group'. 'Incitement', in turn refers to 'statements about national, racial or religious groups that create an imminent risk of discrimination, hostility or violence against persons

---

[42] Art 19 International Covenant on Civil and Political Rights (ICCPR) (1966); Art 10 European Convention on the Protection of Human Rights and Fundamental Freedoms (1950) (ECHR); Art 13 American Convention on Human Rights (1969) (ACHR); Art 9(2) African Charter on Human and People's Rights (1981) ('African Charter').

[43] *Perinçek v Switzerland*, Appl No 27510/08, Judgment, 15 October 2015, §196, available at: http:// hudoc.echr.coe.int ('*Perinçek*'); HRC General Comment 34 §2.

[44] *Handyside v The United Kingdom*, Appl No 54/93/72, Judgment, 7 December 1976, §49, available at: http://hudoc.echr.coe.int ('*Handyside*').

[45] Art 5(1) ICCPR; Art 17 ECHR; Art 29 ACHR; Art 27(2) ACHPR; Art 20(2) ICCPR.

[46] *Kasymakhunov and Saybatalov v Russia*, Appl Nos 26261/05 and 26377/06, Judgment, 14 March 2013, §105, available at: http://hudoc.echr.coe.int ('*Kasymakhunov and Saybatalov*').

[47] HRC General Comment 34, §§50, 52; Rabat Plan of Action on the Prohibition of Advocacy of National, Racial or Religious Hatred that Constitutes Incitement to Discrimination, Hostility or Violence, annex to Report of the United Nations High Commissioner for Human Rights on the Expert Workshops on the Prohibition of Incitement to National, Racial or Religious Hatred, UN Doc A/HRC/22/17/Add.4 (2013), §1; HRC, *Malcom Ross v Canada*, Communication No 736/1997, UN Doc CCPR/C/70/D/736/1997 (2000) §10.6.

[48] Report of the Special Rapporteur on the Promotion and Protection of the Right to Freedom of Opinion and Expression, UN Doc A/67/357 (2012) §43; Report of the Special Rapporteur on the Promotion and Protection of the Right to Freedom of Opinion and Expression ('Special Rapporteur on Freedom of Opinion and Expression'), UN Doc A/74/486 (2019) §§8, 10.

belonging to those groups'. Factors to determine if advocacy amounts to incitement to discrimination, hostility or violence include real and imminent danger of violence resulting from the expression; specific intent of the speaker to incite discrimination, hostility or violence and the context in which hatred was expressed; the status of the speaker; content and form of the speech; extent or reach of the speech act; and likelihood, including imminence, that 'some degree of risk of harm must be identified'.[49]

Article 17 of the European Convention on Human Rights (ECHR) provides for a wider prohibition than Article 20 ICCPR. No state, group or person has a right to engage in any activity or perform any act aimed at the destruction of the rights and freedoms of the Convention. The provision covers acts that are contrary to the text and spirit of the ECHR, that are incompatible with democracy and other fundamental values of the ECHR or that infringe rights recognised in the ECHR.[50] Its purpose is therefore to protect the values of a democratic society against those that use human rights to undermine it.[51] Such fundamental values include justice and peace, effective political democracy and free elections, peaceful settlement of international conflicts and sanctity of human life, tolerance, social peace and non-discrimination, gender equality, and coexistence of members of society free from racial segregation.[52] Article 17 ECHR covers acts whose aim is to promote or justify hatred, violence, xenophobia and racial discrimination, antisemitism, Islamophobia, terrorism and war crimes, negation and revision of clearly established historical facts, contempt for victims of international crimes, war or totalitarian regimes, and political ideas incompatible with democracy.[53] Activities of terrorist groups clearly fall within the scope of Article 17 ECHR because their acts aim to change political, economic or social foundations of a society through violence and intimidation.

Article 17 ECHR covers the right to freedom of expression. Article 17 ECHR has however been inconsistently applied by the European Court of Human Rights and seems to be limited to exceptional situations in which there is a clear hateful intent.[54] The decisive point is whether the statements are manifestly directed against the Convention's underlying values and whether by making the statement, the author attempted to rely on the Convention to engage in an activity or perform acts aimed at the destruction of the rights and freedoms laid down in it.[55] Hence, Article 17 has been invoked in case of a general and vehement attack against a particular group, eg incitement to violence or hate speech against ethnic or religious groups;[56] in situations

---

[49] ibid §46.

[50] European Court of Human Rights, 'Guide on Article 17 of the European Convention on Human Rights, Prohibition of Abuse of Rights' (2021) §21, available at: www.echr.coe.int/Documents/Guide_Art_17_ENG.pdf.

[51] *ROJ TV A/S v Denmark*, Appl No 24683/14, Decision on Admissibility, 17 April 2018, §30, available at: http://hudoc.echr.coe.int ('*ROJ TV*'); *Ayoub and Others v France*, Appl Nos 77400/14, 34532/15 and 34550/15, Judgment, 8 October 2020, §92, available at: http://hudoc.echr.coe.int ('*Ayoub*').

[52] European Court of Human Rights, 'Guide on Article 17 of the European Convention on Human Rights, Prohibition of Abuse of Rights' (2021) §27.

[53] ibid §28.

[54] *Perinçek* §114.

[55] ibid §115; *ROJ TV* §31.

[56] eg *Norwood v The United Kingdom*, Appl No. 23131/03, Decision on Admissibility, 16 November 2004, available at: http://hudoc.echr.coe.int; *Garaudy v France*, Appl No 65831/01, Decision on Admissibility,

where the prohibited aims had a radical and far-reaching character,[57] or when the repeated prohibited aims are repeatedly and systematically displayed.[58]

In *Kasymakhunov and Saybatalov* the European Court of Human Rights applied Article 17 ECHR to reject the application of Article 10 ECHR. Both applicants were active members of Hizb ut-Tahrir al-Islami, a terrorist organisation under Russian law, and were convicted for incitement to participate in the activities of a terrorist organisation. Hizb ut-Tahrir al-Islami advocates the establishment of a caliphate in the Middle East and the introduction of *sharia* law and rejects democracy and civil and political rights.[59] The European Court of Human Rights found that the organisation advocated violence and antisemitism; moreover, the goal of introducing *sharia* law, thereby rejecting democracy and political freedoms, fell within the scope of Article 17 ECHR.[60] Furthermore, the same organisation was banned from operating in Germany. The European Court of Human Rights again applied Article 17 ECHR: the group advocated for the violent destruction of Israel and for the banishment and killing of its inhabitants, and justified suicide bombing against Israeli citizens.[61] In *ROJ TV*, the Court applied Article 17 ECHR to a situation wherein a television station of the PKK, a terrorist organisation, was prosecuted for the broadcasting of incitement to participate in fights and actions, incitement to join the PKK, and the portrayal of deceased guerrilla members as heroes.[62]

Furthermore, in case the advocacy of hatred does not fall within the scope of Article 17, limitations to advocacy may be justified by the general limitations to freedom of opinion and expression.[63] This freedom may be limited by law provided it serves a legitimate purpose and is necessary in a democratic society. Concerning the first requirement, provided by law, the law needs to respect the principle of legality and consequently has to be sufficiently clear as to the scope of the limitation.[64] Concerning the second requirement, legitimate purpose, the protection of public order, national security, public safety, prevention of crime and the rights of others are legitimate grounds to restrict the right of freedom of expression.[65] In particular, the European Court of Human Rights has recognised that the prevention of recruitment of members and supporters of a terrorist organisation through public statements is a legitimate interest.[66] The third requirement, necessary in a democratic

---

24 June 2003, available at: http://hudoc.echr.coe.int; *WP and Others v Poland*, Appl No 42264/98, Decision on Admissibility, 2 September 2004, available at: http://hudoc.echr.coe.int.

[57] eg *Kasymakhunov and Saybatalov* §§106–12; *Hizb Ut-Tahrir v Germany*, Appl No 31098/08, Judgment, 12 June 2012, §73, available at: http://hudoc.echr.coe.int ('*Hizb Ut-Tahrir*'); *Aytoub* §§131, and 133.

[58] eg *ROJ TV* §45; *Belkacem v Belgium*, Appl No 34367/14, Decision on Admissibility, 27 June 2017, §33, available at: http://hudoc.echr.coe.int; *M'Bala M'Bala v France*, Appl No 25239/13, Decision on Admissibility, 20 October 2015, §37, available at: http://hudoc.echr.coe.int.

[59] *Kasymakhunov and Saybatalov* §§5–53.

[60] ibid §§102–15.

[61] *Hizb Ut-Tahrir*, §73.

[62] *ROJ TV*, §§6-17.

[63] Special Rapporteur on Freedom of Opinion and Expression (n 48) §§19–20.

[64] HRC General Comment 34, §46. For an overview of the case law of the European Court of Human Rights: *Perinçek* §§131–36.

[65] Art 19(3) ICCPR; Art 10(2) ECHR; Art 13(2) ACHR; Art 9(2) *juncto* Art 27(2) ACHPR.

[66] *Hogefeld v Germany*, Appl No 35402/97, Decision on Admissibility, 20 January 2000, available at http://hudoc.echr.coe.int.

society, demands that there is a pressing social need to restrict the freedom of opinion and expression.[67] Although states have a margin of appreciation in determining whether such a need exists, the European Court of Human Rights closely scrutinises limitations on the basis of national security,[68] but has given states a broader margin in case of incitement to violence against particular persons.[69] Nevertheless, expressions made in political debate or dealing with matters of public interest have a significant importance and may only rarely be restricted.[70] Furthermore, the limits of permissible criticism are wider with regard to the government than in relation to private citizens.[71] In assessing whether or not states have overstepped their margin of appreciation, the European Court of Human Rights examines whether the interference was proportionate to the legitimate aim pursued and whether the reasons given to justify the limitation were relevant and sufficient.[72] With regard to hate speech, the Court takes into account the factors of the existing political and social background, whether the statements taken in their context were an indirect or direct call for violence or a justification of violence, hatred or intolerance, and the manner in which the statements were made and the indirect or direct capacity to cause harm.[73] The nature and severity of the punishments for illegal speech may be disproportionate and therefore become an infringement of the freedom of opinion and expression.[74]

Most situations dealing with terrorism and incitement to violence are examined under Article 10 ECHR. The prosecution of clear calls to violence, even if they are not likely to cause harm, will not amount to an infringement of Article 10 ECHR. Furthermore, the identifying with and the glorification of terrorist organisations could be regarded as supporting the organisation and incitement to violence and hate; moreover, disseminating messages of praise of terrorists and the denigration of their victims could equally amount to incitement to terrorism.[75] In this regard the European Court of Human Rights looks beyond the actual wording and takes into consideration the immediate and wider context in which the statements are made. Consequently, statements which by their ordinary meaning do not unambiguously call for violence may still be qualified as such.[76] Nonetheless, even in a context of

---

[67] HRC General Comment 34, §22; *Sunday Times v United Kingdom (No 1)*, Appl No 6538/74, Judgment, 26 April 1979, §62, available at: http://hudoc.echr.coe.int ('*Sunday Times*').

[68] *Incal v Turkey*, Appl No 22678/93, Judgment, 9 June 1998, §58, available at: http://hudoc.echr.coe.int ('*Incal*').

[69] *Arslan v Turkey*, Appl No 23462/94, Judgment, 8 July 1999, §46, available at http://hudoc.echr.coe.int.

[70] HRC General Comment 34, §§20, 34; *Féret v Belgium*, Appl No 15615/07, Judgment, 16 July 2009, §63, available at: http://hudoc.echr.coe.int; *Sürek v Turkey* (No 1), Appl No 26682/95, Judgment, 8 July 1999, §61, available at: http://hudoc.echr.coe.int ('*Sürek*').

[71] *Incal* §54.

[72] *Handyside* §§48–50; *Sunday Times* §62.

[73] *Perinçek* §§205–07.

[74] *Sürek* §64; *Leroy v France*, Appl No 36109/03, Judgment, 2 October 2008, §47, available at: http://hudoc.echr.coe.int ('*Leroy*').

[75] *Yavuz and Yaylali v Turkey*, Appl No 12606/11, Judgment, 17 December 2013, §51, available at: http://hudoc.echr.coe.int.

[76] *Zana v Turkey*, Appl No 18954/91, Judgment, 25 November 1997, §§50–60, available at: http://hudoc.echr.coe.int; *Sürek* §§61–65.

societal violence, not all virulent statements will be unprotected under Article 10 ECHR, in particular if they do not incite to violence, but to legitimate means of action.[77]

Concerning glorification of terrorism, in the case of *Leroy v France* the Court did not find a violation of Article 10 ECHR for the conviction of a cartoonist to a fine of €1,500 for complicity in *apologie* of terrorism. The cartoon was published on 13 September 2001 in a Basque weekly and depicted the destruction of the World Trade Centre with the caption 'We have all dreamt about it, … Hamas did it.'[78] The Court found that the cartoon together with the caption did indeed glorify the use of violence against the United States and went further than merely criticising the policies of the United States. It took into consideration the form of the message, a caricature and satire, which by its characteristics meant to provoke, the date of publication, shortly after the actual terrorist attacks, and the volatile situation in the Basque region.[79] In addition, the modest sanction was another reason the limitation of the right of freedom of speech was not disproportionate.[80]

As is clear from *Leroy v France* no form of expression is excluded from amounting to incitement to terrorism, especially when it is distributed through the media. Nonetheless, certain forms of expression will because of their characteristics be less likely to amount to incitement to terrorism. In *Karataş v Turkey*, the European Court of Human Rights found that Article 10 ECHR was infringed by the conviction of the applicant for the publication of an anthology of poems, which could be interpreted as glorifying armed rebellion against Turkey and martyrdom in that fight.[81] Since the nature of poetry is such that it does not appeal to large groups and since it was not spread through mass media, the dangers to national security were limited, and hence together with the excessive penalty imposed on the author, the Court found a violation of Article 10 ECHR.[82]

The Court attaches, therefore, particular importance to the use of the language. In *Erkizia Almandoz v Spain*, the applicant, a former Basque separatist politician, paid tribute at a commemoration service for Mr Argala, a deceased member of the terrorist organisation ETA. For his speech, Mr Erkizia Almandoz was convicted to one year in prison and seven years' suspension of electoral rights.[83] The Court accepted that the speech occurred in a tense political and social climate in which the discussion of Basque independence and the means thereto generated passionate debates.[84] The Court equally acknowledged that the ceremony had the intent to eulogise a fallen member of ETA and that the applicant was the principal speaker

---

[77] *Ceylan v Turkey*, Appl No 23556/94, Judgment, 8 July 1999, §§33–38, available at http://hudoc.echr. coe.int; *Incal* §§49–59.

[78] *Leroy* §§4–17.

[79] ibid §§36–46.

[80] ibid §47.

[81] *Karataş v Turkey*, Appl No 23168/94, Judgment, 8 July 1999, §§8–15, available at: http://hudoc.echr. coe.int.

[82] ibid §§49–54.

[83] *Erkizia Almandoz v Spain*, European Court of Human Rights, No 5869/17, Judgment, 22 September 2021, §§7–12, available at: http://hudoc.echr.coe.int.

[84] ibid §45.

at the event.[85] Nonetheless, the applicant's statements were such that they did not directly or indirectly call for violence or advocated violence, hate and intolerance, despite the applicant ending his speech with 'Viva Argala'. The applicant did not condone terrorist violence; instead, he urged for public reflection geared to creating a new democratic way forward.[86] The active participation in the event as a speaker was in itself not sufficient to be considered a call for violence or glorification of terrorism.[87] Consequently, combined with the severity of the punishment, the conviction violated Article 10 ECHR.

3. INCITEMENT TO TERRORISM IN NATIONAL LEGAL SYSTEMS

The absence of a definition at the international level in Security Council Resolution 1624 (2005) gives UN Member States a certain discretion to introduce incitement to terrorism in municipal criminal law. Although in Europe there is a clear definition of incitement to terrorism in the Convention on the Prevention of Terrorism and Directive (EU) 2017/541, none of these instruments oblige states to incorporate the exact definition in their national legal systems, but require only that this behaviour is in one way or another criminalised.[88] Hence, one may expect a certain variety in how incitement to terrorism is criminalised at the European level as well. Nonetheless, the national implementation of incitement of terrorism may identify common elements of the offence, which may be useful for formulating an international definition of the crime.

3.1. China

A plethora of legal texts regulate terrorism in China.[89] With regard to incitement of terrorism, Amendment IX to the Criminal Law, which entered into force on 1 November 2015, was the first law that criminalised incitement to terrorism as a specific crime. Nonetheless, before Amendment IX entered into force, incitement to terrorism fell within the crime of forming, leading or participating in a

---

[85] ibid §46.
[86] ibid §46.
[87] ibid §47.
[88] CoE Explanatory Report §98. For an overview of the differences in transposition of Council Framework Decision 2008/919/JHA: 'Report from the Commission to the European Parliament and the Council on the Implementation of Council Framework Decision 2008/919/JHA of 28 November 2008 Amending Council Framework Decision 2002/475/JHA on Combating Terrorism', COM(2014) 0554 final, available at: http://eur-lex.europa.eu/legal-content/EN/TXT/?uri=celex:52014DC0554.
[89] Criminal Law of the People's Republic of China, available at: www.mps.gov.cn/n2254314/n2254409/n2254410/n2254417/c3701295/content.html; Amendment III to the Criminal Law, available at: www.npc.gov.cn/npc/lfzt/rlys/2008-08/21/content_1882892.htm; Decision of the Standing Committee of the National People's Congress on Strengthening Counter-Terrorism Work, available at: www.npc.gov.cn/wxzl/gongbao/2011-12/30/content_1686367.htm; Opinions of the Supreme People's Court, the Supreme People's Procuratorate and the Ministry of Public Security on Several Issues Concerning the Application of Law in Handling Criminal Cases of Violent Terrorism and Religious Extremism (Opinions), available at: www.spp.gov.cn/xwfbh/wsfbh/201409/t20140921_80671.shtml.

terrorist organisation,[90] the crime of incitement to split the state,[91] or the crime of incitement of national enmity or discrimination.[92]

In addition, the Anti-terrorism Law, which came into effect on 1 January 2016, equally addresses incitement to terrorism. Unlike Amendment IX, the Anti-terrorism Law is an administrative law,[93] which means that its main function is to build China's anti-terrorism system and to stipulate basic rules on anti-terrorism legislations from macro perspectives.[94] Articles 79 and 80 of the Anti-terrorism Law state the legal liabilities of incitement to terrorism. Anyone advocating terrorism, or inciting others to commit terrorist activities, will be investigated for criminal liabilities in accordance with the law.[95] In line with the Anti-terrorism law, Amendment IX criminalised serious instances of incitement to terrorism. Article 7c Amendment IX introduces Article 120c into the Criminal Code. This provision prohibits the 'advocating of terrorism or extremism by way of preparing or distributing books, audio and video materials or other items that advocate terrorism or extremism or by way of teaching or releasing information, etc or the inciting of terrorist activities'.[96]

The offence of incitement to terrorism includes direct incitement and indirect incitement. Direct incitement only applies to terrorist activities and not to extremist acts.[97] Both direct and indirect incitement do not have to occur in public: a secret sermon, sending books by mail or using private internet chat rooms can also be punished.[98] Concerning indirect incitement through preparing or distributing materials, both the indirect incitement of terrorism and extremism are punishable. 'Preparing' means writing, publishing, printing, copying and other similar behaviour, whereas 'releasing' covers inter alia dissemination through persons or by using mail, text, internet, communication apps, etc.[99] The scope of terrorism related materials is also very wide and can include newspapers, magazines, electronic materials, pictures, leaflets, slogans, symbols, words, costumes, souvenirs, etc, regardless of whether these materials exist on phones, a removable storage medium, an e-reader or the internet.[100] Furthermore, indirect incitement equally includes glorification and

---

[90] Art 120 Criminal Law.

[91] Art 103 Criminal Law.

[92] Art 249 Criminal Law.

[93] Zhao Bingzhi and Niu Zhongzhi, 'On Deficiencies in Coordination between Counter-Terrorism Law and Criminal Law against Terrorism' (2017) 2 *Law Science Magazine* 4.

[94] Jia Yu, *China's Anti-Terrorism Law Textbook* (Beijing, China University of Politic Science and Law Press, 2017) 12–17; Wang Aili, *The Comprehension of Anti-Terrorism Law* (Beijing, China Legal Publishing House, 2016) 311–14; Lang Sheng and Wang Aili, *The Paraphrasing of Anti-Terrorism Law* (Beijing, Law Press China, 2016) 292; Jia Yu, 'The Milestones in China's Rule of Law against Terrorism' (2016) 8 *People Rule of Law* 18.

[95] Art 79 Anti-terrorism Law.

[96] Art 120c Criminal Law (Art 7c Amendment IX).

[97] Lei Jianbin, *The Interpretation and Application of Amendment IX to Criminal Law* (Beijing, People's Court Press, 2015) 80; Shen Deyong, *The Judicial Interpretation of Amendment IX to Criminal Law* (Beijing, People's Court Press, 2015) 95.

[98] Lei (n 97) 81–82; Shen (n 97) 95.

[99] Lei (n 97) 80; Shen (n 97) 95; Zhao Bingzhi, *The Comprehension and Application of Amendment IX to Criminal Law* (Beijing, China Legal Publishing House, 2016) 119.

[100] Lei (n 97) 81–82; Shen (n 97) 95; Zhao (n 99) 120.

justification of terrorism, such as support for *jihad*.[101] The mental element in both offences is direct intent[102] so that indirect intent[103] or negligence are excluded: the perpetrator willingly incites in the awareness that the incitement will cause or may cause dangerous results.[104]

3.2. France

The crime of incitement and glorification of terrorism is penalised in Article 421-2-5 of the Criminal Code, which criminalises direct incitement to terrorist acts and the public glorification of such acts. Incitement to terrorism as well as *apologie* was originally contained in Article 24 Law of 29 July 1881, on the freedom of the press, as a form of abuse of this freedom. However, in 2014 the offence of incitement and glorification of terrorism was lifted out of this law and incorporated in the Criminal Code. The main reason for this decision is that these acts are not considered as a mere abuse of the freedom of the press or expression, but as acts at the origin of terrorist acts. Therefore, they should be prosecuted under the general rules in the Criminal Procedure Code and the special investigation methods for terrorism contained therein, which was not permitted for delicts related to the press.[105]

Incitement to terrorism in French criminal law only covers direct incitement, regardless of the effects of the incitement. The text of the provision seems to indicate that direct incitement is a criminal offence, regardless of the lack of publicity. All forms of indirect incitement fall within the scope of *apologie*, which is much broader than direct incitement; it covers all justifications of a crime that in reality constitute an indirect provocation to commit a terrorist offence.[106] However, a ministerial circular letter issued after the Charlie Hebdo shooting has defined *apologie* more broadly as 'to present or comment upon acts of terrorism with a favourable moral judgment'.[107] French case law has followed this broad meaning of the ministerial

---

[101] Lei (n 97) 78; *People's Republic of China v Yang and Lei*, Kunming Intermediate People's Court, First Instance, No 122, 2 August 2017, available at: wenshu.court.gov.cn/content/content?DocID=187ce1aa-231e-4e47-8c1d-a82a009eedca&KeyWord=%E4%B8%80%E7%99%BE%E4%BA%8C%E5%8D%81%E6%9D%A1%E4%B9%8B%E4%B8%89>.

[102] Pursuant to Art 14 Criminal Law, direct intent means the perpetrator clearly knows that his or her act will cause or may cause harmful consequences to society, but wishes such consequences to occur. See also: Gao Mingxuan and Ma Kechang, *Criminal Law Textbook* (Beijing, Peking University Press, 2016) 109–10.

[103] Pursuant to Art 14 Criminal Law, indirect intent means the perpetrator clearly knows that his or her act may cause harmful consequences to society but allows such consequences to occur. See also Gao and Ma (n 102) 110–11.

[104] Shen (n 97), 95; Zhao (n 99) 119–20.

[105] Assemblée Nationale, 'Projet de Loi no 2110 renforçant les dispositions relatives à la lutte contre le terrorisme' (2014), 6, available at: www.assemblee-nationale.fr/14/pdf/projets/pl2110.pdf; Assemblée Nationale, 'Projet de Loi renforçant les dispositions relatives à la lutte contre le terrorisme, Etude d'impact' (2014), 10–11, available at: www.assemblee-nationale.fr/14/pdf/projets/pl2110-ei.pdf ('Etude d'impact').

[106] Etude d'impact, 43.

[107] Ministère de Justice, 'Principales qualifications susceptibles d'être retenues en matières de racisme, de discrimination, de provocation au terrorisme et d'apologie du terrorisme' (2015), available at: www.justice.gouv.fr/publication/circ_20150113_infractions_commises_suite_attentats201510002055.pdf.

circular letter. Equating victims of terrorism in the Charlie Hebdo attack with the killed perpetrators of that attack constitutes *apologie*.[108] A T-shirt worn by a child named Jihad, born on 11 September 2009, with, on the one side, 'Jihad, born on 11 September' and, on the other side, 'I am a bomb' was equally considered an act of *apologie*.[109] Similarly, calling a terrorist 'courageous', although not supporting the terrorist acts itself, is sufficient to be considered *apologie*.[110] Nonetheless, French law requires an expression of a favourable moral judgment: stating that one is a member of a terrorist organisation and threatening to commit terrorist acts does not amount to *apologie*.[111]

Article 421-2-5 of the Criminal Code includes private and public incitement in order to bring incitement in restricted internet forums within its scope of application, but only public *apologie* is criminalised.[112] The notion of 'public' is very wide: expressions of *apologie* in a loud voice during circumstances which demonstrate an intention to make them public is sufficient.[113] Shouting support for terrorism during a prisoner transport and in the court jail, with only police officers present, satisfies the requirement of public *apologie*.[114] Moreover, wearing a T-shirt glorifying terrorist attacks underneath clothes in a public space suffices.[115] French law does not require that the direct incitement and *apologie* have created a danger, which makes French law significantly broader than incitement to terrorism in the Convention on the Prevention of Terrorism and Directive (EU) 2017/541. Concerning the required *mens rea*, incitement requires that one incites another person to commit a specific crime, in other words, the incited behaviour must contain the constituent elements of a crime.[116] Thus, incitement of terrorism requires that the person has the intention to incite others to commit a terrorist offence. For *apologie* of terrorism no special intent is required: the mere fact that one intentionally justifies a terrorist attack publicly is sufficient, even if one does not have the purpose to actually glorify terrorist acts.[117] French law has therefore a broad definition of *apologie* of terrorism that has been challenged before the Conseil constitutionnel, the French constitutional court. Nonetheless, that Court has upheld the constitutionality of the crime and considers the crime compatible with human rights law.[118]

---

[108] Cour de cassation, Chambre criminelle, Judgment, 25 April 2017, No 16-83.331.

[109] Cour de cassation, Chambre criminelle, Judgment, 17 March 2015, No 13-87.358.

[110] Cour de cassation, Chambre criminelle, Judgment, 27 November 2018, No 17-83.602.

[111] Cour de cassation, Chamber criminelle, Judgment, 4 June 2019, No 18-85.042.

[112] Assemblée Nationale, 'Rapport fait au nom de la commission des lois constitutionelles, de la législation et de l'administration générale de la République sur le projet de loi (no 2110), renforçant les dispositions relatives à la lutte contre le terrorisme, no 2173 (2014), 25, available at: www.assemblee-nationale.fr/14/pdf/rapports/r2173.pdf.

[113] Cour de cassation, Chambre criminelle, Judgment, 11 July 2017, No 16-86.965.

[114] ibid.

[115] Cour de cassation, Chambre criminelle, Judgment, 17 March 2015, No 13-87.358.

[116] Etude d'impact, 43.

[117] Cour de cassation, Chambre criminelle, Judgment, 25 April 2017, No 16-83.331.

[118] Conseil constitutionnel, Decision of 19 June 2020, No 2020-845 QPC, available at: www.conseil-constitutionnel.fr/decision/2020/2020845QPC.htm.

3.3. Spain

Article 18 of the Criminal Code generally criminalises provocation, defined as the direct incitement to perpetrate an offence through means of the press, radio or any other similar means of effective communication, or before a group of persons. The same article defines *apologie* as the expression of ideas or doctrines that extol crimes or glorify the perpetrators thereof in front of a group of individuals or through any means of communication. However, *apologie* in Article 18 is only criminalised as a form of provocation and if its nature or its circumstances amount to direct incitement.[119] Provocation is only punishable if Spanish criminal law expressly provides that provocation of a certain crime is punishable.[120]

Article 579(1) of the Criminal Code criminalises the public dissemination of messages or slogans that are aimed to, or that, by their content, are suitable to, incite others to the commission of terrorist offences. Article 579(3) of the Criminal Code criminalises other forms of incitement. Incitement of terrorism in Article 579 of the Criminal Code is considered as a preparatory act to terrorism.[121] It must be public and direct; that is, incitement to commit a specific terrorist crime.[122] Since in Article 579 of the Criminal Code incitement is a preparatory act and must be aimed at the commission of terrorist offences, the perpetrator must have the special intent to incite others to commit a terrorist offence. This implies that the inciter must have the intent required for terrorist offences. If the provocation leads to the commission of the criminal offence, the person who has provoked will be prosecuted as instigator[123] and punished as principal perpetrator.[124]

Article 578(1) of the Criminal Code criminalises *apologie* of terrorist offences more generally, beyond the scope of Article 18 of the Criminal Code.[125] This provision prohibits any glorification or justification, through any form of public information or communication, of terrorist offences, or of perpetrators of terrorist offences, or the commission of acts tending to discredit, demean or humiliate the victims of terrorist offences or their families. The offence of Article 578(1) of the Criminal Code contains in effect two crimes: the glorification or justification of terrorist offences and the perpetrators thereof, and the humiliation of victims of terrorist offences or their families.[126] The former has the purpose to protect society against the risk

---

[119] Tribunal Supremo, Salo de lo Penal, Recurso No 10071/2017, Sentencia, 5 July 2017, 38, available at: www.poderjudicial.es/search/index.jsp; J Bernal del Castillo, 'Enaltecimiento del Terrorismo y la Humillación a Sus Víctimas como Formas del Discurso del Odio' (2016) 16 *Revista de Derecho Penal y Criminología* 18.

[120] Art 18(2) Criminal Code.

[121] Bernal del Castillo (n 119) 36.

[122] Tribunal Supremo (n 119) 38.

[123] Art 18(2) Criminal Code.

[124] Art 28 Criminal Code; Report of Spain on the Implementation of Security Council Resolution 1624 (2005) on Further Measures to Combat Terrorism, UN Doc S/2007/164 (2007) 2.

[125] Tribunal Supremo (n 119) 37–38.

[126] Report of Spain on the Implementation of Security Council Resolution 1624 (2005) on Further Measures to Combat Terrorism, UN Doc S/2007/164 (2007) 3.

of the commission of terrorist offences, whereas the latter protects the victims of terrorist acts against humiliation, regardless of any risk.[127] Therefore, the latter crime is not relevant in the context of incitement to terrorism. Article 578(1) does not require that the justification or glorification amounts to direct incitement to commit terrorist offences, in which case the justification or glorification would fall under Article 579(1) of the Criminal Code, but prohibits generally the glorification or justification of terrorist offences and their perpetrators.[128] Consequently, the justification or glorification of terrorist offences or terrorists is not a terrorist offence in itself.[129] Nonetheless, the crime requires that glorification must amount to an indirect incitement to violence by creating a climate of hostility and hatred.[130]

Concerning the objective elements of the crime, first, the offence consists of actions or words that glorify or justify. To glorify is to extol or praise, to praise the qualities or merits of someone or something; to justify implies that clearly criminal behaviour is made to appear as lawful and legitimate. Second, the object of glorification or justification is either a terrorist offence contained in Articles 571–577 of the Criminal Code or anyone who has participated in the execution of those offences. It is not necessary to identify one or several such persons specifically, but it suffices that one praises a collective of authors. Third, the glorification or justification has to be carried out by any means of expression or dissemination, such as a newspaper or a public act addressed to a large audience.[131] The case law of the Constitutional Court has added an element of risk to the crime in line with the requirements under constitutional law, human rights law and EU law. Accordingly, an additional element is the risk for persons or rights of third parties or for the system of liberties.[132] When examining whether this risk has materialised, the specific circumstances of the case must be taken into account, such as the author and the recipient of the message, as well as the context in which the act was committed. The importance and credibility of the risk should also be considered.[133] Furthermore, the Tribunal Supremo equally considers the danger that terrorist acts may be committed.[134] With regard to the subjective element, the perpetrator must intend and have knowledge of the dissemination of a message that carries a glorification or justification of terrorist offences or of their perpetrators.[135]

---

[127] Tribunal Supremo, Salo de lo Penal, Recurso No 46/2017, Sentencia, 25 July 2017, 3, available at: www.poderjudicial.es/search/index.jsp; Tribunal Supremo, Salo de lo Penal, Recurso No 1619/2019, Sentencia, 17 February 2021, 19, available at: www.poderjudicial.es/search/index.jsp.

[128] Tribunal Supremo, Salo de lo Penal, Recurso No 46/2017, Sentencia, 25 July 2017, 3.

[129] ibid 3; Tribunal Supremo (n 119) 37–38.

[130] Tribunal Supremo, Salo de lo Penal, Recurso No 3434/2019, Sentencia, 16 July 2021, 39, available at: www.poderjudicial.es/search/index.jsp.

[131] Tribunal Supremo (n 119) 37; Tribunal Supremo, Salo de lo Penal, Recurso No 46/2017, Sentencia, 25 July 2017, 3, available at: www.poderjudicial.es/search/index.jsp.

[132] Tribunal Constitucional, Sentencia 112/2016, 28 July 2016, §§II.3–II.4, available at: hj.tribunalconstitucional.es/en/Resolucion/Show/25026.

[133] Tribunal Supremo, Salo de lo Penal, Recurso No 8/2017, Sentencia, 25 May 2017, 6, available at: www.poderjudicial.es/search/index.jsp.

[134] ibid; Tribunal Supremo, Salo de lo Penal, Recurso No 46/2017, 5, available at: www.poderjudicial.es/search/index.jsp.

[135] Tribunal Supremo, Salo de lo Penal, Recurso No 1619/2016, 6, available at: www.poderjudicial.es/search/index.jsp; Tribunal Supremo, Salo de lo Penal, Recurso No 1998/2016, 29 March 2017, 10, available at: www.poderjudicial.es/search/index.jsp.

3.4. United Kingdom

To implement Security Council Resolution 1624 (2005), the UK Parliament rapidly adopted the Terrorism Act (2006). Section 1 introduced the offence of encouragement to terrorism. Although other provisions have been relied upon to punish the spreading of terrorist propaganda,[136] section 1 of the Terrorism Act 2006 introduced the offence of encouragement to terrorism as a specific offence. After the Terrorist Act 2006, the definitions of terrorist offences[137] and terrorism-related acts[138] all contain the offence of encouragement to terrorism and the offence of dissemination of terrorist publications has been used to combat dissemination of publications that incite, justify or glorify terrorism.[139]

According to the original version of section 1(1) of the Terrorism Act 2006, incitement to terrorism refers to any 'statement that is likely to be understood by some or all of the members of the public to whom it is published as a direct or indirect encouragement or other inducement to them to the commission, preparation or instigation of acts of terrorism or Convention offences'.[140] The Counter-Terrorism and Border Security Act (2019) amended the provision for further clarity. Accordingly, the statement is likely to be understood 'by a reasonable person' as a direct or indirect encouragement or other inducement 'to some or all of the members of the public to whom it is published'.

The material element of the crime consists in the publishing of statements. Publishing consists in publishing a statement in any manner to the public; providing electronically any service by means of which the public have access to the statement; or using a service provided to him electronically by another so as to enable or to facilitate access by the public to the statement.[141] Thus, publishing does not only cover the persons making the statement, but equally internet service providers and persons running websites with fora and message boards.[142] A statement is 'a communication of any description, including a communication without words consisting of sounds or images or both'.[143] The statement must be made to members of the public; if the statement is made at a meeting, the meeting must be open to the public at large.[144] Private conversations are therefore excluded from the scope of the offence.[145]

---

[136] In particular, ss 12, 57 and 58 Terrorism Act 2000; s 2 Terrorism Act 2006. For a brief discussion, see C Walker, 'The War of Words with Terrorism: An Assessment of Three Approaches to Pursue and Prevent' (2017) 22 *Journal of Conflict and Security Law* 529–34.

[137] S 27(1)(d) Counter-Terrorism Act 2008.

[138] Such as conduct which gives encouragement to the commission, preparation or instigation of such acts: s 4(1)(c) Terrorism Prevention and Investigation Measures Act 2011; Schedule 1, s 1(1)(10)(c) Counter-Terrorism and Security Act 2015.

[139] For instance: *R v Brown* [2011] EWCA Crim 2751; *Ahmed Faraz v R* [2012] EWCA Crim 2820; *R v Gul* [2012] EWCA Crim 280; *R v Khan* [2015] EWCA Crim 1341.

[140] 'Convention offences' refer to specified offences in Schedule 1 or equivalent offences under the law of a country or territory outside the UK: s 20(2) Terrorism Act 2006.

[141] S 20(4) Terrorism Act 2006.

[142] A Hunt, 'Criminal Prohibitions on Direct and Indirect Encouragement of Terrorism' (2007) *Criminal Law Review* 444.

[143] S 20(6) Terrorism Act 2006.

[144] S 20(3) Terrorism Act 2006.

[145] C Walker, *Terrorism and the Law* (Oxford, Oxford University Press, 2011) 365; Hunt (n 142) 443.

Nonetheless, it is not required that a majority of the members of the public would be likely incited: 'some' members of the public who receive the message are sufficient, which ranges from one to all members.[146] Whether the statement is likely to be understood as encouragement depends on the content of the statement as a whole and the circumstances and manner of its publication.[147] UK criminal law does not require that the encouragement created a danger that an act of terrorism would be committed.[148] The mental element of the crime is very broad: the perpetrator either intends members of the public to be directly or indirectly encouraged or otherwise induced by the statement to commit, prepare or instigate acts of terrorism, or the perpetrator is reckless in making statements to this effect.[149] Recklessness requires that the defendant 'had knowledge of a serious and obvious risk that a publication will have the effect of encouraging, directly or indirectly, the commission of terrorist offences' and 'in the circumstances known to him, it was unreasonable for him to take that risk'.[150] However, in case of recklessness, the defendant may demonstrate that the published statement did not express his views or have his endorsement and that it was clear in the circumstances that the statement did not express his views or have his endorsement.[151]

Section 1(1) of the Terrorism Act 2006 covers both direct and indirect encouragement. Although the Act does not define indirect encouragement, section 1(3) states that it includes glorification of terrorism, which is partially defined as including 'praise or celebration' in section 20(2). Section 1(3), however, clarifies that glorification needs to be such that members of the public could reasonably be expected to infer that what is being glorified is being glorified as conduct that should be emulated by them in existing circumstances. Unlike Section (1)(1) and other forms of indirect incitement, this is an objective assessment and does not require that an audience actually believes there is glorification.[152] The requirement of emulation in the existing circumstances excludes the glorification of historic acts of terrorism, since these acts are unlikely to lead people to commit terrorist acts.[153] Other acts of indirect incitement, any incitement that has no explicit stimulus, do not require any emulation.[154] Nonetheless, the statement itself, although indirect, must still consist in an incitement so that statements which merely have encouraging effects do not fall within the scope of section 1.[155] Thus, indirect incitement must at least implicitly incite others

---

[146] S 1(1) Terrorist Act 2006; Walker (n 145) 366.

[147] S 1(4) Terrorism Act 2006.

[148] House of Lords & House of Commons, Joint Committee on Human Rights, 'Third Report of Session 2005–06, Counter-Terrorism Policy and Human Rights: Terrorism Bill and Related Matters', HL Paper 75-I/HC 561-I, §34.

[149] S 1(2)(b) Terrorism Act (2006).

[150] *Ahmed Faraz v R* [2012] EWCA Crim 2820, §49; Home Office, *The Terrorism Act 2006*, available at: www.gov.uk/government/publications/the-terrorism-act-2006.

[151] S 1(6) Terrorism Act 2006.

[152] Walker (n 145) 367; J Keiler, 'Terrorist Speech and the Criminal Law – A Comparative Analysis' (2017) 25 *European Journal of Crime, Criminal Law and Criminal Justice* 243.

[153] Home Office (n 150).

[154] Walker (n 145) 368.

[155] Hunt (n 142) 452–53.

to commit acts of terrorism.[156] This is in line with common law which, despite not recognising indirect incitement, has on occasion interpreted encouragement widely.[157] For instance, in *Marlow* the Court of Appeals held that a book that explained how to grow cannabis without encouraging the commitment of the unlawful act constituted encouragement to commit the crime.[158] Similarly, an advertisement for a device that detected police scanners was regarded as an encouragement to commit the crime of excessive speeding.[159] Thus, the broad notion of encouragement may cover indirect incitement which does not amount to glorification, as long as the encouragement consists of words or actions that amount to positive steps aimed at inciting another to commit a crime.[160] In any event, merely showing understanding or explaining terrorist acts would not constitute indirect encouragement.[161]

3.5. United States of America

In the United States the strong protection of freedom of expression in the First Amendment to the Constitution limits the criminalisation of incitement to terrorist acts. In the seminal case of *Brandenburg v Ohio* the Supreme Court stated that 'the constitutional guarantees of free speech and free press do not permit a State to forbid or proscribe advocacy of the use of force or of law violation, except where such advocacy is directed to inciting or producing imminent lawless actions and is likely to incite or produce that action'.[162] This case led to the result that most terrorism glorification or justification cannot be prosecuted under US criminal law. Incitement can only be prosecuted when the speaker intended to incite imminent unlawful action; the speech must be likely to be successful; and the law violation must likely be imminent.[163] Incitement is imminent if the incitement could lead to immediate unlawful action: incitement to unlawful conduct at an undetermined time later in a day or a couple of days or weeks later is therefore beyond the scope of *Brandenburg v Ohio*.[164] Consequently, it is virtually impossible for written incitement to meet the strict *Brandenburg* standard of imminence.[165] This implies that almost all online incitement cannot be prosecuted, since there may be a significant passage of time between the posting and the observing of the message and since advocacy by terrorist

---

[156] ibid 453–54.
[157] Walker (n 145) 368.
[158] *R v Marlow* [1997] EWCA Crim 1833.
[159] *Invicta Plastics Ltd v Clare* [1976] Crim LR 131.
[160] *R v Marlow* [1997] EWCA Crim 1833; Hunt (n 142) 454–55.
[161] D McKeefer, 'The Human Rights Act and Anti-Terrorism in the UK: One Great Leap Forward by Parliament, but Are the Courts Able to Slow the Steady Retreat that has followed?' [January 2018] *Public Law* 128.
[162] *Brandenburg v Ohio*, 447 US 444 (1969) ('*Brandenburg*').
[163] AK Chen, 'Free Speech and the Confluence of National Security and Internet Exceptionalism' (2017–18) 86 *Fordham Law Review* 384.
[164] *Hess v Indiana*, 414 US 105, 106–09 (1973); *NAACP v Claiborne Hardware Co*, 458 US 886, 928 (1982); but see *People v Rubin*, 158 Cal Rptr 488, 493 (Cal Ct App 1979); *US v Timimi* (1:04cr385, 2005).
[165] M Buchhandler-Raphael, 'Overcriminalizing Speech' (2014–15) 36 *Cardozo Law Review* 1685.

groups is focused more on long-term indoctrination.[166] With regard to the second condition, the likelihood that the advocacy incites or produces unlawful conduct, the Supreme Court has not detailed this standard. Doctrine has advanced that the standard is similar to the probable cause standard, which means a substantial chance or fair probability.[167] It is equally unclear whether the *Brandenburg* test covers both public and private incitement.[168] The facts of the case, the recording of a Ku Klux Klan meeting at a farm with only a small group of KKK members present,[169] indicate that the *Brandenburg* standard does not only apply to advocacy of violence before a large audience. In any event, the case law suggests almost no room for prohibitions on speech which justifies terrorist acts or organisations, let alone of incitement to terrorism, or glorification of terrorism.[170] The United States therefore did not enact legislation to respond to the call in Security Council Resolution 1624 to criminalise incitement to terrorism.[171] However, in practice, there are alternatives to punish incitement to terrorism.

One alternative is to prosecute the inciters for conspiracy or another similar offence. The *Brandenburg* test does not apply to threats, solicitation, criminal instructions and conspiracy, which do not benefit from First Amendment protection.[172] Although threats, solicitation, criminal instructions and conspiracy are conceptually different from incitement, the dividing line is not always clear. In the case of *US v Rahman*, Sheik Omar Ahmad Ali Abdel Rahman was found to be a leader of a conspiracy.[173] He referred to the spring 1993 bombing campaign as a 'must' and a 'duty', and advised the members of the conspiracy to seek 'a target (US military installations) for the bombings, and to plan for them carefully'.[174] Furthermore, he frequently contacted the members of the conspiracy which led to the World Trade Center bombing.[175] In the end, the District Court convicted him for attempting to bomb the World Trade Center and to assassinate persons on the basis of 18 USC Section 2384 (Seditious Conspiracy).[176] The Court of Appeals rejected the First Amendment challenge of Rahman, which, he argued, was based on his political and religious beliefs, whereas seditious conspiracy involves a conspiracy to use force, not merely to advocate the use of force. The Court nonetheless found that Rahman's statement amounted to conspiracy to use force and solicitation and confirmed Rahman's conviction.[177] With regard to threats, if the incitement amounts to a 'true threat'

---

[166] Chen (n 163) 395.

[167] T Healey, 'Brandenburg in Times of Terror' (2009) 84 *Notre Dame Law Review* 714–15; Buchhandler-Raphael (n 165) 1727.

[168] Pro inclusion of private incitement: Healey (n 167) 722–26. Contra inclusion of private incitement: RS Tanenbaum, 'Preaching Terror: Free Speech or Wartime Incitement?' (2006) 55 *American University Law Review* 815–19.

[169] *Brandenburg* 445–47.

[170] Barak-Erez and Scharia (n 2) 16.

[171] K Roach, *The 9/11 Effect: Comparative Counter-Terrorism* (Cambridge, Cambridge University Press, 2009) 227.

[172] Healey (n 167) 669. For threats, see: *NAACP v Claiborne Hardware Co*, 458 US 886, 916 (1982).

[173] *US v Rahman*, 189 F3d 88, 125 (2nd Circuit, 1999).

[174] ibid 124–25.

[175] ibid 123–24.

[176] ibid 114–15.

[177] ibid.

and is not regarded as 'political hyperbole',[178] the *Brandenburg* test equally does not apply. True threats are '[t]hose statements where the speaker means to communicate a serious expression of an intent to commit an act of unlawful violence to a particular individual or group of individuals'.[179] For instance, the online publishing of photographs and information of individuals with implicit or explicit calls for violence against those individuals amounts to true threats and therefore falls outside the scope of protection of speech by the First Amendment.[180]

A second alternative is criminalising advocacy that amounts to 'material support'[181] of recognised foreign terrorist groups. In *Holder v Humanitarian Law Project* the Supreme Court held that the federal law prohibiting material support is constitutional, even if it limits speech. The Humanitarian Law Project intended to provide training to designated terrorist groups in how law can be used to peacefully settle disputes. The Supreme Court stated that the provision is not unconstitutional since only speech 'under the direction of, or in coordination with foreign groups that the speaker knows to be terrorist organizations', will amount to material support.[182] In addition, the element of 'in coordination with terrorist organizations' does not require a direct connection: the online posting of English translation of al Qaeda materials and travelling abroad to join a terrorist training camp, even unsuccessfully, fell within the scope of prohibited material support.[183] Advocacy not under the direction of or in coordination with terrorist organisations therefore remains protected under the *Brandenburg* test. However, advocacy, incitement and glorification guided and coordinated with the designated terrorist group will be prohibited.[184]

4. TOWARDS AN INTERNATIONALLY ACCEPTED DEFINITION OF INCITEMENT TO TERRORISM?

Section 3 demonstrated that between states a significant diversity of approaches exists in how incitement to terrorism is criminalised. Consequently, a definition of this offence at the international level is not a sinecure. The European definition of the crime may be used as a starting point, but the definition is broad, which is counterbalanced by the context of a robust human rights protection by the European Court of Human Rights, a context that is absent globally. Therefore, the broad European definition of incitement to terrorism may not be suitable beyond the European context.

---

[178] *Watts v United States*, 394 US 705, 707–08 (1969).

[179] *Virginia v Black*, 538 US 343, 359 (2003).

[180] *Planned Parenthood of Columbia/Willamette, Inc v American Coalition of Life Activists*, 244 F3d 1007 (9th Cir 2001), rev'd en banc, 290 F3d 1058 (9th Cir 2002); *United States v Fullmer*, 584 F3d 132 (2009); *United States v Turner*, 720 F3d 411 (2013).

[181] 18 US Code s 2339B(a)(1).

[182] *Holder v Humanitarian Law Project*, 561 US 1, 21 (2010).

[183] *United States v Mehanna*, 735 F3d 32, 49–50 (1st Cir, 2013).

[184] O Fiss, 'The World We Live In' (2010–11) 83 *Temple Law Review* 296; A Tsesis, 'Terrorist Speech on Social Media' (2017) 70 *Vanderbilt Law Review* 673–74; L Zachary, 'Terror on Your Timeline: Criminalizing Terrorist Incitement on Social Media through Doctrinal Shift' (2017–18) 86 *Fordham Law Review* 814. But see DS Han, 'Terrorist Advocacy and Exceptional Circumstances' (2017–18) 86 *Fordham Law Review* 505–06.

It was precisely to guarantee freedom of expression that the Special Rapporteur on the Promotion and Protection of Human Rights and Fundamental Freedoms While Countering Terrorism opted to replace the words 'whether or not directly advocating terrorism' with 'whether or not expressly advocating terrorism'.[185]

A proposed definition of the offence of incitement to terrorism could find inspiration in other crimes of incitement. Unfortunately, incitement to an international crime is rarely punishable as an autonomous crime, so that analogies are hard to make. There is, however, one exception of an autonomous crime of incitement, namely incitement to genocide. Both incitement to genocide and incitement to terrorism have similarities in that both are necessary prerequisites to the mobilisation of perpetrators to commit genocide or terrorist acts by dehumanising the targeted group,[186] and therefore deserve to be criminalised in similar fashion. The prohibition of incitement to genocide is laid down in Article III(c) of the Convention on the Prevention and Punishment of the Crime of Genocide (Genocide Convention), as an autonomous infraction.[187] The crime is an inchoate offence, with the following elements: the incitement has to be direct, public, intentional and committed with the special intent of destroying in whole or in part a national, racial, ethnic or religious group as such.[188] Incitement to genocide was indirectly prosecuted at Nuremberg[189] and has been applied by the ICTR, which has offered some clarification on the elements and scope of the offence. The definition of incitement to terrorism in the European Convention on the Prevention of Terrorism and in Directive (EU) 2017/541 equally contains the elements of directness, public nature and special intent. It adds the requirement of danger that the incited act may occur.

4.1. Direct and Indirect Incitement

The most controversial aspect of incitement to terrorism is whether the incitement should be limited to direct incitement since the inclusion of indirect incitement may raise concerns on the protection of freedom of expression. Because of this concern, especially in the United States, incitement to genocide was limited to

---

[185] Special Rapporteur on Counter-Terrorism and Human Rights (n 8) §30.

[186] UN Secretary-General Kofi Annan, 'Uniting against Terrorism: Recommendations for a Global Counter-terrorism Strategy', UN Doc A/60/825 (2006) §§22–23; Ronen (n 3) 655–56.

[187] Incitement to genocide was also included in the Rome Statute of the International Criminal Court, but only as a form of individual criminal responsibility, specific to the crime of genocide: Art 25(3)(e) Rome Statute of the International Criminal Court.

[188] Art III(c) Genocide Convention; *Prosecutor v Bikindi*, ICTR-01-72-T, Judgment, 2 December 2008, §419, available at: www.unictr.org/en/cases/ictr-01-72 ('*Bikindi* (Trial Chamber)'); *Nahimana et al v Prosecutor*, ICTR-99-52-A, Judgment, 28 November 2007, §§677–78, available at: www.unictr.org/en/cases/ictr-99-52 (*Nahimana* (Appeals Chamber)); *Prosecutor v Kajelijeli*, ICTR-98-44A-T, Judgment and Sentence, 1 December 2003, §§850–55, available at: www.unictr.org/en/cases/ictr-98-44a (*Kajelijeli* (Trial Chamber)); *Prosecutor v Akayesu*, ICTR-96-4-T, Judgment, 2 September 1998, §§560–62, available at: www.unictr.org/en/cases/ictr-96-4 (*Akayesu* (Trial Chamber)).

[189] Julius Streicher was convicted for incitement to murder and extermination of Jews under the crime against humanity of persecution on political and racial grounds in connection with war crimes: Judgment of the International Military Tribunal (1946), 22 *Nuremberg Trial Proceedings* 549.

direct incitement.[190] In the context of incitement to genocide, direct incitement has been described as 'specifically urging another individual to take immediate action rather than merely making a vague or indirect suggestion'.[191] The ICTR has refused to bring indirect incitement, such as hate speech against certain groups, under the scope of incitement to genocide, even though it recognised that such speech contributes to a climate in which genocide eventually may occur.[192] As a result, it may be argued that at the international level only direct incitement to terrorism should be criminalised. This is in line with Security Council Resolution 1624 (2005),[193] and the opinion of the UN Secretary-General and the Special Rapporteur on the Promotion and Protection of Human Rights and Fundamental Freedoms While Countering Terrorism.[194] The limitation to direct incitement also offers a better guarantee in protecting the human right of freedom of expression and would therefore be acceptable to states with a tradition of strong commitment to freedom of expression, such as the United States. On the other hand, the restriction of the offence of incitement to genocide to direct incitement does not entail that indirect incitement is not punishable pursuant to other human rights conventions.[195] Similarly, indirect incitement to terrorism may as well deserve criminalisation in particular because it creates an environment for radicalisation and acceptance of terrorism as a justified means to achieve certain goals. Various examined states have therefore not hesitated to include indirect incitement to terrorism in their national criminal legislation. Furthermore, the European Court of Human Rights does not consider that convictions for indirect incitement of terrorism necessarily violate the right of freedom of expression.[196]

A solution to the conundrum of indirect incitement may well be found in the content of the speech. Incitement is often not explicit, but couched in euphemisms. The experience of the ICTR has demonstrated that implicit language may well amount to direct incitement to genocide. Whether incitement is direct depends on the cultural and linguistic content, the affiliation of the author, the circumstances, and the understanding of the audience.[197] Poetic language is not excluded either, provided it is unambiguous enough to amount to indirect incitement.[198] A similar approach is adopted by the European Court of Human Rights, which will not only look into the language used, but also whether the language may incite to violence considering

---

[190] WA Schabas, *Genocide in International Law: The Crime of Crimes* (Cambridge, Cambridge University Press, 2009) 319–24.

[191] Report of the International Law Commission on the Work of Its Forty-Eighth Session, 6 May–26 July 1996, (1996) II(2) *Yearbook of the International Law Commission* 22 ('YILC 1996'); *Akayesu* (Trial Chamber) §557.

[192] *Bikindi* (Trial Chamber) §388; *Nahimana* (Appeals Chamber) §§692–93.

[193] See the discussion in s 2.1.1.

[194] UN Secretary-General (n 10) §61; Special Rapporteur on Counter-Terrorism and Human Rights (n 8), §30. See also Counter-terrorism Committee Executive Directorate (n 4) §19.

[195] Art 20 ICCPR; Art 4 International Convention on the Elimination of Racial Discrimination.

[196] In particular, *Leroy* §§36–46.

[197] *Bikindi* (Trial Chamber) §387; *Nahimana* (Appeals Chamber) §701; *Kajelijeli* (Trial Chamber) §853; *Akayesu* (Trial Chamber) §§557–58.

[198] *Bikindi* (Trial Chamber) §421.

the context in which it is made, which includes the location and the passage of time between the crime and the justification or glorification.[199] It equally has examined artistic expressions, which were not excluded per se.[200] Consequently, justification and glorification of terrorism may well amount to direct incitement in light of the context in which they were made and if the intended audience understands that the justification and glorification is a call to action. If justification and glorification do not have such characteristics it is proposed to exclude them from the scope of the future international definition of the offence of incitement to terrorism in order to safeguard the right of freedom of expression against overzealous prosecutions, which have often led to stiff penalties.

4.2. Public Character

What makes public incitement dangerous is that it advocates violence to a large audience, making it more likely that one person will respond to the call; it may equally lead to mob violence.[201] Public incitement has been defined as 'communicating the call for criminal action to a number of individuals in a public place or to members of the general public at large'.[202] This does not require that the inciter is present in the public place, since public incitement can well take place through media, such as newspapers, television and radio.[203] To determine the public character of the incitement, the ICTR considers whether the incitement occurred in a public place and whether or not it was selective or limited.[204] Similarly, incitement to terrorism has to be public, at least according to the definition in the European Convention on the Prevention on Terrorism and Directive (EU) 2017/541. This means that it must be directed at a general audience and not a specific and limited audience and that the place where the speech is made must be accessible by the public at large.[205] Since incitement to terrorism is frequently done through the internet, the question arises when the use of internet and social media is public. According to the explanatory report to the Convention, the dissemination of messages through email or statements made in chatrooms would be considered as being made in public.[206] This is, however, not as clear-cut as the explanatory report seems to pretend. Not all messages online or through social media are made to the public at large since chatrooms are not always open to all and messages on social media are mostly only accessible to a large group of persons who are accepted by the inciter as part of his or her social network. For instance, a Spanish court accepted that messages on an open Facebook profile, and Twitter messages which were not restricted to certain users but accessible to all users,

---

[199] *Zana* §59; *Sürek* §62; *Leroy* §45; *Perinçek* §234.
[200] See *Karataş* §§49–54.
[201] YILC 1996, 22.
[202] ibid.
[203] ibid.
[204] *Akayesu* (Trial Chamber) §556.
[205] Ronen (n 3) 667.
[206] CoE Explanatory Report §104.

were made in public.[207] Had the message not been, the outcome would likely have been different. Furthermore, China and France have precisely criminalised not only public incitement, but equally private incitement as to include private messages in chatrooms. Therefore, it is highly doubtful that direct and public incitement to terrorism would cover closed online forums and restricted social networks.

4.3. Intent

Concerning incitement to genocide, the inciter must have genocidal intent, which will often flow from the content of the statement itself or the context in which the statements were made.[208] The reason for this is simple: the inciter aims to create a state of mind in the persons who are incited that they have to kill persons because they belong to a national, racial, ethnic or religious group as such. Similarly, the European definition requires a specific *mens rea*, namely the intent to incite the commission of a terrorist offence, which entails that he or she needs to have the intent required for a terrorist offence. Consequently, the inciter wilfully aims to spread fear and intimidation through inciting others to commit terrorist acts.[209] Of the examined jurisdictions that have criminalised incitement to terrorism, France and Spain follow the European definition for provocation; the United Kingdom equally requires that the inciter intends to induce the commission of terrorist acts, but adds recklessness. China prescribes a direct intent for incitement, which requires that the inciter intends to see the consequences realised.

4.4. Causal Link

Incitement to genocide, as an inchoate offence, does not require that the incitement causes the genocidal act to occur or that it may in all probability lead to such an act, mainly because the drafters considered incitement to genocide as such a great harm that no risk should be taken.[210] For incitement to terrorism on the other hand, there must be a potential that the harm will occur, which is in line with the European Court of Human Rights case law on the issue.[211] In this regard, both the European Convention on the Prevention of Terrorism and Directive (EU) 2017/541 state that the incitement causes a danger that a terrorist act may be committed. Nonetheless, China, France and the United Kingdom do not require any risk for direct or indirect incitement. Spain does not require any element of risk for direct incitement, but does introduce risk for glorification of terrorism.

---

[207] Audiencia Nacional, Sala de lo Penal, Sentencia No 14/2015, 25 May 2015, SAN 1906/2015, available at: www.poderjudicial.es/search/indexAN.jsp; Audiencia Nacional, Sala de lo Penal, Sentencia No 30/2015, July 2015, SAN 2810/2015, available at www.poderjudicial.es/search/indexAN.jsp.
[208] *Bikindi* (Trial Chamber) §§419–20; *Nahimana* (Appeals Chamber) §677; *Akayesu* (Trial Chamber) §560.
[209] Van Ginkel (n 2) 14; Ronen (n 3) 669.
[210] *Akayesu* (Trial Chamber) §562; *Nahimana et al.*, ICTR-99-52-T, Judgment, 3 December 2003, §1013.
[211] CoE Explanatory Report §100.

The UN Secretary-General has advanced a more rigorous requirement, namely that freedom of speech may be restricted if the speech is 'directly causally responsible for increasing the actual likelihood of a terrorist act occurring' or, in a criminal context, is 'likely to result in a criminal action'.[212] Whereas the standard of the European definition is in line with the case law of the European Court of Human Rights, the European Court never intended to create a strict probability test. In determining the significance of the danger, it takes into account the author and the addressee of the message, and the context in which the offence is committed.[213] Although this standard may be suitable in a human rights context, it is too open-ended and too broad in a criminal context since almost any incitement may, depending on the circumstances, lead to a danger that the incited act may occur. Furthermore, states that attach a great importance to freedom of speech would not be able to accept this requirement. For instance, the United States adopts the strictest standard of risk: incitement is only prohibited if it incites to 'imminent lawless action and is likely to incite or produce such action'.[214] Similar standards have been advanced at the international level as well.[215] The requirements of imminence and likelihood are more objective and therefore more predictable, and at the same time eliminate statements which, although inciting to terrorism, would be unlikely to cause any harm to occur in the circumstances they were made.

5. CONCLUSION

The call of the Security Council to criminalise incitement to terrorism has in the absence of a clear definition led to different descriptions of the crime at the national level. Even in Europe, where an influential definition has been laid down in the Convention on the Prevention of Terrorism and Directive (EU) 2017/541, differences continue to exist. This chapter therefore inquired into a possible definition of the crime at the international level, taking into account human rights law and drawing inspiration from the crime of incitement to genocide. Although a prohibition of incitement to terrorism is not necessarily against the right of freedom of expression, care has to be taken not to draft an overly broad definition of the crime. In this regard, the European definition is too wide to be used at the global level since in the absence of a human rights protection mechanism such as the European Court of Human Rights, the right of freedom of speech may be excessively curtailed. In particular, the inclusion of indirect incitement to terrorism has been found problematic. The crime of incitement to genocide, on the contrary, does not include indirect incitement, although the incitement must not necessarily be explicit. Whether a statement

---

[212] UN Secretary-General (n 10) §§61–62.
[213] CoE Explanatory Report §100.
[214] *Brandenburg* 444.
[215] International Commission of Jurists, 'Response to the European Commission Consultation on Inciting, Aiding or Abetting Terrorist Offences' (2007), 6; 'The Johannesburg Principles on National Security, Freedom of Expression and Access to Information, Article 19' (1995), 9, available at: www.article19.org/data/files/pdfs/standards/joburgprinciples.pdf.

amounts to incitement to genocide will depend on its context, such as the cultural and linguistic content, the affiliation of the author, the circumstances and the understanding of the audience. Identical criteria can be used for establishing whether the message in the context it was made results in direct incitement to terrorism. This chapter also concluded that, like incitement to genocide, incitement to terrorism should be public and have a special intent. In addition, the definition of incitement to terrorism includes a requirement of a causal link. Consequently, the following definition is proposed:

> The distribution, or otherwise making available, of a message to the public, with the intent to incite the commission of a terrorist offence, where such conduct, in light of the context it was made, amounts to direct incitement and causes an imminent danger that a terrorist offence will likely be committed.

16

Towards a Criminal Code for the World?*

PAUL BEHRENS

1. INTRODUCTION

IN NOVEMBER 2007, a teddy bear made headlines. After Gillian Gibbons, a British teacher at a primary school in Sudan, had allowed her class to name the class teddy bear 'Muhammad', complaints were raised with the Education Ministry about her alleged insult to the Prophet Muhammad.[1] Ms Gibbons was arrested on 25 November, then put on trial and sentenced to fifteen days' imprisonment.[2] After intervention by the British government, Ms Gibbons was pardoned and released.[3]

Incidents of this kind fuel the impression that a deep gulf exists between legal systems around the world. The divergence is, arguably, nowhere as apparent as in the field of criminal law which, after all, counts the protection of values among one of its most salient functions. The protection of human rights, the respect a particular religion may enjoy, but also the regulation of matters such as the fight against corruption or illegal drugs, seem to point to considerable variations depending on the perspective adopted by a particular jurisdiction.

In light of this, the search for a universal criminal code, a 'model code' that can be constructed on the basis of common values expressed in criminal justice systems worldwide, seems utopian. The values protected by criminal law appear so closely linked to cultural connotations that it seems poorly suited for the identification of meaningful commonalities. The conclusion, rather, suggests itself that it may be better to respect existing differences rather than to seek the imposition of a framework that cannot hope to accommodate them: to accept the existing criminal laws as good neighbours rather than bad tenants.

That assessment, however, omits salient aspects from the debate. There are, in particular, not only considerations which indicate the usefulness of work on a

---

* I am grateful to Carla Fischer (University of Edinburgh) for her very helpful research assistance.

[1] Elizabeth Day, 'Interview: "I Was Terrified that the Guards Would Come In and Teach Me a Lesson"', *Observer*, 9 December 2007; Alfred de Montesquiou, 'British Teacher Convicted in Sudan Blasphemy Case Involving Teddy Bear Named "Muhammad"', *Associated Press*, 29 November 2007.

[2] Day (n 1).

[3] ibid; 'UK Teacher Jailed over Teddy Row', *BBC News Online*, last updated 30 November 2007, available at: http://news.bbc.co.uk/1/hi/world/africa/7119399.stm.

universal criminal code, but also aspects of international law which positively call at least for the identification of a 'common value system' underlying a criminal code for the world.

The helpfulness of a universal criminal code to individuals who have to deal with criminal justice systems in other countries are, as the Gibbons case demonstrates, difficult to deny. It is not only those who work in other States that are affected by their laws. Today, visitors from other countries may spend a very short period of time in any given State – an odd hour, say, while waiting in an airport lounge for a connecting flight. If they are still held to be able to comply with the legal regulations in every country with which they are in physical contact, then the contemporary world poses challenges to the accessibility and foreseeability of criminal law which are significant.

These are more than mere political considerations. A code that sets out the relevant crimes with clarity and precision also corresponds to legal needs. The right not to be held guilty for an act that did not constitute an offence under the law at the time of its commission is enshrined in the leading human rights treaties,[4] with accessibility and foreseeability being recognised by the European Court of Human Rights (ECtHR) as 'qualitative requirements' of the concept of 'law' in that context[5] and the Court noting also that the rule called for a clear definition of the relevant offences.[6] The existence of a universal criminal code is conducive to the fulfilment of these conditions: such a code can easily be made accessible and provided in translation, thus enabling travellers to adapt their conduct accordingly.

But there is also evidence that, on the international level, at least a rudimentary understanding of a global system of crime categories is required. That is indicated by provisions such as that of Article 41 of the Vienna Convention on Consular Conventions (VCCR) which provides for the general inviolability of consular officers from arrest and detention pending trial,'except in cases of a grave crime and pursuant to a decision by the competent judicial authority'.[7] It is, of course, possible that the appropriate definition of 'grave crime' is to be left to the discretion of the State of jurisdiction, and there is some indication that the phrasing had been selected by the International Law Commission (ILC) to take account of the differences in municipal laws on that point.[8] At the Vienna Conference on Consular Relations, on the other

---

[4] See Art 15 International Covenant on Civil and Political Rights, 19 December 1966, 999 UNTS 171 ('ICCPR'); Art 7 Convention for the Protection of Human Rights and Fundamental Freedoms, 4 November 1950, 213 UNTS 222 ('ECHR'); Art 9 American Convention on Human Rights, 22 November 1969, 1144 UNTS 123 ('ACHR'); Art 7(2) African Charter on Human and Peoples' Rights, 27 June 1981, 1520 UNTS 217. Sudan ratified the ICCPR in 1986. UN Treaty Collection, '4. International Covenant on Civil and Political Rights', https://treaties.un.org/Pages/ViewDetails.aspx?chapter=4&clang=_en&mtdsg_no=IV-4&src=IND.

[5] ECtHR, *Cantoni v France*, Appl No 17862/91, Judgment, 11 November 1996, para 29.

[6] ECtHR, *S W v United Kingdom*, Appl No 20166/92, Judgment, 22 November 1995, para 35. See also Kim Thuy Seelinger, 'Uganda's Case of Thomas Kwoyelo: Customary International Law on Trial' (2017) 8 *California Law Review Online* 30–31, for a direct application of the requirements of 'clarity' and 'specificity' to the ICCPR.

[7] Art 41(1) Vienna Convention on Consular Relations, 24 April 1963, 596 UNTS 261.

[8] UN General Assembly, United Nations Conference on Consular Relations, Vienna 4 March–22 April 1963, *Official Records*, vol 1: *Summary Record of Plenary Meetings and of the Meetings of the First and Second Committees*, A/CON.25/C.1 ('Conference Records 1963/II'), Second Committee, 23rd Meeting, 20 March 1963, 366, para 25 (Mr Žourek).

hand, Romania highlighted the need for 'an objective criterion which would afford a sufficient guarantee of the inviolability of consular officials' and suggested a definition of the offence allowing arrest as one 'for which the maximum penalty is a term of imprisonment of at least five years'.[9] That, too, invites criticism: taking the length of a sentence as a sufficiently objective parameter presupposes the assumption that all criminal justice systems group the same type of crimes into that category.[10] But an entirely subjective approach does not work either: if that had been intended, the ILC might as well have omitted the reference to 'grave crime[s]' altogether, opening the door to the possibility of arrest even for crimes that the sending State, and possibly the international community as a whole, would consider trivial in nature.[11]

Today, the possibility cannot be discounted that the understanding of common values within the international community has consolidated to such a degree that the reference to 'grave crimes' could be answered by customary international law in this field. That, however, would be an assumption of far-reaching consequences: the seemingly simple possibility that general State practice and *opinio iuris* on 'grave crimes' exists would also mean that there is general agreement among States as to how the categorisation of conduct criminalised in their domestic laws is to be performed in view of its respective severity.

These considerations point to a further question. If the establishment of a universal criminal code is seen as desirable, then what evidence can be adduced to the effect that such an undertaking is possible to begin with?

The continued existence in particular of crimes that take into account religious or cultural specificities may appear to militate against the feasibility of such efforts from the outset.

And yet, even in this regard, criminal justice systems may show a greater degree of proximity to one another than might at first appear. Even blasphemy laws are not restricted to a particular region: while a 2012 study found that 13 of 32 countries that retain such laws were in the Middle East and North Africa, no fewer than eight were in Europe,[12] and investigations into cases of blasphemy occurred in several European

---

[9] ibid 361, para 11 Mr Anghel (Romania) and UN General Assembly, United Nations Conference on Consular Relations, Vienna, 4 March–22 April 1963, *Official Records*, vol 2: *Annexes etc*, A/CON.25/16/Add. 1 ('Conference Records 1963/II'), 90, Doc A/CONF.25/C.2/L.149. See also the reference to the term 'serious crime' in Art 2(b) UN Convention on Transnational Organized Crime, 15 November 2000, 2225 UNTS 209 ('UNTOC'); critical on this Boister ('a crude measure of seriousness'): Neil Boister, *An Introduction to Transnational Criminal Law*, 2nd edn (Oxford, Oxford University Press 2018) 136. See also, with regard to the remaining discretion of States Parties in that regard, Andreas Schloenhardt, 'Transnational Organized Crime and International Criminal Law' in M Cherif Bassiouni (ed), *International Criminal Law*, vol 1: *Sources, Subjects and Context*, 3rd edn (Leiden, Brill, 2008) 951.

[10] See, for a critical view, also Conference Records 1963/I, 15th Plenary Meeting, 18 April 1963, 54, para 24, Mr Amlie (Norway).

[11] The danger of arrest for trivial offences was highlighted by the Norwegian delegate when the suggestion was made that arrest of consular officers should be allowed even in cases of their detection 'in flagrante delicto'. ibid, Second Committee, 23rd meeting, 20 March 1963, 366, para 19, Mr Amlie (Norway), with reference to Conference Records 1963/II, 92, Document A/CONF.25/C.2/L.168.

[12] Pew Research Center, 'Laws Penalizing Blasphemy, Apostasy and Defamation of Religion Are Widespread' (11 November 2012) at https://www.pewresearch.org/religion/2012/11/21/laws-penalizing-blasphemy-apostasy-and-defamation-of-religion-are-widespread/.

countries in recent years.[13] In other jurisdictions, insults to the religious feelings of other persons may be covered by more general public order offences.[14]

Outside crimes whose regulations bear witness to strong cultural connections, the commonalities between criminal justice systems can be expected to be even greater. Crimes such as murder, theft, assault and the destruction of property cause the same challenges for any society that wishes to protect its existence, and it would be surprising if the solutions devised did not resemble one another at least to some degree.

There is, therefore, some validity to the exploration of points that make criminal laws around the world members of the same family and to the identification of the minimum consensus that embodies the common values to which the provisions of the various criminal justice systems give expression.

This chapter seeks to approach this understanding of the underpinnings of world criminal law through one particular method: ie, through the systematic analysis of instruments of transnational criminal law that have attracted an extensive degree of approval among members of the international community.

It is a method that carries particular advantages. By ratifying a treaty on transnational criminal law, States Parties agree to criminalise certain forms of conduct in their own domestic legal systems, but these acts and omissions are not necessarily recognised as direct crimes against the international legal order. They thus need not represent behaviour considered by the international community as carrying a particularly severe character, such as genocide, crimes against humanity, war crimes or the crime of aggression.[15] In theory, they may constitute crimes that are considered 'ordinary' by the parties, but find reflection in the relevant treaties because of their transboundary character or because of a perceived need for harmonisation – although this point requires further consideration.[16] At the very least, the incorporation of crimes in certain treaties on transnational criminal law therefore allows for conclusions on the forms of conduct that members of the international community consider punishable acts in their own criminal justice systems.[17] What is more: the incorporation of the relevant crimes in domestic law, and indeed their approval of the treaty that outlines these offences, may, on the level of international law, well contribute to the establishment of customary international law; some treaties at least can be invoked as evidence for general and consistent State practice, accompanied by the legal opinion that this source of international law requires.

That is not to say that the use of transnational criminal law does not invite challenges. The fact in particular that the relevant crimes still need transformation and that

---

[13] See, for instance, 'Spanish Actor Detained After Ridiculing "God and the Virgin Mary"', *The Guardian/AFP*, 12 September 2018, at https://www.theguardian.com/world/2018/sep/12/spanish-actor-detained-after-ridiculing-god-and-the-virgin-mary; and 'Irish Police Drop Stephen Fry Blasphemy Probe', *BBC News Online*, 9 May 2017, at https://www.bbc.co.uk/news/world-europe-39857543.

[14] cf, for the UK, Public Order Act 1986, c 64, ss 4A and 5.

[15] See on these, Arts 6–Art 8bis Rome Statute of the International Criminal Court, 17 July 1998, 2187 UNTS 90.

[16] See below, section 5.2.1.

[17] See on this below at nn 65–69.

States Parties enjoy a certain margin of appreciation where this process is concerned, requires consideration. These are points to which this chapter will return.[18]

The following section (2) provides a brief overview of the development of the concept of a 'universal criminal law' – by reference to theoretical considerations in that regard, but also to certain models, both on the international and the regional level, which have been used in the past to approach the idea of a world criminal code. Section 3 introduces the methodology underlying the current research, focusing in particular on the treaties chosen for consideration and on the rationale behind their selection. Section 4 engages in an analysis of specific findings derived from such treaties and thus includes considerations on the general part of criminal law as apparent from these instruments and the specific crime categories, but also on certain legal consequences on which the treaties allow reflections. Section 5 engages in an analytical evaluation of the relevant findings in light in particular of criticism in relation to the suitability of transnational criminal law as an indicator for world criminal law. The final section (6) provides concluding considerations on the main aspects which this chapter has explored and on their assessment.

The focus of these considerations is on the substantive law as it can be derived from the relevant treaties. The chapter does not explore aspects outside this area, apart from reflections on sentencing and other legal consequences of the relevant crimes.

The result of this study is not a model universal code of crimes as such – not because such a code would be impossible to construct, but because it would inevitably have to rely on other approaches as well if a satisfactory result is to be reached. The aim is rather to gain insight into the universal commonalities which can be derived from an analysis of the relevant treaties and which may thus contribute to the grounds on which a criminal law for the world can be constructed.

2. THE CONCEPT OF UNIVERSAL CRIMINAL LAW

It seems strange that the same decade that witnessed crimes counting among the worst atrocities committed in the history of mankind would also see a renewed belief in the common values of humanity. But it is true – the Atlantic Charter was concluded in 1941, the United Nations were founded in 1945, the Genocide Convention and the Universal Declaration of Human Rights were adopted in 1948. And there was talk of universal values in criminal law too – Robert Jackson, former Chief Prosecutor at Nuremberg, noted in 1949 that, '[i]n making these defendants stand trial before a court of the aggrieved countries we followed an almost universal criminal law'.[19] He was arguably referring to a common rule of procedural law, but there was no shortage of scholars who made the link between a 'universal' or a 'world criminal law' and the part of international law that is today recognised as international criminal law – ie,

---

[18] See below, section 5.1.2.
[19] Robert H Jackson, 'Nurnberg in Retrospect' (1949) 27(7) *Canadian Bar Review* 761–81, 770.

the body of law dealing with offences that are directly recognised as crimes under international law.[20]

That, in fact, appears to be the meaning that had been given by the majority of writers in this field to the concept of universal or world criminal law even prior to the establishment of the International Military Tribunal at Nuremberg (IMT).[21]

Vespasian Pella for one, one of the 'fathers' of modern international criminal law, had, as early as 1935, published a 'Plan d'un code répressif mondial'.[22] This 'Plan for a World Criminal Code' has rightly been interpreted as standing in connection with jurisdiction in international criminal matters,[23] in as far as it included forms of conduct that would have been direct crimes against the international legal order and which would appear, in similar form, at the IMT in 1945 – in particular, the waging of aggressive war.[24]

The IMT itself, together with the International Military Tribunal for the Far East was perceived as lending further strength to this understanding of 'world criminal law'.[25] Such observations seem bolstered by the conclusion of Conventions which expressly envisaged the establishment of an 'international penal tribunal' as an option for their enforcement.[26] And when the International Criminal Tribunal for the

---

[20] See, inter alia, A Schönke in International Law Commission, 'Secretariat Memorandum Concerning a Draft Code of Offences Against the Peace and Security of Mankind' (24 November 1950) A/CN.4/39, Appendix, 218; Bernard VA Röling, 'The Responsibility of the Legislative, Executive and Judical [*sic*] Organs of the State According to International Penal Law' in International Congress of Jurists, *Report of the International Congress of Jurists, Athens, Greece, June 13–20, 1955* (The Hague, 1955) 123; August von Knieriem, *Nuremberg Trials* (Chicago, H Regnery, 1959) 216, but from a critical perspective (see below, at nn 29–39); Quincy Wright, 'The Scope of International Criminal Law: A Conceptual Framework' (1975) 15 *Virginia Journal of International Law* 561–78, 574.

[21] See on this Wm G Hammond, 'Notes of Current European Law' (1877) 2 *Southern Law Review (New Series)* 773–90, 780, 781; Vespasian V Pella (contribution, tr) (1949) 43 *American Society of International Law Proceedings* 109, 112 (with reference to efforts before World War II); Lawrence Preuss, 'Le droit pénal international d'après la législation polonaise. By Kopek Mikliszanski (Paris: Recueil Sirey, 1935. pp. xii, 185)' (1936) 30 *American Journal of International Law* 178.

[22] Vespasian Pella, 'Plan d'un Code Répressif Mondial. Annexe' (1935) *Revue internationale de droit pénal* 366. See, on Pella's work in general, Michelle Pfifferi, 'Chronological Reformism and Transnational Criminal Law' in Neil Boister, Sabine Gless and Florian Jeßberger (eds), *Histories of Transnational Criminal Law* (Oxford, Oxford University Press, 2021) 33–34; and see Neil Boister, 'The Growth of the Multilateral Suppression Conventions in the First Half of the Twentieth Century' ibid 50–51.

[23] Wilbourn E Benton and Georg Grimm (eds), *Nuremberg: German Views of the War Trials* (Dallas, TX, Southern Methodist University Press, 1955) 5.

[24] See on this Pella (n 22), at Titre Deuxième, Chapitre Premier, 1, in conjunction with Chapitre Deuxième, 1. The 1935 Plan did, however, also include certain forms of conduct which would today be seen in the context of internationally wrongful acts by States, see eg Chapitre Premier, 6 ('Immixtion d'un Etat dans les luttes politiques intérieures d'un autre Etat') as well as some acts, such as Chapitre Premier, 1 ('Falsification de monnaies ...') in conjunction with Chapitre Deuxième, 1, which to date remain subject of transnational criminal law (see International Convention for the Suppression of Counterfeiting Currency, 20 April 1929, 112 LNTS 371 ('Counterfeiting Convention 1929'), Arts 1 and 3), but were not included in instruments on international criminal law.

[25] See on this Röling (n 20) 123; JY Dautricourt, 'Nature et Compétence de la Juridiction Belge Pour la Répression des Crimes de Guerre de Lege Ferenda' (1966) 5 *Military Law & Law of War Review* 63, 83.

[26] See Art VI Convention on the Prevention and Punishment of the Crime of Genocide, 9 December 1948, 78 UNTS 277 ('Genocide Convention'); Art V International Convention on the Suppression and Punishment of the Crime of Apartheid, 30 November 1973, 1015 UNTS 243 ('Apartheid Convention'); Stanley W Johnston, 'Problems in the Enforcement of World Criminal Law' (1975) 8 *Australia & New Zealand Journal of Criminology* 87–100, 95.

Former Yugoslavia (ICTY), the International Criminal Tribunal for Rwanda (ICTR) and the International Criminal Court (ICC) were established, it seemed to some that the journey towards world criminal law had almost reached its conclusion.[27]

The reasons for the (apparent) suitability of international criminal law as a template for universal criminal law would have to be seen, not least, in the fact that it serves to protect values shared by the world community, with the preamble to the ICC Statute noting that 'all peoples are united by common bonds, their cultures pieced together in a shared heritage, and concerned that this delicate mosaic may be shattered at any time'.[28] But the understanding of international criminal law as representing, or being a model for, a world criminal law is not free from controversy. Prior to the establishment of the ICC, critics referred, inter alia, to the 'ad hoc' nature of some of the concepts used in the institutions of international criminal justice then in existence – Knieriem, for instance, referring to the concept of 'aiding and abetting' under Control Council Law 10, expressed the view that it did 'not find its foundation in an international criminal law, which simply does not exist, nor is it suitable to serve as the basis for developing a world criminal law'.[29] After the adoption of the ICC Statute, there was criticism that went in the opposite direction: the remit the drafters had given to the treaty was seen as limited,[30] and the list of crimes over which the ICC has jurisdiction, was, by its very nature, selective: the Court, as Fletcher pointed out, 'would not claim the authority to prosecute routine claims of theft, fraud and sexual assault'.[31]

Even the crimes that did make it into the Statute are not necessarily indicative of customary criminal law. Some crimes have already fuelled debate with regard to their nature as offences that represent customary law – such as the war crime of enlisting (as opposed to conscripting) child soldiers.[32] Customary international

---

[27] See on this Leila Nadya Sadat, 'Custom, Codification and Some Thoughts about the Relationship Between the Two: Article 10 of the ICC Statute' (2000) 49 *DePaul Law Review* 909, 923; Kevin Doak, 'Beyond International Law: The Theories of World Law in Tanaka Kotaro and Tsuneto Kyo' (2011) 13 *Journal of the History of International Law* 209–34, 227 (who did, however, express some hesitation as to calling the ICC a '"World Court" in the full sense').

[28] ICC Statute, Preamble, 1st operative para; see also ibid 4th operative para. See also William Schabas, *An Introduction to the International Criminal Court* (Oxford, Oxford University Press, 2020) 82; Kai Ambos, 'Punishment without a Sovereign: The Ius Puniendi Issue of International Criminal Law: A First Contribution towards a Consistent Theory of International Criminal Law' (2013) 33 *OJLS* 293–316, 310–11.

[29] Knieriem (n 20) 216. 'Aiding' is, in fact, not expressly mentioned in that law, although being an 'accessory' is (as well as 'abett[ing]'). Allied Control Council, Control Council Law No 10 (Berlin, 20 December 1945) Art II(2)(b).

[30] Edward M Wise, 'The International Criminal Court: A Budget of Paradoxes' (2000) 8 *Tulane Journal of International & Comparative Law* 261–82, 270.

[31] George P Fletcher, 'Parochial versus Universal Criminal Law' (2005) 3 *Journal of International Criminal Justice* 20–34, 26.

[32] Arts 8(2)(b)(xxvi) and 8(2)(e)(vii) ICC Statute. The debate was given particular impetus through the Hinga Norman appeal before the Special Court for Sierra Leone, whose Statute contains a similar provision (Art 4(c) Agreement between the United Nations and the Government of Sierra Leone on the establishment of a Special Court for Sierra Leone (with Statute), Statute of the Special Court for Sierra Leone 16 January 2002, 2178 UNTS 137, 145–53). See, on the controversy, Matthew Happold, 'International Humanitarian Law, War Criminality and Child Recruitment: The Special Court for Sierra Leone's Decision in *Prosecutor v Samuel Hinga Norman*' (2005) 18 *Leiden Journal of International Law* 283–98, in particular at 289–91. See also Behrens, 'Challenges to Contemporary Criminal Justice' (ch 1 in this volume) at nn 29–33.

law would, at any rate, require State practice that had 'generally been adopted';[33] indeed, according to the International Court of Justice (ICJ), it is an 'indispensable requirement' that within the period in question, the relevant State practice had been 'extensive'.[34] The agreement of States to a treaty may certainly be invoked in evidence for a rule of customary law, and under certain circumstances, a treaty itself may give rise to the development of new customary law.[35] But the fact that, at a time when 193 States were members of the United Nations,[36] no more than 123 were Parties to the ICC Statute[37] raises the question whether the crimes enshrined in it can, on the basis of ratifications alone, be said to be embraced by the general and consistent practice of States. Wise had highlighted that difficulty as early as 2000, noting that the 60 States that would bring the Statute into force would 'constitute slightly less than a third of the membership of the United Nations' and that even 120 States (the number of States voting in favour of the treaty at Rome) would 'account for less than half the world; those reported to have opposed the Statute represent more than half the world's population'.[38] Population figures are not decisive for the determination of customary law, but Wise has a point when he asks 'how a community that excludes half the world can be said to constitute the "international community" – "considered as a community, in its social aggregate capacity"'.[39]

That is not to say that the crimes enshrined in statutory international criminal law do not represent customary international law (and the point of their character as customary law does, of course, arise with regularity in the case law of the international criminal courts and tribunals).[40] Nor does it mean that the codified international criminal law could not serve as a template, and a very good template, for world criminal law. What it means is that the burden of proof for the existence of consensus within the international community on the criminalisation of certain forms of conduct and on the values underlying such measures is not easily discharged by reference to the States Parties to the ICC Statute alone.

---

[33] See on this, International Court of Justice ('ICJ'), *Fisheries Case (United Kingdom v Norway)*, Judgment, 18 December 1951, 1951 ICJ Rep 116, 128.

[34] ICJ, *North Sea Continental Shelf Cases (Federal Republic of Germany v Denmark; Federal Republic of Germany v Netherlands)*, Judgment, 20 February 1969, 1969 ICJ Rep 3, para 74.

[35] ibid, paras 71, 72.

[36] UN Treaty Collection, Charter of the United Nations and Statute of the International Court of Justice (Status 20 July 2021) at https://web.archive.org/web/20210721031525/https://treaties.un.org/pages/ViewDetails.aspx?src=IND&mtdsg_no=I-1&chapter=1&clang=_en.

[37] UN Treaty Collection, Rome Statute of the International Criminal Court (Status 23 July 2021) at https://web.archive.org/web/20210723184655/https://treaties.un.org/pages/ViewDetails.aspx?src=IND&mtdsg_no=XVIII-10&chapter=18&clang=_en.

[38] Wise (n 30) 268.

[39] ibid. The latter quote ('community, in its social aggregate capacity') is to 4 William Blackstone, *Commentaries on the Laws of England 5* (1769).

[40] See eg ICTY, Appeals Chamber, *Prosecutor v Krstić*, IT-98-33-A, Judgment, 19 April 2004, para 25; ICC, Appeals Chamber, *Prosecutor v Bemba Gombo*, ICC-01/05-01/08-3636-Red, Judgment pursuant to Article 74 of the Statute, 8 June 2018, Dissenting Opinion of Judge Sanji Mmasenono Monageng and Judge Piotr Hofmański, para 559; ICC (Trial Chamber), *Prosecutor v Ongwen*, ICC-02/04-01/15, Judgment, 4 February 2021, para 2745, n 7208. See also, in general, Yudan Tan, 'The Identification of Customary Rules in International Criminal Law' (2018) 34(2) *Utrecht Journal of International and European Law* 92–110.

A more obvious basis for the creation of a code of world criminal law could be seen in efforts at harmonisation of provisions of domestic criminal justice systems, initiatives in which the United Nations may be expected to play an important role.

Beginning in 1955, the UN Economic and Social Council hosted Congresses 'on the Prevention of Crime and the Treatment of Offenders'[41] (from 2005, the 'United Nations Congresses on Crime Prevention and Criminal Justice');[42] and these have served to emphasise the importance of coordinated action to prevent and combat crime.

Yet while, at the latest Congress, the representatives of Member States declared their willingness 'to intensify concerted global efforts to prevent and combat crime by facilitating and strengthening international cooperation in criminal matters',[43] the stipulation of such principles has not resulted in a comprehensive code on criminal law with universal applicability. Outside transnational criminal law, to which this chapter will return, global efforts at harmonisation are still a rarity.

More promising efforts exist on the regional level, and the initiatives that have been undertaken in that regard allow for the question whether they can serve as a basis for the identification of universal criminal law, or at least as inspiration for efforts to create a criminal code for the world.

The 'Europeanisation of criminal law' occupies a prominent place in that regard.[44] The developing concept of 'European Criminal Law' is informed by two aspects in particular: on the one hand, by the impact of human rights mandates as identified in particular in the case law of the ECtHR and, on the other hand, by initiatives undertaken by EU institutions to promote the criminalisation of certain forms of conduct.[45]

The first aspect is based not only on the impact of norms which, while phrased as provisions against State intervention, have an impact on the administration of justice – such as the prohibition of torture and inhuman or degrading treatment or punishment (Article 3 ECHR), and indeed on substantive criminal law, such as the prohibition of punishment without a law (Article 7 ECHR). The reading in particular which the ECtHR had given the latter provision, which incorporates the notions of foreseeability and accessibility of the law,[46] has allowed it to declare provisions of national criminal codes which were impermissibly vague incompatible with the *nullum crimen sine lege* principle.[47] Recent years have also seen an increasing focus on

---

[41] See, on their history, Jennifer Peirce, 'Making the Mandela Rules: Evidence, Expertise, and Politics in the Development of Soft Law International Prison Standards' (2018) 43(2) *Queen's Law Journal* 263, 270. The congresses find their basis in General Assembly Resolution 415(V), 1 December 1950, Annex at (d).

[42] See, for an overview of past congresses, United Nations, Office on Drugs and Crime ('UNODC'), 'Previous Congresses', at https://www.unodc.org/congress/en/previous-congresses.html.

[43] UNODC, 14th UN Congress on Crime Prevention and Criminal Justice, *Kyoto Declaration on Advancing Crime Prevention, Criminal Justice and the Rule of Law: Towards an Achievement of the 2030 Agenda for Sustainable Development* (Kyoto 7–12 March 2021), para 5.

[44] Klaus Lüderssen, 'Enlightened Criminal Policy or the Struggle against Evil' (2000) 3 *Buffalo Criminal Law Review* 687–700, 694.

[45] See, in general, Fletcher (n 31) 28.

[46] See above at n 5.

[47] See on this ECtHR, *Liivik v Estonia*, Appl No 12157/05, Judgment, 25 June 2009, paras 100–04; and see Richard Lang, 'Update on Decisions of the European Court of Human Rights Affecting Criminal Law/ Criminal Procedure' (2010) 1 *New Journal of European Criminal Law* 87–118, 92–93 for a discussion.

the positive obligations – such as the duty of Member States 'to secure the right to life by putting in place effective criminal-law provisions'.[48] Fletcher's observation that the 'Strasbourg Court has assumed the remarkable burden of supervising and rewriting the criminal codes of all the Member States'[49] carries the scent of exaggeration – the fact must, after all, be taken into account that in many areas pertaining to the protection of human rights, Member States retain a margin of appreciation – but it would be difficult to deny that the ECtHR case law has been instrumental in the shaping of criminal law on the European continent today.[50]

The second aspect of European Criminal Law – the law as constituted through various instruments adopted by the European Union – extends today to a wide range of areas, including ship-sourced pollution,[51] expressions of racism and xenophobia,[52] the protection of the environment,[53] trafficking in human beings[54] and attacks on information systems.[55] A typical feature of these instruments is the obligation of Member States to declare certain forms of conduct criminal or punishable under their domestic laws;[56] collectively, the relevant instruments therefore make a significant contribution to the harmonisation of criminal law in an increasing number of fields. An instrument that is of particular relevance to the Europeanisation of criminal law is the European Arrest Warrant (EAW), established through a Council Framework Decision in 2002 (EAW Decision),[57] which not only facilitates the surrender of suspects across borders but also refers to no fewer than 32 crime categories for which the requirement of double criminality is waived.[58] That does not mean that full

---

[48] ECtHR, *Osman v United Kingdom*, Appl No 23452/94, Judgment, 28 October 1998, para 115; ECtHR, *Rantsev v Cyprus and Russia*, Appl No 25965/04, Judgment, 7 January 2010, para 218.

[49] Fletcher (n 31), 30.

[50] That finding is reinforced by another consideration that derives from criminal law as an instrument of potential State intervention with the rights of individuals. The fact that such intervention will often have to pass the test of proportionality (see Arts 8(2), 9(2), 10(2), 11(2) ECHR) also gives applicants an opportunity to challenge the very existence of provisions of criminal law when they can show that less intrusive measures had been in existence to protect the legitimate interests which prompted the State to act.

[51] European Parliament and Council, Directive 2005/35/EC (7 September 2005) on Ship-Source Pollution and on the Introduction of Penalties, Including Criminal Penalties, for Pollution Offences, [30 September 2005] OJ L255, 11 ('Pollution Directive').

[52] Council, Framework Decision 2008/913/JHA (28 November 2008) on Combating Certain Forms and Expressions of Racism and Xenophobia by Means of Criminal Law, [6 December 2008] OJ L328, 0055–0058 ('Racism and Xenophobia Decision').

[53] European Parliament and Council, Directive 2008/99/EC (19 November 2008) on the Protection of the Environment through Criminal Law, [6 December 2008] OJ L328, 28–37 ('Environment Directive').

[54] European Parliament and Council, Directive 2011/36/EU (5 April 2011) on Preventing and Combating Trafficking in Human Beings and Protecting its Victims, and Replacing Council Framework Decision 2002/629/JHA, [15 April 2011] OJ L101, 1–11 ('Trafficking Directive').

[55] European Parliament and Council, Directive 2013/40/EU (12 August 2013) on Attacks against Information Systems and Replacing Council Framework Decision 2005/222/JHA, [14 August 2013] OJ L218, 8–14 ('Information Systems Directive').

[56] See eg Arts 5a, 5b Pollution Directive; Arts 1, 2 Racism and Xenophobia Decision; Arts 3, 4 Environment Directive; Arts 2, 3 Trafficking Directive; Arts 3–8 Information Systems Directive.

[57] Council, Framework Decision 2002/584/JHA (13 June 2002) on the European Arrest Warrant and the Surrender Procedures between Member States, [18 July 2002] OJ L190, 0001–0020; European Commission, 'European Arrest Warrant', at https://ec.europa.eu/info/law/cross-border-cases/judicial-cooperation/types-judicial-cooperation/european-arrest-warrant_en.

[58] The crime categories are somewhat arbitrarily appointed and could sometimes be split up into further groups – 'murder' and 'grievous bodily injury', for instance, are grouped together in one category.

harmonisation in these areas is achieved,[59] nor does the EAW Decision even call for the criminalisation of the relevant forms of conduct in the laws of all Member States. Yet the very fact that Member States were able to agree to the omission of the need for double criminality in these cases tells a story about the common values they seek to protect. And while in some areas the relevant crimes reinforce other international obligations (such as the crime of 'unlawful seizure of aircraft'), in others they are primarily seen as offences against the domestic order of individual States (such as murder, grievous bodily injury, trafficking in stolen vehicles and the forgery of administrative documents) and their inclusion is therefore particularly helpful as part of the foundations on which the evaluation of the minimum consensus on values recognised within the European Union rests.

Efforts like those undertaken in the European Union to achieve a degree of harmonisation at least at regional level are, however, still the exception rather than the rule. In light of their suitability as a basis for universal criminal law, the requirement of the 'generality' of criminal law does of course still cause challenges – if doubts had been raised about the suitability of 120 States as representing the 'international community',[60] even more questions can be expected to be raised about the far smaller number of States that, in a particular region, participate in efforts at harmonisation.

By the same token, the best basis on which 'world criminal law' could be identified, would appear to be a review of the criminal laws of all jurisdictions, on the understanding that certain forms of conduct 'could reasonably be expected to appear wrong to all legal systems'.[61] The consideration at the root of such an undertaking would be that certain values have universal status and that all peoples seek to protect the same 'fundamental 'interests'.[62]

That route has indeed been advocated over the years, with some scholars not being shy in suggesting crimes that should be included in this category. Meisel thus speaks of 'universal criminal law proscriptions against homicide, battery, and mayhem';[63] Bagaric and Morss note that 'as a species, we have certain intractable core interests' and that the deprivation of these, as done, for example, through 'murder (and the violation of one's physical autonomy), rape and enslavement should constitute an international crime'.[64]

The 'double criminality' requirement refers to the rule that prohibits the extradition of persons whose conduct did not constitute a crime in the laws of both the State demanding extradition and the one asked to extradite. See, on the concept, Sharon A Williams, 'The Double Criminality Rule and Extradition: A Comparative Analysis' (1991) 15 *Nova Law Review* 581.

[59] Especially with regard to some of the vaguer categories (such as 'sabotage'), that conclusion could not be lightly reached.

[60] See above, n 39.

[61] Fletcher (n 31) 25.

[62] See on this, Mirko Bagaric and John Morss, 'In Search of Coherent Jurisprudence for International Criminal Law: Correlating Universal Human Responsibilities with Universal Human Rights' (2006) 29 *Suffolk Transnational Law Review* 157–206, 206; and Joao Marcello De Araujo, 'International Crimes in Brazilian Domestic Law' (1990) 1 *Touro Journal of Transnational Law* 353–74, 355.

[63] Alan Meisel, 'The Exceptions to the Informed Consent Doctrine: Striking a Balance between Competing Values in Medical Decisionmaking' (1979) *Wisconsin Law Review* 413–88, 419.

[64] Bagaric and Morss (n 62) 355. See, for other attempts by scholars to devise lists of 'international' crimes, Boister (2021) (n 22) 52.

That may well be the case. But 'instinctively feeling' that it is so is not a satisfactory substitute for analysis of such laws which may, after all, yield surprising results depending on the degree of scrutiny (is the required *mens rea* for murder the same in all jurisdictions? Does consent to battery receive the same treatment? At what level does exploitation of an oppressive situation amount to forced labour?) An examination which fulfils the criteria of academic scrutiny, however, is an undertaking of considerable dimensions: it would involve analysis not only of the criminal laws of nearly 200 independent States, together with the potential impact that supranational and international organisations have on these systems, but also the investigation of the relevant provisions in numerous sub-State jurisdictions – as well as the case law that retains its undeniable significance in giving shape to the relevant provisions.

If, however, an examination of the criminal laws of individual States is the 'ideal' way of ascertaining the values they seek to protect and thus identifying the basis for world criminal law, then the second-best way may be an investigation of the values to which States have committed themselves in their international relations and for whose protection they consider – by consensus – criminal justice to be the most suitable tool. That, in other words, is an analysis of those treaties in which members of the international community agreed to criminalise conduct in their domestic legal systems.

These are conventions to which the term 'transnational criminal law' has been applied.[65] In the course of the last century, numerous treaties of that kind have been concluded, with a regulatory remit ranging from counterfeiting activities[66] to psychotropic substances,[67] from 'obscene publications'[68] to acts of nuclear terrorism.[69] As they enshrine the commitment of States not only to prevent the specified forms of conduct, but to reinforce the relevant prohibitions with sanctions of criminal law, at least some of these instruments may serve as evidence for the lowest common denominator on which the international community has been able to agree in the protection of the underlying values.

Depending on the extent to which these treaties have met with the approval of independent States, their ratification may also indicate that general State practice and *opinio iuris* as elements of customary international law in that regard have come into existence. The analysis of the relevant treaties is therefore the subject of the following sections of this chapter.

It is not the first time that an attempt has been made to use instruments of transnational criminal law as the basis for the establishment of a potential code of crimes.

---

[65] It is a usage that differs from that employed by Roger Cotterrell, 'The Concept of Crime in Transnational Perspective' (ch 2 in this volume) section 3. For the purposes of the current chapter, transnational criminal law is seen as composed of those parts of international law by which States adopt an obligation to criminalise certain acts or omissions in their domestic law; international criminal law, in its substantive dimension, refers to acts or omissions that directly constitute crimes against the international order and require no transformation to fulfil this purpose.

[66] Counterfeiting Convention (1929) (n 24).

[67] Convention on Psychotropic Substances, 21 February 1971, 1019 UNTS 175 ('Psychotropic Substances Convention').

[68] Convention for the Suppression of the Circulation of and Traffic in Obscene Publications, 12 September 1923, 27 LNTS 213 ('Obscene Publications Convention').

[69] International Convention for the Suppression of Acts of Nuclear Terrorism, 13 April 2005, 2445 UNTS 89 ('Nuclear Terrorism Convention').

When the ILC in 1994 presented its Draft Code of Crimes against the Peace and Security of Mankind, it included in its Article 20 on the jurisdiction of a future ICC also a category of offences deriving from 'the treaty provisions listed in the Annex' which constituted 'exceptionally serious crimes of international concern'.[70] These were, in the language of the ILC, 'treaty crimes, that is to say, crimes of international concern defined by treaties';[71] and the Annex referred to fourteen instruments of transnational criminal law on which the relevant crimes were based.[72] The current research differs to some extent with regard to the basis of selection, but also in relation to the eventual purpose for which they were employed. It is, after all, theoretically possible that criminalisation which seeks to protect values embraced by international consensus reflects forms of conduct that matter to States even though they do not have 'inevitable international consequences' – one of the alternative criteria which the ILC adopted for its selection process.[73]

The question of methodology is therefore of some importance. Section 3 is dedicated to this matter, while Section 4 provides a more detailed analysis of the aspects of the selected treaties in light of the insights they offer on specific crime categories and on the general structure of the crime as it appears from their provisions.

It is true that the focus on transnational criminal law as a basis for a future world criminal law is not free from critique either. This is a point to which this chapter will return in more detail in Section 5.

3. CHALLENGES AND METHODOLOGY

3.1. The Selection of the Corpus

Initial associations with the term 'transnational criminal law' may invoke treaties that are clearly dedicated to the establishment of offences that Member States seek to criminalise – such as the UN Convention on Transnational Organized Crime[74] and the Protocols thereto[75] – but treaties incorporating provisions of this kind also include

---

[70] International Law Commission ('ILC'), *Draft Code of Crimes against the Peace and Security of Mankind*, (1994) 2(2) *Yearbook of the International Law Commission* ('YILC') 38, Art 20(e).

[71] ibid 41, Art 20, Commentary, para 18.

[72] ibid 67–68, Annex and see also 70–73, Appendix II.

[73] ibid, 41, Art 20, Commentary, para 17. The ILC's reflection on the UN Convention Against Illicit Traffic in Narcotic Drugs and Psychotropic Substances, 20 December 1988, 1582 UNTS 95 ('Narcotic Drugs Convention (1988)') offers an example in this regard. According to the ILC, only offences referred to in Art 3(1) of the Convention were to be included (and only if they were 'crimes with an international dimension' ((1994) 2(2) YILC 68, Annex, at 3(9) and 69, Annex, Commentary at (2)). That limitation rules out, eg, offences covered by Art 3(2) of the Convention. In practice this would have meant that the Draft Code would have extended to (some cases) of intentional sale of the relevant drugs, but not to their possession or purchase.

[74] UNTOC (n 9).

[75] Protocol to Prevent, Suppress and Punish Trafficking in Persons, Especially Women and Children, Supplementing the United Nations Convention against Transnational Organized Crime, 15 November 2000, 2237 UNTS 319 ('Trafficking in Persons Protocol'); Protocol against the Smuggling of Migrants by Land, Sea and Air, Supplementing the United Nations Convention against Transnational Organized Crime, 15 November 2000, 2241 UNTS 507; Protocol against the Illicit Manufacturing of and Trafficking in

those whose main thrust lies, to all appearance, in another area of law. The 1982 Law of the Sea Convention, for instance, includes among its more than 300 articles also a provision under which States Parties agree to make 'the breaking or injury of a submarine pipeline or high-voltage power cable' a punishable offence.[76] The focus in this chapter is on conventions in which the agreement to criminalise certain forms of conduct substantially contributes to the character of the convention – including, however, also the 1949 Geneva Conventions and the relevant Protocols thereto which were considered in light of the considerable influence which their 'Grave Breaches' regime[77] exerted on later instruments that dealt specifically with the criminalisation of certain conduct in armed conflict.[78]

The resulting corpus covers nearly 60 treaties whose provisions have relevance to transnational criminal law and which were concluded between 1910 and 2010.[79] No

Firearms, Their Parts and Components and Ammunition, Supplementing the United Nations Convention against Transnational Organized Crime, 31 May 2001, 2326 UNTS 208.

[76] Art 113 United Nations Convention on the Law of the Sea, 10 December 1982, 1833 UNTS 397 ('UNCLOS').

[77] Each of the four Geneva Conventions contains provisions under which States Parties agree to 'provide effective penal sanctions' under their own laws for certain grave breaches of the Convention. See Arts 49, 50 Geneva Convention for the Amelioration of the Condition of the Wounded and Sick in Armed Forces in the Field, 12 August 1949, 75 UNTS 31 ('Geneva Convention I'); Arts 50, 51, Geneva Convention for the Amelioration of the Condition of the Wounded, Sick and Shipwrecked Members of the Armed Forces at Sea, 12 August 1949, 75 UNTS 85 ('Geneva Convention II'); Arts 129, 130 Geneva Convention Relative to the Treatment of Prisoners of War, 12 August 1949, 75 UNTS 135 ('Geneva Convention III'); Arts 146, 147 Geneva Convention Relative to the Protection of Civilian Persons in Time of War, 12 August 1949, 75 UNTS 287 ('Geneva Convention IV'). (Collectively, 'the four Geneva Conventions'). Art 85 of the First Additional Protocol expands on the grave breaches regime, Protocol Additional to the Geneva Conventions of 12 August 1949, and Relating to the Protection of Victims of International Armed Conflicts (Protocol I), 8 June 1977, 1125 UNTS 3 ('AP1'); with Art 6 of the Third Additional Protocol including a further extension to it, Protocol Additional to the Geneva Conventions of 12 August 1949, and Relating to the Adoption of an Additional Distinctive Emblem (Protocol III), 8 December 2005, 2404 UNTS 261 ('AP3').

[78] See Art 2 Statute of the International Criminal Tribunal for the Former Yugoslavia (adopted 25 May 1993 by SC Res 827); Art 8(2)(a) ICC Statute.

[79] They are the Convention for the Suppression of the White Slave Traffic (1910) 103 British and Foreign State Papers 244–48 and see Protocol Amending the International Agreement for the Suppression of the White Slave Traffic, signed at Paris, on 18 May 1904, and the International Convention for the Suppression of the White Slave Traffic, signed at Paris, on 4 May 1910 (1949) 30 UNTS 23 ('White Slave Convention') and see Convention for the Suppression of the White Slave Traffic, signed at Paris on 4 May 1910, and as amended by the Protocol signed at Lake Success, New York, 4 May 1949 (1949), 98 UNTS 101; the Convention for the Suppression of Traffic in Women and Children (1921) 9 LNTS 415 and see Protocol to Amend the Convention for the Suppression of the Traffic in Women and Children concluded at Geneva on 30 September 1921, and the Convention for the Suppression of the Traffic in Women of Full Age, concluded at Geneva on 11 October 1933 (1947) 53 UNTS 13 and see Convention for the Suppression of the Traffic in Women and Children, concluded at Geneva on 30 September 1921, as Amended by the Protocol Signed at Lake Success, New York, on 12 November 1947 (1947), 53 UNTS 39; the Obscene Publications Convention (n 68) and see Protocol to Amend the Convention for the Suppression of the Circulation of and Traffic in Obscene Publications, concluded at Geneva on 12 September 1923 (1947), 46 UNTS 169 and see Convention for the Suppression of the Circulation of and Traffic in Obscene Publications, concluded at Geneva on 12 September 1923, as Amended by the Protocol signed at Lake Success, New York, on 12 November 1947, 46 UNTS 201; the Slavery Convention (1926), 60 LNTS 254 and see Protocol Amending the Slavery Convention signed at Geneva on 25 September 1926 (1953), 182 UNTS 51, and see Slavery Convention, Signed at Geneva on 25 September 1926 and Amended by the Protocol opened for signature or acceptance at the Headquarters of the United Nations, New York, on 7 December 1953, 212 UNTS 17; the Counterfeiting Convention 1929 (n 24) and see Optional Protocol Regarding the Suppression of Counterfeiting Currency (1929) 112 LNTS 395; the Convention for the Suppression of the Traffic in

claim to complete coverage is made, but the selection does result in the inclusion of some of the most cited treaties in the field, with some attracting a considerable

Women of Full Age (1933) 150 LNTS 431 and see Protocol to Amend the Convention for the Suppression of the Traffic in Women and Children concluded at Geneva on 30 September 1921, and the Convention for the Suppression of the Traffic in Women of Full Age, concluded at Geneva on 11 October 1933 (1947) 53 UNTS 13, and see Convention for the Suppression of the Traffic in Women of Full Age, Concluded at Geneva on 11 October 1933, as Amended by the Protocol signed at Lake Success, New York, on 12 November 1947, 53 UNTS 49; the Convention for the Suppression of the Illicit Traffic in Dangerous Drugs, and Protocol of Signature (1936), 198 LNTS 299 and 320 and see Protocol Amending the Agreements, Conventions and Protocols on Narcotic Drugs concluded at The Hague on 23 January 1912, at Geneva on 11 February 1925 and 19 February 1925, and 13 July 1931, at Bangkok on 27 November 1931 and at Geneva on 26 June 1936 (1946), 12 UNTS 179; the Genocide Convention (n 26); the four Geneva Conventions of 1949 (n 77); AP1 (n 77); AP3 (n 77); the Convention for the Suppression of Traffic in Persons and of the Exploitation of the Prostitution of Others (1950), 96 UNTS 271 and see Final Protocol (1950) 96 UNTS 316; the Supplementary Convention on the Abolition of Slavery, the Slave Trade, and Institutions and Practices Similar to Slavery (1956) 266 UNTS 40 ('Supplementary Slavery Convention'); the Single Convention on Narcotic Drugs (1961) 520 UNTS 151 and see Protocol Amending the Single Convention on Narcotic Drugs, 1961 (1972), 976 UNTS 3 ('Protocol Amending the Single Convention') and see Single Convention on Narcotic Drugs, 1961, as Amended by the Protocol amending the Single Convention on Narcotic Drugs (1975), at https://treaties.un.org/doc/Treaties/1975/08/19750808%20 06-05%20PM/Ch_VI_18p.pdf ('Single Convention on Narcotic Drugs'); the Convention on Offences and Certain Other Acts Committed on Board Aircraft (1963) ('Tokyo Convention'), 704 UNTS 219; the [UNESCO] Convention on the Means of Prohibiting and Preventing the Illicit Import, Export and Transfer of Ownership of Cultural Property (1970) ('UNESCO 1970 Convention'), 823 UNTS 231; the Convention for the Suppression of Unlawful Seizure of Aircraft (1970) ('Hague Hijacking Convention'), 860 UNTS 105 and see Protocol Supplementary to the Convention for the Suppression of Unlawful Seizure of Aircraft (2010), ICAO Doc 9959; the Psychotropic Substances Convention (n 67); the International Convention on the Suppression and Punishment of the Crime of Apartheid (1973) 1015 UNTS 243; the Convention for the Suppression of Unlawful Acts against the Safety of Civil Aviation (1971) ('Montreal Convention'), 974 UNTS 177 and see Protocol for the Suppression of Unlawful Acts of Violence at Airports Serving International Civil Aviation, Supplementary to the Above-mentioned Convention (1988), 1589 UNTS 474; the Convention on International Trade in Endangered Species of Wild Fauna and Flora (1973), 993 UNTS 243 ('CITES') and see Amendment to the Convention on International Trade in Endangered Species of Wild Fauna and Flora (Bonn, 1979), TIAS 11079 and see Amendment to the Convention on International Trade in Endangered Species of Wild Fauna and Flora (Gaborone, 1983), reproduced in Richard L Wallace (ed), *The Marine Mammal Commission Compendium of Selected Treaties, International Agreements, and Other Relevant Documents on Marine Resources, Wildlife, and the Environment*, vol 1 (Washington DC, 1994) 656; the International Convention for the Prevention of Pollution from Ships (1973), 12 ILM 1319 ('MARPOL') and see Protocol of 1978 Relating to the International Convention for the Prevention of Pollution from Ships (1978), 1340 UNTS 61; the Convention on the Prevention and Punishment of Crimes against Internationally Protected Persons, including Diplomatic Agents (1973) ('Internationally Protected Persons Convention'), 1035 UNTS 167; the Convention on the Physical Protection of Nuclear Material and Nuclear Facilities (1979), 1456 UNTS 101 ('CPPNM') and see Amendment to the Convention on the Physical Protection of Nuclear Material (2005) IAEA Doc. INFCIRC/274/Rev.1/Mod.1 ('ACPPNM'); the International Convention Against the Taking of Hostages (1979), 1316 UNTS 205 ('Hostages Convention'); the Convention against Torture and Other Cruel, Inhuman or Degrading Treatment or Punishment (1984), 1465 UNTS 85; the Convention for the Suppression of Unlawful Acts against the Safety of Maritime Navigation (1988), 1678 UNTS 201 ('SUA Convention') and see Protocol to the Above-mentioned Convention for the Suppression of Unlawful Acts against the Safety of Fixed Platforms Located on the Continental Shelf (1988) ('SUA PROT', 'Fixed Platforms Protocol'), 1678 UNTS 304 and see Protocol of 2005 to the Convention for the Suppression of Unlawful Acts against the Safety of Maritime Navigation, LEG/CONF.15/21 ('SUA 2005') and see Protocol of 2005 to the Protocol for the Suppression of Unlawful Acts against the Safety of Fixed Platforms Located on the Continental Shelf, LEG/CONF.15/22 ('SUA PROT 2005'); the Narcotic Drugs Convention (1988) (n 73); the International Convention Against the Recruitment, Use, Financing and Training of Mercenaries (1989), 2163 UNTS 75 ('Mercenaries Convention'); the Convention on the Marking of Plastic Explosives for the Purpose of Detection (1991), 2122 UNTS 359; the Convention on the Safety of United Nations and Associated Personnel (1994), 2051

number of ratifications. But not all of them: some, like the Beijing Convention have, that far, only few Parties.[80]

That raises the question of the evaluation of treaties which are not widely supported by States. The matter is of relevance: the fact that a treaty deals with serious crimes of potentially far-reaching international dimensions does not necessarily mean that it has near universal approval. The Supplementary Slavery Convention has 124 Parties,[81] the Apartheid Convention has 109.[82] The conclusion, however, that apartheid,[83] debt bondage or serfdom[84] are not considered crimes by States that did not ratify the relevant treaties would be a non sequitur. There may be a range of reasons why a State has not become party to a treaty other than its opposition to provisions on criminalisation that the treaty may enshrine: there may be objections to other provisions, there may be resource implications, a newly concluded treaty may still have to clear parliamentary hurdles, and so forth.

All the same, if a treaty has been able to attract only few ratifications, the challenge outlined in the context of the ICC Statute above[85] re-emerges: evidence for the view that the relevant conduct is embraced as a crime in the collective consciousness of the international community is, on the basis of such an instrument alone, difficult to adduce. Neither would the existing list of parties demonstrate that 'general State practice' as an element of customary law has come into existence, nor would it be suitable as evidentiary basis for a sufficiently strong international consensus on which a future world criminal code could be based.

3.2. Selection of Treaties for Analysis

In light of the above, it appears there are two requirements which, in the selection of the relevant treaties are indispensable. One relates to a formal aspect: the fact that a significant number of States need to have become party to the relevant treaty; the

---

UNTS 363 and see Optional Protocol to the Convention on the Safety of United Nations and Associated Personnel (2005), 2689 UNTS 59; the International Convention for the Suppression of Terrorist Bombings (1997), 2149 UNTS 256 ('Terrorist Bombings Convention'); the International Convention for the Suppression of the Financing of Terrorism (1999), 2178 UNTS 197 ('Terrorist Financing Convention'); UNTOC (n 9) and its three supplementary protocols (n 75); the United Nations Convention against Corruption 2003, (2005) 2349 UNTS 41 ('UNCAC'); the Nuclear Terrorism Convention (n 69); the Convention on the Suppression of Unlawful Acts Relating to International Civil Aviation (2010), ICAO Doc 9960 ('Beijing Convention'). Protocols to the relevant conventions are counted as pertaining to transnational criminal law only if they contain provisions affecting criminal justice measures.

[80] As of 1 September 2021, the Beijing Convention had 37 Parties. ICAO, 'Convention on the Suppression of Unlawful Acts Relating to International Civil Aviation', https://www.icao.int/secretariat/legal/List%20 of%20Parties/Beijing_Conv_EN.pdf.

[81] UN Treaty Collection, 'Supplementary Convention on the Abolition of Slavery, the Slave Trade, and Institutions and Practices Similar to Slavery', https://treaties.un.org/pages/ViewDetailsIII.aspx?src= TREATY&mtdsg_no=XVIII-4&chapter=18&Temp=mtdsg3&clang=_en.

[82] UN Treaty Collection, 'International Convention on the Suppression and Punishment of the Crime of Apartheid', https://treaties.un.org/Pages/ViewDetails.aspx?src=IND&mtdsg_no=IV-7&chapter=4& clang=_en.

[83] See Arts I and II Apartheid Convention.

[84] Arts 1(a) and (b) Supplementary Slavery Convention.

[85] See above at nn 38–39.

other to a substantive aspect: the fact that the treaty must indeed deal with matters of criminalisation.

With regard to the formal aspect, two questions require considerations: firstly, the question of the aggregate sum – what is the totality of which the States that are parties to the relevant treaties form a percentage? – and secondly, the question of the threshold criterion – what is the percentage that allows us to talk about the treaty as having attracted a 'sufficient' amount of ratifications?

For the purposes of the current research, the assessment of the totality is informed by the international treaty that has attracted the largest number of parties – most widely recognised as being the Vienna Convention for the Protection of the Ozone Layer (1985) and the Montreal Protocol on Substances that Deplete the Ozone Layer (1987),[86] which have 198 Parties each.[87] If not providing a precise figure of all States on the planet,[88] this does give an indication as to the maximum number of parties that, to this date, have been able to commit to an international treaty.

The question of the applicable threshold of participating States invites an even greater degree of subjectivity. It is clear that, if doubts are cast on the acceptability of 120 States as representing the international community,[89] a simple majority of States would not suffice (nor, it appears, would 60%, where 198 is taken as the totality of possible parties).

In the ILC's selection of 'treaty crimes' for the Draft Code of Crimes against the Peace and Security of Mankind,[90] numerical significance appears to have played a role as well. Certain instruments, for instance, which were then at development stage or were not yet in force were deliberately omitted,[91] and the treaty crimes that were included derived from conventions which had attracted a substantial number of ratifications. But they did not in all cases reach even the number of 120 States: the Apartheid Convention, for instance, has even today no more than 109 Parties (and stood in 1994 at 99 Parties).[92] If the Apartheid Convention were discounted, then

---

[86] See Geneva Environment Network, 'Briefing to the Permanent Missions on the 24th Meeting of the Parties to the Montreal Protocol' (7 November 2012) https://www.genevaenvironmentnetwork.org/events/briefing-to-the-permanent-missions-on-the-24th-meeting-of-the-parties-to-the-montreal-protocol/ and UN Environment Programme, 'Most Widely Ratified Protocol in UN History Marks 25th Anniversary', 16 September 2012, https://www.unep.org/news-and-stories/press-release/most-widely-ratified-treaty-un-history-marks-25th-anniversary.

[87] Vienna Convention for the Protection of the Ozone Layer, 22 March 1985, 1513 UNTS 293; see UNTC, Vienna Convention for the Protection of the Ozone Layer (1985) https://treaties.un.org/pages/ViewDetails.aspx?src=IND&mtdsg_no=XXVII-2&chapter=27&clang=_en#:~:text=The%20Convention%20was%20adopted%20by,1985%20until%2021%20March%201986. For the Montreal Protocol on Substances that Deplete the Ozone Layer, 16 September 1987, 1522 UNTS 3, see UNTC, Montreal Protocol on Substances that Deplete the Ozone Layer (1987) https://treaties.un.org/PAGES/ViewDetails.aspx?src=TREATY&mtdsg_no=XXVII-2-a&chapter=27&clang=_en.

[88] The European Union, for instance, is Party to both instruments; Taiwan, on the other hand, is not.

[89] See above at n 38.

[90] See above at nn 70–72.

[91] See (1994) 2(2) *YILC* 41, Art 20, Commentary, para 23; ibid, 68, Annex, Crimes Pursuant to Treaties, Commentary.

[92] UN Treaty Collection, 'International Convention on the Suppression and Punishment of the Crime of Apartheid' (1973) https://treaties.un.org/Pages/ViewDetails.aspx?src=IND&mtdsg_no=IV-7&chapter=4&clang=_en. There is, however, reason to believe that at least some ILC members relied on additional evidence as a basis for its inclusion in the draft, see (1994) 2(2) *YILC* 40, Art 20, Commentary, para 16 (referring to the 'widespread ratification' of the treaty, but also 'the even more widespread condemnation of the practice of apartheid as a crime').

the instrument with the lowest number of ratifications that was still considered by ILC, would be the Fixed Platforms Protocol of 1988[93] which, even today, has no more than 156 Parties,[94] amounting to a threshold of 78.78%.

For the purposes of the current research, only treaties are included to which nine-tenths of the possible total have declared their consent to be bound. It is a high threshold, but it appears justified in light of the ICJ's requirement of evidence of 'extensive' State practice as an element of customary international law.[95] The acceptance of a two-thirds threshold, for instance (amounting to 132 States) would allow the consideration of a treaty that was not ratified by any Council of Europe State; a four-fifths threshold (more than 158 States) would allow the consideration of a treaty boycotted by the entire Latin American and Caribbean region. The threshold of 90% ensures that such discrepancies do not arise: where ratification by more than 178 parties is required, situations in which large legal families do not support a particular treaty are not likely to emerge.[96]

In relation to the substantive aspect of selection, it is necessary that the treaty contains a commitment to criminalisation – a point that may appear straightforward, but which, on closer scrutiny, invites challenges. Evidence for a duty of criminalisation, for example, may not always be entirely clear. It may be tempting to include instances such as the ban on 'violence to life and person, murder of all kinds, mutilation, cruel treatment and torture' which Common Article 3 of the Geneva Conventions of 1949 envisages and which it endows with strict prohibitions ('shall remain prohibited at any time and in any place whatsoever')[97] – not least because the article did form the basis of provisions of international criminal law.[98] It is tempting, too, to establish similar reasons for the inclusion of the Chemical Weapons Convention of 1992 on account of its prohibition on the use of chemical weapons,[99] or of the Law of the Sea Convention 1982 on account of its reference to piracy, the classical crime against the international order.[100]

In its Draft Code of Crimes against the Peace and Security of Mankind,[101] the ILC took a stricter approach. Piracy, on which, apart from questions of definitions, the Law of the Sea Convention mainly provides jurisdictional rules, rules on the retention and loss of nationality and the duty of cooperation in the repression of

---

[93] (1994) 2(2) *YILC* 72 (Appendix); Fixed Platforms Protocol (n 79).

[94] International Maritime Organization, 'Status of Treaties', https://wwwcdn.imo.org/localresources/en/About/Conventions/StatusOfConventions/StatusOfTreaties.pdf.

[95] *North Sea Continental Shelf Cases* (n 34), para 74.

[96] See also Judge Lachs's opinion in the *North Sea Continental Shelf Cases*, noting that for the 'formation of a new rule of general international law' the fact had to be taken into account that 'States with different political, economic and legal systems' had participated in the process. *North Sea Continental Shelf Cases* (n 34), Dissenting Opinion of Judge Lachs, 1969 ICJ Rep 219, 227.

[97] Common Art 3 of the Four Geneva Conventions.

[98] See on this Art 4 Statute of the International Criminal Tribunal for Rwanda (adopted 8 November 1994 by SC Res 955); Art 8(2)(c) ICC Statute; and see, for Art 3 ICTY Statute, ICTY, Appeals Chamber, *Prosecutor v Kunarac et al*, IT-96-23&IT-96-23/1-A, Judgment, 12 June 2002, para 68.

[99] Art 1(1)(b) Convention on the Prohibition of the Development, Production, Stockpiling and Use of Chemical Weapons and on their Destruction, 3 September 1992, 1975 UNTS 45.

[100] See Arts 100–105 UNCLOS.

[101] See above, at nn 70–72.

this conduct,[102] was deliberately excluded from the list of treaty crimes.[103] The Chemical Weapons Convention was likewise omitted, with the ILC noting that it did 'not create criminal offences or extend the jurisdiction of any State, and contains no provisions relating to extradition'.[104] The First Additional Protocol to the Geneva Conventions of 1949[105] did make it into the list of treaty crimes,[106] but the Second Additional Protocol[107] did not: while the ILC acknowledged that it prohibited certain forms of conduct, it found that it contained 'no clause dealing with grave breaches, nor any equivalent enforcement provision'.[108]

That appears to be the better way. For one, the prohibition of a certain form of conduct primarily concerns the external relationship of the State as a member of the international community only, relating principally to its obligations as a party to the relevant treaty under international law. And prohibitions cover a wide range of areas: while Common Article 3 of the Geneva Conventions of 1949 may seem a persuasive basis for criminalisation, the same will arguably not hold true of Article 34 of the Second Geneva Convention, which contains the prohibition on hospital ships to 'possess or use a secret code for their wireless or other means of communication'.[109] The fact remains that States have, in these cases, a wide range of options at their disposal which allow them to comply with their international commitments: the obligations cited above might, for instance, be implemented through instruments of administrative, rather than criminal, law. Some treaties, in fact, make express reference to that possibility: Article 8 of the UNESCO 1970 Convention thus obliges States to 'impose penalties *or administrative sanctions*' on persons responsible for infringements of some of its provisions.[110]

Not all treaty provisions are as clear as that: Article 4 MARPOL, for instance, dealing with violations of requirements of that Convention, seems to employ the language of criminal law: MARPOL parties do assume the duty not only to prohibit such violations but also to establish 'sanctions' for them, and the 'penalties' which their domestic laws specify pursuant to that article 'shall be adequate in severity to discourage violations' of the Convention.[111] Even that, however, is not conclusive on the duty of criminalisation: the laws of some countries do, after all, provide for penalties for administrative offences as well, while retaining the distinction to sanctions under criminal law.[112]

---

[102] See Arts 104, 105, 100 UNCLOS.

[103] (1994) 2(2) *YILC* 68, Annex, Commentary at (d).

[104] ibid at (h).

[105] See above, n 77.

[106] (1994) 2(2) *YILC* 68, Annex, Crimes Pursuant to Treaties, at 1(e).

[107] Protocol Additional to the Geneva Conventions of 12 August 1949, and Relating to the Protection of Victims of Non-international Armed Conflicts (Protocol II), 8 June 1977, 1125 UNTS 609 ('AP2').

[108] (1994) 2(2) *YILC* 69, Annex, Commentary at (j).

[109] Art 34 Geneva Convention II. See also Wolff Heintschel von Heinegg, 'Article 34: Discontinuance of Protection of Hospital Ships' in Knut Dörmann et al (eds), *Commentary on the Second Geneva Convention* (Cambridge, Cambridge University Press 2017) 837 (doubting the continued 'practical relevance' of the norm).

[110] Emphasis added. UNESCO 1970 Convention (n 79).

[111] See Arts 4(2) and 4(4) MARPOL.

[112] See, for instance, the German Act on Regulatory Offences, Ordnungswidrigkeitengesetz, 30 May 1968 (33) BGBl I/431, English version at https://www.gesetze-im-internet.de/englisch_owig/ and cf the German

For the purposes of this study, therefore, the question whether the provisions of a treaty had a clear impact on the criminal justice system was decisive for the selection process at the level of the substantive law.[113]

The Conventions which, on the basis of the two requirements named above, were selected, are the following fifteen instruments (subsequently referred to as 'the fifteen Conventions' or 'the Conventions'):

(1)–(4)	The Four Geneva Conventions (1949)	(196 Parties)[114]
(5)	The Single Convention on Narcotic Drugs, 1961, as amended by the Protocol amending the Single Convention on Narcotic Drugs (1975) ('Single Convention on Narcotic Drugs')	(186 Parties)[115]
(6)	The Tokyo Convention (1963)	(187 Parties)[116]
(7)	The Hague Hijacking Convention (1970)	(185 Parties)[117]
(8)	The Psychotropic Substances Convention (1971)	(184 Parties)[118]

(Continued)

Criminal Code, Strafgesetzbuch, 13 November 1998 (BGBl I/3322), English version at https://www.gesetze-im-internet.de/englisch_stgb/.

[113] Even then, problematic situations can arise. The ILC, for instance, declined to include provisions of the Tokyo Convention in its *Draft Code of Crimes against the Peace and Security of Mankind*, finding that '[t]he Convention applies to offences against *national* penal law (including minor offences) as well as to conduct which may interfere with air safety whether or not it involves an offence', (1994) 2(2) *YILC* 68–69, Annex, Commentary at (f) (emphasis added). But the Convention is not without its impact on the criminal justice systems of States Parties, an impact which becomes particularly clear through its limitation on the kinds of domestic criminal law whose violation may be considered as establishing a right to take counter-measures aboard aircraft (see below at nn 310–11), and it is for that reason that it is included in the current study. The ILC also did not include the Psychotropic Substances Convention for the purpose of establishing 'treaty crimes', noting that the Convention was 'merely regulatory' and did 'not treat use or traffic in psychotropic drugs as a crime of an international character', (1994) 2(2) *YILC* 69, Annex, Commentary at (g). That, however, appears to be based on an imprecise reading of the treaty. While the Convention does refer to a range of administrative measures, its Art 22 also provides that 'any action contrary to a law or regulation adopted in pursuance' of obligations under the Convention is to be treated by the relevant Party 'as a punishable offence', and that the Party 'shall ensure that serious offences shall be liable to adequate punishment, particularly by imprisonment or other penalty of deprivation of liberty'. It is for that reason that this Convention is included in the current study as well.

[114] United Nations Treaty Collection ('UNTC'), Geneva Convention I, https://web.archive.org/web/20211012064052/https://treaties.un.org/Pages/showDetails.aspx?objid=080000028015847c; ibid, Geneva Convention II, https://web.archive.org/web/20211012064059/https://treaties.un.org/Pages/showDetails.aspx?objid=08000002801591b0; ibid, Geneva Convention III, https://web.archive.org/web/20211012064111/https://treaties.un.org/Pages/showDetails.aspx?objid=0800000280159839; ibid, Geneva Convention IV, https://web.archive.org/web/20211012064119/https://treaties.un.org/Pages/showDetails.aspx?objid=0800000280158b1a.

[115] UNTC, 'Single Convention on Narcotic Drugs, 1961, as amended by the Protocol amending the Single Convention on Narcotic Drugs, 1961', https://web.archive.org/web/20220122014636/https://treaties.un.org/Pages/ViewDetails.aspx?src=IND&mtdsg_no=VI-18&chapter=6&clang=_en.

[116] See International Civil Aviation Organization ('ICAO'), 'Convention on Offences and Certain Other Acts Committed on Board Aircraft', https://web.archive.org/web/20210731071806/https://www.icao.int/secretariat/legal/List%20of%20Parties/Tokyo_EN.pdf.

[117] See ICAO, 'Convention for the Suppression of Unlawful Seizure of Aircraft', https://web.archive.org/web/20210828125419/https://www.icao.int/secretariat/legal/list%20of%20parties/hague_en.pdf.

[118] UNTC, 'Convention on Psychotropic Substances', https://web.archive.org/web/20210628132410/https://treaties.un.org/pages/ViewDetails.aspx?src=TREATY&mtdsg_no=VI-16&chapter=6.

(Continued)

(9)	The Montreal Convention (1971)	(188 Parties)[119]
(10)	CITES (1973)	(183 Parties)[120]
(11)	The Internationally Protected Persons Convention (1973)	(180 Parties)[121]
(12)	The 1988 Narcotic Drugs Convention (1988)	(191 Parties)[122]
(13)	The Terrorist Financing Convention (1999)	(189 Parties)[123]
(14)	UNTOC (2000)	(190 Parties)[124]
(15)	UNCAC (2003)	(187 Parties)[125]

4. FINDINGS

In examining the provisions of the fifteen Conventions that engage with criminalisation, particular focus was placed on aspects relating to the structure of the crime and on provisions dealing with sentencing and other legal consequences; other aspects (such as questions of cooperation) did not inform the main analysis.

In this section, issues relating to the structure of the crime are discussed. Section 4.1 deals with the *actus reus*, section 4.2 with the *mens rea* and section 4.3 with other aspects relating to the substantive law: defences, modes of liability and inchoate crimes. Section 4.4 is dedicated to sentencing provisions and provisions dealing with other legal consequences of the crimes.

The relevant instruments do not, as a general rule, contain many provisions dealing with the 'general part' of criminal law. That was not their purpose: in that regard, the existing treaties on transnational criminal law are truly 'ad hoc' instruments, designed to address a particular problem at hand. Almost any insights on the general part thus have to be derived from the regulation of the more specific issues to which

---

[119] See ICAO, 'Convention for the Suppression of Unlawful Acts Against the Safety of Civil Aviation signed at Montreal on 23 September 1971', https://web.archive.org/web/20210524151601/https://www.icao.int/secretariat/legal/List%20of%20Parties/Mtl71_EN.pdf.

[120] See CITES, 'Parties of the Convention', https://web.archive.org/web/20210826123520/https://cites.org/eng/disc/what.php.

[121] UNTC, 'Convention on the Prevention and Punishment of Crimes against Internationally Protected Persons, including Diplomatic Agents', https://web.archive.org/web/20210724133437/https://treaties.un.org/pages/ViewDetails.aspx?src=IND&mtdsg_no=XVIII-7&chapter=18&clang=_en.

[122] UNTC, 'United Nations Convention against Illicit Traffic in Narcotic Drugs and Psychotropic Substances', https://web.archive.org/web/20210825004047/https://treaties.un.org/Pages/ViewDetails.aspx?src=IND&mtdsg_no=VI-19&chapter=6.

[123] UNTC, 'International Convention for the Suppression of the Financing of Terrorism', https://web.archive.org/web/20210731095647/https://treaties.un.org/pages/ViewDetails.aspx?src=TREATY&mtdsg_no=XVIII-11&chapter=18&clang=_en. See, generally on that Convention, Kimberly Prost, 'The Intersection of AML/SFT and Security Council Sanctions' in Colin King, Clive Walker, Jimmy Gurulé (eds), *The Palgrave Handbook of Criminal and Terrorism Financing Law* (Cham, Palgrave, 2018) 907–26.

[124] UNTC, 'United Nations Convention against Transnational Organized Crime' https://web.archive.org/web/20210412183402/https://treaties.un.org/pages/ViewDetails.aspx?src=IND&mtdsg_no=XVIII-12&chapter=18&clang=_en.

[125] UNTC, 'United Nations Convention against Corruption', https://web.archive.org/web/20210729152451/https://treaties.un.org/pages/ViewDetails.aspx?src=TREATY&mtdsg_no=XVIII-14&chapter=18.

the treaties are dedicated. By the same token, the treaties do not reveal very much about the prevailing understanding of the general principles of criminal law.[126]

4.1. Findings Relating to the *Actus Reus* of the Crime

In view of the above observations, it may not be surprising that an explicit dissection of elements of the *actus reus* of the relevant crimes – for instance, into distinct parts of conduct, consequence, circumstance and causation – is absent from most of the Conventions. UNCAC offers an exception, in as far as it provides a rare reflection on the element of consequences, noting that, for the purposes 'of implementing this Convention it shall not be necessary, except as otherwise stated herein, for the offences set forth in it to result in damage or harm to state property' (Article 3(2) UNCAC). For the most part, the Conventions are, on the side of the *actus reus*, concerned with aspects relating to conduct than other characteristics of this part.

Most of all, it is on the side of the *actus reus* that the 'special part' of substantive transnational criminal law is thrown into relief. That is not surprising: the objective aspects of certain forms of conduct – such as trade in illicit drugs, behaviour that aids terrorism or acts that are dangerous to the safety of aviation – are the ones that initially tended to attract the attention of those seeking criminalisation. Considerations on the *mens rea* might make their appearance only later in the debate – although, as will be seen, they are of some importance to transnational criminal law as well and provide important insights.

Even in private initiatives to establish a world criminal code, the special part of criminal law traditionally occupied a place of prominence. Nor should such considerations be lightly dismissed: when de Araujo refers to slavery and piracy[127] and Eagleton to traffic 'in women and children'[128] as crimes whose incorporation in a world criminal code has or can be suggested, they highlight aspects which considerations based on only a limited number of treaties selected on the basis of the significant number of their parties may omit, while the existence of widespread agreement of the international community on the relevant crimes may well be suspected.

Yet at the margins of these lists, some of the problems to which reference has been made above reappear.[129] For some forms of conduct, such as 'breaking of cables',[130] it is much more difficult to establish consensus among a sufficiently large number of States regarding their criminalisation – quite apart from the fact that some offences (such as 'crimes involving the use of computers'[131]) give little insight into the specific aspects of the conduct that are meant to be covered.

---

[126] See also Anneke Petzschke, 'A Historical Perspective on Modes of Liability in Transnational Criminal Law' in Boister et al (n 22) 253. Some references to general principles are contained in the Geneva Conventions (see eg Arts 86 and 99 Geneva Convention III, Art 67 Geneva Convention IV), but they appear not in sections on criminalisation, but in those dealing with trials of prisoners of war (Geneva Convention III) and trials by an Occupying Power (Geneva Convention IV), respectively.

[127] De Araujo (n 62) 355.

[128] Clyde Eagleton, *International Government* (New York, Ronald Press, 1932) 174.

[129] See above, after n 64.

[130] See Eagleton (n 128) 174.

[131] De Araujo (n 62) 355.

The forms of conduct that received criminalisation in the fifteen Conventions are much more limited and do in fact exclude prominent crimes to which reference is made in works on transnational criminal law (such as maritime safety offences, human trafficking and cybercrimes).[132] The remaining crimes can be grouped in eight categories:

1. Corruption and bribery,[133]
2. Transnational organised crimes,[134]
3. Financing of terrorism,[135]
4. Drugs-related crimes,[136]
5. Crimes against internationally protected persons or property,[137]
6. Crimes relating to endangered species,[138]
7. Aircraft related crimes[139] and
8. Crimes committed against protected persons and property in armed conflict.[140]

Under each of these categories, a range of individual crimes exists, leading to a total of 112 offences that are addressed.[141]

Some Conventions, especially those of a more recent date, have provisions on the specific forms of conduct falling under the same crime category; and in those cases, a distinction between principal and ancillary offences may be possible. That applies to certain drugs-related offences where, for instance, the Narcotic Drugs Convention (1988) not only imposes the obligation on States to provide for the establishment of criminal offences for the manufacture, sale, importation etc of illegal narcotic drugs or psychotropic substances,[142] but also for the 'acquisition, possession or use of property' which was derived from one of the principal offences.[143] Similarly, UNCAC not only obliges States to criminalise acts such as the promising of an 'undue advantage' to a public official in order that that official 'act or refrain from acting in the exercise of his or her official duties',[144] but also contains a provision on the laundering of

---

[132] See on these points Boister (n 9) 45–55, 62–68, 187–99.

[133] See UNCAC (2003) (n 79). See also Dimiris Ziouvas, 'International Asset Recovery and the United Nations Convention Against Corruption' in King et al (n 123) 594.

[134] See UNTOC (2000) (n 9).

[135] See Terrorist Financing Convention (1999) (n 79).

[136] See the Single Convention on Narcotic Drugs (1961) (n 79); the Psychotropic Substances Convention (1971) (n 67); the Narcotic Drugs Convention (1988) (n 73).

[137] See the Internationally Protected Persons Convention (1973) (n 79).

[138] See CITES (1973) (n 79).

[139] See the Tokyo Convention (1963) (n 79); the Hague Hijacking Convention (1970) (n 79); the Montreal Convention (1971) (n 79).

[140] See the four Geneva Conventions (1949) (n 77).

[141] An element of subjectivity unavoidably inhabits this categorisation. For instance, for purposes of the current study, 'production' and 'manufacture' of narcotic drugs (Art 3(1) Narcotic Drugs Convention (1988)) are treated as falling within different categories of crimes (see also Arts 1(1)(n) and (t) of the Single Convention on Narcotic Drugs (1961); Neil Boister, *Penal Aspects of the UN Drugs Conventions* (The Hague, Kluwer, 2001) 79 and Boister (n 9) 94), even though the terms tend to be used synonymously in the pharmaceutical industry; see Henri Mazaud, John F Scott, William C. Gilmore and David McClean, *Commentary on the United Nations Convention against Illegal Traffic in Narcotic Drugs and Psychotropic Substances 1988* (New York, United Nations, 1998) E/CN.7/590, 53.

[142] See Art 3(1)(a)(i) Narcotic Drugs Convention (1988).

[143] ibid Art 3(1)(c)(i).

[144] Art 15(a) UNCAC (2003).

proceeds of crime and lays down the duty of States to criminalise the 'acquisition, possession or use of property' that is the proceeds of the principal crime.[145] The Convention even expressly acknowledges the existence of crimes that live in a relationship of dependence on other offences. In its interpretive article, it thus defines 'proceeds of crimes' as 'any property derived from or obtained, directly or indirectly, through the commission of an offence', and a 'predicate offence' as 'any offence as a result of which proceeds have been generated that may become the subject of an offence as defined in article 23 of this Convention'.[146] Article 23, in turn, obliges States, for instance, to criminalise the transfer of property for the purpose of helping a person who is 'involved in the commission of the predicate offence to evade the legal consequences of his or her action'.[147]

If the *actus reus* thus occupies a place of such prominence in the fifteen Conventions, it is tempting to reach the conclusion that it retains an important position in the shared understanding of the international community on the relevant aspects of criminal justice. The view, however, that the relevant crimes are included as representative of consensus on the need for their criminalisation is not free from critique and invites further evaluation. It is a point to which this chapter will return.[148]

4.2. Findings Relating to the *Mens Rea* of the Crime

If the *actus reus* is the part that principally drew the attention of States Parties to the underlying problems, the concomitant *mens rea* can be expected to have played only a secondary role in their considerations. That understanding would mirror the critique that has been voiced in the literature about the state of international criminal law: there, Fletcher in 2005 expressed the view that the subjective side of the crime represented one of the 'weakest areas' in the field, finding that international criminal law 'desperately' needed 'serious work on why and when intention should be required and, even more acutely, on the meaning of intentionality and recklessness'.[149]

That seems an uncharitable view: the ICC Statute at least contains, in Article 30, a detailed expression of its understanding of the default *mens rea* of international crimes – which is more than some jurisdictions (especially within the common law family) provide. It is also more than transnational criminal law provides, which, in the absence of a consolidated treaty in the field, cannot offer an article on *mens rea* with applicability to all offences.

But the requirement of the existence of a subjective element can also be derived from the mandate of individual criminal responsibility, which, as part of *nulla poena*

---

[145] ibid Art 23(1)(b)(i).
[146] ibid Art 2(e) and (h).
[147] ibid Art 23(1)(a)(i). See also, on the scope of predicate offences, Badr El Banna, 'Article 23: Laundering of Proceeds of Crime' in Cecily Rose, Michael Kubiciel and Oliver Landwehr (eds), *The United Nations Convention Against Corruption: A Commentary* (Oxford, Oxford University Press, 2019) 251–58, 255–57.
[148] See below at section 5.2.
[149] Fletcher (n 31) 33.

sine culpa – a principle of customary international law[150] – has in turn been seen as directly derived from the principle of legality.[151] The reason for this link to the demands of individual criminal responsibility appears even stronger when the fact is taken into account that it is arguably the mens rea that gives shape to *culpa* rather than the *actus reus* – *acti rei*, after all, can be the same for accidents and for intentional crimes.

Yet transnational criminal law, perhaps surprisingly, does tend to reflect on the subjective element. In the fifteen Conventions, references to various forms of *mens rea* are therefore found, ranging from intent[152] to the 'wanton' commission of crimes[153] and to 'knowledge' of certain specified material elements.[154]

Nor can it be said that these references were inserted in an arbitrary fashion: several Conventions make clear that the drafters were aware of the distinctions between the various forms of *mens rea* they included; in particular, those between knowledge, intent and purpose.[155]

Of the particular forms of *mens rea* addressed, intent is certainly the most common, as indicated by references to obligations to criminalise the relevant acts 'when committed intentionally' or through the use of the words 'intentional' or 'intentionally'.[156] The terms 'wilful' or 'wilfully' arguably go further and also embrace the concept of recklessness.[157]

---

[150] The Tadić Appeals Chamber noted on the principle *nulla poena sine culpa* that 'in international law as much as in national systems', nobody 'may be held criminally responsible for acts or transactions in which he has not personally engaged or in some way participated', ICTY, Appeals Chamber, *Prosecutor v Duško Tadić*, IT-94-1-A, Judgment, 15 July 1999 ('*Tadić* (Appeals Chamber)'), para 186, with further reference as to its derivation. See also for an express acknowledgment of that principle, ECtHR, *Russian Conservative Party of Entrepreneurs and Others v Russia*, Appl Nos 55066/00 and 55638/00, Judgment, 11 January 2007, para 66 and ECtHR, *GIEM SRL and others v Italy*, Appl Nos 1828/06, 34163/07, 19029/11, Judgment, 28 June 2018 ('ECtHR *GIEM*'), para 242. On the link between criminal culpability and *mens rea*, see also ICTY, Trial Chamber, *Prosecutor v Zejnil Delalić et al*, IT-96-21-T, Judgment, 16 November 1998, paras 424–25.

[151] See on this, ECtHR *GIEM*, Partly Concurring, Partly Dissenting Opinion of Judge Pinto de Albuquerque, para 23 (with references to ECtHR case law). See, however, for a view that would allow the permissibility of strict liability offences in certain contexts, n 173 below.

[152] See, for instance, Art 15 UNCAC.

[153] See, for instance, Art 147 Geneva Convention IV.

[154] See, for instance, Art 6(1)(a)(ii) UNTOC.

[155] See Arts 5(2) and 6(2)(f) UNTOC, Art 28 UNCAC; Art 3(3) Narcotic Drugs Convention (1988).

[156] See Arts 36(1)(a) and 36(2)(a)(ii) Single Convention on Narcotic Drugs; Arts 3(1) and (2) Narcotic Drugs Convention (1988); Arts 5(1), 6(1), 8(1), 23 UNTOC; Arts 15, 16(1) and (2), 17–22, 23(1), 24–25 UNCAC; Arts 22(1)(a) and 22(2)(a)(ii) Psychotropic Substances Convention; Art 1(1) Montreal Convention; Art 2(1) Internationally Protected Persons Convention; Art 2(5)(c) Terrorist Financing Convention. See also, for money laundering offences under UNTOC, Stefano Betti, 'The European Union and the United Nations Convention against Transnational Organised Crime', Working Paper LIBE 116 EN (European Parliament, Directorate-General for Research 2001) 15.

[157] See Art 50 Geneva Convention I; Art 51 Geneva Convention II; Art 130 Geneva Convention III; Art 147 Geneva Convention IV; Art 2(1) Terrorist Financing Convention. On this interpretation of 'wilful', see Knut Dörmann and Eve La Haye, 'Article 50: Grave Breaches' in Knut Dörmann et al (eds), *Commentary on the First Geneva Convention* (Cambridge, Cambridge University Press, 2016) 1053, 1061, 1076; Knut Dörmann and Eve La Haye, 'Article 51: Grave Breaches' in Dörmann (2017) (n 109) 1077, 1086, 1101; Knut Dörmann and Eve La Haye, 'Article 130: Grave Breaches' in Knut Dörmann et al (eds), *Commentary on the Third Geneva Convention* (Cambridge, Cambridge University Press, 2021) 1884, 1893, 1909, 1916.

A particularly interesting feature is the fact that specific intent – a form of intent that introduces a subjective element in addition to those that merely mirror the objective parts of the crime – makes a common appearance. Phrases such as 'in order that' in UNCAC and UNTOC are indications of that: under UNTOC, for instance, the offering of an undue advantage to a public official is to be criminalised where such offering is done 'in order that the official act or refrain from acting in the exercise of his or her official duties',[158] with a similar duty being enshrined in UNCAC.[159] In other provisions, the terms 'for the purpose of',[160] 'with the aim',[161] 'for his or her benefit',[162] 'with the intention' (where this exceeds an intention corresponding to an objective element)[163] or indeed the mere particle 'to'[164] contain indications that specific intent is a condition of the crime.

It is the more interesting, as specific intent – precisely because of the lack of a corresponding element on the objective side of the crime – can cause considerable difficulties for the prosecution. The crime of genocide, which does require specific intent, is an example. It has become common to refer to the evidentiary difficulties that this element poses: SàCouto outlines one of the problems when noting that '[v]ery infrequently is there a smoking gun evidence of intent'.[165] Nor were these difficulties unknown at least when some of the Conventions were concluded: as early as 1998

---

[158] Art 8(1)(a) UNTOC, see also ibid Art 8(1)(b).

[159] See Art 15(a) UNCAC and see Boister (n 9) 156, referring to this as 'specific intention'. See also Art 15(b), Art 16(1) and (2), Art 18(a) and (b), Art 21(a) and (b) UNCAC. See also, for the required subjective connection between, on the one hand, 'offer or advantage' and, on the other hand, inducing an official to act or to refrain from acting (in the context of Art 15), Michael Kubiciel, 'Article 15: Bribery of National Public Officials' in Rose et al (n 147) 165–74, 172. On the importance of the subjective element in relation to Art 18 of that Convention, see Aloysius Llamzon, 'Article 18: Trading in Influence' ibid, 192–209, 196 ('[t]he crime only requires the intent to "abuse" influence; that influence need not actually be asserted'). See also Michael Kubiciel, 'Article 21: Bribery in the Private Sector', ibid 238–44, 243 in relation to Art 21 (not requiring that the act or omission has taken place and arguing that the words 'in order to' refer to 'intention rather than to completed conduct').

[160] See Art 3(1)(a)(ii) ('for the purpose of the production of narcotic drugs') and Art 3(1)(b)(ii) ('for the purpose of concealing or disguising the illicit origin of the property') Narcotic Drugs Convention (1988); Art 6(1)(a)(i) ('for the purpose of concealing or disguising the illicit origin of the property') UNTOC; Art 19 ('for the purpose of obtaining an undue advantage') and Art 23(1)(a)(i) ('for the purpose of concealing or disguising the illicit origin of the property') UNCAC, see Cecily Rose, 'Article 19: Abuse of Functions' in Rose et al (n 147) 210–18, 215; Banna (n 147) 251–58, 254.

[161] See Art 2(c)(i) Terrorist Financing Convention. On specific intent in the context of provisions on terrorism, see also Sten Idris Verhoeven and Yi Zhang, 'The Offence of Incitement to Terrorism' (ch 15 in this volume), at nn 39–40.

[162] See Art 17 UNCAC.

[163] See Art 2(1) Terrorist Financing Convention.

[164] In particular where obstruction of justice is concerned. See Art 23(a) ('to induce false testimony or to interfere'), Art 23(b) ('to interfere with the exercise of official duties') UNTOC; Art 25(a) ('to induce false testimony or to interfere'), Art 25(b) ('to interfere with the exercise of official duties') UNCAC. See, in general on the requirement of 'ulterior intentions' in transnational criminal law, Boister (n 9) 26. Dörmann and La Haye also read specific intent into torture under the grave breaches regime of the Geneva Conventions; Dörmann and La Haye (2016) (n 157) 1053; Dörmann and La Haye (2017) (n 109) 1079; Dörmann and La Haye (2021) (n 157) 1885.

[165] Susana SàCouto, 'Advances and Missed Opportunities in the International Prosecution of Gender-Based Crimes' (2006–07) 10 *Gonzaga Journal of International Law* 49, 51. See also Florian Jessberger, 'Corporate Involvement in Slavery and Criminal Responsibility under International Law' (2016) 14 *Journal of International Criminal Justice* 327, 331, fn 1; Marko Milanović, 'State Responsibility for Genocide' (2006) 17 *European Journal of International Law* 553, 574.

did the *Akayesu* Trial Chamber note, in the particular context of specific intent, that 'intent is a mental factor which is difficult, even impossible, to determine'.[166]

Yet the reason for the inclusion of specific intent in transnational crimes may well be that, to the drafters, this may have been the element that gave them their particular identity. That is nowhere as clear as where the relevant crime is done in furtherance of another offence: such as, in UNTOC, the laundering of proceeds of crime. Article 6(1) (a)(i) UNTOC provides in that regard that the transfer of property, knowing that such property is the proceeds of crime, is to be criminalised, for instance, when the perpetrator did this 'for the purpose of concealing' the illicit origin of the property.[167] Still – the result is an element that may cause considerable difficulties to those charged with its evaluation at trial stage.

Below the level of intent, the fifteen Conventions do not contain many reflections on the relevant elements of *mens rea*. In that regard, another parallel to contemporary international criminal law exists: Article 30 ICC Statute does not explicitly refer to advertent or inadvertent negligence and appears to omit recklessness as well.[168] Knowledge, however, (to which Article 30 does make reference) does appear as a mental element in the Conventions. It matters in two respects, of which the first is knowledge of material elements that are not necessarily the result of the perpetrator's own actions (elements which the ICC Statute would have termed 'circumstantial' elements) – for instance, knowledge of the fact that certain property is the proceeds of crime,[169] or is derived from certain offences.[170] The other context in which the cognitive element appears, relates to knowledge of certain subjective elements of other persons: knowledge, for instance, of a particular group intention,[171] or of the purpose for which funds, equipment, material or substances are to be used.[172]

Reference to recklessness appears to be made in the 'Grave Breaches' regime under the Geneva Conventions and in the Terrorist Financing Convention, where it is indicated by the word 'wilful', but also in provisions in the Geneva Conventions which require certain conduct to be carried out 'wantonly'.[173] Neither advertent nor inadvertent negligence are mentioned in the fifteen Conventions.

---

[166] ICTR, Trial Chamber, *Prosecutor v Jean-Paul Akayesu*, ICTR-96-4-T, Judgment, 2 September 1998, para 523.

[167] See Art 6(1)(a)(i) UNTOC.

[168] In that regard, Art 30(2)(b) and Art 30(3) ICC Statute, using the phrase 'will occur in the ordinary course of events', appear to impose a standard that is closer to oblique intent than to recklessness.

[169] See Arts 23(1)(a)(i), 23(1)(a)(ii) UNCAC; Arts 6(1)(a)(i), 6(1)(a)(ii), 6(1)(b)(i) UNTOC.

[170] See Arts 3(b)(i), 3(b)(ii), 3(c)(i) Narcotic Drugs Convention (1988); Arts 24 UNCAC. See, on the interpretation of intent in the context of Art 2 Internationally Protected Persons Convention (which encompasses knowledge of the status of the victim), Louis M Bloomfield and Gerald Francis Fitzgerald, *Crimes against Internationally Protected Persons: Prevention and Punishment. An Analysis of the UN Convention* (New York, Praeger, 1975) 79.

[171] See Art 2(c)(ii) Terrorist Financing Convention; see also Art 5(1)(a)(ii)b UNTOC.

[172] See Art 2(1) Terrorist Financing Convention; Arts 3(1)(a)(iv), 3(1)(c)(ii) Narcotic Drugs Convention (1988).

[173] On 'wilful', see n 157 above. On the term 'wantonly', see Art 50 Geneva Convention I, Art 51 Geneva Convention II, Art 147 Geneva Convention IV and see Dörmann and La Haye (2016) (n 157) 1079; Dörmann and La Haye (2017) (n 109) 1104. The ICC Statute considers this element to refer to '[e]xtensive destruction and appropriation of property' only, Art 8(2)(a)(iv) ICC Statute. See, however, also, with regard to the option at the disposal of States Parties to UNTOC to include recklessness and negligence (as well as, in McClean's view, strict liability), John David McClean, *Transnational Organized Crime: A Commentary on*

The Conventions do, however, recognise the evidentiary difficulty that the establishment of mental elements causes. In some treaties, therefore, explicit reference is made to permissible inferences which may aid those charged with the application of the law. The Narcotic Drugs Convention (1988) thus provides that 'knowledge, intent or purpose' may be 'inferred from objective factual circumstances',[174] a rule which is reproduced in UNTOC[175] and in UNCAC.[176]

4.3. Other Aspects of the Crime

If the structure of a crime is considered to follow the paradigmatic tripartite model that distinguishes between *actus reus*, *mens rea* and defences stricto sensu, it is the third part which, in some legal systems, has attracted charges of being particularly poorly developed. With regard to international criminal law, Fletcher thus raises the critique that the ICC Statute 'does not even recognize the distinction between justification and excuse' and may have to 'compensate for [an] overly restrictive definition by adding new "grounds for excluding criminal behaviour" under Article 21(2) ICCSt'.[177]

Yet the point can be made that the ICC Statute does at least, in Articles 31–32, contain rules on defences with general applicability for all crimes under the jurisdiction of the ICC. That is more than is provided in some jurisdictions, where the applicability of certain justifications or excuses has to be confirmed for each crime separately.[178]

It is also more than is done in transnational criminal law; and in this case, it is also difficult to draw inferences on such defences from the special crimes contained in the fifteen Conventions: the Conventions contain hardly any reflections on them.

Some Conventions do restrict the concept of the relevant offences to acts that have been carried out 'unlawfully': the Hague Hijacking Convention, for instance, provides that anybody commits an offence who 'by force or threat thereof, or by any other form of intimidation', seizes an aircraft, if that is done 'unlawfully' on board an aircraft in flight.[179] The use of these terms thus leaves open the possibility

---

the UN Convention and its Protocols (Oxford, Oxford University Press, 2007) 62; see also Betti (n 156) 14. Similarly, for the Narcotic Drugs Convention (1988), Mazaud et al (n 141) 51 and, critical on the option at the disposal of States Parties to the drugs conventions to include a negligence or even a 'no fault' standard, Boister (2001) (n 141) 519. For UNTOC, see Cecily Rose, 'Article 17: Embezzlement, Misappropriation or other Diversion of Property by a Public Official', in Rose et al (n 147) 182–91, 188 and Cecily Rose, 'Article 19: Abuse of Functions' (ibid) 210–18, 215. See also Boister (n 9) 26.

[174] Art 3(3) Narcotic Drugs Convention (1988). See on this Mazaud et al (n 141) 83.

[175] See Arts 5(2) and 6(2)(f) UNTOC.

[176] Art 28 UNCAC. See on this Kubiciel, 'Article 15' (n 159) 172. See also, on the influence that the original wording in the Narcotic Drugs Convention (1988) had on international and European materials, McClean (n 173) 65.

[177] Fletcher (n 31) 34. Art 21(2) ICC Statute allows the Court to 'apply principles and rules of law as interpreted in its previous decisions'.

[178] An example in English criminal law is the defence of duress, which is available for some, but not all crimes, see David Ormerod and Karl Laird, *Smith and Hogan's Criminal Law*, 14th edn (Oxford, Oxford University Press, 2015) 405–09. On the whole, international criminal law provides a more coherent system, although it, too, is not free from inconsistencies: the superior orders defence, for instance, is available for war crimes, but not for orders to commit crimes against humanity and genocide (Art 33(2) ICC Statute).

[179] Art 1(a) Hague Hijacking Convention. See also Art 50 Geneva Convention I; Art 51 Geneva Convention II; Art 147 Geneva Convention III; Art 1(1) Montreal Convention; Art 2(1) Terrorist Financing Convention.

that the relevant act can in theory be carried out lawfully – one may think of actions undertaken by security services of the State of registration in a situation of duress, whose conduct is thus covered by a justification.

Geneva Conventions I, II and IV also provide, in a rare departure in transnational criminal law, for a defence in their 'Grave Breaches' regime, by expressly recognising 'military necessity' at least as a justification to the extensive destruction and appropriation of property.[180]

A negative approach to justifications is provided in the Terrorist Financing Convention: the Convention obliges States Parties to take the necessary measures to ensure that 'considerations of a political, philosophical, ideological, racial, ethnic, religious or other similar nature' do in no case render criminal acts under the scope of the Convention 'justifiable'.[181]

Apart from that, however, the Conventions leave the determination of applicable defences to the domestic laws of the States Parties. The Narcotic Drugs Convention (1988) includes an explicit reference to that effect, noting that the description of the 'legal defences' to the offences to which the treaty refers 'is reserved to the domestic law of a Party';[182] UNTOC, similarly, provides that 'the applicable legal defences or other legal principles controlling the lawfulness of conduct is reserved to the domestic law of a State Party',[183] a rule that is reproduced in UNCAC.[184]

Where modes of liability are concerned, the fifteen Conventions offer a plethora of terms to cover the relevant conduct, including organising,[185] directing,[186] participation,[187] association,[188] aiding and abetting,[189] being an accomplice,[190] assisting,[191] facilitating,[192] being an instigator,[193] inducing[194] and counselling.[195]

---

[180] See Art 50 Geneva Convention I; Art 51 Geneva Convention II; Art 147 Geneva Convention III. This reading (limiting the defence to these particular crimes) is the one which the ICC Statute followed: see Art 8(2)(a)(iv) ICC Statute. See also Dörmann and La Haye (2016) (n 157) 1078; Dörmann and La Haye (2017) (n 109) 1103.

[181] Art 5 Terrorist Financing Convention.

[182] Art 3(11) Narcotic Drugs Convention (1988).

[183] Art 11(6) UNTOC; but see on this also McClean (n 173) 135.

[184] Art 30(9) UNCAC.

[185] See Art 2(b) Terrorist Financing Convention; Art 5(1)(b) UNTOC.

[186] See Art 2(b) Terrorist Financing Convention; Art 5(1)(b) UNTOC.

[187] Art 22(2)(a)(ii) Psychotropic Substances Convention; Art 36(2) Single Convention on Narcotic Drugs; Art 3(c)(iv) Narcotic Drugs Convention (1988); Art 6(1)(b)(ii) UNTOC; Art 23(1)(b)(ii) UNCAC.

[188] Art 3(1)(c)(iv) Narcotic Drugs Convention (1988); Art 6(1)(b)(ii) UNTOC; Art 23(1)(b)(ii) UNCAC. See Boister (2001) (n 141) 122.

[189] Art 3(1)(c)(iv) Narcotic Drugs Convention (1988); Art 5(1)(b) UNTOC; Art 23(1)(b)(ii) UNCAC.

[190] Art 1(b) Hague Hijacking Convention; Art 1(2)(b) Montreal Convention; Art 2(1)(e) Internationally Protected Persons Convention; Art 2(5) Terrorist Financing Convention; Art 8(3) UNTOC; Art 27(1) UNCAC.

[191] Art 27(1) UNCAC.

[192] Art 3(1)(c)(iv) Narcotic Drugs Convention (1988); Arts 5(1)(b), 6(1)(b)(ii) UNTOC; Art 23(1)(b)(ii) UNCAC.

[193] Art 27(1) UNCAC.

[194] Art 3(1)(c)(iii) Narcotic Drugs Convention (1988). On the relationship between inducement and incitement, see Mazaud et al (n 141) 74.

[195] Art 3(1)(c)(iv) Narcotic Drugs Convention (1988); Arts 5(1)(b), 6(1)(b)(ii) UNTOC; Art 23(1)(b)(ii) UNCAC. See also, in general, on divergences among national systems on modes of participation in criminal activity, McClean (n 173) 64. On the relationship between counselling and inciting, see Mazaud et

For some of these terms – say, 'directing' on the one hand and 'assisting' on the other – the literal interpretation will convey some clarity on the distinctions that inhabit them. For other terms – for instance, 'facilitating' and 'aiding and abetting' – the differentiation is far less clear, even though the terms are used in the same Conventions.[196] Nor does the Convention text give any indication as to the characteristics with which the drafters may have endowed the different concepts.

The result is an inflation of codified modes of liability – a phenomenon not unknown in the field of international criminal law, where numerous terms are employed in the statutes of international criminal courts and tribunals to encapsulate the criminal responsibility of individual perpetrators.[197] That would not be expected to yield problematic consequences in criminal justice systems where the same sentence is available for principal perpetrators as for other participants. Where differences can be made at sentencing level, the matter is more complicated, and the making of exact distinctions is unavoidable. In that regard, the continuous piling on of modes of liability, without delineating their boundaries, is a regrettable aspect of modern transnational criminal law and does not help to establish sufficiently clear international consensus.

Two of the more recent Conventions contain a provision approaching a concept that, in international criminal law, would be understood as acting in furtherance of a joint criminal enterprise. The Terrorist Financing Convention refers to contributions to one or more of the relevant offences when they are committed by a group acting with common purpose, if such contribution is intentional and made either 'with the aim of furthering the criminal activity or criminal purpose of the group' or 'made in the knowledge of the intention of the group' to commit an offence.[198] These words are, in their material parts, identical to those used in the ICC Statute to capture joint criminal enterprise (JCE).[199] It is, however, interesting to note that the Terrorist Financing Convention does not expressly refer to the controversial 'third form' of JCE – ie, the possibility of attributing liability to a participant for a specific crime that did not form part of the group's 'common criminal purpose' but whose commission by members of the group was foreseeable to the defendant.[200] While that form of JCE has been embraced by the international criminal tribunals,[201] it is questionable whether, given prevailing distinctions within domestic legal systems on

---

al (n 141) 74, and on distinctions between incitement, induction and counselling in the Narcotic Drugs Convention (1988), Boister (2001) (n 141) 121.

[196] See at nn 189, 192 above.

[197] See Art 7(1) ICTY Statute; Art 6(1) ICTR Statute; Art 25(3)(a)–(c) ICC Statute. For a more positive assessment, see Boister (2001) (n 141) 123.

[198] Art 2(c) Terrorist Financing Convention. On the comparably recent appearance of joint enterprise liability in transnational criminal law, see Boister (n 9) 26.

[199] See Art 25(1)(d) ICC Statute. On the understanding of this provision as covering JCE, see Marko Milanović, 'An Odd Couple' (2007) 5 *Journal of International Criminal Justice* 1139, 1144. But see, for a critical approach, Jens David Ohlin, 'Joint Criminal Confusion' (2009) 12 *New Criminal Law Review* 406, 407.

[200] See *Tadić* (Appeals Chamber), para 220.

[201] ibid and see ICTR, Appeals Chamber, *Prosecutor v Elizaphan Ntakirutimana and Gérard Ntakirutimana*, ICTR-96-10-A and ICTR-96-17-A, Judgment, 13 December 2004, paras 465, 468.

this matter,[202] a convention on transnational criminal law which obliged States to encode the third form of the JCE in their criminal laws would have met with the same level of acceptance as one limiting itself to the type of JCE addressed in the Terrorist Financing Convention.

UNTOC (2000), similarly, confers the duty on Parties to criminalise conduct of a person that is carried out 'with knowledge of either the aim and general criminal activity of an organized criminal group or its intention to commit the crimes in question' where it results in that person's participation in '[c]riminal activities' of that group.[203] But UNTOC goes further than the Terrorist Financing Convention: it expressly embraces also participation in 'other activities of the organized criminal group' if such activities are carried out 'in the knowledge' that the participation 'will contribute to the achievement of the above-described criminal aim.[204] In that case, therefore, participation does not need to be participation in activities that are criminal themselves; the blameworthiness of the conduct is borrowed from the fact that the participant seeks to contribute to the achievement of a criminal aim.

The fifteen Conventions also contain provisions on inchoate forms of conduct. Conspiracy is frequently mentioned: the Psychotropic Substances Convention thus obliges Parties to make conspiracy to commit any of the relevant offences a punishable offence.[205] It is, however, worth noting that Conventions referring to conspiracy invariably acknowledge limitations to criminalisation which may apply due to 'constitutional limitations',[206] 'constitutional principles'[207] or the 'basic concepts' of the Parties' 'legal system'.[208] Art 5(1) UNTOC clarifies the difficulty: the Article recognises that an agreement between persons 'to commit a serious crime for a purpose' relating to obtaining 'a financial or other material benefit' may, under the laws of some States, require the involvement of an 'act undertaken by one of the participants in furtherance of the agreement or involving an organized criminal group'.[209] In light of this expressly acknowledged restriction, it would be difficult to assert that the consensus of the international community extends to conspiracy per se as an inchoate form of committing the crime.

---

[202] See on this Milanović (n 199) 1144, who also doubts whether the third form of the JCE can in fact be based on a reading of the ICC Statute, ibid.

[203] Art 5(1)(a)(ii)a. UNTOC. See, on the origins of that provision, Boister (n 9) 139 and Serena Forlati, 'Organized Crime. The Road to the Palermo Convention' in Boister et al (eds) (2021) (n 22) 184.

[204] Art 5(1)(a)(ii)b. UNTOC.

[205] See Art 22(2)(a)(ii) Psychotropic Substances Convention. See also Art 36(2)(a)(ii) Single Convention on Narcotic Drugs; Art 3(1)(c)(iv) Narcotic Drugs Convention (1988); Art 6(1)(b)(ii) UNTOC; Art 23(1)(b)(ii) UNCAC (but see Boister (n 9) 161).

[206] See Art 22(2)(a)(ii) Psychotropic Substances Convention; Art 36(2)(a)(ii) Single Convention on Narcotic Drugs.

[207] Art 3(1)(c)(iv) Narcotic Drugs Convention (1988).

[208] Art 6(1)(b)(ii) UNTOC; Art 23(1)(b)(ii) UNCAC. On divergences among individual jurisdictions regarding conspiracy (in the context of the drugs conventions), see Boister (2001) (n 141) 73, 87 and 519 (with reference to 'exotic common law notions').

[209] Art 5(1)(a)(i) UNTOC. See on this McClean (n 173) 63. See also, on the debates about the inclusion of 'conspiracy' in both the Internationally Protected Persons Convention and the Montreal Convention and the difficulties which such proposals faced, Bloomfield and Fitzgerald (n 170) 78. See also Mazaud et al (n 141) 72.

Attempts are likewise frequently addressed by the duty of criminalisation in the fifteen Conventions.[210] In this context, too, safeguard clauses have been added to take into account the 'constitutional limitations', the 'legal system and domestic law' of a party,[211] the 'basic concepts of its legal system'[212] or simply its 'domestic law'.[213] But not always: several Conventions seek criminalisation without expressly referring to any such restrictions,[214] suggesting that international consensus may be wider with regard to attempt than with regard to conspiracy.

The appearance of other inchoate acts is less frequent. The Narcotic Drugs Convention (1988) makes reference to public incitement to commit any of the relevant offences,[215] the Internationally Protected Persons Convention obliges States to criminalise 'threats' to commit the attacks to which the Convention refers.[216] The Single Convention on Narcotic Drugs and the Psychotropic Substances Convention also refer to 'preparatory acts',[217] while UNCAC provides that a State Party 'may' adopt measures 'as may be necessary to establish as a criminal offence, in accordance with its domestic law, the preparation' of a relevant offence.[218]

In some cases, the interpretation of the conduct that is to be criminalised may be assisted by findings from the international criminal courts and tribunals. For the determination of 'public incitement' and 'conspiracy', for instance, guidance can be derived from case law which considered the corresponding forms of conduct, for example, in judgments in the context of genocide.[219] It is true that strict interpretation, as a general principle of human rights law, applies to construction in the context of the fifteen Conventions as well; care must therefore be taken that the resulting understanding does not constitute an extension of the crime to the detriment of the defendant.[220] Within these parameters, however, it may be possible to take advantage

---

[210] Art 1 Hague Hijacking Convention; Art 22(2)(a)(ii) Psychotropic Substances Convention; Art 1(2) Montreal Convention; Art 2(1)(d) Internationally Protected Persons Convention; Art 36(2)(a)(ii) Single Convention on Narcotic Drugs; Art 3(1)(c)(iv) Narcotic Drugs Convention (1988); Art 2(4) Terrorist Financing Convention; Art 6(1)(b)(ii) UNTOC; Arts 23(1)(b)(ii) and 27(2) UNCAC. See, however, Michael Kubiciel and Cornelia Spörl, 'Article 27: Participation and Attempt' in Rose et al (n 147) 282–91, 289, with regard to the non-mandatory character of Art 27(2) UNCAC.

[211] Art 36(2)(a)(ii) Single Convention on Narcotic Drugs; Art 22(2)(a)(ii) Psychotropic Substances Convention.

[212] Art 3(1)(c)(iv) Narcotic Drugs Convention (1988); Art 6(1)(b)(ii) UNTOC; Art 23(1)(b)(ii) UNCAC.

[213] Art 27(2) UNCAC. The term 'safeguard clause' had been suggested by Mazaud et al (n 141) 72 in the context of Art 3(1)(c) Narcotic Drugs Convention (1988). See also Michael Elliot and Felix Lüth, 'Corporate Liability' in Boister et al (eds) (n 22) 212.

[214] See Art 1 Hague Hijacking Convention; Art 1(2) Montreal Convention; Art 2(1)(d) Internationally Protected Persons Convention; Art 2(4) Terrorist Financing Convention. But see also Bloomfield and Fitzgerald (n 170) 77. On the wider currency of the concept of attempts, see Boister (2001) (n 141) 88.

[215] See Art 3(1)(c)(iii) Narcotic Drugs Convention (1988). This is again subject to the 'constitutional principles and the basic concepts' of the Party's legal system.

[216] Art 2(1)(d) Internationally Protected Persons Convention, without reference to constitutional or other limitations in the legal systems of the State Parties. See, however, Bloomfield and Fitzgerald (n 170) 76, on views advanced against a common international position on the criminal concept of 'threat'.

[217] See Art 22(2)(a)(ii) Psychotropic Substances Convention; Art 36(2)(a)(ii) Single Convention on Narcotic Drugs, both with reference to the 'constitutional limitations of a Party, its legal system and domestic law'.

[218] Art 27(3) UNCAC. See on this Kubiciel and Spörl (n 210) 290–91.

[219] ICTR, Appeals Chamber, *Nahimana, Barayagwiza and Ngeze v Prosecutor*, ICTR-99-52-A, Judgment, 28 November 2007, paras 677 and 894.

[220] See on this ECtHR, *Kokkinakis v Greece*, Appl No 14307/88, Judgment, 25 May 1993, para 52 and ECtHR, *Vasiliauskas v Lithuania*, Appl No 35343/05, Judgment, 20 October 2015, para 154.

of the benefits derived from the clear definition of the relevant concepts in the field of international criminal law, as long as due consideration is given to the differences and specificities of that body of law.[221]

4.4. Sentencing and Other Legal Consequences

An interesting facet of the fifteen Conventions is the fact that some of the treaties also reflect on the legal consequences of the relevant offences. Where sentencing is concerned, there is often a strong retributivist element that appears to have guided the drafting of the instruments. It appears in articles that provide that the 'gravity'[222] or the 'grave nature'[223] is to be taken into account in the determination of the relevant sanctions or that oblige States Parties to ensure 'that serious offences shall be liable to adequate punishment'.[224] The Montreal Convention arguably goes farthest by imposing the duty on Contracting States 'to make the offences mentioned in Article 1 punishable by severe penalties'.[225] Deterrence, too, is mentioned as a purpose: the Narcotic Drugs Convention (1988) thus obliges Parties to ensure that discretionary legal powers 'are exercised to maximize the effectiveness of law enforcement measures' in relation to the relevant offences 'and with due regard to the need to deter' their commission;[226] and similar wording is found in UNTOC and UNCAC.[227]

In light of these considerations, it is then, perhaps, not surprising that imprisonment is mentioned in several Conventions as an exemplary form of punishment,[228]

---

[221] ICTY, Trial Chamber, *Prosecutor v Kunarac et al*, IT-96-23-T & IT-96-23/1-T, Judgment, 22 Feb 2001, paras 467–71.

[222] See Art 11(1) UNTOC; Art 30(1) UNCAC.

[223] Art 2(2) Internationally Protected Persons Convention; Art 4(b) Terrorist Financing Convention. The grave nature of the relevant offence and its link to retributive responses is also apparent in Art 3(4)(c) Narcotic Drugs Convention (1988), according to which certain rehabilitative measures are available 'as alternatives to conviction or punishment' (as opposed to being merely additional measures) only in 'appropriate cases of a minor nature'. See also Mazaud et al (n 141) 87.

[224] Art 36(1) Narcotic Drugs Convention (1988). On retributivism in the drugs convention in general, see Boister (2001) (n 141) 137, 150, 189.

[225] Art 3 Montreal Convention.

[226] Art 3(6) Narcotic Drugs Convention (1988). See also Boister (n 9) 40. Mazaud et al, however, suggest that 'the touchstone' of the provision is the need to secure the 'effectiveness of law enforcement measures' and that therefore considerations such as the 'promise of reduced penalties [which] may persuade an accused person to provide information implicating others' may be given weight in the decision-making: Mazaud et al (n 141) 94.

[227] Art 11(2) UNTOC (and see, on this, McClean (n 173) 133); Art 30(3) UNCAC. On the question of the degree of severity as a factor in sentencing considerations in the context of Art 30 UNCAC, see Thea Coventry, 'Article 30: Prosecution, Adjudication and Sanctions' in Rose et al (n 147) 301–18, 305. See also, on the general trust in the effectiveness of deterrence as exhibited by the drafters of the Internationally Protected Persons Convention, Bloomfield and Fitzgerald (n 170) 83. However, for a differentiating assessment of the phrase 'effective penal sanctions' in the grave breaches regime of the Geneva Conventions, see Paola Gaeta, 'Grave Breaches of the Geneva Conventions' in Andrew Clapham, Paola Gaeta and Marco Sassòli, *The 1949 Geneva Conventions* (Oxford, Oxford University Press, 2015) 624–25.

[228] See Art 22(1)(a) Psychotropic Substances Convention; Art 36(1)(a) Single Convention on Narcotic Drugs; Art 3(4)(a) Narcotic Drugs Convention (1988).

while in UNTOC the maximum duration of the relevant deprivation of liberty is taken as a benchmark for the definition of 'serious crime' under that Convention.[229] The Narcotic Drugs Convention (1988) also refers to 'pecuniary sanctions' which State Parties can adopt in their efforts to enact measures that take the grave nature of the offences into account.[230]

The fifteen Conventions, however, also provide criteria which are instrumental in the assessment of the relevant sentences, and it is the consideration of these criteria that brings a certain suppleness to the determination of the legal consequences. The Narcotic Drugs Convention (1988), UNTOC and UNCAC all refer to the possibility of early release, albeit in a restrictive way: by obliging the State authorities to bear in mind the 'serious nature' of the offences',[231] their 'grave nature'[232] or 'gravity'[233] when considering early release or parole. But both UNTOC and UNCAC also refer to the possibility of mitigating sentences[234] or even granting immunity from prosecution,[235] where a person has provided 'substantial cooperation' in investigations or prosecutions. The obligation of Parties is, in that regard, however, weak: States are merely held to 'consider' these options, and where immunity is concerned, both Conventions expressly make reference to the 'fundamental principles' of a State's domestic law which may consequently restrict the availability of that option.[236] The need to assess recidivism which exists in some jurisdictions is likewise reflected in some of the treaties: both the Psychotropic Substances Convention and the Single Convention on Narcotic Drugs thus provide that foreign convictions for the relevant offences are to be taken into account where the establishment of recidivism is concerned.[237]

In spite of the strong position of retributivism, States Parties showed, from a comparably early stage on, awareness of the need to reach beyond these aims. It is, perhaps, not surprising that such considerations arose in particular where the subject matter indicated the need for a wider range of legal tools. In treaties dealing with drugs-related offences, therefore, consequences were formulated which targeted the particular position of the persons involved, with the Single Convention on Narcotic Drugs formulating (following an amendment in 1972) the need for 'rehabilitation',[238]

---

[229] Art 2(b) UNTOC. On the debate relating to this way of determining the element of 'serious crime', see McClean (n 173) 42.

[230] Art 3(4)(a) Narcotic Drugs Convention (1988). See, however, Mazaud et al (n 141) 85, stressing that the sanctions listed in this provision are 'neither exclusive nor necessarily cumulative'.

[231] Art 3(7) Narcotic Drugs Convention (1988).

[232] Art 11(4) UNTOC; See Betti (n 156) 30. On the relevance of national distinctions relating to early release and parole for this provision, see McClean (n 173) 134.

[233] Art 30(5) UNCAC. See, on this, Coventry (n 227) 312–13.

[234] Art 26(2) UNTOC; Art 37(2) UNCAC. See also, on the influence of the example of national jurisdictions on the provision of mitigation, Betti (n 156) 80 and on the rationale behind mitigation in UNCAC, Philip M Nichols, 'Article 37: Cooperation with Law Enforcement Authorities' in Rose et al (n 147) 374–82, 376.

[235] Art 26(3) UNTOC; Art 37(3) UNCAC. See, on the controversy around the granting of immunity, Nichols (n 234) 376–377.

[236] Art 26(3) UNTOC; Art 37(3) UNCAC.

[237] See Art 22(2)(a)(iii) Psychotropic Substances Convention; Art 36(2)(iii) Single Convention on Narcotic Drugs.

[238] See Art 36(1)(b) in conjunction with Art 38(1) Single Convention on Narcotic Drugs and see Arts 14 and 15 Protocol Amending the Single Convention; Mazaud et al (n 141) 86, n 193.

an aim that also appears in the Psychotropic Substances Convention[239] and the Narcotic Drugs Convention (1988).[240] The corresponding obligations of States Parties, however, differ: they are, arguably, strongest in Article 20 of the Psychotropic Substances Convention and in Article 38(1) of the Single Convention on Narcotic Drugs, under which Parties 'shall' adopt 'all practicable measures […] for […]rehabilitation' of the relevant persons;[241] whereas the other provisions mentioned above are merely 'may' provisions: the Parties 'may provide' measures of rehabilitation.[242]

References to treatment,[243] education[244] and aftercare[245] likewise make an appearance in Conventions dealing with drugs-related offences. As does 'social reintegration',[246] and there, the drugs-related Conventions are joined by UNTOC and UNCAC, which oblige States Parties to 'endeavour to promote the reintegration into society of persons convicted' of the relevant offences.[247]

UNCAC, in particular, contains references to further sanctions tailored to particular perpetrators, such as the possibility of the use of disciplinary powers against civil servants,[248] procedures for disqualification from holding public office or holding 'office in an enterprise owned in whole or in part by the State' which States Parties shall consider[249] as well as the possible removal, suspension or reassignment of public officials accused of a relevant offence.[250]

In other provisions, legal consequences attach to particular objects that were used in the crimes under consideration or were the results of such crimes. Confiscation is a

---

[239] Art 20(1) and 22(1)(b) Psychotropic Substances Convention; see Boister (2001) (n 141) 147.

[240] Art 3(4)(b)–(d) Narcotic Drugs Convention (1988). Mazaud et al, however, suggest that, under this provision, 'additional or alternative treatment and care measures' are not limited to drug users and may indeed be seen 'in the wider context of measures for the treatment of offenders in general, designed to reduce the likelihood for their offending again', Mazaud et al (n 141) 87. On alternatives to punishment in the drugs conventions in general, see Boister (n 9) 102.

[241] Art 20(1) Psychotropic Substances Convention; Art 38(1) Single Convention on Narcotic Drugs.

[242] See Art 22(1)(b) Psychotropic Substances Convention, see Boister (2001) (n 141) 147; Art 36(1) Single Convention on Narcotic Drugs; Art 3(4)(b)–(d) Narcotic Drugs Convention (1988). On the adoption of alternatives to conviction and punishment in the context of the Single Convention on Narcotic Drugs in practice, see International Narcotics Control Board, *Celebrating 60 Years of the Single Convention on Narcotic Drugs of 1961*, E/INCB/2020/1/Supp.1 (Vienna, International Narcotics Control Board, United Nations 2021) 24.

[243] Arts 20(1), 22(1)(b) Psychotropic Substances Convention; Arts 36(1)(b), 38(1) Single Convention on Narcotic Drugs; Arts (3)(4)(b), 3(4)(d) Narcotic Drugs Convention (1988). On the controversy surrounding the provision of treatment as an alternative to punishment and as a condition to avoiding a custodial sentence, see Mazaud et al (n 141) 88.

[244] Arts 20(1), 22(1)(b) Psychotropic Substances Convention; Arts 36(1)(b), 38(1) Single Convention on Narcotic Drugs; Arts 3(4)(b), 3(4)(c), 3(4)(d) Narcotic Drugs Convention (1988).

[245] Arts 20(1), 22(1)(b) Psychotropic Substances Convention and see Boister (2001) (n 141) 47; Arts 36(1)(b), 38(1) Single Convention on Narcotic Drugs; Arts 3(4)(b), 3(4)(d) Narcotic Drugs Convention (1988).

[246] Arts 20(1), 22(1)(b) Psychotropic Substances Convention; Arts 36(1)(b), 38(1) Single Convention on Narcotic Drugs; Arts 3(4)(c), 3(4)(d) Narcotic Drugs Convention (1988). On the differentiation between rehabilitation and social integration, see Mazaud et al (n 141) 88.

[247] Art 31(3) UNTOC; Art 30(10) UNCAC. See Coventry (n 227) 317–18 and see Betti (n 156) 98 on the concept of reintegration at the European level. On the concepts of identification, treatment, education, after-care, rehabilitation and social re-integration in the drugs conventions, see Boister (2001) (n 141) 152–53, 158–59, 180.

[248] Art 30(8) UNCAC. See Coventry (n 227) 316–17.

[249] Art 30(7) UNCAC; see also Art 31(2)(d)(ii) UNTOC (possible disqualification from 'acting as directors of legal persons'). See Coventry (n 227) 315–16.

[250] Art 30(6) UNCAC, see Coventry (n 227) 313–14.

consequence that is frequently mentioned in that regard: under CITES, Parties must adopt measures to prohibit trade in specimens (ie, animals or plants) in violation of the Convention, including measures to 'provide for the confiscation or return to the State of export of such specimens'.[251] The object of confiscation can also be illegal drugs or psychotropic substances,[252] as well as proceeds of the relevant crimes[253] and property used or destined to be used in the relevant crimes.[254] Similarly, the seizure[255] and freezing[256] of certain items or assets is envisaged in several Conventions. Some of the treaties dealing with illegal drugs also provide for the destruction of particular plants: the Single Convention on Narcotic Drugs obliges Parties to 'destroy the coca bushes if illegally cultivated',[257] while the Narcotic Drugs Convention (1988) more generally imposes the duty on Parties 'to prevent illicit cultivation of and to eradicate plants containing narcotic or psychotropic substances'.[258]

5. EVALUATION OF THE FINDINGS

The fact that the fifteen Conventions contain provisions on the particular crimes on which international consensus exists does not mean that aspects of the general part of criminal law are not at all embraced by such a consensus. What it means is that the relevant conclusions mostly have to be drawn from insights gained from rules on specific crimes.

A perhaps unexpected result of this examination is the identification of a significant number of provisions dealing with subjective elements. Many of the treaties thus require the existence of intent, while several also refer to a knowledge element. Some also stipulate the need for specific intent, which indeed lends certain crimes their particular characteristics. Few provisions, however, deal with *mens rea* below intent – the Geneva Conventions do include recklessness for particular crimes, but none of the Conventions appears to deal with negligence. The more recent treaties (the 1988 Narcotic Drugs Convention, UNTOC and UNCAC) also are cognisant of

---

[251] Art VIII(1)(b) CITES. See also ibid Arts VIII(2) and VIII(4). See also Willem Wijnstekers, *The Evolution of CITES*, 9th edn (Budapest, International Council for Game and Wildlife Conservation, 2011) 261–98. For confiscation under Art 12 UNTOC, see Ziouvas (n 133) 596.

[252] Art 37 Single Convention on Narcotic Drugs, and see Boister (2001) (n 141) 348–351; Art 22(3) Psychotropic Substances Convention, and see Boister (2001) (n 141) 351–353.

[253] See Art 5 Narcotic Drugs Convention (1988), in particular para 1. See also ibid Art 3(4)(a) for confiscation in general. See also Arts 12–14 UNTOC; Arts 31 and 57 UNCAC.

[254] See Art 5 Narcotic Drugs Convention (1988); Arts 12–14 UNTOC; Arts 31 and 57 UNCAC. For a critical assessment of confiscation (in the context of the drugs conventions), in view in particular of its potential effect on innocent parties, the right to privacy, but also of the doubtful efficiency of that measure, see Boister (2001) (n 141) 186, 363, 395, 397.

[255] Art 22(3) Psychotropic Substances Convention; Art 37 Single Convention on Narcotic Drugs; Art 5(2) Narcotic Drugs Convention (1988); Art 8 Terrorist Financing Convention; Art 12(2) UNTOC; Art 31(2) and (3) UNCAC.

[256] Art 5(2) Narcotic Drugs Convention (1988), and see Boister (2001) (n 141) 366–67 on the differentiation between 'seizure' and 'freezing' in that context; Art 8 Terrorist Financing Convention; Art 12(2) UNTOC; Art 31(2) and (3) UNCAC. See Ziouvas (n 133) 602–03.

[257] Art 26(2) Single Convention on Narcotic Drugs.

[258] Art 14(2) Narcotic Drugs Convention (1988). See, on the limits which are placed on the eradication of certain plants, in particular due to the need to take into account the protection of the environment, Mazaud et al (n 141) 301.

the difficulty of proving mental elements and expressly allow inferences to be drawn from 'objective factual circumstances'.

Other aspects are addressed in a far less satisfactory manner. Justifications and excuses hardly feature at all. For modes of liability, a wide range of terms has been employed, without, however, sufficient clarification on conceptual distinctions. At the same time, it is worth noting that international agreement apparently can be established on these modes, including on joint criminal enterprise (though not in its third, and most controversial, form).

Similarly, some inchoate forms of the relevant crimes are nearly universally accepted. That certainly applies to attempt, whose concept is embodied in several treaties without expressly referring to a margin of appreciation in that regard. Conspiracy constitutes a more difficult case: there, the conventions do acknowledge domestic restrictions that may apply with regard to the implementation of the relevant conduct, indicating that divergences in this context still prevail.

The Conventions also allow insights on international consensus regarding certain legal consequences of the relevant offences. The fairly wide range of these consequences is interesting – as is the fact that retribution, while still, arguably, the default purpose for sentencing in many treaties, is not the only consequence recognised. It is joined by measures aiming at rehabilitation and measures seeking social reintegration. Several Conventions also refer to consequences that take into account specific characteristics of perpetrators (such as disqualification) or of the relevant objects (such as confiscation or destruction).

When considered in their entirety, it is possible to detect distinct evolutionary stages in the development of the Conventions. The early treaties did not show signs of particular sophistication: the four Geneva Conventions which principally addressed a different area of law (the law of armed conflict), only contained one article each on the forms of conduct which Parties agreed to criminalise, and in these provisions, several crimes were lumped together, with scant reflection on aspects such as modes of liability and inchoate forms of commission.[259] Nor did all of the subsequent Conventions provide satisfactory insight into common understandings within transnational criminal law: as late as 1963 did the Tokyo Convention limit itself to certain duties (for instance, the establishment of jurisdiction) which Parties had with regard to 'offences and acts committed on board' aircraft, without in any way specifying what these offences would entail.[260]

And yet, at that time, another stage in the development had already begun to manifest itself. The Single Convention on Narcotic Drugs, for instance, included an extensive article on 'penal provisions'[261] which not only contained details on the conduct to be criminalised, but also a reflection on the relevant *mens rea* (requiring intention for the relevant acts), on forms of liability as well as on conspiracy and attempt – rules on which the later treaties on drug-related offences expanded.[262]

---

[259] See Art 50 Geneva Convention I; Art 51 Geneva Convention II; Art 130 Geneva Convention III; Art 147 Geneva Convention IV.
[260] See Art 3(1) Tokyo Convention. See also above, n 113.
[261] Art 36 Single Convention on Narcotic Drugs.
[262] See, in particular, Art 22 Psychotropic Substances Convention; Art 3 Narcotic Drugs Convention (1988).

The third treaty in this particular area, the Narcotic Drugs Convention (1988), also signalled the beginning of the final and most useful stage where the fifteen Conventions are concerned. Here, the provisions on criminal law were advanced to a significant degree – the 1988 Convention and certain subsequent treaties, especially UNTOC and UNCAC, provide rules whose level of detail sets them apart from previous conventions. That includes their reflection on evidentiary questions relating to the establishment of *mens rea*[263] and, for the first time, a recognition of the general role that 'legal defences' play in the evaluation, even though their 'description' is left to regulation by domestic law.[264] These Conventions also contain a more extensive range of modes of liability for the commission of the relevant acts,[265] culminating in the recognition at least of one form of joint criminal enterprise.[266] The Conventions dealing with drugs-related offences also provide for a wider range of legal consequences of the relevant acts,[267] with the aim of social reintegration being explicitly adopted in UNTOC and UNCAC as well.[268]

And yet, in spite of the commitment by a large number of States on these aspects, some questions still remain which may cast doubt on the suitability of transnational criminal law as a basis for a universal criminal code or as evidence for customary international criminal law.

Such an understanding would presuppose the existence of an international consensus on the protected interests, at least to the extent that those violating the relevant norms are considered as acting contrary to values embraced by the international community as a whole. Not everybody is content with this interpretation: Cotterrell, in this volume, voices the view that 'transnational crime in general cannot be seen as an affront to some all-embracing transnational collective consciousness', noting that the idea of 'such a global consciousness as a basis of universal cultural authority for criminalisation is a myth'.[269] He would, at the same time, give room for the possible existence of 'limited transnational networks' and names as an example the European Union, where it might be possible to speak of a belief in 'European values'.[270]

Even there, the assumption of a 'value-based' consensus on the provisions of transnational criminal law invites critical reflection. The fact, for instance, may be recalled that, in December 2002, 109 Members of the European Parliament asserted, in a Proposal for a Recommendation, 'that the policy of prohibiting drugs, based on the UN Conventions of 1961, 1971 and 1988', was 'the true cause of the increasing damage' that the relevant substances were inflicting on 'whole sectors of society' and called on the Council and the EU Member States to begin a process of revising these

---

[263] See Art 3(3) Narcotic Drugs Convention (1988); Arts 5(2) and 6(2)(f) UNTOC; Art 28 UNCAC.
[264] Art 3(11) Narcotic Drugs Convention (1988); Art 11(6) UNTOC; Art 30(9) UNCAC.
[265] See, for instance, Art 3(1)(c)(iv) Narcotic Drugs Convention (1988); Arts 5(1)(b) and 6(1)(b)(ii) UNTOC; Art 23(1)(b)(ii) UNCAC.
[266] See Art 5(1)(a)(ii) UNTOC, but see also earlier Art 2(c) Terrorist Financing Convention.
[267] See above at nn 243–46.
[268] See Art 31(3) UNTOC; Art 30(10) UNCAC. On the historical background and codification history of UNCAC, see Cecily Rose, 'The Origins of International Anti-Corruption Law. The Failed Negotiation of an International Agreement on Illicit Payments' in Boister et al (eds) (n 22) 188–200.
[269] See Cotterrell (n 65) at n 46.
[270] See ibid, after n 46.

treaties, 'with the aim of repealing or amending the 1961 and 1971 Conventions', with a view also 'to repealing the 1988 Convention'[271] (of which the European Union is a Party).[272]

The reliance on treaties of transnational criminal law for the construction of the above named consensus would appear to benefit from more detailed assessment. The main points of discussion in this regard can be considered in two categories.

There is, firstly, the matter of the 'unreflected law' (discussed in section 5.1), referring to the difficulty that, in spite of their increasingly detailed provisions on criminal law, certain aspects with which legal observers are well familiar from domestic criminal justice systems, are still missing in the Conventions – partly because they may simply be omitted (section 5.1.1), but partly also because of the margin of appreciation from which States Parties benefit (section 5.1.2).

But the 'reflected law' too – aspects that did make it into the Conventions – can cause challenges (section 5.2). The matters that arise in this context concern, for one, the question whether the relevant crimes were indeed included because of an existing position on the protected values, shared by the international community (section 5.2.1). A related question pertains to the impact which the potential existence of political or other reasons for the conclusion of the relevant treaties may exercise (section 5.2.2).

5.1. The Unreflected Law

5.1.1. *Legal Aspects not Enshrined in the Conventions*

In the fifteen Conventions, certain elements that make regular appearances in domestic criminal legal systems receive no mention or only references that have to be considered incomplete. Some treaties, like the Hague Hijacking Convention[273] and CITES,[274] do not make any reference to *mens rea* as part of the relevant offences at all; others, like the Montreal Convention, provide *mens rea* elements for some acts but not for others.[275] Most of the treaties do not mention specific justifications or excuses that could apply, although several of them provide that the relevant conduct must have been carried out 'unlawfully',[276] thus opening the possibility that conduct that prima facie fulfils the conditions of the relevant offences may, because of special circumstances, still be considered lawful in nature. But the references to mental disease or defect, intoxication, self-defence and duress, which the ICC Statute makes,[277] are

---

[271] European Parliament, 'Proposal for a Recommendation Pursuant to Rule 49(1) of the Rules of Procedure', Session Doc B5-0541/2002 (23 December 2003), paras 1 and 4.

[272] UNTC (n 122).

[273] See Art 1 Hague Hijacking Convention.

[274] See Art VIII(1) CITES.

[275] Under Art 1(1) Montreal Convention, the principal offences have to be committed 'intentionally', but that element is missing in the second paragraph, which provides for liability for attempts and liability of accomplices.

[276] See above, n 179, and accompanying text.

[277] See Art 31(1) ICC Statute.

not present in any of the Conventions, nor are those to mistake of law or fact[278] or the age of criminal responsibility.[279] In the field of specific criminal law, only selected crimes are addressed by the Conventions and important forms of conduct which, for instance, have found their way into international criminal law do not form part of their regulations.

Such omissions can be based on a range of reasons. They may have come about precisely because the negotiating States were not able to establish consensus on a particular element. It may also be the case that the relevant treaty possessed a scope that was deliberately limited – a Convention dealing with drugs-related offences would not be expected to also address the question of enforced disappearances. It is also possible that the relevant treaty dealt with criminalisation as a 'side effect' only – a point that applies where the Geneva Conventions are concerned, which, in the main, provide rules on the law of armed conflict.[280] Given their primary thrust, it is, arguably, understandable that they do not provide the degree of detail on criminalisation that UNTOC and UNCAC were able to offer.[281] In light of that, however, the question remains how these instances of silence on particular aspects are to be evaluated. If, for instance, CITES does not mention the *mens rea* of the perpetrator or justifications and excuses, does that mean that the international community does not recognise these features of criminal law?

To a degree, the high standard imposed on the selection of the Conventions counteracts conclusions of this kind. It allows for a cumulative perspective, so that it is, for instance, in light of the fact that several Conventions do refer to *mens rea* and indeed mention specific subjective elements,[282] reasonable to conclude that general awareness and recognition of *mens rea* by the international community does exist. Yet the question whether this condition also exists for, say, trade in specimens in violation of CITES[283] still remains.

The possible range of reasons behind the relevant omissions militates against the conclusion that silence of the negotiating States must necessarily indicate a lack of consensus. At the same time, it appears equally perilous to read presumed elements of the law into a treaty even though no clear reference has been made to them. It is sometimes done: the ICJ did so, for instance, in the 1989 *ELSI* case which turned on a 1948 Treaty of Friendship, Commerce and Navigation between the United States and Italy, finding that the 'important principle' of the exhaustion of local remedies could not be 'held to have been tacitly dispensed with', even though it was not expressly mentioned in that treaty.[284] But, as will be seen, even in that case, the Court did not proceed without a legal basis.[285]

---

[278] See ibid Art 32.
[279] See ibid Art 26.
[280] See above, at nn 77–78.
[281] See above, at nn 263–68.
[282] See above, at nn 152–176.
[283] See Art VIII(1)(a) CITES.
[284] ICJ, *Case Concerning Elettronica Sicula SpA (ELSI) (United States of America v Italy)*, Judgment, 20 July 1989, 1989 ICJ Rep 15, 42, para 50 ('*ELSI* Case').
[285] See below, at n 288.

In the field of transnational criminal law, however, two particular considerations impose limits on such an extensive reading of treaty provisions. For one, by the very nature of this field of international law, the reference to particular offences in the treaty is not the final step in the application of the law: the relevant offences still require implementation by the States Parties, and it is entirely possible that the regulation of the 'missing' aspects of the crimes is left to them and subject to their discretion (see section 5.1.2 below). Reading the pertinent aspects into the treaty would restrict such discretion and may go against the intentions of the drafters.

The other consideration concerns the fact that the provisions under consideration deal with matters of criminal law and are thus subject to the applicable principles of that field – in particular that of *nullum crimen sine lege*, which militates in favour of strict interpretation of the relevant offences.[286] That does not mean that every interpretation of elements of criminal law that avails itself of insights not directly derived from the text of the treaty is impermissible – but such interpretive efforts do meet their limits where they lead to results which disadvantage the defendant.

In light of these considerations, it would appear that lacunae caused by omissions cannot always be filled through interpretive efforts – and where that is the case, the result has to be that international consensus on the affected points of law simply cannot be established.

On the other hand, the assertion that silence *invariably* means that there is no international consensus on the relevant topic ignores the nature of contemporary international law, which is marked by an increasing trend towards fragmentation.[287] Consensus within the international community might therefore be established through the impact of fields other than transnational criminal law and through sources other than the Conventions. That, ultimately, is the way the ICJ followed in *ELSI* as well: it was prepared to read the 'important principle' of the exhaustion of local remedies into the treaty precisely because it found that it already led an existence in customary international law.[288]

Similar considerations apply at least in some areas of transnational criminal law as well. The lack of a reference to a subjective element in CITES may be revisited here: the silence of States Parties on this point does not necessarily mean that they wanted to exclude this important element, nor does it mean that they would have been permitted to do so. *Mens rea*, after all, finds its basis not only in express regulations in treaties of transnational criminal law, it also derives from the principle *nulla poena sine culpa*, and thus from human rights principles rooted in customary international law.[289] The approach taken to silence in this context thus is not dissimilar to that followed by the ICJ: here, too, the consensus of the international community can be established through customary international law, and in both cases it cannot be assumed that a principle of overarching importance would have been silently

---

[286] See above at n 220.

[287] See, on the problem, ILC, Study Group on Fragmentation of International Law, Report *Fragmentation of International Law: Difficulties Arising from the Diversification and Expansion of International Law*, 18 July 2006, A/CN.4/L.702, 3–4, in particular at para 6.

[288] See *ELSI* Case, para 50.

[289] See above, at nn 150–51.

dispensed with – it constitutes a default, whose derogation (if it were permitted in the first place) would be expected to be done in an explicit manner.

5.1.2. The Margin of Appreciation

The second point relating to instances of 'unreflected law' has its basis in the very nature of transnational criminal law. The fifteen Conventions are not instruments of international criminal law and thus do not address conduct that directly constitutes crimes against the international order. The offences to which they refer require implementation, and if States are then expected to enjoy a margin of appreciation in this process,[290] the provisions contained in the Conventions, by necessity, have to stay somewhat general. It is for that reason that they tend not to stipulate exhaustive rules on the given aspects of criminal law.

The Conventions employ a range of phrases to clarify that a margin of appreciation exist. In some instances, even criminalisation itself is left to the discretion of the State, as indicated by articles that call on States to 'consider' adopting measures to establish the relevant offences,[291] and there are other phrases, such as references to 'fundamental principles' of the Parties' domestic laws[292] or to their 'constitutional limitations'[293] which indicate that a potential restrictive effect of the domestic framework is recognised.[294] But several Conventions also allow Parties to adopt stricter measures than those provided in the treaty,[295] while the Hague Hijacking Convention, the Montreal Convention and the Internationally Protected Persons Convention contain express references to the fact that the treaty 'does not exclude any criminal jurisdiction exercised in accordance' with

[290] See, for an affirmation of that principle, Art 3(11) Narcotic Drugs Convention (1988); Art 11(6) UNTOC; Art 30(9) UNCAC. See also, with regard to the Geneva Conventions, Gaeta (n 227) 620. Generally on the discretion of States enjoyed in that regard, see International Narcotics Control Board (n 242) 23; Petzschke (n 126) 251. On the use of the phrase 'margin of appreciation' with application to the discretion enjoyed by States Parties in this field, see Boister (n 9) 23.

[291] See Arts 16(2), 18–22, 24 UNCAC. See also, on that phrasing in the context of Art 8 UNTOC, McClean (n 173) 119.

[292] Art 34(1) UNTOC; Art 37(3) UNCAC. Art 5(1) Terrorist Financing Convention contains two disclaimers: for one, States shall take the necessary measures to enable legal entities to be held liable, but only 'in accordance with [their] domestic legal principles', and, secondly, the article provides that such liability 'may be criminal, civil or administrative'. See also Arts 10(1) and (2) UNTOC and Arts 26(1) and (2) UNCAC. See also Art 2(1) Narcotic Drugs Convention 1988 ('in conformity with the fundamental provisions of their respective domestic legislative systems') and Art 2(2) of that Convention ('consistent with the principles of sovereign equality'), described by Boister as a 'blanket escape clause' which served as the 'ultimate consensus builder' for the convention, Boister (2001) (n 141) 523.

[293] Art 36(1)(a) and (2) Single Convention on Narcotic Drugs. On the difference between 'constitutional limitations' and 'fundamental principles', see McClean (n 173) 77. See also Art 3(1)(c) Narcotic Drugs Convention (1988) and Boister (2001) (n 141) 117 on the distinction between 'constitutional principles' and 'constitutional limitations'.

[294] See also Art 27 UNCAC and ibid Art 23(1)(b). See also above, nn 206–08.

[295] Art 23 Psychotropic Drugs Convention; Art 39 Single Convention on Narcotic Drugs; Art XIV(1)(a) CITES; Art 24 Narcotic Drugs Convention (1988); Art 34(3) UNTOC. See, for the Single Convention on Narcotic Drugs, International Narcotics Control Board (n 242) 23. The provision in CITES has given rise to diverging assessments, see JM Hutton, 'Who Knows Best? Controversy over Unilateral Stricter Domestic Measures", in Jon Hutton and Barnabas Dixon (eds), *Endangered Species, Threatened Convention. The Past, Present and Future of CITES, the Convention on International Trade in Endangered Species of Wild Fauna and Flora* (London, Earthscan Publications, 2000) 57–66 and RB Martin, 'When CITES Works and When It Does Not' ibid 29–37, 32. See also Wijnstekers (n 251) 431–34.

the domestic law of the relevant State.[296] The Psychotropic Substances Convention, on the other hand, also allows Parties to provide, 'either as an alternative to conviction or punishment or in addition to punishment' measures of 'treatment, education, aftercare, rehabilitation and social integration'.[297]

At times, concepts employed by the conventions, due to their very nature, indicate that an effort at implementation is still required. Thus, Article 23 UNCAC obliges Parties, where the laundering of proceeds is concerned, to adopt criminalisation 'to the widest range of predicate offences',[298] while CITES calls on States to take 'appropriate measures' to prohibit trade in specimens in violation of the Convention (although it follows this up by noting that such measures 'shall include' penalisation).[299]

The existence of a margin of appreciation as a general rule underlying treaties on transnational criminal law is nowhere more clearly expressed than in the Narcotic Drugs Convention (1988), UNTOC and UNCAC, which all contain an article affirming 'the principle that the description' of the relevant offences and of the relevant legal defences 'is reserved to the domestic law' of the Parties, and that 'such offences shall be prosecuted and punished in conformity with that law'.[300]

The existence of this general principle highlights the danger of a reading of the Conventions which yields the prima facie result that a lacuna does not exist, since the relevant treaty may make provision for a particular element of the crime in question. It is only by taking into account the margin of appreciation that the understanding emerges that international consensus might not necessarily be established, at least where the detailed interpretation of the relevant element is concerned.

However, for the evaluation of instances where the margin of appreciation applies, two further considerations come into play.

For one, the margin itself does, at times, give space for critical analysis. It is true that, in certain Conventions, the margin may be considerable: the Tokyo Convention offers a prime example for that.[301] In other Conventions, however, it is considerably restricted. If a treaty, like UNCAC, provides rules on the subjective elements of the crime, including evidentiary considerations,[302] an extensive range of modes of liability and inchoate forms of conduct,[303] and no fewer than 26 principal[304] and 16 ancillary offences,[305] one may wonder how much discretion a State Party, in spite of the assurance that the 'description of the offences' is 'reserved to the domestic law',[306] really has. There is always *some* discretion, but in some areas it appears that

---

[296] Art 4(3) Hague Hijacking Convention; Art 5(3) Montreal Convention; Art 3(3) Internationally Protected Persons Convention.

[297] Art 22(1)(b) Psychotropic Substances Convention.

[298] Art 23(2)(a) UNCAC.

[299] Art VIII(1) CITES. See also Art 9(1) UNTOC.

[300] Art 3(11) Narcotic Drugs Convention (1988); Art 11(6) UNTOC; Art 30(9) UNCAC, with minor stylistic variations between the provisions.

[301] See n 113.

[302] See Art 28 UNCAC.

[303] ibid Art 23. See, however, for a critical evaluation of modes of liability in the Conventions, above at nn 196–197.

[304] Arts 15–22 UNCAC.

[305] ibid Arts 23–25.

[306] ibid Art 30(9).

the remaining margin is not much more extensive than the space that, for instance, is enjoyed by judicial interpreters of the law.

Secondly, the above considerations about the potential of the impact of rules from other areas of international law[307] have equal applicability here. Here, too, provisions – especially the general principles of criminal law which find their bases in human rights law – can develop their force. In this context, they constitute a cap on the margin of appreciation, a limit which the discretion of the national lawmaker may not exceed.

What is more: the concept of a cap on discretion is expressly recognised in several Conventions. Reference has already been made to an example in CITES: the Convention, while granting a margin of appreciation by allowing States to take 'appropriate measures' to prohibit trade in specimens in violation of the treaty, restricts the margin again by imposing the obligation that such measures must include penalisation.[308] Similarly, UNTOC accepts that the legislation of some States Parties may set out 'a list of specific predicate offences', but then emphasises that 'at a minimum', such lists have to include 'a comprehensive range of offences associated with organized criminal groups'.[309]

Arguably the most direct indication of a cap is provided in the Tokyo Convention. The Convention, while generally allowing for the definition of the relevant offences that may be committed on board aircraft by the State of registration,[310] stipulates at the same time that the Convention is not to be interpreted 'as authorizing or requiring any action in respect of offences against penal laws of a political nature or those based on racial or religious discrimination'.[311] It is an interesting provision – a seemingly administrative safeguard in a Convention which otherwise gives significant leeway to States Parties. But by adopting this phrase, the international community declared its agreement to the view that State sovereignty, in the field of criminal law, is not unlimited: it finds its boundaries where it endangers certain values shared around the world, where it collides with what could be termed 'fundamental human rights guarantees'.

Both instances of the 'unreflected law' – situations of simple omissions and situations in which the further implementation is left to the States Parties – thus appear, at least at first sight, to indicate that international consensus on the relevant points is lacking. But the interpretation of the Conventions allows for closer inspection, and the result may be a more interconnected criminal justice system than might at first have been expected. Margins of appreciation, for instance, may be restricted by the detailed rules on which the negotiating States themselves were able to find agreement, and both forms of lacunae may in turn be impacted by rules from other fields of international law which may thus fill the gaps or indeed limit the freedom which States Parties would otherwise enjoy in transnational criminal law. By so doing, these rules, too, contribute to a system which reveals the consensus that, among an overwhelming number of members of the international community, does exist.

---

[307] See above, at nn 287–89.
[308] See above at n 299.
[309] Art 6(2)(b) UNTOC.
[310] See above at n 301.
[311] Art 2 Tokyo Convention. See n 113; see also Boister (n 9) 108.

5.2. The 'Reflected Law'

Where aspects of criminal law are concerned that did make it into the Conventions, it may at first sight appear that a strong case for the assumption of substantial international consensus exists. But this aspect – the 'reflected law' – invites critical observation too. For one, the question has been asked whether the incorporated provisions can indeed be said to represent efforts to protect common values of the international community (discussed in section 5.2.1). Secondly, the impact of other factors, in particular political considerations on the agreement that States gave to these instruments, requires consideration: does the existence of such factors affect their suitability for the establishment of world criminal law? That aspect will be discussed in section 5.2.2.

5.2.1. *Does the Reflected Law Allow for the Identification of Common Values?*

The assertion that international agreement on the criminal nature of certain forms of conduct corresponds to an intention of States Parties to enshrine certain values into law has at times met with criticism. Cotterrell, for one, addressing the example of piracy – the classical crime acknowledged on the international plane – questions whether criminalisation in this regard is 'supported by a genuinely universal (global) network of community', and finds that that is not the case: in his view, what supports criminalisation here is 'not a global community of belief or ultimate values (perhaps focused on universal human rights and dignity) but rather the existence of common or convergent interests in transnational trade'.[312] His conclusion is that the 'relevant transnational communal network' is thus 'primarily economic in nature' – States act 'on behalf of transnational trading networks from whose welfare and success they benefit'.[313] From this perspective, it would appear that efforts at criminalisation that transcend the boundaries of one State are undertaken not because of a sense of shared values, but simply because certain issues, in particular those of an economic kind, do require cross-boundary regulation.

There are, however, considerations which may justify a repositioning of these reflections. For one, the need for cross-boundary regulation can of course arise in a wide range of situations – driving without a valid licence can be a transboundary concern (and one that can easily endanger economic interests as well). Yet there is no treaty with the same high number of States Parties that provides for the criminalisation of this form of conduct. The comparison to the fifteen Conventions rather suggests that a particular degree of severity inhabits the crimes slated for criminalisation, and this in turn indicates that the drafters sought to go beyond the regulation of particular 'interests' and may indeed have imposed the corresponding obligations on States because such commitment responded to deeply held concerns about matters that affected them, and the individual victims, on a more fundamental level.

---

[312] See Cotterrell (n 65) at n 43.
[313] ibid. See also, for similar criticism with regard to European Criminal Law, Fletcher (n 31) 31.

Secondly, even if, *arguendo*, the reason for the conclusion of the Conventions had been principally economic in nature, the question arises why this would militate against the assumption of a value-based approach. Economic interests, after all, represent values, too, and the rights in which they are manifested are, as such, recognised by instruments of international law – such as the right to property,[314] the freedom to choose an occupation[315] and the right to work,[316] let alone the fact that both the International Covenant on Civil and Political Rights (ICCPR) and the International Covenant on Economic, Social and Cultural Rights (ICESCR) make reference to the free pursuit of 'economic' development as one of the aspects of the right of all peoples to self-determination[317] – a point that is of considerable importance not least to materially disadvantaged countries. Rights such as that to join a trade union, which several human rights treaties expressly recognise as part of the freedom of association,[318] demonstrate that protected interests in this field do not invariably favour large entities with particular concerns about the safety of trade routes, but may benefit individuals as well; and yet, the link between this right and economic matters is undeniable.[319]

A third consideration derives from the nature of the subject matters themselves. The fifteen Conventions cover a wide range of issues – they engage with the protection of internationally protected persons,[320] the prohibition of drugs-related conduct,[321] the protection of prisoners of war[322] and of persons and property in occupied territories.[323] It is true that, if even the pirate as *hostis humanis generis* is seen more as a threat to trade networks than to human rights and the safety of individuals, then no area of international law is safe from being considered an 'economic matter'. Still – it would seem quite a stretch to say that rules seeking (as in CITES) to protect wild fauna and flora have the primary purpose of protecting economic interests. If anything, CITES can be expected to work in the opposite direction – Hutton, for one, observes that its whole purpose is 'to achieve the protection of particular species through trade regulation including, where necessary, the total prohibition of trade whose purpose is "primarily commercial"' and mentions doubts about the compatibility of CITES with the General Agreement on Tariffs and Trade.[324]

---

[314] See Art 1 First Protocol to the European Convention on Human Rights, on the Enforcement of Certain Rights Not Included in Section I of the Convention (20 March 1952), 213 UNTS 262; Art 17 GA Res 217(III), International Bill of Human Rights, 10 December 1948 ('Universal Declaration of Human Rights').

[315] See Art 15 Charter of Fundamental Rights of the European Union, [7 June 2016] OJ C202 389–405.

[316] See Art 23 Universal Declaration of Human Rights; Art 6 International Covenant on Economic, Social and Cultural Rights, 16 Dec 1966, 993 UNTS 3 ('ICESCR'); Art 1 European Social Charter, 18 October 1961, ETS 35.

[317] Common Art 1 ICCPR and ICESCR.

[318] See Art 11(1) ECHR; Art 22(1) ICCPR.

[319] See, on that connection, Art 16(1) ACHR and Art 8(1)(a) ICESCR.

[320] Internationally Protected Persons Convention.

[321] Psychotropic Substances Convention, Single Convention on Narcotic Drugs, Narcotic Drugs Convention (1988).

[322] Geneva Convention III.

[323] Geneva Convention IV.

[324] General Agreement on Tariffs and Trade, 30 October 1947, 55 UNTS 194; Hutton (n 295) 61. See also, on the various reasons that may give rise to provisions of transnational criminal law, Boister (n 9) 20.

Fourthly, even treaties which might be considered as protecting international trade, contain provisions which extend far beyond the safeguarding of economic interests. UNCAC – a treaty that seeks to combat corruption and bribery – certainly appears to be exemplary for an instrument informed by economic considerations. But even there, the objectives of the treaty reach far beyond these rationales. When the treaty obliges States Parties to criminalise the offering of an 'undue advantage' to public officials, so that they act or refrain from acting in the exercise of their official duties, it addresses a problem that extends beyond financial matters.[325] A corrupt official is a problem to individuals and the general public alike: corruption can obstruct a citizen who wishes to register to vote or applies for social housing or an asylum seeker requesting a professional and impartial decision on the right to remain in a particular country.

Most of all, however, it is the understanding of the text of the Conventions itself that does not easily allow for the conclusion that the protection of values was not embraced by the intention of the parties. If it had been their principal purpose to remove obstacles to transboundary traffic – in particular, for economic reasons – one would expect that the impact that the relevant crime had on the economic infrastructure would occupy centre place, regardless of the severity of the conduct. Indeed, the question may be raised why, in that case, it was felt necessary to employ tools of criminal law to begin with. A treaty could thus simply provide for the prohibition of any obstacle to 'trade networks' and leave the detailed regulation to States Parties – the rationale for references to the severity of the conduct, on the other hand, lies in the fact that the Parties were dealing with behaviour that, in their collective view, was deemed offensive.

And yet, the treaties are replete with references of this kind. The Internationally Protected Persons Convention obliges Parties to make the relevant forms of conduct punishable 'by appropriate penalties which take into account their grave nature';[326] under the Narcotic Drugs Convention, the courts of the States Parties must 'bear in mind the serious nature of the offences enumerated';[327] under the Terrorist Financing Convention, the 'grave nature' of the offences must be taken into account when providing penalties for them;[328] and so forth.[329] Where the intention of the Parties is concerned, the provision on the implementation of UNTOC is likewise of interest: the Convention, while dedicated to 'transnational organized crime' obliges States to criminalise certain offences 'independently' of the 'transnational nature',[330] thus offering further indication that concern about the protection of transnational trade networks cannot be considered an exhaustive explanation for the adoption of the relevant rules.

The existing wording of the Conventions, the wide range of problems which they sought to address and their understanding of the severity of the conduct they sought

---

[325] Art 15(a) UNCAC. See, on the 'common ground' underlying the considerations of this provision which, in his view, extends to 'proper management of public affairs' and 'respect for human rights', Kubiciel, 'Article 15' (n 159) 167.

[326] Art 2(2) Internationally Protected Persons Convention.

[327] Art 3(7) Narcotic Drugs Convention (1988).

[328] Art 4(b) Terrorist Financing Convention.

[329] See also Art 3(4)(a) Narcotic Drugs Convention (1988); Art 11(4) UNTOC.

[330] Art 34(2) UNTOC.

to regulate does not suggest that they constitute mere instruments of 'administrative criminalisation', constructed to aid economic interaction.[331] A careful reading yields a different impression: they are Conventions which give voice to the concern felt by the international community on forms of conduct which were damaging to values they cherished, and they are not only values representing economic interests. They include a wide range of fundamental concerns, extending to an individual's enjoyment of health (as expressed in treaties on drugs-related offences), the integrity of person and possessions of victims of armed conflict (as in the Geneva Conventions), the inviolability of diplomats (as in the Internationally Protected Persons Convention) and the integrity, too, of the natural environment (as expressed in CITES).

5.2.2. The Impact of Extra-legal Factors on the Evaluation of the Conventions

The fact that diverse interests are protected through the fifteen Conventions does not mean that reasons other than legal considerations could not have been at the root of the decision of Parties to ratify them. If such reasons can be established, the question appears what impact, if any, this has on the evaluation of the Conventions: does it make their provisions pertaining to criminalisation less suitable for consideration as a basis for consensus within the international community on a world criminal code?

The examination especially of some older Conventions indeed invites the observation that the rationale for their adoption may be somewhat more complex than might at first be expected. Societal and other perceptions of certain concepts in the Conventions are subject to change over the years; but if States are still willing to ratify a treaty – sometimes more than fifty years after its conclusion – reasons other than the persuasiveness of the text may, at times, have played a role in the decision-making. That is perhaps nowhere as clear as in the case of the Geneva Conventions – it is questionable whether States joining in the 1990s or 2000s were entirely impressed by the monthly pay rates that the Third Geneva Convention provides for prisoners of war (8 Swiss francs for prisoners below the rank of sergeants)[332] or by the obligation of Detaining Powers under the Fourth Geneva Convention to enable, in places of internment, purchases by internees of 'articles of everyday use, including [...] tobacco, such as would increase their personal well-being and comfort'.[333] Different reasons may have played a role in their ratification: apart from the fact that other treaty articles may have appeared more acceptable, there may have been political considerations,

---

[331] See Cotterrell (n 65) at n 44.

[332] Art 60 Geneva Convention III. See, on this point, Silvia Sanna, 'Treatment of Prisoners of War' in Clapham et al (n 227), noting that, 'with regard to most belligerents, the figures set forth in Article 60 certainly need to be updated' as well as Wolff Heintschel von Heinegg, 'Article 60: Advances of Pay' in Dörmann et al (2021) (n 157) 1068–69, noting that Detaining Powers must 'consider in good faith an adequate increase' and basing this on the 'intent behind the provision'.

[333] Art 89 Geneva Convention IV. Oswald and Iapichino refer in this regard to challenges which may arise from the simultaneous application of the WHO Framework Convention on Tobacco Control, 21 May 2003, 2302 UNTS 166. Bruce Oswald and Lucrezia Iapichino, 'Treatment of Internees' in Clapham et al (n 227) 1355. See also, on the similar provision in Art 26 Geneva Convention III, Sanna (n 332) 998 and Bruce Oswald, 'Article 26: Food' in Dörmann et al (2021) (n 157) 773.

including the wish to adhere to a common position in a particular group of States or the wish not to turn oneself into a pariah on the international stage.[334]

Nor are such reasons necessarily without significance for the evaluation of sources of international law. Where customary international law is concerned, the establishment of a subjective element – the *opinio iuris sive necessitatis*,[335] ie, the legal opinion that there is an obligation or an entitlement to adopt the relevant practice[336] – is a prerequisite for its existence, and international courts have for a long time taken a strict position on the fulfilment of that condition: in cases where 'convenience', 'political expediency' or considerations of 'international policy' were decisive for the relevant State practice,[337] they are less likely to find that *opinio iuris* has come into being.

At the same time, the difficulty of establishing *opinio iuris* must be considered one of the key differences between treaty and customary law. Treaties are, by their very definition, legal agreements, and, as the ILC made clear, the 'intention to create obligations under international law' is inherent to the very concept of this source.[338] Contemporary multilateral treaties also tend to require ratification for the establishment of 'consent to be bound',[339] giving national parliaments (and legal departments of the executive) a chance to consider the legal repercussions of the relevant agreement.[340] Once such consent is established, the existence of other considerations leading to the conclusion of the treaty does not carry great relevance. An exception exists in the case of coercion (treaties procured by coercion are void ab initio[341]), but this refers to a very limited situation: while some members of the ILC sought to include 'a threat to strangle the economy of a country' as falling within this concept,[342] this was a step too far for the Commission as a whole, which did not follow this extensive view.

In light of these considerations, the mere existence of political (or other) reasons that may have influenced a State's decision to be bound does not militate against the

---

[334] At times, a particular international event may likewise impact ratification numbers. See, on the ratification development of the Terrorist Financing Convention after the terrorist attacks in the United States on 11 September 2001, Marieke de Goede, 'Counter-Terrorism Financing Assemblages after 9/11' in King et al (n 123) 762; Clive Walker, 'Terrorism Financing and the Governance of Charities' ibid 1086; Boister (n 9) 114.

[335] ICJ, *Case Concerning Military and Paramilitary Activities in and against Nicaragua (Nicaragua v United States of America)*, Judgment, 27 June 1986, (1986) ICJ Rep 14 ('*Nicaragua* Case'), 109, para 207.

[336] See on this Paul Behrens, *Diplomatic Interference and the Law* (Oxford, Hart, 2016) 8.

[337] See on this ICJ, *Asylum Case (Colombia v Peru)*, Judgment, 20 November 1950, (1950) ICJ Reports 1950, 266, 286; *Nicaragua* Case, 109, para 207. See also, generally, Permanent Court of International Justice, *The Case of the 'SS Lotus'*, Judgment, 7 September 1927, PCIJ Series A No 10, 28.

[338] The ILC read this element into the phrase 'governed by international law', which it had included in the definition of 'treaty' in Art 2(1)(a) of its Draft Articles on the Law of Treaties. See ILC, *Draft Articles on the Law of Treaties* (1966) 2 *YILC* 189, Art 2, Commentary, para 6. The definition in the Vienna Convention on the Law of Treaties is identical, see Art 2(1)(a) Vienna Convention on the Law of Treaties, 23 May 1969, 1155 UNTS 331('VCLT'), and it is suggested that here, and in the following references to the VCLT, the treaty represents customary international law.

[339] See Arts 24(2) and 14 VCLT.

[340] See (1966) 2 *YILC* 197, Draft Art 11, Commentary, para 2, on historical constitutional shifts leading to the requirement of ratification.

[341] See Art 52 VCLT (1969); (1966) 2 *YILC* 247, Draft Art 49, Commentary, para 6.

[342] (1966) 2 *YILC* 246, Draft Art 49, Commentary, para 3.

existence of the required legal intention[343] – in fact, the treaty in whose conclusion political reasons did not play a role would be a rarity. A difference, it appears, has to be drawn between the intent to be legally bound and the reasons behind such intent; not all that different from the differentiation recognised in criminal law between intent as part of the *mens rea* and motives behind intent.[344] Here, and there, the general rule is that intent is the decisive point; motives underlying intent are largely irrelevant.

If that is the case, however, it is a valid conclusion that Parties to a treaty that professes to protect certain values of international concern have given their genuine commitment to this purpose, as long as their consent is not vitiated. That observation holds valid no matter whether the underlying motives were political, economic or exclusively legal in nature.

*

Both aspects of the 'reflected law' thus suggest that the wholesale dismissal of a value system that was instrumental for the establishment of the relevant offences in the fifteen Conventions does not appropriately account for the complexities of the matter. While a value system would exist even if the values in question were 'merely' economic in nature, the reach of the Conventions and the subject matters reflected in them are, in fact, more extensive than that. The emphasis they place on the 'gravity' of the relevant acts suggests that they do indeed affect values that occupy a fundamental place in the international community. The willingness of States Parties to enforce the corresponding provisions through international commitments is demonstrated through their provision of consent to be bound in the form required under treaty law. That being the case, however, the large number of ratifications carries importance in its own right: it affirms the assertion that they represent perhaps the clearest available evidence for the existence of an international value system and thus allows the conclusion that, to the degree to which they reflect on particular aspects of criminal law, they form a strong basis for the construction of a universal criminal code.

6. CONCLUSION

A world criminal code does not exist. But little doubt attaches to the desirability of an instrument that could, with authority, identify those parts of criminal law on which the international community as a whole is able to agree. The resulting instrument would be of help not only to lawmakers who yet have to fulfil their obligations of implementation, but also to those charged with the application of the law and to individuals as addressees of criminal law. Beyond that, there are instances in which international law indeed appears to work on the assumption that the existence of

---

[343] See above at n 338.
[344] See, on this problem in general as well as on the difficulty of the distinction between 'intent' and 'motive' in particular situations, Paul Behrens, 'Genocide and the Question of Motives' (2012) 10(3) *Journal of International Criminal Justice* 501–23.

certain concepts of criminal law (such as that of a 'grave crime') is embraced by the international community.[345] A world criminal code thus may serve an important purpose in the interpretation of international law itself.

The examination of transnational criminal law is an important starting point for any attempt to construct a world criminal code, and, as this analysis has shown, can be a fruitful endeavour. It is in this body of international law that not only a clear abhorrence of certain forms of conduct by the international community can be identified, but that opportunity is also provided for conclusions about the existing international consensus on particular areas of general criminal law that emerges from its provisions.

That transnational criminal law as a basis for universal criminal law has its limitations is true. The relevant restrictions are owed, not least, to the very nature of this area of international law which, by necessity, leaves a margin of appreciation to the States Parties to the individual treaties.

Yet this margin cannot mask the fact that the Conventions also possess an impressive level of detail. That is true not only of the specific offences enshrined therein; it is true also of certain aspects of general criminal law. The rules on inchoate crimes, on the interrelationship between *mens rea* and evidence, on sentences and other legal consequences and even on certain modes of liability go a long way in establishing consensus beyond the 'minimum content' that, given the particular topics of the individual Conventions, might have been considered as strictly required.

Given the large number of parties to the Conventions, there is reason to understand them as evidence not only for widespread consensus, but indeed for customary international law in this field. The fact that the relevant parts of criminal law still require implementation does not in all cases defeat this argument. In most instances, extensive State practice and *opinio iuris* at least on a general level can be established for the fifteen Conventions, even though differences on a more specific level may still exist. Very often, too, the level of detail that the Conventions provide on aspects of criminal law exercises a limiting impact on the discretionary space that is retained by the States Parties.

The particular position that transnational criminal law occupies in the consideration of a world criminal code does not mean that the work on the identification of the rules pertaining to such a code is limited to this area of international law.

But it is difficult to see how a world criminal law could dispense with a reflection on conclusions derived from the fifteen Conventions. In fact, work on such a code is likely to expand on the existing quasi-universal transnational criminal law and extrapolate from it. It would be strange, for instance, if severe attacks on the physical integrity of a person, which States have to criminalise in certain situations of armed conflict,[346] when committed against an internationally protected person[347] or when committed on board an aircraft in flight 'if that act is likely to endanger the

---

[345] See above, at nn 7–11.
[346] See Art 50 Geneva Convention I; Art 51 Geneva Convention II; Art 130 Geneva Convention III; Art 147 Geneva Convention IV.
[347] See Art 2(1)(a) Internationally Protected Persons Convention.

safety of that aircraft',[348] would not, outside these contexts, be also considered crimes embraced by the collective consciousness of the international community.

Even as they currently stand, the relevant provisions of the fifteen Conventions are testament to a consensus that challenges stereotypes that still prevail where the consideration of criminal justice systems around the world is concerned. The view that the use of drugs is 'part of the culture' in certain States has to overcome the extensive agreement that three treaties dealing with drugs-related offences attract; the opinion that 'corruption is an accepted part of life' in this or that State faces the objection that the international community, by a very large majority, embraces detailed obligations to criminalise corruption in the public sector; the understanding that this or that State 'resorts to draconian sanctions of criminal law' has to engage with the fact that an overwhelming majority of States recognise the social reintegration of persons convicted of certain offences as an aim they seek to promote.

What States intend and what States do are different things. But no injustice is done if a State is held to the commitments which it freely and after due deliberation accepted. It is here that the subjective aspect of the treaties under consideration has its greatest significance. For what its analysis yields is the conclusion that there is, in the end, considerably more that unites us than divides us, and that the protection of the fundamental interests that the international community holds dear reveals values that truly compose the common hymnsheet of humanity.

---

[348] See Art 1(1)(a) Montreal Convention.

Part 5

Concluding Thoughts

17

Criminal Justice in an Age of Uncertainty

PAUL BEHRENS

1. CRIMINAL LAW BETWEEN CHALLENGES AND ASPIRATIONS

A BOOK DEDICATED to contemporary challenges to criminal justice inevitably invites challenges itself. The point can be raised that such a study presents an unduly pessimistic view – criminal law, after all, is also the fruit of certain ambitions with regard to its impact in the wider community; focusing on its inherent difficulties only may convey a slanted perspective.

Any attempt, however, to subject these ambitions (and their potential realisation) to closer scrutiny offers room for more discerning consideration. As in the case of the challenges that were explored above,[1] the aspirations can be traced to aspects that lie at the very foundations of the law – even to the basic understanding that criminal law is meant to represent a system that aims to achieve justice within a community.

None of these points is free from doubt. The very concept of 'justice' is notoriously difficult to approach; the question whether it is realised through criminal law invites further challenges. Nor is the presumed link between criminal law and the community beyond question: what is the relevant community to begin with, and can criminal law really be said to fulfil its communicative function? More fundamentally still: does criminal law even fulfil the requirements of a 'system' to begin with?

These are aspects which are reflected in several of the chapters of this volume, and the following examination will make reference to them, where this is indicated. Above them all, however, there remains the question raised at the outset: once the relevant analysis is done, is the resulting picture one of irreconcilable difficulties, or does, in the end, a message of hope emerge?

---

[1] Paul Behrens, 'Challenges to Contemporary Criminal Justice' (Chapter 1 in this volume).

2. THE ASPIRATIONS AND THE REALITY

2.1. Criminal Law as a System

The understanding of criminal law as a 'system' is, with regard to some elements of that term, not straightforward. A system presupposes a form of organisation, especially where complex collections of concepts are concerned,[2] and it is therefore with some justification that coherence has been outlined as one of its characteristics. In the words of Elliot and de Than: 'if the rules of law fitted together randomly and bore no relationship to each other then there would be no system at all'.[3]

And consistency is required for other reasons as well: a consistent application of the laws which a State enacts has been considered part of the principle of legal certainty which in turn is linked to the rule of law.[4] Consistency is also essential for the requirement of foreseeability[5] – if inconsistency inhabits the law, it is not possible for its addressees to understand what exactly is required of them and to adapt their conduct accordingly.

And inconsistency can be a sign of something worse: the existence of inconsistent rules may well indicate that the uniting aspect of criminal law[6] has lost much of its force and that the relevant society is, in fact, marked by a measure of fragmentation.[7]

And yet, consistency is not a feature that can be taken for granted in every criminal justice system. In the United Kingdom, the Law Commission, in its 1989 recommendations on a criminal code for England and Wales, referred to inconsistencies relating to terminology and substance as a 'serious problem' in English criminal law (which it sought to address through codification).[8]

Inconsistency can arise at various levels. It can emerge when different courts lend different interpretations to the same provision, and, with even greater probability (and not always with good reason) where the interpretation (or indeed the codification) of different provisions of criminal law is concerned. Prominent examples that have been cited in English law in this regard include its treatment of recklessness across various crime categories,[9] its treatment of consent,[10] of the combination of preliminary

---

[2] Among the various definitions which the Oxford English Dictionary employs for the noun 'system', that of an 'organized scheme or plan of action, esp. one of a complex or comprehensive kind; an orderly or regular method of procedure, government, administration, etc.' is, in light of the examples provided, arguably the most apt in this context. Oxford English Dictionary, 'system, n.', 3rd edn (Oxford, Oxford University Press, June 2015), at II.14.

[3] Catherine Elliott and Claire de Than, 'The Case for a Rational Reconstruction of Consent in Criminal Law' (2007) 70 *Mod L Rev* 225, 226.

[4] See on this European Commission for Democracy Through Law (Venice Commission), *Report on the Rule of Law* (4 April 2011) CDL-AD(2011)003rev, paras 41–42.

[5] See on this Behrens (n 1), at n 11.

[6] See ibid, section 2.3.

[7] See on this Arlie Loughnan, 'Drink Spiking and Rock Throwing: The Creation and Construction of Criminal Offences in the Current Era' (2010) 35 *Alternative LJ* 18, 21.

[8] Law Commission, *A Criminal Code for England and Wales. Volume 1: Report and Draft Criminal Code Bill* (Law Com No 177), at 2.9 and 1.16.

[9] Ibid at 2.9 and see, for more recent developments, Elliott and de Than (n 3) 228.

[10] In view in particular of the assessment of capacity to consent and indeed of the relevance of consent itself, which can be performed differently for different crime categories, but may at times even differ within the same category. See Elliott and de Than (n 3), in particular at 235, 241, 247 and 250.

offences[11] and of the subjective element underlying similar justifications.[12] But inconsistencies can also arise where one factual situation invites assessment under various systems of the law which have adopted different approaches to the same subject matter.

Difficulties can also emerge at trial level – for instance, in relation to the conduct of trial participants. A problem that has been outlined in that context is the possibility of the prosecution advancing conflicting positions on their factual assessment of the same incident in two separate trials that arise from it – or indeed conflicting arguments on the same substantive legal issues.[13] A prominent problem on the procedural side concerns also the conflicting message that may be sent out in the sentencing framework of a State:[14] the juvenile justice system in the United Kingdom has come under particularly harsh criticism in this regard for the 'competing views' that it disseminates.[15] Inconsistencies regarding sentencing policy take on a particularly dramatic shape where, within the boundaries of one State, different jurisdictions send out diverging messages and starkly differing sentences. 'It should be abhorrent to judicial minds', noted Tillim, writing from an American perspective, 'that any human being might suffer legal death by the sheer accident of residence in a particular jurisdiction.'[16]

Nor are such inconsistencies restricted to the level of domestic law – international criminal law had its experiences with them as well. Genocide provides an example, both on the systemic level and with regards to varying interpretations of the same crime. On the systemic level, the position of intent has attracted differing and confusing messages. Where the commission of genocide by the principal perpetrator is concerned, long-standing case law affirms the particular importance of establishing specific intent: this, after all, is the element that 'characterises the crime'.[17] But that assessment takes on a very different shape in relation to superior responsibility: a military commander, for instance, can be expected to be found liable for genocide committed by forces under his control where he 'knew or, owing to the circumstances at the time, should have known that the forces were committing or about to commit such crimes';[18] in other words, the *mens rea* standard may be reduced to one of inadvertent negligence.

---

[11] Law Commission (n 8) at 2.9.

[12] Elliott and de Than (n 3) 230.

[13] J Vincent II Aprile, 'Criminal Justice Matters' (1999) 14 *Crim Just* 56, in particular at 57, 59, 60.

[14] See DA Thomas, 'The Criminal Justice Act 1991' (1993) 1992 *Inter Alia* 40.

[15] Stephanie J Millet, 'The Age of Criminal Responsibility in an Era of Violence: Has Great Britain Set a New International Standard?' (1995) 28 *Vand J Transnat'l L* 295, 301–302.

[16] Sidney J Tillim, 'Mental Disorder and Criminal Responsibility' (1950–1951) 41 *J Crim L & Criminology* 607–608.

[17] See ICTY, Trial Chamber, *Prosecutor v Radoslav Brđanin*, IT-99-36-T, Judgment, 1 September 2004, para 695 and earlier ICTR, Trial Chamber, *Prosecutor v Jean-Paul Akayesu*, ICTR-96-4-T, Judgment, 2 September 1998, para 517.

[18] And did not take the relevant steps to prevent or repress their commission or 'to submit the matter to the competent authorities for investigation and prosecution', Rome Statute of the International Criminal Court, 17 July 1998, 2187 UNTS 90, Art 28(a). Different views have been put forward on the categorisation of superior responsibility as a mode of liability for the principal offence or as a 'mere' supervisory offence, see ICTY, Appeals Chamber, *Prosecutor v Milorad Krnojelac*, IT-97-25-A, Judgment, 17 September 2003, para 171; contra Court of Bosnia and Herzegovina, *Prosecutor's Office of Bosnia and Herzegovina v Miloš Stupar*, First Instance Verdict, 29 July 2008, 162 ('to be held *liable* for the crime of genocide', emphasis added).

On the level of interpretation, difficulties arise due to different approaches which the ad hoc tribunals have adopted in relation to the fact that genocidal intent needs to embrace the destruction of a protected group in whole or in 'substantial' part. In this context, a defendant might thus be acquitted of genocide where thousands of victims have been targeted, if they constituted less than 2% of the relevant protected group and the Trial Chamber followed a strictly numerical approach, while another defendant might be convicted of the crime over the killing of three community leaders, if his judges favoured the functional approach.[19]

On the procedural level, inconsistencies arise, inter alia, in the field of plea bargaining – a method which not only received different treatment at different stages in the development of international criminal justice, but is also capable of disseminating diverging messages. In the early days of the ad hoc tribunals, plea bargaining had been rejected as incompatible with the aims of international criminal justice; at later stages, however, it was an objective that was 'aggressively pursue[d]'.[20]

Why, then, do these inconsistencies arise?

The increased use of criminal law, in particular on the domestic level, as a tool to address social ills and the sheer number of offences that are the consequence of this certainly have created ample opportunity for divisions among codified crimes and interpretive approaches.[21] More specifically, it appears to be the very specific, 'ad hoc' nature of the offences that invites the possibility of contradiction – the feature which Horder described as 'particularism' in the drafting process: 'the inclusion of definitional detail that merely exemplifies rather than delimits wrongdoing'.[22]

And then there is the fact that different objectives may be pursued by different provisions of the law, both at the substantive and at the sentencing level.[23] The phenomenon of plea bargaining offers an example for instances in which divergent interests have an impact on the same situation – the interests of judicial economy and the need to save time and resources find themselves opposed to the interests of the victims.[24] But there also remains the uncomfortable question whether plea bargaining really can be said to provide justice for the offender – the existence of the 'trial penalty', which Candace McCoy's chapter in this book explored, casts doubt on that.[25]

The problem of diverging aims is even clearer where different legal systems have an impact on the same situation. The simultaneous applicability of human rights and norms of the criminal justice system – the coinciding, say, of the freedom of belief, guaranteed under Article 9 of the European Convention on Human Rights (ECHR),

---

[19] See Paul Behrens, '"A Matter of Utmost Gravity": Approaching the Magnitude of Genocide' (Chapter 14 in this volume).

[20] Michael P Scharf, 'Trading Justice for Efficiency – Plea-Bargaining and International Tribunals' (2004) 2 *J Int'l Crim Just* 1070, at 1071–1072.

[21] See also Loughnan (n 7) 21.

[22] Jeremy Horder, 'Rethinking Non-Fatal Offences against the Person' (1994) 14 *Oxford J Legal Stud* 335; see Loughnan (n 7) 20.

[23] Jack P Gibbs, 'Deterrence, Penal Policy, and the Sociology of Law' (1978) 1 *Rsch L & Soc'y* 103.

[24] Scharf (n 20) 1071, 1076.

[25] See Candace McCoy, 'Pleas without Bargains: Guilty Plea Discount or Coercive Trial Penalty?' (Chapter 7 in this volume).

with laws against blasphemy[26] – illustrates this point. In this book, Sten Verhoeven and Yi Zhang have outlined the impact that human rights law may have on situations in which the crime of incitement to terrorism is alleged, and underlined the need to take care to codify a crime that is not so broad as to violate freedom of expression.[27]

It is well possible that attempts to achieve a total removal of inconsistencies from the criminal justice system are futile. It is certainly true that a measure of flexibility in the application of the law is required, as is a certain discretion on the part of the judges in the interpretation of legal norms.[28] It is instructive that the European Court of Human Rights (ECtHR) itself warned against 'excessive rigidity': the law, it felt, 'must be able to keep pace with changing circumstances'.[29] But keeping pace with circumstances is one thing. Providing widely differing interpretations on what is essentially the same situation is another, and it is difficult to see how such a development would not open the doors wide to arbitrariness and obstruct the foreseeability of the law.

It is also true that the existence of different objectives is not particularly surprising where different systems of the law are concerned – where, for instance, both civil and criminal law are called upon to evaluate the same situation. But there, too, the danger exists of accepting the resulting contradictions too readily as 'inevitable features of the systems'. Their interrelationship often benefits from closer scrutiny. Civil law and criminal law certainly pursue different objectives, and the distinction between them – for example, the elevated standard of proof for prosecution under criminal law – appears justified because of the incomparably graver consequences that a defendant may face within that framework. But if that is the case, it would seem strange if, as a consequence of the same set of circumstances, a conviction for a crime may be more easily obtained than the establishment of liability to pay civil damages. Yet it is that situation that has been found to exist with regard to certain crimes under English law.[30]

That does not mean that inconsistencies can never be resolved. Judicial interpretation, in particular, can not only be the cause for contradictions, but also serve to overcome them; especially if a judgment is rendered with the authority of the highest judicial body that has a say in the matter. Such decisions can also consider diverging systems of the law and incorporate their messages in their findings. With regard to the United Kingdom, for instance, the fact may be recalled that courts have to take into account judgments of the ECtHR and must, '[s]o far as it is possible to do so', read legislation and give effect to it in a way compatible with ECHR rights.[31]

---

[26] See, eg, ECtHR, *ES v Austria* (Application no 38450/12), Judgment, 25 October 2018, para 52 (distinguishing Art 188 of the Austrian Criminal Code from laws incriminating blasphemy and noting that 'a religious group must tolerate the denial by others of their religious beliefs and even the propagation by others of doctrines hostile to their faith, as long as the statements at issue do not incite to hatred or religious intolerance').

[27] See Sten Idris Verhoeven and Yi Zhang, 'The Offence of Incitement to Terrorism' (Chapter 15 in this volume).

[28] See on this ECtHR, *SW v United Kingdom* (Application no 20166/92), Judgment, 22 November 1995, para 36.

[29] ECtHR, *Bakir and Others v Turkey* (Application no 46713/10), Judgment, 10 July 2018, para 53.

[30] Elliott and de Than (n 3) 240, see also 232.

[31] ss 2(1)(a) and 3(1) Human Rights Act 1998, c 42.

The suggestion has also been made that certain other difficulties deriving from inconsistencies in the system can, at least in theory, be resolved at the procedural level. Thus Scharf, writing about plea bargaining in international criminal law, notes that the need for this mechanism could have been avoided if the prosecution had been 'more selective in issuing indictments, charging only a handful of the highest-level perpetrators instead of so many foot soldiers, prison guards and mid-level military personnel'.[32] It is an interesting approach and one which seems well suited to an understanding of international criminal justice which, in particular, takes into account the resource limitations which international institutions face. More selective prosecutions, however, come with their own problems. The difficulty of selective prosecutions and the criticism they invite have certainly haunted international criminal justice ever since Nuremberg – a point which Schabas analysed in his chapter in this book.[33] Nor is it inevitably easier to focus on 'a handful of the highest-level perpetrators'. The chapter by Karnavas, Pettay and Al-Malt has highlighted the very difficulty that had arisen in that regard in the Extraordinary Chambers in the Courts of Cambodia (ECCC), whose jurisdiction was indeed found to be limited to senior and non-senior 'leaders of the Khmer Rouge who are among the most responsible'.[34]

Better hope for the resolution of the problem may arguably lie in its treatment at the legislative level. It is there that the system as a whole can be effectively considered, as well as the potential contradictions which may arise due to messages which a particular criminal justice system sends out to other fields of the law. Some good examples exist: Loughnan refers to coordinating efforts made between various Australian jurisdictions, especially with regard to the offence of food and drink spiking,[35] but also to certain 'systematising projects' regarding other crime categories.[36] To a degree, the need for a more systemic approach is recognised at the international level too – some of the more recent conventions on transnational criminal law thus contain provisions that do at least contain an obligation of 'cooperation',[37] which may thus facilitate the coordination of various systems in the field. More detailed systemic approaches have come into existence on a regional level – such as the move towards harmonisation of criminal law that is discernible within the European Union and among its Member States.[38]

Legislative action is certainly a hopeful venue: it allows the adoption of a broader perspective that is not easily available to judges assigned to issue a ruling in a

---

[32] Scharf (n 20) 1080.

[33] See William Schabas, 'Victor's Justice? Selecting Targets for Prosecution' (Chapter 10 in this volume).

[34] See Michael G. Karnavas, Tanya Pettay, and Noah Al-Malt, 'Defining "Senior Leaders" and "Most Responsible" for Prosecution at the Extraordinary Chambers in the Courts of Cambodia: A Jurisdictional Conundrum or a Policy-Driven Discretionary Diktat' (Chapter 12 in this volume).

[35] Loughnan (n 7) 18.

[36] ibid, 19, in particular at n 11.

[37] See eg Art 18 International Convention for the Suppression of the Financing of Terrorism, 9 December 1999, 2178 UNTS 197 and Art 63(1) United Nations Convention against Corruption, 31 October 2003, 2349 UNTS 41.

[38] See, eg, Carolina Villacampa Estiarte, 'The European Directive on Preventing and Combating Trafficking in Human Beings and the Victim-Centric Treatment of This Criminal Phenomenon' (2012) 2 *Eur Crim L Rev* 291, 299, and, for a critical assessment, André Klip, *European Criminal Law. An Integrative Approach* (Cambridge, Intersentia, 2012) 23–27.

particular case. That does not mean that all efforts at codification bring with it the promise of a well-ordered approach: the current multitude of criminal offences in the United Kingdom, often created on an ad hoc basis, is an example for the opposite direction.[39] A more hopeful approach is the adoption of a single, unified criminal code as the result of detailed debate which takes into account the potential of inherent contradictions and seeks to reduce it. That may seem a daunting task. But it has been done – not only by Law Commissions (such as the 1989 Criminal Code suggested by the Law Commission for England and Wales),[40] but also by national parliaments, seeking the provision of a single code where previously individual criminal laws had existed for various regions – such as the German *Strafgesetzbuch* of 1871. Modern efforts at comprehensive codification also benefit from the opportunity of taking into account the impact of other legal systems (such as human rights law) on domestic criminal law as well as the consequences of individual provisions of criminal law on other systems (such as civil law).

2.2. The Claim that Justice Be Done

The second aspiration that inhabits the concept of criminal law is that it is a system which provides justice.

The concept of justice, however, is one that is no less elusive than the concept of truth had been to Pilate.[41] At times, it may appear as if consensus can be found only in the negative: that, whatever the concept of justice may entail, it does not seem to work.[42]

Yet if agreement can at least be found in the very basic notion that criminal law is supposed to be a tool to reduce crime, one aspect would seem to gain clarity: the safety of victims, and of society as a whole, is an element that has to be achieved if criminal law is supposed to have done 'justice by' these constituencies. But it is clear that the position of the perpetrator plays a role in the criminal justice system too: punishments that constitute an 'abuse of power' would hardly be perceived as 'just'[43] – a consideration which is thus capable of introducing certain safeguards into the penal system, such as the requirement of a reasonable link between the criminal act and its legal consequences, and a prohibition of excessive sentences.

The question about the reasons for punishment tends to invite the consideration of various approaches, chief among them retribution, general and specific deterrence, and incapacitation. Yet measured against the above mentioned aspects of justice, none of them can claim to come without inherent challenges.

---

[39] See Behrens (n 1) at nn 4–8.

[40] Law Commission (n 8) Appendix A. Criminal Law Bill, 25–154.

[41] John 18:38.

[42] Cf Gibbs, with regard to the particular question of the goals of punishment: 'Diogenes could find an honest man more readily than he could identify an American who is content with what he or she takes to be U.S. penal policy', Gibbs (n 23) 104.

[43] See on this Richard Lowell Nygaard, 'On the Philosophy of Sentencing: Or, Why Punish' (1996) 5 *Widener J Pub L* 237, 248.

It is arguably true to say that retribution is still, at least among the general public, one of the most popular reasons underlying punishment. There is a reason why James Fox's phrase that '[m]any Senators believe in the three Rs: retribution, revenge and retaliation',[44] has become popular, and far beyond its application to US lawmakers.[45] What is more: the retributive character appears to inhabit the very concept of criminal law, with the severity of the sentence being one of the factors which the ECtHR is prepared to consider in ascertaining whether proceedings in a State qualify as 'criminal proceedings'.[46]

And yet, if retribution is seen as associated with the notion of 'just deserts'[47] and with society 'getting even' for the perpetrator's misconduct, the principle cannot be said to fulfil even its own promise. The retribution that is meted out is hardly ever 'like for like';[48] imprisonment and fines are ill suited to mirroring offences, say, against the physical integrity of a person. On the international level, this inherent contradiction becomes clearer still: those sentenced by international criminal courts and tribunals may well be responsible for atrocities involving thousands of victims. The passing of a fixed-term or a life sentence is hardly an adequate reflection of the magnitude of the crimes that were committed.[49]

Among other, interrelated problems,[50] retribution also raises questions about the position of punishment within societal cycles of violence, a problem highlighted by Nygaard with particular regard to sentences exceeding 'just deserts'.[51] It would indeed be naïve to accept that spirals of violence limit themselves to situations where private actors or military operations are concerned and cannot manifest themselves in relationships between offenders, offender communities and the criminal justice system.

That, however, raises uncomfortable questions about certain aspirations of criminal justice outlined above. Especially where the safety of victims and of society is concerned,[52] challenges remain. There is, in fact, no reason why retribution, by itself, would be concerned with considerations of this kind. That, however, puts a rather different light on its societal value: far from seeking to provide a 'cure for society's ills',[53] retribution offers no more than a sedative for society's nightmares.[54]

---

[44] W John Moore, 'Shooting in the Dark', *The National Journal*, 12 February 1994.

[45] See Nygaard (n 43) 268 and, in adapted form, Amy Maguire, 'Murdering Myths: The Story behind the Death Penalty. By Judith W. Kay (Book Review)', (2006) 46 *Brit J Criminology* 532, 533.

[46] See on this ECtHR, *Engel and Others v Netherlands* (Application nos 5100/71; 5101/71; 5102/71; 5354/72; 5370/72), Judgment, 8 June 1976, para 82 and see also para 80 (on the distinction between criminal and disciplinary proceedings). See also ECtHR, *Demicoli v Malta* (Application no 13057/87), Judgment, 27 August 1991, para 34.

[47] See on this Marina Aksenova, 'Symbolism as a Constraint on International Criminal Law' (2017) 30 *LJIL* 475, 487.

[48] See Erin I Kelly, 'What is Justice?' (2020) 18 *Geo JL & Pub Pol'y* 889.

[49] See also Luke Moffett, 'Meaningful and Effective? Considering Victims' Interests through Participation at the International Criminal Court' (2015) 26 *Crim LF* 255, 277.

[50] One difficulty that has also been outlined in that regard concerns the perception of punishment by the perpetrators themselves – ie, their acceptance of the relevant punishment as a 'reasonable' consequence of their acts. See on this Kelly (n 48) 902.

[51] Nygaard (n 43) 266, 263.

[52] See above after n 42.

[53] See Behrens (n 1) after n 3.

[54] See also Nygaard (n 43) 251. And even that feature of the retributive function may be doubted, as it is not able to mete out sanctions that mirror the initial conduct (see above at n 48) and is thus unable, at least

Deterrence, the second ground that is often employed as a rationale for punishment, experiences similar problems. It tends to be understood as a concept with two dimensions: general deterrence is premised on the belief that society itself will refrain from undertaking particular acts if they witness the reactions which the criminal justice system visits on persons who engaged in them; specific deterrence enshrines the concept that a particular person will refrain from engaging in the relevant act to avoid the consequences that he knows criminal justice has in store for him.

Deterrence certainly has maintained its position as a popular theoretical ground for the imposition of punishment,[55] and it, too, can be linked directly to the very nature of criminal law.[56] It is, at the same time, based on assumptions that invite critique.

General deterrence presupposes an appropriate level of understanding of criminal law by the general public – as well as society's capacity to reach correct conclusions as to the application of the individual rules;[57] it presupposes, in other words, that the law has fulfilled its communicative function.[58] What is more: it requires society to establish a minimum link between the perpetrator's conduct and their own situation. That, however, cannot easily be presumed – especially given the fact that the message conveyed by criminal law is, inevitably, discriminatory in character: it sets aside the 'us' group of law-abiding citizens from the 'them' group of criminal perpetrators.[59] Tillim's analogy to the framework of religion is apt: while religion too, provides consequences for misconduct, even the threat of 'everlasting punishment for grave sins has not effectively discouraged criminal activity even in religious persons'.[60]

Specific deterrence, on the other hand, presupposes that potential criminals consider the consequences of their actions before they embark on them. That, too, is a point that cannot be taken for granted – at least not for all persons whom criminal law seeks to address. Some perpetrators may not give much thought to the consequences at all; and where they do, there is evidence that they may be moved more by expectations of their social peer group than by the impact that legal rules may have.[61]

The third rationale for punishment which has been mentioned above – incapacitation – is based on the understanding that keeping perpetrators away from society is a way of preventing them from committing further crimes.

It, too, is a rationale that has lost none of its popularity – in this book, Nelken referred in this regard to the significant employment of incapacitation as a method

---

on this basis, to provide a remedy for society's grievances. The debate is not a new one. Dumas' Count of Monte Cristo, in a conversation with Franz d'Epinay, referred to the fact that conduct causing years of suffering was inadequately reflected in the passing of a death sentence. '"Yes I know," said Franz, "that human justice is insufficient to console us. She can give blood in return for blood, that is all; but you must demand from her only what it is in her power to grant."' Alexandre Dumas, *The Count of Monte Cristo* (1845/1846, reprinted in Oxford, OUP Oxford World's Classics series, 1990) 346.

[55] See Nygaard (n 43) 253.

[56] See ECtHR, *Oztürk v Germany* (Application no 8544/79), Judgment 21 February 1984, para 53; ECtHR, *Benedenoun v France* (Application no 12547/86), Judgment, 24 February 1994, para 47.

[57] See on this Gibbs (n 23) 112.

[58] See on this also below at n 102 et seq.

[59] See Behrens (n 1), section 2.3.

[60] Tillim (n 16) 605.

[61] See Nygaard (n 43) 254, 256.

in the United States.[62] Similar observations can be made about the United Kingdom, whose prison population in 2001 had reached 131 inmates per 100,000 of the national population, with an occupancy level of more than 100%.[63] Like deterrence and retribution, incapacitation, too, is closely linked to the nature of criminal law and recognised as such by the ECtHR.[64]

Incapacitation, however, invites the criticism that it is based on a myopic perspective of criminal justice. If it is a purpose of justice to keep victims and society safe,[65] then difficulties arise which are similar to those mentioned in the context of retribution:[66] at least in the long term, incarceration does not provide a cure to the relevant societal problems. Erin Kelly, writing about the US criminal justice system, refers to the difficulties that former prisoners have in reintegrating into the employment system and finding their way in life after release; noting the temptation to commit crimes and the generally high recidivism rates.[67] Incapacitation thus does not seem to offer a solution to the underlying difficulties – it rather represents their deferment.[68] Its effects may be even worse than that: prison provides a chance for more seasoned criminals and promoters of extremist ideologies to connect with first-time prisoners and, by providing an environment that is seemingly more welcome to them than that of society in general, inculcate them with messages and attitudes that render them an even greater danger upon release than they had been before.[69]

At the international level, the problems relating to the traditional rationales for punishment are exacerbated by the conditions that characterise the international criminal justice system. Reference has already been made to the challenge of applying the rationale of retribution at this level.[70] Pragmatic considerations of resource limitations constitute another difficulty which has an impact on several of the above named rationales: ever since Nuremberg, international criminal justice had to accept that it would be able to try only a selected few perpetrators involved in the situations with which it dealt. And while limited resources are a recognised problem on the domestic level as well,[71] the symbolic character of convictions plays an undeniably greater role on the international stage.[72]

---

[62] See David Nelken 'Understanding (and Reforming) Criminal Justice in the Former Soviet Union' (Chapter 9 in this volume).

[63] World Prison Brief, 'United Kingdom: England and Wales' https://prisonstudies.org/country/united-kingdom-england-wales.

[64] See, on this *Engel* (n 46), para 80, with regard to impositions of deprivations of liberty; see also *Benedenoun* (n 56), para 47.

[65] See above after n 42.

[66] see above at nn 52–54.

[67] Kelly (n 48) 897.

[68] Nygaard (n 43) 261.

[69] See on that problem also Paul Behrens, 'Why Not the Law? Options for Dealing with Genocide and Holocaust Denial', in Paul Behrens, Nicholas Terry and Olaf Jensen (eds), *Holocaust and Genocide Denial. A Contextual Perspective* (Abingdon, Routledge, 2017) 230, 240–241.

[70] See text at n 49 above.

[71] That, in fact, is a point that must be counted among the main reasons for the increased use of plea bargaining at the domestic level, see Scharf (n 20) 1076.

[72] See, on the whole problem, Aksenova (n 47).

That means that other considerations tend to occupy centre place where international criminal justice is concerned. Rather than retribution and specific deterrence,[73] considerations such as the 'restoration and maintenance of peace' and the message conveyed through the trial of high-level defendants assert themselves.[74]

Aspirations of this kind come with their own challenges – reference has been made to some of them in individual chapters of this book. The very selection of defendants deemed suitable to stand trial can be fraught with doubt and invites criticism.[75] But even once a trial of a high-ranking official takes place, mechanisms such as plea bargaining are capable of exerting an impact on the message which the criminal justice system is expected to send out. The case of Biljana Plavsić, a former acting co-President of the Serb Republic of Bosnia-Herzegovina, is an illustration: in 2002, she had been charged, inter alia, with crimes of genocide and extermination.[76] Following an Agreement in which she pleaded guilty to persecution and the Prosecution dismissed the other counts, she was sentenced to eleven years' imprisonment.[77] While still serving her sentence in Sweden, she gave an interview in which she stated that she had entered the guilty plea 'so I could bargain for the other charges' and noted: 'I sacrificed myself. I have done nothing wrong.'[78] In cases like these, the question does not appear groundless whether international criminal justice has fulfilled even its symbolic function.

If principal challenges relating to the delivery of justice, especially on the domestic level, are formed by rationales traditionally associated with the concept of punishment, a resolution might be seen in a repositioning of our approaches to the very aspirations of the criminal justice system. In line with that, a more auspicious starting point may be to consider what approaches have 'worked' in practice, when measured against parameters associated with the concept of justice. If the safety of victims and society is one of them,[79] then the question of recidivism unavoidably plays a role in that assessment.

It is for that reason that the Norwegian criminal justice system is an often quoted example for 'best practices' in the field: there, the two-year reconviction rate reportedly stood in 2005 at about 20%, while that for the United States (federal), for the same year, was 60%.[80] In England and Wales, the reconviction rate after one year stood at 48%.[81] But the situation had not always been thus: in the 1980s and 1990s,

---

[73] See ibid 491. But see, contra, ICTY, Trial Chamber, *Prosecutor v Drazen Erdemović*, IT-96-22-T, Sentencing Judgment, 29 November 1996, para 64.

[74] See on this Scharf (n 20) 1072.

[75] See above at n 33–34; Schabas (n 33); Karnavas et al (n 34).

[76] ICTY, *Prosecutor v Momcilo Krajisnik and Biljana Plavsić*, IT-00 39 & 40-PT, Amended Consolidated Indictment, 7 March 2002, paras 15–17, 24–25.

[77] ICTY, Trial Chamber, *Prosecutor v Biljana Plavsić*, IT-00-39&40/1-S, Sentencing Judgment, 27 February 2007, paras 5, 134.

[78] *UPI*, 'Jailed Plavsic Recants Hague Confession', 27 January 2009.

[79] See above after n 42.

[80] Denis Yukhnenko, Shivpriya Sridha and, Seena Fazel, 'A Systematic Review of Criminal Recidivism Rates Worldwide: 3-year update' (2020) 4:28 *Wellcome Open Research* 8, Table 3 (Year 2005), https://www.ncbi.nlm.nih.gov/pmc/articles/PMC6743246/pdf/wellcomeopenres-4-17992.pdf.

[81] In 2015/16. Ibid, Table 2.

the recidivism rate in Norway reportedly was between 60 and 70%, and it was only after a deliberate effort by the Norwegian government to analyse the failures of the existing system that changes were implemented.[82] The resulting system adopted as a core principle that of 'normality', described as an effort to give prisoners 'as close an experience to normal life as possible'.[83] It is a system which thus provides prisoners with particular functions and daily purpose[84] – in Halden prison, for instance, a range of facilities exist to prepare inmates for life outside the prison walls, including woodworking and assembly workshops and a recording studio,[85] while prison officers are seen less as guards than, in the words of one observer, as 'role models, coaches and mentors all in one'.[86] It is treatment that is well aligned with the 2015 UN Standard Minimum Rules for the Treatment of Prisoners (the Nelson Mandela Rules) which provide in Rule 99(1) that organisation and method of work in prisons 'shall resemble as closely as possible those of similar work outside of prisons, so as to prepare prisoners for the conditions of normal occupational life'.[87]

It is also well aligned with the views of those writers on criminal justice and criminology who, for a long time, have advocated an approach that places greater emphasis on rehabilitation, proposed 'truly corrective measures' in the treatment of offenders[88] and have considered the educative function to lie at the centre of the criminal justice system.[89]

Where the security of society is concerned, rehabilitation may indeed prove to be one of the most effective approaches yet – it is in fact one of the few rationales that adopts a forward-looking perspective and considers the ability of prisoners to reintegrate into society in the future.[90]

What it also means is that a correct understanding of the minds of the offenders is essential, including an understanding of the factors that contributed to the commission of the crime.[91] In Norway, a 'needs assessment' of new prisoners is carried out, in the course of which questions about substance abuse problems, about the need for job training and education and about the form of behaviour that led to the arrest are raised.[92] In a similar manner, the American Warren Report of 2007 highlights the

---

[82] Dave Davies, 'Psychiatrist: America's "extremely punitive" prisons make mental illness worse [transcript of interview with Christine Montross]', *NPR Fresh Air*, 16 July 2020.

[83] Ibid.

[84] *Newstex Blogs, Alaska Dispatch*, 'Can Alaska Learn from Norway's "radically humane" prisons?', 11 October 2017.

[85] Christina Sterbenz, 'Why Norway's Prison System is so Successful', *Business Insider*, 11 December 2014, at https://www.businessinsider.com/why-norways-prison-system-is-so-successful-2014-12?r=US&IR=T.

[86] *Financial Express* (Bangladesh), 'Reforming Correction Centres', 17 August 2020.

[87] General Assembly, 'United Nations Standard Minimum Rules for the Treatment of Prisoners (the Nelson Mandela Rules)', Annex, Rule 99(1) (17 December 2015).

[88] See Nygaard (n 43) 264.

[89] See also Kelly (n 48) 899, with reference to Plato, and see Scharf (n 20) 1072.

[90] See also Nelson Mandela Rules (n 87), Rule 107. Other considerations play a role in an efficient implementation of rehabilitation. Reference has, for instance, been made to the intensive training that candidates for the position of prison officer have to undergo in Norway, see *Financial Express* (n 86).

[91] See Tillim (n 16) 605.

[92] Davies (n 82).

importance of 'cognitive-behavioral programs rooted in social learning theory' as the 'most effective in reducing recidivism'.[93]

Rehabilitation is not the only rationale that has been suggested as a more feasible alternative to traditional approaches to punishment. Restorative justice, an approach that places victims' interests in a more central position, has likewise found its supporters; and it does indeed appear to hold promise of hope, especially in situations involving crimes that are well suited for 'mediated victim–offender' encounters which can promote healing and involve the making of amends by the perpetrator.[94] That does not mean that this approach is free from criticism. In this book, Drumbl has cast concerns about the 'politics of victims' rights', which may tend to lead to a more retributivist perspective.[95]

That, however, is a point which allows debate. Mitchell, in the context of sentences for murder, has raised the possibility that the public may not always be 'as punitive as may have traditionally been assumed'.[96] Sterbenz, referring to the case of Anders Breivik, who in 2011 had killed 77 people in Norway and a year later was sentenced to 21 years' imprisonment – a conviction that seemed to put the Norwegian policy of rehabilitation to a harsh test – notes that Norwegians in general, including some parents of the killed children, 'seemed satisfied with the sentence' and suggests that most of the outrage about the sentence 'came from the US'.[97]

It would, in any event, not appear tenable to exclude victims' interests altogether from the considerations underlying punishment – a system that excludes those whose suffering informs the concept of crime to begin with would be hard to justify. But what the above considerations show is that an understanding of justice that focuses on one constituency only, is of little help in achieving the aspiration of the system to return 'justice' to a situation that suffered a disturbance. Divergences among the interests of the affected parties may, however, arise even where they are less expected: not only between interests of victims and perpetrators, but also between those of victims and society. In the Cambodian context, for instance – as mentioned in Chapter 13 above, reference had been made by the Prime Minister of that country to the danger of civil war emerging if 'all the lower-level' cadres were prosecuted,[98] a view that highlights the tension between competing interests in a judicial assessment of the crimes. The interests of both parties can diverge from those of the chambers in trial efficiency,[99] and so forth.

---

[93] Roger K Warren, *Evidence-Based Practice to Reduce Recidivism: Implications for State Judiciaries* (The Crime and Justice Institute and the National Institute of Corrections, Community Corrections Division 2007).

[94] See on this Kelly (n 48) 896.

[95] See Mark Drumbl, '"The Mob is Fickle, Brother" – Bringing "Public Morality" into Sentencing Policy' (Chapter 3 in this volume).

[96] See Barry Mitchell, 'Murder, the Mandatory Life Sentence, and the Question of Perceived Legitimacy' (Chapter 6 in this volume).

[97] Sterbenz (n 85). See, on the case, Martin Sandbu, 'Breivik Given 21 Years for Norway Killings', *Financial Times Online*, 24 August 2012, at https://www.ft.com/content/118e4bbc-edc3-11e1-8d72-00144feab49a.

[98] Karnavas et al (n 34) at n 186.

[99] As highlighted, inter alia, by the phenomenon of plea bargaining, see above at n 20.

It may, in the end, only be through a comprehensive appreciation of the interests of all affected parties that the application of criminal law can be achieved to the extent that its characterisation as a system of justice is truly merited. In his chapter in this book, Doak referred to the objective of realising a more 'holistic form of criminal procedure, which better encapsulates the range of harms that stem from criminal acts'.[100] There may be reason to go further and call for a holistic understanding of the aspiration of criminal justice in its entirety; one that includes the legitimate interests of all concerned by its application. They embrace those of society, which become particularly clear in the field of international criminal justice where, often after situations of long-standing internal turmoil, the aspiration of justice includes its contribution to the maintenance of peace and security in the country. They cannot exclude those of the perpetrators themselves who have the right to be free from excessive penalties, but to whom a fair chance should also be offered to acknowledge reasonable punishment as a consequence of their actions.[101] And they must include those of the victims – to whom restitution needs to be available where that is possible and appropriate, but who also have a legitimate expectation in the manifestation of another aspect of justice that goes to the very essence of criminal law: the provision of solidarity on the part of the community with those, who, through no fault of their own, had been made to suffer at the hands of the perpetrators.

2.3. A System within the Community

The third aspiration to which reference has been made above concerns the fact that criminal justice is a system which works 'within the community'. By defining particular acts as crimes, as Duff had it, the law 'formally declares that they are wrongs in terms of the community's own values and, further, that they are "public" wrongs that properly concern the whole community and that must be formally recognized and condemned as such by the community'.[102]

'Formal recognition' and 'condemnation' indicates the existence of a dialogue between law and society. In this context, the term of the 'communicative function' of the law has been coined;[103] based on the view that the enactment of the appropriately labelled crime and its legal consequences convey the societal and moral condemnation of the relevant conduct.[104] As such, this consideration has received a similar degree of support on the international level: for sentences issued by the ad hoc tribunals, the *Aleksovski* Appeals Chamber thus noted that they 'should make plain the condemnation of the international community of the behaviour in question [...] and show "that the international community was not ready to tolerate serious violations of international humanitarian law and human rights"'.[105] As a message of moral

---

[100] Jonathan Doak, 'Mainstreaming Redress in Criminal Justice' (Chapter 5 in this volume), after n 85.

[101] See on that Kelly (n 48) 902.

[102] RA Duff, *Punishment, Communication, and Community* (Oxford, OUP, 2000) 58.

[103] See on this AP Simester, JP Spencer, Findlay Stark, GR Sullivan and GJ Virgo, *Simester and Sullivan's Criminal Law*, 6th edn (Oxford, Hart, 2016) 32–33.

[104] See on this Gibbs (n 23) 108.

[105] ICTY, Appeals Chamber, *Prosecutor v Zlatko Aleksovski*, IT-95-14/1-A, Judgment, 24 March 2000, para 185.

condemnation, the communicative function is indicative of a relationship between criminal law and the values of the community which it seeks to protect; as a message that is targeted at society as a whole, it also embraces an educative component, be it through the law itself or through its application in practice.[106]

As such, it is one of its essential components that society has a sufficiently accurate understanding of the law and of the consequences of its actions within the legal framework; an aspect which carries an evident connection to the Rule of Law[107] and human rights mandates.[108]

Yet the communicative objective, too, invites more discerning assessment. At the most basic level, the premise underlying it is subject to doubt. The relationship in particular between consequence and causation is not always apparent. That certain forms of conduct are considered repugnant by society is beyond question. But does that feeling arise because of the norms of criminal law, or might different reasons be at its root? When James Fitzjames Stephen observes that '[t]he fact that men are hanged for murder is one great reason why murder is considered so dreadful a crime',[109] he does not seem far removed from the pastor who, in a sermon to his congregation, offered this argument for the existence of God: 'If there were no God, why would there be a pastor?'

Attributing societal condemnation to the impact of criminal law gives credit to the communicative function of that system that might not be deserved and ignores the influence of other messages – messages that do not stem from criminal law but which society doubtlessly recognises at the same time.

At the same time, the role that the communicative function plays within the framework of relations between the messages disseminated by criminal law and those sent by authors outside the legal system (or by other parts of the legal system) is likewise a factor which merits more critical analysis. Once it can be positively established that criminal law, at least in some parts, fulfils its communicative function, the danger may exist that, by doing so, it drowns out legitimate messages coming from any of these other sources. Loughnan, writing in the context of the creation of new offences (where that is accompanied by the expansion of police powers), thus notes that, by resorting to that means, 'the sense of inadequacy of existing law enforcement powers and procedures' is reinforced.[110] That is an important consideration: it emphasises the point that the impact of the communicative function of criminal law may not always be beneficial in a complex system marked by mandates issued by a range of different societal actors.[111]

---

[106] See also Scharf (n 20) 1072 on the educative function associated with international criminal trials.

[107] See on this Simester et al (n 103) 21.

[108] See Behrens (n 1) at n 11.

[109] Quoted in Rudolph J Gerber, 'Death Penalty We Can Live with' (1974) 50 *Notre Dame Law Review* 251, at 253. See, for a very different assessment, Hershovitz: '[...] we expect people to refrain from murder because murder is wrong, not because the law prohibits it, and certainly not because the law punishes it. Indeed, it would be perverse to avoid murder on legal rather than moral grounds', Taylor Scott Hershovitz, 'The Authority of Law', in Andrei Marmor (ed), *The Routledge Companion to Philosophy of Law* (Abingdon, Routledge, 2012) 65–75, at 66.

[110] Loughnan (n 7) 19.

[111] This problem is exacerbated further by the possibility not only of a diminution of the impact of messages by other authors, but by the possibility of contradictory messages. See on this point also above, in particular at n 30.

Difficulties also arise at the level of the addressees of criminal law. Criminal law tends to address various audiences: at the very least, it speaks to the general public on the one hand and, on the other, to legally trained persons and jurors who are involved in the trial process (a distinction that led Robinson et al to moot the possibility of two distinct codes to allow criminal law to perform its functions 'more efficiently and successfully').[112] It also speaks, at least if the thinking behind deterrence as a rationale for punishment is followed, to offenders and potential offenders. Depending on the circle of the addressees, however, different challenges arise.

Where the general public is concerned, different aspects of criminal law allow for the question whether a correct understanding of the relevant legal mandates can invariably be assumed to be in existence. The employment of vague terms is one of them. The temptation, for instance, to have recourse to adjectives such as 'reasonable' is entirely understandable: it provides the lawmaker with a flexible formula which allows the relevant provision to cover a multitude of situations. But it comes at a cost. '[T]o some extent', as Simester and Sullivan note in the context of negligence-based liability, which, under English criminal law, often turns on the 'unreasonableness' of the conduct, 'the individual must judge the law's standard for himself, and risk the Court disagreeing with him'.[113] The risk of diverging assessments is, in these instances, apparent, and the communicative function of criminal law may thus fail to be fulfilled.

It is also at risk where 'obscure' offences are concerned. Obscure offences have, for a long time, been the staple of more or less humorous consideration, and it is true that some of them – such as the prohibition on firing a cannon within 300 yards of a dwelling house[114] – may be of limited practical significance in the 21st century. Situations covered by other offences, however – such as carrying a plank 'upon any footway'[115] or being drunk in a 'public place',[116] still do arise, and the relevant laws owe their 'obscurity' to their lack of application in practice rather than to their subject matter.[117] It is, in any event, doubtful whether knowledge of the relevant offences can truly be said to be widespread. Nor would it be possible to claim, with any certainty, that the communicative function is satisfied where the relevant offences were created in common law only and never received codification to begin with.[118]

Challenges to the communicative function are also owed to the significant proliferation, in certain jurisdictions, of provisions of criminal law – a point which has been mentioned before.[119] While the sheer number of offences makes it difficult for

---

[112] Paul H Robinson, Peter D Greene and Natasha R Goldstein, 'Making Criminal Codes Functional: A Code of Conduct and a Code of Adjudication' (1996) 86 *J Crim L & Criminology* 304–305.

[113] Simester et al (n 103) 30.

[114] s 55 Metropolitan Police Act 1839, c 47.

[115] Ibid, s 54.

[116] s 12 Licensing Act 1872 c 94.

[117] In 2013, the Law Commission of England and Wales published a document that reflects on the above named and other 'Legal Oddities'. Law Commission, 'Legal Curiosities: Fact or Fable?' (March 2013) https://www.lawcom.gov.uk/app/uploads/2015/03/Legal_Oddities.pdf.

[118] See on this also Behrens (n 1), after n 8.

[119] See ibid at nn 4–12.

anybody to maintain a workable awareness of the expectations of the legal system, there is another problem that the large-scale extension of criminal law invites. The inordinate increase of provisions in this field is, like any inflationary development, likely to reduce the value of the relevant currency. Loughnan points to that effect when noting that the frequent recourse to criminalisation appears to 'squander the moral and social power of criminal law prohibitions'.[120] And in this book, Weinstein, discussing the large number of regulatory offences reportedly on the books of the US federal government, referred to observations that the considerable increase in these offences serves to undercut the moral force of criminal law.[121]

But challenges also arise on a more basic level. Who, one may ask, is 'the public' to begin with? The question whether the public can be considered a monolithic bloc is not without its justification, and the conclusion may well be, at least with regard to some crime categories, that public awareness of the law, as Gibbs has it, 'varies from one social unit to the next'.[122] The problem is particularly apparent in international criminal law: there – especially where customary international criminal law is concerned – the entire world can be considered to be addressee of the relevant norms. Yet, as Cotterrell has pointed out above, the premise of the existence of 'transnational networks of community united [...] by shared beliefs' is open to challenge: the possibility looms large that there are, instead, individual networks and that what might be seen in one of them as criminal, 'could be seen in another as normal and necessary practice'.[123]

If the notion of deterrence as a rationale underlying criminal justice is given credence,[124] the addressees of its communicative function would extend to individual offenders as well as potential offenders within society. And yet, at that point, too, questions about the communicative function arise. The concerns voiced above about deterrence in general retain their validity here: justifiable doubt exists regarding the willingness of both past and potential offenders to receive the relevant message in the first place.[125]

In addition to that, the problem manifests itself again that messages sent out by other authors – in particular those within the social circles of the addressees – may also exert an impact on them[126] and quite possibly a stronger one than that of the law. Even where these messages go in the same direction – to the degree that they all acknowledge the power of criminal law to evaluate a particular form of conduct – the understanding of the precise mandate of the law may differ considerably. Gibbs uses the example of aggravated assault: behaviour that lawyers may

---

[120] Loughnan (n 7) 21.

[121] Stuart Weinstein, 'OFAC's Strict Liability Regime: Blackstone and Holmes were Right' (Chapter 8 in this volume) at n 53.

[122] Gibbs (n 23) 113.

[123] See Roger Cotterrell, 'The Concept of Crime and Transnational Networks of Community' (Chapter 2 in this volume). But see, for a differentiating assessment, Paul Behrens, '"A Matter of Utmost Gravity": Approaching the Magnitude of Genocide' (Chapter 14 in this volume), n 15 and Paul Behrens, 'Towards a Criminal Code for the World?' (Chapter 16 in this volume), section 5.2.1.

[124] See above at nn 55–61.

[125] See above at nn 60–61.

[126] See on this above after n 109.

categorise thus, 'may be thought of by a private citizen as nothing more than the legal "protection of private property"'.[127]

If the trial stage in international criminal justice is taken into account as well, another dimension to the challenge of multiple messages appears. International criminal trials often deal with situations in which defendants still have a certain following in their own countries. Coupled with the fact that international criminal courts and tribunals tend to focus on high-profile defendants, there is a distinct possibility that the message of the law is not the only communication that is sent out and that the accused persons themselves turn the defendant's box into a pulpit from which a divergent evaluation of the events is promoted to their supporters in the room and in front of the television screens.[128]

Addressing these deficiencies is a challenging task. To a degree, efforts at the codification level can help – but they cannot be limited to the promulgation of new provisions on an ad hoc basis (which has the likely effect of exacerbating the problem). Clear communication is required and, above all, a systematic approach[129] that takes into account the way in which the relevant message can be expected to be received by its addressees. Insights from international criminal law can be helpful: from the Statute of the International Criminal Court, for one, standing at the conclusion of a learning process in which the international community had to take aboard similar difficulties regarding the lack of clarity on existing crimes. For all the faults that still remain, it is testament to a successful effort at providing a unified criminal code covering nearly the entire field of substantive international criminal law; and in spite of the large amount of individual crimes it had to accommodate, it still managed to reflect a degree of clarity and concision that is missing in the scattered criminal laws of various domestic legal systems.

Even if systematic codification were achieved, however, the need to give appropriate publicity to the law remains. That goes far beyond publishing legal texts in official gazettes and involves community work. The teaching of at least the key messages of the law in schools is a significant step which can be expected to be particularly effective. Beyond that, the work of authorised 'language brokers', persons knowledgeable about the law but able to convey it to the general public in an accessible way, is of significant help for the dissemination of the legal message; be it through bodies that are accessed on an ad hoc basis, such as citizen advice bureaux, or through more dedicated outreach work carried out with the specific mandate of bringing the law to the communities.

And it is not only the wider group of non-lawyers that can be expected to benefit from increased efforts to enhance the communicative function of criminal law. There is certainly room for a critical assessment of the teaching of law to lawyers, down to the level of the particular subjects that form part of the curriculum. In this book, Kyriakides has rightly pointed out the dangers of not including ethics as a compulsory element of LLB degrees – given the risk of solicitors being exposed to

---

[127] Gibbs (n 23) 112.

[128] See on this John Lloyd, 'International Law on Trial', *Financial Times*, 25 July 2008 (with regard to the trial of Vojislav Šešelj before the International Criminal Tribunal for the Former Yugoslavia (ICTY)).

[129] See on this also above, at nn 39–40.

complaints in disciplinary or other types of proceedings – and argued in favour of law students being taught the skills necessary to handle difficult situations, including those presented by ethical dilemmas.[130]

The task of empowering the communicative function of criminal law will, at the international level, have to be fulfilled primarily through members of the international community, including international organisations. That does not mean that there is no part for civil society to play: as Cotterrell has pointed out above, intercultural dialogue fulfils an important role in the 'transnationalisation of the idea of crime'.[131] In a world marked by considerable, and at times seemingly irreconcilable, cultural and political differences, that may seem a tall order. Yet the alternative – not doing anything, trusting that the message will somehow reach its audience because a copy of the law is available in the Peace Palace Library of the Hague, carries its own costs: it means that the criminal justice system is deprived of one of its most essential characteristics and that the communicative function remains seriously impaired – with all the consequences that this generates for society and victims alike.

3. AN ARC THAT BENDS TOWARDS HOPE

The above considerations are not offered with the pretence that they represent a comprehensive overview of all challenges arising from the aspirations of the criminal justice system. It is sobering, however, to reflect on the difficulties that emerge if, as above, even three of its most fundamental objectives are considered in detail.

There are, however, two perspectives that provide helpful considerations for any attempt to contribute to the realisation of these aspirations. The first is a reflection that looks back to the original reasons from which they arose and subjects them to scrutiny. If, for instance, the safety of society is seen as one of the aspects of the justice that criminal law seeks to pursue, then a consideration of the traditional rationales for the *ius puniendi* – of retribution, deterrence and incapacitation – may well require repositioning.[132]

The other perspective is informed by the consequences of methods associated with the relevant aspiration: by taking into account their effects, it is possible to discern which approaches 'worked' in practice and which showed less convincing results.[133] At this stage, too, lessons derived from other frameworks of criminal justice render particular help in assessing the system in question. International criminal law and its application illustrates this point; it is in that context that Roberts noted above that 'international criminal proceedings might be looked upon as laboratories of juridical innovation and potential models for domestic legal reform'.[134] And international criminal law, in turn, can take helpful inspiration from other legal systems – and has

---

[130] See Klearchos Kyriakides, 'Ethics, Education and Employment: Criminal Defence Solicitors, Law Schools and the Legitimacy of the Criminal Justice System' (Chapter 4 in this volume).

[131] See Cotterrell (n 122), after n 49.

[132] See above at nn 44–78.

[133] See above, in particular at nn 79–93.

[134] See above, Paul Roberts, 'Mr Seferović's Pigeons – An Encounter with International Criminal Evidence' (Chapter 11 in this volume), section 6.

done so in the past. In this book, Fournet, talking about the particular matter of the *actus reus* of genocide and the interpretation of the group element, pointed out that international criminal tribunals appear to have made a loan of methods advanced by the ECtHR, resorting, in particular, to the 'living instrument doctrine' it adopted.[135] Approaches of this kind help overcome what would otherwise have remained a dichotomy of divergent systems, with the application of different methods of interpretation and possibly the dissemination of different messages to the same group of addressees.

What emerges from these considerations is that the analysis of the aspirations of criminal law share this point with the examination of its challenges: in both cases, the look at one system in isolation will often fail to provide a comprehensive understanding of the problems and the most effective solutions they may invite. An approach which takes into account other systems of criminal law – and indeed certain legal systems which have a different primary focus (such as human rights law) – not only allows new insights to emerge, but may indeed be required to provide an appropriate evaluation of the legal framework within which the assessment of a particular situation has to be placed.

It is for that reason that it is appropriate that this *liber amicorum*, which is informed by this understanding, is dedicated to Ralph Henham, whose work reflects this extensive approach to the evaluation of criminal justice, incorporating insights from a large range of systems and legal areas, from sentencing considerations on the domestic level to plea bargaining and the role of the prosecution in international criminal trials. And, indeed, beyond criminal justice – thus leading the way towards an understanding of the field that takes into account its position in the wider system of the law and is able to critique the impact which the message of criminal law exerts from a truly contextual perspective.

That approach sets a high bar for the rest of us. The challenges of making acquaintance with a new system (and, in the process, gaining distance from the one with which we possess familiarity) can be considerable. But the results are rewarding. They consist not only in the procurement of knowledge of a different framework and of parameters by which our own system may be measured. At the end of the process is also the acquisition of new insights and original pathways, offering not only a fruitful field of scholarly endeavour, but providing benefits for all parties upon whom criminal justice leaves its mark.

---

[135] See above, Caroline Fournet, 'Standing the Test of Time: The Dynamic Interpretation of the Genocide Convention' (Chapter 13 in this volume), section 5.

Part 6

Ralph Henham: Life and Work

Reflections on Ralph Henham

ACROSS FIVE DECADES

AMAZING AS IT now seems, my links with Ralph Henham stretch back more than fifty years. He started as an undergraduate in the law faculty at Leicester University in 1968, and I arrived there the following year as a young lecturer in my first academic job. The faculty at this time was housed in dark, dingy offices next to the university's new architectural wonder, its prize-winning, glass-and-steel Engineering Building (immortalised on a 1971 postage stamp).

In Ralph's graduation year (1970–71) I lectured and tutored him in jurisprudence. By then the law faculty had moved into College House, a large detached residence on campus. It had been home for the Attenborough family, when naturalist David and actor/director Richard were children and their father was Principal of the then Leicester University College. I liked to imagine that my small first-floor office had once been a bedroom of one of the Attenborough boys. I loved my four years at Leicester – everything was new, the faculty was tiny, and I was just two or three years older than my first students – but Ralph told me later that he had felt unengaged with undergraduate law studies except, as I was very pleased to hear, jurisprudence.

It would be nice to think that this subject, taught at Leicester in a way strongly sympathetic to social science, encouraged his scholarly ambition, which certainly flourished once he found the right vehicle for it. After graduation he decided that the life of a high-street solicitor was not for him, studied criminology and eventually began lecturing. He found that the subject of sentencing was a good focus for his widening intellectual horizons, and set his research direction to become an innovative, imaginative and prolific criminal justice scholar.

Around the time Ralph started his teaching career we renewed contact and have since maintained it. He sent draft papers and many times over the years he travelled from Nottingham to London to lunch with me and discuss his ideas and plans. I enjoyed our discussions and looked forward to them. Perhaps he felt a little isolated intellectually at times and needed a sounding board. As his interest in theory grew he was attracted to some of my sociolegal and theoretical ideas, and I valued his opinions on how my research orientations might intersect with his interests.

We met, often at the Old Amalfi restaurant in Bloomsbury, talking happily for hours. And Ralph sent copies of his books as they appeared, and kept me informed of his projects. He soon became much more than a link with the old Leicester days;

rather, someone with whom it was fun to engage in mutual learning (and share a bit of academic shop talk). I am happy that our relationship evolved that way, becoming a highly valued, long-term one for both of us.

Roger Cotterrell

RALPH'S VOICE AND ENERGY

One of the first articles I ever coauthored was with Ralph. It was about plea bargaining at the international criminal tribunals. Back in the day, notably at the International Criminal Tribunal for the Former Yugoslavia, a widespread practice of plea bargaining had arisen. This struck us as somewhat paradoxical given that much of this approach was superimposed from ordinary criminal justice systems to the context of collective crimes against humanity. In a sense, this uploading was ill-conceived, as it applied norms for deviant individual crimes in regulated criminal justice systems to the very different context of collective mass crimes in anarchic international systems. And, whatever the merits of this superimposition, the process of plea bargaining was more one of celerity than considered thinking and drained the expressive value of international prosecutions. Writing together with Ralph was a joy. Whereas I was about numbers and doctrine and individual cases, Ralph was about big ideas, theory and connectivities with the world beyond the courtroom. In the end, the piece hit on many cylinders. And with that collaboration as a start, a friendship grew. Ralph is thoughtful, gentle, brilliant and funny. He is a wonderful colleague, gracious with his time, and a partisan of fine dining and good cheer. He spent time at my university, Washington and Lee, as a Visiting Scholar, and here, too, was enthusiastic and energetic. Although he wrote about the darkest aspects of the human condition – violence and the carceralism of the state – he always maintained great faith in that same human condition for betterment, growth and aspiration. His is precisely the kind of voice desperately needed in criminal justice studies: aware of the abuses, and embracing of possibilities and potentialities. His voice, to be sure, remains in his writings and his teachings, he continues to inspire and guide, and I am ever grateful for having had the opportunity to learn from him, to share with him, and to laugh with him. I know he will continue to engage and be engaged, wherever his many upcoming years take him, and I am looking forward to many more of his thoughts, ideas, and vivacity.

Mark A Drumbl

A CASE STUDY IN COLLEGIALITY

When Dr Paul Behrens extended an invitation to me to contribute a chapter to a book dedicated to Professor Ralph Henham, I had no hesitation in accepting it. In common with so many other people, I am indebted to Professor Henham. In 2005, I co-delivered a paper at a memorable conference hosted by Nottingham

Trent University, his long-standing academic home. The conference marked the sixtieth anniversary of the establishment of the International Military Tribunal at Nuremberg in 1945.[1] Back in 2005, I was simultaneously a practising solicitor in London and a novice university lecturer at the University of Hertfordshire. I had never previously met Professor Henham; nor had I had any other prior dealings with him. Even so, during the course of the conference, he found the time to advise, encourage and inspire me. In so doing, he displayed the civic duty, humanity, kindness and wisdom that every academic needs to possess. At the same time, he effectively brought home to me that academia is nothing without a spirit of collegiality. Indeed, his selflessness reminded me that this cherished concept must not only apply amongst academics within the same university, but amongst academics across all universities. Despite our different institutional affiliations, we all belong to the same family of thinkers who are following in the footsteps of Socrates, Plato, Aristotle and the other pioneers of academia. For these and for other reasons, I thank Professor Henham. I also congratulate him for all that he has achieved and wish him all the very best as the future unfolds.

Klearchos A Kyriakides

A VALUED AND ADMIRED COLLEAGUE

It was an absolute privilege to be invited to contribute to this *Festschrift*. I first met Ralph when I joined Nottingham Law School in November 2007. At that time, I was at a relatively early stage in my career. I was in awe of his highly sophisticated and nuanced understanding of both domestic and international criminal justice. In particular, his books with Mark Findlay, *Transforming International Justice* and *Beyond Punishment*, served as highly informative exemplars of what outstanding rigorous and critical legal scholarship should be like. Although a giant in the field, I was immediately struck by Ralph's modesty and approachability. I recall how he was extremely generous with his time, reading drafts and providing sage and inspiring words of advice. I learnt a huge amount from him in terms of how to shape my own research agenda and how to construct robust academic arguments.

He also paid a crucial role in supporting and developing what was then a relatively small community of researchers at Nottingham Law School. He also played a pivotal role in developing the School's then fledging suite of LLM courses, developing a new stream in international criminal justice underpinned by his flagship modules, 'Foundations of International and Comparative Criminal Justice' and 'Comparative Sentencing and Penology'.

Fifteen years later, and having rejoined Nottingham Law School as Associate Dean of Research, I am delighted that Ralph remains a highly valued member of staff on a fractional contract; we were most fortunate to have submitted his exceptionally

---

[1] The paper resulted in the following publication: Klearchos Kyriakides and Stuart Weinstein, 'Nuremberg in Retrospect' (2005) 5(3) *International Criminal Law Review* 373–86, https://doi.org/10.1163/1571812054940094 (last accessed 1 August 2021).

strong outputs as part of our recent Research Excellence Framework return. We still use examples of his work as part of our staff development work with early-career researchers; his work is an epitome of what world-leading research looks like.

A *Festschrift* often signals the end of a long and distinguished career, but I am certain this is not the case with Ralph. While he has left a firm footprint in national and international criminal justice, he continues to work on a number of highly innovative and exciting projects which no doubt will also be highly impactful upon the discipline.

Jonathan Doak

HENHAM AHEAD OF THE CURVE

In 1998, Ralph Henham travelled to the United States to attend the annual meeting of the Law and Society Association and present the findings of his research paper on the 'trial tax' (which is also called the trial penalty, confession reward, trial tariff, guilty plea discount, or – should the speaker be a criminal defence attorney – any of a variety of curses). As it turned out, I also was presenting a paper on the same panel on the exact same topic from the US side of things. I recall Ralph and I locked eyes when the panel's organiser announced the near-identical titles. Like the aspiring journalist I had once been, my first thought was 'oh no, scooped again'. Ralph later told me that his first thought was 'Aha! Research is finally underway on this topic in other common law countries. Maybe we'll be able to leverage it and get some traction so practition-ers will recognise what a denial of due process the trial tax is.'

Ralph is obviously a better strategist than I am.

He quickly turned his excellent research paper into a law review article,[2] published a year later and cited in thirty-three American law review articles since then – which is the count from only American law reviews listed in HeinOnLine. I leave it to British readers to run a citation count on that article and am certain you will find it had great influence in placing the trial penalty problem on the policy agenda. Ralph placed it there over three decades ago.

Now, at least on this side of the Atlantic, bar associations and criminal procedure reform organisations are agitating to rein in the excesses of the trial penalty.[3] Deeply concerned that innocent people are coerced to plead guilty when sentences imposed after conviction at trial are grossly disproportionate to the punishment offered in

---

[2] Ralph Henham, 'Bargain Justice or Justice Denied – Sentencing Discounts and the Criminal Process' (1999) 62 *MLR* 515.

[3] New York County Lawyers Association, 'Solving the Problem of Innocent People Pleading Guilty' (2019), available at www.nycla.org/resource/board-report/solving-the-problem-of-innocent-people-plead-ing-guilty/; National Association of Criminal Defense Lawyers, 'The Trial Penalty: The Sixth Amendment Right to Trial on the Verge of Extinction and How to Save It' (2019), available at https://www.nacdl.org/Document/TrialPenaltySixthAmendmentRighttoTrialNearExtinct; New York State Association of Criminal Defense Lawyers, 'The New York State Trial Penalty: The Constitutional Right to Trial Under Attack' (2021), available at https://nysacdl.org/page/NYTrialPenalty21 (URLs accessed 20 August 2021).

return for a guilty plea, and convinced that this is one important driver of the death of the jury trial, they have inserted the topic into wider justice system reform efforts.

This sort of development becomes possible only when legal scholars recognise a systemic injustice, research and publish about it, shape practitioner and scholarly understanding of it, and continually refine the empirical research and policy ramifications of it. Ralph got there first and he did all that. I don't mind that he accomplished the scholar's equivalent of the journalist's scoop.[4] After another three decades has passed, let us hope that the work he did and that so many people are doing right now will have produced fundamental changes in the excesses of the guilty plea process.

Candace McCoy

RALPH HENHAM – HUMANISING CRIMINAL JUSTICE FOR ALL

It is my pleasure to participate in this tribute to Professor Ralph Henham. Ralph's work in the field of international criminal justice and criminal law has been instrumental in making the case for reform and rethinking perspectives on the most significant problems faced. I need not reiterate here what so many of my more eloquent co-contributors have said about Ralph's exceptional corpus of works as they do far greater justice to him than I can. For my part, it is my hope that this volume brings out to all who read it the unique gifts and cherished temperament that Ralph brought to his engagement as a mentor, colleague and inspirational educator. Encouraging scholars and students to challenge themselves and to make sure they are not afraid to ask themselves the hard questions – the ones for which there are no easy answers. In doing so Ralph has brought out the best in all of us and for that all of us are immensely grateful.

Stuart Weinstein

A PIONEER OF INTERNATIONAL AND TRANSNATIONAL CRIMINAL JUSTICE

I am delighted to contribute to this *Festschrift* for Ralph Henham. Ralph has been a pioneer in imaginatively pushing the boundaries of the academic study of criminal law and criminal justice at a time where the challenges have never been greater. Can we find global, or at least regional solutions, to crime problems that transcend national boundaries? What forms do they take? What forms should they take? What can and what should be the goals of international criminal justice? It was a special pleasure, some years back, to be invited by Ralph (and Mark Findlay) to take part in their methodologically sophisticated efforts to rethink the role of 'context' and

---

[4] Unlike Ralph with his one-year turnaround time, it took me six years to publish an article from the Law and Society conference paper, and it was in a Canadian law review. The Canadians are deeply concerned about this problem as well. See: Candace McCoy, 'Plea Bargaining as Coercion: The Trial Penalty and Plea Bargaining Reform' (2005) 50 *Criminal Law Quarterly* 67.

'comparison' in the search for international criminal justice (see, for example, Ralph Henham, 'Criminal Trials: A Plea for Empirical Research' (2007) 5(7) *Journal of International Criminal Justice* 757–78, and Mark Findlay and Ralph Henham, 'Integrating Theory and Method in the Comparative Contextual Analysis of Trial Process' in Mike McConville (ed), *Research Methods for Law* (Edinburgh, Edinburgh University Press, 2007) 134–62).

David Nelken

TWO NOTTINGHAM LAW SCHOOLS, ONLY ONE RALPH HENHAM

When I joined the University of Nottingham in 1993 institutional relations with Nottingham Trent University (NTU) were somewhat strained, owing to a difference of opinion as to whether 'Nottingham Law School' was a confusingly misleading name for a new venture in professional legal education. Such matters were – and still are – way above my pay grade, though I do know that several of my visitors have ended up lost on Chaucer Street over the years, and to this day some of my mail still gets routed via NTU. I suppose it didn't help that my Department of Law was located in the Trent Building, nor did changing our name to the School of Law presumably mitigate any confusion. Happily, none of this institutional frostiness chilled relations between individual members of staff working in the fields of criminal law and criminal justice, which in my experience have been unfailingly warm, collegial and collaborative. For two decades and up to his retirement, Ralph Henham was a central figure in this informal Nottingham network, and we would soon become firm friends as well as academic colleagues. Particularly in the early years after my arrival in the leafy Beeston suburbs, I would regularly find myself driving the few miles along Derby Road and down into the city centre to attend lectures and seminars at NTU, including, in due course, Ralph's own inaugural professorial lecture. Frequent return visits were made in the opposite direction. Ralph was a stalwart of our termly Criminal Justice Discussion Group meetings, a tireless reader of material in draft, and an astute sparring partner for knocking unformed ideas into shape.

Two features of Ralph's own research and extensive publications stand out, to me, as particularly admirable. First, whether exploring plea bargaining, sentencing, victimology or general penal policy, Ralph's writing is informed by a strong sociological sensibility, inherited from Durkheim via Roger Cotterrell. This strand of thought constitutes a significant, and sometimes challenging, corrective for those of us inclined to more austerely normative perspectives, analyses and argumentation. Interdisciplinarity, and the close attention to methodological questions to which it almost inevitably leads, are a second notable feature of Ralph's scholarship. Shifting focus from (primarily) domestic to international criminal justice might appear, in retrospect, an obvious extrapolation from existing penal theorising, but this is an illusion cast by the speed with which new disciplinary genres – when timely and successful – coalesce, solidify and institutionalise. When Ralph originally saw the potential connections, in the days before International Criminal Law was a recognised subject, his publications (many in collaboration with Mark Findlay) mapped out bold and original new directions for criminal justice research and international penal policy.

I have tried to reflect both features of Ralph's scholarship in my contribution to this celebration of his professional life's work, albeit with a topic and methodological approach more characteristic of my research agenda than his. Personal relationships between scholars are perhaps, after all, not so different from relations between institutional neighbours. If we sometimes disagree, explicitly and in public, this is only the logical consequence of a shared commitment to deeper intellectual projects and values. The creative tensions of academic debate, when conducted in the generous spirit exemplified by Ralph Henham throughout his long and distinguished career, cement enduring friendships and keep the conversation alive.

Paul Roberts

PERSONAL REFLECTION ON PROFESSOR RALPH HENHAM

An academic journey can be punctuated with key encounters. If we are very lucky, we meet academics who somehow follow our paths, interact with us with kindness, respect and understanding, and support us at every opportunity they have.

I first met Ralph Henham during my very first month as an academic, that is to say in September 2004. Together with Paul Behrens, he was organising at Nottingham Trent University an academic workshop of experts on 'The Criminal Law of Genocide'; I contacted them and they were kind enough to let me – the junior of juniors – attend. A year later, I travelled back to Nottingham to contribute to an international conference Ralph and Paul were organising on the very same topic. Once again, they were giving me an opportunity to share my thoughts and present my work as a junior academic and, once again, they allowed me to meet with them and other experts in the field. With the humbleness that characterises him, Ralph certainly has no idea of how much his trust and encouragements meant to me. And he did not leave it at that. On two occasions, Ralph and Paul included my research within a volume they were editing – *The Criminal Law of Genocide: International, Comparative and Contextual Aspects* (Ashgate, 2007) and *Elements of Genocide* (Routledge, 2012). With Mark Findlay, Ralph invited me to contribute to another edited volume – *Exploring the Boundaries of International Criminal Justice* (Ashgate 2011). Both even agreed to publish one of my monographs in their International and Comparative Criminal Justice Series (Ashgate). Much later on, Ralph kindly agreed to act as one of my referees in support of my professorship.

I consider myself very lucky: my academic journey has been marked by key encounters and Ralph was definitely one them. I thus feel truly privileged to have been invited by Paul to write a chapter in this volume. My modest contribution is a way of expressing my sincere gratitude and of saying 'thank you' to Ralph. Thank you for having been among the first to give me a chance, thank you for your thoughtfulness, thank you for all your help and thank you for having been such an inspiring mentor.

Caroline Fournet

MEMORIES OF A FRIEND

If the first of our Reflections on Ralph Henham recalled a friendship stretching over fifty years, it may be appropriate to close them with memories of a more recent date (and even that is relative!).

I first met Ralph under somewhat daunting circumstances. I had applied for a Research Assistantship (my first permanent post in academia) at the Nottingham Law School, and as the successful candidate would be reporting directly to Professor Henham, he was a member of the interviewing panel. What I remember most clearly was that the others asked a fair few questions, but that there was also this man with the formidable mane of silver hair who would not say a word. He rather reminded me of Theodor Mommsen, the German jurist and historian (always portrayed as a brooding curmudgeon). That did not seem to augur well!

Needless to say, I shouldnae have worried. Ralph could not have been a kinder or more supportive employer – one who led by example and only the gentlest hint of advice, who was always happy to give younger colleagues (not just me!) space to develop and to foster their creativity.

Ralph was, at that time, researching fields of international criminal law – a topic which I found fascinating but which, that far, I had little chance to explore. A successful funding application led to a project on the law of genocide, two conferences and two books which we edited.[5] It is wonderful to see the names of so many good colleagues who contributed to these books as authors of this *liber amicorum* as well. These projects gave us the opportunity to work with a range of fascinating experts, some of whom are no longer with us – I remember in particular Henry T King, erstwhile Prosecutor at the main Nuremberg trial, and his comments on meeting Raphael Lemkin, the father of the law of genocide. ('I thought he was a crank!' he said.)

After my work at Nottingham Law School came to an end, our ways went in different directions (although my next post was at Ralph's alma mater, the University of Leicester!). Now we are even in different countries (just about – he in England, I in Scotland), but we managed to stay in touch, tell each other about our life and work and compare notes about our different institutions. When the opportunity arose to edit this *liber amicorum*, I was delighted to embark on this task, and it came as no surprise that many of Ralph's friends were very happy to contribute. No doubt it will embarrass him to read it, but throughout these well-nigh twenty years, I have never experienced Ralph other than as a wonderful friend (come rain or shine), a source of wisdom and gentle counsel, a fount of knowledge – a scholar and a gentleman alike.

Paul Behrens

---

[5] Ralph Henham and Paul Behrens (eds), *The Criminal Law of Genocide* (Aldershot, Ashgate, 2007); Paul Behrens and Ralph Henham (eds), *Elements of Genocide* (Abingdon, Routledge, 2012).

Ralph Henham's Life and Work

PAUL BEHRENS

THE CONNECTION BETWEEN law – in its professional and academic sense – and the Henham family spans several generations. John Alfred Henham, Ralph's father, was a County Court and Circuit Judge based in Sheffield during the 1980s and 1990s. Some of his cases were matters to which readers today can easily relate – such as that of a retired naval commander who brought an action against the rail unions over the cancellation of a train (which resulted in an award of £153 for his expenses, and, perhaps more importantly, a *Guardian* article entitled 'A Passenger's Victory').[1]

Ralph's mother, Suzanne, was born in Brussels. She and John met during World War II when he was on leave whilst serving with the RAF in Germany. They married in 1946 and came to England. Following John's career, Suzanne was whisked away to Yorkshire in 1947. Ralph himself – Ralph Jean Henham – was born in Doncaster on 20 July 1949. Following a spell in Walsall, where Ralph's brother Marc was born, the young family moved to Goring-by-Sea in West Sussex, John having been appointed Clerk to the Justices for Worthing, Arundel and Chichester.[2] Sadly, Suzanne passed away very suddenly in 1972. In 1974 John decided to return north as Stipendiary Magistrate for South Yorkshire and was eventually elevated to the Sheffield Bench in 1985. He retired in 1995.

Ralph's father John loved his work and was a fine lawyer and much-respected judge. The heavy responsibility of being a judge is not generally appreciated, or borne lightly. In particular, he would agonise over sentencing more than any other issue. His deliberations made a lasting impression on Ralph. In later years, John enjoyed commenting on Ralph's work and retained his love of the law until his death in 2008.

Ralph studied law at Leicester Law School, joining the first generations of students of that department (the Law School had been founded in 1965). Whilst he enjoyed his legal studies, Ralph became increasingly interested in the relationship between law and society. He was much influenced by Roger Cotterrell, whose lectures and tutorials in what was then called Jurisprudence Ralph found especially inspiring. Roger has continued to help and inspire Ralph as a colleague and friend throughout his

---

[1] Martin Wainwright, 'A Passenger's Victory', *The Guardian*, 18 May 1986.
[2] During this period John engaged in the difficult task of producing and updating a summary of Magistrates' sentencing powers in a handy pocket-sized format that could easily be referred to during proceedings: see John A Henham, *Magistrates' Summary Jurisdiction: A Guide to Sentencing Powers*, 2nd edn (Chichester, Barry Rose, 1968).

academic life. So Ralph developed an interest in the Sociology of Law, socio-legal approaches to the study of law and the then fledgling subject of Criminology whilst at Leicester.

In 1971, Ralph graduated with an LLB (Hons); three years later, he was admitted as Solicitor of the Supreme Court of England and Wales. But academia continued to call to Ralph – he pursued postgraduate studies and obtained, only one year after his admission as a solicitor, an MA in Criminology from the University of Keele (1975), following this up with an MPhil in Social Administration and Law from the University of Nottingham in 1985. By that time, Ralph had already decided to settle on a career in academia.

In 1978 Ralph married Annemarie in Southampton, where Annemarie's parents lived, and, after a brief spell in Kent, they moved to Nottinghamshire where they pursued their respective careers and raised their three children, Nicole, Marc and Marie-Louise, two of whom went on to enter the legal profession. Ralph and Annemarie remained in Nottinghamshire for thirty-seven years before moving to West Dorset in 2016.

From 1977 to 1979, Ralph was a Lecturer in Law at the University of Greenwich, switching in 1979 to Nottingham Trent University, an institution to which he would remain faithful for more than half a century (and counting!). In 1979, too, his first two articles were published, on topics that those familiar with his work today may not immediately associate with him, but which demonstrate the considerable breadth of his academic interests: the enforcement of outsider rights under the Companies Act 1948, and the subject of actions against limited companies.[3] Longer peer-reviewed articles followed, including, in the 1980s, Ralph's first forays into the field of sentencing policy, which was to remain such an important part of his work.[4] Books followed, too, starting with *Sentencing Principles and Magistrates' Sentencing Behaviour* in 1990.[5] And every few years, more would be added to an ever growing publication list, some edited, but most authored by Ralph himself, until (by the time of writing), he had reached the biblical age of twelve books, released by such prominent houses as Ashgate, Routledge and Oxford University Press. As well as more than seventy articles, firmly establishing his reputation in fields ranging from trial justice to genocide, but in particular in the theoretical, comparative and policy-related aspects of sentencing policy.

His achievements were recognised by his university as well: in 1985 he was promoted to Senior Lecturer in Law, in 1995 to Reader, and in 1998, he became Professor of Criminal Justice, a post he would hold until his retirement in 2015. Other universities also appreciated his expertise, leading to numerous visiting positions over the years, at the Universities of Oxford and Cambridge, at the European University

---

[3] Ralph Henham, 'The Enforcement of Outsider Rights under Section 20(1) of the Companies Act 1948' (1979) 76 *Law Society Gazette* 203; Ralph Henham, 'Actions against Limited Companies: Is the Rule in *Foss v Harbottle* Still Viable?' (1979) 76 *Law Society Gazette* 1006.

[4] See eg Ralph Henham, 'The Influence of Sentencing Principles on Magistrates' Sentencing Behaviour' (1986) 25(3) *Howard Journal of Criminal Justice* 190; Ralph Henham, 'The Importance of Background Variables in Sentencing Behaviour' (1988) 15(2) *Criminal Justice and Behaviour* 255.

[5] Ralph Henham, *Sentencing Principles and Magistrates' Sentencing Behaviour* (Aldershot, Avebury, 1990).

Institute in Florence and other institutions of higher education.[6] His membership in scholarly societies was equally impressive and included, among others, a Fellowship of the Royal Society of Arts.[7]

The consistent theme underlying Ralph's writing is that trial justice should be conceived as a recursive reproductive system. Furthermore, that the constituent elements of that system – the theory, practice and outcomes of sentencing – are contextualised, so that understandings, interpretations and explanations must always be treated as relative to time and place. The most important implication of this perspective is that the State should ensure that penal interventions have social value. Ralph's fullest elaboration of these ideas came with *Sentencing Policy and Social Justice*, a monograph which was published by Oxford University Press in 2018.[8]

The path taken always owes much to unforeseen events, and the direction of Ralph's career is no exception. First, came the appointment of Peter Kunzlik, who was charged with establishing a research culture within the Law School post-1992. Ralph had been on the brink of returning to private practice when Peter appointed him to the embryonic 'research team'. Had he not done so, things would have been very different. Secondly, came a chance encounter with Mark Findlay, an Australian academic seconded to Nottingham Law School from the University of Sydney. Mark's imaginative thinking and positivity helped to rekindle Ralph's enthusiasm and drive.

Ralph also drew inspiration from working with other distinguished colleagues,[9] many of whom are represented within these pages. This work reinforced his interest in the comparative aspects of sentencing, and, more particularly, whether perspectives more associated with international criminal justice and transitional justice have any relevance for domestic sentencing, and vice versa.

In 2002, while already well established as Professor at Nottingham Trent University, Ralph completed his PhD at the University of Keele, an experience which, as everybody who does a PhD while in full-time employment can appreciate, was not without its challenges.

A recurring feature of Ralph's work was his engagement with friends and colleagues from various areas of the law – through conferences which he attended or hosted at Nottingham Trent, through his guest scholarships, through co-written articles, book chapters and books. His many editorial achievements ought to be seen in the same light,[10] and they began at an early stage: he was deputy editor of the *Nottingham Law Journal* from 1990 to 1992 and member of its editorial board from 1999 to 2012. He became member of the editorial advisory group of the *Howard Journal of Criminal Justice* in 2000 and remained in that capacity for the following twelve years, was a member of the editorial board of the *International Journal of Law, Crime and Justice* until recently and remains co-editor (together with Mark Findlay) of the International and Comparative Criminal Justice Series at Routledge.

---

[6] See Paul Behrens, 'Ralph Henham – A Homage' (in this volume), after n 73.

[7] ibid.

[8] Ralph Henham, *Sentencing Policy and Social Justice* (Oxford, Oxford University Press, Clarendon Studies in Criminology, 2018).

[9] See Behrens (n 6) nn 74–78.

[10] See on this also Behrens (n 6) after n 78.

In 2015, upon his retirement, Ralph was made Emeritus Professor of Criminal Justice at the Nottingham Trent University. He became Research Fellow in Criminal Justice at Nottingham Trent in 2015 and Senior Research Fellow in 2020.

Today, Ralph lives with his wife in Dorset where he enjoys the more relaxed pace that comes with his emeritus position (and the less relaxed pace that comes with being a grandfather). It does, in any case, give him an opportunity to dedicate more time to his hobbies, which include painting, music, reading and walking in the beautiful Dorset countryside. It might also be true to say (to adapt the words of a former politician) that retirement from university also gave him more time for academia. That, at least is a wish that we, his friends and colleagues, sincerely hope has come true for him and will remain so in the future!

Ralph Henham: A Bibliography

1. BOOKS

1.1. Authored Books

Sentencing Principles and Magistrates' Sentencing Behaviour (Aldershot, Avebury, 1990)

Criminal Justice and Sentencing Policy (Aldershot, Dartmouth 1996)

Sentence Discounts and the Criminal Process (Aldershot, Ashgate 2001; Abingdon, Routledge [hardback edition 2017; paperback edition 2019])

(with M Findlay) *Transforming International Criminal Justice: Retributive and Restorative Justice in the Trial Process* (Cullompton, Willan, 2005; Abingdon, Routledge [paperback edition 2012])

Punishment and Process in International Criminal Trials (Aldershot, Ashgate, 2005; Abingdon, Routledge [paperback edition 2016])

(with M Findlay) *Beyond Punishment: Achieving International Criminal Justice* (Basingstoke, Palgrave Macmillan, 2010) [nominated for the SLS Hart Socio-Legal Book Prize 2011]

Sentencing and the Legitimacy of Trial Justice (Abingdon, Routledge 2011; [paperback edition 2013])

Sentencing: Time for a Paradigm Shift (Abingdon, Routledge, Key Ideas in Criminology Series, 2013)

Sentencing Policy and Social Justice (Oxford, Oxford University Press, Clarendon Studies in Criminology, 2018)

1.2. Edited Books

(with P Behrens, eds) *The Criminal Law of Genocide: International, Comparative and Contextual Aspects* (Aldershot, Ashgate, 2007; Abingdon, Routledge [paperback edition 2016])

(with M Findlay, eds) *Exploring the Boundaries of International Criminal Justice* (Aldershot, Ashgate, 2011; Abingdon, Routledge [paperback edition 2016])

(with P Behrens, eds) *Elements of Genocide* (Abingdon, Routledge, 2012 [paperback edition 2014])

2. CHAPTERS IN BOOKS

'Victims of Economic Crime and the Criminal Process' in L de Koker, BAK Rider and JJ Henning (eds), *Victims of Economic Crime* (Centre for Business Law, Faculty of Law, University of the Free State, Bloemfontein, 1999)

'Sentencing Policy and Guilty Plea Discounts' in N Hutton and C Tata (eds), *Sentencing and Society: International Perspectives* (Aldershot, Ashgate, 2002)

'The Normative Context of Sentencing for Genocide' in R Henham and P Behrens (eds) *The Criminal Law of Genocide: International, Comparative and Contextual Aspects* (Aldershot, Ashgate, 2007)

(with M Findlay), 'Integrating Theory and Method in the Comparative Contextual Analysis of Trial Process' in M McConville and WH Chui (eds), *Research Methods for Law* (Edinburgh, Edinburgh University Press, 2007)

'Evaluating Sentencing as a Force for Achieving Justice in International Criminal Trials' in R Henham and M Findlay (eds), *Exploring the Boundaries of International Criminal Justice* (Aldershot, Ashgate, 2011)

'International Sentencing as a Force for Achieving Peace through Justice' in Oxford Transitional Justice Research (eds), *Critical Perspectives in Transitional Justice* (Cambridge, Intersentia, 2012)
'Sentencing Perpetrators of Genocide' in P Behrens and R Henham (eds), *Elements of Genocide* (Abingdon, Routledge, 2012)
'Exploring the Relationship between Social Rehabilitation and Social Justice in Sentencing' in F Coppola and A Martufi (eds), *Social Rehabilitation and Criminal Justice* (Abingdon, Routledge [forthcoming])

3. ARTICLES

3.1. Peer-Reviewed Journal Articles

'The Influence of Sentencing Principles on Magistrates' Sentencing Behaviour' (1986) 25(3) *Howard Journal of Criminal Justice* 190
'The Importance of Background Variables in Sentencing Behaviour' (1988) 15(2) *Criminal Justice and Behaviour* 255
'Evaluating the United States Federal Sentencing Guidelines' (1992) 21(4) *Anglo-American Law Review* 399
'The European Context of Sentencing Violent Offenders' (1993) 21 *International Journal of the Sociology of Law* 265
'Attorney General's References and Sentencing Policy' [1994] *Criminal Law Review* 499
'Criminal Justice and Sentencing Policy for Drug Offenders' (1994) 22 *International Journal of the Sociology of Law* 223
'Criminal Justice and the Trial and Sentencing of White Collar Offenders' (1995) 59(1) *Journal of Criminal Law* 83
'Dangerous Trends in the Sentencing of Mentally Abnormal Offenders' (1995) 34(1) *Howard Journal of Criminal Justice* 10
'Sentencing Policy and the Court of Appeal' (1995) 34(3) *Howard Journal of Criminal Justice* 218
'Due Process, Procedural Justice and Sentencing Policy' (1995) 23 *International Journal of the Sociology of Law* 233
'Cumulative Sentencing and Penal Policy' (1995) 59(4) *Journal of Criminal Law* 420
'Harm, Sentence Severity and Serious Motoring Offenders' (1996) 1 *Web JCLI*
'Drug Offenders and Sentencing Policy' (1996) 2 *Web JCLI*
'Sentencing Policy and Serious Motoring Offenders' (1996) 60(2) *Journal of Criminal Law* 208
'Truth in Sentencing: Some Problems of Enforcement Strategy' (1996) 3 *Web JCLI*
'Sentencing Policy, Appellate Guidance and Protective Sentencing' (1996) 60(4) *Journal of Criminal Law* 424
'Back to the Future on Sentencing: The 1996 White Paper' (1996) 59(6) *Modern Law Review* 861
'Protective Sentences: Ethics, Rights and Sentencing Policy' (1997) 25 *International Journal of the Sociology of Law* 45
'Anglo-American Approaches to Cumulative Sentencing and the Implications for UK Sentencing Policy' (1997) 36(2) *Howard Journal of Criminal Justice* 261
'Child Victims and Sentencing Policy for Violent and Sexual Crimes' (1997) 5 *Web JCLI*
'Sentencing Policy and the Abolition of Parole and Early Release' (1997) 25 *International Journal of the Sociology of Law* 337
'Dangerousness, Rationality and Sentencing Policy' (1997) 26(4) *Anglo-American Law Review* 495
'Sentencing Sex Offenders: Some Implications of Recent Criminal Justice Policy' (1998) 37(1) *Howard Journal of Criminal Justice* 70
'Making Sense of the Crime (Sentences) Act 1997' (1998) 61(2) *Modern Law Review* 223
'Attorney-General's References Revisited' (1998) 62(4) *Journal of Criminal Law* 468
'Human Rights, Due Process and Sentencing' (1998) 38(4) *British Journal of Criminology* 592
'Sentencing Policy and Economic Crime' (1998) 6(1) *Journal of Financial Crime* 15
(with PE Morris), 'The Prisons Ombudsman: A Critical Review' (1998) 4 *European Public Law* 345

(with PE Morris), 'The Scottish Prisons Complaints Commission: A Preliminary Study' (1999) 28(3) *Anglo-American Law Review* 365

'Bargain Justice or Justice Denied? Sentence Discounts and the Criminal Process' (1999) 62(4) *Modern Law Review* 515

'Dangerousness and Sentencing Policy in Great Britain' (1999) 20(3) *Policy Studies* 173

'Theory, Rights and Sentencing Policy' (1999) 27(2) *International Journal of the Sociology of Law* 167

'Truth in Plea Bargaining: Anglo-American Approaches to the use of Guilty Plea Discounts at the Sentencing Stage' (2000) 29(1) *Anglo-American Law Review* 1

'Problems of Theorizing Sentencing Research' (2000) 28(1) *International Journal of the Sociology of Law* 15

'Reconciling Process and Policy: Sentence Discounts in the Magistrates' Courts' (2000) *Criminal Law Review* 436

'Some Alternative Strategies for Improving the Effectiveness of the English Prisons Ombudsman Scheme' (2000) 39(3) *Howard Journal of Criminal Justice* 29

'Sentencing Theory, Proportionality and Pragmatism' (2000) 28(3) *International Journal of the Sociology of Law* 239

'On the Philosophical and Theoretical Implications of Judicial Decision Support Systems' (2000) 14(3) *International Review of Law, Computers & Technology* 283

'Sentencing Dangerous Offenders: Policy and Practice in the Crown Court' (2001) *Criminal Law Review* 693

'Theory and Contextual Analysis in Sentencing' (2001) 29(3) *International Journal of the Sociology of Law* 253

'Further Evidence on the Significance of Plea in the Crown Court' (2002) 41(2) *Howard Journal of Criminal Justice* 151

'The Internationalisation of Sentencing: Reality or Myth?' (2002) 30 *International Journal of the Sociology of Law* 265

(with M Findlay), 'Criminal Justice Modelling and the Comparative Contextual Analysis of Trial Process' (2002) 2 *International Journal of Comparative Criminology* 162

'The Policy and Practice of Protective Sentencing' (2003) 3(1) *Criminal Justice* 57

'Some Issues for Sentencing in the International Criminal Court' (2003) 52(1) *International and Comparative Law Quarterly* 81

'The Philosophical Foundations of International Sentencing' (2003) 1(1) *Journal of International Criminal Justice* 64

(with G Mannozzi), 'Victim Participation and Sentencing in England and Italy: A Legal and Policy Analysis' (2003) 11 *European Journal of Crime, Criminal Law and Criminal Justice* 278

'Conceptualising Access to Justice and Victims' Rights in International Sentencing' (2004) 13(1) *Social and Legal Studies* 27

'Procedural Justice and Human Rights in International Sentencing' (2004) 4 *International Criminal Law Review* 185

'Theorising the Penality of International Criminal Trials' (2004) 8(4) *Theoretical Criminology* 429
Reprinted in N Larsen and R Smandych (eds), *Global Criminology and Criminal Justice: Current Issues and Perspectives* (Calgary, AB, Broadview Press, 2005)

'Some Reflections on the Role of Victims in the International Criminal Trial Process' (2004) 11 *International Review of Victimology* 1

'The Ethics of Plea Bargaining in International Criminal Trials' (2005) 26(3) *Liverpool Law Review* 209

(with M Drumbl), 'Plea Bargaining at the International Criminal Tribunal for the former Yugoslavia' (2005) 16(1) *Criminal Law Forum* 49

'Plea Bargaining and the Legitimacy of International Trial Justice: Some Observations on the Dragan Nikolic Sentencing Judgement of the ICTY' (2005) 5(4) *International Criminal Law Review* 601

(with G Mannozzi), 'Il ruolo delle vittime nel processo penale e nella commisurazione della pena: un'analisi delle scelte normative e politico-criminali effettuate nell'ordinamento inglese e in quello italiano' (2005) 2 *Rivista Italiana di diritto e procedura penale* 706

'Some Reflections on the Legitimacy of International Trial Justice' (2007) 35(2) *International Journal of the Sociology of Law* 75

'International Sentencing in the Context of Collective Violence' (2007) 7 *International Criminal Law Review* 449

'Developing Contextualised Rationales for Sentencing in International Criminal Trials: A Plea for Empirical Research' (2007) 5 *Journal of International Criminal Justice* 757

'Atrocity, Punishment and International Law' (2007) 8(2) *Melbourne Journal of International Law* 477 (review article)

'Theorising Law and Legitimacy in International Criminal Justice' (2007) 3(3) *International Journal of Law in Context* 257

'Punishment and the Role of the Prosecutor in International Criminal Trials' (2008) 19 *Criminal Law Forum* 395

'Exploring the Relationship between Sentencing and the Legitimacy of Trial Justice' (2009) 37 *International Journal of Law, Crime and Justice* 65

(with J Doak and B Mitchell), 'Victims and the Sentencing Process: Developing Participatory Rights?' (2009) 29 *Legal Studies* 651

'Towards Restorative Sentencing in International Criminal Trials' (2009) 9 *International Criminal Law Review* 809

'Penal Ideology, Sentencing and the Legitimacy of Trial Justice' (2012) 57(1) *Crime, Law and Social Change* 77

'Evaluating the Contribution of Sentencing to Social Justice: Some Conceptual Problems' (2012) 12(3) *International Criminal Law Review* 361

'The 2020 White Paper on Sentencing: a Missed Opportunity for Reform' (2021) *Criminal Law Review* 374

'Sentencing Policy, Social Values and Discretionary Justice' (2022) 42(4) *Oxford Journal of Legal Studies* 1093

'Re-Thinking Notions of Evidence and Proof for Sentencing: Towards a More Communitarian Model' (2023) *International Journal of Evidence and Proof* https://doi.org/10.1177/13657127231172207

3.2. Shorter Articles

'The Enforcement of Outsider Rights under Section 20 (1) of the Companies Act 1948' (1979) 76 *Law Society Gazette* 203

'Actions against Limited Companies: Is the Rule in Foss v Harbottle Still Viable?' (1979) 76 *Law Society Gazette* 1006

'Sentencing the Violent Offender: The Need for a Fresh Approach' (1989) 139(6437) *New Law Journal* 1744

'Anomalies in Sentencing Violent Offenders' (1990) 9 *The Criminal Lawyer* 3

'Drunkenness and Addiction' (1991) 135(48) *Solicitors Journal* 1343

'The Use and Abuse of Sentencing Guidelines' (1992) 25 *The Criminal Lawyer* 3

'Sentencing Policy and Mentally Abnormal Offenders' (1995) 60 *The Criminal Lawyer* 4

(with PE Morris), 'The English Prisons Ombudsman Scheme: A Preliminary Assessment' (1998) 9 *The Ombudsman* 8

(with PE Morris), 'The Scottish Prisons Complaints Commission: An Initial Study' (1998) 10 *The Ombudsman* 6

4. REVIEWS

Review of Bing, *Criminal Procedure and Sentencing in the Magistrates' Courts* (1992) 20(1) *International Journal of the Sociology of Law* 353

Review of Munro and Wasik (eds), *Sentencing, Judicial Discretion and Training* (1995) 23(1) *International Journal of the Sociology of Law* 161

Review of Ashworth, *Sentencing and Criminal Justice* (1996) 24 *International Journal of the Sociology of Law* 448

Review of Tonry, *Sentencing Matters* (1997) 36(1) *Howard Journal of Criminal Justice* 119

Review of Walker and Padfield, *Sentencing Theory, Law and Practice*, 2nd ed (1997) 25 *International Journal of the Sociology of Law* 189

Review of Tonry and Hatlestad (eds), *Sentencing Reform in Overcrowded Times* (1999) 62(1) *Modern Law Review* 470

Review of Worrall, *Punishment in the Community* and Brownlee, *Community Punishment* (1999) 8(1) *Nottingham Law Journal* 69

Review of Walker, *Aggravation, Mitigation and Mercy in English Criminal Justice* (2000) 40(3) *British Journal of Criminology* 534

Review of Drumbl, *Atrocity, Punishment and International Law* (2007) 8(2) *Melbourne Journal of International Law* 477

Review of Wandall, *Decisions to Imprison: Court Decision-Making Inside and Outside the Law* (2009) 49 *British Journal of Criminology* 421

Review of D'Ascoli, *Sentencing in International Criminal Law* (2012) 51(2) *Howard Journal of Criminal Justice* 237

5. CONFERENCE PAPERS AND LECTURES

'Sentencing Violent Offenders: A European Dimension', British Society of Criminology Conference, York University, July 1991

'Sentencing Policy and the Court of Appeal', Prisons 2000 Conference, Leicester University, April 1994

'Sentencing Policy for Drug Offenders', British Society of Criminology Conference, Loughborough University, July 1995

'Recidivist Sentencing in the United States: The Implications for UK Sentencing Policy', Socio-Legal Studies Association Conference, Southampton University, April 1996

'Sentencing Policy after the 1996 White Paper', Centre for the Study of Public Order, Leicester University, September 1996

'Protective Sentences: Ethics, Rights and Sentencing Policy', Human Rights 2000 Conference, Leicester University, September 1996

'Theory, Rights and the Sentencing Process', Socio-Legal Studies Association Conference, University of Wales, Cardiff, April 1997

'Judicial Policy-making and Sentencing', ISA Annual Meeting of the Research Committee on the Sociology of Law, University of Antwerp, Belgium, July 1997

'Reflections on the Crime (Sentences) Act 1997', SPTL Annual Conference, Warwick University, September 1997

'Dangerousness and Sentencing Policy in Great Britain', American Society of Criminology, 49th Annual Conference, San Diego, California, USA, November 1997

'Some Problems of Theorizing Sentencing Research', Law and Society Association, Annual Meeting, Aspen, Colorado, USA, June 1998

'Victims of Economic Crime and the Criminal Process', Sixteenth International Symposium on Economic Crime, Jesus College, Cambridge, September 1998

'The English Prisons Ombudsman: A Comparative Analysis', American Society of Criminology, 50th Annual Conference, Washington DC, USA. November 1998

'Sentence Discounts and the Criminal Process', Socio-Legal Studies Association Conference, Loughborough University, April 1999

'On the Philosophical and Theoretical Implications of Judicial Decision Support Systems', Second International Workshop on Judicial Decision Support Systems, University of Oslo, Norway, June 1999

'Sentencing Policy and Guilty Plea Discounts', Sentencing and Society: An International Conference, University of Strathclyde, Scotland, June 1999

'Victorian and Modern Parallels in Sentencing: Some Theoretical and Methodological Issues', Third Meeting of the Working Group on Law, Culture and the Humanities, Georgetown University Law Centre, Washington, DC, USA, March 2000

'Conceptualising Rights and Norms in Sentencing Theory', Canadian Law and Society Association, Annual Meeting, Lake Louise, Banff National Park, Alberta, Canada, June 2000

'Guilty Plea Discounts and Protective Sentencing in the Crown Court', Crown Prosecution Service, Nottingham, July 2000

'Sentencing Dangerous Offenders: Policy and Practice in the Crown Court', British Society of Criminology Conference, Leicester University, July 2000

'The Policy and Practice of Protective Sentencing in the Crown Court', SPTL Annual Conference, University College London, September 2000

'Social Theory, Rights and Criminal Justice', Australian and New Zealand Society of Criminology, 15th Annual Conference, University of Melbourne, Australia, February 2001

(with M Findlay), 'Theory and Methodology in the Comparative Contextual Analysis of Trial Process', International Criminal Trial Project Seminar, Nottingham Law School, Jockey's Fields, London, March 2001

'Developing a Theoretical Framework for the Contextual Analysis of the Relationship between Sentencing Law and Policy', European Society of Criminology Conference, University of Lausanne, Switzerland, September 2001

'Developing Conceptions of Theory, Policy and Practice for Internationalised Sentencing Praxis', Sentencing & Society: Second International Conference, University of Strathclyde, Glasgow, Scotland, June 2002

'The Need for Rationality in International Sentencing', European Society of Criminology Conference, University of Castilla-La Mancha, Toledo, Spain, September 2002

(with M Findlay), 'Integrating Theory and Methodology in The Comparative Contextual Analysis of Trial Process', Workshop on Socio-Legal Research Methods, International Institute for the Sociology of Law, Onati, Spain, April 2003

'Developing Theory for the Contextual Analysis of Trial Process', Socio-Legal Studies Association Annual Conference, Nottingham Trent University, April 2003

(with M Findlay), Colloquium on the International and Comparative Criminal Trial Project, Max Planck Institute for Foreign and International Criminal Law, Freiburg, Germany, September 2003

'Promoting and Rewarding Research in a University Law School', Kingston University Law School Research Day, January 2004

'The Role of Victims in International Criminal Trials', International Criminal Justice Short Course, Human Rights Law Centre, University of Nottingham, February 2004

'A Philosophical Perspective on International Criminal Justice', Third International Conference, International Criminal Justice: A Transatlantic Dialogue, organised by the Katholieke Universiteit, Leuven, Faculty of Law and Northwestern University School of Law at the European Parliament and the Royal Flemish Academy for Sciences and Arts, Brussels, May 2004

(with M Findlay), 'Comparative Contextual Analysis: Theory, Method and Use', Workshop on Sentencing Research: Theory, Methodology and Perspective, Max Planck Institute for Foreign and International Criminal Law, Freiburg, Germany, June 2005

'The Normative Context of Sentencing for Genocide', International Conference, The Criminal Law of Genocide: International, Comparative and Contextual Aspects held at Nottingham Law School, Nottingham Trent University, September 2005

'Understanding the Concept of Plea Bargaining in International Criminal Trials', Law School Research Seminar, University of Exeter, May 2006

'Human Rights, Accountability and the Legitimacy of Punishment in International Trials', International Conference, Accountability for Human Rights Violations by International Organisations, Brussels, March 2007

'Exploring the Relationship between International Sentencing and Governance in International Criminal Justice', Research Seminar, University of Oxford, Centre for Criminology, June 2007

'Problems of Researching International Criminal Justice', Nottingham Trent University, College Research Students Conference, December 2007

'Understanding the Significance of Sentencing in International Criminal Justice', Public Seminar, University of Sydney, Institute of Criminology, February 2008

(with M Findlay), 'Transforming International Trial Justice: From Theory to Practice', WUN Colloquium, International and Comparative Criminal Justice: Policy Convergence, Divergence and New Justice Paradigms, Centre for Criminal Justice Studies, University of Leeds, June 2008

'Deconstructing Punishment and Sentencing in International Criminal Justice', Research Seminar, Faculty of Law, Queen Mary, University of London, October 2008

'The Role of Sentencing in Achieving Justice in International Criminal Trials', Inaugural Professorial Lecture, Nottingham Trent University, 26th November 2008

'International Sentencing as a Force for Achieving Peace Through Justice', Taking Stock of Transitional Justice Conference, Oxford Transitional Justice Research, University of Oxford, June 2009

'Punishment in Transition: Re-thinking the Role of Punishment and Sentencing for Transitional Justice', Research Seminar, Oxford Transitional Justice Research, Centre for Socio-Legal Studies, University of Oxford, February 2010

'Re-conceptualising the Relationship between International Trial Justice and Transitional Justice: Time for a Paradigm Shift', International Conference, Restoration, Transition and Society, University of Durham, March 2010

'Legitimacy and the Role of International Trial Justice during Transition: Towards a More Constructive Engagement', Research Seminar, Cambridge Transitional Justice Research Network, Faculty of Law, University of Cambridge, February 2011

'Evaluating the Contribution of Sentencing to Social Justice: Some Conceptual Problems', International Conference, Transitional Justice and Restorative Justice: Potential, Pitfalls and Future, Durham Law School, St John's College, University of Durham, September 2011

'Researching International Criminal Justice: Some Conceptual and Methodological Issues', Nottingham Trent University, College Research Students Conference, May 2012

'Penal Ideology, Sentencing and Globalisation', WG Hart Legal Workshop on Globalisation, Criminal Law and Criminal Justice, The Institute of Advanced Legal Studies, University of London, June 2012

'Penal Ideology, Sentencing and Social Values', Research Seminar, Centre for Responsibilities, Rights and the Law, Sussex Law School, University of Sussex, February 2013

Index